INSIDE THE REVOLUTION

This Large Print Book carries the
Seal of Approval of N.A.V.H.

INSIDE THE REVOLUTION

JOEL C. ROSENBERG

THORNDIKE PRESS

A part of Gale, Cengage Learning

Detroit • New York • San Francisco • New Haven, Conn • Waterville, Maine • London

ALL RIGHTS RESERVED

Thorndike Press® Large Print Inspirational.

The text of this Large Print edition is unabridged.

Other aspects of the book may vary from the original edition.

Set in 16 pt. Plantin.

LIBRARY OF CONGRESS CATALOGING-IN-PUBLICATION DATA

Rosenberg, Joel C., 1967–
  Inside the revolution / by Joel C. Rosenberg. — Large print ed.
    p. cm.
  Originally published: Carol Stream, Ill. : Tyndale House Publishers, c2009.
  Includes bibliographical references.
  ISBN-13: 978-1-4104-3385-5 (lg. print : hardcover)
  ISBN-10: 1-4104-3385-4 (lg. print : hardcover)
    1. Middle East—Politics and government—1979– 2. Jihad. 3. Islamic fundamentalism. 4. Terrorism. I. Title.
  DS63.1.R67 2011
  956.05'4—dc22   2010050775

Published in 2011 by arrangement with Trident Media Group, LLC.

Printed in the United States of America
1 2 3 4 5 6 7 15 14 13 12 11

"The Rank-and-File represent the vast middle ground of the Muslim world. They are going about their day-to-day lives without much of a desire to be Revolutionaries of any kind. But they are the audience to which the Radicals, the Reformers, and the Revivalists are speaking. If any of these three major movements ever gains the majority — or even a working plurality — of the Rank-and-File, the entire world will be forever changed, for good or ill."

from the introduction

To Caleb, Jacob, Jonah and Noah,
our revolutionaries in training

CONTENTS

NOTE TO READERS

Though there are a number of different ways to spell the name of the founder of Islam, I have chosen for clarity and simplicity to use the standard spelling "Muhammad." In the case of those individuals cited in the book who go by the same name, I use the spelling of their choice. Some prefer "Mohammed"; others prefer "Mohammad."

In addition, while there are several ways to spell the name of the book Muslims believe contains their Islamic scriptures, I have chosen for clarity and simplicity to use the standard spelling "Qur'an." The specific edition cited throughout this book is *The Qur'an with Annotated Interpretation in Modern English* by Ali Unal, produced by Light Publishers in New Jersey in 2006. This edition was both given to me and recommended to me as the best English translation by my friend Dr. Ahmed Abaddi, one of the top Muslim scholars in Morocco.

Unless otherwise noted, citations from the Bible throughout this book are from the New American Standard translation of *The Holy Bible.* I note the use of other translations with the abbreviation

13

"NIV" for the New International Version and "KJV" for the King James Version.

INTRODUCTION:
NOT "IF" BUT "WHEN"

On April 1, 1979, Iran became the first Islamic republic in history.

Three decades later, the shock waves from the Iranian Revolution are still being felt around the globe. Iran today is the most dangerous terrorist state on the face of the planet. What's more, we are rapidly approaching the most dangerous moment in the history of the Iranian Revolution.

Iran's senior leaders have taught in recent years that the Revolution is now reaching its climax. They have stated publicly that the end of the world is "imminent." They have taught that the way to hasten the arrival or appearance on earth of the Islamic messiah known as the "Twelfth Imam," or the "Mahdi," is to destroy Israel, which they call the "Little Satan," and the United States, which they call the "Great Satan." They have vowed to annihilate the United States and Israel and have urged Muslims to envision a world without America and Zionism. They have come to believe that Allah has chosen them to create chaos and carnage on the planet.

The key leaders in Iran seem hell-bent on accomplishing their apocalyptic, genocidal mission. They are feverishly trying to build, buy, or steal

15

nuclear weapons. Iran is actively testing advanced ballistic missiles capable of delivering nuclear warheads. Tehran is building alliances with Russia, China, and North Korea — all nuclear-armed powers — and has cooperated on the development of offensive and defensive weapons systems with those countries.

Iran's leaders are building a network of thousands of suicide bombers ready to strike American targets. They are sending suicide bombers and other insurgents, money, and weapons into Iraq to kill Iraqis as well as American and Coalition forces. They are harboring scores of al Qaeda terrorists and leaders inside Iranian cities and allowing terrorists to crisscross their territory. They are making a concerted effort to enlarge the reach of terrorist operations by building strategic alliances with other jihadist organizations, regardless of their theological differences.

The Iranian leaders are digging hundreds of thousands of new graves in Iran itself to bury the enemies of Islam. They are calling for the unification of the Islamic world politically and economically, including the creation of a single currency. They are aggressively exporting their Islamic Revolution to countries throughout the Middle East and around the world.

Put simply, the leaders of Iran believe that Allah is on their side, the wind is at their back, and the end of Judeo-Christian civilization as we know it is near.

I believe just the opposite. As an evangelical Christian with a Jewish father and a Gentile mother, I worship the God of the Bible — the God of Abraham, Isaac, and Jacob, who is also the God of the New Testament. I do not believe that God is on the side of the zealots that run Iran. Rather, I believe that the end of their reign of terror is increasingly close at hand. Every day I pray for the peace of Jerusalem. Every day I pray for peace throughout the Middle East. What's more, I pray for the salvation of the leaders of Iran and the salvation of their terrorist allies, and I encourage others to do the same. And because I serve a prayer-hearing and prayer-answering God, a wonder-working God of miracles, I firmly believe that God in His grace can change the leadership in Iran.

That said, the God of the Bible may have other plans. If, in His sovereignty, He chooses not to remove the Radicals from Iran peacefully, then I believe a major, cataclysmic war or series of wars is coming soon as a direct result of the Iranian Revolution that was set into motion by the Ayatollah Khomeini in 1979. The United States, NATO, Israel, or some combination thereof could initiate a preemptive strike to neutralize the Iranian nuclear threat. If they do not, Iran will soon be poised to launch the apocalyptic war required by its theology to destroy the West and usher in the end of days. The question we all must be asking is not *if* there will be war with Iran but *when* it will begin and *who* will strike first.

A Clear and Present Danger

Iran, however, is not the only threat.

Osama bin Laden and his al Qaeda terrorist network remain a clear and present danger to the national security and economic vitality of the United States, the State of Israel, and our Western allies. While al Qaeda has certainly been badly damaged by U.S. and Coalition forces in recent

17

years, they are by no means defeated. Rather, they are doing everything they can to reconstitute themselves in Afghanistan, Iraq, Pakistan, North Africa, and elsewhere around the world. They are building new alliances, recruiting new jihadists, raising more money, acquiring more weapons, and plotting new attacks.

For the past several years, many Americans, Canadians, Europeans, and others have asked, "Why are the Americans at war in Iraq and Afghanistan when they have not been hit by any terrorist attacks inside the borders of the United States since September 11, 2001? What's the point of all this fighting if the American people are no longer in danger?" This sentiment reveals a fundamental misunderstanding of the history of the last eight years and of the jihadists' intentions and preparations. True, as of this writing, the U.S. homeland has not been hit with terrorist attacks since 9/11, but that is not because the jihadists are not trying.

There are actually three reasons we have not been hit again — not yet, at least.

First, the U.S. and our allies are getting significantly better at identifying terrorist plots early and intercepting them before they can be set into motion. Indeed, dozens of terror plots have been foiled by U.S. and allied intelligence and law enforcement agencies in recent years. I will recount several of those disrupted operations along the way, and I have included more such successes in an appendix to this book.

Second, after 9/11, the U.S. and our allies remained on offense against the jihadists throughout the years President George W. Bush served in office. We were not waiting to be hit, as we seemed

18

to be doing prior to 9/11. We took the fight to the enemy in Iraq and Afghanistan rather than wait for the jihadists to come to us. In the process, we effectively created in Iraq and Afghanistan two magnets that drew local and international jihadists into contact with the best-trained and best-equipped militaries in the history of mankind. These battles have not been easy. Thousands of brave American and Coalition men and women have sacrificed their lives to defeat the jihadists overseas. But to date we have been winning. From 2003 to 2008, for example, our forces killed nearly 20,000 terrorists and insurgents and captured more than 25,000 in Iraq alone.[1] That means some 45,000 Radical Islamic jihadists are now unable to travel west, infiltrate the United States, and strike inside our borders.

That said, there is a third reason why we have not yet been hit again, and it is a sobering one, to say the least: al Qaeda is planning larger attacks. Senior al Qaeda leaders no longer want to merely frighten us; they want to annihilate us. They no longer seek only to inflict minor damage on planes, trains, buses, restaurants, malls, and other "soft targets" that have little or no external security. Rather, they are plotting to inflict catastrophic damage on the U.S. and our allies.

To accomplish their objectives, the Radicals need weapons of mass destruction. They need more accurate ballistic missiles and long-range missiles capable of reaching all of Europe and the United States. They need followers who are religiously and ideologically committed to helping them carry out their plans and — if at all possible — infiltrate the American homeland and set off catastrophic attacks from the inside.

19

What they need most — what they pray for most of all — is Western ignorance, apathy, and lack of moral clarity. If the West can be lulled to sleep, if free people the world over can somehow be prevented from understanding the true goals and objectives of the Radicals and mobilizing to take all necessary actions to prevent their success, then the Radicals will soon be able to pull off a series of attacks that make 9/11 pale by comparison and could leave millions dead, not thousands.

Not One Revolution but Three

Thirty years after the rise of the Ayatollah Khomeini to power in Iran, it has become clear to me that there is not simply one Revolution under way; there are three. Each is pursued with equal passion and vigor by groups I define as the "Radicals," the "Reformers," and the "Revivalists." And with the stakes so high — and time so short — there are important questions to be answered, and fast.

How, for example, can citizens and leaders in the West properly understand and counter the threat Islamic Radicals pose to Judeo-Christian civilization? How can we understand what is really going on inside the minds of the Radicals? When they read the Qur'an, what verses drive them to rob, kill, and destroy? Is there any way to persuade them to not carry out their apocalyptic agendas? Diplomacy has not worked so far, but might direct negotiations at the highest possible level — president to president — work? Or is that a fool's errand?

At the same time, are there any Muslim leaders pushing back against the jihadists? Are there any leaders who think the Radicals are crazy and

20

dangerous and who are willing to say so? If so, who are they? What verses in the Qur'an do these Reformers point to in making their case that Islam is a "religion of peace"? What are their personal stories? How did they climb to power, and why don't we hear more about them in the media? Do such Reformers really have any chance at remaking the modern Middle East and winning the war of ideas — as well as the war of bullets and bombs — with the Radicals?

What's more, are war and politics the only prescriptions for what ails the people of the Middle East today? Are there any sources of true hope? Is Christianity really dying out in the lands of its birth, as many claim, or is it true that more Muslims are coming to faith in Jesus Christ today than at any other time in history? Is there any evidence that Christianity is surging in the epicenter? Who are the Revivalists, and what is the message of spiritual hope and change they are trying to spread? And if Muslims are converting to Christianity in record numbers as some have suggested, what are the implications of this trend for the Church in the West and around the world?

These are questions I have often been asked since the 9/11 attacks, as I have written fiction and nonfiction books about events in the Middle East, been interviewed hundreds of times by U.S. and foreign media outlets, and had the honor of speaking to audiences around the world. What follow are the answers I have found and the conclusions I have drawn after traveling to Iraq, Afghanistan, Egypt, Jordan, Turkey, Morocco, the United Arab Emirates, central Asia, Israel, the West Bank, Europe, and Canada, as well as throughout the U.S., doing research and meeting with key participants inside these ongoing Revolutions.

In the pages ahead, you will hear key leaders of each movement making their own cases and speaking in their own words. You will read direct quotes taken from the speeches, textbooks, memoirs, manifestos, Web sites, and videos written or produced by the Radicals, Reformers, and Revivalists themselves. You will see verses from the books they consider holy. You will find excerpts from captured and intercepted memos and diaries they have written. I have also quoted transcripts of previously classified interrogation sessions and from exclusive, never-before-published interviews, many of which I conducted myself. You will also hear from those who have devoted their lives to hunting or confronting the Radicals, including presidents, prime ministers, CIA directors, intelligence operatives, military leaders, and members of Congress, as well as Americans who have been directly impacted by terrorist attacks.

Among those whom I had the privilege of personally interviewing during the course of researching this book:

Porter Goss, Director of the Central Intelligence Agency (2004–2006) and chairman of the House Permanent Select Committee on Intelligence (1997–2004)

Lieutenant General (ret.) William "Jerry" Boykin, U.S. Deputy Undersecretary of Defense for Intelligence and Special Warfighting (2003–2007), former commander of Delta Force, and author of *Never Surrender: A Soldier's Journey to the Crossroads of Faith and Freedom*

L. Paul Bremer III, presidential envoy to

Iraq and first U.S. administrator after liberation (2003–2004), and author of *My Year in Iraq: The Struggle to Build a Future of Hope*

Fred Schwien, senior advisor to U.S. Homeland Security Secretary Michael Chertoff

Lynn Derbyshire, chief spokeswoman for the families of the U.S. Marines killed in the Beirut truck bombing of 1983

Alireza Jafarzadeh, Iranian dissident and author of *The Iran Threat: President Ahmadinejad and the Coming Nuclear Crisis*

Mala Bakhtyar, spokesman for Iraqi president Jalal Talabani

Qubad Talabani, son of Iraqi President Jalal Talabani and the official representative in Washington, D.C., for the Kurdistan Regional Government

Samir Sumaida'ie, Iraq's ambassador to the United States

Falakaddin Kakaye, Minister of Culture, Kurdistan Regional Government of Iraq

Dr. Ahmed Abaddi, Morocco's Director of Islamic Affairs

Dr. Ahmed Khamlichi, director of Morocco's leading Islamic seminary

Khalid Zerouali, Director of Border Security, Morocco's Interior Ministry

Abdelsalam al-Majali, Prime Minister of Jordan (1993–1995 and 1997–1998)

Benjamin Netanyahu, Prime Minister of Israel (1996–1999)

General Moshe Ya'alon, Chief of Staff of the Israeli Defense Forces (2002–2005)

Dore Gold, Israeli ambassador to the United Nations (1997–1999) and senior advisor to Prime Minister Ariel Sharon (2001–2003)

Hormoz Shariat, member of the Iranian Revolution in 1979 who later converted to Christianity, set up a satellite television ministry, and is now one of the best-known evangelists in Iran

Taysir Saada, former Palestinian terrorist who converted to Christianity and now runs an evangelical ministry called Hope for Ishmael

Over 150 Arab and Iranian pastors and ministry leaders, including former Islamic jihadists who have converted to Christianity

Dozens of Arab and Iranian prodemocracy dissidents

Western and Middle Eastern intelligence officials, both active and retired

Western and Middle Eastern diplomats, both active and retired

Some of these spoke to me specifically for *Inside the Revolution.* Others spoke to me for other books and articles I have written over the years. As with my previous nonfiction book, *Epicenter,* I should note that not all of these sources will agree with the analysis and conclusions found in the pages ahead, but I am exceedingly grateful for their valuable time and helpful insights. I have no doubt this book is richer for the assistance they provided.

A Final Note

Before you begin your journey inside the Revolution, allow me to briefly describe three other groups of people that are important to our story. They do not receive much direct attention in this book as they are not in and of themselves Revolutionaries. But at least a cursory awareness of who these groups are and how they fit into the overall picture is vital, I believe, in understanding the broader context of the current dynamics in the Middle East. I speak here of groups I call the "Resisters," the "Reticent," and the "Rank-and-File."

The Resisters are leaders of Muslim-majority countries who show little evidence of wanting serious social or ideological change of any kind. While Muslim themselves, they do not want the kind of fundamental, sweeping changes advocated by the Radicals, Reformers, or Revivalists. To the contrary, they resist change; generally speaking, their mission is to hold power for as long as possible.

Most modern Arab regimes fall into this category. The royal family and senior leaders of Saudi Arabia are classic Resisters. As Sunni Wahhabi Muslims, some may theologically identify with the Radicals, but they part paths politically. Some of their schools are certainly producing a new generation of extremists, and their oil wealth often funds groups of Radicals, but the House of Saud wants to remain in political power and wants to retain the enormous revenues that come from selling oil to the West and the East. Thus Saudi leaders try to remain vigilant so as not to let Radicals take over their kingdom. They do not want a revolution on the Arabian peninsula. Nor do they want Osama bin Laden, himself a Saudi, and his al Qaeda movement to destroy the West and establish a global caliphate. Moreover, they are absolutely terrified by the notion that Iranian Shia Muslims will attempt to blow up the world to hasten the coming of the Mahdi — an eschatology they as Sunnis do not share. So they maintain close ties to the U.S. and the European Union and pursue geopolitical stability at almost all costs.

President Hosni Mubarak of Egypt — nominally a Muslim but more of a secular Arab nationalist at heart — is also a classic Resister. His predecessor, Anwar Sadat, was the region's first bold Reformer: a Muslim who made peace with the Israelis, broke with the Soviets, and embraced the United States. But he was assassinated by Radicals for his efforts, and Mubarak never forgot that. Mubarak was Egypt's vice president at the time and was sitting next to Sadat the day he was killed. Mubarak has never appointed another vice president and has resisted fundamental changes in Egypt of almost any kind ever since.

Other Resisters tend to be secular Arab nationalists as well, not interested in creating a Radical Islamic caliphate, though they certainly want to rule as dictators and seize as much wealth, power, and territory as they can. At times they align themselves with Radicals if they think they can gain material or territorial advantages in the process. But they are not "true believers." Indeed, they are just as likely to round up and kill or imprison Radicals as join forces with them. It often depends on their mood and their sense of self-interest. Resisters also tend to imprison, torture, and sometimes execute Reformers and Revivalists because, in their view, change is dangerous. Stability is all-important. Syria's Bashar al-Assad is a classic Resister. So is Libya's Moammar Ghaddafi, along with the leaders of Algeria and Tunisia.

The Reticent include leaders of Muslim-majority countries or territories who have leanings toward

26

one movement or another but have not fully committed. They do the two-step, dancing for a season with one partner, then shifting to another.

Palestinian chairman Mahmoud Abbas is, in many ways, a charter member of the Reticent. Once the number-two man next to Yasser Arafat, he wrote his doctoral dissertation denying the Holocaust. He is a Sunni Muslim but has operated historically much more like a secular Arab nationalist and even like a Marxist. Since rising to power in the wake of Arafat's death, however, Abbas has shown some small but noteworthy signs of shifting away from Arafat's worldview and toward actually wanting to make peace with Israel through a two-state solution. But he is politically weak. He is surrounded by Radicals and Resisters. The jihadists of Hamas have seized control of Gaza — fully a third of his territorial "kingdom" — and threatened to assassinate him, his family, and everyone else he knows if he makes peace with Israel or embraces true democratic reforms in the West Bank. So he dances.

Pakistani president Pervez Musharraf was also a member of the Reticent, until he resigned his post in August 2008. Before 9/11, Musharraf's intelligence services helped build and strengthen the extremist Taliban government in Afghanistan. But after 9/11, to his credit, Musharraf made a significant course correction. Unfortunately, he made little effort or progress to clean up Pakistan's rampant corruption problems. But in other ways he did begin remaking himself as a Reformer, however imperfect. He became an important and useful ally in the war against the Radicals, directing his security forces to hunt down and arrest hundreds of terrorists and extremist leaders, including Khalid Sheikh Mohammed, the mastermind of the 9/11 attacks, and Dr. A. Q. Khan, the father of Pakistan's nuclear weapons program, who would later confess to selling blueprints, equipment, and technical advice to Iran, Libya, and North Korea to help them develop their nuclear weapons programs. He took steps to protect the Pakistani Christian community from jihadist attacks and even reached out to Israel, once shaking Prime Minister Ariel Sharon's hand at the United Nations and delivering a major address to a gathering of the American Jewish Congress in New York in 2005. It was no wonder, then, that al Qaeda and other Radical groups tried to assassinate him so many times.

The Rank-and-File, finally, comprise the vast majority of the world's 1.3 billion Muslims. They do not run countries. Individually, they generally have little or no wealth or power. But they are enormously important. First, they are souls created in God's image. Second, they are suffering. As I will detail later in the book, many live in absolute, destitute poverty and see no future and no hope for their lives, their children's lives, or their grandchildren's lives. Third, they are searching. They want a better life. They know their nations and their regions are failing. But they are not sure which way to turn.

When it comes to the social, economic, and spiritual crises plaguing the Islamic world, the Rank-and-File wonder, *Who has the right diagnosis? Who has the right prognosis? Are the Radicals right in teaching that a purer form of Islam is the answer and that violent jihad is the way? Are the Reformers right in thinking that Islam is good but*

28

that more freedom, openness, and democracy are the way forward? Or are the Revivalists right, that Islam is not the answer, that Jesus is the answer, and that only by accepting Christ's death on the cross and resurrection from the dead can a person be forgiven and saved and filled with hope and joy here in this life and in the life to come?

The Rank-and-File represent the vast middle ground of the Muslim world. They are going about their day-to-day lives without much of a desire to be Revolutionaries of any kind. But they are the audience to which the Radicals, the Reformers, and the Revivalists are speaking. If any of these three major movements ever gains the majority — or even a working plurality — of the Rank-and-File, the entire world will be forever changed, for good or ill.

Understanding these three Revolutionary movements — including the crises they are responding to and the answers they are offering — is of absolutely critical importance. Those who ignore these trends do so at their peril.

Joel C. Rosenberg
WASHINGTON, D.C.
NOVEMBER 11, 2008

■ ■ ■ ■

PART ONE:
THE RADICALS

■ ■ ■ ■

CHAPTER ONE:
WORST-CASE SCENARIO

My conversation with the
former commander of Delta Force

I first met him at the Pentagon in February 2007.

At the time, William G. "Jerry" Boykin was a three-star lieutenant general in the United States Army, serving as deputy undersecretary of defense for intelligence. As such, he was responsible for overseeing the gathering and analysis of all military intelligence related to the global War on Terror. He had read my first nonfiction book, *Epicenter: Why the Current Rumblings in the Middle East Will Change Your World,* and had invited my wife, Lynn, and me for lunch to discuss my research and conclusions.

After taking us and some mutual friends on a tour of the Pentagon and showing us the memorial chapel where Flight 77 hit on 9/11, General Boykin took us to a private dining room where we began to chat. We talked about his family and his years in the military. We talked about his thoughts on the ongoing battles in Iraq and Afghanistan and about the rising Iranian nuclear threat. He asked me about my assessment of Iranian president Mahmoud Ahmadinejad and why I believed the president's Shia eschatology, or end times theology, was driving Iranian foreign policy. It was not a subject that was being discussed much inside the Pentagon's higher echelons at the time, and he was curious. It was the beginning of a friendship that would soon deepen between our two families.

Few men I have ever met in Washington understand the mind-set and mission of the Radicals better than Boykin. He has, after all, been hunting Radicals for nearly thirty years, and his firsthand knowledge and insight were invaluable.

Two Propaganda Windfalls . . . and a Third

When the Iranian Revolution erupted in 1979, Boykin was a thirty-one-year-old commando training with the U.S. Army's newly formed and highly classified counterterrorism team known as Delta Force. In November of that year, Radicals seized the American Embassy in Tehran and took dozens of American diplomats and Marines hostage. Boykin and his boss, Col. Charlie Beckwith, the legendary Delta commander, were ordered to the Pentagon. There they were briefed on the latest intelligence and began planning a rescue.

This was America's first direct confrontation with Radical Islamic jihadists. No one in Washington had ever encountered a crisis quite like this. In the months that followed, Boykin and his colleagues studied everything they could find on the Ayatollah Khomeini, the nature and loyalty of his followers, the students that had stormed the embassy compound, and the religious and political beliefs that drove them to wage jihad against the West. When President Carter finally ordered the rescue of the hostages, Boykin was one of the Delta team leaders penetrating Iranian airspace in the dark of night. The mission, as I will detail in a later chapter, was a disaster, not simply due to failures of equipment and human error, but because it emboldened the Radicals and gave them a sense of divine choosing and invincibility.

"I'll say two things, Joel," Boykin told me when we sat down for a formal interview in the winter of 2008, several months after he retired from the Army. "First of all, that failed rescue attempt was the greatest professional disappointment of my thirty-six-plus years in the military. In our view, we had not only failed the fifty-three Americans in the embassy, we'd failed the nation. And it was a tremendous burden that we all still carry today. But the second thing is that the hostage crisis was the beginning of our focus on the Islamic Revolution. That was when we really started paying attention to what was happening among the Radical jihadists."[1]

"What was the impact of that failure?" I asked Boykin.

"If you stop and think about it, that was one of the two most significant propaganda windfalls in Radical Islam's recent history," he replied. "The fact of the matter is the jihadists were able to say with some credibility to the rest of the Islamic world, 'We have just defeated the Great Satan. We held their hostages for 444 days, and they were inept. Allah has shown us favor. Allah is with us.' "

"What was the second?" I asked.

"The second was when the Russians left Afghanistan and went home defeated, and the Soviet Union disintegrated," Boykin replied immediately. "Now, Osama bin Laden used that for propaganda

35

purposes. He said, 'We have defeated the world's great infidel power. Now the effeminate Americans will be easy.' "

The combination of those two events, Boykin told me, became the greatest recruiting tool in the history of the Radicals and dramatically swelled their ranks in the years to come.

I noted that there was a third event that aided the growth of the Radicals: Hezbollah's suicide truck bombing attack against the Marine barracks in Beirut, Lebanon, in 1983.

Boykin agreed. "That was a devastating day for America when they killed our Marines at the barracks," he said, noting that before 1983, U.S. forces had never encountered a suicide bombing. "People who would blow themselves up? This was something we didn't understand."

The incident was horrifying for the entire Marine Corps and specifically for the families of the men who were directly involved. But compounding the disaster, the Reagan administration chose to cut and run, pulling all U.S. military forces out of Lebanon.

"The great tragedy of that whole thing geopolitically," Boykin argued, "is that we immediately withdrew our forces. What did that say? What did it say to the Islamists? What did it say to the extremists? It made them think, 'We won; you lost.' And they were able to make that point with some credibility. After all, they blew up our Marines, we withdrew, and Beirut was back in their hands."

"We Have a Black Hawk Down"
Ten years later, Boykin again found himself at the vortex of a battle between the U.S. and Radical

Islam, which became yet another propaganda windfall for the Radicals. The time: August 1993. The location: Mogadishu, Somalia. The enemy: the jihadist militia run by Somalian warlord Mohammed Farrah Aidid, supported by al Qaeda jihadists, financed and trained by none other than Osama bin Laden.

"Almost 4.5 million people, more than half the total number in the country, were threatened with starvation, severe malnutrition, and related diseases," reported a U.N. assessment team. "The magnitude of suffering was immense. Overall, an estimated 300,000 people, including many children, died. Some two million people, violently displaced from their home areas, fled either to neighboring countries or elsewhere within Somalia. All institutions of governance and at least 60 percent of the country's basic infrastructure disintegrated."[2]

At the order of President Bill Clinton, U.S. special forces were sent to capture General Aidid and stop the bloodletting. This time, Boykin was no longer just a member of the Army's most elite fighting force. He was now the Delta Force commander, and he was horrified by what he found.

"We went into Mogadishu not fully realizing the difficulty of our task," Boykin explained. "Given that this was a lawless society, this was anarchy in its purest form — it was nothing but sectarian violence, clan against clan. And they were all, in one form or another, extremists — Islamic extremists. They were doing things that were alien to us. They were using unarmed women as shields as they would approach our positions. When we would go into certain facilities, they would throw their children up in front of them as a shield. It is

37

difficult for us as Americans to understand that kind of mentality."

On October 3, U.S. forces received intelligence that a small group of Aidid's closest associates were having a meeting in an area called the Bakara Market, euphemistically known as the "Black Sea." It was known to be the most violent part of the Somalian capital, and one that Boykin and his men had not gone into previously. "In a situation like that, you don't choose your locations; the people you're after do," Boykin told me. "The intelligence was credible. We knew they were there. We were expecting about half a dozen of them. So we went in."

Major General Bill Garrison was responsible for the overall operations of Task Force Ranger, as well as for coordinating U.S. strategy with the U.N. forces. Boykin had the specific tactical responsibilities for going after the targets in Mogadishu.

"We made our assault, captured roughly twenty-one people, and then loaded them on trucks and started back to our base to bring them in for interrogation," Boykin recalled. "As we were trying to get out of the city, one of our helicopters was shot down, and it changed everything."

With the crash of a Black Hawk helicopter in the middle of a Radical no-man's-land, the Americans had suddenly lost the initiative. Now, rather than a quick strike and rapid extraction operation, U.S. forces had to literally fight their way house by house, street by street, block by block just to get to the crash site and try to recover the dead and wounded that were there. Thousands of heavily armed jihadists poured into the streets and began converging on the site. As the hours passed and night fell, the firefight intensified. Neither the Delta teams nor the Rangers were having success in extracting the bodies of the chopper's two crew members.

The battle lasted eighteen hours. Eventually the Delta operators and Army Rangers were able to reassemble their team and fight their way out of the city. But they were completely unprepared for what they would see next.

"If you remember the news footage of our soldiers," Boykin recalled, "their bodies were dragged through the streets and mutilated. And some of the stories have never even been told. It would be too painful for the families to tell the whole story, but the abuse and mutilation, particularly by the women in Mogadishu, was something that just is incomprehensible to us. What causes someone to be that way? Is it just a tribal thing? Is it just a cultural thing? Or is it part of their theology?

"By military standards, it was a victory for us," Boykin concluded. "We captured more than the six [of General Aidid's top commanders] that we went after — we captured about twenty-one of them. We lost eighteen Americans dead and over seventy wounded. It seems like a high casualty count. But then compare it to the casualties on the other side. Conservative estimates by the Red Cross are that we killed and wounded 1,100 people in an eighteen-hour battle. Now, by any standards, that's a victory. However, that was when we realized you can win the battle and lose the war."

"How so?" I asked.

"First, because the American media called it a disaster — a huge military failure," Boykin

39

explained. "Second, the Clinton administration pulled all of Task Force Ranger out of Mogadishu before we had completed our mission, before we had captured Mohammed Aidid."

"What was the effect of the White House decision to withdraw prematurely?" I asked.

"The extremists there were encouraged, particularly Osama bin Laden," Boykin replied without hesitation. "Now, I am one who does not believe Osama bin Laden was there, involved in that battle. I've seen no evidence of that. But he was certainly associated with it. He was certainly tied to it in terms of probably providing material and financial support to those people, but certainly ideological support, moral support. And then we gave him an opportunity, as a result of our withdrawal, to once again proclaim that Allah had shown them favor and that more good Muslims should come to the Islamic extremist cause. And they did."

How Serious a Threat?

I asked General Boykin to take these four examples — the U.S. failure to rescue our hostages in Iran, the U.S. withdrawal from Lebanon after the Marine barracks attack, the Soviets pulling out of Afghanistan, and the U.S. pulling out of Somalia — and put them into a broader context. What were the implications of these events? What was the Big Picture?

"Well, first of all, there are 1.3 billion Muslims around the world," Boykin told me. "And I'll just tell you right now, Joel, I don't think that every Muslim is a threat to America or to the West. I think there are many who really would like to see this extremism go away because it in fact is causing more problems for them than it is helping their cause. But if only one percent of the 1.3 billion are extremists and jihadists, do the math. That's frightening. I mean particularly when they are willing to die for their cause, when they believe that martyrdom is the surest way to heaven — that's frightening. If that one percent all turned into suicide bombers, just think what a threat that would be.

"As we look at every time that we have been up against these extremists, we've either been unsuccessful in our objectives or, more importantly, we've not been willing to stay the course and see it through and to fight to win, which is exactly what happened in Mogadishu. It's exactly what happened after the Beirut bombing in 1983. And it's exactly what many advocate in terms of our operations in Iraq and even Afghanistan today. All that has done is emboldened the extremists. All that has done is given them fodder for their propaganda. It has given them credibility as they use the Internet, use the broadcast media, use every outlet to broadcast their propaganda, to say that Allah has shown them favor, to say, 'You need to now align yourself with our cause.' It has allowed them credibility to bring more young Radicals into the cause.

"That's one of the reasons that I think that staying the course — and I don't mean tactically, I don't mean necessarily using exactly the same methodologies that we're using today, but staying the course strategically — in Iraq is very critical. Why? Because if we give the Radicals this opportunity for more propaganda by pulling out and not fighting this radicalism, all we're going to do is increase their recruiting, increase their opportunities for finding more young Radicals."

I asked, "With all your years of experience in the Pentagon, commanding Delta Force, hunting jihadists around the globe, in your judgment, how serious to U.S. national security is the threat of Radical Islam in the twenty-first century?"

"When I came into the Army in 1971, we were focused on the Soviet Union," Boykin replied. "Even though we were fighting in Vietnam, our real threat was the Soviet Union. But I would say to you, Joel, that the threat that Radical Islam presents to not only America but to the world today is an even more serious threat than when we were in a nuclear standoff during the Cold War. And it's more concerning to me because this is an enemy that is hard to understand. It is an enemy that is easy to ignore, and it is an enemy that is absolutely relentless."

"What's the mind-set of the jihadist movement? What do they want? What's driving them?"

"Well, first of all, I think their mind-set is very clearly based on their own manifesto that they are adhering to — a very radical, extreme interpretation of the Qur'an. They clearly believe that infidels — infidels defined as those that do not serve Allah — must either be converted or killed."

The "Top Five" List

"What, then, is the worst-case scenario?" I asked.

"I think the worst-case scenario is that the jihadists continue in their pursuit of weapons of mass destruction," Boykin said without hesitation. "Weapons of mass destruction are available to them now, particularly chemical and biological, and those are not hard to make. But the worst-case scenario is, I think, that they have nuclear capabilities within these terrorist organizations, within the jihadist movement; that they intimidate Europe to the point that Europe is no longer capable of standing against them as they have done historically; and that they take their extremism to the entire world, and people start to buckle under the intimidation and pressure of what I would see as a huge Islamic movement."

How exactly would the Radicals hit us?

Boykin gave me his "top five" list of scenarios that deeply trouble him and his colleagues in the military and intelligence community.

Worst-Case Scenario No. 1: Once Iran acquires operational nuclear weapons, they could attach these warheads to short-to-medium-range ballistic missiles, hide such missiles in commercial containers (used to transport cars, farm equipment, toys from China, and so forth), and then launch those missiles off the backs of container ships approaching major American port cities. As portrayed in my novel *Dead Heat,* this would give the enemies of the United States the decisive element of surprise. A missile fired at Manhattan, Los Angeles, Seattle, or Washington, D.C., would take less than five minutes to impact, giving civilians no effective warning and no time to evacuate, and giving U.S. military forces precious little opportunity to intercept those missiles — even if we had a missile-defense system guarding the homeland, which we currently do not.

Iranian forces would not have to carry out such attacks themselves, of course. They could provide nuclear weapons and missiles to terrorist groups such as al Qaeda, Hezbollah, or some other Radical group as proxies to carry out their

43

apocalyptic agenda.

Worst-Case Scenario No. 2: Iran or other Radical states or groups could load nuclear weapons onto private planes taking off from Canada, Mexico, or another foreign country, bound for the United States. Once inside our airspace, they could then fly kamikaze missions into American cities or simply detonate the nuclear weapon inside the plane itself — over their intended target — without initiating a dive-bombing sequence or making any other obviously hostile moves that might alert air-traffic controllers to the threat. Passengers and cargo on private planes receive few if any security clearances before entering U.S. airspace. No ID checks. No metal detectors. No luggage screening. All this creates enormous holes in our homeland security defense systems, which Radicals may soon take advantage of.

Worst-Case Scenario No. 3: Radicals could load nuclear weapons onto private yachts or other boats entering the harbors of major American cities and detonate these weapons close to population centers, airports, and naval bases.

Worst-Case Scenario No. 4: Radicals could smuggle nuclear weapons or other weapons of mass destruction into the U.S. through Canada or Mexico to be detonated deep in the interior of the country. People, drugs, and weapons are smuggled into the U.S. all the time. U.S. homeland security has improved significantly since 9/11, but in many ways, our borders are still Swiss cheese, making us extremely vulnerable to catastrophic attacks of this nature.

Worst-Case Scenario No. 5: Even without access to fully developed, state-of-the-art nuclear bombs and nuclear warheads, Radicals could still hit us hard. They could, for example, build and detonate "dirty bombs" — bombs made with conventional explosives such as dynamite, mixed with waste from nuclear power plants or other radiological substances — inside the United States. Experts say such devices would not cause the same magnitude of catastrophic death or destruction as a true nuclear weapon, but they would still be psychologically and economically devastating.[3] We are also vulnerable, Boykin noted, to chemical and biological weapons in subways and water systems.

"The fifth scenario is my greatest concern," Boykin would later elaborate in an e-mail to me, although he added that the combination of elements from several of these scenarios is very worrisome. "All the others are real possibilities, but they require a fair amount of logistics and consequently a fair number of people who know what is happening. That means there is a greater chance of one of the intel services finding out and preventing it. But dirty bomb (or chemical or biological) materials could come in across the Mexican border fairly easily, I am sad to say.

"The other way is for the terrorists to recruit a local in the North Carolina or South Carolina coastal region to bring things in aboard his sport fishing vessel, to which no attention is paid, and put it in his pickup and drive it to D.C. A dirty bomb would shut down our government even though it would not kill millions of people. In the confusion inside D.C., other conventional bombs could be used to destroy much of the U.S. govern-

45

ment infrastructure. I am concerned about the growing number of Americans who have been recruited to Islam. They are usually angry young men with a sense of hopelessness. Even if they are not suicidal, they may very well be genocidal as well as eager to seek revenge for what they see as injustice. These people could make several scenarios more feasible. Think of the devastating psychological effects of a dirty bomb disrupting our government. The recruiting of the Radicals would go off the scale and embolden every radical Muslim in America to support the 'soon return of the Mahdi and the soon rise of the caliphate.' "[4]

Longer term, Boykin also worries about a sixth scenario. Once Iran or another Radical state is able to build long-range, intercontinental ballistic missiles and attach nuclear warheads to them, such states could fire these missiles at the U.S. and our allies. We are working hard on building missile-defense systems capable of stopping such attacks, but these systems are not yet fully operational and continue to arouse enormous resistance from some members of Congress, from some of our allies, and most notably from the Russians.

The Iranian Bomb

How close is Iran to having nuclear weapons?

Boykin told me that based on everything he had seen and heard during his tenure at the Pentagon, he believes that "within two years, maybe three," the Iranians will "develop a nuclear weapon, a deliverable nuclear weapon."

Translation: 2010 or 2011.

"We know that Ahmadinejad has centrifuges spinning. We know that he has the technology. He has the scientists, and he certainly has the deter-

46

mination. Ahmadinejad is a very, very dangerous man in my view. I believe that the world should pay close attention to what he has said. Some would say, 'Well, that's just rhetoric.' But let's go back and look at Hitler's rhetoric in 1933 and what ultimately occurred."

"Given all that you know about the Ayatollah Khomeini from the 1970s and Mahmoud Ahmadinejad today," I asked, "which one is more dangerous?"

For Boykin, it was not a close call. "I think Ahmadinejad is far more dangerous than the Ayatollah Khomeini was because he has more resources," he told me. "Certainly he has more money as a result of the oil in Iran. He has greater weapons capabilities. He has a more sophisticated army and military in general. And regardless of what the 2007 National Intelligence Estimate says, he is developing nuclear capabilities."

"In your view," I asked, "can the West successfully deter or negotiate with Ahmadinejad and his regime in the kind of classic balance-of-power approach that worked with the Soviets?"

"My view is that negotiating with Ahmadinejad is a waste of time," Boykin replied. "I don't think there's anything that you can appeal to in Ahmadinejad's view of geopolitics, of life in general, that would result in any kind of meaningful agreement with the West. I think Ahmadinejad sees himself as a man who is supposed to hasten the arrival of the Mahdi. He has even indicated that in his speeches. Ahmadinejad believes that the Mahdi will come as a result of his efforts, part of which includes destroying or at least subjugating Israel. And so I think the threat goes beyond just nuclear weapons. I think the threat really is a threat of growing Radicalism within Iran, which is influencing much of the thinking in the rest of the Islamic world. And ultimately, when a man is that driven — when a man is that convinced that Allah is holding him accountable to do that [destroy Judeo-Christian civilization] — I think to believe that we could negotiate with him in any meaningful way is just inane."

A Grand Finale

Is General Boykin correct?

Are Radical Islamic jihadists in general — and the Ahmadinejad regime in Iran in particular — actively seeking weapons of mass destruction and specifically nuclear weapons to destroy Western civilization and usher in the end of days?

Kamal Saleem certainly thinks so. "Ahmadinejad is in a race to create nuclear weapons," this former Lebanese terrorist — once a member of the Muslim Brotherhood — told me. "Ahmadinejad is a true Muslim zealot. You know in the Muslim world he is a hero. Why? Because he's fulfilling his duty to usher in the Mahdi. The Mahdi is the Muslim Messiah who would usher in a Muslim one-world order, which is ruled by one Muslim man. And that's his heart's desire. If you ask anybody on the street in the Middle East, they know this. But when you ask somebody in the United States of America about this, they have no clue. They don't know what Ahmadinejad is all about. It's world domination, to take over the world — one world order — that's it."[5]

Walid Shoebat agrees. "They want a grand finale," this former Palestinian terrorist told the producer of our *Epicenter* documentary film. "They don't want to simply put a bomb in a bus or in a mall. They want a grand finale; they want one operation that kind of cripples America once and for all — be it dirty bomb, or be it a real nuke."[6]

Porter Goss, director of the Central Intelligence Agency from 2004 through 2006, thinks so as well. "There's no question in my mind that Ahmadinejad and people in the military in Iran are seeking the Persian Bomb for military purposes," he told me as I researched this book. "If that is allowed to happen, we're talking about a nuclear weapon in the hands of a Radical. That would be a huge, huge watershed in the geopolitical world."[7]

"Will the CIA know when Iran has the Bomb *before* they use it?" I asked.

Goss was not so sure. Back in 1998, he noted, India and Pakistan stunned the world by testing nuclear weapons within days of each other when not a single Western intelligence agency — including the CIA — had any idea either country was so close to having the Bomb. Calling it "the biggest intelligence failure" in the CIA's history to that point, Goss warned that "the intelligence community had failed to give sufficient priority to the development of nuclear weapons by sovereign states. I think we had been lulled into the fraternity of the nuclear club and [into thinking] that the folks in the International Atomic Energy Agency had things under control and were doing their job effectively. It turned out not to be true."

"Could such a catastrophic intelligence failure happen again?" I asked. "Is it possible that the CIA and other U.S. and Western leaders might fundamentally misunderstand Iranian intentions and misread Iran's technological capabilities and suddenly be confronted with a nuclear-armed

Islamic regime well ahead of their current assessments?"

"Yes," Goss conceded, "there could be another surprise."

Alireza Jafarzadeh, a leading Iranian dissident who strongly opposes the Ahmadinejad regime, also believes Tehran is feverishly pursuing nuclear weapons. "This is the nightmare scenario," he told me when I interviewed him in 2008, "that the most Radical Islamic extremist regime — which is already the world's leading state sponsor of terrorism; which is now fully entrenched in the most violent way in Iraq, killing thousands of innocent people; which has called for wiping Israel off the map and an end to the United States; and which has this global Islamic rule agenda and believes in the end of the world — would now get the nuclear bomb."[8]

Jafarzadeh certainly knows what he's talking about. An outspoken advocate of a "non-nuclear, secular, democratic state" in the country of his birth, it was Jafarzadeh who on August 14, 2002, held a press conference in Washington to reveal the existence of two top secret Iranian nuclear weapons research facilities. Up to that point, both facilities — a uranium enrichment plant in Natanz, about 100 miles north of Isfahan, and a heavy-water uranium production plant in Arak, about 150 miles south of Tehran — were completely unknown to U.S. or Western intelligence agencies. But the existence and significance of both have now been confirmed by the CIA and the International Atomic Energy Agency (IAEA), intensifying Western fears that Iran is hiding advanced nuclear weapons research facilities and could be closer to the Bomb than previously

50

believed. During his 2002 news conference, Jafarzadeh also revealed that in a closed session of the Iranian regime's Supreme National Security Council earlier that year, it had been agreed that "access to [a] nuclear bomb is the most important guarantor of our survival and in case of having the bomb, the Western countries will not be able to block penetration and expansion of the Islamic Revolution."[9]

Senator John McCain is also deeply concerned about Iran's nuclear ambitions and the implications of the mullahs getting the Bomb. "There's only one thing worse than using the option of military action [to stop Iran], and that is the Iranians acquiring nuclear weapons," the Arizona Republican said on NBC's *Meet the Press* while gearing up to run for president. If Iran gets the Bomb, he said, "I think we could have Armageddon."[10]

The Clock Is Ticking

The bottom line: time is running out.

Western diplomatic efforts to persuade Tehran to abandon its feverish bid for nuclear weapons have not succeeded as of this writing. Nor have economic sanctions. By the fall of 2008, Iran claimed to have upwards of 6,000 operational centrifuges, sophisticated machines that can turn low-grade uranium into highly enriched, weapons-grade, bomb-making material.

Senior Israeli intelligence officials tell me they now fear Iran could have operational nuclear weapons by the end of 2009 or sometime in 2010. Senior U.S. intelligence and military officials tell me they think we have a bit more time. Some believe Iran will not have the Bomb until perhaps

2011. Others believe it could be as late as 2015.

Hopefully, those who say Iran is still quite a few years off from having nuclear weapons are right. But all the military and intelligence officials I interviewed for this book readily acknowledge that no one knows for certain how close Iran is to getting the "Islamic Bomb" and either holding hostage every power in the Middle East or actually carrying out their apocalyptic agenda.

In the end, it may not matter if U.S. and European intelligence analysts believe the world has more time before Iran gets the Bomb. It may not even matter if they are correct in their analysis. Why not? Because if the U.S. and NATO refuse to take military action to neutralize the Iranian nuclear threat, and if Israel thinks that time has run out, leaders in Jerusalem may feel as if they are in the same situation their fathers were in 1967.

Then, Israel's enemies threatened to "throw the Jews into the sea" while they amassed state-of-the-art military forces on the borders of the Jewish state. Israeli officials faced an existential threat, and they concluded that they had no choice but to launch a preemptive strike in the hopes of neutralizing, if not eliminating, that threat. If they waited to be attacked, they feared they could be hit so hard, so fast, with so much firepower that they could never recover. So strike they did. Miraculously, the war lasted only six days.

Today, Israel faces an even more dangerous scenario than that of 1967. If Iran's Ayatollah Khamenei and President Ahmadinejad are able to acquire nuclear warheads and attach them to the high-speed ballistic missiles already in their possession, they would be in a position to accomplish in about six minutes what it took Adolf Hitler nearly six years to do: kill six million Jews.

Israeli leaders may, therefore, choose a strategy similar to the one their predecessors chose in 1967. In this case, they may launch a massive air and missile strike against Iranian nuclear facilities, air bases, missile launchers, air defense systems, and possibly government offices and critical infrastructure facilities before Iran has the opportunity to strike Israel first.

Such a move may prove necessary in the end, but it could also set the whole region on fire. Israel could face hundreds of incoming retaliatory missiles from Iran as well as tens of thousands of incoming ballistic missiles and rockets from Syria, from Hezbollah in Lebanon, from Hamas in Gaza, and possibly from the West Bank, as well. Some of these missiles could be carrying chemical or biological warheads, even if the nuclear warheads in Iran were not in the picture. Ballistic missiles could also be fired from Iran at the oil fields in Saudi Arabia and the Gulf States, at oil tankers in the Persian Gulf and the Strait of Hormuz, and at U.S. bases and forces in Iraq. Thousands of suicide bomber cells could be activated in the region, particularly against Iraq and Israel. At the same time, sleeper terrorist cells could be activated in Western Europe, Canada, and the United States.

Meanwhile, terrorist efforts to topple pro-Western Middle Eastern leaders, such as Jordan's King Abdullah II and Egypt's President Hosni Mubarak, in favor of Radical Islamic regimes friendly to Tehran could also be set in motion. Amid such global carnage and chaos, oil prices could soar to $300 a barrel or more. U.S. gas prices could spike to $10 a gallon or more, with horrific domestic and international economic repercussions. Worst of all, tens of millions of innocent civilians could be caught in the cross fire of a war they don't want but cannot prevent.

The View from Jerusalem

General Moshe Ya'alon, former chief of staff of the Israeli Defense Forces, sees a major war with Iran coming soon because the West has been so feckless and unconvincing in confronting the regime in Tehran. When I met with him in his office in Jerusalem, he was clear and direct. "The confrontation with the Iranian regime is inevitable, and it is going to be a military one rather than a political one because of the lack of determination when it comes to the international community to deal with it [the Iranian threat] by political or economic means. And we can't avoid it, unless we are going to give up our way of life, our values, our culture."[11]

"How much time does the West have to make a decision about how to stop Iran?" I asked.

"When it comes to the Iranian military nuclear project," he said, "it is in terms of a couple of years — might be a couple of months."

That was March of 2007.

"Can the West successfully stop Iran?" I pressed.

It can, he insisted, if it gets serious — quickly. "In military terms, the Iranians are not so strong." The problem, he said, is that "the West has a lack of determination. There are few leaders today who really understand that we are engaged in World War III."

Like Generals Boykin and Ya'alon, former Israeli prime minister Benjamin Netanyahu is also worried about the rising Iranian nuclear threat and the West's inability or unwillingness thus far to confront the crisis effectively. And he, too, believes the day of reckoning is fast approaching.

"I think the West misunderstood, and still misunderstands, the threat of Radical Islam," he told me in his Tel Aviv office in March of 2007. "It is a fanatic, messianic ideology that seeks to have an apocalyptic battle for world supremacy with the West. It seeks to correct what its disciples see as an accident of history, where the West has risen and Islam has declined. The correction is supposed to be accomplished by the resurrection of an Islamic empire and the acquisition and use of nuclear weapons, if necessary, to obliterate Islam's enemies, and to subjugate the rest. This is a pathological ideology, much like Nazism was. And it poses a threat, in my judgment, in many ways bigger than Nazism because Hitler embarked on a world conflict and then sought to achieve nuclear weapons, whereas the leading radical Islamic regime, Iran, is seeking to first acquire nuclear weapons and then embark on a world conflict. And that is what is not yet understood in the West, and certainly, if it's understood, it's not acted upon.

"Once Iran has nuclear weapons," Netanyahu continued, "they could threaten the West in ways that are unimaginable today. They could take over the Persian Gulf on all its sides and take control of the oil reserves of the world, most of them. They could topple Saudi Arabia and Jordan in short order. And, of course, Iraq. All your internal debates in America on Iraq would be irrelevant, because nuclear-armed Iran would subordinate Iraq in two seconds. And, of course, they threaten

55

to create a second Holocaust in Israel and proceed on their idea of building a global empire, producing twenty-five atomic bombs a year — 250 bombs in a decade — with missiles that they are already working on, to reach the eastern seaboard of the United States. Everything else pales in comparison to this development. This has to be stopped."

How much time, I asked him, does the West have to act decisively to stop Iran?

"Not much," he replied. "We are running out of time. I can't tell you if it's a period of months or a few years. Certainly no more than a few years."[12]

CHAPTER TWO:
"ISLAM IS THE ANSWER; JIHAD IS THE WAY"

Who are the Radicals, and what do they want?

Over the course of researching this book, I read hundreds of books, speeches, articles, and Web sites written and produced by Radicals themselves. For weeks on end I would come out of my office at night and slump down at the kitchen table for dinner with my wife, Lynn, and our boys, feeling gloomy and depressed. When you read what the jihadists are actually saying and begin to comprehend the evil they have in their hearts, it is sobering to say the least.

But equally distressing, I have to say, is the fact that there are far too many in positions of American national leadership and in the media who either are not studying the Radicals carefully or simply are not taking them seriously. Inexplicably, they are stuck in a pre–9/11 mind-set and seem unwilling or unable to see or comprehend the dangers that lie just ahead.

In the midst of the 2008 presidential campaign, for example, Senator Barack Obama, the Illinois Democrat, made a shocking statement at a town hall in Oregon. He argued that Iran was a tiny country, not a "serious threat" to the United

57

States, Israel, or our allies in the Middle East. "I mean, think about it," he explained. "Iran, Cuba, Venezuela — these countries are tiny compared to the Soviet Union. They don't pose a serious threat to us the way the Soviet Union posed a threat to us. You know, Iran — they spend one one-hundredth of what we spend on the military."[1]

The press was stunned. American Jewish leaders were stunned. So were many supporters of Senator Obama. Was this a gaffe? Or did Obama actually believe that Iran was not a serious threat? Sen. John McCain, the Republican presidential candidate, sharply criticized his rival. "Such a statement betrays the depth of Senator Obama's inexperience and reckless judgment," he argued in an address in Obama's hometown of Chicago. "The threat the government of Iran poses is anything but tiny."[2]

The next day, Senator Obama did an about-face. He changed his tune during a speech in Billings, Montana. "Iran is a grave threat," he said, reading from a prepared text. "It has an illicit nuclear program. It supports terrorism across the region and militias in Iraq. It threatens Israel's existence. It denies the Holocaust."[3]

Obama's new statement certainly conformed to accepted international opinion. It echoed views expressed by Senator Hillary Rodham Clinton, the New York Democrat and Obama's chief rival at the time. It also echoed the views of then president Bush. But did it express what Senator Obama really believed? Had he misspoken one day and given his real view the next? Or was it possible that Obama's initial, unscripted comment in Oregon provided a more accurate window into how the forty-six-year-old political novice

58

truly viewed the Iranian nuclear threat?

If it is the latter, Obama would certainly not have been alone. The world is replete with skeptics about the Iranian leadership's intentions and capabilities, from diplomats to intelligence professionals, to academics, to journalists.

Russian foreign minister Sergey Lavrov, for example, insisted in 2007 that "North Korea poses a fundamental threat, but Iran does not."[4]

Scott Ritter, a former Marine Corps intelligence officer and former United Nations weapons inspector in Iraq, argued in 2007 that "Iran has never manifested itself as a serious threat to the national security of the United States, or by extension as a security threat to global security. . . . Iran as a nation represents absolutely no threat to the national security of the United States, or of its major allies in the region, including Israel."[5]

Nikki R. Keddie, history professor at the University of California at Los Angeles and author of *Modern Iran: Roots and Results of Revolution,* wrote in 2006 that "Ahmadinejad's statements have an audience in the Muslim world, perhaps even more than in Iran, but they do not mean that Iran intends aggressive acts. Ahmadinejad is far from insane."[6]

Ted Koppel, the former host of ABC's *Nightline,* has also belittled the Iranian nuclear threat. He even suggested — in a 2006 op-ed in the *New York Times,* no less — that the world should *allow* Iran to get the Bomb. "Washington should instead bow to the inevitable," he insisted. "If Iran is bound and determined to have nuclear weapons, let it."[7]

CNN founder Ted Turner went even further. "They [Iran] are a sovereign state — we have

59

28,000 [nuclear warheads] — why can't they have 10?" he argued in 2006. "They aren't usable by any sane person."[8]

What the Radicals Say They Want

Are such "experts" correct?

Should we permit the Radicals to have a nuclear weapon, or ten?

Before we do, it might be worth a closer examination of the ambitions of the Radicals in general and the Iranian regime in particular. After all, the Radicals are not shy about explaining their goals and rallying millions to help them accomplish those plans.

> "The governments of the world should know that . . . Islam will be victorious in all the countries of the world, and Islam and the teachings of the Qur'an will prevail all over the world." — *Ayatollah Ruhollah Khomeini in January 1979*[9]
>
> "We must strive to export our Revolution throughout the world." — *Ayatollah Khomeini on March 21, 1980*[10]
>
> "We don't shy away from declaring that Islam is ready to rule the world. . . . We must believe in the fact that Islam is not confined to geographical borders, ethnic groups, and nations. It's a universal ideology that leads the world to justice. . . . We must prepare ourselves to rule the world." — *Iranian president Mahmoud Ahmadinejad on January 5, 2006*[11]
>
> "I meet with you today . . . under the banner of the blessed awakening of the *Ummah* [Islamic nation] that is sweeping the

60

world. . . . The world's largest infidel military force [the Soviet Union] was destroyed. The myth of the superpower withered in the face of the Mujahideen's [Islamic jihadists] cries of 'God is great!' Today, we work from the same mountains to free the *Ummah* from the injustice that has been imposed on it by the Zionist-Crusader alliance . . . [and create] the forthcoming pan-Islamic state. . . . Our Lord, shatter our enemies, divide them among themselves, shake the earth under their feet, and give us control of them." — *Osama bin Laden on August 23, 1996*[12]

"We have ruled the world before, and by Allah, the day will come when we will rule the entire world again. The day will come when we will rule America. The day will come when we will rule Britain and the entire world." — *Sheikh Ibrahim Mudeiris, a leading Palestinian cleric in Gaza, on May 13, 2005*[13]

"Our mission: world domination" — *Slogan featured on the front page of a Muslim Brotherhood publication in London in 2001*[14]

Restoring the caliphate and building an Islamic empire that literally encompasses the entire globe is, without question, the expressed goal of the Radicals, be they Shia Muslims or Sunnis. It has been a goal since the seventh century, when Muhammad, whom Muslims revere as a prophet, walked the earth. But whereas once this notion was a dream — desired but far off — many Radicals now believe it is actually achievable as history, in their view, draws to a conclusion and the end of the world approaches.

In 1979, there were three countries that, in the

eyes of the Radicals, stood in the way of world domination: the Soviet Union, Israel, and the United States. The collapse of the U.S.S.R. on Christmas Day 1991 dramatically emboldened the Radicals. "One down, two to go," they reasoned, and Israel was widely perceived as the next target.

"It is the mission of the Islamic Republic of Iran to erase Israel from the map of the region." — *Iranian Supreme Leader Ayatollah Ali Khamenei in January 2001*[15]

"One bomb is enough to destroy Israel. . . . In due time the Islamic world will have a military nuclear device." — *Iranian president Rafsanjani in December 2001*[16]

"Rafsanjani Says Muslims Should Use Nuclear Weapon against Israel." — *Headline from the Iran Press Service, December 14, 2001*[17]

"Israel must be wiped off the map." — *Iranian president Mahmoud Ahmadinejad on October 26, 2005*[18]

"Like it or not, the Zionist regime is heading toward annihilation. . . . The Zionist regime is a rotten, dried tree that will be eliminated by one storm . . . [because] its existence has harmed the dignity of Islamic nations." — *Ahmadinejad on April 14, 2006*[19]

"I must announce that the Zionist regime [Israel], with a 60-year record of genocide, plunder, invasion, and betrayal is about to die and will soon be erased from the geographical scene." — *Mahmoud Ahmadinejad on June 2, 2008*[20]

"If they [Jews] all gather in Israel, it will save us the trouble of going after them worldwide." — *Hezbollah leader Sheikh Hassan Nasrallah on October 23, 2002, alluding to Shia Muslims' end times belief that it is God's will to create Israel briefly so that it can be destroyed*[21]

"One of the central reasons for creating Hizbullah was to challenge the Zionist program in the region. Hizbullah still preserves this principle, and when an Egyptian journalist visited me after the liberation and asked me if the destruction of Israel and the liberation of Palestine and Jerusalem were Hizbullah's goal, I replied: 'That is the principal objective of Hizbullah, and it is no less sacred than our [ultimate] goal.' " — *Sheikh Hassan Nasrallah in May 2000*[22]

"All spears should be directed at the Jews, at the enemies of Allah, the nation that was cursed in Allah's book. Allah has described them as apes and pigs, the calf-worshipers, idol-worshipers. . . . Whoever can fight them with his weapons, should go out [to the battle]. . . . Nothing will deter [the Jews] except for us voluntarily detonating ourselves in their midst. . . . We blow them up in Hadera, we blow them up in Tel Aviv and in Netanya, and in this way, Allah establishes us as rulers over these gangs of vagabonds." — *Palestinian Sheikh Ibrahim Madhi, Sheik 'Ijlin Mosque in Gaza on August 3, 2001*[23]

"Have no mercy on the Jews, no matter where they are, in any country. Fight them, wherever you are. Wherever you meet them, kill them. Wherever you are, kill those Jews and those Americans who are like them — and those who stand by them — they are all in

63

one trench, against the Arabs and the Muslims — because they established Israel here, in the beating heart of the Arab world, in Palestine." — *Dr. Ahmad Abu Halabiya preaching at a mosque in Gaza on October 13, 2000*[24]

Israel, however, is not the ultimate objective. In the eyes of most top Radical leaders, the Jewish state is the "Little Satan." The United States is considered the "Great Satan" and thus the most desired target.

"God willing, with the force of God behind it, we shall soon experience a world without the United States and Zionism." — *Mahmoud Ahmadinejad on October 26, 2005*[25]

"Today, the time for the fall of the satanic power of the United States has come, and the countdown to the annihilation of the emperor of power and wealth has started." — *Mahmoud Ahmadinejad on June 2, 2008, marking the nineteenth anniversary of the death of Ayatollah Khomeini*[26]

"Get ready for a world minus the U.S." — *Mahmoud Ahmadinejad on June 4, 2008*[27]

"The judgment to kill and fight Americans and their allies, whether civilian or military, is an obligation for every Muslim who is able to do so — in any country. In the name of Allah, we call upon every Muslim who believes in God and asks for forgiveness, to abide by God's order by killing Americans and stealing their money anywhere, anytime, and whenever possible." — *Osama bin Laden on February 2, 1998*[28]

"We now predict a black day for America —

and the end of the United States as the United States, God willing." — *Osama bin Laden interview with ABC News in May 1998*[29]

"We call on the Muslim nation . . . to prepare for the Jihad imposed by Allah and terrorize the enemy by preparing the force necessary. This should include a nuclear force." — *Osama bin Laden on May 14, 1998*[30]

"Let the entire world hear me. Our hostility to the Great Satan [America] is absolute. . . . I conclude my speech with the slogan that will continue to reverberate on all occasions so that nobody will think that we have weakened. Regardless of how the world has changed after 11 September, Death to America will remain our reverberating and powerful slogan. Death to America." — *Hezbollah leader Sheikh Hassan Nasrallah on September 27, 2002*[31]

"Allah willing, America will soon be annihilated, just like the USSR was annihilated. We are convinced of this. . . . Allah willing, we will reach America. The men of this nation will reach America." — *Muhammad Taher Al-Farouq, leader of the Islamic Movement of Uzbekistan, in a Web posting on December 3, 2007*[32]

"Allah will drown the little Pharaoh, the dwarf, the Pharaoh of all times, of our time, the American president. Allah will drown America in our seas, in our skies, in our land. . . . America will be destroyed." — *Sheikh Ibrahim Mudeiris, a leading Palestinian cleric in Gaza, on March 21, 2003*[33]

"Allah, destroy the U.S., its helpers and its agents." — *Sheikh Ikrimeh Sabri, the Islamic*

Note carefully the language of the leading Radicals. At this point in the Revolution — post-1979, and post–9/11 — the jihadists do not simply seek to frighten or terrorize the American people; they seek to utterly destroy them. They do not simply seek to repudiate or humiliate; they seek to annihilate.

How would such Radicals accomplish their mission? Both Iran's Shia leaders and al Qaeda's Sunni leaders are explicit: they will use any means necessary, including weapons of mass destruction and particularly nuclear weapons, should they become available.

In his manifesto published in 2001, *Knights under the Prophet's Banner,* Dr. Ayman al-Zawahiri, bin Laden's top deputy, made al Qaeda's strategy crystal clear: "Cause the greatest damage and inflict maximum casualties on the opponent, no matter how much time and effort these operations take, because this is the language understood by the West."[35]

In June 2002, Suleiman Abu Ghaith, a Kuwaiti-born spokesman for al Qaeda, went even further when he openly declared, "Al-Qa'ida has the right to kill four million Americans — two million of them children — and to exile twice as many and wound and cripple hundreds of thousands. Furthermore, it is our right to fight them with chemical and biological weapons."[36]

Even a cursory study of the statements made by leading Radicals leaves no doubt as to their motive. This, in turn, raises serious doubts about the knowledge, wisdom, and judgment of U.S. and foreign leaders, academics, and journalists who say such extremists pose no serious threat to Western security and that radicalized countries such as Iran should be permitted to acquire even one operational nuclear bomb or warhead, much less several or more. The risks are simply too great, the stakes too high.

The Roots of Their Rage

What accounts for such genocidal anger and ambition? What drives the Radicals to such ends, and what are the roots of such rage?

The answer, at its core, lies in the deep-seated feeling of shame, humiliation, failure, and impotence in the modern world that many Muslims feel today.

Once, the Islamic peoples were understandably considered the greatest military and economic powers on the planet. Muslim militaries and merchants spanned the globe and dominated nearly everywhere they went, from North Africa and Spain in the West to India, China, and ultimately Indonesia — today the most populous Muslim country in the world — in the East. Muslim armies and preachers penetrated deep into Africa in the south and far into Russia in the north. It was Muslims who controlled the great trading routes of gold and silver and silk and slaves from Asia to Europe. It was Muslims who brought India's system of mathematics to Europe. It was Muslims who led the world in science and medicine and architecture and music and literature and poetry for a thousand years or more.

Today, Islamic journalists, academics, and politicians themselves say that the Muslim world is best known for tyranny, abject poverty of all but the

67

elite, rampant corruption, violence, and terrorism. Despite the discovery of oil and fantastic wealth in Islamic territories, despite the rise of nationalism and the creation of nation-states after the departure of colonial Britain and France from the Middle East and North Africa, despite the widespread introduction of elementary and secondary schools and at least a basic education for hundreds of millions of children, the Islamic world at the dawn of the twenty-first century is mired in hopelessness and despair. The Muslim powers are not winning wars. The Muslim peoples are not making medical breakthroughs. They are not creating dramatic new technologies. Indeed, many Muslims note that their governments are barely able to feed their people or provide them with enough meaningful jobs.

"What is wrong with us? How did it all come to this?"

Such is the lament you hear in conversations among Muslims in the Middle East, in Europe, and throughout North America. It is the angst that comes across in innumerable speeches and books and blogs and e-mails that Muslims author these days.

Bernard Lewis, the noted Princeton University scholar on Islamic and Middle East history, has written two insightful and provocative books on this very subject.[37] In them, he makes the fascinating and quite compelling case that it was actually the early successes of the Muslims that planted the seeds of their own decline. When Islam was powerful and dominated the epicenter of the earth, travel through Muslim territories was treacherous and thus enormously costly for European traders. So the Europeans became

68

determined to find a way to circumvent the Islamic world altogether. Hoping to find a way around the Horn of Africa and on to India and East Asia, they began exploring sea routes that could take them south from England, France, Spain, and Portugal along the African coastlines.

Such long and arduous naval voyages required more of the Europeans — more education, more technology, more risk-taking. They required building better ships, creating more accurate maps, and developing navigational skills. They required crafting more precise weather instruments and developing a deeper understanding of meteorology. To protect their men and ships from pirates, bandits, and competing colonialists, the Europeans had to develop better weapons and war-fighting techniques and technologies as well.

There were many mistakes and failures, to be sure. But the Europeans proved persistent and resilient. Through long periods of trial and error, they developed an educational and technological infrastructure at home that enabled them to master the perilous seas and find their way east by sailing south. Eventually, Eastern wealth, spices, and other treasures returned to European nations via increasingly advanced shipping companies and navies.

The more European Christians worked to circumvent Middle Eastern Muslims, the more knowledge and experience was gained. They learned about gunpowder and explosives from the Chinese. They discovered medicines and herbal remedies throughout the Orient. They came back with new ideas and a thirst for further insights.

Success bred success. Innovation led to more innovation, and this spirit of exploration blazed across Europe, leading men like Christopher Columbus to sail west to get to the East. In time, wooden ships gave way to steel. Wind power gave way to steam. Steam propulsion gave way to engines using fossil fuels. The Wright brothers discovered flight. Then came jumbo jets and fighter jets. Oil- and gas-powered engines gave way to nuclear-powered submarines and aircraft carriers. Then came space travel. The Russians put a man in orbit. The Americans landed a man on the moon.

By the dawn of the third millennium, global travel was possible in a way never before known in human history. Knowledge was increasing exponentially. It all seemed to fulfill the words of the Hebrew prophet Daniel when he wrote that in the end of time, "many will go back and forth, and knowledge will increase" (Daniel 12:4).

The Islamic world was being left behind. Yet, for the better part of three hundred years, Muslims had no idea. They perceived themselves as the masters of the universe and Europeans as infidels and barbarians. They had little interest in noticing, examining, or caring about the tremendous advances in science and engineering that Western Christians were making. But eventually the invention and rapid spread of radio and television and global communications made it increasingly clear even to the uneducated masses within the Muslim world how enormous the gaps were between their world and the West.

And so a despondent cry has been rising from deep inside the Muslim world for the better part of a century, certainly ever since the collapse of the Ottoman Empire and the end of the Islamic caliphate in Istanbul, Turkey, in 1924.[38] This collective groaning intensified after the Arabs were defeated by Israel in 1948, 1956, 1967, and again in 1973. It seemed to reach a crescendo during the Islamic Revolution in Iran in 1979. It dramatically worsened in the wake of the 9/11 attacks, and now it has reached a deafening roar.

In an essay entitled "Islamic Failure," which he wrote for a British intellectual journal in February 2002, Pervez Amir Al Hoodbhoy — a leading Pakistani scientist and a professor of physics in Islamabad — decried the fact that "you will seldom see a Muslim name as you flip through scientific journals and, if you do, the chances are that this person lives in the West." Noting that "today's sorry situation contrasts starkly with the Islam of yesterday," Al Hoodbhoy pointed out that "between the ninth and thirteenth centuries — the golden age of Islam — the only people doing decent work in science, philosophy, or medicine were Muslims." But by the thirteenth century, "Islam choked," and "the rest of the world moved on." The Renaissance, Al Hoodbhoy observed, "brought an explosion of scientific inquiry in the West," and the Islamic world was left behind. "For Muslims, it is time to stop wallowing in self-pity: Muslims are not helpless victims of conspiracies hatched by an all-powerful malicious West. The fact is that the decline of Islamic greatness took place long before the age of mercantile imperialism. The causes were essentially internal. Therefore, Muslims must be introspective and ask, 'What went wrong?' "[39]

In a series of essays he wrote for an Arabic-language Web site in June 2003, Al-Afif al-Akhdar, a Tunisian Muslim journalist now living in exile in Paris, asked, "Why is it that the Arab world is so

71

wealthy in natural resources and poor in human resources? Why does human knowledge elsewhere steadily grow while in the Arab world what expands instead is illiteracy, ideological fear, and mental paralysis? Why do expressions of tolerance, moderation, rationalism, compromise, and negotiation horrify us, but [when we hear] fervent cries for vengeance, we all dance the war dance? . . . Why do other people love life, while we love death and violence, slaughter and suicide, and call it heroism and martyrdom?"[40]

In an article entitled "What's Wrong with the Arab World?" published in *The Arab American News* in January 2008, author Jamal Bittar wrote emotionally about "the deterioration of the political, social, and economic order in most countries in the Arab world" and the "self-made Arab failures" that were destroying the dreams and aspirations of millions. "Every regime in the Arab world has proved a failure," he concluded. "Not one has been able to provide its people with realistic hopes for a free and prosperous future. The regimes have found no way to respond to their people's frustration other than by a combination of internal oppression and propaganda to generate rage against external enemies. . . . What are the Arab leaders doing?"[41]

And it is not just reporters and academics who are asking these questions. Major political leaders in the region are asking as well. Consider, for example, the words of Pakistani president Pervez Musharraf, delivered in a stunningly frank address to senior Muslim officials from Muslim-majority countries at a conference on science and technology held in Islamabad in February 2002, not long after the 9/11 attacks: "Today we are the poorest, the most illiterate, the most backward, the most unhealthy, the most unenlightened, the most deprived, and the weakest of all the human race," Musharraf said.[42]

He noted that the *collective* gross national product of *all* Muslim countries stood at just $1.2 trillion, compared to Germany, whose GNP alone was $2.5 trillion at the time, and Japan, whose GNP was then $5.5 trillion. Why? One reason he cited was that "none of the Muslim countries had ever paid any [serious] attention to educational and scientific development."[43]

This was not a "Johnny-come-lately" revelation for Musharraf in hopes of placating the West with moderate language in the wake of al Qaeda's devastating attack on the U.S. This had been a theme of the Pakistani leader since he came to power in 1999. Indeed, in one of his first addresses to the 170 million Muslims in his country on October 17, 1999, Musharraf did not mince words:

Fifty-two years ago, we started with a beacon of hope, and today that beacon is no more and we stand in darkness. There is despondency and hopelessness surrounding us with no light visible anywhere around. The slide down has been gradual but has rapidly accelerated in the last many years. Today, we have reached a state where our economy has crumbled, our credibility is lost, state institutions lie demolished, provincial disharmony has caused cracks in the federation. . . . In sum, we have lost our honor, our dignity, our respect in the comity of nations. Is this the democracy [our leaders] had envisaged? Is this the way to enter the new

73

millennium?[44]

"The Setback"

Then came the rebirth of the State of Israel in 1948.

Three hundred million Muslims in the Middle East expected the Arab armies of Egypt, Syria, Jordan, Lebanon, and Iraq to strangle the newborn Jewish state in its crib. But when the relatively tiny Israeli army defeated the combined Arab armies, the growing sense of failure and humiliation Muslims were feeling only intensified. The 1956 showdown between Israel and Egypt, in which Israel not only survived but prevailed, further exacerbated Muslim shame and their sense of military impotence.

Then in June 1967 came a stunning and cataclysmic defeat for the Muslims known throughout the Arabic-speaking world as *an-Naksah,* "The Setback." In just six days, the Israelis more than tripled their land, regained the strategic Jordan Valley, gained the strategic Golan Heights, and reunified Jerusalem — without direct help from the Americans, the British, the French, or any other ally. How was this possible? the Islamic world wanted to know. How could Muslims lose to the "infidels"? The pain in the region was palpable, and the soul-searching accelerated.

For men like Yasser Arafat, the largely secular nationalist leader of the newly created (in 1964) Palestine Liberation Organization, the lesson of the Six-Day War was simple: *Don't trust the Arab dictators; rather, take measures into your own hands. Use guerrilla terrorist tactics to make the Jews suffer, fear, die, and eventually flee.* For many Arab Muslims also caught up in the spirit of nationalism that spread around the globe in the latter half of the twentieth century, this was a compelling and intoxicating diagnosis and prognosis. Arabs were failing, went the argument, because they were essentially outsourcing their own security. But the Arab dictators were betrayers. The only way to win was to sign up for the PLO's revolution and get into the fight oneself.

But there was another, competing analysis too. It was less prominent in the region at the time but nonetheless more compelling to many who heard it. Radical Islamic preachers argued that the Arabs were losing to the Jews — as well as failing in so many other areas of life — not because they were bad people or bad soldiers but because they were bad Muslims. They had wandered from the true path of Islam. They had become weak, even secularized. They had put their faith in the Arab states, not in God. Their only hope, these clerics argued, was for Muslims throughout the region to purify themselves, recommit themselves to Allah, and wage an Islamic jihad based on the principles of the Qur'an, not a secular political revolution based on the principles of Karl Marx, Gamal Abdel Nasser, or anyone else. Only then would Allah show them favor again. Only then would they regain the glory of their history. Only then would they regain their honor and their pride.

"I can tell you what the war of '67 did to the region," observed Essam Deraz, an Egyptian army reconnaissance officer at the time who would later join the mujahadeen (Islamic jihadists) in Afghanistan and fight with Osama bin Laden. "We saw the army of our country destroyed in hours. We thought that we could conquer Israel in hours. . . . It wasn't Israel that defeated us, but it was [Nasser's] regime that defeated us, and I started to be against the regime. It wasn't a military defeat. It became a civilizational defeat. We didn't know that we were so backward, we were so retarded, so behind the rest of modern civilization. There was an earthquake in the Arab-Islamic personality, not only in Egypt but in the entire Arab world."[45]

"Why were we defeated in 1967?" asked Sheik Yussef Al-Qaradhawi, head of the Islamic law faculty at Qatar University and a spiritual leader of the Muslim Brotherhood movement. "Officers stated that we had vast amounts of weapons, but we did not provide the warrior with mental preparation. We did not prepare him to fight for religious belief and for defending religious sanctuaries."[46]

It was precisely this conclusion that Dr. Ayman al-Zawahiri, himself an Egyptian, came to as well. And this was a central reason that in the aftermath of the "setback" of the Six-Day War he founded a terrorist organization known as Egyptian Islamic Jihad, which would later merge with bin Laden and al Qaeda. "[A] serious factor that affected the march of the Jihad movement [was] the 1967 setback," he would write. "The myth of the Leader of Arab Nationalism who would throw Israel into the sea was destroyed. . . . This movement spawned a new generation a few years after the 1967 defeat. This generation returned to the field of Jihad."[47]

Their Mantra

In 1973, Arab fortunes went from bad to worse.

The Israelis were nearly destroyed by a surprise attack from Egypt and Syria on Yom Kippur, the holiest day in Judaism. But with the help of a

76

round-the-clock American airlift of arms to the Israelis, the Jewish state decisively turned the tide. Soon, the Soviet-armed, -trained, and -supplied Arab forces were being routed and demanding a cease-fire at the United Nations. Their defeat further compounded the humiliation of secular Arab nationalists. But it simultaneously added fuel to the Radicals' argument.

As long as the Muslim world continues to embrace corrupt Arab dictators and refuses to return to the principles of the Qur'an and ways of violent jihad, they will never defeat the Zionists, the Radicals argued. *What could be more humiliating than losing to Jews again and again and again?* they taunted. *When will the Muslims learn and turn back to Allah?*

"We have arrived at the end of the world," warned Mohammed Taki al Moudarrissi, an Iraqi-born Shia terrorist leader operating out of his headquarters in Tehran, as the Radical movement was gaining strength. "The presidents and the ministers [in the Islamic world] are devouring themselves. The armies are traitors. Society is corrupt. The privileged, the notables do not concern themselves with the poor. Only Islam can give us hope."[48]

"We must wipe away the shameful stain whereby some people imagine that violence has no place in Islam," concluded Muhammad Taghi Mesbah Yazdi, a high-ranking Iranian cleric who would later become a spiritual advisor to Mahmoud Ahmadinejad. "We have decided and are determined to argue and prove that violence is at the heart of Islam."[49]

In a fatwa (religious ruling) issued by an Islamic conference in Sudan, Hassan al-Turabi, Sudan's spiritual leader, declared, "Those Muslims

77

who . . . try to question or doubt the Islamic justifiability of jihad are hereby classified as 'hypocrites' who are no longer Muslims, and also 'apostates' from the religion of Islam; and they will be condemned permanently to the fire of Hell."[50]

More and more, Muslims in the region began listening to the Radical preachers and shifting their allegiances away from what they saw as reprobate politicians. The jihadist movement was growing, and they now had a mantra, which was in essence: *"Islam is the answer, and jihad is the way."*

This mantra was repeated across the Middle East from Egypt to Iran, among Sunnis and Shias alike, and it spread like wildfire. The slogan of the Muslim Brotherhood — emblazoned on its literature and publications — became "Allah is our objective. The Prophet is our leader. [The] Qur'an is our law. Jihad is our way. Dying in the way of Allah is our highest hope."[51] Al-Zawahiri fanned the flames, writing one manifesto after another that declared, "There is no solution without Jihad"[52] and "the only solution is to confront the tyranny . . . and perform Jihad in the Path of Allah. We shall only be able to live in honor if we learn how to die as martyrs."[53]

But what changed the fortunes of the Radicals was not Sunni strategists like those in the Muslim Brotherhood and Egyptian Islamic Jihad. What poured gas on the fire and changed the destiny of the modern Middle East — and the history of the Western world — forever was the rise of an obscure Shia cleric in Iran by the name of Ruhollah Musavi Khomeini, who declared, "By means of *Jihad,* [we] must expose and overthrow tyran-

78

nical rulers." It was not just a threat. It was a promise.

In chapter four, we will examine Khomeini's dramatic rise to power and the effect it had on Radicals throughout the region. First, however, it is important to better understand just what the Radicals believe theologically and how these beliefs drive them to use violence to achieve their objectives.

CHAPTER THREE:
THE THEOLOGY OF THE RADICALS

What they believe, verse by verse

On September 17, 2001, just six days after the horrific terrorist attacks that killed nearly three thousand Americans, President George W. Bush traveled in a heavily guarded motorcade to the Islamic Center of Washington, D.C. There he made a statement to reporters that would be carried across the nation and around the world.

"The face of terror is not the true faith of Islam," said the president, surrounded by an extraordinary phalanx of well-armed and highly alert Secret Service agents. "That's not what Islam is all about. Islam is peace. These terrorists don't represent peace. They represent evil and war. When we think of Islam, we think of a faith that brings comfort to a billion people around the world. Billions of people find comfort and solace and peace."

The president went on to note that "America counts millions of Muslims amongst our citizens, and Muslims make an incredibly valuable contribution to our country. Muslims are doctors, lawyers, law professors, members of the military, entrepreneurs, shopkeepers, moms and dads. And they need to be treated with respect. In our anger and emotion, our fellow Americans must treat each other with respect."[1]

Three days later, the president told a joint session of Congress that "the terrorists are traitors to their own faith, trying, in effect, to hijack Islam itself."

During a November 15, 2001, message to American Muslims in celebration of Ramadan, the president stated unequivocally that "the Islam that we know is a faith devoted to the worship of one God, as revealed through the Holy Qur'an" and "teaches the value and the importance of charity, mercy, and peace."

The following year, during a discussion with Muslim leaders at the Embassy of Afghanistan in Washington, D.C., the president reiterated, "All Americans must recognize that the face of terror is not the true face of Islam. Islam is a faith that brings comfort to a billion people around the world. It's a faith that has made brothers and sisters of every race. It's a faith based upon love, not hate."[2]

During a November 2003 press conference, Bush was asked, "Mr. President, when you talk about peace in the Middle East, you've often said that freedom is granted by the Almighty. Some people who share your beliefs don't believe that Muslims worship the same Almighty. I wonder about your views on that." The president replied, "I do say that freedom is the Almighty's gift to every person. I also condition it by saying freedom is not America's gift to the world. It's much greater than that, of course. And I believe we worship the same God."[3]

These were not anomalies. President Bush

continued to describe Islam as a religion of peace throughout his tenure in office and argued consistently that the Radicals were "hijacking" true Islam.

And he was not alone. Other Western leaders have made similar arguments. British prime minister Tony Blair, for example, often discussed the "monumental struggle going on worldwide between those who believe in democracy and moderation, and forces of reaction and extremism" and insisted that the "forces of extremism" were basing their convictions regarding jihad against the West "on a warped and wrongheaded misinterpretation of Islam."[4]

Likewise, French president Nicolas Sarkozy argued that "those who kill in the name of Islam and want to push the world into a global religious war smear Islam by speaking its name."[5]

A Religion of Peace, or of Jihad?
Such statements have been enormously controversial in the West.

So let me be clear about my own views: The vast majority of the 1.3 billion Muslims on the planet are not Radicals. They do not believe in waging jihad against the West. They do not condone sending their sons and daughters to be suicide bombers to kill Christians, Jews, and apostate Muslims, among others. They do not want to annihilate Judeo-Christian civilization as we know it or take over the world. They are, by and large, quiet, peaceful people. They want to raise their children in decent schools to get decent jobs and live respectable, productive, God-honoring lives.

Second, Western leaders should be commended

— not condemned — for affirming the peaceful nature of most Muslims. Why insult Muslims who are unengaged in jihad?

Third, critics should keep in mind that Western leaders are making these points, in part, both to build and to strengthen political and military alliances with government leaders throughout the Muslim world who are willing to side with Western governments against the Radicals.

That said, let us now consider the central question. While it is certainly accurate to say that the vast majority of Muslims are peaceful *people,* is it also true that Islam itself is an intrinsically peaceful *religion?* In other words, are Muslim and Western leaders accurate in asserting that Islam is a religion of peace, not a religion that calls for jihad against the infidels? Are the Radicals, in fact, "hijacking" Islam and in the process "smearing" its good name? If so, how can the Radicals claim that "Islam is the answer, and jihad is the way" if there is no basis for their beliefs in the Qur'an, the guidebook for all Muslims?

In Part 2 of this book, I will explain the moderates' case in detail. I will give the Reformers the opportunity to explain in their own words the theology that drives them and the verses in the Qur'an they use to justify their notion that Islam is a religion of peace, not violence. But for the moment, let us examine the case the Radicals make, consider the theology that drives them, and learn the verses from the Qur'an and other Islamic writings that inspire them to wage jihad.

Greater Jihad Versus Lesser Jihad
Many Islamic scholars teach that there are two different forms of jihad. There are, therefore, two

different definitions of jihad. One is considered the "greater" form; the other is the "lesser" form. This dual nature is attributed to Muhammad himself, who is believed to have said on his return from a battle, "We are finished with the lesser jihad; now we are starting the greater jihad," although this saying was not recorded in the Qur'an.[6]

To these scholars, Greater Jihad — also known as "inner jihad" — represents the highest and most important form. It can best be defined as a spiritual and intellectual striving to do the will of Allah and abstain from sin and temptation. It is, in other words, an internal battle or "holy war" against one's sinful nature, and it can be a fierce battle at that. It is to many Muslims the most important form of jihad because it involves a daily, ongoing, never-ending battle between the Muslim and his all-too-human desires to lie, steal, commit adultery, or commit other forms of sin.

Islamic theology teaches that a person can go to heaven only if his good deeds outweigh his sinful deeds. Waging an effective jihad against one's sinful nature is thus a matter of eternal life and death. Sura 29:6 of the Qur'an, for example, teaches that whoever "strives hard" or wages jihad against his carnal nature "strives for the good of his own soul." Likewise, speaking in Sura 29:69, Allah assures the reader that "those who strive hard for Our sake, We will most certainly guide them to Our ways. Most assuredly, God is with those devoted to doing good, aware that God is seeing them."

This, then, is the peaceful version of jihad. It is the one many Muslims point to in saying that Westerners misunderstand the notion of jihad.

When my first novel, *The Last Jihad,* was published in November 2002, I was speaking at an event at the Tattered Cover, a major independent bookstore in Denver, Colorado. During the Q&A session, a Muslim man from the Middle East stood up and chastised me for misusing the word *jihad.* It did not, he insisted, signify a violent man-versus-man battle between Muslims and the infidels. Rather, it spoke of a man-versus-himself conflict regarding purification and self-control. I appreciated his comments and readily conceded that this was certainly one of the definitions of jihad. But it is not the only one.

Lesser Jihad — also known as "outer jihad" — can best be defined as Muslims using violent means or "holy war" to accomplish the will of Allah in punishing infidels and expanding the kingdom of Allah on earth. To many Muslim scholars, this form of pleasing Allah, while vitally important, is not as important as the Greater Jihad or "inner jihad." Nevertheless, as I explained to the man in Denver along with the rest of the audience that was listening in on our discussion, it is this definition — violence in Allah's service — that Radicals such as the Ayatollah Khomeini, Osama bin Laden, and others have used to justify their actions.

The Radicals also use this definition to persuade members of the Islamic Rank-and-File — particularly young people — to join their movement and engage in the Revolution. This form of violent jihad is particularly critical, according to one form of Muslim eschatology, in the end of days as the Day of Judgment approaches, something I will explain in more detail in chapter twelve, which discusses the coming of the Islamic messiah known as the Mahdi.

Even a brief survey of the writings and speeches of Radicals reveals numerous citations of verses from the Qur'an, some taken out of context. Consider the following passages, which Radicals draw upon to call Muslims to violent action:

"Prescribed for you is fighting, though it is disliked by you. It may well be that you dislike a thing but it is good for you." — *Sura 2:216*

"[Jews and Christians] are the ones whom God has cursed, and he whom God excludes from His mercy, you shall never find one to help and save him." — *Sura 4:52*

"The recompense of those who fight against God and His Messenger . . . they shall either be executed, or crucified, or have their hands and feet cut off alternately, or be banished from the land." — *Sura 5:33*

"O you who believe! Take not the Jews and Christians for guardians and confidants. . . . Surely God does not guide such wrongdoers." — *Sura 5:51*

"Kill them [infidels, namely Christians and Jews] wherever you may come upon them, and seize them, and confine them, and lie in wait for them at every conceivable place." — *Sura 9:5*

"Fight with the leaders of unbelief." — *Sura 9:12*

"Fight against those among the People of the Book who do not believe God and the Last Day . . . until they pay the *jizyah* (tax of protection and exemption from military service) with a willing hand in a state of submission. And those Jews say, 'Ezra is God's son'; and the Christians say: 'The Messiah is God's son.' . . . May God destroy them!" — *Sura 9:29–30*

"For those who disbelieve, garments of fire are certain to be cut out for them, with boiling water being poured down over their heads, with which all that is within their bodies, as well as their skins, is melted away." — *Sura 22:19–20*

"Pay no heed to (the desires of) the unbelievers, but engage in a mighty striving against them." — *Sura 25:52*

"When you meet those who disbelieve in war, smite them at their necks." — *Sura 47:4*

Regarding enemies, "God only forbids you . . . to take them for friends and guardians. Whoever takes them for friends and guardians, those are the wrongdoers." — *Sura 60:9*

"O Prophet! Strive hard against the unbelievers and the hypocrites, and be stern against them. Their final refuge is Hell." — *Sura 66:9*

Clearly, then, according to the Radicals, the Qur'an is adamant about certain things:

- Violence is good.
- Jews and Christians are cursed and are not supposed to be helped or saved or befriended.
- Actually, Jews and Christians are to be killed — whenever and wherever Muslims find them — because they are loathsome, filled with evil, and destined for hell.
- Infidels can (and sometimes should) be

crucified, beheaded, have their hands and feet cut off, or tortured in all manner of ways.

Radicals and the Hadiths

The Qur'an is not the only source of inspiration and justification for the Radicals. They also draw on the "hadiths" — the sayings of Muhammad and oral traditions of the events of his life that were collected and written down for posterity by several of his devoted followers. Douglas Streusand, a respected scholar of Islamic history, has noted that "in hadith collections, jihad means armed action; for example, the 199 references to jihad in the most standard collection of hadiths — *Sahih al-Bukhari* — all assume that jihad means warfare."[7]

The collection Streusand was referring to is the writings of Muhammad ibn Ismail al-Bukhari, who in the ninth century recorded one of the six most trusted Sunni collections of hadiths. (Shias have separate collections.) Al-Bukhari recorded, for example, one of the Radicals' most often quoted passages, in which Muhammad said, "The Hour [of the end of days] will not be established until you fight with the Jews, and the stone behind which a Jew will be hiding will say, 'O Muslim! There is a Jew hiding behind me, so kill him' " (Bukhari, 52:177).

Sunan Abu Dawud recorded another of the six most trusted Sunni collections of hadiths, including a passage central to Radical theology: "Jihad will be performed continuously since the day Allah sent me as a prophet until the day the last member of my community will fight with the Dajjal (Muslim version of the Antichrist)" (Abu Dawud, 14:2526).

In 1968, shortly after Egypt's crushing defeat to Israel in the Six-Day War, Sheikh Muhammad Abu-Zahra — a Radical theologian based at al-Azhar University, the Harvard of the Sunni world, located in a suburb of Cairo — used this verse to urge Muslims around the world to follow the path of jihad, not the path of Arab nationalism, to realize their dreams and ambitions, and to never surrender. "Jihad will never end," he declared, drawing inspiration from the hadiths. "It will last to the Day of Judgment."[8]

To what extent do these teachings influence the way young Muslims view the world in general and the Jews in particular? Consider what Walid Shoebat, a one-time Palestinian Radical and author of *Why I Left Jihad,* told the producer of the *Epicenter* documentary film:

We learned many things about the Jewish people in the [Islamic] school and the religious curriculum. [We were taught that] the Jews first of all were prophet killers, the Jews spread disease, the Jews put infertility drugs [in the water supply] for the Palestinians so they'll not have children, the Jews caused tsunamis, the Jews run the Congress, the Jews own the media, the Jews created the protocols of the elders of Zion. Everything under the sun was always accused towards what is called international Zionism, which has its tentacles all over the whole globe in which they influence the West and they run America, and they run Europe and they run everything. So basically, that the Jew was a conspirator that needs to be destroyed and eliminated. And then the eschatological teaching in the Islamic studies

89

department focused [on] the Jews gathering in Israel and the surrounding nations [so that] the Muslims [could] attack them [more easily]. And then the trees will cry out and the stars will come out — there is a Jew hiding behind me; come, O Muslim, come and kill him. That's a well-known thing in all our schools that we learn. So the elimination of the Jew finally will happen in Israel, and it will be carried out by the Muslims. And this is what we see — [Iranian president] Ahmadinejad calling for the destruction of Israel, [Hezbollah leader Hassan] Nasrallah calling for the destruction of Israel. All of a sudden the fantasy has become reality. All of a sudden they are carrying out this eschatological dogma that is being taught all over the Middle East to fruition, when you see Nasrallah and his military war machine marching with goose steps on the streets of Beirut and all over Lebanon, exactly as the Nazis were doing, you know, the same gestures of Nazis. . . . What has been a dream to us and what we've learned in the schools have all of a sudden become real. And what that does, it builds the confidence for the Muslims, that this is not a dream anymore; this is real. So the confidence level builds up in Iran, the confidence level builds up in Lebanon, the confidence level builds up among the Palestinians [that we will] force the Jews to leave Israel.

It should be noted that some prominent Radicals completely reject the notion of the two different forms and definitions of jihad. They insist there is only one definition: violent action to advance Allah's kingdom. For example, Abdullah Azzam, a Palestinian cleric who was an early intellectual mentor to Osama bin Laden, once wrote, "The saying, 'We have returned from the lesser jihad (battle) to the greater jihad (jihad of the soul)' which people quote on the basis that it is a hadith, is in fact a false, fabricated hadith which has no basis. It is only a saying of Ibrahim Ibn Abi 'Abalah, one of the Successors [of Muhammad], and it contradicts textual evidence and reality. . . . The word *jihad*, when mentioned on its own, only means combat with weapons. . . . Jihad is the zenith of Islam. . . . Jihad today is individually obligatory by self and wealth, on every Muslim, and the Islamic community remains sinful until the last piece of Islamic land is freed from the hands of the Disbelievers, nor are any absolved from the sin other than the Mujahideen [wagers of jihad]." Azzam went on to write that violent jihad "is a collective act of worship."[9]

The Ayatollah Khomeini, however, was one who both believed in the concepts of inner jihad and outer jihad and taught them to his disciples. Indeed, during one nationally televised sermon he delivered after returning to Iran in February 1979, Khomeini told the millions of Iranians watching him, "Those who engaged in jihad in the first age of Islam advanced and pushed forward without any regard for themselves or their personal desires, for they had earlier waged a jihad against their selves. Without the inner jihad, the outer jihad is impossible. Jihad is inconceivable unless a person turns his back on his own desires and the world."[10]

91

Radicals and Assurance of Salvation

Religiously driven Radicals believe their violent actions will bless their families and neighbors. They believe that the only way of economic, political, and social salvation for the Muslim *Ummah*, or Islamic nation at large, is to return to the purest form of obedience to the teachings of Muhammad as expressed through the Qur'an and the hadiths. If Muhammad tells them to kill infidels, then they want to obey faithfully because they believe only then will Allah once again show mercy on the Muslim people and once and for all establish a global Islamic government to complete all of human history.

But Radicals are not driven simply by a desire to bless all Muslims. They are also driven by the belief that obedience to the way of jihad is the only path to personal salvation.

As you study the Qur'an, you will find that Islam is a works-based religion. Therefore, Radicals — and all religious Muslims who take the Qur'an seriously — constantly have to be thinking about a "51 percent solution." They must constantly strive to do more good works than bad, lest they be damned for eternity.

The problem is that the Qur'an does not provide a way for Muslims to assess how they are doing throughout their lives. There are no quarterly report cards. There are no annual performance reviews. How, then, can a Muslim — Radical or otherwise — know for certain whether he will go to heaven? How can he find the assurance of salvation that every thoughtful soul seeks *before* death? This lack of clarity about the quality of their earthly performance — and thus the lack of assurance of their eternal salvation — is a source of great angst, fear, and insecurity for many Muslims, Sunnis and Shias alike.

To better understand this works-based salvation system, consider the following verses from the Qur'an:

"Every soul is bound to taste death. So you will be repaid in full on the Day of Resurrection (for whatever you have done in the world). Whoever is spared the Fire and admitted to Paradise has indeed prospered and triumphed . . . if you are patient, steadfast, and keep within the limits of piety." — *Sura 3:185–186*

"God has promised those who believe and do good, righteous deeds that for them is forgiveness and a tremendous reward." — *Sura 5:9*

"O you who believe! If you keep from disobedience to God in reverence for Him and piety to deserve His protection, He will . . . blot out from you your evil deeds, and forgive you." — *Sura 8:29*

"He responds with acceptance to those who believe and do good, righteous deeds. . . . However, as to the unbelievers, for them is a severe punishment." — *Sura 42:26*

"We will set up balances of absolute justice on the Day of Resurrection, and no person will be wronged in the least. Even though it be a deed so much as the weight of a grain of mustard seed, We will bring it forth to be weighed. We suffice as reckoners." — *Sura 21:47*

"Those whose scales (of good deeds) are heavy, they are prosperous, while those

93

whose scales (of good deeds) are light, they will be those who have ruined their own selves, in Hell abiding. The Fire will scorch their faces, their lips being displaced and their jaws protruding." — *Sura 23:102–104*

These last two verses give us a clear image of the divine scales of justice. On the Day of Judgment, Islamic theology teaches, Allah weighs a Muslim's good deeds and bad deeds and determines who will spend eternity in paradise and who will be cast into the fires of hell to be punished and tortured for all of eternity. It should not be surprising, therefore, that Radicals — who at their core are purists — take the verses about waging jihad and killing infidels very seriously. Why shouldn't they? To disregard the command to jihad would be to disobey, and such disobedience could tip the scales of justice against them in the final reckoning.

But continue with this theological logic for a moment. Even if a Muslim is fully obedient to the command to wage jihad, this alone is not a *guarantee* of eternal salvation. According to the Qur'an, it adds more deeds to the "good" side of the scales. But what if a Muslim's life before becoming a jihadist was filled with sin? What if he commits sins during his time waging jihad? What if he commits sins that he does not even fully realize he is committing? Or what if certain sins weigh more heavily than certain good deeds? The truth is, even a fully devoted follower of jihad knows in his heart of hearts — if he is truly honest with himself — that he will not know for sure if his good works will tip the scales in his favor until the Day of Judgment itself. But who wants to wait until then? That really is gambling with one's eternal security.

Which brings us to the only way in the theology of the Radicals that a Muslim can be sure of his eternal destiny.

The Supremacy of Martyrdom

Radicals believe the only true assurance or secure promise of eternal salvation for a Muslim is to be a martyr — and ideally a suicide bomber — in the cause of jihad.

"The call to Jihad in God's name," wrote Osama bin Laden and his colleagues in 1984 in the first issue of their recruiting magazine, *Jihad,* "leads to eternal life in the end, and is relief from your earthly chains."[11]

"A martyr will not feel the pain of death except like how you feel when you are pinched," bin Laden told his followers in 1996 in his formal declaration of war against the United States. "A martyr's privileges are guaranteed by God; forgiveness with the first gush of his blood, he will be shown his seat in Paradise, he will be decorated with the jewels of [belief], married off to the beautiful ones . . . assured security in the Day of Judgment . . . [and] wedded to seventy-two of the pure [virgin women of Paradise]."[12]

Bin Laden went on to assert that "without shedding of blood, no degradation and branding can be removed from the forehead."[13]

Put another way, bin Laden both believes and preaches that if a Muslim sheds his blood and loses his life in the cause of jihad, then he will have all his bad deeds removed from the scales. What's more, he uses the concept of the assurance of salvation through martyrdom as a recruiting tool, offering hope to Muslims who fear hell more than death.

Bin Laden is not the only one preaching this. Many Radicals do.

"Blessings to those who wage [jihad] with their body," proclaims Sheikh Ibrahim Mudeiris, a leading Radical preacher in Gaza. "Blessings to our *Shahids* [martyrs] who sacrifice their souls easily for the sake of Allah. . . . Blessings to the happy *Shahids* within the entrails of the green bird in Paradise. Blessings to the *Shahids* whose sins are forgiven with the first drop of their blood."[14]

Some clerics go even further and argue that a martyr not only attains his own forgiveness and eternal salvation but can save the souls of as many as seventy of his family members. "The martyr, if he meets Allah, is forgiven with the first drop of blood," proclaims Sheikh Isma'il Aal Radhwan, another leading Radical preacher in Gaza. "He is saved from the torments of the grave; he sees his place in Paradise; he is saved from the Great Horror [of the Day of Judgment]; he is given seventy-two black-eyed women; he vouches for seventy of his family to be accepted to Paradise; he is crowned with the Crown of glory, whose precious stone is better than all of this world and what is in it."[15]

To be clear, the Qur'an does not actually promise seventy-two virgins to suicide bombers and other martyrs. The number seventy-two comes from various sayings ascribed to Muhammad that were recorded by ancient Islamic scholars. Still, there are verses in the Qur'an that bin Laden and other Radicals cite to make their point. Among them:

"As for those who are killed in God's cause, He [Allah] will never render their deeds vain. He will guide them. . . . He will admit them into Paradise that He has made known to them." — *Sura 47:4–6*

"For him who lives in awe of his Lord and of standing before his Lord [in the Hereafter], there will be two Gardens. . . . Reclining on beds lined with silk . . . are pure, chaste-eyed spouses whom no man or Jinn [devil] has touched before . . . maidens good in character and beautiful . . . pure maidens assigned for them in secluded pavilions." — *Sura 55:46, 54, 56, 70, 72*

"For the God-revering pious there will surely be triumph: Gardens and vineyards, and youthful, full-breasted maidens of equal age, and a cup [of wine] full to the brim. . . . A reward from your Lord, a gift according to [His] reckoning in full satisfaction." — *Sura 78:31–36*

"WWMD?"

What would Muhammad do?

That is the question the Radicals are asking. A casual examination of the Qur'an and the hadiths reveals that Muhammad commanded his followers to wage violent holy war in the name of Allah against infidels, be they Jews, Christians, idol worshipers, apostate Muslims, agnostics, atheists, or others who refused to confess that "Islam is the answer, and jihad is the way." Muhammad conducted such wars during his lifetime. His disciples after him did so as well. It should not be surprising, therefore, that Radicals are waging the very

97

jihad to which they are commanded in their sacred writings.

"Allah wanted Muhammad's life to be a model," noted Sheik Yussef Al-Qaradhawi, head of the Islamic law faculty at Qatar University and a spiritual leader of the Muslim Brotherhood movement, just a few months before the 9/11 attacks in the United States. "Allah has made the prophet Muhammad into an epitome for religious warriors since he ordered Muhammad to fight for religion." By contrast, the scholar noted, "the Christian is incapable of imitating Jesus regarding war . . . since Jesus never fought."[16]

Chapter Four:
"We Were Asleep"

How Washington missed the Iranian Revolution

On November 15, 1977, President Jimmy Carter hosted the shah of Iran, Mohammad Reza Pahlavi, and his wife, Empress Farah, at a sumptuous state reception on the South Lawn of the White House. Despite thousands of Iranian students protesting outside the White House gates, denouncing the shah's human rights abuses and restrictions on personal freedom in the country of their birth, the president spoke warmly of his "close personal friendship" with the shah and called Iran "an island of stability" in the Middle East, reflecting on the personal and strategic ties between the two men and the nations they led.[1]

Carter was the eighth American president to know the shah personally. The first was Franklin Delano Roosevelt, who had met the Persian monarch in the Iranian capital of Tehran in 1943 at a summit with Josef Stalin and Winston Churchill, seeking a way to stop Adolf Hitler and his Nazi war machine, which was rampaging through Europe and the Middle East.

Since that summit and the subsequent conclusion of World War II, Iran had emerged as a key

99

and trusted ally of the United States and the Western alliance, as a bulwark against Soviet expansionism in the Middle East, and as a major supplier of oil to American industries and families. Washington feared Moscow's desire to seize the oil fields of the Middle East and control the Persian Gulf and the oil shipping routes to the West. It was a fear the shah and his top advisors shared. They had no desire to become a Kremlin satellite, so they turned to the Americans for help, and Washington readily responded.

Over the next three decades, the U.S. sold Iran advanced American fighter jets, naval assets, and all manner of others arms, in addition to a state-of-the-art radar system to safeguard Iranian airspace from Soviet bombers. The U.S. also trained Iranian pilots and built several intelligence-gathering outposts in the northern mountains of Iran, designed to track Soviet missile tests and intercept Soviet military communications. During the coldest years of the Cold War, the relationship with Tehran was one the White House and the Pentagon valued deeply.

In December of 1977, merely a month after hosting the shah and his wife at the White House, President Carter and his wife, Rosalyn, accepted the shah's reciprocal invitation to visit Tehran. Moments after Air Force One touched down in Tehran on New Year's Eve, the president restated on Iranian television what he had expressed to the people of the United States.

"Iran is an island of stability in one of the more troubled areas of the world," Carter said without any apparent reservation and without any sense of what was coming. "This is a great tribute to you, Your Majesty, and to your leadership and to the respect, admiration, and love which your people give to you."[2]

A year later, the shah's regime had been toppled, the Pahlavi family had fled into exile, a radical Islamic jihadist was in power and in command of billions of dollars' worth of advanced American weaponry, and oil had stopped flowing into the U.S. from Iran.

And top officials in Washington had not seen it coming.

"We knew there was some resentment [to the shah]," Carter's national security advisor, Zbigniew Brzezinski, would later comment. "We knew somewhat of the history of the country, but we were not conscious, nor were we informed, of the intensity of the feelings."[3]

How was that possible? How could the best and brightest minds in the White House, State Department, and Central Intelligence Agency have missed the lead-up to the Islamic Revolution in Iran? And thirty years later, is it possible that Washington could miss the danger rising in Iran once again?

Seeds of the Revolution

It was not hard to find evidence of anti-shah sentiment building in Iran in the mid-1970s. Ruhollah Khomeini, the fiery Shia Islamic cleric widely known as "the ayatollah," had been railing against the shah for decades at that point, often from exile in Turkey, Iraq, or France.

First and foremost, Khomeini despised the fact that since ascending to the throne in 1941, the shah had sought to turn Iran into a modern, pro-Western society. For several decades the shah appeared to be trying to follow the secular demo-

101

cratic reforms set into motion in Turkey by Mustafa Ataturk, who founded and built the modern Turkish state following the collapse of the Islamic caliphate in Istanbul in the early 1920s. Like Ataturk, the shah banned women from wearing Islamic veils, required men to wear Western clothes in all government offices, permitted women to enroll in classes at Tehran University, and gave women the right to vote.[4] In October 1962, the shah did away with the requirements that candidates for political office had to be men and had to be Muslims. Khomeini vehemently protested the shah's move and worked closely with clerics and their followers around the country to push for the Islamic requirements to be reinstated.[5] Eventually they were, but the tensions between Khomeini and the shah only intensified.

"The Shah . . . has embarked on the destruction of Islam in Iran," warned Khomeini. "I will oppose this as long as the blood circulates in my veins."[6]

In nearly every sermon and in almost every book and article that he wrote, Khomeini denounced the shah as a traitor to Islam and a betrayer of the Iranian people, and he found he was touching a nerve. The more forcefully he preached against the shah's regime, the more Iranians responded to his message and called for change. As the number of Khomeini's followers increased dramatically in the early 1970s, the shah grew increasingly worried. He feared an Islamist movement that could topple his regime — or at the very least destabilize it — was rising. So he began moving in the opposite direction, rolling back some of his earlier democratic reforms and restricting personal freedoms. In March 1975, for example, the shah ended Iran's multiparty democracy and imposed a one-party system — his own.[7] When students and other dissidents protested, the shah cracked down, using the police to attack crowds with water cannons and tear gas. He used his secret police force, known as SAVAK, to round up, interrogate, and at times torture political opponents.

The following year, in an attempt to appeal to Persian nationalism and put the Islamic fundamentalists in their place, the shah unilaterally abolished the use of the Islamic (lunar) calendar and instead required Iranians to use the Persian calendar that had been developed under the reign of Persian leader Cyrus the Great.[8]

The move backfired. Increasingly, the shah was perceived as a cruel dictator rather than the benevolent monarch that had long been his public persona. Khomeini's anger, meanwhile, was growing, and more and more Iranians were paying attention. "He is against the Islamic calendar," railed the ayatollah during a February 1978 speech. "To be against the Islamic calendar is to be against Islam itself. In fact the worst thing that this man has done during his reign is to change the calendar."[9]

Targeting Christians and Jews

Khomeini and his followers had other grievances beyond the shah's hostility toward their brand of Radical Islam. They despised, for example, his overt alliance with the United States, the epicenter of modern Christendom in their eyes, and his barely disguised alliance with Israel, the epicenter of Judaism. Israel, after all, was a "Little Satan" in their eyes, while the U.S. was the "Great Satan." Yet the shah was doing business with both.

As early as 1951, the shah began permitting Iraqi Jews to emigrate to the newly formed Jewish state through direct — though secret — flights from Tehran to Tel Aviv.[10] Iran under the shah sold and shipped oil to Israel. The shah bought fighter jets from Israel. He also allowed Israeli fighter pilots to train jointly with Iranian pilots. What was more, from 1961 to 1978, every Israeli prime minister from David Ben-Gurion to Menachem Begin visited Tehran and met directly with the shah.[11]

All this made the Radicals apoplectic. "Our wretched people subsist in conditions of poverty and hunger, while the taxes that the ruling class extorts from them are squandered," Khomeini bellowed during one speech. "They [the shah and his advisors] buy Phantom jets so that pilots from Israel and its agents can come and train in them in our country. So extensive is the influence of Israel in our country — Israel, which is in a state of war with the Muslims, so that those who support it are likewise in a state of war with the Muslims — and so great is the support the regimes gives it, that Israeli soldiers come to our country for training! Our country has become a base for them!"[12]

By October 1964, the alliance between the U.S. and Iran had become so strong and so vital to the Iranian economy and military that the shah gave American military advisors and their families, as well as technical and administrative staff, legal immunity for any and all criminal offenses they might commit in Iranian territory. To Khomeini, this smacked of American imperialism. No longer was Iran a sovereign, strong, respectable country, he argued. It was now subservient to its Washington master.

"They [the shah and his advisors] have reduced the Iranian people to a level lower than that of an American dog," cried Khomeini during a speech in Qom, Iran, on October 27, 1964. "If someone runs over a dog belonging to an American, he will be prosecuted. Even if the Shah himself were to run over a dog belonging to an American, he would be prosecuted. But if an American cook runs over the Shah, the head of state, no one will have the right to interfere with him. . . . The government has sold our independence, reduced us to the level of a colony, and made the Muslim nation of Iran appear more backward than savages in the eyes of the world! . . . This is high treason!"[13]

And Khomeini was just warming up. "Muslim peoples! Leaders of the Muslim peoples — come to our aid! Are we to be trampled underfoot by the boots of America simply because we are a weak nation and have no dollars? . . . Let the American president know that in the eyes of the Iranian people, he is the most repulsive member of the human race today because of the injustice he has imposed on our Muslim nation. Today the Qur'an has become his enemy, the Iranian nation has become his enemy! . . . All of our troubles today are caused by America and Israel. . . . O God, remedy the affairs of the Moslems! O God, bestow dignity on this sacred religion of Islam! O God, destroy those individuals who are traitors to this land, who are traitors to Islam, who are traitors to the Qur'an."[14]

Khomeini's words infuriated the shah. Rather than allow the ayatollah to denounce his policies right under his nose, the shah proceeded to have

105

Khomeini arrested and deported from the country.

Once Khomeini was gone, the shah accelerated and intensified Iran's ties to the U.S. in the years that followed, culminating in January 1978, when President Carter granted Iran "most favored nation" status to increase U.S.-Iranian trade.[15]

To the ayatollah in exile — and his followers inside Iran — the trade deal exemplified the very core of the problem. They did not want to be seen as favored by the infidels in the United States. They had had enough. They desperately wanted a confrontation with the U.S. and the shah, and they were about to get both. "We are fighting against America," Khomeini said bluntly. "Soon the whole nation will realize that this Shah is an American agent."[16]

The Gathering Storm

On February 18, 1978, antigovernment protests — encouraged by Khomeini and his allies — broke out in the Iranian city of Tabriz. Iranian security forces attacked the protestors, and many were killed and wounded.

Ten days later, during a speech in the Iraqi Shia capital of Najaf, Khomeini denounced "the criminal massacres and bloodshed that have taken place in Tabriz" and called on Allah and the people to "remove the evil of the oppressors," noting, "the people of Iran have chosen their path, and they will not rest until they have overthrown these criminals and avenged themselves and their fathers on this bloodthirsty family."[17]

On March 29, anti-shah demonstrations broke out not in one Iranian city but in fifty-five.

By May 10, violent demonstrations had spread

to an additional twenty-four cities. The shah ordered the army to restore order using tanks and tear gas.

Several senior Shia clerics in Tehran called for people to engage in "peaceful demonstrations" that would not provoke the shah's forces. Many listened. There was a surge in commercial and educational strikes throughout the country. Merchants sympathetic to the Revolution refused to open their shops for business on days specified by Khomeini's grassroots leaders, while the Rank-and-File members of the Revolution refused to shop at stores that did open their doors. On certain days, parents were told by Khomeini activists not to send their children to school, while growing legions of university students stopped attending classes, held anti-shah rallies, and handed out anti-shah leaflets throughout their campuses and their cities.

The ayatollah himself, however, did not approve of the notion of peaceful demonstrations. He wanted a direct confrontation, and he urged his followers to overthrow the "pagan regime." Ever larger anti-shah demonstrations quickly followed.[18]

August 19, 1978, was a turning point. Someone set fire to the Cinema Rex movie theater in the petroleum port city of Abadan. While it was clearly a case of arson, it is not clear to this day who was responsible. But the impact was horrific. Some 377 people were killed, and many suspected the shah's secret police forces of setting the blaze. News of the fire and conspiracy theories about SAVAK's involvement spread like wildfire throughout the country. On August 21, Khomeini delivered a speech in which he directly accused "the criminal hand" of the shah's "tyrannical regime" of setting the fire and murdering those within. "Lighting a ring of fire around the cinema and then having its doors locked by the cinema staff was something only the authorities had the power to do," Khomeini said in the city of Najaf.[19]

Tens of thousands — and then hundreds of thousands — of enraged Iranians soon began pouring into the streets, denouncing the shah and his regime and calling for the immediate return of the ayatollah. As the riots spread from city to city, people began throwing Molotov cocktails at the police, and the police fired back. Over the course of the next few months, an estimated three thousand Iranian protestors were killed by the forces of the shah.[20]

Incredibly, however, that same August CIA Director Stansfield Turner's top Iran experts were telling him that "the Shah would survive another ten years."[21] Worse, the CIA sent a written analysis to President Carter arguing that Iran "is not in a revolutionary or even a prerevolutionary situation."[22]

Gary Sick, a staffer on the Carter National Security Council as the Iranian Revolution began, would later admit that "the notion of a popular [Islamic] revolution leading to the establishment of a theocratic state seemed so unlikely as to be absurd."[23]

Ken Pollack, a Middle East specialist on President Clinton's National Security Council, would later concede that "virtually all of the Iran experts in Washington . . . believed that the Shah would be able to weather the storm."[24]

New York Times intelligence correspondent Tim

Weiner, in his 2007 book, *Legacy of Ashes: The History of the CIA,* concluded after years of research that "the idea that religion would prove to be a compelling political force in the late twentieth century was incomprehensible" to Washington officials at the time and that "few at the CIA believed that an ancient cleric could seize power and proclaim Iran an Islamic republic."[25]

Mark Bowden, the award-winning journalist and author of *Black Hawk Down* and *Guests of the Ayatollah: The First Battle in America's War with Militant Islam,* drew a similar, sobering conclusion after years of his own research: "By 1978, the Peacock Throne was teetering. Not that American intelligence and military assessments realized it; it was uniformly predicted that the shah would weather the storm. What the Western intelligence reports missed was the awakening giant of traditional Islam, a grassroots rebellion against the values of the secular, modern world. The rise of Khomeini and the mullahocracy took everyone by surprise."[26]

The Crescendo

Despite Washington insiders' unconcern and the CIA's bizarre take on the situation, on September 7, more than a half million Iranians demonstrated in the streets of Tehran, shouting "Death to the Pahlavis!" and "Khomeini is our leader!" and "We want an Islamic Republic!" and "America out of Iran!"

The next day, the shah imposed martial law. Iranian security forces attacked a crowd of five thousand in a southern section of Tehran. An estimated two hundred demonstrators were killed, and hundreds more were wounded in this attack

109

and others like it throughout the capital.[27]

It is true that such police violence against the protestors only intensified sympathy and support for Khomeini and his followers, dramatically enlarging their base of support. But it is also true that many Iranians read the police's actions, which could have been far worse, as a sign that the shah did not have the stomach to slaughter his enemies. Many had fully expected the police to massacre everyone in sight. The fact that the response, while aggressive, was not as aggressive as it could have been — and certainly not as aggressive as other Middle Eastern dictators had been against enemies of the regime throughout the centuries — was quickly perceived by Khomeini's followers as evidence of the shah's weakness and the beginning of the end for the monarch and the "Peacock Throne."

On November 26, more than a million people turned out for a demonstration in Tehran against the shah and his regime. On December 10 and 11, upwards of nine million Iranians — well over a quarter of the population — demonstrated and rioted around the country in what one historian has dubbed "the largest protest event in history."[28]

As the uprising reached its crescendo, the shah could read the handwriting on the wall. His day was over. The day of the Ayatollah Khomeini had begun. The only question now was whether the shah wanted to wait to be captured by Khomeini's crowds and executed in public or flee the country while there was still time. On January 16, 1979, the shah made his choice. Exactly one year after President Carter declared Iran "an island of stability" and just five months after the CIA's top Iran analysts had concluded the shah would last

110

another ten years, Mohammad Reza Pahlavi, his wife, and their three children fled Iran into exile, traveling first to Egypt and then to Morocco.

"The Holy One Has Come!"

On February 1, 1979, the Revolution came home. The chartered Air France 747 touched down in Tehran at Mehrabad International Airport at precisely 9:33 a.m. local time and was immediately greeted by a rapturous welcome. An estimated fifty thousand Iranians had converged on the terminal, tarmac, and grounds, some weeping, some wailing, all desperate to get a glimpse of the man they suspected might, in fact, be the Twelfth Imam they had so long awaited.

"The holy one has come!" the crowds chanted as the Ayatollah Khomeini, tall and slender with a long gray beard and dark, brooding eyes, draped in black robes and his signature black turban, stepped out into the morning air. Now seventy-eight, he looked somewhat tired at first, even tearful, as he waved a bit feebly to the cheering throngs. But as the roars grew and people screamed, "He is the light of our lives!" the firebrand seemed to draw energy and resolve from the crowd.[29] The shah was gone, Khomeini was back, and the country was his for the taking.

As he descended the stairs to the tarmac below, the crowd began to chant, "Khomeini, O Imam! Khomeini, O Imam!" and *Allahu akbar,"* or "God is great!"

"A personality cult was in the making," the head of the BBC's Persian broadcasting service would later write. "Khomeini had been transformed into a semi-divine figure. He was no longer a grand ayatollah and deputy of the Imam, one who

111

represents the Hidden Imam, but simply 'The Imam.' In Arabic [and Sunni theology and common usage], the term "Imam" is used to describe a leader or prayer leader, but in Shi'i Iran, where the title was reserved for the twelve infallible leaders of the early Shi'a, among ordinary people it carried awe-inspiring connotations. In encouraging its use, some of Khomeini's supporters clearly wanted to exploit popular religious feelings and to imply that he was the long-awaited Hidden Imam."[30]

And Khomeini certainly did nothing to discourage the people from thinking he was the One.

"I thank the various classes of the nation for the feelings they have expressed toward me," Khomeini said in remarks broadcast around the country. "The debt of gratitude I owe to the Iranian people weighs heavily upon my shoulders, and I can in no way repay it." Then, in an ominous foreshadowing of events still ten months away, Khomeini added, "Our triumph will come when all forms of foreign control have been brought to an end and all roots of the monarchy have been plucked out of the soil of our land. The agents of the foreigners during the recent events have been trying desperately to restore the Shah to power. . . . I say that their efforts are in vain. . . . Unity of purpose is the secret of victory. Let us not lose this secret by permitting demons in human form to create dissension in the ranks."[31]

The massive crowd went wild.

Iranian security forces had never seen anything like it. But this was only the beginning.

What really terrified the security people were the quarter of a million Iranians waiting at Khomeini's next stop, a cemetery for Islamic martyrs, and the estimated five million more frenzied Shia Muslims lining the roads from the airport into the heart of Tehran.[32] More than one in seven people living in Iran at the time turned out to catch a glimpse of their new leader. The security officials knew they could not afford to allow the leader of the Revolution to be swallowed up and crushed by the unprecedented crowds. The country had already been through so much.

They had to change their plans. As *Time* magazine would later report, "the crush stalled the Ayatollah's motorcade, so that he had to be lifted out of the crowds, over the heads of his adulators, by helicopter."[33]

"This Is the First Day of God's Government"

On February 14, 1979 — just two weeks after the Ayatollah Khomeini had returned to Iran — 150 or so Islamic Radicals stunned American officials by storming the U.S. Embassy compound in Tehran and taking hostages. It was a tense and terrifying time for the nearly one thousand diplomats, Marines, and support staff who had already witnessed more than a year of massive demonstrations, riots, and violent anti-shah and anti-American protests.

Fortunately, the situation had a happy ending. Only a few hours after it began, the Radicals — under pressure from Khomeini loyalists — released their hostages and retreated from the embassy grounds. Breathing a sigh of relief, the staff referred to the incident as the "St. Valentine's Day Open House."

But events in Iran were clearly going from bad to worse, and the State Department recalled most of its diplomatic team, leaving fewer than seventy

113

employees on site.

The Central Intelligence Agency, however, did not seem troubled. "Don't worry about another embassy attack," the chief of the Iran branch in the CIA's Directorate of Operations in Langley, Virginia, calmly assured his team back in Tehran. "The Iranians have already done it once so they don't have to prove anything. Besides, the only thing that could trigger an attack would be if the Shah was let into the States — and no one in this town is stupid enough to do that."[34]

Actually, that wasn't quite true.

Within days of the release of the hostages, Khomeini named a provisional prime minister to run the day-to-day affairs of state and moved quickly to authorize a national referendum that would change the very nature of the Iranian system of government from a constitutional monarchy to a nation governed by Sharia law. On March 30 and 31, millions of Iranians went to the polls, and then, on April 1, 1979, Khomeini officially announced that the referendum had passed overwhelmingly, with 97 percent of the vote. Iran was now the first true Islamic Republic in the history of the world.

"I declare to the whole world that never has the history of Iran witnessed such a referendum," Khomeini noted that day from his home in Qom, "where the whole country rushed to the polls with ardor, enthusiasm, and love to cast their affirmative votes and bury the tyrannical regime forever in the garbage heap of history. . . . By casting a decisive vote in favor of the Islamic Republic, you have established a government of divine justice, a government in which all the segments of the population shall enjoy equal consideration, the

114

light of divine justice shall shine uniformly on all, and the divine mercy of the Qur'an . . . shall embrace all, like life-giving rain. . . . Tyranny has been buried. . . . This day [is] the first day of God's government."[35]

The Fuse Is Lit

In January, the shah and his family had settled briefly in Morocco after fleeing into exile, but that did not last long. By March, King Hassan was growing increasingly worried that Islamic Radicals might use the shah's presence as an excuse to launch violent attacks inside his kingdom or even attempt to overthrow his regime. He asked the shah to leave.

Without much choice, the Pahlavis flew to the Bahamas, then to Mexico. By October, however, the shah had been diagnosed with malignant lymphoma. His body was beginning to shut down, and his doctors worried that without better treatment he might not live more than eighteen months. On October 22, President Carter agreed to allow the shah and his wife entry into the U.S. for medical treatment. The next day, they arrived. But neither the president nor his top aides fully appreciated the fuse they were lighting or the firestorm that was coming.

Khomeini had just called on "all grade-school, university, and theological students to increase their attacks against America."[36] A second embassy takeover plot was already in advanced planning stages by a group of university students eager to play their part in the Revolution, and now the students' leaders felt they had two critical elements for success. First, they had a blessing from their Supreme Leader to strike the "Great Satan,"

115

indirect though that blessing was since Khomeini at that point was not even aware of their plans. Second, they had a perfect pretext to strike since Iranians throughout the country were deeply outraged by Carter's decision to show hospitality to a man they felt was a traitor to Islam and thus worthy of death.

On November 1, more than two million Iranians demonstrated at Tehran University, not far from the embassy grounds, shouting, *"Death to America! Death to America!"* What more incentive did they need, the plot leaders surmised, than the fact that the Imam and his people were with them?

That same day, U.S. National Security Advisor Zbigniew Brzezinski met secretly with Iranian prime minister Mehdi Bazargan. His deputy, Robert Gates — who would later become the director of central intelligence under President Bush 41 and the secretary of defense under President Bush 43 — was in the meeting.

"Brzezinski flew to Algiers to represent the United States at the twenty-fifth anniversary of the Algerian revolution," Gates later recalled. "I accompanied him. It was an extraordinary experience. A highlight of the celebrations was a reception for the foreign guests and a lavish banquet. The reception was an intelligence officer's dream come true. All the principal thugs in the world were present — Assad of Syria, Qaddafi of Libya, Yasir Arafat of the PLO, General Giap of Vietnam, Admiral Gorshkov of the Soviet Navy — and a remarkable collection of lesser-known terrorists, guerrilla leaders, and representatives of various liberation movements."

When Brzezinski received word that the Iranian delegation wanted to meet with him, he agreed, taking Gates along to the meeting as a note-taker. Recalled Gates, "Our hosts were Prime Minister Bazargan, a wizened little guy with wisps of white hair floating around his head; Foreign Minister Ibrahim Yazdi; and Defense Minister Mustafa Ali Chamran. Their greeting and the tone of the entire meeting were surprisingly friendly under the circumstances."[37]

What happened next is astounding. In a stunning display of the Carter administration's complete lack of understanding of the forces they were dealing with, Brzezinski told Iran's new prime minister that the U.S. government was ready to find a way to work together and actually offered to sell the Radicals new weapons systems. "[Brzezinski] assured them of American acceptance of their revolution," Gates observed, "discussed the reality of a common foe in their Soviet neighbor to the north, the need to cooperate on security matters relating to the Soviets, and left open the possibility of resuming military sales."

Brzezinski confirmed all this in his own memoirs, noting that he specifically promised not to try to overthrow Khomeini's regime but rather to work closely with the ayatollah and his team. "I made the point that the United States was not engaged in, nor would it encourage, conspiracies against the new Iranian regime," he wrote. He further recalled that he said specifically to Bazargan, "We are prepared for any relationship you want. . . . The American government is prepared to expand security, economic, political, and intelligence relationships at your pace."[38]

Bazargan apparently did not laugh, but he might as well have. To say he was not impressed with the "Great Satan's" offer would be putting it mildly.

117

The prime minister insisted the U.S. hand over the shah for trial in Iran. Brzezinski said no. There were many ways the two governments could co-operate, he replied, but "to return the Shah to you would be incompatible with our national honor."[39]

News of the secret meeting leaked the next day. Back in Iran, anti-American sentiment — already red-hot — erupted. Iranians were enraged by the notion that their prime minister was even in the same room with, much less talking to, a top White House official.

Incredibly, however, few in Washington sensed imminent danger. On Saturday, November 3, President Carter went fishing up at Camp David, apparently oblivious to the enormous damage that was about to be done to America's "national honor."[40]

The Explosion

Dawn had not yet broken in Washington.

It was Sunday morning, November 4, when an urgent "Flash Traffic" message from Embassy Tehran arrived in the State Department's top secret communications center: "Demonstrators have entered embassy compound and have entered the building."[41]

More than three thousand Radicals, most of them students, had climbed over the embassy's walls, penetrated the compound's internal security fences and doors, disarmed the Marines (who had been ordered by their superiors not to shoot), and were holding sixty-six Americans hostage while rifling through whatever files they could get their

118

hands on.*

Staffers in the White House Situation Room immediately awoke the president at Camp David with a phone call at 4:30 a.m. The president spoke with Brzezinski, just back from Algiers, and Secretary of State Cyrus Vance. Both were concerned, to be sure, but neither was overly worried, believing the situation would be corrected quickly, as it had been on Valentine's Day. The president, therefore, went back to sleep. It was the last half-decent sleep Carter would get until after he left office on January 20, 1981.

U.S. intelligence officials soon had a translated copy of the students' first communiqué, which blasted "the world-devouring America" and stated, "We Muslim students, followers of the Imam Khomeini, have occupied the espionage embassy of America in protest against the ploys of the imperialists and the Zionists. We announce our protest to the world; a protest against America for granting asylum and employing the criminal shah while it has its hands in the blood of tens of thousands of women and men in this country."[42]

Top officials at the CIA and State all expected Khomeini to order the students to free the Americans and their compound in short order. It never happened.

To the contrary, the ayatollah quickly issued a statement praising the students. He then appointed his son, Ahmad, to serve as the liaison

*Initially, sixty-six U.S. Embassy staffers were taken hostage. Thirteen women and African-Americans were released in late November. One hostage was released in July 1980 for seriously declining health. The remaining fifty-two hostages spent a total of 444 days in captivity.

with the students holding the embassy.

Ahmad would later write that his father expected "thunder and lightning" from Washington, a quick and fierce military operation that would both rescue the embassy staffers and punish the new regime. But weeks turned into months without such a response. Instead, in Ahmad's view, the Carter White House churned out feckless, limp-wristed statements and showed no serious interest in a military confrontation. President Carter's envoy to the United Nations, Ambassador Andrew Young, publicly implored the ayatollah to show "magnanimity and compassion."

Khomeini smelled weakness. He mocked the Carter administration as acting "like a headless chicken," and exploited Carter's indecision to the fullest.[43]

Humiliation

For well over a year, fifty-two American citizens were subjected to torture, interrogation, and all manner of physical and psychological abuse at the hands of Islamic Radicals.

Some of the hostages were blindfolded and paraded before the Iranian media in pictures that would be flashed around the world. Others were repeatedly kicked and beaten. Some had guns put to their heads while students threatened to blow their brains out if they did not open safes or answer questions. At other times, the students played Russian roulette with them. At one point, a group of students forced a diplomat to the floor. One pulled out a knife, positioned it mere centimeters from the diplomat's face, and threatened to cut out his eyes, one by one, if he refused to divulge classified information. And all the while, the Ayatollah Khomeini gave his full approval to such activities, and his son oversaw the terrorists' day-to-day operations.

Back home, Americans felt a growing sense of humiliation and outrage as they saw the crisis in Iran play out on the evening news night after night with seemingly no light at the end of the tunnel. Most people did not understand the motivation of the Radicals who had seized the embassy or the ayatollah whom they apparently worshiped. Nor did they understand why President Carter looked so weak in the face of such a serious threat to U.S. national security. All they saw were millions of Iranians chanting, "Death to America! Death to Israel!" and violent, fanatical mobs burning the American flag and burning President Carter in effigy. As the crisis worsened, Carter's approval rating plummeted to a mere 25 percent.

Muslims around the world — Sunnis and Shias alike — were stunned by such a dramatic turn of events. Radicals were energized. Reformers were horrified.

Officials in Washington were stupefied. In less than a year, the White House, the State Department, and the Central Intelligence Agency had missed the Islamic Revolution in Iran, the rise of Khomeini, the fall of the shah, and the takeover of the U.S.'s own embassy in a country central to its national security and sharing a 1,600-mile border with the Soviet Union.

Admiral Stansfield Turner, the director of the Central Intelligence Agency under President Carter, would later admit in his memoirs, "We in the CIA served the president . . . badly with respect to our coverage of the Iranian scene. . . . We had not appreciated how shaky the Shah's political foundation was; did not know the Shah was terminally ill; did not understand who Khomeini was and the support his movement had; did not have a clue as to who the hostage-takers were or what their objective was; and could not pinpoint within the embassy where the hostages were being held and under what conditions. . . . We were just plain asleep."[44]

CHAPTER FIVE:
TRAGEDY AT DESERT ONE

The inside story of Delta Force's
attempt to rescue the hostages

Delta Force had been in existence for only two years.

After watching Radicals throughout the Middle East and Europe hijack civilian jetliners, blow up buses and elementary schools, murder Israeli hostages at the Munich Olympic Games, and bomb U.S. military bases and other sensitive Western installations throughout the early 1970s, Colonel Charlie Beckwith, Delta's legendary creator and longtime commander, had fashioned the Army's new, elite, top secret counterterrorist unit after the highly successful British Special Air Services (SAS). Beckwith had long believed the American military — a leader in air supremacy and massive ground operations — was woefully unprepared for a new age of terrorism, and he had all but begged his superiors to give him a shot at creating an answer. But neither Beckwith nor any of his men had any idea how quickly they would be needed.

On the eve of the embassy takeover, Delta's operators were undergoing their final evaluation by the Pentagon's top brass to be declared operationally ready for duty. Jerry Boykin, a founding member of the force, described for me that fateful day.

"On the fourth of November, we had just finished our evaluation and were declared prepared by a group of evaluators. Some of the guys went out to celebrate. But having not slept for nearly seventy-two hours, I crashed in a deep and desperately needed sleep. Suddenly, someone was shaking me and saying, 'Jerry, Jerry, can you hear me?' I thought I was dreaming. When they finally woke me up, they told me the Embassy had been seized and Americans had been taken hostage."[1]

Beckwith regathered his Delta operators and sent them to the Farm, a top secret CIA training facility, to rest up and await further instructions. Then he told Boykin to head to D.C. with him to start planning a possible rescue operation.

"It was my first ever visit to the Pentagon," Boykin recalled. "And I must tell you there was just a sense of disbelief — disbelief that these Radicals would again seize hostages in an American embassy, which by international law is U.S. sovereign territory. And no one really understood at that point that we were seeing the beginning of the Islamic Revolution. No one really understood the nature of the threat that we were up against."

On November 8, Beckwith and Boykin were taken into Room 2C840, a highly secure war planning room in the Pentagon, where they met Secretary of Defense Harold Brown, Joint Chiefs chairman David Jones, the rest of the service chiefs, and several intelligence specialists.

"What do we know? What kind of intel do we have?" Secretary Brown asked.

124

The answer: very little.

"Who, exactly, are the hostage-takers, and what do they want?" Brown pressed.

Again, the intel was sketchy at best. It was clear Iranian students were involved and that they were loyal to Khomeini. But their demands were unclear, and no one in the Pentagon knew if they had outside help.

"Has the Iranian government made any public statements?" asked Chairman Jones.

Yet again, he was told there was little to go on.

On and on it went. There were far more questions than answers, and the questions were daunting, to say the least.

What kind of aircraft might they use to mount a rescue operation? Planes, helicopters, or both?

How many would be needed?

How would they refuel?

Where would they land?

How would they penetrate Iranian airspace undetected?

Would they need fighter jet escorts?

Once in the country, how would the Delta operators actually get to the embassy? The hostages were, after all, being held in the heart of Tehran, deep inside the center of the country, hours from Turkey, Iraq, Afghanistan, or an aircraft carrier operating in the Persian Gulf.

And Tehran wasn't exactly a friendly city. Delta would be heading into a city of five million people, all of whom hated America and would love nothing more than to kill American military forces who were "invading" their capital.

Were all the hostages being held at the embassy, or were they being moved around the city?

How many guards were holding them?

What kind of arms did they use?

How often did they rotate the guards?

Each question generated dozens more. But there was one question that haunted the men in that room more than any other: what would they do tomorrow or next week or next month if the Iranians began executing the hostages one by one?

Operation Eagle Claw

In his extraordinary book *Guests of the Ayatollah*, journalist Mark Bowden cites a list of requirements and conditions one of Boykin's colleagues wrote down at the time, describing just how challenging was their task. Among the requirements: "Enter Tehran undetected"; "Breach the embassy and rescue the hostages"; "Don't hurt any civilians"; and "Do not permit the Iranian forces to be aware of or react to our presence." Among the conditions: "No country will help you"; "The entire training program must be kept secret"; and "The entire operation must take place in darkness."[2]

The task was overwhelming. But Beckwith, Boykin, and their men had no other choice. No one had much confidence that the diplomacy of the Carter administration would be able to resolve the crisis peacefully. Even given their limited understanding of radical Islam at the time, they realized that the ayatollah was a jihadist at heart and was loving every moment of his standoff with the "Great Satan." Delta had to be ready, and they had to deliver. So much was on the line.

Soon, a concept emerged. It was code-named Operation Eagle Claw.

"As we started our planning," Boykin explained to me, "the first thing we looked for was who in the region would support us. We had hoped that Turkey would, but Turkey chose not to. We had hoped that Pakistan would, but Pakistan made the same decision. It was only Egypt and Oman that agreed to support us in the region, so we had to launch our operation from one of those two places.

"As it turned out, we launched from Oman. Our plan was to fly our assault troops — roughly a hundred Delta, with some support from the Rangers — on Air Force C141 Starlifters from a base in Wadi Kena, Egypt, to Masirah, Oman. Then we would put everyone on C-130 Talons [enormous Army cargo planes] and secretly fly into a location about a hundred miles from Tehran, where we would offload in the desert in a remote spot known as Dasht-e-Kavir.

"Meanwhile, eight empty RH-53D Sea Stallion troop transport helicopters would launch off of the deck of the *Nimitz* [an aircraft carrier operating in the Indian Ocean] with nothing but their crews on them. They would link up with us at this area that we would call Desert One. We would refuel the helicopters. All of the troops from Delta would then board the helicopters and fly into a second location, which we called Desert Two, where we would hunker down and get some rest."

The next night, Boykin explained, three Delta teams — designated Red, White, and Blue — aided by some Farsi-speaking CIA agents, would board large trucks (disguised as though they were carrying fruits, vegetables, and canned goods to market) obtained and driven by Iranians who had been recruited by the CIA. The trucks would be driven into Tehran and right up to the embassy under the cover of darkness. Around midnight, Blue Team — commanded by Boykin — would

127

bolt from one of the trucks and, using .45 caliber grease guns fitted with silencers, take out the guards at two posts along Roosevelt Avenue. Blue Team would then secure the perimeter as Red and White teams scaled the compound walls, quietly dropped onto the other side, and stormed the embassy, taking out all the hostiles they encountered.

Red Team was to assault a warehouse on the embassy grounds known as "Mushroom Inn," where some of the hostages were believed to be. White Team, meanwhile, would blast their way into the chancery, where the majority of the hostages were holed up.

Once the operation was successfully under way, the plan was for Boykin's Blue Team to race across the street to storm and hold a soccer stadium. They would position snipers on rooftops where they could see and stop any military reinforcements that might be heading to the embassy. The stadium would also serve as the site where the rescue helicopters would land, load up all the hostages and the Delta operators, and then fly out of the city with a fighter jet escort.

The choppers would then fly to an Iranian airfield in Manzariyah that would be seized during the rescue operation by a separate Ranger element. C-130 Talons would fly in, pick up all the Americans, and get them out of the country, after the Rangers and Delta operators had destroyed all of the helicopters.

On November 19 and 20, the Delta planners got some good news. The Iranians had released thirteen women and African-American hostages in a bid to win some international sympathy. They didn't get much sympathy, but U.S. intelligence officials got a treasure trove of fresh and detailed information. Suddenly, some of Delta's hundreds of previously unanswered logistical and operational questions were getting answered. Using details gathered from the released hostages, Delta was soon able to construct and fine-tune a precise mockup of the embassy compound at the Farm. There, they practiced their assault, made their mistakes, corrected them, and tried again, day after day, week after week.

"We presented our concept to our president," Boykin recalled. "We were anxious to go, because frankly we needed as much darkness as possible, and obviously, as the spring and summer approached, we were running out of hours of darkness. I'm sad to say that the president waited until the very last minute until we said, 'Beyond this point our plan will have to be revised and we'll have to come up with a new concept or wait until fall until we start to get the proper hours of darkness again.' "

In his book *Never Surrender,* Boykin noted, "Just after the embassy takeover, President Carter declared publicly that America wouldn't do anything to endanger the lives of the hostages. What he should have said was: 'We will go to any length to get our people back. All options are on the table.' . . . It didn't build confidence in us that Carter was unwilling to state that publicly. Most of us saw him as a weak president before the hostage crisis. Now, all of us interpreted his public comments as revealing that he didn't have the stomach for armed conflict, even if it meant global humiliation of the nation he meant to lead. . . . I was disappointed in Jimmy Carter. I knew he was a man of faith, and I didn't understand his interpretation of his God-given responsibility to defend the defenseless."[3]

"Eight off the Deck"

After months of White House hand-wringing and fruitless State Department back-channel negotiations with the Iranians, Carter finally gave the "go" order in early April of 1980.

The actual operation date was set for April 24. Beckwith took his men to Egypt on the twenty-first to pre-position them for the mission and wrap up final details. On the morning of the twenty-fourth, he gathered them together for one last briefing and pep talk, then asked Boykin to lead the men in prayer.

Boykin was stunned. The colonel was as rough and tough a special forces soldier as he had ever met. Beckwith had never discussed faith or religion in his presence, much less prayed. Most of the time he was screaming at his men, cursing them, and telling them he was going to fire them if they didn't improve, not encouraging them to look to God. Nevertheless, the task before them was almost impossible, and even Beckwith seemed to recognize their need for divine intervention. Boykin was honored and humbled by the moment.

"You know, guys, about three thousand years ago, right in this very desert where we're standing, God led the Israelites out of bondage," Boykin told his band of brothers. "They traveled across this same desert to a new freedom. And I believe God has called us to lead fifty-three Americans out of bondage and back to freedom."

With that, he bowed his head, closed his eyes, and led the men in a prayer.

"Almighty God," he began, "we've placed ourselves in Your hands. And we ask You to lead us and guide us so that we might liberate our fellow Americans. We ask for Your hand of mercy to be upon us. We ask for wisdom and strength and courage. We ask that You keep us safe, and keep safe the people we're going after. Bring us all home to our families. And I pray this in Christ's name. Amen." Together, the men sang "God Bless America." Then they grabbed their gear, boarded the transport planes, and headed for Iran.

The flight was long, and it was quiet but for the radio transmission from the *Nimitz* — "Eight off the deck" — meaning the eight helos had been successfully launched and were en route to the rendezvous point.

Eventually, the transport planes filled with American special forces and a whole lot of extra fuel penetrated Iranian airspace undetected using gaps in Iran's coastal radar system — gaps that the American contractors who had designed the system for the shah had purposely created for unforeseen future contingencies. This was certainly one of those unforeseen contingencies. But it was about the last good thing that happened on this mission.

On final approach to the makeshift landing strip at Desert One, Boykin saw a massive explosion erupt in the distance. *What in the world could that be?* he and his men wondered. They were in the middle of nowhere, hours from civilization.

Only moments later, they learned that a group of smugglers had been driving a fuel tanker, probably filled with stolen gasoline, through the desert. The smugglers had stumbled upon a detachment of U.S. Army Rangers who were providing perimeter security for the rest of the incoming Talons. When the Rangers tried to stop the fuel truck, the smugglers — obviously not expecting to find anyone in their path — had panicked and tried to escape. The Rangers dared not take the risk that the smugglers might alert others to their presence, so they had fired a light antitank weapon at the tanker, blasting it to smithereens. Now, however, the entire team worried the explosion itself might give them away. That, it turned out, was the least of their problems.

Soon afterward a passenger bus filled mostly with women drove by. The bus passengers were just as startled as the smugglers had been to find foreign troops on Iranian soil, along with burning wreckage. The Rangers fired warning shots at the bus and forced it to stop. Now they had nearly fifty temporary prisoners to deal with. And the hits just kept coming.

The inbound helicopters now reported they were experiencing a *haboob,* an intense sandstorm common to the Iranian wastelands but rarely experienced by American chopper pilots. "That created a delay," said Boykin, "and I think the helicopters were somewhere around an hour and a half late. Again, we were running out of the hours of darkness that we needed. We had very little margin to work with."

And when Boykin and his colleagues finally heard the helos approaching, they saw only six, not the eight that had been launched; two had encountered mechanical difficulties and turned back.

Disaster

This was a grave development.

When the helos landed, however, there was more devastating news. One of the six remaining helicopters now had hydraulic problems. They were down to five.

During their planning meetings back at the Pentagon, Beckwith and his logisticians had determined that they absolutely, positively needed a minimum of six helicopters to complete the mission and get all the hostages, soldiers, advance teams, and equipment out of Tehran. Fewer than six would require Beckwith to abort the whole mission.

Now they were deep inside enemy territory with a green light from their commander in chief to rescue fifty-three American souls, but they were suddenly in danger of having to head home empty-handed.

Sure enough, Beckwith came over to Boykin and his team a few moments later. "We're going to have to scrub the mission," he said.

Boykin couldn't believe it. "His words hit me like a punch in the gut. My mind flashed to the hostages. We'd all studied their faces for months. We'd memorized every detail. We knew their stories. And I also knew that if we didn't go forward to get them now, we'd never go at all."

He was prepared to argue, but it became readily apparent that Beckwith would not budge. He could not, after all, risk the lives of his entire team. They had made the six-helo minimum for a reason — back at home, without emotion, without adrenaline — and Beckwith was sticking with it. He ordered his men to start reloading the C-130s with all of their equipment.

"People have questioned the wisdom of not going forward with the five that we had," Boykin told me. "And here's the fact: we needed every single man that we had to assault a twenty-seven-acre compound, plus assault the Ministry of Foreign Affairs, which is where three of the hostages were being held. But more importantly, we needed all of the lift capacity we could get to bring out the hostages. If we went forward with a reduced force and succeeded in retaking our hostages, we were going to be in a dilemma because the helicopters simply wouldn't lift everybody out. So we were going to exchange one set of hostages for another, and that was not a good option either."

Boykin and his men moved quickly. Light would be dawning soon, and they did not want to be found in Iran, exposed in the open desert, when the sun came up. But just then, disaster struck. Boykin watched as one of the helicopters that had just been refueled lifted off the ground and prepared to reposition itself away from the transport planes. But as a blinding amount of dust and sand was stirred up by the rotors, the helo's pilot experienced vertigo. The pilot lost command of where he was and and began setting down directly on top of one of the C-130s.

A moment later, another massive fireball lit up the predawn sky as the chopper and transport plane collided. Boykin felt a wave of searing heat wash over him, and then he realized dozens of his colleagues were trapped inside the burning plane. Worse, the plane was filled with thousand of pounds of additional fuel, which would erupt any second. Boykin, choking on sand and smoke, shouted out a desperate prayer to save his men.

134

"Father, please don't let these men die!" he pleaded. "We put ourselves in Your hands, and now they're all going to die unless You perform a miracle!"

Almost before he could say "Amen," Boykin watched one of the Talon's emergency doors, already engulfed in flames, burst open and his colleagues start leaping out and running from the plane as fast as they possibly could. "As the men approached me," he recalled, "I shouted for them to get behind the C-130 that was behind me, to protect themselves from the heat and the new blast that was just moments away." Then sure enough, the Talon exploded, along with the ammunition and various rockets and shoulder-mounted missiles that were packed inside.

Impact

When it was all over, eight U.S. servicemen were dead. Seven American helicopters had been lost, along with a C-130. The hostages were still in the hands of the Radicals. And the whole world was about to find out.

Beckwith radioed the devastating news back to the National Military Command Center, the high-tech, nuclear-bomb-proof war room deep underneath the Pentagon. David Jones, the chairman of the Joint Chiefs, then called the president, who was stricken, as was his senior staff. Hamilton Jordan, the White House chief of staff, promptly excused himself, stepped into the president's private bathroom, and threw up.[4]

At 7:00 eastern time, the president broke the news to the nation in a live, televised address from the Oval Office.

The nation was stunned.

In the months to come, right or wrong, Carter would get the blame both for the hostage crisis and for his administration's failure to get the hostages out. And then voters would drive him out of office, replacing him with Ronald Reagan, the anti-Communist former actor and former California governor who promised to rebuild the American military, stare down her enemies, and restore her pride.

Throughout the presidential campaign, Carter and his advisors tried to scare the electorate into thinking Reagan was a radical, right-wing warmonger. The strategy did not work in the States. Reagan won in a landslide.

But Carter's rhetoric did seem to work in Tehran. All fifty-three American hostages were released on January 20, 1981, just hours after Reagan took the oath of office.

But the political implications of the tragedy at Desert One were not on Boykin's mind at the time. What bothered him most was the evil he saw being unleashed through the Ayatollah Khomeini and his followers, an evil neither he nor most Americans had ever experienced before.

"What is really important," Boykin insisted to me, the pain of those memories still evident on his face and in his voice, "is to realize that the Iranians recovered the bodies of eight of our people that were killed there and desecrated them, mutilated them. The U.S. media was unwilling to show what they were doing. We saw it because we saw it on international networks. But that was something that we had never experienced. That was something that we couldn't understand — the inhumanity of it. What drives people to take such pleasure in mutilating and desecrating the bodies of fallen warriors?"*

*It is important to note that the U.S. military in general and Delta Force in particular learned a great deal from the tragedy at Desert One and the mistakes that were made there. In time, they corrected those mistakes and have had tremendous successes in counterterrorism operations and in full-blown combat operations in the Middle East and around the world, including the liberation of Grenada from Soviet-backed Communists, the liberation of Panama from the drug-running dictatorship of Manuel Noriega, the liberation of Kuwait from the Iraqis, the liberation of Iraq from Saddam Hussein's reign of terror, and the liberation of Afghanistan from Taliban and al Qaeda control. I highly recommend Boykin's book *Never Surrender,* as he was intimately involved in a number of those missions.

CHAPTER SIX:
"WE MUST EXPORT
OUR REVOLUTION"

Iran, Hezbollah, and the tragedy in Lebanon

At 6:25 local time on the morning of October 23, 1983, agents of the ayatollah used a suicide bomber to plow a truck filled with explosives into the U.S. Marines barracks in Beirut, Lebanon.

The attack resulted in "the largest non-nuclear explosion that had ever been detonated on the face of the earth," according to a U.S. federal court judge who found the Islamic Republic of Iran liable for perpetrating the crime.[1] Locked doors on a building nearly three hundred feet away were ripped off their hinges. All the trees in the surrounding area were stripped completely bare of their leaves. The windows in the control tower at Beirut's international airport were blown out. And the four-story cement and steel Marine facility collapsed into fifteen feet of rubble, ash, and smoke.

When my wife and I got married in the summer of 1990 and settled in the Washington, D.C., area, we soon met Charlie and Lynn Derbyshire, a couple at church who had experienced the evil of the Iranian Revolution firsthand. Lynn lost her oldest brother — Marine Captain Vincent Smith

— in the Beirut bombing. Charlie was still helping her heal from the loss when we met. But the horrors of 9/11 and the subsequent deaths of American and Israeli forces in Iraq, Afghanistan, and Lebanon in the years that followed ripped open those wounds afresh. Through Lynn and Charlie, my wife and I have gotten a personal and painful glimpse at the lasting emotional scars left by the jihadists.

When I set out to write this book, I wrestled with whether or not to even ask Lynn if I could share her story. In the end, however, I did ask. I felt it was important for others to understand the human impact of the Revolution and to realize that for the victims of terrorism, the trauma is in many ways as real today as it was so long ago.

Graciously, Lynn and Charlie agreed.

"He Made Sure I Was Safe"

"I loved Vince," Lynn explained as we sat in her living room and talked over coffee. "Vince was my hero, my protector, my friend. He was so much more than a brother. I have six brothers and two sisters, and he was the oldest. And he was always the one who would come in and stop the family fights. He was always the one who would tell my brothers, 'Okay, quit pickin' on her; enough is enough.' You know, whatever practical joke they were playing — putting frogs in my pockets or whatever. Vince would just swoop in and rescue me from this kind of sibling fun. I always looked to Vince as my savior. Vince was always the one who made sure I was safe."

Vince graduated with honors from high school, then headed off to the Naval Academy. He played football. He sang in the glee club. He also became a follower of Jesus Christ while at the Naval Academy through long conversations with Lynn's cousin, a strong believer, who was there as well.

In time, Vince fell in love, got married, and then went off to basic training and flight school before becoming a pilot, most often flying Cobra attack helicopters.

In May of 1983, he was sent to Beirut to serve as the air liaison officer for the group, making sure that when ground troops needed air support — whether for transporting supplies or for a combat mission — they got what they needed.

"This Can't Be Happening"

In October of that year, Lynn was living in New Mexico. Newly married, she and her husband had just come home from church on a beautiful Sunday morning when her neighbor ran to meet her. Tears were streaming down her neighbor's face. She grabbed at Lynn's arm as Lynn was getting out of the car. "You've gotta come in the house," she said. "Something terrible has happened! You gotta come watch the news."

"It was about ten in the morning," Lynn recalled. "I kept saying, 'Well, just tell me what's happened — just tell me.' We went into her house — and this was before they had 24/7 coverage of news events, so we had to wait through whatever the program was until the next time they broke in with their special report — and I kept saying to her, 'Tell me what's wrong; tell me!' We were both crying, and I just couldn't conceive of what was happening. So then when the news came on, I was obviously prepared that there was a huge tragedy, but I just didn't . . . I just couldn't think. And so when the news came on the television, it

140

was almost like being physically hit. I kind of sat back in the chair — 'This can't be happening, this can't be true.' "

Network newscasters reported that suicide bombers had attacked the Marine barracks in Beirut as well as the barracks housing French peacekeepers. There were 241 Americans dead, 56 dead from the French barracks, and many more wounded.

Lynn rushed back home and called her parents, who were living at the Marine Corps base in Cherry Point, NC, but they were not home. Nobody had cell phones back then, so she had no way of reaching them.

She then called Vince's wife, also in Cherry Point, and found her parents already there, trying to comfort her and her young son. Lynn asked her father, who was an active duty major general in the Marine Corps at the time, "Dad, don't you know what's happening? Can't you tell us anything?"

"We just don't know anything yet," her father replied, noting that his colleagues were saying a massive search-and-rescue operation was under way because there were so many men still unaccounted for.

"That was a Sunday," Lynn remembered, "and it was two and a half, almost three weeks later before they were able to identify Vince's body. So it was just every day — going into my neighbor's house to watch the television and calling my parents every day. My dad finally said, after about the fourth day, 'Honey, I know it's hard, but I promise I'll call you if I find anything out. I'm not gonna leave you out. I promise I'll call.'

"I was a schoolteacher, and I went to school

141

and was trying to teach, and I just couldn't even function. I would be writing on the blackboard and forget midsentence what I was writing. I would turn around and look at these little sixth graders, and I just kept leaving the room. But I couldn't *not* go to work, because that's even worse. So if you can just imagine . . . waiting — nineteen days — to find out whether someone you love is dead or alive. It was torture."

"How did you finally get the news?" I asked her.

"My father called me on a Thursday morning. It was about 5:00 a.m., I think. And when the phone rang, I knew. I just knew. You know, you have a sixth sense about that stuff. I answered the phone, and he said, 'It's time to come home. They've identified Vince, and it's time to come home to bury him.'

"That was a whirlwind in itself, trying to get from a tiny little town in central New Mexico back to Washington, D.C., and see to the funeral arrangements, and it was just surreal. They buried him in Quantico Cemetery. It was the first time I had been back together with most of my family since my wedding day. So to go from the joy of seeing your family at your wedding and then to be together at a funeral, it was just terrible.

"And I really couldn't believe it. I spent a long time in that first stage of grief, where you say, 'This isn't happening; this can't be real; this isn't me.' Because I was accustomed to Vince being gone for a long time. He was seven years older than me. When I was eleven, he went away to the Naval Academy, and I was accustomed to not seeing him. He would be gone for long stretches, and then we would get letters and hear whatever was going on with him. Then he would be home for a few days, and then he'd be gone again for six months. So I just had this surreal feeling that, 'He's gonna come home. He's gonna come home.'

"Of course it was a closed casket, so I had to talk myself into believing that he was in that box. I remember when we went to the funeral home the night before the funeral. They had the casket in a room and you could go in and kneel down and pray, and they gave each of us an opportunity to do that. Here's this flag-draped casket and all these flowers, and there's nothing there that was Vince. It couldn't be — it just couldn't be. I remember kneeling down and praying, 'Lord, how could You do this? If You really are a loving God, how could You let this happen?'

"And as strange as it sounds, I really couldn't believe it even through the whole funeral. I flew back to New Mexico still feeling that it wasn't real, because there were men who had survived the bombing who weren't identified for a long time, who were airlifted to a hospital in Germany or somewhere. They were bandaged head to toe and were recovering, and it was weeks before they figured out who these people were because they were so badly banged up. They were unrecognizable. And I kept dreaming. I'd wake up in the middle of the night sitting up, like you see in Hollywood films, screaming his name, because I was just convinced that he couldn't have died. It wasn't possible."

"I'd Never Heard of Suicide Bombing"

In time, U.S. authorities reconstructed the chain of events that led to the bombing.

They learned that after months of monitoring operations at the barracks housing the 24th

Marine Amphibious Unit, Hezbollah operatives had ambushed a truck that was headed to the compound to deliver fresh water. The operatives then quickly replaced that truck with one they had painted to look like the one Marine guards were expecting. This nineteen-ton vehicle, however, had been outfitted with some 2,500 pounds of high-tech explosives.

The driver, the U.S. later learned, was a devout jihadist, eager to give up his life to kill Americans and thus, he hoped, secure his place in paradise.

As the sun was just beginning to rise on a gorgeous autumn day in the Lebanese capital, "the driver drove past the Marine barracks" and "circled in the large parking lot behind the barracks." He then pushed the accelerator to the floor, "crashed through the concertina wire barrier and a wall of sandbags, and entered the barracks." The force of the explosion was equivalent to between 15,000 and 21,000 pounds of TNT.[2]

At the time, of course, Lynn and her family knew almost none of the details. They were operating in the fog of war, amid rumors and scraps of information. Moreover, they were dealing with a kind of warfare that had never been used against Americans before.

"I'd never heard of suicide bombing," Lynn recalled. "And up until Vince went there, I had never heard of Lebanon. I'm embarrassed to say I was one of the average Americans who doesn't know anything about geography. We had to look it up on a map. I had never heard of terrorists, of course. I had heard of Muslims, but I'd never heard of this whole idea of radical Muslims and jihad and all of that sort of stuff. None of us had ever heard of that."

Lynn was not alone; this was the first known suicide bombing by Muslims against American targets in history.

Many Americans were unsure why we had forces in Lebanon in the first place and demanded that we pull out. We were not there *making* peace, they argued. We obviously were not *keeping* the peace. There was no peace. So what was the point?

Unfortunately, the U.S. government offered no answers. In my view, the Reagan administration should have attacked Hezbollah camps with a vengeance, making it clear that killing Americans would not pay. They also should have given the Marines clearer rules of engagement. Incredibly, at the time Marine "peacekeepers" in Lebanon weren't allowed to carry weapons with live rounds in them. The Marine guards on duty the morning of the attack had not even been allowed to chamber rounds of ammunition in their weapons, making them helpless to stop the suicide bomber as he sped toward them. They were sitting ducks.

All of that should have changed immediately. But instead of showing strength in the face of the jihadist challenge, the Reagan administration cut and ran. On February 7, 1984, President Ronald Reagan announced that he was pulling the Marines out of Lebanon.

Not a few Americans breathed a sigh of relief. But among jihadists throughout the region, there was elation. The "Great Satan" had just been dealt a significant blow. The Americans were now in retreat, all because of one driver willing to give up his life to kill others. This was a model, they concluded, that had to be replicated.

Iran's Involvement

And then the story took a curious twist.

"Right after the bombing," Lynn explained, "Hezbollah came forward and claimed credit for having done this, and in a very bragging, grandiose way: *'We killed all these Americans! We're gettin' 'em! We're gettin' 'em where it counts, and we're the ones; we did it!'* But by pretty early in 1984, it became clear that Hezbollah was doing this at the behest of the Iranian government."

Sure enough, over the next few years, as the U.S. government continued to investigate the attack, it became increasingly clear that the entire operation had been set into motion not by Hezbollah alone but with the direct assistance of the Khomeini regime in Tehran. The mounting evidence was so compelling, the families of the slain Marines eventually decided to join together and file a wrongful death suit against the Islamic Republic of Iran. In so doing, they hoped to prove once and for all in a court of law that Iran was, in fact, responsible for the deaths of their loved ones. They also hoped to punish the regime in the only way they could, since neither the Reagan administration nor any U.S. administration that followed had punished anyone for the wanton murder of American Marines.

"I'm just a soccer mom," Lynn demurred. "Really, I'm just trying to raise my children and keep my household running. I'm going to the grocery store and doing the laundry and those kind of things, so most of this about radical Islam I don't really understand. It's way above my pay grade. It wasn't until we were actually at the trial and I was hearing the testimony they had gathered that I understood how cut-and-dried the case

really was, how completely and thoroughly responsible the government of Iran was for the death of
my brother and the other 240 Americans that were
killed that day."

Overwhelming Evidence

Lynn was right. During the court case, which the
families ultimately won, many facts came to light
that proved beyond a doubt that Iran was behind
the attack. Consider the following excerpts from
the trial judge's written opinion:[3]

"The post-revolutionary government in Iran . . .
declared its commitment to spread the goals of
the 1979 revolution to other nations. Towards that
end, between 1983 and 1988, the government of
Iran spent approximately $50 to $150 million
financing terrorist organizations in the Near East.
One of the nations to which the Iranian government directed its attention was the war-torn
republic of Lebanon.

"Dr. Michael Ledeen, a consultant to the
Department of Defense at the time of the Marine
barracks bombing and an expert on U.S. foreign
relations, testified at the trial that 'Iran invented,
created, funded, trained, and runs to this day
Hezbollah, which is arguably the world's most
dangerous terrorist organization.'

"The fake water delivery truck . . . [was] driven
by Ismalal Ascari, an Iranian.

"On October 25, 1983, the chief of naval intelligence notified Admiral [James A.] Lyons of an
intercept of a message between Tehran and Damascus that had been made on or about September 26, 1983. . . . The message directed the
Iranian ambassador to contact . . . the leader of
the terrorist group . . . and to instruct him to

147

have his group instigate attacks against the multinational coalition in Lebanon, and *'to take a spectacular action against the United States Marines."* (Emphasis added.)

"Based on the evidence presented by expert witnesses at trial, the Court finds that it is beyond question that Hezbollah and its agents received massive material and technical support from the Iranian government."

An Order from the Top
One of the judge's conclusions was that "the sophistication demonstrated in the placement of an explosive charge in the center of the Marine barracks building and the devastating effect of the detonation of the charge indicates that it is highly unlikely that this attack could have resulted in such loss of life without the assistance of regular military forces, such as those of Iran."[4]

Which brings up the question: would the Ayatollah Khomeini have been required to give approval to such a plan?

At one point in the trial, lawyers questioned Dr. Patrick Clawson, an Iran expert at the Washington Institute for Near East Policy, on this very issue. Clawson said there was no doubt in his mind that such a massive attack against American forces had to have been approved at the highest possible level of the Iranian regime, specifically by Khomeini himself. Otherwise, he argued, Hezbollah would never have even considered making a move against the U.S.

Q: In the fall of 1983, was there anything of a significant nature, and especially a terrorist attack [of] the dimensions of the attack on the

148

Marine barracks of October 23, 1983, which would or could have been undertaken by Hezbollah without material support from Iran?

Clawson: Iran's material support would have been absolutely essential for any activities at that time, and furthermore, the politics of the organization [were such] that no one in the organization would have thought about carrying out an activity without Iranian approval and almost certainly Iranian orders.

Q: Is that opinion within a reasonable degree of certainty as an expert on Iran?

Clawson: Absolutely, sir.

Q: Would any such operation as the October 23rd, 1983, attack require the approval within Iran of the Ministry of Information and Security?

Clawson: Yes, sir.

Q: What about [Iranian prime minister] Rafsanjani?

Clawson: There would have been a discussion in the National Security Council, which would involve the prime minister, Mr. Rafsanjani. . . . It would also have required the approval of Iran's supreme religious leader, Ayatollah Khomeini.[5]

Justice for the Survivors

When the trial was over and all the evidence had been examined and thoroughly reviewed, the Honorable Royce C. Lamberth, the U.S. district judge for the District of Columbia, ruled that agents acting on behalf of the Islamic Republic of Iran "caused the deaths of over 241 peacekeeping servicemen at the Marine barracks" in a "willful and deliberate act of extrajudicial killing." Moreover, Judge Lamberth concluded that Hezbollah, the Islamic Republic of Iran, and the Iranian Ministry of Information and Security "are jointly and severally liable to the plaintiffs for compensatory and punitive damages."[6]

I asked Lynn what her reaction was when she heard the verdict.

"I sank to my knees in gratitude," she replied instantly. "I was so grateful. To me, it was a piece of justice that had finally been done. To be able to finally say, 'Here's the guilty party; we can name somebody who has done this' was a huge step down the road to justice."

"No order from this Court will restore any of the 241 lives that were stolen on October 23, 1983," Judge Lamberth wrote in the closing section of his opinion. "Nor is this Court able to heal the pain that has become a permanent part of the lives of their mothers and fathers, their spouses and siblings, and their sons and daughters. But the Court can take steps that will punish the men who carried out this unspeakable attack, and in so doing, try to achieve some small measure of justice for its survivors, and for the family members of the 241 Americans who never came home."[7]

On September 7, 2007, after reviewing the

merits of each individual member of the class action suit, Judge Lamberth ordered Iran to pay more than $2.6 billion to the nearly one thousand survivors and family members of those killed. "The cost of state-sponsored terrorism," he said, "just went up."[8]

The families of the victims know that the chances of their ever actually receiving any of the settlement money are very low. And even victory cannot heal all the wounds.

"Twenty-four years later, the wound in my heart over Vincent's death is still gaping wide," Lynn shared with me as our conversation drew to a close. "Now why is that? It's because the criminals are getting away with their crime. And it's because they're continuing to commit similar crimes and other people are suffering and dying at their hands. So there's a sense of hopelessness. There's a sense that this is never going to end, that our world has changed completely and we'll never be able to go back to feeling safe. You know, we're not safe in the United States, we're not free in the United States. We're in bondage to our fear — the fear of terrorism. Now you just look around Washington, look around the airports, all those security measures, all the big barricades, the concrete barriers. All that stuff is a result of terrorism, because we're afraid of terrorists."

Hezbollah's Continuing Threat

Sadly, Lynn is right. Those responsible for the Marine barracks attack continue to get away with their crimes and to plot new ones. Hezbollah is widely regarded in intelligence circles as the most dangerous Shia Muslim terrorist organization in the world. Former U.S. Deputy Secretary of State

151

Richard Armitage has said that "Hezbollah may be the A team of terrorists," while "al Qaeda is actually the B team."[9]

Sheikh Hassan Nasrallah, the leader of Hezbollah, continues to breathe murderous threats against Americans and Israelis and to recruit and train jihadists while working closely with Tehran to prepare for the Islamic messiah known as the Mahdi to come and bring about the end of the world. Consider a mere sampling of Nasrallah's statements:

"Let the entire world hear me. Our hostility to the Great Satan [America] is absolute. . . . Regardless of how the world has changed after 11 September, 'Death to America' will remain our reverberating and powerful slogan: 'Death to America.' "[10]

"We do not believe in multiple Islamic republics; we do believe, however, in a single Islamic world governed by a central government."[11]

"Jerusalem and Palestine will not be regained with political games but with guns."[12]

"America will remain the nation's chief enemy and the greatest Satan of all. Israel will always be for us a cancerous growth that needs to be eradicated."[13]

"We pledge to persevere on the path [our founders] had chosen, the path of Khomeini and Khamenei."[14]

"I ask Almighty Allah . . . to make you the men who would clear the way for the Mahdi of this earth to establish divine justice."[15]

Nasrallah, the oldest of nine children, was born on August 31, 1960, in an East Beirut slum. He was only eighteen when the Islamic Revolution unfolded in Iran. But he quickly proved to be a powerful orator, a magnetic leader, and a highly effective organizer. He helped found Hezbollah in 1982 with direct Iranian funding, training, and organizational assistance, and he helped build it into an enormous force with aid and ongoing strategic and tactical guidance from Iran.*

By 1983, Nasrallah and his team had already

*Nasrallah has stated publicly that Hezbollah was founded upon the orders of the Ayatollah Khomeini. He has said on the record that in 1982, "the faithful were of the opinion that a revolutionary and Islamist current should be established to adequately confront the new challenge facing Lebanon. This current was to have a clear Islamist political vision, and operate through a consistent ideology based on the principles and political line of Imam Khomeini. . . . This is how Hezbollah came to be" (cited by Noe, p. 26). In an interview on Iranian television on April 16, 2007, Sheikh Naim Qassem, the number two leader of Hezbollah, admitted that "when Hezbollah commenced activities in 1982, it did so according to the opinion and religious ruling of Imam Khomeini." He went on to explain that Hezbollah follows the religious directives and tactical military orders from the religious and political leadership in Iran, specifically the current ayatollah, Khamenei. The leaders of Hezbollah can, he explained, ask Khamenei for direction on what is acceptable and what is forbidden in carrying out jihadist operations against Israel, to make sure they do not sin or commit a crime (cited and translated from Arabic into English by the Intelligence and Terrorism Informa-

recruited and trained some two hundred jihadists and launched the Marine barracks attack, killing more Americans at one time than any terrorist had before that point. Within a decade, Nasrallah had at least two thousand trained jihadists at his command, though most were "reservists," not full-time paid operatives.[16] By the time of the Second Lebanon War against Israel in 2006, Hezbollah had between 6,000 and 10,000 trained jihadists in their network compared to 170,000 IDF forces and over 400,000 Israeli reservists, yet under Nasrallah's leadership, Hezbollah was widely perceived to have all but defeated the Israelis in that thirty-four-day showdown.[17]

Terrorist attacks by Hezbollah (sometimes spelled "Hizballah" or "Hizbullah") have extended far beyond the suicide truck bombings of the U.S. Embassy and U.S. Marine barracks in Beirut in 1983. According to the U.S. State Department's 2008 *Patterns of Global Terrorism* report, Hezbollah was also behind the 1984 attack on the U.S. Embassy annex in Beirut; the 1985 hijacking of TWA flight 847, during which a U.S. Navy diver was murdered; the kidnapping, detention, and murder of Americans and other Westerners in Lebanon in the 1980s; the 1992 attacks on the Israeli Embassy in Argentina; the 1994 attack on the Argentine-Israeli Mutual Association (AMIA) in Buenos Aires; and the 2000 kidnapping of three Israeli soldiers and an Israeli noncombatant."[18]

At least since 2004, Nasrallah's forces have also

---

tion Center on April 29, 2007, based on excerpts from the interview as cited by *MEMRI* and Israeli TV Channel 2. See www.terrorism-info.org.il).

been training members of the Iraqi "Mahdi Army" — the Shia terrorist group run by Moqtada al-Sadr — to attack and kill U.S., Coalition, and Iraqi military forces, as well as Iraqi civilians.[19] Senior Iraqi and U.S. military and intelligence officials say that several thousand Mahdi Army insurgents have traveled to Lebanon to receive Hezbollah training, returning to Iraq as "the best-trained fighters in the Mahdi Army."[20] Boasted one twenty-six-year-old Mahdi Army fighter: "We have formal links with Hizbollah. We do exchange ideas and discuss the situation facing Shiites in both countries. . . . It is natural that we would want to improve ourselves by learning from each other. We copy Hizbollah in the way they fight and their tactics. We teach each other and we are getting better through this."[21]

Now Nasrallah is building what he believes will be the ultimate fighting force to destroy the U.S. and Israel in the "end of days." According to Hezbollah documents captured by Israeli soldiers during the 2006 war, Nasrallah has recruited forty-two thousand Muslim children ages eight to sixteen into a jihadist youth movement known as "the Imam al-Mahdi Scouts." The children are immersed in understanding Shia eschatology — end times theology — about the coming of the Islamic Messiah known as the Mahdi. They study the lives and teachings of Nasrallah and current Iranian ayatollah Khamenei, whom they refer to as their "commander-leader." They wear camouflage suits, paint their faces black, and swear an oath to participate in jihad against Jewish and Christian infidels. According to official organization documents, 120 members have already died in terrorist actions, including as suicide bombers.

Once they turn seventeen, they join Hezbollah's formal military units.[22]

Yet, inexplicably, despite Hezbollah's history of killing Americans, Israelis, and Iraqis — and their clear plans to kill many more — the U.S. has done precious little to crush Hezbollah as it has sought to crush al Qaeda. Nor has it done much to bring Hezbollah leader Sheikh Hassan Nasrallah or his forces to justice. This has served to embolden Nasrallah, who is convinced that Allah is with him and that the Mahdi is on his way.

CHAPTER SEVEN:
CHRISTMAS IN KABUL

How the Soviet invasion of Afghanistan
led to the rise of Osama bin Laden

1979 was not a good year for the CIA.

On February 14, Adolph Dubs, the U.S. ambassador to Afghanistan, was kidnapped and killed by Radicals in Kabul. Aghanistan had been imploding for much of the previous year, with a bloody coup, assassinations, violent antigovernment demonstrations, and numerous bombings rocking the country. A pro-Soviet Marxist by the name of Nur Mohammad Taraki was newly in charge, having seized power in April of 1978.

Having effectively missed the Islamic Revolution in Iran just weeks earlier, the CIA's Middle East analysts were busy trying to catch up and understand the implications of the fall of the shah and the rise of Khomeini. On the day Dubs died, Langley's Near East Division was primarily focused on the U.S. Embassy in Tehran, which had just been seized for the first time by followers of Khomeini, though the Valentine's Day siege ended after just a few hours.

The Soviet KGB's Near East analysts, however, were fixed primarily on the rising chaos in Afghanistan. Yes, Taraki was a Soviet ally. Yes, he and Soviet premier Leonid Brezhnev had signed the Soviet-Afghan friendship treaty in December of 1978, binding the two countries together more formally than ever before. And yes, Taraki was a student of Stalinesque methods of torture and repression. But KGB analysts were watching their would-be puppet create anarchy along the Soviet southern border, not establish and maintain stability. In less than a year since coming to power, Taraki had already executed three thousand political prisoners, had another seventy thousand rotting in Afghan jails, and had allowed internecine warfare to leave nearly a hundred thousand civilians dead.[1]

"We Cannot Lose Afghanistan"

In addition to this horrific violence, Taraki had seized some 3 million acres of farmland, planning to redistribute it to those he deemed most worthy. Now Afghanistan's Islamic clergy had been awakened to the Communist threat. They were railing against the godless atheists who were supporting Taraki and his brutal tactics, and they were mobilizing to take Taraki down.

The Kremlin was worried. Though Afghanistan was a poor, uneducated, and nearly resourceless country, it was strategically important to them. Why? Location, location, location. By fully controlling Afghanistan, the Soviets effectively controlled two borders of Iran, which gave the Soviet military an excellent launching pad to take over that oil-rich country and dominate if not outright control the economically vital Persian Gulf region. With a Revolution already under way in Iran and the U.S. having just lost its key ally in the shah,

158

the Soviets believed they might soon have an opportunity to seize Iran for themselves, and this was far too valuable a prize to allow a pawn like Nur Mohammad Taraki to lose.

Moreover, Moscow deeply feared the possibility of 40 million Muslims in the central Asian republics becoming radicalized if they saw Islamic Radicals successfully rolling over the Soviets and their puppets in Afghanistan. The stakes for the Kremlin were just too high, and on March 17, in a closed-door meeting of the Politburo, Soviet intelligence chief Yuri Andropov told senior officials point-blank: "We cannot lose Afghanistan."[2]

Already Moscow was considering the steps necessary to maintain control of Afghanistan, including an invasion if necessary. They began moving some thirty thousand combat troops to the Afghan border as a precautionary measure. But analysts at Langley completely misread the situation. On March 23, 1979, the CIA's top secret daily intelligence report to senior officials at the Carter White House, the Pentagon, and the State Department stated categorically: "The Soviets would be most reluctant to introduce large numbers of ground forces into Afghanistan."[3]

In July, President Carter authorized a half million dollars in covert financial aid to the Islamic rebels known as the mujahadeen (wagers of jihad) to help them resist Taraki's pro-Soviet regime. The funds were not for weapons. Rather, they were "for insurgent propaganda, and other psychological operations in Afghanistan; establishment of radio access to the Afghan population through third-country facilities; and the provision, either unilaterally or through third countries, of support to the Afghan insurgents, in the form of either

159

cash or non-military supplies," recalled Robert Gates, then a member of Carter's National Security Council staff.[4]

The money was not nearly enough to overthrow Taraki or drive out Soviet influence. Six weeks later, the money was gone. But then again, it was really just a gesture of tepid support by the Carter administration, not the makings of a real anti-Soviet strategy. After all, neither the White House nor the CIA accurately saw the growing Soviet threat. On August 24, for example, a CIA report to the president stated that the majority of Agency analysts "continue to feel that the deteriorating situation does not presage an escalation of Soviet military involvement in the form of a direct combat role."[5]

But even without American weapons, the mujahadeen were attacking Taraki's forces with ever-increasing frequency, and the Soviets were clearly getting edgy. Then, on September 14, Taraki was assassinated. CIA Director Stansfield Turner finally wrote to the president that day, warning him that "the Soviet leaders may be on the threshold of a decision to commit their own forces to prevent the collapse of the regime and to protect their sizable stakes in Afghanistan." But Turner concluded his memo by saying that though such a decision was being contemplated, it still seemed unlikely.[6]

Hafizullah Amin — Moscow's man — took over after Taraki's death and eagerly launched attacks against the mujahadeen, killing more than a thousand in just a few weeks. But by December, mujahadeen operations against Amin's regime were growing more effective. The Soviets, afraid the newly installed Amin might soon be toppled,

160

moved more than five thousand combat troops and several high-ranking Soviet military commanders into the theater to join the growing number of forces already pre-positioned along the border.

Yet on December 17, Director Turner told the National Security Council that "the CIA does not see this as a crash buildup" or evidence of an imminent Soviet invasion of Afghanistan.[7] Even as late as December 19, the CIA's top analysts concluded, "The pace of Soviet deployments does not suggest . . . urgent contingency."[8]

On December 25, 1979 — Christmas Day — eighty-five thousand Soviet combat troops invaded Afghanistan. Two days later, Soviet special forces assassinated Hafizullah Amin. They installed a new puppet and sent in another twenty thousand troops to crush the mujahadeen and secure the country for themselves once and for all.

Once again, President Carter and senior White House officials were stunned, as were the American people. Two nations, Iran and Afghanistan, had fallen within a short period of time. Radical Islam and Soviet imperialism were on the rise. The U.S. had been blindsided by both developments and seemed powerless to affect events.

In his State of the Union address delivered on January 23, 1980, the president captured the gravity of the situation. "The implications of the Soviet invasion of Afghanistan could pose the most serious threat to the peace since the Second World War," a sober commander in chief told a joint session of Congress and the nation, adding that "the crises in Iran and Afghanistan" posed "a clear and present danger" to U.S. national security, in part because jihadists and Communists now threatened

161

to control U.S. and Western access to Middle Eastern oil supplies.[9]

And still the CIA stonewalled. "The CIA not only missed the invasion," noted *New York Times* intelligence reporter Tim Weiner, "it refused to admit that it had missed it. Why would anyone in his right mind invade Afghanistan, graveyard of conquerors for two thousand years?"[10]

Robert Gates, who in 1979 had just returned to the CIA after a five-year stint with the National Security Council, concurred. "Between summer and December, CIA's Soviet analysts just couldn't believe that the Soviets actually would invade in order to play a major part in ground combat operations. They saw all the reasons why it would be foolish for the Soviets to do so — the same reasons many in the Soviet leadership saw — and simply couldn't accept that Brezhnev or the others might see the equation differently. The analysts thought that the Soviet leaders thought as they did. It was not the first or the last time they would make this mistake."[11]

The Turning Point

Enter Osama bin Laden, a shy, lanky, awkward, underachieving twenty-two-year-old management student in Saudi Arabia.

When the Ayatollah Khomeini established in Iran the first Islamic republic in history and the Soviets invaded Afghanistan and began killing Muslims en masse, few who knew bin Laden could ever have imagined him emerging one day as the undisputed leader of Sunni Islamic jihadists, the architect of the deadliest terrorist attacks in American history, and the charismatic hero of

162

Radicals around the globe, be they Sunnis or Shias.

Without question, 1979 was the turning point. Bin Laden quickly became obsessed with both Khomeini's Iran and the Soviet invasion. He examined their causes and their implications, and it was these two events that changed his destiny forever, leading him to conclude that Allah had chosen him for a very specific mission: to help destroy the Soviet Union and the United States and to reestablish a global Islamic caliphate on earth.

Born in late 1957 or early 1958 (the record is not entirely clear), Osama — which means "lion" in Arabic — was the seventeenth of at least fifty-four children born to Mohammed bin Laden, a wealthy Saudi who was the founder of one of the largest construction companies in the Middle East.* Osama's mother, Alia Ghanem, was a Syrian of Palestinian origin and met Mohammed in Jerusalem when he was doing renovations work on the Dome of the Rock. She was only fourteen years old when she married Mohammed, becom-

*There is a dispute over just how many children Mohammed bin Laden really had. The 9/11 Commission Report, Section 2.3, says fifty-seven. But Lawrence Wright, author of *The Looming Tower,* an absolutely exceptional book that was indispensable in drafting this chapter, says fifty-four (see note on p. 444 of Wright's book). CNN's Peter Bergen, meanwhile, cites an interview with a childhood friend of bin Laden's, confirming fifty-four. See Bergen's *The Osama bin Laden I Know: An Oral History of al Qaeda's Leader,* another excellent and vitally helpful book, p. 17.

ing one of his twenty-two wives.

Osama was the only child Alia had with Mohammed, and the boy received little if any attention from his father. When Osama was only four or five years old, Mohammed divorced Alia and forced the two to move out of his house — away from all of Osama's brothers and sisters — into a small home a few blocks away. It was a traumatic moment for the little boy, now effectively an only child, being raised by a single mother in the rigid, antiwoman, fundamentalist culture of Saudi Arabia.

But it was about to be terribly compounded. Not long after the divorce, Osama learned that his father had died in a plane crash.[12] Later, Osama's brother Salem would also die in a horrific plane crash.[13] Planes and death, it would seem, became inextricably intertwined in Osama's psyche at a fairly young age.

Eventually, his mother married again, this time to an employee of the bin Laden construction empire named Attas, and bore him three sons and a daughter, giving Osama new brothers and a sister to grow up with. But in June of 1967, as he approached his tenth birthday, Osama and the rest of the Arab world experienced another major trauma. They watched the tiny State of Israel devastate the Soviet-funded, -trained, and -armed military forces of Egypt, Syria, and Jordan in just six days.

Why? the emotionally devastated Osama and his friends asked themselves. *What was going wrong? Why was Allah turning his back on the Arab forces?* They were not the only ones asking such questions, of course. It seemed as if everyone in the Islamic world was asking what was going wrong.

Joining the Muslim Brotherhood

The first time Osama bin Laden heard an answer that made sense to him seems to have been around 1972, in his freshman year of high school. It was then that he met a Syrian gym teacher who was a member of the Muslim Brotherhood, the Islamic jihadist group founded in Egypt in 1928 by a charismatic radical Sunni cleric named Hassan al-Banna.[14]

Applying the teachings of al-Banna to the disaster of the Six-Day War, the gym teacher explained to bin Laden that the Arabs had turned their back on Allah by embracing the godless Soviets, so Allah was turning his back on the Arabs. Apostasy was crippling the Arab people. Only if the Arabs purified themselves, turned wholly and completely to following the teachings of the Qur'an, and engaged in holy war against the Jews and the Muslim apostates could they ever regain Allah's favor and the glory that was once theirs.

The more bin Laden heard, the more he began to buy into the Radicals' ideology. As he did so, he experienced a religious and political awakening, concluded Lawrence Wright in his landmark book, *The Looming Tower: Al-Qaeda and the Road to 9/11.* "Osama stopped watching cowboy shows. Outside of school, he refused to wear Western dress. Sometimes he would sit in front of the television and weep over the news from Palestine. . . . He began fasting twice a week, on Mondays and Thursdays, in emulation of the Prophet. . . . In addition to the five prayers a day, he set his alarm for one in the morning and prayed alone every night."[15]

As he approached his sixteenth birthday in 1973

— and underwent a massive growth spurt that left him six feet six inches tall and 160 pounds — bin Laden was again stunned and horrified to see the Jews of Israel defeat Egypt and the Syrians during the Yom Kippur War. Now the Muslim Brotherhood argument made even more sense. The Arabs were getting slaughtered and utterly humiliated by the Israelis and by the West because they had lost their way and forgotten the path of the prophets. Islam was the answer, he concluded, and jihad was the way.

Bin Laden soon became a member of the Brotherhood himself. He began reading the collected works of Sayyid Qutb, the radical Sunni theologian and Muslim Brotherhood activist who was executed by Egyptian authorities in 1966 but whose books became wildly popular among young jihadists, selling millions of copies after his death. Bin Laden married for the first time in 1974 to a devout fourteen-year-old Muslim girl who was a cousin of his from Syria.* Following high school,

*Intelligence analysts believe bin Laden is currently married to four wives, including one who is a descendant of the founder of Islam. He has also divorced one wife along the way. He is believed to be the father of at least fifteen children. Bin Laden once described his view of the benefits of polygamy, which was, of course, practiced by the founder of Islam and encouraged in the Qur'an. "One [wife] is okay, like walking," bin Laden told a friend. "Two [wives] is like riding a bike: it's fast but a little unstable. Three is a tricycle, stable but slow. And when we come to four, ah! This is the ideal. Now you can pass everyone!" (cited by Lawrence Wright in *The Looming Tower,* p. 94.)

he enrolled at King Abdulaziz University in Jeddah, ostensibly to study management and economics but also to find and make common cause with like-minded jihadists.

All the while, one geopolitical event after another kept forcing him to think more deeply about his worldview and how committed he was to it.

In 1975, for example, Saudi king Faisal was assassinated by his nephew. The assassination rocked the kingdom and was widely perceived by Islamic Radicals as a judgment against the king's love of the U.S. and Western Europe.

In 1977, Egyptian president Anwar Sadat made his dramatic visit to Jerusalem, and he began talking about making peace with the Israelis, horrifying young Radicals who saw Sadat as an apostate worthy of assassination himself (something they accomplished four years later).

In early 1979, the Ayatollah Khomeini led his Islamic Revolution to victory in Iran, electrifying Radicals throughout the region, including Sunnis like bin Laden who disagreed with Khomeini's theology but loved his tactics and envied his accomplishments.

On November 20, 1979, more than 1,300 radical Islamic jihadists seized control of the Grand Mosque in Mecca. Their leader declared himself the Mahdi and called for the overthrow of the apostate House of Saud and the establishment of a global Islamic caliphate. Saudi police eventually stormed the sacred facility to expel the extremists, killing 250 people, wounding 600, and infuriating Muslims who had been sympathetic to the extremists' cause.

And then the Soviet invasion of Afghanistan

closed out 1979 with a bang.

Bin Laden found himself wrestling with hard questions. How serious was he about his religious faith and his political views? If he had to decide between following his steadily developing convictions and becoming obscenely wealthy, which would he choose? Though he had been cast out of the bin Laden family at an early age, he still bore his father's name. He was still entitled to tens of millions of dollars in inheritance. He still had the opportunity to be a key figure in a multi-billion-dollar family construction business. Which path would he choose?

Finding a Mentor

Osama bin Laden went through his college years not only seeking education but searching for a father figure who would be willing to be his mentor and spiritual guide. He wanted to sit at the feet of a man who would give him the personal attention he so desperately craved, teach him the ways of Allah, and model for him a life of jihad. He wanted someone to help him choose the right direction for his life. He believed deeply that Allah had chosen him for a special mission. But he was not sure he could find it on his own.

In 1981, bin Laden finally found a Radical sheikh by the name of Abdullah Azzam who was all too happy to take the young and hungry student under his wing.

Azzam had been born in Jenin, a town in the West Bank, in 1941. During the 1967 war, he fled to Jordan, then moved to Cairo, where he earned a doctorate in Islamic jurisprudence from al-Azhar University. Later, he took a job leading prayers at King Abdulaziz University in Jeddah, Saudi Ara-

168

bia, where he met bin Laden.

Bin Laden was attracted, in part, to the fact that Azzam was a fellow member of the Muslim Brotherhood and a Palestinian with an intense desire to liberate Jerusalem from the Jews. He was also intrigued by the intense fervor with which Azzam preached his message and his absolute commitment to the use of violence.

"Jihad and the rifle alone" was the way to liberate the Holy Lands from the infidels, Azzam once insisted. "No negotiations, no conferences, no dialogues."[16] Another time, Azzam argued, "Jihad must not be abandoned until Allah *alone* is worshiped. . . . Jihad is the way of everlasting glory."[17] In his book *Defense of Muslim Lands,* Azzam wrote, "Pay close attention to the hadith: 'To stand one hour in the battle line in the cause of Allah is better than sixty years of night prayer.' "[18]

But the charismatic cleric did not just talk jihad; he lived it, and this galvanized bin Laden all the more. In 1981, Azzam went to Pakistan to teach the Qur'an at the International Islamic University in Islamabad. There, he met leaders of the Afghan mujahadeen. Entranced by the passion of these jihadists for death and for victory over the Soviets, Azzam visited Afghanistan. When he returned to Saudi Arabia, he told bin Laden and his other students, "I reached Afghanistan, and I could not believe my eyes. I felt as if I had been reborn."[19] Azzam was convinced it was in Afghanistan that Muslims should make a stand against the Communists, and he was eager to get his young Saudi protégé involved.

"Azzam returned to Jeddah frequently, staying in bin Laden's guest flat on his trips to the Kingdom," journalist Lawrence Wright has noted.

"He held recruiting sessions in bin Laden's apartment, where he magnetized young Saudis with his portraits of the suffering of the refugees and the courage of the mujahadeen. 'You have to do this!' he told them. 'It is your duty! You have to leave everything and go!' "[20]

By the early 1980s, there were 3,000 to 3,500 Arabs fighting in Afghanistan, a number that quickly grew to somewhere between 16,000 and 20,000 by the mid-1980s.[21]

"I Felt Closer to God Than Ever"

Osama bin Laden was convinced. His mentor wanted to take him on a journey to wage jihad against the Soviets in Afghanistan, and he desperately wanted to say yes. But bin Laden's mother told him he could not go. So did the Saudi government.

At first, bin Laden complied, promising his mother he would not travel into harm's way. But Azzam was relentless, part exhorting, part shaming his protégé into coming with him on his next trip into the battle zone.

By June 1984, Azzam's strategies had succeeded. He finally persuaded bin Laden to leave the family construction business behind, defy his family and many of his less devout friends, and join him in Afghanistan.

Upon arriving in the barren, rugged Afghan mountains, bin Laden was stunned by the squalor and the wretched state of affairs his fellow Muslims found themselves in. "I was surprised by the sad state of the equipment and everything else — weapons, roads, and trenches," he later recalled. "I asked forgiveness from God Almighty, feeling that I had sinned because I listened to those who advised me not to go. . . . I felt that this four-year delay could not be pardoned unless I became a martyr."[22]

Bin Laden had an epiphany in Afghanistan when he watched jihadists shoot down four Soviet aircraft. The experience moved him deeply. "I saw with my own eyes the remains of [one of] the pilots. Three fingers, a part of a nerve, the skin of one cheek, an ear, the neck, and the skin of the back. Some Afghan brothers came and took a photo of him as if he were a slaughtered sheep! We cheered. . . . I felt closer to God than ever."

Bin Laden had found his calling. True, he could not yet preach with the same intellect, experience, and charisma that Azzam possessed. Indeed, he was still a very shy and reclusive man. But he eagerly wanted to emulate his mentor. Perhaps, he thought, he could help finance the battle against the Soviets with his own money and with funds raised from kindred spirits back in Saudi Arabia. He resolved to return to Jeddah and find willing financial allies. By the end of the year he had raised nearly $10 million for the mujahadeen.[23]

At the same time, he did not want to simply write checks. He wanted to help in practical, tangible ways. He wanted to get his hands bloody. So he continued making trips to Afghanistan to visit those to whom he was supplying weapons, ammunition, food, and medical supplies, and he soon put his family's engineering experience to work, helping design, finance, and construct new roads, underground bunkers, and various facilities for the mujahadeen. And as he gained more in-country experience, he even began to try his hand at commanding small units of Arab jihadists in battles against the Soviets.

Views of bin Laden's military skills, even by close associates, were mixed at best. Bin Laden lost many men during his few clashes with the enemy. But there was absolutely no question that he was building a deeply devoted following of both Arabs and Afghans who admired his commitment to their overall success and were grateful for his personal and financial support. "He not only gave his money, but he also gave himself," recalled Hamza Muhammad, a Palestinian who signed up to help the mujahadeen and along the way became enamored of bin Laden. "He came down from his palace [in Arabia] to live with the Afghan peasants and the Arab fighters. He cooked with them, ate with them, dug trenches with them. That was bin Laden's way."[24]

The Birth of Al Qaeda

By the late 1980s, bin Laden could see the handwriting on the wall. The Soviets were getting their clocks cleaned by the mujahadeen, and he suspected Moscow might soon withdraw. When they did, bin Laden wanted to be able to boast that Allah had defeated one of the world's two infidel superpowers and was now ready to take down the other.

But bin Laden knew he could not possibly take on the "Great Satan" alone. He needed to build a team, an organization, and a movement. And the son of one the region's savviest businessmen soon realized he did not need to start from scratch. A merger would do just fine.

Bin Laden turned to Dr. Ayman al-Zawahiri, the head of an up-and-coming terrorist movement known as Egyptian Islamic Jihad, an offshoot of

172

the Muslim Brotherhood. The two had met sometime in 1984 or 1985, and bin Laden was intrigued with his story.

Zawahiri — about six years older than bin Laden — was born in Egypt in June 1951. Heavily influenced by the Brotherhood and the writings of Sayyid Qutb, he had formed his first jihad cell group in 1966, when he was only fifteen years old.

Recruitment was slow going at first. But a year later, Egypt lost the Six-Day War with Israel. Three years later, Egyptian president Gamal Abdel Nasser died of a heart attack. Three years after that, then president Anwar Sadat lost the 1973 war with Israel.

By this time, Zawahiri was twenty-two. The case he had been making to his emotionally devastated Egyptian friends was finally winning him converts. Secular nationalist movements such as Nasser's and Sadat's, he argued, were never going to help Arabs regain their honor or lost glory. Nor were such movements ever going to liberate Jerusalem. Islam was the only answer, he argued. Violent jihad was the way. And now was the time.

By the time he finished medical school in 1974, Zawahiri had forty members in his cell. But he was not nearly satisfied. Soon, he adopted four smaller cells operating in the Cairo area.

Then came the Islamic Revolution in Iran and the Soviet invasion of Afghanistan. Zawahiri was captivated by Khomeini's vision of a global jihadist movement, not just one limited to a single country. He also became intoxicated by accounts of the "miracles" of the mujahadeen destroying the Soviets with Allah's help.

Zawahiri wanted to learn everything he could in

173

order to take the lessons back to Cairo, overthrow Sadat's regime, create a Sunni version of the Islamic Revolution, and then export the Revolution throughout North Africa and the Sunni Middle East.

It became clear to bin Laden that Zawahiri had a bold and sweeping vision, a detailed strategy, and a ready-made organization of highly educated and well-trained warriors and experienced cell commanders. It was, in short, a turnkey scenario enabling bin Laden to establish what would effectively become "Jihad, Inc.," a multinational corporation dedicated to destroying Judeo-Christian civilization and imposing Sharia law on the entire planet.

Zawahiri needed money and a safe base of operations to train more men, plan terrorist actions, and launch attacks without being under the constant watchful eye of the Egyptian authorities. For bin Laden money was no object. His family had decided to bless him and his efforts rather than disown him. Thus, his own personal fortune was now estimated at between $60 million and $300 million. He also had thousands of names and addresses of donors who had helped him as he helped the mujahadeen.

Meanwhile, Afghanistan seemed to bin Laden like an ideal place to set up training camps and his global headquarters. Once the Soviets were gone, it would essentially be a no-man's-land, teeming with unemployed but experienced mujahadeen looking for new work and a new target.

On September 10, 1988, therefore, with help from Zawahiri and Egyptian Islamic Jihad, Osama bin Laden formed a new jihadist organization known as al Qaeda (Arabic for "the base"). Bin Laden was only thirty years old.

CHAPTER EIGHT:
DECLARING WAR ON AMERICA

The birth and growth of al Qaeda

"I am only one person," Osama bin Laden told fifteen colleagues at their first planning meetings in September of 1988.[1] They had to build a movement of Sunni jihadists, and they had to build fast, he told them. Bin Laden's plan was to have 314 trained terrorists on the payroll in Afghanistan and ready to embark on missions within six months.

By 1990, al Qaeda had established cells, recruiters, and fund-raising operations in fifty countries, including the United States.[2] By 1993, al Qaeda had trained more than six thousand Arabs to export jihad throughout the world.[3]

"New recruits filled out forms in triplicate, signed their oath of loyalty to bin Laden, and swore themselves to secrecy," reported Lawrence Wright. "In return, single members earned about $1,000 a month in salary; married members received $1,500. Everyone got a round-trip ticket home each year and a month of vacation. There was a health care plan and — for those who changed their mind — a buyout option: they received $2,400 and went on their way. From the beginning, al-Qaeda presented itself as an attractive employment opportunity for men whose education and careers had been curtailed by jihad."[4]

What accelerated the growth of the fledgling organization so quickly?

The Soviet withdrawal from Afghanistan, plain and simple. In nine years, more than fifteen thousand Soviet soldiers and airmen were killed in Afghanistan, and another thirty thousand or so were injured. Hundreds of Soviet jets and helicopters were shot down. And all the while bin Laden passionately argued that the mujahadeen's victories against the Soviet infidels were proof that Allah was on their side.*

*Bin Laden conveniently left out two major elements of the story of the Soviet defeat in Afghanistan: President Ronald Reagan and Rep. Charlie Wilson (D-Texas). Together, Reagan and Wilson persuaded Congress to increase funding to provide massive amounts of arms to the mujahadeen, including shoulder-launched ground-to-air missiles capable of destroying Soviet fighter jets and helicopters. Without U.S. funding and equipment, the mujahadeen never would have been able to defeat the Soviets. Some have questioned whether these funds ended up going directly to Osama bin Laden. The answer is no. Bin Laden used the mujahadeen victories to his advantage, but he himself was never a recipient of U.S. funding. After years of investigative reporting, CNN correspondent Peter Bergen concluded, "The Agency [CIA] directed around three billion dollars to the Afghan mujahadeen during the war against the Soviets, but there is no

But in bin Laden's mind, the defeat of the Soviets was only the beginning. He knew he needed to seize the momentum from this perceived victory and channel it into future operations. So no sooner had the Soviets retreated than bin Laden returned to Saudi Arabia and took a victory lap.

"The praise and media attention made bin Laden a sought-after celebrity," reported Youssef Bodansky, author of *Bin Laden: The Man Who Declared War on America,* one of the best biographies written about the enigmatic jihadist. "He spoke at countless mosques and private gatherings. Some of his fiery speeches were recorded; well over a quarter of a million official cassettes were sold, and countless illegal — and later,

---

evidence that any of that money went to the Afghan Arabs, nor is there any evidence of CIA personnel meeting with bin Laden or anyone in his circle." For more on covert CIA efforts to defeat the Soviets in Afghanistan, see Robert Gates, *From the Shadows,* pp. 319–321; Peter Bergen, *The Osama Bin Laden I Know,* pp. 60–61. Some would also point to George Crile's book, *Charlie Wilson's War: The Extraordinary Story of How the Wildest Man in Congress and a Rogue CIA Agent Changed the History of Our Times,* upon which the movie with Tom Hanks, Julia Roberts, and Philip Seymour Hoffman was based. While it is an extraordinary story told by key participants in these covert operations, readers and viewers should be warned that both the book and the film are filled with obscenities and debauchery. I cannot in good conscience, therefore, recommend them.

underground — copies were also made and distributed."[5]

"Allah . . . granted the Muslim people and the Afghani mujahedeen, and those with them, the opportunity to fight the Russians and the Soviet Union," bin Laden preached to anyone and everyone who would listen, including American journalists. "They were defeated by Allah and were wiped out. There is a lesson here. The Soviet Union entered Afghanistan late in December of '79. The flag of the Soviet Union was folded once and for all on the twenty-fifth of December, just ten years later. It was thrown in the waste basket. Gone was the Soviet Union forever. We are certain that we shall — with the grace of Allah — prevail over the Americans and over the Jews, as the Messenger of Allah promised us in an authentic prophetic tradition when he said the Hour of Resurrection shall not come before Muslims fight Jews and before Jews hide behind trees and behind rocks."[6]

Competing Visions

Al Qaeda was now a fast-growth company.

Money and new recruits were pouring in, but tensions within the organization were mounting as well, particularly between bin Laden's two mentors and ideological guides. Abdullah Azzam strongly disagreed with Ayman al-Zawahiri's vision of a global jihadist movement, believing it was a waste of time and money to build on such a large and expensive scale. Instead, Azzam implored bin Laden to turn his attention exclusively to helping Palestinians build an Islamist movement and muscle the secular nationalist Yasser Arafat and his Palestine Liberation Organization

179

out of the way. In his spare time, Azzam had helped create Hamas, the Islamic Resistance Movement of the Palestinians, in 1987. With bin Laden's money and intellectual leadership, Azzam believed together they could liberate Jerusalem and the Holy Land just as they had liberated Afghanistan.

Zawahiri, however, pushed back hard. The Palestinian issue was important, he argued, but al Qaeda was not ready. Liberating Palestine was simply too difficult for their next mission. Yes, Allah would be with them, but they had to play it smart. They needed to find more donors. They had to recruit more jihadists. They needed to build their organization and gain more experience. Moreover, they needed to focus on toppling apostate Arab leaders such as those in Egypt, Saudi Arabia, and Jordan. If they could surround the Jews with Islamist states and muster a massive army of mujahadeen, not just a ragtag band of blessed but exhausted warriors, then they could pull off something truly spectacular.

Both men competed vigorously for bin Laden's attention and resources. With his Palestinian background, bin Laden was sympathetic to Azzam's vision. But his heart was with Zawahiri. He certainly wanted to help liberate Jerusalem and destroy the Jewish and Christian infidels that had created and were actively supporting the modern State of Israel. But he wanted more. He now had a vision of building the largest and most aggressive Radical jihadist organization in the world. He wanted to take down the United States. And he agreed with Zawahiri that this would take more time and planning than Azzam, apparently, had patience for.

Azzam was deeply offended. He believed bin Laden would not have become the rock star of Sunni Radicals if it had not been for him, and he resented Zawahiri's claim to his protégé's time and affections.

Zawahiri, in turn, was livid. He worried that Azzam was trying to hijack al Qaeda and could, in the process, doom them to failure. Zawahiri was not about to let that happen. Something had to give.

On November 24, 1989, the problem was solved. Azzam and his two sons were killed by a roadside bomb on the way to a mosque in Peshawar, Pakistan. No one ever claimed credit. But the tensions were no more.

Building a Movement

For the next decade, bin Laden and Zawahiri built the "company" of their dreams.

When opportunities arose to recruit new men, they took advantage.

In the summer of 1989, for example, they watched General Omar al-Bashir seize power in a military coup in Sudan, and they noticed that Bashir was close with Hassan Abdallah al-Turabi, a radical Sunni cleric. Before long, it became clear that Bashir was dramatically changing Sudan's course from a historic alliance with Libya — led by Moammar Ghaddafi, a secular Arab nationalist — to a daring new alliance with the revolutionary mullahs in Iran.*

*By December 1991, 157 members of the Iranian parliament, as well as then Iranian president Ali Akbar Hashemi-Rafsanjani, visited Khartoum in a show of the new Iranian-Sudanese alliance. Soon, Iranian weapons

Bin Laden and Zawahiri were impressed. Deciding this was a man and a regime with which they could do business, they flew to Khartoum, met with Bashir, and offered to help set up new terrorist recruitment and training bases, working side by side with the Iranians. Bashir readily agreed, and for years, bin Laden and many of his top advisors actually lived in Sudan.

The al Qaeda leadership was also on the lookout for opportunities to give their "employees" experience in attacking infidels in high-profile ways, which was good for publicity and thus allowed more fund-raising and recruiting. In 1992, they noticed that U.S. Navy ships en route to Somalia were docking in Yemen's port city of Aden for refueling and to give the American sailors a short breather before going back into harm's way. Bin Laden, whose father was originally from Yemen, was enraged. He ordered his team to hit the Americans, and on December 29, 1992, al Qaeda launched its first terrorist attack, bombing two hotels in Aden. No Americans were actually killed in the operation, but the Navy did stop making port visits there for a while. Bin Laden considered it a small but important first victory. The Americans, he concluded, were weaker than most Muslims thought.

Throughout 1992 and 1993, al Qaeda funneled money, weapons, and even some personnel into Somalia, a country they considered Muslim territory. "In 1993, bin Laden issued a fatwa (religious

---

and advisors began flowing into Sudan, a trend that has continued right up through the regime of Mahmoud Ahmadinejad.

edict) calling for Somalis to attack U.S. forces and drive them out of the country," recalled James Phillips, the senior Middle East analyst at the Heritage Foundation, a D.C.-based think tank.[7]

Phillips has also noted that al Qaeda members were suspected of teaching the Somalian militia "how to shoot down U.S. helicopters by altering the fuses of rocket-propelled grenades so that they exploded in mid-air. This tactic [was] developed by the Afghan mujahideen in their war against the Soviets."[8]

As former Delta Force commander Jerry Boykin has noted, the al Qaeda operation in Somalia proved phenomenally successful in terms of propaganda, fund-raising, and recruiting after Washington was seen as cutting and running following the "Black Hawk Down" events.

"After our victory in Afghanistan and the defeat of the oppressors who had killed millions of Muslims, the legend about the invincibility of the superpowers vanished," bin Laden would later gloat in an interview on American television. "Our boys no longer viewed America as a superpower. . . . America had entered [Somalia] with 30,000 soldiers in addition to thousands of soldiers from different countries in the world . . . [but] the American soldier was just a paper tiger. He was unable to endure the strikes that were dealt to his army, so he fled. . . . I was in Sudan when this happened. I was very happy to learn of that great defeat that America suffered; so was every Muslim."[9]

"Kill Americans . . . and Their Allies"

By 1996, Sudanese officials were under pressure from the U.S. and the Saudis not to harbor al

Qaeda any longer, and President Bashir told bin Laden he had to leave. Unable to return to his home country due to all his rhetoric denouncing the Saudi royal family, bin Laden and his team returned to the mountains of Afghanistan, where they were warmly received by the leadership of the Taliban, the Radical Islamic group that had recently seized control of Afghanistan.*

Buoyed by early successes and once again in a secure base of operations, bin Laden, now thirty-nine, revealed the object of his fondest wishes and most fervent prayers. He issued a formal "Declaration of War against the United States" on August 23, 1996.

O you who believe, be careful of your duty to Allah. . . .

It should not be hidden from you that the people of Islam have suffered from aggression, iniquity, and injustice imposed on them by the Zionist-Crusaders alliance and their collaborators. . . . [Muslim] blood was spilled in Palestine and Iraq. . . . Massacres in Tajikistan, Burma, Kashmir, the Philippines . . . Somalia, Eritrea, Chechnya, and in Bosnia-Herzegovina took place, massacres that send shivers in the body and shake the conscience. . . .

The latest and the greatest of these aggressions . . . is the occupation of the land of the two Holy Places [referring to Mecca and Medina in Saudi Arabia] by the armies of the American Crusaders and their allies. . . .

Today, your brothers and sons [the al Qaeda

*I describe the Taliban in more detail in Part 2, during the chapters on Afghan president Hamid Karzai.

forces] . . . have started their Jihad in the cause of Allah, to expel the occupying enemy from [Saudi Arabia]. . . .

A few days ago the news agencies reported that the Defense Secretary of the Crusading Americans [William Perry] said that "the explosion at . . . the Khobar [Towers]* had taught him one lesson: that is, not to withdraw when attacked by coward terrorists." We say to the Defense Secretary that his talk can induce a grieving mother to laughter and shows the fears that have enshrined you all. Where was this false courage of yours when the explosion in Beirut took place on 1983? . . . You were turned into scattered pits and pieces at that time [when] 241 mainly Marine soldiers were killed. And where was this courage of yours when two explosions made you leave Aden in less than twenty-four hours!

But your most disgraceful case was in Somalia, where — after vigorous propaganda about the power of the USA and its post–Cold War leadership of the New World Order — you moved . . . 28,000 American soldiers into Somalia. However, when tens of your soldiers were killed in minor battles and one American pilot was dragged in the streets of Mogadishu,

*This refers to the June 25, 1996, attack on the Khobar Towers housing complex near Dhahran, Saudi Arabia, by members of the Saudi Hezbollah. Terrorists detonated a tanker truck filled with plastic explosives, all but destroying the nearest building. The attack killed 19 U.S. servicemen and one Saudi citizen and wounded 372 others.

you left the area carrying disappointment, humiliation, defeat, and your dead with you. . . . You have been disgraced by Allah, and you withdrew; the extent of your impotence and weaknesses became very clear. It was a pleasure for the heart of every Muslim and a remedy to the chests of believing nations to see you defeated in the three Islamic cities of Beirut, Aden, and Mogadishu.

[Our forces] have no intention except to enter paradise by killing you [Americans]. . . . The most honorable death is to be killed in the way of Allah.[10]

Clearly bin Laden's objective at that point was to drive the Americans out of Saudi Arabia. But over the next two years, he came to the conclusion that hitting Americans solely on the Arabian Peninsula was a mistake. Thus, on February 23, 1998, bin Laden issued a new fatwa declaring that every Muslim in the world was now obligated to attack and kill Americans anywhere and everywhere and to liberate not only Saudi Arabia but Jerusalem and Palestine as well.

We — with God's help — call on every Muslim who believes in God and wishes to be rewarded to comply with God's order to kill the Americans and plunder their money wherever and whenever they find it. We also call on Muslim [nations], leaders, youths, and soldiers to launch the raid on Satan's U.S. troops and the devil's supporters allying with them, and to displace those who are behind them so that they may learn a lesson.[11]

Going Operational

The fatwas were not mere bluster. Bin Laden, Zawahiri, and their team began to make good on their threats as well.

First, they accelerated their training of as many jihadists as they possibly could, both for their own organization and for other Radical groups. According to U.S. intelligence insiders, between the time bin Laden moved his operations to Afghanistan and the deadly attacks on the U.S. on September 11, 2001, al Qaeda trained between ten and twenty thousand jihadists in their camps.[12]

"In addition to training fighters and special operators, [al Qaeda's] network of guesthouses and camps provided a mechanism by which [bin Laden and his senior leaders] could screen and vet candidates for induction into its own organization," noted *The 9/11 Commission Report*. "From the time of its founding, al Qaeda had employed training and indoctrination to identify 'worthy' candidates. Al Qaeda continued meanwhile to collaborate closely with the many Middle Eastern groups — in Egypt, Algeria, Yemen, Lebanon, Morocco, Tunisia, Somalia, and elsewhere — with which it had been linked when bin Laden was in Sudan. It also reinforced its London base and its other offices around Europe, the Balkans, and the Caucasus."[13]

Second, they began to launch actual operations against U.S. interests outside of Saudi Arabia.

On the morning of August 7, 1998, two truck bombs exploded in front of the U.S. embassies in the African cities of Nairobi, Kenya, and Dar es Salaam, Tanzania, within minutes of each other. The Nairobi attack killed twelve Americans and 201 others, mostly Kenyan citizens, and injured some five thousand more. The attack in Tanzania killed eleven people, though none of them turned out to be Americans. Bin Laden did not hesitate to take credit for the attacks. He said publicly that if calling for jihad against Americans and Jews "is considered a crime," then "let history be a witness that I am a criminal."[14]

In December of 1999, Jordanian officials intercepted a phone conversation between senior al Qaeda operatives and members of a jihadist cell group based in the Hashemite Kingdom. They were hatching a plot they referred to as "the day of the millennium." Jordanian police units moved quickly, arresting sixteen terrorists who were planning to launch a chemical weapons attack by releasing hydrogen cyanide in a crowded movie theater in the capital of Amman, blow up tourists at the SAS Radisson Hotel in Amman, and attack Christian pilgrims at John the Baptist's shrine along the Jordan River.[15]

On October 12, 2000, al Qaeda used a small fishing boat to launch a suicide bombing attack against the USS *Cole,* a billion-dollar guided-missile destroyer, in the port of Aden, Yemen, which was once again being used by U.S. Naval forces. Seventeen American sailors were killed, and another forty were wounded in the blast, which tore a massive hole in the side of the ship, nearly sinking it. Bin Laden's senior staff had wanted to hit an oil tanker or some other commercial ship, but the al Qaeda terror master insisted they target an American warship.[16]

All the while, however, senior al Qaeda operatives were planning the most daring and deadly attack on U.S. soil in history.

CHAPTER NINE:
UNLEASHING THE ISLAMIC BOMB

What bin Laden and al Qaeda really want

On March 1, 2003, Khalid Sheikh Mohammed (aka "KSM") — al Qaeda's chief of external operations and the co-mastermind with bin Laden of the 9/11 attacks — was arrested in a daring raid near Islamabad, Pakistan.

The operation was led by CIA and Pakistani operatives who had been hunting KSM for years. It constituted the capture of the highest-ranking al Qaeda leader to that point. After being interrogated extensively by U.S. officials on multiple occasions over many months, KSM was eventually brought back to the United States to face a military tribunal at the U.S. Naval Base at Guantanamo Bay, Cuba. Eventually, previously classified notes of his interrogations were made available to the public.* So was the transcript of his interrogation by military prosecutors at Gitmo.[1]

*These notes are available in an official document entitled "Substitution for the Testimony of Khalid Sheikh Mohammed," which contains detailed information gleaned from previously classified U.S. intelligence interrogations of the senior al Qaeda terrorist. The

For me, reading both documents felt like I was actually sitting in the room with sheer evil, comparable perhaps to being in the presence of Charles Manson or Adolf Hitler, men clearly plagued by demons, spiritual or emotional or both. It was also a chilling window into the mind and heart of Osama bin Laden, who approved everything KSM did.

When I say *evil,* what I mean is that Khalid Sheikh Mohammed expressed absolutely no remorse for the fact that he has personally helped murder, maim, and injure well over ten thousand people in his lifetime. To the contrary, he was proud of it. He eagerly described all of the terrorist actions against innocent civilians that he planned and executed, up to and including the 9/11 attacks, as well as those following. At one point, he even boasted about cutting off the head of a *Wall Street Journal* reporter he had taken hostage in the months following 9/11. "I decapitated with my blessed right hand the head of the American Jew, Daniel Pearl, in the city of Karachi, Pakistan," he told U.S. officials without shame. "For those who would like to confirm, there are pictures of me on the Internet holding

---

document was made available to federal prosecutors for legal proceedings against Zacarias Moussaoui, an al Qaeda sleeper agent arrested inside the United States. Moussaoui was recruited and trained by KSM to conduct "second wave" attacks in the aftermath of 9/11. To read the full document online, go to http://www.rcfp.org/moussaoui/pdf/DX-0941.pdf, accessed July 18, 2008.

his head."[2] If this is not evil, I do not know what is.

One thing that certainly emerged from KSM's testimony was a clear and deeply disturbing portrait of the planning process that led up to September 11, 2001, and the deaths of nearly three thousand people in New York, Virginia, and Pennsylvania. The story really begins back in 1996, around the time bin Laden issued his declaration of war against the United States. KSM said he met with the Sunni terror master in the caves of Tora Bora, Afghanistan, and laid out his dream. He wanted enough men and money to hijack ten planes *inside* — not en route to — the United States and unleash them on kamikaze missions of murder and terror into American cities.

Having just met the man, bin Laden was hardly convinced KSM could pull off such a mission, but he was intrigued. And the more he learned about KSM, the more he liked.

Born in Pakistan sometime in 1964 or 1965, KSM was raised in Kuwait in a devout, fundamentalist family. He became a member of the Muslim Brotherhood at the age of sixteen and, much like bin Laden, became convinced at an early age that violent jihad was the only way to restore the glory of the Muslim world. KSM had fought with the mujahadeen in Afghanistan. He had fought against the West with the jihadist forces in Bosnia. And he had helped raise money for both causes.

But there was something else about this Radical that drew bin Laden to him: he had lived in the United States and understood how to operate in an "infidel" environment. According to *The 9/11 Commission Report,* after graduating from high school, "KSM left Kuwait to enroll at Chowan

191

College, a small Baptist school in Murfreesboro, North Carolina. After a semester at Chowan, KSM transferred to North Carolina Agricultural and Technical State University in Greensboro. . . . KSM earned a degree in mechanical engineering in December 1986."[3]

Bin Laden also appreciated KSM's fanatical desire to kill as many Americans as possible. KSM and his nephew, Ramzi Yousef — three years his junior — had helped plot and execute the truck bomb attack on the World Trade Center in 1993.*

So bin Laden agreed to let KSM begin researching such an operation in more detail, but only if he would help al Qaeda design and launch other high-profile terrorist attacks, an assignment KSM accepted with relish. Over the next few years, he developed "Operation Bojinka," a plot to hijack as many as a dozen jumbo jets in the Philippines and throughout Asia and then blow them up over the Pacific en route to the United States.[4] While the operation was foiled by police in Manila before it could be executed, it did give KSM extensive insight into how best to get men and weapons on board planes and how to handle many of the logistical questions that were bound to come up.

Meanwhile, he successfully masterminded the bombings of the U.S. embassies in Africa. This impressed bin Laden and convinced him that KSM was not only serious about killing Americans

*Ramzi Yousef was captured by Pakistani security forces in 1995 during a raid of a suspected al Qaeda safe house. He was later handed over to U.S. authorities, then tried in a federal court, convicted, and sentenced to life in prison without parole for his role in the 1993 World Trade Center attack.

but tactically savvy enough to pull off a complex operation in multiple cities on another continent.

"I Swear Allegiance to You for Jihad"

In April of 1999, KSM — who typically operated not in Afghanistan but out of Pakistan, Kuwait, or other parts of the Middle East and Asia — was back in the caves of Tora Bora, meeting with bin Laden and trying to persuade him and Dr. Ayman al-Zawahiri to embrace his audacious scenario. This time, bin Laden gave the green light, saying he believed the plot could work and that KSM had the organization's blessing and financial backing.

Thrilled, KSM set out to recruit the right men — that is, those capable of successfully entering the United States and living there undetected, capable of keeping their mouths shut, capable of training for a mission that they would not be told the final details of until the last possible moment, and — perhaps most important — capable of murder. KSM later told interrogators that he required each man selected to pledge the following oath of loyalty to bin Laden personally: "I swear allegiance to you, to listen and obey, in good times and bad, and to accept the consequences myself; I swear allegiance to you for jihad, and to listen and obey, and to die in the cause of God."[5]

By early 2001, the plot had advanced to the point where KSM was ready to review a list of targets with bin Laden. The emir, or prince, of al Qaeda insisted they hit the two World Trade Center towers, the Pentagon, and the U.S. Capitol, at a minimum. But bin Laden also gave KSM latitude to hit other targets as well, including the White House, the Sears Tower in Chicago, and a

193

foreign embassy of his choosing in Washington, D.C. When Mohammed Atta (one of the Egyptian cell commanders who would eventually hijack American Airlines Flight 11 and fly it into one of the World Trade Center towers) suggested hitting a nuclear power plant in Pennsylvania, bin Laden agreed to add the target to the list.

"After the 1993 attacks on the World Trade Center, I decided that explosives and bombs could be problematic, and so I focused on using airplanes as weapons," KSM told interrogators. "The most attractive targets were high buildings, both for their relative ease of targeting as well as for the symbolic impact. Bin Laden expressed his desire to simultaneously hit the Pentagon, the White House, and the U.S. Capitol building."[6]

Bin Laden personally and specifically chose the cell leaders to carry out the operation. But it was KSM whom bin Laden trusted for all the operational details. It was KSM, for example, who designed the rigorous training regime each cell member would undergo, including basic physical conditioning, English lessons, and instruction in how to conduct a hijacking, how to disarm an air marshal, and the use of explosives. The men also were required to butcher sheep and camels as practice for killing anyone who got in their way on board the planes.

It was KSM who gave the cell commanders the cash they needed for the mission. It was KSM who helped his men acquire "clean" passports without Pakistani and Afghan stamps. He told them where in the U.S. to live. He told them what to study (more English and how to fly a jumbo jet). He forbade them to speak to other Muslims while in the U.S., lest they be tempted to confide their plans to someone they might consider a kindred spirit. He told them how to communicate with headquarters.

Everything was "compartmentalized." Only KSM, bin Laden, and a handful of other al Qaeda senior operatives knew all the details.

As the time of the operation approached, KSM said bin Laden kept pushing for faster action. Three times bin Laden pressured him to launch sooner, but KSM insisted they were not quite ready. That summer, for example, bin Laden heard that Israeli prime minister Ariel Sharon was heading to the White House. He urged KSM to move fast in order to kill Sharon and President Bush and their top advisors at the same time. But again KSM resisted, saying his team was close but still not ready to strike. Moreover, KSM believed the final decision on choosing a strike date should be in the hands of the senior cell commander to whom he had given this authority.

Thus, it was not until August that KSM himself finally learned of the date of the operation. He immediately informed bin Laden. But he was horrified that as the date of the attack approached, bin Laden began telling colleagues and even high-level visitors to his camp in the mountains of Afghanistan that something big was coming. KSM urged bin Laden not to say anything more or risk compromising the operation.

Eventually, of course, the 9/11 attacks were carried out and were actually far more successful than either bin Laden or KSM had imagined. "We sat down to calculate the amount of losses within the enemy and we expected the number to be those inside the plane, and for the [World Trade Center] towers, the number of people that the plane would actually hit," bin Laden told friends at a November 2001 dinner in Kandahar that was recorded on someone's personal video camera and later recovered by U.S. intelligence. "I was the most optimistic of all because of my expertise in this profession and in this business. I said the fuel on the plane would melt the iron and the iron would lose its properties." Bin Laden said he had predicted that the building would be destroyed from the point of impact upward. But the total destruction of the buildings, he said, "was a lot more than we expected."[7]

Bin Laden formally claimed credit for the 9/11 attacks in 2003 during an eighteen-minute video released to the Al Jazeera news network. In the tape, the al Qaeda leader said he decided "we should destroy towers in America" because "we are a free people . . . and we want to regain the freedom of our nation."[8]

KSM later shed more light on his and bin Laden's motivations. According to the notes of his interrogations, "Sheikh Mohammed said that the purpose of the attack on the Twin Towers was to 'wake the American people up.' Sheikh Mohammed said that if the target would have been strictly military or government, the American people would not focus on the atrocities that America is committing by supporting Israel against the Palestinian people and America's self-serving foreign policy that corrupts Arab governments and leads to further exploitation of the Arab [and] Muslim peoples."[9]

What Al Qaeda Really Wants
During his military tribunal at Gitmo, KSM admitted that he was not only responsible for the

196

9/11 attacks but also the mastermind of "second wave" attacks and other planned mega-attacks in the United States, Israel, and around the globe. In a written statement given to interrogators, KSM went on to confess to no fewer than thirty-one separate terrorist attacks. Some had already been carried out. Others were foiled by U.S. and foreign security forces or by KSM's arrest. Each provided a sobering insight into what Osama bin Laden and his al Qaeda network really want:

1. I was responsible for the 1993 World Trade Center Operation.
2. I was responsible for the 9/11 Operation, from A to Z.
3. I decapitated with my blessed right hand the head of the American Jew, Daniel Pearl. . . .
4. I was responsible for the Shoe Bomber Operation to down two American airplanes.
5. I was responsible for the Filka Island Operation in Kuwait that killed two American soldiers.
6. I was responsible for the bombing of a nightclub in Bali, Indonesia, which was frequented by British and Australian nationals.
7. I was responsible for planning, training, surveying, and financing the New (or Second) Wave attacks against the following skyscrapers after 9/11:
   Library Tower, California
   Sears Tower, Chicago
   Plaza Bank, Washington State
   The Empire State Building, New York City

8. I was responsible for planning, financing, and follow-up of operations to destroy American military vessels and oil tankers in the Straits of Hormuz, the Straits of Gibraltar, and the Port of Singapore.

9. I was responsible for the planning, training, surveying, and financing for the operation to bomb and destroy the Panama Canal.

10. I was responsible for the surveying and financing for the assassination of several former American Presidents, including President Carter.

11. I was responsible for the surveying, planning, and financing for the bombing of suspension bridges in New York.

12. I was responsible for planning to destroy the Sears Tower by burning a few fuel or oil tanker trucks beneath it or around it.

13. I was responsible for the planning, surveying, and financing for the operation to destroy Heathrow Airport, the Canary Wharf Building, and Big Ben on British soil.

14. I was responsible for the planning, surveying, and financing for the destruction of many nightclubs frequented by American and British citizens on Thailand soil.

15. I was responsible for the surveying and financing for the destruction of the New York Stock Exchange and other financial targets after 9/11.

16. I was responsible for the planning, financing, and surveying for the destruction of buildings in the Israeli city of Elat by using airplanes leaving from Saudi Arabia.

17. I was responsible for the planning, survey-

ing, and financing for the destruction of American embassies in Indonesia, Australia, and Japan.

18. I was responsible for the surveying and financing for the destruction of the Israeli embassy in India, Azerbaijan, the Philippines, and Australia.

19. I was responsible for the surveying and financing for the destruction of an Israeli El-Al Airlines flight on Thailand soil departing from Bangkok Airport.

20. I was responsible for sending several mujahadeen into Israel to conduct surveillance to hit several strategic targets deep in Israel.

21. I was responsible for the bombing of the hotel in Mombasa that is frequented by Jewish travelers via El-Al airlines.

22. I was responsible for launching a Russian-made SA-7 surface-to-air missile on El-Al or other Jewish airliner departing from Mombasa.

23. I was responsible for planning and surveying to hit American targets in South Korea, such as American military bases and a few nightclubs frequented by American soldiers.

24. I was responsible for providing financial support to hit American, Jewish, and British targets in Turkey.

25. I was responsible for surveillance needed to hit nuclear power plants that generate electricity in several U.S. states.

26. I was responsible for planning, surveying, and financing to hit NATO headquarters in Europe.

27. I was responsible for the planning and

surveying needed to execute the Bojinka Operation, which was designed to down twelve American airplanes full of passengers. I personally monitored a round-trip, Manila-to-Seoul Pan Am flight.

28. I was responsible for the assassination attempt against President Clinton during his visit to the Philippines in 1994 or 1995.
29. I shared responsibility for the assassination attempt against Pope John Paul II while he was visiting the Philippines.
30. I was responsible for the training and financing for the assassination of Pakistan's President Musharraf.
31. I was responsible for the attempt to destroy an American oil company owned by the Jewish former Secretary of State, Henry Kissinger, on the Island of Sumatra, Indonesia.

The Ultimate Objective

As horrifying as these operations were, they pale in comparison to what al Qaeda has been praying for and planning for at least a decade: acquiring weapons of mass destruction (WMDs) — ideally nuclear weapons — to be used against the United States to kill between four and ten million Americans.

Asked in 1998 if al Qaeda had nuclear or chemical weapons, bin Laden told *Time* magazine that "acquiring weapons for the defense of Muslims is a religious duty. If I have indeed acquired these weapons, then I thank God for enabling me to do so."[10] The timing of that statement was significant, for 1998 was the year that Pakistan tested nuclear weapons.

Since then, many more disturbing details have emerged about bin Laden's feverish hunt for WMDs and his deep-rooted belief that Allah has commanded him to use them to kill Christians and Jews. In the summer of 2002, Suleiman Abu Ghaith, a Kuwaiti-born spokesman for al Qaeda, posted the following statement on the Internet: "Al-Qa'ida has the right to kill four million Americans, including one million children, displace double that figure, and injure and cripple hundreds of thousands."[11] In May 2003, al Qaeda unveiled a fatwa from a leading Saudi cleric that sanctioned the use of nuclear weapons against the U.S. and permitted the killing of up to ten million Americans.[12]

In 2007, FBI director Robert Mueller made the following statement at a conference on nuclear terrorism: "By some estimates, there is enough highly enriched uranium in global stockpiles to construct thousands of nuclear weapons, and it is safe to assume that there are many individuals who would not think twice about using such weapons. The economics of supply and demand dictate that someone, somewhere, will provide nuclear material to the highest bidder, and that material will end up in the hands of terrorists. Al Qaeda has demonstrated a clear intent to acquire weapons of mass destruction. In 1993, Osama bin Laden attempted to buy uranium from a source in the Sudan. He has stated that it is Al Qaeda's duty to acquire weapons of mass destruction. And he has made repeated recruiting pitches for experts in chemistry, physics, and explosives to join his terrorist movement."[13]

Former CIA director George Tenet at first wasn't sure just how seriously to take bin Laden's

WMD threats. But over time, he became convinced. He now believes that bin Laden's top priority is to acquire nuclear weapons and detonate them inside the United States.

"Although we had his own statements to give us great concern, the consensus inside and outside our own government could be boiled down to this: 'Guys in caves can't get WMD,' " Tenet wrote in his 2007 memoirs, *At the Center of the Storm: My Years at the CIA.* "But this was an issue about which we could not afford to be wrong. So soon after 9/11, I directed CIA's CTC [Counterterrorism Center] to establish a new capability to focus exclusively on terrorist WMD. . . . We began to review the historical record. We combed our files and sent teams around the world to share our leads and ask foreign intelligence services about information in their possession. We interrogated al-Qa'ida prisoners and pored over documents found in safe houses and on computers captured in Afghanistan. What we discovered stunned us all. The threats were real. Our intelligence confirmed that the most senior leaders of al-Qa'ida are still singularly focused on acquiring WMD. Bin Laden may have provided the spiritual guidance to develop WMD, but the program was personally managed at the top by his deputy, Ayman al-Zawahiri. Moreover, we established beyond any reasonable doubt that al-Qa'ida had clear intent to acquire chemical, biological, and radiological/nuclear (CBRN) weapons, to possess not as a deterrent but to cause mass casualties in the United States."[14]

"Of all al-Qa'ida's efforts to obtain other forms of WMD, the main threat is the nuclear one," Tenet stressed. "I am convinced that this is where [bin Laden] and his operatives desperately want to go. They understand that bombings by cars, trucks, trains, and planes will get them some headlines, to be sure. But if they manage to set off a mushroom cloud, they will make history. Such an event would place al-Qa'ida on a par with the superpowers and make good on bin Ladin's threat to destroy our economy and bring death into every American household. Even in the darkest days of the Cold War, we could count on the fact that the Soviets, just like us, wanted to live. Not so with the terrorists. Al-Qa'ida boasts that while we fear death, they embrace it."[15]

CHAPTER TEN:
TERROR HIGH

How the Radicals are infiltrating
the U.S. and Europe

How serious is the Radical threat today?

Many Americans — perhaps most — simply have no idea how aggressively Radicals are trying to infiltrate the United States, recruit Americans into terrorist cell groups, and gather the weaponry they need to pull off catastrophic attacks inside this country. Consider, then, a case that occurred not that long ago right here in Washington, D.C., the city Lynn and my boys and I call home.

Meet Ahmed Ali

Ahmed Omar Abu Ali was born in 1982, three years after the Iranian Revolution. His family moved to the Washington, D.C., area when he was four years old, and he was raised in Falls Church, Virginia. He studied at an Islamic school in Alexandria, Virginia, and graduated with honors in 1999, having been named his class's valedictorian.

Sometimes I wonder if I ever crossed paths with him, or if my wife or kids did. On the outside, Ahmed seemed like a poster child for the Reformers — a friendly, bright, successful young Muslim

American man who seemed to love his country, love his family, and be eager to pursue his dreams of building a life for himself in a land of liberty. But things are not always what they seem. On the inside, Ahmed was a Radical in the making, seething with hatred.

In the fall of 1999, Ahmed entered the University of Maryland to study electrical engineering. The following year, however, he changed his mind. He transferred to the University of Medina in Saudi Arabia to study Islamic law and theology and quickly gravitated to those who shared his belief that Islam was the answer and jihad was the way. In 2002, not long after the attacks on the World Trade Center and the Pentagon, Ahmed joined a clandestine al Qaeda cell group operating inside the kingdom.

Ahmed was a recruiter's dream come true. He had full American citizenship, an American passport, and a respectable cover as a university student. His al Qaeda handlers quickly sent him for training in the tradecraft of terror, including firing various weapons, building and detonating explosives, and forging documents. Then they told him to return to the U.S., marry a Christian woman, and assimilate into the community. They also told him he would be provided with operatives to carry out spectacular attacks.[1]

Like a scene from one of the novels I was writing at the time, the plot Ahmed and senior al Qaeda leaders were developing half a world away involved a conspiracy to assassinate the president of the United States and trigger apocalyptic destruction in the nation's capital. Ahmed told friends he believed George W. Bush was "the leader of the infidels."[2] He and his colleagues, therefore, planned to use multiple snipers and suicide bombers to kill the president, while other al Qaeda sleeper cell operatives simultaneously hijacked planes outside the U.S. and used them to launch kamikaze attacks against American targets.[3] What was more, Ahmed met with a high-ranking al Qaeda leader who asked him to research the feasibility of attacking nuclear power facilities inside the U.S. homeland.[4] The goal: to unleash horrors equivalent to actually having their own weapon of mass destruction.

But for the grace of God and the hard work of Homeland Security officials at home and abroad, the plots might very well have succeeded. In the summer of 2003, after a series of terrorist bombings throughout Saudi Arabia, authorities there launched a series of raids against suspected Radical compounds throughout the country. Swept up in the dragnet was Ahmed, although the Saudis were not specifically looking for him and were barely aware that he existed, much less posed a threat. Once the Saudis began interrogating him, however, it quickly became evident just how serious a suspect they had in their hands, and they turned him over to U.S. officials.

At Ahmed's trial, Justice Department lawyers argued that he had "joined an al Qaeda terrorist cell . . . in order to engage in jihad against the United States."[5] What's more, they described the case as "one of the most dangerous terrorist threats that America faces in the perilous world after September 11, 2001: an al Qaeda operative born and raised in the United States, trained and committed to carry out deadly attacks on American soil."[6]

Ahmed's family laughed in the courtroom when

206

the charges were explained, insisting Ahmed was innocent. "Everything the government has said is lies upon lies upon lies," Ahmed's father told the *Washington Post,* describing his son as a peaceful student of Islam who was arrested while taking his final exams.[7]

The jury didn't buy it. Ahmed Omar Abu Ali was convicted on November 22, 2005, and sentenced to thirty years in a maximum-security federal prison.

Stopping the Next Ali

Now meet Fred Schwien.*

Born in 1957 in WaKeeney, Kansas, a town of only two thousand people today and far smaller then, Fred grew up watching the counterculture revolution of the '60s and '70s at home and horrific wars and revolutions unfolding abroad, including the trauma of America's involvement in Vietnam. Raised in a Lutheran home, Fred was an evangelical Christian by the age of sixteen.

Fred saw the turbulence of the times and felt a calling to defend his country against all enemies, foreign and domestic. He received an appointment to attend college at the United States Military Academy at West Point, graduated in June of 1979 during the early stages of the Iranian Revolution, and began his active duty in the Army the following month.

Over the course of the next two decades, Fred served as an Airborne Ranger infantry officer and in various command and staff positions in the U.S., Europe, and Panama. He served at the Pentagon on the Army Staff, working on counter-

*Pronounced "Shween."

terrorism issues. He served on the Joint Staff, working on arms-control issues. Later, he worked at NATO's Supreme Headquarters in Mons, Belgium, as the deputy U.S. national military representative. Along the way, he was blessed with a wonderful Christian wife, and together they began to raise a family. Fred retired from the Army in 1999 as a lieutenant colonel, and he and his family eventually moved back from Europe to D.C.

That's when Lynn and I met them. Actually, Lynn first met Fred's wife and family in a kids' ministry they were involved in at our church. At the time, Fred was serving as an aide to U.S. Commerce Secretary Don Evans, but in 2005, he was hired as a senior advisor to U.S. Homeland Security Secretary Michael Chertoff.

"You've really got to meet this guy," Lynn kept insisting. "His wife thinks you two would really hit it off, and I think she's right. He's read your books. He's given them to the secretary and others in the office. Plus, he's not writing about the War on Terror, he's actually living it."

As is almost always the case, Lynn was right. Fred and I began to get together for an occasional lunch or cup of coffee, and the more I got to know him, the more impressed I became. Whether jumping out of planes as a Ranger or flying into Baghdad on a Black Hawk helicopter to coordinate Homeland Security operations with his Iraqi counterparts, Fred Schwien had spent all of his professional life protecting people like my family and me from people like Ahmed Omar Abu Ali, and I was deeply grateful.

In the winter of 2008, I sat down with Fred and asked him to take me inside the Revolution from his vantage point — a world few Americans ever really see.

First of all, I asked Fred his perspective on the threat that America faces today from radical Islam. "Just how serious is that threat to the American people?"

"The threat is very real," he replied. "In the past few years, there have been a number of attacks that were successful in London and Madrid. And then there have been a number of attacks that we disrupted abroad. An airline plot in the summer of 2006 was disrupted before the terrorist could blow airliners up coming across to the U.S. from the U.K. There was a case at JFK airport where some Radicals were planning to blow up the fuel lines, hoping to cause really mass destruction near JFK. We know that al Qaeda and like-minded groups would love to cause great damage and cause massive casualties within the United States. So the threat is very real, and the ones that I've mentioned are ones that have been in the press, but there are others that the public doesn't know about. There are people at the border that are stopped every day trying to come into the United States that have something about them in their background, or with their connections, that the Customs and Border Protection agents look at and say, 'This person isn't coming in the United States.' Or we deny people visas when they apply . . . because we believe they have some connection [to terrorism]."[8]

"Can you give me an example," I asked, "of a case where Homeland Security denied someone entry into the U.S. and that action actually saved lives?"

"Absolutely," he replied. "One guy we stopped

209

coming across because a border agent didn't feel that he was legitimate. We didn't know what this fellow was up to, but he was stopped at the border. We denied his entry into the country, and he was sent home. Two years later he was found to have been a suicide bomber. His hands were found attached to the steering wheel after a suicide truck bombing in Iraq."

U.S. authorities in Iraq took the fingerprints from those hands and ran them through the Homeland Security database to see who he was. The system worked. They not only tracked down the bomber's identity, they were able to confirm that he had tried to enter the U.S. at one point but had been refused.

Thank God, I thought, *for that alert border agent — he may have only been going by instincts at the time, but those instincts had proven right.*

"When it comes to the threat of radical Islamists," Fred noted, "you have to keep in mind the stakes are very high. We have to be right every time; they only have to get it right once." A Radical that slips into the country would be poised to carry out his murderous and possibly genocidal objectives.

"What worries you most these days, Fred?" I asked.

"The worst-case scenario that we worry about is some type of nuclear or improvised nuclear device, or some type of biological weapon," he explained. "Those are our two biggest fears. We have fifteen planning scenarios and a number of plans applied against those planning scenarios to react to them if something were to happen. These could involve a pandemic influenza. They could involve a nuclear device. They could involve a chemical attack. So if, God forbid, one of those things happens, the government is in a much better position now to respond than we were before September 11."

"Based on all your years of experience, Fred, help me understand the mind-set of the radical Islamic jihadist that makes him so dangerous to the American people."

"What makes jihadists so dangerous is that they really do hate us and in many ways they hate our way of life," he replied. "And they work very hard at recruiting other people to believe their ideas. When I've spoken with Muslim leaders, with Imams — the moderate ones, Reformers — they believe that Radicals take the Qur'an completely out of context and use it to brainwash young people, in many cases, to believing in a cause that really is very, very violent and very anti-Western, very anti-American."

Fred then pointed to the two countries he worries about most for Radical recruiting: Iraq and the United States.

"In my personal view, there is nothing the Radicals want more than to see the United States fail in Iraq," he told me. "They want us to fail to show that they can beat us. And we really have to get Iraq right. We need to get a functioning democratic society working there. It may take Iraq years to get it right, but we have to make sure that it's a success, because the consequences of Iraq becoming a failed state and a massive breeding ground for terrorists are too horrific to even imagine."

Then he added, "Self-radicalization by Muslims living in the United States is also something that Homeland Security is very concerned about.

211

Young men in particular are vulnerable if they feel marginalized in society. In fact, when I was visiting Morocco, one of the officials said young jihadists are like the Columbine shooters. These kids are out there. They get on the Internet, they get on a jihadist Web site, and they look at something and they go, 'Ah, that's something I can belong to,' and they get sucked into Radical thought and a jihadist mentality. And that's when they can become very dangerous because they, in essence, self-radicalize right where they are, and it's tough to know who they are and tough to find and stop them."

Indoctrinating the Next Ali

Which brings us back to Ahmed Omar Abu Ali.

Yes, he was an American citizen. Yes, he was bright. Yes, he was a high school valedictorian. But what was he learning? What was he being taught? And what are the chances that there are others like him out there being indoctrinated or self-radicalized?

Ahmed graduated from the Islamic Saudi Academy (ISA), a private Muslim elementary and secondary school located in Alexandria, Virginia, just across the Potomac River from the White House and the Capitol building, the epicenter of American democracy. The school opened its doors back in 1984 with a handful of a students but a passionate mission to educate a new generation of Muslim young people capable of studying at American universities, working in American jobs, and influencing American society with the values of the Qur'an. It soon became a highly prestigious institution, sought out by Muslims from Saudi Arabia and the U.S. "The Saudi ambassador to the United States is chairman of the school's board of directors," reported the *Washington Post,* "and the kingdom subsidizes expenses beyond the academy's $3,000 annual tuition for non-Saudi students. Saudi students attend free."[9]

By 2008, ISA had two campuses — the original in Alexandria and another in Fairfax, Virginia — educating about a thousand children from pre-K through twelfth grade. Al Jazeera has called it "the largest institution teaching the Arabic language and Islamic education on the East Coast of the U.S.," but its critics have since dubbed it "Terror High."[10]

Why? Aside from the fact that its most famous graduate was convicted of trying to assassinate the president, a *Washington Post* investigation also found that ISA "used textbooks as recently as 2006 that compared Jews and Christians to apes and pigs, told eighth-graders that these groups are 'the enemies of the believers,' and diagrammed for high school students where to cut off the hands and feet of thieves." Saudi officials admitted to the *Post* that "the textbooks used at the Islamic Saudi Academy had contained inflammatory material since at least the mid-1990s." They claimed to have ordered revisions in 2006, but the *Post* found that in the 2006–07 school year, "at least one book still contained passages that extolled jihad and martyrdom, called for victory over one's enemies, and said the killing of adulterers and apostates was 'justified.' "[11]

ISA administrators and Saudi officials now insist they are doing everything they can to change the textbooks and safeguard the curriculum against violent teachings. But some experts say what has been happening there is just the tip of the iceberg.

The Saudi government and radicalized Saudi clerics, such experts claim, are actively exporting their vision of the Revolution to the U.S. and Europe and using Islamic training institutes known as madrassas at home and abroad to indoctrinate young people and prepare them for recruitment into terrorist cells.

Exporting the "Wahhabi Islam" Way

"It is not an accident that 15 of the 19 terrorists who attacked us on September 11, 2001, were Saudis," noted former CIA director James Woolsey during congressional testimony in 2002. "A poll conducted by Saudi intelligence and shared with the U.S. government [found] that over 95 percent of Saudis between the ages of 25 and 41 have sympathy for Osama bin Laden."[12] Such sympathies, combined with extremist ideology being taught in Islamic schools, are creating a breeding ground for a new wave of radical Islamic terrorists.

But Woolsey argued that this dangerous situation was not isolated to the Arabian Peninsula. "The Saudi-funded, Wahhabi-operated export of hatred for us reaches around the globe," he warned. "It is well known that the religious schools of Pakistan that educated a large share of the Taliban and al Qaeda are Wahhabi. But Pakistan is not the sole target." Woolsey noted that "a substantial percentage of American mosques have Wahhabi-funded Imams." A dangerous ideology of sheer hatred and violence, he said, is being "proliferated by the Wahhabis within the American homeland."[13]

Wahhabi Islam is a strict, purist form of Sunni theology developed by Muhammad Ibn 'Abd al-

Wahhab on the Arabian Peninsula in the eighteenth century. Today, it is the dominant form of Islam practiced in Saudi Arabia, Qatar and the Gulf states, Egypt, and much of North Africa, with the exception of Morocco, and it is an intensely aggressive, missionary religion. While al-Wahhab probably never used such a simplistic slogan, he was in many ways one of the earliest adherents and preachers of the notion that "Islam is the answer, and jihad is the way."

In the mid-1700s, just as Thomas Jefferson and his colleagues were laying the groundwork for the American Revolution to create freedom and democracy in the West, al-Wahhab and his colleagues were laying the groundwork for their own Revolution in the Middle East. They feared Sunnis were losing their religious zeal, moral holiness, and military effectiveness, and they urged Muslims to rededicate themselves to a radically fundamental version of Islam. For the next century and a half, they and their descendants and disciples after them embarked on a series of military conquests in the region, culminating in the establishment of the Kingdom of Saudi Arabia in 1932.*

Today there are an estimated 1,200 mosques in the U.S., and between 50 and 80 percent are believed to be under Wahhabi control or dominated by Wahhabi theology.[14] Between 1990 and 2000, the number of mosques in the United States increased 42 percent, and one in five mosques

*Wahhabi Islam is also often referred to as Salafi Islam. Salafi in Arabic means "a pious or righteous ancestor." Salafists, therefore, follow the fundamental, Radical version of Islam taught by their devout forefathers, such as Mohammad Ibn 'Abd al-Wahhab.

now run full-time elementary, middle, and secondary schools, meaning that far more attention is being paid by Muslims of all sects and theological distinctions to raising up a new generation of fully devoted Muslim leaders.[15]

There are also a growing number of mega-mosques being built in major American cities — full-service, one-stop-shopping Islamic super-centers designed to meet a wide variety of spiritual and educational needs. The 48,000-square-foot Dearborn Mosque in Dearborn, Michigan, not far from Detroit (home of some three hundred thousand people of Middle Eastern descent) is three stories high, takes up an entire city block, and is the largest Sunni mosque in the U.S. Meanwhile, the $12-million-plus Islamic Center of America — also in Dearborn — not only is the largest Shia mosque in the country, it was also described by the Associated Press as "the largest Arab American religious and cultural facility in North America." Besides a new worship facility, "the center's 120,000-square-foot complex . . . feature[s] an auditorium, library, and community center."[16]

Don't get me wrong. I am not saying that either of these specific mega-mosques should necessarily be classified as a threat. Nor should those who attend them. Nevertheless, the problem of Radical indoctrination in mosques and Islamic schools is real and widespread. In 2005, the highly respected human rights organization known as Freedom House set out to examine the influence of Saudi-sponsored Wahhabi Islam on American life. Their researchers analyzed more than two hundred books and publications collected from more than a dozen mosques and Islamic centers throughout

American cities such as Washington, D.C., New York, Los Angeles, Oakland, Chicago, Dallas, and Houston. Ninety percent of the material was originally published in Arabic, though some books and tracts analyzed were in English, Urdu (the major language of Pakistan), Chinese, or Tagalog (the major language of the Philippines). All of the publications had been printed by a Saudi government ministry, distributed by the Saudi Embassy, or distributed through a mosque or Islamic center sponsored by the Saudi royal family.

What the researchers found was that Saudi-sponsored materials used in hundreds of mosques throughout the U.S. propagated "a religious ideology that explicitly promotes hate, intolerance, and other human rights violations, and in some cases violence, toward members of other religious groups, both Muslims and non-Muslims." Furthermore, the study concluded that "Saudi-connected resources and publications on extremist ideology remain common reading and educational material in some of America's main mosques."[17]

Consider a few examples from the researchers' report:

"Muslims who convert out of Islam, of course, are apostates . . . and, under Saudi law, they are to be put to death. An Urdu-language publication, published by the Saudi Ministry of Religious Affairs [and found in a Saudi-financed mosque inside the U.S.] quotes Sheik Bin Uthaimin preaching this policy: '[O]ur doctrine states that if you accept any religion other than Islam, like Judaism or Christianity, which are not acceptable, you become an unbeliever. If you do not repent, you are an apostate and you should be killed because you have denied the Qur'an.' "[18]

"In a book published by the Ascension Printing House in Saudi Arabia and distributed to a number of mosques in the United States, including the King Fahd Mosque in Los Angeles, California, which was built with $8 million in direct donations from Saudi King Fahd and his son, the issue of Christian missionary activity is linked to a continuation of the Crusades. The Wahhabi text reads: 'He is wrong who thinks that the Crusaders' hate for Islam and the Muslims was over with at the end of the Crusades; it remains with us even today if only in a different form from that which it had before. Converting Muslims into Christians is one of the most obvious faces of this malicious movement, which started spreading in some Muslim countries to finally uproot Islam from its people.' "[19]

"Saudi state education teaches children from an early age the virtues of jihad. State elementary and high school curricula have been replete with examples of jihad indoctrination, and many of these same writings are now available to an expanding Muslim audience in America. One example is a book for third-year high school students published by the Saudi Ministry of Education that was collected from the Islamic Center of Oakland in California. The text, written with the approval of the Saudi Ministry of Education, teaches students to prepare for jihad in the sense of war against Islam's enemies, and to strive to attain military self-sufficiency: 'To be true Muslims, we must prepare and be ready for jihad in Allah's way. It is the duty of the citizen and the government. The military education is glued to

218

faith and its meaning, and the duty to follow it.' "[20]

"According to the Wahhabi view, it is a Muslim's religious duty to cultivate enmity between oneself and unbelievers. Hatred of unbelievers is the proof that the believer has completely disassociated from them. A work entitled *Loyalty and Dissociation in Islam,* compiled by the Ibn Taymiya Library in Riyadh and distributed by the King Fahd–supported Islamic Center of Washington, D.C., states emphatically: 'To be dissociated from the infidels is to hate them for their religion, to leave them, never to rely on them for support, not to admire them, to be on one's guard against them, never to imitate them, and to always oppose them in every way according to Islamic law.' "[21]

How Many Radicals Are There in the U.S.?

All that said, let me again be crystal clear: not all Muslim children who attend Islamic schools in the U.S., Europe, or the Middle East are being indoctrinated with violent jihadist theology. To the contrary, the vast majority of the 1.3 billion Muslims in the world are peaceful, friendly people who pose no threat to the U.S. or to Western lives or interests. Indeed, it is the very premise of this book that while Radicals who believe and preach that "Islam is the answer, and jihad is the way" are incredibly dangerous, they represent only one segment of the Muslim world and need to be understood within the context of other powerful regional and global trends.

The big question is, just how many Radicals are out there, compared to the number of Muslims who are peaceable and nonthreatening?

To get a handle on the answer, let us look first

219

at the situation inside the U.S.

In 2007, the Pew Research Center published the largest and most comprehensive study of Muslim American opinion ever done, involving nearly sixty thousand interviews with Muslim Americans conducted in English, Arabic, Farsi, and Urdu. The study, entitled "Muslims in America: Middle Class and Mostly Mainstream," found that there are an estimated 2.35 million Muslims in the U.S. and that they are "largely assimilated, happy with their lives, and moderate with respect to many of the issues that have divided Muslims and Westerners around the world." The study also found that "Muslims in the United States reject Islamic extremism by larger margins than do Muslim minorities in Western European countries." For example, nearly seven in ten Muslims in America (68 percent) had a "somewhat unfavorable" or "very unfavorable" view of al Qaeda.[22]

This was good news, to be sure. But in the current environment, it must be asked: why was it not 100 percent? Deeply troubling, in fact, was that fully 5 percent of all Muslims in America admitted to the pollsters that they had a favorable view of al Qaeda. This included 7 percent of American converts to Islam and 9 percent of African-American Muslims. Moreover, nearly three in ten (27 percent) said they either didn't know or refused to answer the question about their view of al Qaeda. Out of 2,350,000 Muslims, this means there are at least 117,500 Muslims inside the U.S. who like what Osama bin Laden and his colleagues are doing and have a favorable view of their terrorist network. If those who refused to answer the question were disguising their own support for al Qaeda, there could be another 600,000 or more Radical Muslims or Radical-leaning Muslims or sympathizers inside the country.

To their credit, the Pew researchers pushed further, trying to clarify the issue. They asked whether Muslims in the U.S. believed suicide bombings against civilian targets were ever justified. Again, the good news was that the majority said no, never. The bad news was that this majority was only 78 percent. A stunning 9 percent refused even to answer the question. The remainder — some 13 percent — indicated they believed suicide bombings against innocent civilians are justified sometimes (7 percent), often (1 percent), or rarely but not never (5 percent). Also troubling was that the study found younger Muslims — those between the ages of eighteen and twenty-nine — were more religiously observant and more Radical. Fully 7 percent of younger Muslims held favorable views of al Qaeda, and a terrifying 15 percent of them said they believe suicide bombings are sometimes or often justified.

Now, translate those percentages into numbers of real people, and you can begin to see the potential magnitude of the Radical threat inside the United States:

- 23,500 Muslims in America believe suicide bombings against civilians are often justified.
- 164,500 Muslims in America believe suicide bombings against civilians are sometimes justified.
- 211,500 Muslims in America refused to answer the question.

How Many Radicals Are There in Europe?

The U.S. is not the Radicals' only target, of course. Great Britain also faces an enormous threat.

On July 7, 2005, a series of suicide bombings ripped through London's subway and bus systems during morning rush hour traffic, leaving fifty-two dead and some seven hundred wounded. It was a horrifying tragedy, as well as a bracing wake-up call to British authorities who for too long had seemed to ignore the magnitude of the problem.[23]

British intelligence and homeland security services immediately launched a massive counter-terrorism research effort — code-named Project Rich Picture — to determine just how many Radicals they were dealing with. The results were chilling. Of the roughly 1.6 million Muslims in the U.K. today, an estimated one-half of one percent are al Qaeda sympathizers. While that may not seem like a large number at first glance, British officials are quick to note that it means there are as many as eight thousand future terrorists and suicide bombers in Great Britain today.[24]

MI5 — Britain's equivalent of the FBI — which has seen its staff grow from less than two thousand in 2001 to thirty-five hundred in 2008, "is trying to drill down and identify those who may be coming into contact with radical sources," a British security source told the *Independent.* "You only have to look at the background of the 7 July London terrorists to see the speed to which radicalization can take place. Some of those who blew themselves up were spotted, recruited, and radicalized within a year."[25]

Of further concern is the fact that as many as three thousand British-born or British-based

Radicals have already been trained in al Qaeda training camps.[26]

But MI5 may actually be understating the magnitude of the threat. A confidential report on "Young Muslims and Extremism," produced by the U.K. Foreign and Commonwealth Office/Home Office and presented to then prime minister Tony Blair in 2004, found that some ten thousand Brits have attended Islamic extremist conferences and that "compared with the population as a whole, Muslims have three times the unemployment rates, the lowest economic activity rates . . . and a higher concentration in deprived areas."[27]

The prime minister's advisors analyzed six British public opinion surveys conducted between November 2001 and March 2004 to better understand the attitudes of British Muslims on a variety of topics. The good news, the report found, was that "the great majority of British Muslims (up to 85 percent) regarded terrorist attacks on Western targets, including the 9/11 attacks, as unjustified. The great majority (up to 87 percent) felt loyal to Britain. A majority felt patriotic (67 percent) and thought it wrong for British Muslims to fight against allies in Afghanistan (62 percent). A survey of young Muslims in 2001 showed strong feelings of outrage at the 9/11 attacks and that the majority believed that Islam either prohibited or discouraged such attacks."

But as in the American study conducted by the Pew Research Center, there was bad news in the British surveys as well.

- "A minority of [British] Muslims defend terrorism (up to 13 percent) . . . and a minority did not feel loyal to Britain (up to 26 percent)."

- "Between 7 and 15 percent [of British Muslims] thought the September 11 attacks were justified."
- "Between 7 and 13 percent thought further terrorist attacks would be justified."
- "Between 15 and 24 percent thought it was okay for British Muslims to fight with the Taliban."

The study concluded that "the number of British Muslims actively engaged in terrorist activity, whether at home or abroad, or supporting such activity is extremely small and estimated at less than one percent."

Less than one percent is indeed an "extremely small" number in terms of percentages. But, it should be noted, advisors to the British prime minister indicated that there could be upwards of sixteen thousand possible terrorists or terrorist supporters operating inside the U.K. at this very moment.

Some in Britain are losing hope, believing that Radicals are taking over and that there may be no way to stop them. In February 2008, for example, Dr. Rowan Williams, the Archbishop of Canterbury, told the BBC that it was time for the British people to "face up to the fact" that eventual adoption of Sharia law in the United Kingdom "seems unavoidable."[28]

Others, including widely respected scholars and historians, worry that all of Europe is in danger of being controlled by Islam. In January 2007, renowned Middle East historian Bernard Lewis shocked the Western world by warning that Muslims "seem to be about to take over Europe."

The real question, he said, is this: "Will it be an Islamized Europe or Europeanized Islam?" In other words, will the Europe of the future be run by the Radicals or the Reformers? "Europeans are losing their own loyalties and their own self-confidence," Lewis said. "They have no respect for their own culture." Europeans, he added, have "surrendered" on every issue with regard to Islam.[29]

Today, 16 million Muslims live in Europe, and the risk of more Radical-driven terrorism in Europe remains. It may even be growing.[30] Polling conducted throughout Europe in 2006 and 2007, for example, indicated that:

- 15 percent of Muslims in the U.K. believed suicide bombings against civilian targets were sometimes or often justified.
- 16 percent of Muslims in France believed suicide bombings against civilian targets were sometimes or often justified.
- 16 percent of Muslims in Spain believed suicide bombings against civilian targets were sometimes or often justified.
- 7 percent of Muslims in Germany believed suicide bombings against civilian targets were sometimes or often justified.[31]

Another survey found the following:

- 40 percent of Muslims in Great Britain believe Iran should have nuclear weapons.
- 29 percent of Muslims in France believe Iran should have nuclear weapons.
- 14 percent of Muslims in Germany believe Iran should have nuclear weapons.[32]

225

How Many Radicals Are There Worldwide?

In 2007, authors John Esposito and Dalia Moga-hed published a book entitled *Who Speaks for Islam? What a Billion Muslims Really Think.* Esposito is a professor of Islamic studies at Georgetown University and founding director of the school's Prince Alwaleed Bin Talal Center for Muslim-Christian Understanding. Mogahed, herself a devout Muslim, is executive director of the Gallup Center for Muslim Studies.

As they stated in their introduction, "This book is the product of a mammoth, multiyear Gallup research study. Between 2001 and 2007, Gallup conducted tens of thousands of hour-long, face-to-face interviews with residents of more than 35 nations that are predominantly Muslim or have substantial Muslim populations. . . . In totality, we surveyed a sample representing more than 90 percent of the world's 1.3 billion Muslims, making this the largest, most comprehensive study of contemporary Muslims ever done."[33]

What these two scholars discovered was fascinating . . . and sobering.

First, the good news. After asking scores of different questions to test attitudes and intentions, the Gallup poll revealed that upwards of 93 percent of Muslims worldwide fit Esposito and Mogahed's definition of a "moderate" — that is, peaceable, nonviolent, and traditionally religious but unlikely to pose a threat to Western security interests. In Egypt, for example, 94 percent of Muslims said they would like to have a constitution that would guarantee "allowing all citizens to express their opinion on the political, social, and economic issues of the day." In Iran, 93 percent said they wanted such personal and political freedom, as did 90 percent of Muslims in Indonesia, the world's largest Islamic country. In Turkey, 93 percent of Muslims believe women should have the right to vote, as do 89 percent of Muslims in Iran and 90 percent in Bangladesh. Nine in ten Muslims in Indonesia, Bangladesh, Turkey, and Lebanon believe that women should have the same legal rights as men.[34] All very good news, indeed.

Now the bad news. While the overwhelming majority of Muslims worldwide are moderates, about 7 percent would be classified as Radicals. That is, they are supportive of anti-American and anti-Western terrorism, believe it is fully justified, and thus are sympathetic of and potentially helpful to violent Islamic extremists. This is the pool from which current Radical jihadists are recruiting future jihadists, and thus they pose a serious threat to Western security interests.

"According to the Gallup poll, 7 percent of [Muslim] respondents think that the 9/11 attacks were 'completely' justified and view the United States unfavorably," Esposito and Mogahed concluded. "By focusing on the 7 percent, whom we'll call 'the politically radicalized,' we are not saying that all in this group commit acts of violence. However, those with extremist views are a potential source for recruitment or support for terrorist groups. . . . They are also more likely to view other civilian attacks as justifiable."[35]

At first glance, 7 percent may seem like a relatively small number. But the implications of such results are staggering. Seven percent of 1.3 billion Muslims equals 91 million people. It may comfort people to know that the vast majority of the world's Muslims are peaceful people. But how comforting is it to know that 91 million Muslims are "politically radicalized"? After all, were these 91 million people to form their own country — the Islamic Republic of Radicalstan, say — they would represent the twelfth largest country on the planet, having twice the population of Spain, nearly three times the population of Canada, almost ten times the population of Sweden, and more than twelve times the population of Israel.★

Extensive polling also found that the Radicals were not necessarily more religious than moderate Muslims; nor did they necessarily attend mosque more frequently or read the Qur'an more often. They were simply *differently* religious. That is, they were fully devoted to a radicalized interpretation of the Qur'an, such as the theologies taught by the Ayatollah Khomeini, Sayyid Qutb, and Osama bin Laden.

Moreover, these Radicals do not tend to be poor, uneducated, unsophisticated people living in some hovel somewhere, though there are

★Other research suggests the 7 percent Radical figure may actually be too low. According to a 2007 Pew Research Center poll, 28 percent of Egyptian Muslims say they believe suicide bombings against civilian targets are sometimes or often justified; 17 percent of Turkish Muslims agree, along with 10 percent of Indonesian Muslims, 14 percent of Pakistani Muslims, 29 percent of Jordanian Muslims, and 46 percent of Nigerian Muslims. See Andrew Kohut, "Muslims in America: Middle Class and Mostly Mainstream," Pew Research Center, May 22, 2007, http://pewresearch.org/assets/pdf/muslim-americans.pdf, accessed June 24, 2008.

certainly Radicals who come from impoverished backgrounds. According to the Gallup poll data, the typical profile of a Radical today is actually very much like Ahmed Omar Abu Ali — young, male, smart, college educated, financially well-off, technologically literate, highly mobile, deeply determined, and thus incredibly dangerous. According to the study:

- 49 percent of political Radicals are between the ages of eighteen and twenty-nine.
- 62 percent are male, while 37 percent are female.
- 67 percent have secondary education or higher.
- 65 percent say they have average or above-average income.[36]

MUSLIMS IN AMERICA

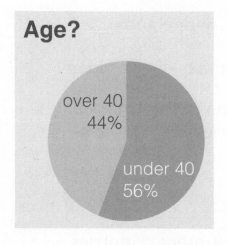

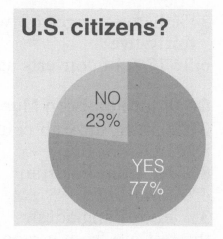

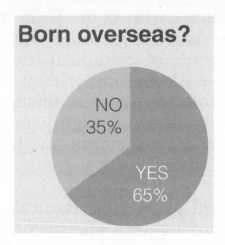

Born overseas?

NO
35%

YES
65%

23% of Muslims in America are converts
59% of converts are African-Americans
34% are white
7% other
55% of converts become Sunnis
6% of converts become Shias
49% converted before the age of twenty-
  one
34% between ages of twenty-one and
  thirty-five
only 17% of converts are thirty-six or older

Of all foreign-born Muslims in the U.S.:
24% are from Arab countries
8% are from Iran
8% are from Pakistan
4% from India
3% from Bangladesh
the rest are from a range of other countries

Why did they come?
26% of foreign-born Muslims say they came
  to the U.S. for educational opportunities
24% for economic opportunities

24% for family reasons
20% because of conflict or persecution

What kind of Muslims are they?
50% of Muslims in America say they are Sunnis
16% say they are Shias
22% say they have no affiliation
the rest were a potpourri of other traditions or
  would not say

53% say it has gotten harder to be a Muslim in the U.S. since 9/11
25% say they have been personally discriminated
  against in the U.S.
73% say they have suffered no discrimination in
  the U.S.

How devout?
41% pray five times a day
40% attend mosque once a week or more
26% go less than once a week
34% never go
77% of Iranian Muslims never go to mosque —
  only 7% go once a week
57% of Pakistani Muslims go to mosque more
  than once a week — 14% never go

How political?
63% are Democrats or lean Democratic (71%
  voted for Kerry in 2004)
11% are Republican or lean Republican (only
  14% voted for Bush in 2004)
26% are independents
43% believe mosques should express political

views, while 49% say they should stay out of political issues★

★Source: Andrew Kohut, "Muslims in America: Middle Class and Mostly Mainstream," Pew Research Center, May 22, 2007

CHAPTER ELEVEN:
REVOLUTION 2.0

The rise of Ayatollah Khamenei and Mahmoud Ahmadinejad

The secret of success is successors.

The Islamic Revolution could have come to a screeching halt on June 3, 1989, when the Ayatollah Khomeini died of cancer just shy of his eighty-seventh birthday. But Khomeini never saw himself as a one-man show. He had invested his life in building a movement of disciples to embrace his Radical vision, export it around the world, and carry it on long after his death. In so doing, he had carefully groomed an inner circle of trusted, loyal, and ideologically pure protégés to whom he felt he could entrust the movement's leadership.

When one of these protégés, the Ayatollah Hussein Ali Montazeri — one of Khomeini's closest friends and his designated heir — betrayed him, daring to take public issue with the regime's human-rights record, Khomeini turned instead to another disciple, giving the keys to the kingdom, as it were, to the Ayatollah Ali Khamenei.

Khamenei was born in 1939 in the town of Mashhad to a poor but devoutly religious family who were descendants of Muhammad. In 1958, at the age of nineteen, he entered seminary in Qom, where he met his mentor while attending his classes on Islamic mysticism and jurisprudence. Khomeini immediately took a liking to the bright and eloquent young Ali, taking him under his wing not only to teach him the intricacies of Sharia law but also to instill in him a hatred for the shah and a passion for waging jihad to purify Iranian society and one day establish an Islamic state.

Ali was an eager and devoted follower. He translated the books of Sayyid Qutb, the Egyptian Radical, into Farsi. He wrote a number of books of his own. He also became so immersed in underground, subversive political activities that by 1979 he had been arrested, imprisoned, and tortured by the shah's secret police at least a half dozen times. Through it all, Ali Khamenei emerged as one of Khomeini's most trusted deputies inside Iran during the ayatollah's exile in Turkey and Iraq.

When Khomeini finally returned home and rose to power, he made Ali, who was only forty at the time, a member of his Revolutionary Council, then promoted him rapidly. Khomeini often tapped him for the honor of delivering Friday sermons and prayers to the teeming masses in Tehran. By 1980, Khomeini had named him defense minister, just as the Iran-Iraq War was breaking out. By October of 1981, Ali Khamenei had been elected president of Iran, where he served until his mentor's death and his surprise promotion to the nation's Supreme Leader, having narrowly survived several assassination attempts along the way.

A Confrontation with the U.S. Is "Unavoidable"

One of the most striking features of the Ayatollah Ali Khamenei is just how few strikingly unique features he really has.

Few have questioned his religious devotion, but no one in Iran — least of all his fellow clerics — sees him as a game-changing theologian, the way his mentor was. No one questions his intelligence, but neither does anyone see him as a brilliant political strategist, as his mentor was. He has been widely described as an impressive orator — that was one trait Khomeini picked up early on — but as Iran's Supreme Leader he has mostly shied away from being perceived as the public face or voice of the Revolution, preferring instead to play the behind-the-scenes puppet master to whoever is serving as the nation's president at any given moment.

He has, in many ways, seemed to suffer an inferiority complex, as if he knows he is not up to the monumental task of leading the Revolution forward that was laid upon him and fears everyone around him knows this as well. He actually signaled such self-doubts during his inaugural speech as Supreme Leader. "I am," he said, "an individual with many faults and shortcomings and truly a minor seminarian. However, a responsibility has been placed on my shoulders, and I will use all my capabilities and all my faith in the Almighty in order to be able to bear this heavy responsibility."[1]

In his new role, therefore — a role I don't think he ever really believed he was qualified for or was actually going to get (or perhaps last in for very long) — Khamenei made clear he was sticking to his mentor's message: anti-American, anti-Zionist,

235

and fully committed to exporting the Revolution and confronting the West, whatever the cost. Consider a small sampling of Ali Khamenei's more troubling quotes:

"The end of the U.S. will begin in Iraq. As the Imam said, 'One day the U.S., too, will be history.' "[2]

"The bitter and venomous taste of Western liberal democracy, which the United States has hypocritically been trying to portray through its propaganda as a healing remedy, has hurt the body and soul of the Islamic Ummah [community] and burned the hearts of Muslims."[3]

"It is natural that our Islamic system should be viewed as an enemy and an intolerable rival by such an oppressive power as the United States, which is trying to establish a global dictatorship and further its own interests by dominating other nations and trampling on their rights. It is also clear that the *conflict and confrontation between the two is something natural and unavoidable*"[4] (emphasis added).

"A day will come that the current U.S. president [George W. Bush] . . . . will be tried in an international supreme court for the catastrophes they caused in Iraq. Americans will have to answer for why they don't end occupation of Iraq and why waves of terrorism and insurgency have overwhelmed the country. It will not be like this forever, and someday they will be stopped as happened to Hitler."[5]

"Today more than ever, the Muslim peoples

are disgusted and furious with the Americans. . . . The American regime can expect a resounding slap and a devastating fist-blow from the Muslim nation for its support of the Zionist crimes and criminals. . . . America's and Israel's aggressive character and conduct revives the spirit of resistance in the Islamic world, [now] more than ever, and makes the value of Jihad clearer than ever."[6]

"There is no way to confront the barbaric Zionist wolves and the aggression of the Great Satan except through martyrdom."[7]

"The Iranian people have been defeating America for the past twenty-five years. The world of Islam has been mobilized against America for the past twenty-five years. The people call, 'Death to America!' "[8]

"There is a great resemblance between the behavior of today's Americans and the behavior of the Nazis. . . . The Americans are infected today with satanic pride and arrogant egotism."[9]

"It is the mission of the Islamic Republic of Iran to erase Israel from the map of the region."[10]

"Regarding atomic energy, we need it now. Our nation has always been threatened from outside. The least we can do to face this danger is let our enemies know that we can defend ourselves. Therefore, every step you [members of Iran's nuclear scientific community] take here is in defense of your country and your evolution. With this in mind, you should work hard and at great speed."[11]

"A wave of Islamic revival has swept through

the Islamic world, and Muslim nations are expressing a strong desire to return to Islam and practice this lofty religion. This awakening has stemmed from the great Islamic revolution of the Iranian people under the leadership of our late magnanimous Imam. . . . The enemies told us not to export our Islamic revolution! . . . However, our Islamic revolution [is] like the scent of spring flowers that is carried by the breeze [and has] reached every corner of the Islamic world."[12]

It is worth noting that while Khamenei has talked tough (and has continued to fund terrorist groups throughout the Middle East), he has done little to rock the boat in real and practical ways. He permitted virtually no serious and lasting reforms at home; nor did he launch any new wars abroad. Rather, he spent much of his first fifteen years as Supreme Leader building the domestic political base that he sorely lacked when he came to power, and he built critical new international alliances — notably with nuclear powers Russia, China, and North Korea — that he believed would eventually help Iran accomplish its national objectives.

And then, in 2005, he chose an unexpected and virtually unknown protégé of his own to install as president and carry his own message of radical change to the nation . . . and the world.

"The Little Street Sweeper"
No one saw Mahmoud Ahmadinejad coming.

When he announced his candidacy for president in April 2005, the five-foot-four-inch Radical received almost no media coverage. He received

238

no newspaper endorsements. No political parties supported him. He had few political credentials and almost no experience.

Born to a poor but devoutly religious family on October 28, 1956, in Aradan, a small town in central Iran, he had no personal wealth or family connections going for him. The son of a grocer, Ahmadinejad was only twenty-two when the Revolution unfolded. He had not been close to the Ayatollah Khomeini. He had not studied political science, public policy, history, or even Islamic theology in college. Instead, he held a doctorate in traffic management and had been a professor for a few years after his time in the military. He had not married into a political family; his wife was also a professor.

Ahmadinejad was not the head of a trade union or some other nationwide organization. He had come in twenty-third in his 1999 campaign for a seat on the Tehran City Council. He had barely been elected mayor of Tehran in 2003, when only 12 percent of the city's eligible voters had turned up to the polls. He had then tried to endear himself to the city's poor by occasionally donning an orange jumpsuit and helping the municipal street cleaners sweep up trash in one neighborhood or another.[13]

After more than a thousand candidates had been denied the right to run for president by the central government, one early poll put Ahmadinejad second to last in a contest among the eight remaining candidates, drawing a paltry 2.8 percent support.[14]

The front-runner in the race was Akbar Hashemi Rafsanjani, one of the most respected clerics and politicians in the country and the man who had succeeded the Ayatollah Khamenei as president in 1989 and served until 1997. The chairman of the Tehran City Council — a close political ally of the mayor — told reporters, "There is widespread pressure on Ahmadinejad to withdraw. Everyone wants him to leave the race, but he himself is not prepared to go."[15] Ahmadinejad later joked, "They said to me, 'No one has heard of you, you won't win votes.' I told them, 'If no one has heard of me, then don't worry — if I lose, no one will notice.' "[16]

Two months later, however, everyone noticed Mahmoud Ahmadinejad. On June 17, 2005, the Iranian political class felt blindsided when Ahmadinejad won 19.5 percent of the vote, while Rafsanjani failed to secure a victory with only 21 percent, falling well short of the necessary threshold of 50 percent. The BBC reported that Ahmadinejad's campaign staffers were so shocked by the results, they "had not even prepared a podium for him to speak from in response to the results."[17]

Then, one week later — on June 24 — the entire world was stunned when Ahmadinejad not only won the runoff with Rafsanjani but did so in a landslide, winning 62 percent to 36 percent, with the government claiming that about six in ten eligible voters, some 28 million Iranians, had actually voted.

AHMADINEJAD STUNS WORLD
— Arab News, June 26, 2005

THE IRANIAN SURPRISE
— Al-Ahram, July 7, 2005

U.S. MULLS SHOCK RESULT IN IRANIAN

Agence France-Presse rightly characterized the election as a "political earthquake" whose tremors were being felt around the world.[18]

"Today is the beginning of a new political era," Ahmadinejad declared upon learning of his astounding victory. "I am proud of being the Iranian nation's little servant and street sweeper."[19]

In just two months, the militant mayor had gone from virtually no press coverage to global saturation coverage, and he immediately used his new media platform, vowing to accelerate Iran's nuclear program and provoke direct confrontations with the United States and with Israel. And that was just the beginning.

Chosen by Allah or the Ayatollah?

Rafsanjani immediately cried foul.

"All the means of the regime were used in an organized and illegal way to intervene in the election," the former president insisted.[20]

Rafsanjani's supporters alleged — with no small amount of evidence — that the Ayatollah Khamenei had hand-picked Ahmadinejad and thrown his enormous political weight behind him. Khamenei, after all, controlled the millions of current and former members of the Iranian Revolutionary Guard Corps, an elite branch of the Iranian Army. He also controlled the hundreds of thousands of current and former members of the Basij, a vast Iranian network of paramilitary operatives that helps Iran's uniformed and secret police forces maintain order and serves as a reserve force in

241

time of war or internal crisis. If Khamenei chose to signal these and other networks not only to vote for someone but also to round up millions of other votes, he certainly had the power to do so, and allegations of ballot box stuffing by the Revolutionary Guards and many other forms of election fraud were rampant throughout that summer.[21]

Ahmadinejad, however, refused to admit being chosen by the ayatollah. Rather, he believed he was chosen by Allah.

In an October 14, 2006, speech to the Union of Islamic Engineers, for example, Ahmadinejad claimed a divine connection to Allah and suggested he had been chosen for a unique mission: to launch the second and final round of the Islamic Revolution, to make Iran a nuclear power, and to usher in the reign of the Twelfth Imam. He claimed to be directly and personally inspired by Allah and suggested that only Allah's favor on his life could account for his meteoric rise to power and his ability to constantly stymie the foreign policy objectives of the United States and other Western powers vis-à-vis the Middle East.

"I told you that the second wave of the Revolution has already begun with my election to the presidency, and that it is bigger and more terrible than the first," Ahmadinejad told the gathering "On the nuclear issue, I have said to my friends on many occasions, 'Don't worry. They [the West] are only making noise.' But my friends don't believe [me], and say, 'You are connected to some place!' I always say: 'Now the West is disarmed vis-à-vis Iran [on the nuclear issue], and does not know how to end this matter.' But my friends say: 'You are uttering divine words!' . . . Someone asked me: 'So-and-so said that you have a connection.' I said: 'Yes, I have.' He asked me: 'Really, you have a connection? With whom?' I answered, 'I have a connection with God.' "[22]

Ahmadinejad then contrasted his direct inspiration from Allah with his claim that President Bush was directly inspired by the devil and thus doomed to defeat. "The president of America is like us. That is, he too is inspired. . . . But [his] inspiration is of the satanic kind. Satan gives inspiration to the president of America."[23]

Four years after Ahmadinejad was elected the sixth president of Iran, the evidence is now quite clear that the Ayatollah Khamenei chose him, blessed him, and gave him enormous latitude to make apocalyptic pronouncements and bring Iran to the verge of war. The real question is, why? Who is Mahmoud Ahmadinejad? What does he believe? Where does he believe Iran and the world are headed?

The answers I found to these questions were surprising, in part because while Ahmadinejad speaks so highly of the Iranian Revolution's founder, he has a distinctly different theology, one that has dramatically changed the course of Iran, perhaps forever.

A Follower of the Mahdi

Mahmoud is the fourth of seven children — three boys, four girls — but *Ahmadinejad* is not his actual given surname. His father's name was Ahmad Sabaghian. The name Sabaghian* means "dye-master," suggesting that the family was at one time engaged in dying wool for Persian

*Some biographers spell it "Saborjhian."

carpets. But according to a relative, when Ahmad moved his family to Tehran when Mahmoud was a year old, he decided to change the family name, perhaps to sound less like rural peasants and more intensely religious. *Ahmadinejad,* the name he chose, is a combination of two Persian words, *Ahmad* and *Nejad.* Together, the words mean "of the Ahmadi race" or "of the race of the righteous" or, more broadly, "of the race of the Prophet Muhammad," a reference to the fact that one of the names of Muhammad was Ahmad, meaning "righteous one."[24]

Ahmad was originally a teacher of the Qur'an but could not earn enough money teaching to support his family. He ran a grocery store that failed. For years he ran a barber shop in Aradan, a town of about ten thousand people. Then he became a grocer again in Narmak, a community on the outskirts of Tehran, and later a blacksmith and metalworker when a construction boom in the capital took off during the 1950s. His wife was a descendant of Muhammad and all her life wore a full-length black dress and head-covering known as a chador that hid everything but her eyes.

Mahmoud Ahmadinejad may not have had money or a well-connected family, but he had a powerful intellect and deep religious convictions, and both have helped him advance significantly. After high school, he placed 132nd out of some one hundred fifty to two hundred thousand students who were competing for only about ten thousand freshman openings in Iranian universities. He eventually chose to attend the University of Science and Technology in Narmak. When he was twenty-two, the Revolution broke out, and he and his brothers became deeply involved in pro-Khomeini political activities on campus. Ahmadinejad helped found the Islamic Students Union and worked for a politically active student religious publication called *Jeegh va Daad,* which is Farsi for "Scream and Shout."

During this same period, it appears Ahmadinejad was also involved in a shadowy Islamic society known as the Hojatieh, whose leaders taught that the Twelfth Imam was coming soon and whose members believed they were required to take spiritual (but not political) actions to hasten his coming.[25]

Even in the intensely religious environment Khomeini was creating at the time, many believed the Hojatieh was a religious cult. Worse, from Khomeini's perspective, the movement discouraged people from being fully devoted to creating an Islamic state, preferring instead to wait for it to come from the sky. In 1983, therefore, Khomeini actually banned the Hojatieh, and Ahmadinejad seems to have subsumed his sympathies for the group to protect his opportunities for career advancement.

In 1980, Ahmadinejad married a devoutly religious mechanical engineering student he had met while in university, and the couple had three children, a daughter and two sons, the last of whom was born in 1987. But for the first half of the 1980s, at least, Ahmadinejad was not home much. Millions of Iranian men were being sent to the front to fight the war Saddam Hussein had launched in 1980. Khomeini was also sending hundreds of thousands of small children to the front to walk across minefields, blowing themselves to smithereens, "martyring" themselves in

245

the cause of jihad and thus clearing a path for trained soldiers to follow and advance against the Iraqis.

Ahmadinejad had no choice but to fight in the war, and he may have believed that doing so was preparing the way for the revelation of the Hidden Imam, but his precise role during the war is murky. His official biography states that "during the war imposed on Iran, Dr. Ahmadinejad was actively present as a member of the volunteer forces (Basij) in different parts and divisions of the battlefronts particularly in the war engineering division until the end of the war."[26] That may be true in part, but Western intelligence sources, along with numerous media and academic accounts, say Ahmadinejad eventually became a senior commander in the Qods [Jerusalem] Force, a unit of the Revolutionary Guard Corps known for assassinations and terrorist attacks throughout Iran, the Middle East, and Europe.[27]

When Ahmadinejad completed his military service, he began to serve in various positions in provincial government throughout Iran, eventually becoming a close personal friend and disciple of an aging but very influential ultraradical Shia theologian by the name of Ayatollah Muhammad Taghi Mesbah-Yazdi.

Born in 1934, Mesbah-Yazdi has arguably become Iran's leading clerical voice proclaiming the coming of the Mahdi and the urgency of preparing the way for his arrival and appearance on the earth. Nicknamed "Professor Crocodile" because of "a notorious cartoon that depicted him weeping false tears over the jailing of a reformist journalist," he fiercely opposes democracy, opposes free speech, hates the U.S. and Israel, supports the use of suicide bombings against innocent civilians to advance an Islamic agenda, and supports the assassination of critics of Islam such as Salman Rushdie.[28]

"The prophets of God did not believe in pluralism," Mesbah-Yazdi once said, voicing his hatred for representative government and Reformers. "They believed that only one idea was right. What is being termed as 'Reform' today is in fact corruption. What is being promoted in the name of Reforms and the path of the prophets is in fact in total conflict with the objectives of the prophets."[29] A fierce proponent of violent jihad as a means of preparing the way for the Mahdi's arrival, Mesbah-Yazdi has argued that "we must wipe away the shameful stain whereby some people imagine that violence has no place in Islam. We have decided and are determined to argue and prove that violence is at the heart of Islam."[30]

Just to give you a sense of how dangerous this guy is, one of Mesbah-Yazdi's disciples, Mohsen Gharavian — a teacher of Shia theology in Qom — once issued a fatwa that declared "for the first time that the use of nuclear weapons may not constitute a problem, according to Sharia." He then asserted that "when the entire world is armed with nuclear weapons, it is permissible to use these weapons as a countermeasure."[31]

Did Ahmadinejad distance himself from his mentor before or after the issuing of the fatwa, or based on any of the other positions the professor has taken? To the contrary, Ahmadinejad has said publicly, "I regard Ayatollah Mesbah-Yazdi as one of the great leaders of Islam and Shi'ism. . . . I sincerely respect him as one of the leading

247

scholars of Islam."[32]

Not surprisingly, when he was elected mayor of Tehran in 2003, Ahmadinejad brought his dual passion for the Mahdi and for martyrdom to office. "Today our nation's great duty and prophetic mission is to prepare for the formation of the universal rule of the Mahdi," he insisted.[33] He called for the people of Tehran to prepare to fulfill their "historical prophetic mission," that of establishing a "global Islamic government."[34] He forced men and women to take separate elevators in Tehran, created separate parks for men and women, demanded that billboards of British soccer heartthrob David Beckham be taken down, sharply critized Western movies and music, passed a city ordinance exempting mosques and religious organizations from paying taxes and fees, visited Radical mosques frequently, and encouraged religious zealotry, eventually earning the nickname "the Iranian Taliban."[35]

In a speech to religious activists, he said, "This is the time for a cultural war. We have to direct the minds of our youth towards the basic principles, methods, and values of the Revolution."[36] In another speech, he declared, "Any society that has the spirit of martyrdom will remain undefeatable. . . . If we want to resolve today's social problems, we must return to the culture of the martyrs."[37] He even ordered an enormous billboard that depicted a female Palestinian suicide bomber holding a boy in one hand and a machine gun in the other erected along one of the business streets in Tehran. The caption read: "My children I love, but martyrdom I love more."[38]

Along the way, he captured the imagination of the Ayatollah Khamenei, who decided Ahmadine-

jad was just the man to take the Revolution to the
next level.

Campaigning for the Mahdi

From the beginning of his campaign for president,
Ahmadinejad started his speeches by praying for
the reemergence of the Twelfth Imam, calling for
the reinvigoration of the Islamic Revolution, and
insisting that Iran should oppose the Western powers of "global arrogance" and lead the way in
establishing one world government under Sharia
law.

Ahmadinejad insisted that Khomeini's Revolution was not meant to have solved all of Iran's
social and economic problems. Only the Mahdi
could solve mankind's problems, he argued. Of
course there was poverty. Of course there was
unemployment. Of course there were political
scandals and crime and prostitution and cultural
pollution from the West corrupting their young
people. Of course the Americans and the Zionists
were running the world and enslaving oppressed
peoples of the world, particularly the Muslims.
These were not failures of the Ayatollah Khomeini
— or, more importantly, the Ayatollah Khamenei
— but rather evidence of the last days. Now was
not the time to be weak, he said. Now was the
time to finish the Revolution. Now was not the
time to reach out to the West, as Rafsanjani suggested. Now was the time to take them on. History was on Iran's side, he promised. The Americans and the Israelis would be judged in due time.
So would all other apostates and infidels. Now,
therefore, was the time to prepare the way for the
Mahdi to come and make it all right. But who
was going to do that? he asked. A near-apostate

like Rafsanjani, or a true believer like him?

Piling on, Ahmadinejad played the class warfare card. Attacking Rafsanjani as an out-of-touch politician of wealth and privilege, Ahmadinejad dressed in plain trousers, an open shirt, and a simple, tan, zip-up jacket (which he would come to refer to as his signature "Ahmadinejad jacket"), vowing to care for the poor and needy because he understood their plight firsthand. Again and again he told his personal story of growing up with almost nothing, the son of a father who constantly had to change jobs and look for work but who always taught him from the Qur'an.

Ahmadinejad's rhetoric was a potent and provocative cocktail of fundamentalist religion mixed with a dash of revolutionary Marxism, and it had a strong appeal with a significant minority of Iranians. But was it really enough to intoxicate 62 percent of the Iranian people into voting for him in June of 2005 when most of the country had barely heard of him two months earlier? It does not seem likely, particularly given that the vast majority of Iranians — some experts I have spoken to say 70 percent or more — have turned against Islam and are now quite secular in private, even if they are cautious about expressing their dissent in public. This is why neither Rafsanjani nor the political and media elites in Tehran (or outside the country for that matter) saw Ahmadinejad coming. They dismissed him as a zealot buffoon, not an international statesman, and little worried that he had a chance of overtaking the front-runner.

But Ahmadinejad's campaign strategy, in retrospect, was a very shrewd one. He was not trying to win over 62 percent of the country. He had an

250

audience of one. The Supreme Leader had, after all, liked what he had seen and heard when Ahmadinejad was mayor. If Khamenei continued to like what he saw throughout the campaign, Ahmadinejad knew that the ayatollah could throw the levers of power in his favor. That was what he was betting on, and in the end, his bet paid off. The more strident Ahmadinejad became on the stump — explaining that the Revolution was not a failure but rather that the Mahdi was coming to solve everything — the more energized the Supreme Leader became. Khamenei heard the message and quietly chose the man.

When Khamenei then turned to the fundamentalist leaders in the military and paramilitary — men the ayatollah had been actively courting and winning over since 1989 — and whispered that Ahmadinejad was "the one," it was not a hard sell. Indeed, such Radicals, burrowed into key positions throughout the Iranian government and society, could read between the lines. They could see Ahmadinejad was speaking their language, making the case that Islam was the answer and jihad was the way. They were also beginning to believe the time was ripe for the Mahdi to return. And so they did whatever they had to do to put the ayatollah's man over the top.

Governing for the Mahdi

No leader in the history of Iran had ever been so fully devoted to the notion that the Mahdi was coming soon and that it was his responsibility to prepare the Iranian people and the world for his increasingly imminent arrival. Such beliefs were actually a sharp departure from the teachings of the Ayatollah Khomeini, who certainly believed in the concept of the Mahdi and referred to him occasionally but never believed his reappearance on earth was close at hand. As we saw earlier, Khomeini believed it was his job — not the Mahdi's — to establish a global Islamic government aggressively and proactively, not to wait for it to "come down from the sky." But Ahmadinejad was about to change everything.

Upon the election of his protégé as president, Ayatollah Mesbah-Yazdi said Ahmadinejad had won because of "the special kindness of the Mahdi."[39] Ahmadinejad, in turn, increased government funding for his mentor's messianic institute 1,000 percent to $3.5 million.[40] He also began conferring with his mentor more regularly and appointed no fewer than four of Mesbah-Yazdi's disciples to key cabinet positions, bringing others into the government to serve as advisors and in other critical posts, including in the Ministry of Intelligence and Security and the Ministry of the Interior.

From day one, Ahmadinejad made it clear he was the Mahdi's man. In fact, he seemed to see himself as a John the Baptist figure — not the Islamic messiah himself but the one appointed to lay the groundwork and herald his coming. The question was whether Ahmadinejad intended to baptize the world by water or by fire.

Before his inauguration, Ahmadinejad told Khamenei that he was only a temporary steward of the presidency and would soon be handing over the reigns of power to the Mahdi. The Ayatollah asked, "What if he doesn't come by then [the end of your term]?" Ahmadinejad was adamant. "I assure you; I really believe this. He will come soon."[41]

At his first cabinet meeting, Ahmadinejad required every government minister to sign a statement pledging loyalty not to him but to the Mahdi.[42] He told his senior advisors in July 2005 that his mission was "the establishment of a global Islamic government, with the assistance of the Mahdi."[43] He publicly announced that his mission as president was to establish a government and society that would be "a blueprint for the people of the world and thus [one that] ultimately serves as a platform for the reappearance of the Mahdi."[44] He visted the Jamkaran Mosque near Qom and prayed at one of the two wishing wells where Iranian Shias believe the Mahdi once appeared, then committed millions of dollars for improving the facilities around the well and additional sums to build new roads and rail lines that would bring people to the site from all over the country.[45] He then declared the Mahdi's birthday — September 9 — a national holiday. This, in turn, triggered a wave of one million Iranian pilgrims who visited the well on that day in 2005, most of whom tossed small scraps of paper with their prayers scrawled on them into the well, hoping for the Mahdi to read and answer them.[46]

For the Western world, the first public hint of just how central Islamic eschatology would be to Ahmadinejad's governance came during his first address to the United Nations General Assembly in New York in September of 2005. Ahmadinejad stunned the audience of world leaders and diplomats by ending his speech with this prayer: "O mighty Lord, I pray to you to hasten the emergence of your last repository, the Promised One, that perfect and pure human being, the One that

253

will fill this world with justice and peace."[47]

As the fall progressed, reports were beginning to surface in the Iranian media that Ahmadinejad was telling associates he was in direct communication with the Mahdi and was one of a select group of men specifically chosen by the Mahdi to be his representatives and helpers in the world prior to his return. Whether this communication was supposed to have come in the form of prayer, through some sort of spiritual vision or manifestation, or by an actual physical visitation was not clear. But some reports have indicated that Ahmadinejad has slipped away from official duties for several hours to have secret conversations with the Hidden Imam.[48]

What's more, Ahmadinejad began speaking of a specific time frame, telling associates and even foreign ministers of Islamic countries that he believed the end of the world was just two or three years away and that the way to hasten the coming of the Mahdi was to annihilate two countries: Israel and the United States. According to the widely respected Iranian-born journalist Amir Taheri, Ahmadinejad started boasting "that the Imam gave him the presidency for a single task: provoking a 'clash of civilizations' in which the Muslim world, led by Iran, takes on the 'infidel' West, led by the United States, and defeats it."[49]

Ahmadinejad later stunned a group of senior Islamic clerics by claiming that during his U.N. speech he was surrounded by a light until the end and felt the presence of Allah speaking through him. A colleague told him that when he began his speech, "I saw a celestial light come and surround you and protect you." Ahmadinejad then told the clerics, "I felt it myself, too. Suddenly, the

254

atmosphere changed. [All the people in the room] sat there and for the duration of the twenty-seven or twenty-eight minutes, they did not blink. I am not exaggerating. I looked up and I saw them. They were transfixed. It was as if a hand was holding them."[50]

In October, Ahmadinejad laid his eschatological cards on the table when he gave a speech in Tehran in which he further clarified his objectives. He vowed to wipe Israel "off the map" and urged Muslims to imagine a world without the United States. "Is it possible for us to witness a world without America and Zionism?" he asked a gathering of leaders from Hamas and Islamic Jihad. "You had best know that this slogan and this goal are attainable, and surely can be achieved." He urged Muslims all over the world — Shias and Sunnis alike — to prepare for the day when "our holy hatred expands" and "strikes like a wave."[51]

Next Ahmadinejad began publicly denying the Holocaust even while calling for another. "Some European countries are insisting on saying that Hitler burned millions of oppressed Jews in crematoria," he said at an Islamic conference in Mecca. "They insist so much on this issue that if someone proves the opposite, they convict him and throw him into prison. Although we do not accept this claim, let's assume that it is true, and we ask the Europeans: Does the killing of oppressed Jews by Hitler [justify] their support for the regime that is occupying Jerusalem?"[52] Later, in a nationally televised speech in Iran, Ahmadinejad said that the Zionists "have fabricated a legend under the name, 'Massacre of the Jews.' "[53]

It was not just talk. Ahmadinejad was simultaneously making a number of aggressive moves to build up Iran's military and accelerate its bid to go nuclear. That fall Iran purchased $1 billion worth of missiles from Russia, building on years of buying submarines and other advanced weapons systems from Moscow.[54] Iran also received a dozen cruise missiles with a three-thousand-kilometer range, each of which was capable of carrying nuclear warheads.[55] Iran's parliament voted to block international inspections of its nuclear facilities.[56] And Ahmadinejad "placed the military firmly in control [over] his nation's nuclear program, undercutting his government's claim that the program is intended for civilian use," according to a report in the Pakistani *Daily Times.*[57]

Ahmadinejad's actions and remarks understandably ignited an international firestorm of protest. Curiously, numerous senior Iranian clerics and political leaders were outraged as well. Some opposed the president's call for genocide on principle. Others, even though they privately agreed with the president, publicly opposed him for making remarks in a way that would risk Iran's international reputation and trade status with the West — and, by extension, Iran's economy. Former Iranian president Mohammad Khatami, for example, said Ahmadinejad and his fellow Radicals aspired "to imitate bin Laden" and argued that "they are competing with the Taliban in calling for violence and in carrying out extremist crimes that are counter to the [Islamic] religion."[58]

Such pushback was a useful reminder that even in a Radical government there are many differences and crosscurrents — some policy-driven and some personal — operating in tandem. But in the end, the important thing to note is that none of the harsh criticism of Ahmadinejad, either external or internal, silenced his voice. The Ayatollah Khamenei could very well have reined in his hand-picked president, but he chose not to do so. To the contrary, he actually demanded that Ahmadinejad's critics be quiet and show deference. "Khamenei," noted one shrewd Mideast analyst, "took up a position next to Ahmadinejad, praising him and his functioning, requesting that none criticize him, and calling for the support of all the political forces in the government. Khamenei pointed out that Iran is now in a sensitive stage, and called for putting aside political rivalries — and indeed, Khatami's comments were not subsequently reported in the Iranian press."[59]

This was significantly instructive for anyone who was watching closely and listening carefully. What we learned in the summer and fall of 2005 was not just what Mahmoud Ahmadinejad believed but what the Ayatollah Khamenei believed, whom he wanted speaking for him, and what he wanted the world to hear.

Apocalyptic rhetoric about the end of the world.

A fatwa approving the use of nuclear weapons.

A vow to annihilate the U.S. and Israel.

And a rapid acceleration of Iran's nuclear research program.

For those willing to connect the dots, this was a dangerous and disturbing package.

The problem: almost no one in the West was watching closely or listening carefully.

CHAPTER TWELVE:
MAKING WAY FOR THE MAHDI

How Shia eschatology has driven Iranian foreign policy

In the fall of 2006, Mahmoud Ahmadinejad returned to New York to address the United Nations. This time, however, he launched a charm offensive.

First came his "exclusive" interview with Mike Wallace on CBS's *60 Minutes* in August. Next, he appeared on the cover of *Time* magazine in September. This was followed by a lengthy interview with Brian Williams for *NBC Nightly News* and a twenty-minute prime-time interview with CNN's Anderson Cooper. Then came Ahmadinejad's speech at the United Nations — concluding once again with a prayer that Allah would hasten the coming of the Mahdi — which garnered the Iranian president wall-to-wall coverage.[1]

Yet, as I pointed out at the time in two articles on National Review Online and on my blog, something was curiously absent from all this media coverage. Not one of these major American journalists asked Ahmadinejad about his Shia religious beliefs or his fascination with the coming of the Mahdi. They did not ask about his critique

258

of President Bush's faith in Jesus Christ in an eighteen-page letter he had sent the president. They didn't mention his encouragement that President Bush convert to Islam or his ten-page letter to German chancellor Angela Merkel on essentially the same topic.*

Wallace actually took the time to ask Ahmadinejad about his jacket and about what he does for leisure. But he took no time to ask how Ahmadinejad's eschatology has been driving Iranian foreign policy. *Time*'s cover story and exclusive print interview with Ahmadinejad never broached the subject of his eschatology. Nor did Williams in his interview. Nor did Cooper. Nor did almost any of the saturation coverage Ahmadinejad received during his U.S. visit.[2]

---

*Ahmadinejad sent his letters to President Bush and Chancellor Merkel in May 2006. In both letters, he urged the leaders to convert to Islam and accept his vision of world events. "Ahmadinejad hoped to follow in the footsteps of many great men in history who urged world leaders and opponents to submit to the will of Allah and convert to Islam," wrote one biographer. "These attempts had begun 1,400 years earlier when the Prophet Mohammed sent emissaries to kings and emperors far and wide to invite them to embrace Islam. More recently, Ayatollah Khomeini had written to President Mikhail Gorbachev in 1989 to suggest, 'Islam could fill the intellectual gap that the demise of Communism has created for the Soviet Union.' " (Kasra Naji, *Ahmadinejad: The Secret History of Iran's Radical Leader,* p. 197.)

Bewitched or Befuddled?

American journalists are not typically shy about asking tough, probing questions about the world-view of international leaders. President Bush was often asked about how his evangelical Christianity informed his foreign policy as president, particularly with regard to Israel and the Middle East. Why was there such hesitancy, then, when it came to questioning the religious beliefs of an Islamic leader who has called for the Jewish state to be wiped off the planet and urged fellow Muslims to envision a world without the United States?

As I complete this manuscript in the fall of 2008, not a single Western reporter who has interviewed Ahmadinejad — one of the most dangerous men in the world — has *ever* asked him directly about his eschatology. Yet he *wants* to talk about what he believes and why he believes it. His religion shapes who he is and what drives him. He unapolegetically talks about it all the time. He talked about it as mayor of Tehran. He talked about it while campaigning for president of Iran. He has repeatedly prayed about it before the entire U.N. General Assembly and a phalanx of cameras and international reporters. He gives major addresses on it at eschatology conferences. He talks about it with small groups of friends and religious leaders. He references it in letters to world leaders.

Nevertheless, the mainstream media refuses to ask him about it. Are journalists somehow bewitched in Ahmadinejad's presence? Or are they so slavishly devoted to their own secularism that they are befuddled, unable to comprehend the notion that a man's private religious beliefs could so profoundly and completely affect his public persona and political decision-making?

In a 2006 column for National Review Online, I offered five questions Mike Wallace and/or his colleagues should have asked the president of Iran. So long as Ahmadinejad or someone holding similar views remains in office, the questions remain valid. Asked politely, not provocatively, I have no doubt they would unlock a door into an intriguing and internationally significant story. I remain curious, therefore, to see who will ask them first.

1. Mr. President, you are telling colleagues in Iran that you believe the end of the world is rapidly approaching. Why do you believe this? How are these views shaping your foreign policy?

2. Could you tell us in the West more about your belief that the "Twelfth Imam" (or "Hidden Imam") will soon reappear and why you believe that the way to hasten the coming of this Islamic messiah is to launch a global jihad against Israel and the U.S.?

3. Mr. President, in Islam, Jesus Christ is considered a great prophet and teacher. In your lengthy letter to President Bush, you talked a lot about Jesus Christ. You criticized the president for, in your view, not following the teachings of Jesus. What are some of your favorite teachings of Jesus? Do you believe Jesus was Jewish? Do you believe that He lived and taught and performed His miracles in Israel? Do you believe Jesus wished for Israel to be wiped "off the map"? In the current crisis, what would Jesus do, in your opinion?

261

4. You have told colleagues that when you were speaking at the United Nations in the fall of 2005, you were surrounded by a light from heaven and that for about twenty-seven or twenty-eight minutes everyone in the General Assembly was mesmerized by your speech — that not a single person blinked for that entire time. Would you describe that experience for us? Do you believe that God or an angel was with you at that moment? Do you believe Allah has chosen you to be the leader of Iran at this moment in history?
5. You say that the era of bombs is over. Why then did you sign a $1 billion deal with Moscow in December 2005 to buy Russian missiles and other arms? Why are you sending missiles, bombs, and $100 million a year to Hezbollah? Why are you sending bombs and bombers into Iraq?[3]

Though the media elite have not shown much curiosity either in these kinds of questions or in the answers to them, fortunately the same cannot be said of a small but growing number of American policy makers and national security officials. As Ahmadinejad's statements and actions have become more outrageous — and as economic sanctions and diplomacy have proved increasingly ineffective — interest in the religious motivations of Iran's leaders has grown steadily among government insiders.

Since 2006, I have been invited to Capitol Hill and the Pentagon numerous times to speak privately and informally with Congressmen and Senators of both major parties, chiefs of staff from both the House and the Senate, legislative policy advisors, and generals and other high-ranking military leaders. I have also had the privilege of being invited to meet with past and present officials from the Central Intelligence Agency and the Department of Homeland Security, as well as with foreign ambassadors, diplomats, and political leaders. Some of these have been one-on-one meetings. Some have been in small groups of a dozen or so.

In the fall of 2007, I had the honor of addressing about 125 officials at the Pentagon on "Why Mahmoud Ahmadinejad's Eschatology Is Driving Iranian Foreign Policy: An Evangelical Christian Perspective." All of these meetings have been off the record, meaning I am not at liberty to share who was in the meetings or what they said. I can, however, share what I said. On most occasions, my message was an executive summary of the material that follows.

Welcome to Shia Eschatology

The Twelfth Imam was a real, flesh-and-blood person who lived during the ninth century AD. Like the eleven Shia leaders who went before him, he was an Arab male who, as a direct descendent of the founder of Islam, was thought to have been divinely chosen to be the spiritual guide and ultimate human authority of the Muslim people. His name was Muhammad Ibn Hasan Ibn Ali, and it is generally believed by Shias that he was born in Samarra, Iraq, in AD 868, though few details of his brief life are certain or free from controversy. Sunnis, for example, believe he was born later.

Before he could reach an age of maturity, when

he could teach and counsel the Muslim world as was believed to be his destiny, Ali vanished from human society. Some say he was four years old, while others say five and some say six.[4] Some believe he fell into a well in Samarra but his body was never recovered. Others believe the Mahdi's mother placed him in the well to prevent the evil rulers of the time from finding him, capturing him, and killing him — and that little Ali subsequently became supernaturally invisible. This is where the term "Hidden Imam" is derived, as Shias believe that Ali is not dead but has simply been hidden from the sight of mankind — Shias refer to this as "occultation" — until the end of days, when Allah will reveal him once again.

It is worth noting that on February 22, 2006, Sunni Radicals blew up the golden dome of the Al-Askari Mosque in Samarra, the mosque that houses the tombs of the tenth and eleventh Shia Imams and marks the site of the well where the Twelfth Imam mysteriously vanished.

Shias believe the Mahdi will return at the end of history — during a time of chaos, carnage, and confusion — to establish righteousness, justice, and peace. When he comes, they say, the Mahdi will bring Jesus with him. Jesus will be a Muslim and will serve as his deputy, not as King of kings and Lord of lords as the Bible teaches, and he will force non-Muslims to choose between following the Mahdi or death. "The spiritual position of the Mahdi is higher than that of Jesus in Shiism, but Jesus will appear when the Mahdi rises," notes Mehdi Khalaji of the Washington Institute for Near East Policy, author of *Apocalyptic Politics*. "According to the tradition, Jesus will: perform jihad under the Mahdi's commandership and kill

264

Dajjal — the Muslim concept close to that of the Christian 'Devil'; [he will] invite people to Islam, killing Christians and destroying churches; and also die before the Mahdi."[5]

By most accounts, Shia scholars believe the Mahdi will first appear in Mecca and conquer the Middle East, then establish the headquarters of his global Islamic government — or caliphate — in Iraq. But there is not universal agreement. Some believe he will emerge from the well at the Jamkaran Mosque in Iran and then travel to Mecca and Iraq. Some say that he will conquer Jerusalem before establishing his caliphate in Iraq. Others believe Jerusalem must be conquered as a prerequisite to his return. "When the Mahdi returns he will fight with Jews and kill all of them," wrote a Shia cleric in 1409. "Even if a Jew hides behind a rock, the rock speaks and says, 'O Muslim! A Jew is hiding behind me. Kill him!' "[6]

None of this is actually written in the Qur'an, and Sunnis reject this eschatology, so there is little clarity and plenty of room for debate and disagreement. But one thing that is fairly well agreed upon among devout "Twelvers" is that the Mahdi will end apostasy and purify corruption within Islam. He is expected, therefore, to conquer the Arabian Peninsula, Jordan, Syria, and "Palestine," and then he and Jesus will kill between 60 and 80 percent of the world's population, specifically those who refuse to convert to Islam.[7]

Signs of the Mahdi's Return
The Bright Future Institute in Qom is a theological think tank established by Shia scholars in 2004 to study "Mahdism" in depth and to prepare Shias for the return of the Islamic Messiah.[8] The

Institute teaches that five "distinct signs" will precede the arrival or the revelation of the Hidden Imam:[9]

1. The first [sign] is the rise of a fighter from Yemen called the Yamani, who attacks the enemies of Islam.
2. The second sign is the rise of an anti-Mahdi militant leader named Osman Ben Anbase, who will also be known as Sofiani. He will be joined by another anti-Mahdi militant called Dajal, whom many Muslim clerics have compared to the Antichrist. The uprising of Sofiani will precede the reappearance of the Mahdi in Mecca by exactly six months. These two forces, known as the forces of evil, will occupy Syria and Jordan and advance from there. The forces of good in this battle will be led by a man from Khorasan, a province in Iran, and the opponents will meet for an epic battle near the city of Kufa, in the Shiite heartland of southern Iraq.
3. The third distinct sign will be voices from the sky. The most distinctive voice will be that of the angel Gabriel, who will call the faithful to gather around the Mahdi.
4. The fourth sign will entail the destruction of Sofiani's army.
5. The fifth and final sign is the death of a holy man by the name of Muhammad bin Hassan, called Nafse Zakiye, or the pure soul. Fifteen days after he is killed, the Mahdi will appear in Mecca. [Then] the Mahdi will appoint Jesus Christ as his deputy. People will recognize the Mahdi

266

because there will be an angel above his head shouting, "This is the Mahdi. Follow him." The Mahdi will be wearing a ring that belonged to King Solomon and will hold the wooden stick that Moses held when he parted the Red Sea. His army of 313 will grow into ten thousand, fifty of whom will be women.

A similar perspective is taught by the Ayatollah Ibrahim Amini, a professor at the Religious Learning Centre in Qom and one of Iran's most respected Shia scholars. In his book *Al-Imam al-Mahdi, the Just Leader of Humanity*, Amini described the signs of the coming of the Mahdi in great detail.[10] Chief among them are a massive earthquake and the launching of a global war to kill or subjugate Jews, Christians, and other "infidels." In one passage, Amini quotes Muhammad (from a hadith, not from the Qur'an), saying: "Listen to the good news about the Mahdi! He will rise at the time when people will be faced with severe conflict and the earth will be hit by a violent quake. He will fill the earth with justice and equity as it is filled with injustice and tyranny. He will fill the hearts of his followers with devotion and will spread justice everywhere."

Wrote Amini:

When the world has become psychologically ready to accept the government of God and when general conditions have become favorable to the idea of the rulership of the truth, God will permit the Mahdi to launch his final revolution. . . .

A few selected individuals . . . will be the

first ones to respond to his call, and will be drawn to him like iron to a magnet in that first hour of his appearance. . . . On seeing the fulfillment of many of the signs promised in the traditions, a large number of unbelievers will turn towards Islam. Those who persist in their disbelief and wickedness shall be killed by the soldiers of the Mahdi. The only victorious government in the entire world will be that of Islam, and people will devotedly endeavor to protect it. Islam will be the religion of everyone, and will enter all the nations of the world. . . .

The Mahdi will offer the religion of Islam to the Jews and the Christians; if they accept it they will be spared, otherwise they will be killed. . . . It seems unlikely that this catastrophe can be avoided. . . . Warfare and bloodshed [are] inevitable. . . .

The Imam of the Age and his supporters will overcome the forces of disbelief and godless materialism by undertaking jihad. It will be with the power of just warfare that the forces of God's enemy and the supporters of disbelief and injustices will be exterminated. There are numerous traditions that speak about the impending use of force to achieve the goal.

Preparing People for the End

Muslim leaders and scholars tell me an unprecedented number of books, articles, pamphlets, and Web sites have been produced since the end of the 1980s, and specifically in the last few years, teaching people how to prepare for the end of days. Many such books have been huge best sellers in Iran and throughout the Middle East.

But Ahmadinejad and his advisors want everyone to be ready, not just those who can or want to read Islamic eschatology. Toward that end, a documentary film series called The World Towards Illumination was launched on Iranian television in the fall of 2006, designed to help answer the many questions Iranians have about the end of the world as we know it. Echoing the Bright Institute, the Ayatollah Amini, and other noted Shia scholars, the series explained the signs of the last days and what to expect when the Islamic messiah arrives. Among the key points the series made:[11]

- The world is now in its "last days."
- The Mahdi will first appear in Mecca, then in Medina.
- The Mahdi will conquer all of Arabia, Syria, and Iraq, destroy Israel, and then set up a "global government" based in Iraq, not Iran.
- Jesus will come back to earth, but not as the Son of God or even as a leader. Rather, He will serve as a deputy to the Mahdi to destroy the infidels.
- The Mahdi will send ten thousand of his troops to the east and west to uproot the "oppressors." During this time, "God will facilitate things for him, and lands will come under his control one after the other."
- "He will appear as a handsome young man, clad in neat clothes and exuding the fragrance of paradise. His face will glow with love and kindness for the human beings. . . . He has a radiant forehead, black piercing eyes, and a broad chest. He very much resembles his ancestor [the] Prophet Muhammad. Heavenly light and justice ac-

company him. He will overcome enemies and oppressors with the help of God, and as per the promise of the Almighty, the Mahdi will eradicate all corruption and injustice from the face of the earth and establish the global government of peace, justice, and equity."

- Before the Mahdi appears to the world, "a pious person . . . a venerable God-fearing individual from Iran" will meet with him. This individual will pledge allegiance to the Mahdi as he "fights oppression and corruption and enters Iraq to lift the siege of Kufa and holy Najaf and to defeat the forces of [Islam's enemies] in Iraq."*

An Israeli news site was the first to pick up the story and its significance to Israeli national security, noting that the program also said that the Mahdi will soon "form an army to defeat Islam's enemies in a series of apocalyptic battles" and "will overcome his archvillain in Jerusalem."[12]

What I found particularly interesting was the attention that the series gave to the parallel surge in interest in eschatology among Muslims and evangelical Christians, though it also noted the numerous and profound theological differences between the two.

"The apocalypse is a deep belief among humans regarding the end of the world," said the program's narrator. "One of the characteristics of the West in the current era is obsession with the end of time. Experts say discussions about the savior and the 'end of time' have not been so prevalent

* The series did not specify whether this person was President Ahmadinejad or someone to come.

270

before as they are now in the West. . . . They [evangelicals] believe the Messiah [Jesus] will re-appear and will establish his global rule with its center in [Jerusalem], with the help of born-again Christians. This sect's religious leaders in the 1990s strongly propagated their beliefs in the U.S. and European societies. In the past two years dozens of books have been published in this field. . . . These extremist Christians believe that certain events must be carried out by the Protes-tants in the world so as to prepare the grounds for the Messiah's reappearance. The followers of this school believe they have a religious duty to ac-celerate these events, for example planting the il-legal Zionist state of Israel for the Jews of the world, in Palestine."[13]

The program and its accompanying Web site even went so far as to suggest that the Mahdi might come to earth in 2007 and could be revealed to the world as early as the spring equi-nox.

That, of course, did not happen.

"Imminent"

Not all Muslims — nor even all Shias — share the brand of eschatology I have just outlined. Even Shias who do believe what Ahmadinejad believes are not all convinced that such events are going to happen in their lifetime, much less soon. Indeed, many Iranians are horrified by what Ahmadinejad has been saying and doing. But the point is that Ahmadinejad and his close aides and advisors are driven by the deeply rooted belief that the Islamic messiah will appear soon and that by launching a war to annihilate Judeo-Christian civilization, they can hasten that day. So is the Supreme Leader

271

Khamenei.

Hasten is a key word here. Ahmadinejad and his team do not believe they are supposed to be sitting around, twiddling their thumbs, *waiting* for the Mahdi. They believe they have been given specific tasks to speed up his arrival, and they are determined to accomplish those tasks, whatever the cost to themselves or their country. "The Hidden Imam has no tangible presence among us, but he is always [here], and we must prepare the ground for his speedy appearance," Ahmadinejad said at a 2006 eschatology conference on the occasion of the Mahdi's birthday. "We must rush towards him and hasten to prepare the ground for his appearance. *[He will not appear] if we sit idly. Mankind must hurry towards the Hidden Imam in order to reach him*"[14] (emphasis added).

Soon is another key word. Western leaders may not notice or care, but Ahmadinejad has operated in office as if the clock were ticking and time running out. As I noted earlier, shortly after his election in June 2005, Ahmadinejad began telling colleagues that the end of the world was just two or three years away. It was significant, therefore, that two years later he gave a speech to the International Seminar on the Doctrine of Mahdism in Tehran in which he warned that the West's day was almost finished. On August 25, 2007, Ahmadinejad said, "Our enemies naturally feel threatened by the call to [believe in] the Mahdi, for they do not want people to think about justice. But our reply to them is that the era of the aggressive has come to an end. We believe that it is time for the righteous to rule." Then he added that the preparations for the Hidden Imam "will soon be complete."[15]

A few days later, on August 28, Ahmadinejad said that "the current problems faced by the world result from [the rule] of unworthy rulers" and that "the ultimate solution is to replace these unworthy regimes and rulers, and to establish the rule of the Hidden Imam." He then reemphasized that the Mahdi's return "is imminent."[16]

On August 29, he said, "The Iranian nation and the Islamic Revolution have a pivotal role in preparing the ground for the coming of the Hidden Imam. . . . *We must rapidly develop Iran in order to create the [right] conditions for his coming,* and we must also help the rest of the world's nations [to prepare for his return], in order to precipitate this great event. . . . The responsibility that currently rests on Iran's [shoulders] is very heavy; it is the kind of mission [with which] the divine prophets [were entrusted]. It does not permit us to rest or slumber even for a moment. Have you ever seen a prophet take a rest from the fulfillment of his mission?"[17] (emphasis added).

A few weeks later, during his third visit to the U.S., rather than close his speech before the U.N. General Assembly with a prayer for Allah to bring the Mahdi quickly as he had on his two previous visits, Ahmadinejad chose to begin his speech with prayer. "O God," he prayed before hundreds of world leaders, "hasten the arrival of Imam al-Mahdi and grant him good health and victory and make us his followers and those to attest to his rightfulness."[18]

Ideas Have Consequences: Creating Chaos in Iraq

If all this were just talk, that would be one thing. But ideas have consequences. Ahmadinejad's

273

religious beliefs have driven Iranian policy in a variety of significant areas. In this section and the next, I will note two of the most important.

The first was Iran's policy toward Iraq following the U.S. and Coalition effort to liberate the country from Saddam Hussein's reign of terror. Some American politicians have suggested that Tehran has a real and vital interest in helping create a calm and peaceful Iraq, even if they are not happy with efforts to create a pro-Western democracy there. Such leaders have, therefore, strenuously advocated that the U.S. enter into direct negotiations with Ahmadinejad's regime to find ways to end the sectarian violence throughout Mesopotamia.

In their *Iraq Study Group Report* released in 2006, for example, former secretary of state James A. Baker III, former House Foreign Affairs Committee chairman Lee Hamilton, and a distinguished group of foreign policy veterans argued the following: "The United States must build a new international consensus for stability in Iraq and the region. In order to foster such consensus, the United States should embark on a robust diplomatic effort to establish an international support structure intended to stabilize Iraq . . . including all of Iraq's neighbors — Iran and Syria among them. Despite the well-known differences between many of these countries, they all share an interest in avoiding the horrific consequences that would flow from a chaotic Iraq, particularly a humanitarian catastrophe and regional destabilization."[19]

At first glance, such analysis looks good, particularly coming from such eminently qualified experts. But look at it again through the lens of

Shia eschatology. Are leaders who feel called by Allah to create chaos, carnage, and confusion throughout the Middle East likely to feel it is in their strategic national interest to ameliorate the "horrific consequences" of war and insurgency? Moreover, are leaders who believe the Mahdi will soon establish Sharia law in Iraq and set up the seat of a global Islamic government there likely to believe that it is in their best interest to help the Americans, the British, the French, and other Judeo-Christian powers establish freedom and democracy in Iraq? Or over time are they more likely to send terrorists, money, and weapons into Iraq to kill Americans, Coalition forces, and Iraqis; destroy infrastructure; disrupt the economy; hinder the flow of oil and gas coming from Iraq; and generally make life miserable for everyone in the country?

In 2005, Iran poured an estimated $1 billion into activities aimed at interfering with Iraqi internal affairs.[20] By mid-2006, 80 percent of foreign insurgents being arrested in Iraq (1,577 out of 1,972) had come from Iran.[21] In June of 2006, former Iranian president Rafsanjani said bluntly, "If Iran and Iraq become united, the enemies will not be able to force anything against Islam in the region."[22] By May of 2007, an estimated 70 percent of foreign insurgents were still coming from Shia Gulf states, including Iran.[23] That summer, as he was claiming the Mahdi's arrival was "imminent," Ahmadinejad was also tipping his hand regarding Iran's aspirations, telling reporters, "The political power of the occupiers [U.S. and Coalition forces in Iraq] is collapsing rapidly. Soon, we will see a huge power vacuum in the region. . . . We are prepared to fill

275

the gap."[24]

In April of 2008, Iraqi security forces uncovered the largest cache of Iranian weapons to date, including more than a thousand roadside-bomb components, more than three thousand pounds of explosives, and forty-five Katusha rockets, along with scores of rounds of ammunition, mortars, and mortar stands.[25] Not surprisingly, that same month, General David Petraeus testified on Capitol Hill that Iranian-backed terrorist groups such as the Mahdi Army — run by Iraqi Shia firebrand Moqtada al-Sadr — posed the "greatest long-term threat to the viability of a democratic Iraq."[26] The following month, CIA director Michael Hayden said point-blank, "It is my opinion [that] it is the policy of the Iranian government, approved to highest level of that government, to facilitate the killing of Americans in Iraq. Just make sure there's clarity on that."[27]

It should be noted here that in mid-2008, Tehran began to call off the Mahdi Army and stopped sending as much support to the Shia insurgents. As a result, violence in Iraq dropped dramatically. But I believe Ahmadinejad and his advisors made a tactical decision to calm things down in Iraq. It was not that they agreed with the Baker-Hamilton Commission and thought, "Oh my goodness, violence on our borders and chaos in Baghdad is a bad thing." To the contrary, the Iranian leaders hate the Iraqis. They feel Arabs are ethnically, racially, and morally beneath Persians. They want revenge for Saddam's invasion of Iran in 1980 and the horrors of the eight-year Iran-Iraq War. More to the point, strategically they want to create the conditions in Iraq that will hasten the coming of the Mahdi, and they saw that the chaos they were producing was very effective. But tactically they faced a question: would it not be more effective to inflict more carnage in Iraq *after* U.S. and coalition forces had left the region? Of course it would. What, then, would be the best way to get U.S. and coalition forces out of Iraq as fast as possible? Simple — let Washington feel as if the war had been won.

That required ratcheting down the violence, and quickly. Less violence in Iraq, the leadership in Tehran hoped, might help the presidential campaign of Barack Obama, who was advocating a speedy withdrawal of U.S. troops.* It might also hurt the campaign of John McCain by providing less of a felt need for Americans to elect a war hero and experienced veteran to the role of Commander in Chief. Furthermore, less violence in Iraq would give Congress and the Bush administration a reason to pull U.S. troops out of Iraq as quickly as possible, which is what all the polls of American public opinion indicated the country wanted.

But make no mistake: this was a tactical deci-

*In March 2008, Ahmadinejad actually told a Spanish newspaper that he would have no problem seeing Barack Obama elected president of the United States instead of John McCain. After it became clear that he had gone too far and might actually damage Obama's chances, Ahmadinejad had to publicly state that he had not intended to endorse the junior senator from Illinois. (See "Ahmadinejad: I Never Endorsed Obama," Press TV, March 5, 2008. See also "Iran Avoids Support for US Presidential Hopefuls," Fars News Agency, March 11, 2008.)

sion. If Iran is not dealt with — and if Khamenei, Ahmadinejad, and leaders who hold similar theological views remain in power — Tehran will eventually do everything it possibly can to make Iraq hell on earth in order to create the conditions for the coming of the Mahdi.

Ideas Have Consequences:
Acquiring Nuclear Weapons

The second major policy arena driven by Shia eschatology is Iran's feverish desire to build, buy, or steal nuclear weapons.

In December 2007, a ferocious international debate erupted over just how soon Iran would be able to go nuclear against Israel or any other country. The debate was triggered by the release of an American document known as the "National Intelligence Assessment," or NIE. Written in cooperation with sixteen U.S. spy agencies, the NIE suggested that the U.S. had hard evidence that Iran halted its program to develop nuclear weapons back in 2003.

"Tehran is most likely keeping its options open with respect to building a weapon," reported the *International Herald Tribune,* drawing upon the unclassified version of the report, but intelligence agencies "do not know whether it currently intends to develop nuclear weapons. . . . Iran is continuing to produce enriched uranium . . . a program that the Tehran government has said is designed for civilian purposes. The new estimate says that the enrichment program could still provide Iran with enough raw material to produce a nuclear weapon sometime by the middle of the next decade, a timetable essentially unchanged from previous estimates. But the new estimate declares with 'high confidence' that a military-run Iranian program intended to transform that raw material into a nuclear weapon has been shut down since 2003, and also says with high confidence that the halt 'was directed primarily in response to increasing international scrutiny and pressure.' "[28]

The big questions: Was this U.S. intelligence assessment correct? Has Iran given up trying to build nuclear weapons?

"Maybe" was my response at the time, "and let's hope so." It would be wonderful to know that Iran is not the increasingly worrisome nuclear threat the U.S. and other intelligence agencies had been saying it was right up to the release of the NIE.

But there is, of course, always the possibility that the U.S. assessment is wrong.

The accuracy of some of our intelligence reports in the Middle East has certainly been called into question in recent years, and rightly so. What's more, we must always remember May 1998, when India and Pakistan conducted multiple nuclear weapons tests, stunning U.S. and other Western intelligence agencies, which had absolutely no idea either country was so close to getting the Bomb. At the time, Sen. Richard Shelby (R-AL), then the chairman of the Senate Intelligence Committee, called this a "colossal failure" of the U.S. intelligence community, and he was right.[29]

God forbid we should have a similar failure with regard to Iran. A new intelligence failure concerning the current apocalyptic regime in Tehran could be a *cataclysmic* failure, not merely a *colossal* one.

And even if Iran did, in fact, briefly halt development of nuclear weapons in 2003, much has happened since then that could have changed the calculus in Tehran.

For one thing, the United States and our allies liberated Iraq in 2003. Is it possible Iran restarted its nuclear weapons program for defensive reasons after major ground operations ended, trying to prevent Iran from ever being "liberated" by the U.S. or any other country or coalition? For another thing, Ahmadinejad came to power in August 2005. Is it possible that Iran restarted its nuclear weapons program for offensive reasons, hoping to set the stage for the Islamic messiah to appear?

NIE skeptics abounded, then and now. Numerous former U.S. diplomats, intelligence analysts, and military experts at home and abroad doubted whether the assessment of Iran's intentions and capabilities was accurate.[30] And in a rare unanimous convergence of agreement, the editorial pages of the *New York Times, Wall Street Journal,* and *Washington Post* expressed similar doubts.

The *Times* warned that the NIE "is not an argument for anyone to let down their guard when it comes to Iran's nuclear ambitions."[31]

The *Journal* pointed out that "as recently as 2005, the consensus estimate of our spooks was that 'Iran currently is determined to develop nuclear weapons' and do so 'despite its international obligations and international pressure.' This was a 'high confidence' judgment. The new NIE says Iran abandoned its nuclear program in 2003 'in response to increasing international scrutiny.' This too is a 'high confidence' conclusion. One of the two conclusions is wrong, and casts considerable doubt on the entire process by which these 'estimates' — the consensus of 16 intelligence bureaucracies — are conducted and accorded

280

gospel status."[32]

The *Post,* as skeptical as the others, rightly highlighted the fact that "while U.S. intelligence agencies have 'high confidence' that covert work on a bomb was suspended 'for at least several years' after 2003, there is only 'moderate confidence' that Tehran has not restarted the military program." Furthermore, the *Post* noted — somewhat ominously, I might add — that "Iran's massive overt investment in uranium enrichment meanwhile proceeds in defiance of binding U.N. resolutions, even though Tehran has no legitimate use for enriched uranium" and "the U.S. estimate of when Iran might produce enough enriched uranium for a bomb — sometime between late 2009 and the middle of the next decade — hasn't changed."[33]

And new information has come to light since the NIE was written. At the close of 2007, an investigation by the International Atomic Energy Agency (IAEA) revealed that Iran has obtained on the black market blueprints to build nuclear warheads. "Both the IAEA and other experts have categorized the instructions outlined in the blueprints as having no value outside of a nuclear weapons program," reported the Associated Press. "Senior IAEA officials were refused interviews with at least two top Iranian nuclear officials suspected of possible involvement in a weapons program, they said. One was the leader of a physics laboratory at Lavizan, outside Tehran, which was razed before the agency had a chance to investigate activities there. The other was in charge of developing Iran's centrifuges, used to enrich uranium."[34]

By February of 2008, the IAEA told top U.S.

officials that it had received from multiple member states "extensive documentation that detailed Iran's past attempts to develop a nuclear warhead."[35] Shortly thereafter, the U.N.'s chief nuclear weapons inspector told a closed-door meeting of international diplomats that "the agency had gathered intelligence from around ten countries suggesting Iran was engaged in weaponization studies." He specifically noted the discovery of a fifteen-page Iranian document that described the process of machining uranium metal into two hemispheres of the kind used in nuclear warheads, which he found "alarming," noting that "there was no reason why a country would need to possess such a document unless they wanted to produce uranium hemispheres for a nuclear weapon."[36]

In the summer of 2008, Ahmadinejad announced that Iran possessed six thousand centrifuges, machines capable of enriching uranium to weapons-grade standards, almost double the number the U.N. had said Iran was using just a few months earlier.[37]

Meanwhile, that summer Iran tested missiles with a range of at least 1,250 miles — capable of hitting sections of eastern and southern Europe — each of which was capable of carrying nuclear warheads once those were ready.[38] Iran also launched their *Omid* ("hope") satellite into orbit, raising concerns that if they had the technical expertise to put rockets into space, they were also closing in on the day when they could launch a long-range, intercontinental ballistic missile capable of hitting North America.[39]

Can We Live with the Persian Bomb?

As Iran under Ahmadinejad accelerated its pursuit of nuclear weapons and the missiles to deliver them, a growing chorus of voices in the foreign policy community suggested this might not be such a terrible thing, claiming that the West would be able to successfully deter or contain a nuclear-armed Iran much as we did with the Soviet Union during the Cold War and have done with the People's Republic of China.

Michael Eisenstadt, senior fellow and director of security studies at the Washington Institute for Near East Policy, delivered testimony before the House Armed Services Committee on February 1, 2006, entitled, "Deter and Contain: Dealing with a Nuclear Iran."

Barry R. Posen of the MIT Center for International Studies wrote an op-ed for the *New York Times* on February 27, 2006, entitled, "We Can Live with a Nuclear Iran."

In a column published in *National Journal* on May 19, 2006, journalist Paul Starobin wrote, "In thinking about a new deterrence structure, some analysts advocate a global approach in which nuclear states — including the U.S., Britain, France, Russia, and China, the five permanent members of the U.N. Security Council — would in effect cover the greater Middle East region with a protective nuclear umbrella. The proposition would be simple: If the mullahs [of Iran] use or even threaten to use nukes, they would face the prospect of retaliation from these powers." Starobin also argued that "Iran's acquisition of a bomb would probably improve the chances of the U.S. and Iran renewing a dialogue after all these years" because, as one Mideast analyst told him, "they see acquisition of a nuclear weapon as a precondition of having talks with the U.S."

In the fall of 2007, former CENTCOM commander John Abizaid joined the growing crowd as well, saying, "There are ways to live with a nuclear Iran. I believe we have the power to deter Iran if they go nuclear," just as we deterred the Soviet Union and China. "Iran is not a suicidal nation," he added. "Nuclear deterrence would work with Iran."[40]

Throughout the 2008 presidential primaries, deterrence and containment were the themes of the Democratic contenders. As I noted in chapter two, Senator Barack Obama dismissed the seriousness of the Iranian threat during his campaign, saying it was nothing compared to the threat the Soviet Union posed during the Cold War and arguing that we had successfully deterred Moscow from doing something catastrophic.

Former U.N. Ambassador Bill Richardson made a similar case, stating during one of the debates, "As we know from the Cold War, deterrence is above all a matter of clarity and credibility. We need to be absolutely clear that a nuclear Iran is unacceptable, and we need to be absolutely credible when we say what we will do about it if the Iranians continue to disregard the will of the international community. The clear message must be this: develop nukes and you will face devastating global sanctions."[41]

Senator Hillary Rodham Clinton was even more explicit during an interview on ABC's *Good Morning America* on the morning of the Pennsylvania primaries. She threatened to wipe Iran out *after* an Iranian nuclear attack, hoping that such strong language would deter the Iranian regime from launching such an attack.

"You said, 'If Iran were to strike Israel, there would be a massive retaliation,' " noted host Chris Cuomo. "Scary words, Mrs. Clinton. Does 'massive retaliation' mean you go into Iran, you would bomb Iran? Is that what that's supposed to suggest?"

"Well, the question was if Iran were to launch a nuclear attack on Israel, what would our response be?" Clinton replied. "And I want the Iranians to know that if I'm the president, we will attack Iran, and I want them to understand that, because it does mean that they have to look very carefully at their society. Because at whatever stage of development they might be in their nuclear weapons program, in the next ten years, during which they might foolishly consider launching an attack on Israel, we would be able to totally obliterate them. That's like a terrible thing to say, but those people who run Iran need to understand that because that perhaps will deter them from doing something that would be reckless, foolish, and tragic."[42]

It certainly sounded tough, and it may have helped Clinton defeat Senator Obama in the Pennsylvania primary that day, 55 percent to 45 percent. But there were two serious flaws in what Clinton said.

First, by offering a reactive rather than a proactive military strategy vis-à-vis Iran, she was allowing for the possibility of another Holocaust. If Iranian leaders get nuclear warheads and can attach them to the high-speed ballistic missiles they already have, Ahmadinejad could kill some six million Jews in about six minutes. What good is it to say that the U.S. would obliterate Iran *after* Ahmadinejad or a successor accomplishes another

Holocaust?

Second, Clinton and her like-minded colleagues believe their tough talk will deter Iran's leaders from launching a nuclear attack against Israel. But will it? Remember, Iranian leaders believe they are supposed to create global chaos and carnage in order to bring about the optimal conditions for the return of the Mahdi. They believe they have been chosen by Allah to annihilate the U.S. and Israel and export the Islamic Revolution. Is it not true that the only way that is remotely possible, humanly speaking, is for Iran to acquire nuclear weapons and the means to deliver them against America and Israel? How then could the West successfully deter or contain them? If they die, these Radicals believe they are going directly to paradise. What could we possibly offer them as either carrots or sticks that would keep them from what they see as their God-given duty when their failure to obey could, in their minds, be disobedience punishable by an eternity in the fires of hell?

Many in Washington cannot or will not see the problem here. Delaware Senator Joe Biden, for example, said during his presidential campaign, "My concern is not that a nuclear Iran some day would be moved by messianic fervor to use a nuclear weapon as an Armageddon device and commit national suicide in order to hasten the return of the Hidden Imam. My worry is that the fear of a nuclear Iran could spark an arms race in the Middle East, with Saudi Arabia, Egypt, Syria, and others joining in."[43]

That second issue is certainly a real concern. But based on the evidence, why would Biden be so quick to dismiss the first issue? Mahmoud Ah-

madinejad is not just another power-hungry dictator in the mold of the Soviet or Chinese leaders of
yore. Neither is the Ayatollah Khamenei or the
Ayatollah Mesbah-Yazdi or their many colleagues
in the upper echelons of Iranian leadership. They
are not Communists. They are not atheists. They
do not believe that this world is all there is. They
are Shia Islamic fascists. They believe they are
Shia John the Baptists, forerunners of the soon-
coming Islamic messiah. They believe their life
mission is to kill millions of Jews and Christians
and usher in an Islamic caliphate. If they die, they
are convinced they know where they are going.

But they do not really believe they are going to
die — not at the hand of the infidels, at any rate.
They believe instead that they have been chosen
for a divine appointment and that nothing can
stop them. That is what makes them so dangerous. Unfortunately, too many Washington politicians — Obama, Clinton, and Biden included —
do not understand this.

And that is a serious problem. To misunderstand
the nature and threat of evil is to risk being blindsided by it. To misunderstand the nature and
threat of the Second Iranian Revolution could be
the prelude to genocide. We dare not be blindsided.

Chapter Thirteen:
The Road Ahead

My conversation with the
former director of Central Intelligence

It was a beautiful Sunday morning in downtown Baghdad when a boy named Amar entered a crowded polling station without attracting much attention. Though he was nineteen, Amar had been born with Down syndrome and was believed to have the mind of a four-year-old.

This was an exciting day in Iraq — January 30, 2005 — the day of the first truly free and democratic elections in the country's long and troubled history. Despite intense sectarian violence that had plagued the country since the fall of Saddam Hussein in the spring of 2003, there were long lines of people waiting to cast their ballots, and there was a buzz of excitement around the voting boxes. This was a big deal. People wanted to be part of it. Indeed, more than eight and a half million people all across the country — 58 percent of those eligible to vote — showed up that day at neighborhood polling stations like this one to make their voices heard. No one in their wildest imaginations would have ever worried that Amar might be a suicide bomber.

But before anyone realized what was happening, Amar disintegrated in an explosion that could be heard for miles.

His parents were at the home of some friends, celebrating the fact that they had just voted for the first time. But they heard the explosion, and soon they heard a rumor moving quickly through their Shia neighborhood that the bomber had been a disabled boy. Panic-stricken, they raced home, only to find Amar missing. "They got neighbors to search, and one of them identified Amar's head where it lay on the pavement," the boy's cousin told an Australian reporter. "His body was broken into pieces. I have heard of [the jihadists] using dead people and donkeys and dogs to hide their bombs, but how could they do this to a boy like Amar?"[1]

Iraqi authorities suspected that insurgents had kidnapped Amar when his parents went to vote, quickly fitted him with a suicide bomber vest, then sent him to the polling station. "They must have kidnapped him," his cousin said. "He was like a baby. He had nothing to do with the resistance, and there was nothing in the house for him to make a bomb. He was Shiite — why bomb his own people? He was mindless, but he was mostly happy, laughing and playing with the children in the street. Now, his father is inconsolable; his mother cries all the time."

Iraqi interior minister Falah al-Naqib was beside himself with anger. "A handicapped child was used to carry out a suicide attack on a polling site," he seethed. "This is an indication of what horrific actions they [the followers of jihad] are carrying out."[2]

Unfortunately, this was not the first time Radicals who say they want to become martyrs for Allah had preyed upon those unable to choose their own fate. Nor would it be the last.

On the morning of February 1, 2008, two mentally handicapped women strolled through the crowded streets of Baghdad. Unbeknownst to those around them, under their full-length Islamic body coverings they wore suicide bombers' vests. One entered the bustling al-Ghazl market in the center of the city. The other made her way to a bird market in a neighborhood in the southeastern section of the capital and gathered people around her, saying she had birds to sell.

At precisely 10:20 a.m. local time, the first woman blew up, killing forty-six people and injuring at least one hundred others. Twenty minutes later, the second woman blew up, killing twenty-seven people and wounding another sixty-seven.

"Police initially said the bomb . . . was hidden in a box of birds," reported the Associated Press, "but determined it was a suicide attack after finding the woman's head."[3]

As the investigation unfolded, the police realized that both bomber vests had been detonated by remote control, suggesting that these poor women probably did not even realize what they were doing — or what was being done to them in the name of Allah. Rather, authorities said they were likely used by Radicals precisely because they were women, unlikely to be searched at checkpoints where male soldiers and police officers are forbidden by Islamic law to search women and where there are simply too few female officers to do the job.* The fact that these particular women were

*Female suicide bombers are becoming more common

290

mentally challenged just made the Radicals' job that much easier.

"By targeting innocent Iraqis, they [the jihadists] show their true demonic character," said a military spokesman in Baghdad. "They care nothing for the Iraqi people. They want to subjugate them and forcefully create a greater Islamic Sharia state."[4]

I agree, and I hope that spokesman got a promotion and a raise for telling the truth. Too many innocents have died for us to remain quiet. How dare the world keep silent about what is being done by Radicals in the name of God? Silence betrays and dishonors the memories of the innocents who were killed without cause.

So let's call a spade a spade: What was unleashed upon humanity by the Islamic Revolution of 1979 was sheer, unbridled evil in the form of cold-blooded, ruthless killers who feast on death, who are aroused and energized by the thought and sight of human blood, and who privately — and increasingly publicly — fantasize about unleashing another Holocaust because murdering mere hundreds or thousands no longer slakes their unholy lust.

Three decades later, this evil has not been contained. Nor has its threat diminished. Rather, it has worsened, for today the Radicals — be they Shia disciples of the Ayatollah Khomeini or Sunni disciples of Osama bin Laden — are on the verge

---

in Radical operations. Between 1985 and 2006, more than 220 women were suicide bombers worldwide, about 15 percent of the total, according to Mia Bloom, author of *Dying to Kill: The Allure of Suicide Terror*.

of acquiring the very technology necessary to make their genocidal fantasies come true.

Why is the West sleeping? Can it be awakened? What does the future hold, and what should we be watching for on the road ahead?

"There Is No Sanctity of Life in Their Playbook"

A few days after the February 1 attacks in Baghdad, I had the privilege of discussing these very questions with one of America's most experienced and highest ranking intelligence officials.

Born in 1938, Porter Goss began his post-Yale career in 1960 as a U.S. Army intelligence officer during some of the coldest years of the Cold War, including the Cuban Missile Crisis, before being recruited by the Central Intelligence Agency's Directorate of Operations. There, he served as a clandestine operative in Latin America, the Caribbean, and Europe from 1962 until 1972, when a serious illness forced him to retire.

He and his wife, Mariel, resettled in southern Florida, where Goss ran some businesses, was elected mayor of his town, and eventually won a seat in Congress in 1989. For eight of his sixteen years in the House, Goss was chairman of the House Permanent Select Committee on Intelligence, before President Bush nominated him to be the director of Central Intelligence in August of 2004, replacing George Tenet. Goss retired from the Agency and political life on May 26, 2006, after nearly a half century of service to his country.

Lynn and I first met Porter and Mariel over dinner in December of 2007 at a quaint little country inn not far from the Shenandoah mountains in rural Virginia. Mutual friends of ours had arranged the evening after learning that the Gosses not only had a copy of my book *Epicenter* but had both read it several times. When they called to see if we wanted to get together, we did not hesitate for an instant. To the contrary, we considered it an honor.

The Gosses could not have been more gracious or down-to-earth as Lynn and I plied them for stories and insights of their remarkable years of knowing what few others know and seeing what few others see.

Porter told us that, as chairman of the House intelligence committee, he had been to the Pakistan-Afghanistan border with Pakistani intel officials in August of 2001 to learn more about the terrorist risks coming from the region. Then he described how he had been in a meeting with the director of Pakistani intelligence in a secure conference room in the U.S. Capitol on the morning of 9/11 when an aide slipped him a note saying a plane had just hit one of the World Trade Center towers. Like many, he did not think much of it at first, believing it was probably a small private plane gone astray. But when an aide stepped back in the room a few moments later to slip him another note, one that said the second tower had just been hit, Goss instantly knew it was terrorism. He gave the note to his committee cochair, Sen. Richard Shelby of Alabama, who then handed the note to the Pakistani intel chief. All color drained from the man's face. This was al Qaeda. There was no doubt in their minds. The Radicals' war to destroy the United States had finally come home.

When we sat down in February 2008 for an interview in a room overlooking the Capitol, I asked Goss just how serious he believed the threat from Radical Islam and the followers of jihad was to U.S. national security.

"It's an extraordinarily serious threat," he replied. "It's something that we have been very slow to address as a nation — and it's going to take generations to solve. . . . I think that the Beirut bombings is when we began to suddenly think about terrorism as a national security threat, along with hostages being taken in Lebanon, including a chief of station who was badly treated and brutally murdered back in the early '80s.* Suddenly the lexicon of national security included the words *terrorism* and *terrorist.*

"Then we've had a whole litany of other attacks, all the explosions and bombings, the attack on the *Cole,* attacks on our embassies. The jihadist threat is different and more dangerous in some ways from other historic threats — most notably the suicide martyr. They use suicide bombers in this asymmetric warfare that they have. Human ordnance — especially young women — is a new experience for us. Think of that — *human* ordnance. They're spending human lives to go out and blow up other people. There is no sanctity of life in their playbook. Martyrdom and its rewards trump the U.S. Code of Military Justice, to say nothing of our Constitution and Bill of Rights. It's all about Allah and whatever is the will of Allah in their eyes. We don't know how to cope with that. We have to learn new ways to deal with what

*Goss was referring to William Buckley, the CIA's Beirut station chief, who was kidnapped by Hezbollah on March 16, 1984, and later died in captivity due to illness and torture in June of 1985.

the Radicals do, but first we have to begin to understand how they think, and we haven't got that first step done."[5]

Goss told me that "the ingredients are all in place for the Radical Islamists to recruit and expand and do damage. They generally understand our vulnerabilities. Their desire to hurt us will not abate. Radical teaching will continue. Resources will flow — including money from oil — to arm and train martyrs. They will continue to take advantage of our open society to attack us, and they will continue to exploit our sensitivity to tolerance and human rights to brutalize us, all the while claiming they are the 'victims' of the 'Evil Satan.' The jihadists seek to destroy our core values and beliefs and to replace them with their own. They are energized and determined, and they know how to exploit asymmetric warfare to their purpose. They have resiliency, substantial support, timeless patience. If they are allowed more strength, particularly some form of WMD, we face a fatal and urgent time."

The Big Seven

I asked Goss, based on all his experience and all that he has seen — classified and open-source — what countries or trends in the epicenter worried him most thirty years after the Islamic Revolution. Goss laid out seven threats he is tracking closely.

Threat No. 1: Iran

The biggest threat to U.S. national security, to Israel's security, and to the security of our allies in Europe and the Middle East is the Islamic Republic of Iran, so long as Radicals continue to run the show there, Goss argued.

"Mahmoud Ahmadinejad is a populist charismatic energized by a surreal vision," Goss warned. "He is dangerous. There is not the slightest doubt in my mind that Iran is actively pursuing a nuclear military weapon capability that includes a long-range delivery system. They seek the know-how and the hardware from multiple sources and have bought years of time by stringing out less-than-sincere negotiations with the E.U., the U.N., the IAEA. They have played Chinese, Russian, and French self-interest to their advantage. There's no question in my mind that Ahmadinejad and people in the military in Iran are seeking the Persian Bomb for military purposes. It's not just about peaceful nuclear power. They have plenty of oil to start with, so that's a bit of a joke, but that is a very, very dangerous situation. Ahmadinejad really wants to be a player in the nuclear club. If that is allowed to happen, suddenly we're talking about a nuclear weapon in the hands of a Radical in the caliphate. That would be a huge, huge watershed in the geopolitical world."

"How long until Iran actually has operational nuclear weapons?" I asked.

"It depends on how they get it," he replied. "If they cheat and buy one, anything is possible. But my guess is that if they didn't go out and buy one, if they couldn't find somebody to buy one from, then I believe the answer is that you could see a weapon, all other things being equal, in the five- to ten-year range. Whether they go the uranium route or the plutonium route doesn't really much matter. We're looking at Iran having the know-how in a couple of years, an actual weapon in perhaps five to ten, and then perhaps a capability that makes them a bigger player if the rest of the world stands by and lets it happen, and that's a piece I cannot judge at this point. I do not know what the rest of the world is going to do. My estimate is formed by some conflicting views and reappraisals over the recent years. But it is not *if,* it is *when.*"

"When you think about Iran over the next few years, then, what worries you most?" I asked.

"That somebody who has got passion and no restraint is going to get a nuclear weapon, and the most likely candidate for that right now is Ahmadinejad," he said.

"Right now" was the most important phrase in that sentence. However, Goss noted that Ahmadinejad's popularity has been slipping in Iran and that this Persian Radical may not be around much longer.

"This fellow Ahmadinejad is hardly a seasoned politician," he explained. "He is a bit of a populist. The trouble is it's not working anymore. . . . His lack of real-time management skills is eroding his appeal among the Iranian citizenry as his campaign platform deliverables are nowhere in sight. . . . Every day, Iranians are much more interested in their daily bread than they are in the return of the Twelfth Imam. So there is now beginning to be a disconnect. That disconnect is being exaggerated by technology today, the Internet. He's not quite as popular or quite as esteemed as he thinks he should be. I think Ahmadinejad is on a downslope. I don't think what he's doing is sustainable."

In this context, it is important to note that while Ahmadinejad may increasingly be in political trouble, he is not the only leader in Iran who

297

could soon pass from the political scene. The country's Supreme Leader, the Ayatollah Khamenei — born July 17, 1939 — is in poor and declining health and has looked more and more enfeebled in public appearances over the past several years. He reportedly has cancer and may have suffered a stroke in December 2006 or January 2007.[6] Moreover, both leaders face the possibility of assassination, a coup, a popular rebellion, or regime change by some other means.

At some point in the not-too-distant future, therefore, we could see a dramatic change in Iranian politics. The question is, when Khamenei and Ahmadinejad are no longer in power, which direction would a new Iranian government go? Would a new ayatollah and president continue to export the Revolution; complete Iran's nuclear weapons development program; do more publicly and privately to hasten the coming of the Mahdi; attempt to seize the "holy lands" of Mecca and Medina from the Sunnis; and launch genocidal attacks against Israel, the United States, and others? Or would they reverse the Radicalism set into motion in 1979, abandon the quest for the Persian Bomb, and either temper the Islamic fanaticism coming from the mullahs or eliminate the Radical threat completely by transforming Iran into a secular, nonviolent, democratic republic or constitutional monarchy?

It all depends, of course, on who would follow Khamenei and Ahmadinejad. But Goss is right — the stakes are high, and for the foreseeable future Iran is one of the most important countries in the Islamic world to watch.

Threat No. 2: Al Qaeda and Osama bin Laden

Osama bin Laden and his organization ranked a close second on Goss's threat list.

"There actually are some people who still don't think Osama bin Laden exists, that he is just a myth, a Hollywood character or something. I remember the president of the United States after 9/11 had a very hard time convincing some of our close allies that there was a person named Osama bin Laden. But bin Laden is a huge danger. He is now an icon, of course. He has a vision. He has charisma. And he has coupled himself with a magnificent manager/manipulator, a very devious guy who feels like he's the great victim of all times, a fellow named Zawahiri, from Egypt.

"Some jihadists are true believers, but other motivators such as family or tribal honor, nationalism, schisms in Islam, desperate living conditions, perceived victimization, injustice, and the like can all be involved. But for the top leadership of al Qaeda and many of the Radical imams, it is simply a quest for power based on a hijacked version of the Qur'an. What bin Laden and Zawahiri want is their own way, which includes pursuit of power, revenge, some earthly reward, and a return of Islam to purer Sunniism. Destroying apostates, removing infidels from the holy lands [of Saudi Arabia and Israel], and eventually subjugating infidels elsewhere — including the United States — seems to be the game plan."

"You were essentially in charge of hunting bin Laden for almost three years," I noted. "Why has he been so hard to catch? Would you have expected that more than six years after 9/11 he would still be on the run?"

"Why haven't we caught [bin Laden] after so

many years? Well, there are a lot of answers," Goss sighed. "In the first place, the geography [along the Afghanistan-Pakistan border] is so harsh that you can't even explain it. Even when you see it you can't believe it. There are places where the cliffs are so steep, they're so close together, and the chasm is so narrow that the sun only shines for a few minutes a day at the actual bottom of the chasm. Even with a helicopter you have to sort of peer over and look down. I've seen that terrain. I don't know how anybody wanders around there. But, of course, there are caves all over the place. There are no reference landmarks. Everything looks like everything else. There's no cover [for U.S. agents or commandos] to be out and about. So this is a very tough area to get into, a very tough area to survive. And you just don't go in and say, 'I think I'll take a room at that lodge over there and see if I can find bin Laden.' It's not that kind of place at all. So he's got himself a built-in surveillance system to keep the bad guys out. The geography works beautifully for him. He also has a message system that he uses that is very hard for us to deal with because he's learned the hard way about what we can do and what we can't do, so they've taken defensive measures and countermeasures that are very helpful."

The other part of the story of how bin Laden has been able to elude capture, Goss noted, was that the U.S. is severely limited by the kind of force it can use, and where it can use such force.

"Let me explain that if I may," Goss told me. "Say I got a message in my office that said, 'Mr. Director, we know where Osama bin Laden is; we can pinpoint it right here. We have actual intelligence that is 100 percent certain that Osama bin

Laden is right in this place.' Then you have to ask, can somebody go in and arrest him? I mean, what's the situation? I've just explained that he's in a very hostile geographic area. Let's say I've got the cave pinpointed and know it's him. Who goes to the cave? How do you get there? Well, what country is it in? Let's say it's Pakistan, because it's been suggested in the newspapers that he might actually be in the northwest frontier of Pakistan. If that's true, we have to go to Pakistan if we're going to use our military. Now, is our military going to be allowed to come into Pakistan to go hunt bin Laden? No, they're not. Can they go without the Paks' permission? No, they're a sovereign state. We've signed treaties. So our military is not a player in this unless they're invited in by the Paks. If the president of Pakistan invited the United States military to come into Pakistan to catch Osama bin Laden, I think he would be the *former* president very quickly. That stability factor would disappear, and he would have chaos on the streets. So the United States military is not the action agent in all likelihood. Okay, does the United States of America have a capability other than military that they could bring to bear if you had actual intelligence on where Osama bin Laden is? The answer is yes, we do actually have some capabilities. Now the question is, can we use them? And the answer, often, is no."

On this, Goss declined to elaborate further. He was clearly suggesting that America's clandestine services — of the sort he himself was once a member — could theoretically raid a safe house along the Pakistan border, but again, operating in the no-man's-land along the Afghanistan-Pakistan

301

border without the support of the Pakistani government is enormously problematic.

That said, however, Goss was optimistic, believing that the mission would be accomplished. "I think Osama bin Laden will be taken out eventually," he said. "He'll be captured or neutralized in some way."

Threat No. 3: Pakistan

Pakistan loomed large on Goss's list of threats. A country of 170 million-plus people, Pakistan is a center for extreme Sunni fundamentalism. It has nuclear weapons. And it is not exactly the most politically stable country. Should Radicals suddenly seize control of the country, or should the country disintegrate into chaos or civil war, Pakistan could in a matter of hours or days become the most dangerous country on the face of the planet.

"I feel this is now the new Doomsday Scenario, if one of these nuclear weapons or this capability falls in the hands of irresponsible people who have declared that they want to wipe out our Western form of civilization because it is apostate," Goss explained. "The all-too-possible nightmare of assassination, chaos, and anarchy in Pakistan could lead to the country's nuclear capability falling into wrong hands. The 'wrongest' of those hands would be the Taliban and related fanatical religious groups who are currently restrained primarily by lack of firepower. It would be a disaster if the Pak military lost control of the serious weaponry in Pakistan — including WMD — and it is worth noting that fissures do exist inside the military itself. It seems to be not unusual for sensitive strategic and tactical information to find its way

302

into the hands of our enemies via the Pak Army and/or intelligence members who are more sympathetic to that [Radical] cause than to ours. Regrettably, some are more sympathetic to the Taliban, especially about Kashmir and ages-old tribal distinctions."

Should Pakistani nuclear weapons be sold to — or stolen by — al Qaeda or the Taliban and moved to the lawless regions on the Afghanistan-Pakistan border, or even into the mountains of Afghanistan itself, Goss said we could be facing "at least the next big war." Another risk, he noted, was Pak nukes winding up in the hands of the Iranians. "They have somebody who is in control of the Iranian Revolutionary Guards who is hardly responsible as a world player," Goss said of the current regime in Tehran. "Nobody would want to see a nuclear weapon in their hands."

Washington is "betting Pakistan will evolve successfully along 'democratic' norms before the crazies can grab control," Goss noted, but he added that "progress toward free assembly, women's rights, parliamentary elections, etc. has been spotty." This has fueled ever more political instability, and the situation could get much, much worse.

"How big of a disaster, intelligence-wise, was it when Pakistan and India tested nuclear weapons in 1998 and the CIA had no idea they were ready?" I asked. "And what does that tell us about the danger of the CIA not knowing when Iran has the Bomb?"

"The fact that we've missed the development of nuclear capability in sovereign states is very worrisome," Goss conceded. "I think we've beefed up our intelligence capability, but it could happen

303

again. The possibility of somebody emerging as a nuclear power or events happening that surprise us on the nuclear stage is still a possibility. It always will be because there's an awful lot going on behind the scenes. Our intelligence just has to get better on that score."

At the time I interviewed Goss, Pervez Musharraf was still president of Pakistan, and I asked Goss to evaluate Musharraf's ability to maintain stability in his country, as well as his ability to evolve into a true Reformer.

"We are a heartbeat away from anarchy in Pakistan if somebody actually has a successful assassination attempt of President Musharraf," Goss said bluntly. "Now whether you think President Musharraf was the best president or not doesn't matter. . . . He has tried to be a little bit progressive toward democracy, but his 'street' [popular opinion among the Rank-and-File] doesn't allow him to go too far. He's got a very, very difficult parade to try and lead over there. He has done a pretty good job, I think, of bringing a measure of stability, of giving the country an opportunity to go forward. At the same time we [in Washington] are being very serious about containing any nuclear proliferation, and we have his cooperation on that, on bringing to a stop what the A. Q. Khan* organization was doing with other irresponsible people, and in dealing with terrorists. Now, if somebody gets lucky and Musharraf gets

*Dr. Abdul Qadeer Khan was the father of Pakistan's nuclear weapons program. In 2004, he confessed to selling blueprints, equipment, and technical advice to Iran, Libya, and North Korea to develop their nuclear weapons programs.

304

taken out, we will have anarchy. Who will emerge from the pile when it's all over is hard to say. One hopes that the Pak military would be able to keep control of the nuclear suitcase in Pakistan. One assumes that that can happen, and one does what one can to make sure it does happen. But that is not necessarily going to happen. So the question remains: if we have chaos in Pakistan, who emerges with the weapons? And the answer is: it can't be the wrong people."

Having survived repeated assassination attempts throughout his tenure — events he recounted so vividly in his memoirs, *In the Line of Fire* — Pervez Musharraf finally resigned in August of 2008, under tremendous pressure from his political enemies. Perhaps more than ever, then, Pakistan is a country to watch closely.

Threat No. 4: Iraq

Iraq remains a critically important country to U.S. national security and the overall security of Western civilization. Should it implode, this would be seen throughout the Islamic world as a catastrophic defeat for the United States and a success of miraculous proportions for both Shia and Sunni extremist groups that have been waging jihad against Coalition forces since shortly after the liberation of Iraq in 2003. Radical recruitment would soar. Fund-raising for the Radicals would reach new highs. And Iraq could become a new base camp for terrorists who would then fan out all over the world to attack American and Western interests with renewed vengeance and ferocity.

"Iraq has to come out right," Goss said. "There are no choices other than to get Iraq right, because if we don't get Iraq right, everything else goes wrong in the region. So whether or not it is the center of the struggle between Radicalism and Reform, it's the most important chapter today. And we cannot afford to walk away from Iraq without having that country moderated and resolved with a degree of stability and progress, quality of life, and so forth, and assurances that we will continue to be their friends toward those goals. I think that will have a huge benign effect on the area. Not having that would have such a catastrophic effect on the area that I think other progress of the area would come unraveled very quickly in nearby states."

That said, Goss was optimistic about Iraq's future in February 2008, and he remained so throughout the year. He was opposed to any rapid reduction in U.S. and Coalition troop levels in Iraq that could be perceived as a policy of "cut and run." But he was encouraged by steady reduction in violence there and, unlike scores of critics and naysayers in Washington, was deeply convinced that Iraq would in time emerge as a peaceful, prosperous country.

"I expect Iraq can evolve into a responsible sovereign nation in the near future," Goss told me, happily bucking the conventional wisdom at the time. "It is blessed with location, resource, water, fertile soil, and rich history and culture, and it is not particularly vulnerable to foreign enemy invasion. Sorting out the levers of power and sharing the blessings among the Sunni, Shia, and Kurds are not insurmountable tasks. Rebuilding the badly depleted infrastructure and resisting some bad habits from the old days will take time and goodwill. I think the majority of Iraqis would agree today that an investment in time and goodwill is a much better idea than their recent past experience. Positive signs do exist, notably voting and forming a government, getting some businesses up and running, better street security, and confidence that friends in the West can be trusted to assist them. Government services are being reestablished on a professional level, albeit unevenly. Professional military and police training is taking hold, albeit unevenly. I think for us Iraq will be a fairly stable, reliable ally in a tough neighborhood in the decade ahead."

So long as, he insisted, we do not do something stupid.

Threat No. 5: Saudi Arabia

The Saudis have been key suppliers of oil to the West for the better part of a century, and the royal family has generally been close to officials in Washington, hoping to maintain the stability of their regime and keep the petrodollars from the U.S. flowing. But Saudi Arabia is also:

- the home of Mecca and Medina
- the birthplace of Muhammad, the founder of Islam
- the place where the Qur'an was written
- the birthplace of Osama bin Laden
- the birthplace of fifteen of the nineteen 9/11 hijackers, responsible for the deaths of nearly three thousand Americans
- the site of the Khobar Towers bombing in 1996 that killed nineteen Americans and wounded 372 others
- the source of enormous transfers of wealth to terrorist organizations such as al Qaeda, Hamas, and Hezbollah

307

Goss argued that ultimately we are going to have to deal with the Saudis, one way or the other.[7]

"Even though Iraq is historically a vital spot, I do not think it is necessarily the central or last battleground of the struggle between Radicals and Reformers," he told me. "My candidate for where the major battle may well occur between Radicals and Reformers in Islam is not far from where it all started back in 600 AD — Saudi Arabia. If you are going to settle questions of what is true Islam, you need to go to the wellspring. I am not optimistic that a peaceful solution can be found. Wealth and Wahhabism flow from Saudi Arabia as do countless 'homicide bombers' into epicenter hotspots. The regime's arrangement with the fanatical clerics as well as its 'family matter' approach to captured terrorists suggests a very hard landing when the post-octogenarians come back to earth."

Threat No. 6: Hamas and Hezbollah

Do not forget about the twin sisters of Radicalism, both of which are backed by Iran and seeking to annihilate Israel with some sort of cataclysmic event, Goss urged. He warned specifically of "daily fuse-lighting events in Gaza" by the Sunni Radicals of Hamas that could trigger an Israeli invasion and possible reassertion of control over Gaza. He also warned of "a big blast" by the Shia Radicals of Hezbollah that could "further inflame the fanatics" against "any tolerance of Israel" by the government of Lebanon or "any moderate policies at all" in Beirut. A violent seizure of the Lebanese government by Hezbollah or an effective takeover via rigged elections are very real possibilities.

"Oil cannot be ignored when talking about security," Goss told me, rounding out his list of top threats to watch in the coming months and years. "Yes, there is plenty of oil for the foreseeable needs of the near future, but much of it seems to be in the wrong places or in unreliable hands. Conserving on air-conditioning or heating oil voluntarily — or cutting back because of high prices at the pump — are not the issues. Production in troubled areas and distribution via vulnerable channels raise issues of availability, price notwithstanding."

The big question, he said, was this: "How far forward will any nation with military power lean to ensure delivery of energy to sustain quality of life and/or political viability at home?"

Goss was not offering policy prescriptions of how, exactly, the U.S. or any other country should maximize energy security for the next generation. He was simply noting that our enemies are using oil as a weapon against us.

Two weeks after our interview, Michael McConnell, the U.S. director of national intelligence, made the same point before Congress. "OPEC countries earned an estimated $690 billion from oil exports last year, nearly three times the revenues earned in 2003," McConnell noted. "The increased revenues also have enabled producers like Iran, Venezuela, Sudan, and Russia to garner enhanced political, economic, and even military advantages and complicated multilateral efforts to address problems such as the tragedy in Darfur and Iran's nuclear program."[8]

Few Americans realize that the leaders of al Qaeda and Iran have explicitly been pursuing a policy of economic jihad against the United States:

"If their economy is destroyed, they will be busy with their own affairs rather than enslaving the weak peoples. It is very important to concentrate on hitting the U.S. economy through all possible means." — *Osama bin Laden, December 2001*[9]

"We will also aim to continue, by the permission of Allah, the destruction of the American economy." — *Dr. Ayman al-Zawahiri, September 2002*[10]

"Alongside the mujahadeen in Afghanistan, we bled Russia for ten years until it went bankrupt and was forced to withdraw in defeat. . . . We are continuing this policy to bleed America to the point of bankruptcy. . . . Al Qaeda spent $500,000 on [the 9/11 attacks], while the incident and its aftermath have cost America more than half a trillion dollars. This meant that, by the Grace of God, every dollar al Qaeda spent cost America a million dollars and a huge number of jobs. . . . [T]his demonstrates the success of the bleed-until-bankruptcy plan." — *Osama bin Laden, October 2004*[11]

"No politician can be found in the United States who is capable of saving the U.S. economy from this move toward the valley of downfall." — *Mahmoud Ahmadinejad, April 2008*[12]

"These days, [although] no incident has as yet occurred, oil prices have risen from $12 to $120 a barrel. Now try to calculate how high [the price] of this essential commodity will rise if the enemy acts in a foolhardy man-

310

ner." — *Mohammad Ja'far Assadi, commander of the Iranian Revolutionary Guard Corps, August 2008*[13]

As Commander Assadi noted, this policy of economic jihad against the U.S. and the West has been working, especially when it comes to driving up the price of oil and thus forcing Westerners to transfer their wealth to states controlled by the Radicals. Consider the following trend lines:[14]

- **1973:** Oil was less than $5 a barrel when the Arab oil embargo against the West began. Gas was just 39 cents a gallon.
- **1979:** Oil was $13 a barrel when the Iranian Revolution began. Gas was 90 cents a gallon.
- **1981:** Oil was $37 a barrel when the Iran-Iraq War was fully under way. Gas was $1.38 a gallon.
- **1988:** Oil dropped to $15 a barrel as the Iran-Iraq War ended. Gas was 95 cents a gallon.
- **1998:** Oil dropped to only $10 a barrel in the aftermath of the first Gulf War, a peace treaty between Israel and Jordan, and a moderate regime in power in Iran under President Mohammad Khatami. Gas was $1.06 a gallon.
- **2000:** Oil rose to $30 a barrel after al Qaeda attacks against U.S. embassies in Africa and against the USS *Cole,* the collapse of the Arab-Israeli peace talks at Camp David, and the explosion of the second intifada, along with growing demand from China and India. Gas was $1.51 a gallon.

- **June 2008:** Oil rose to a record high of $135 a barrel after the 9/11 attacks; the war in Afghanistan; the war in Iraq; the insurgency in Iraq; repeated al Qaeda terrorist attacks throughout the world; the election of Mahmoud Ahmadinejad; Iran's threats to wipe Israel off the map; the Hezbollah war against Israel; growing talk of a possible preemptive strike by the U.S. or Israel against Iran; and Iranian threats to destroy oil tankers and U.S. naval ships passing through the Straits of Hormuz, the strategically vital chokepoint between the Indian Ocean and the Persian Gulf, through which some 17 million barrels of oil are transported each and every day. Gas was $4 a gallon.[15]

While global oil and gas prices will continue to go up and down in the years ahead for a variety of reasons, some geopolitical and some related to supply and demand, a critical question has to be asked: what is the United States doing to protect our energy security, wean ourselves off Middle Eastern oil, and insulate our economy from the strategies of the Radicals who hope to bleed us dry?

So far, very little.

We should, however, be doing everything we can to become more energy efficient and find alternative energy sources.

We should also be drilling for more oil in our country.

Incredibly, since the Iranian Revolution, U.S. crude oil production has *fallen* 37 percent. In 1979, U.S. domestic crude oil production was 8.552 million barrels per day. By 2006, we were down to 5.136 million barrels per day.[16] In 1982, the U.S. actually imposed a federal ban on drilling for oil on the Outer Continental Shelf. But prices, technology, and geopolitical conditions have changed drastically since then.[17]

It is time to drill. According to the U.S. Department of the Interior, "assuming existing technology, there are approximately 112 billion barrels of technically recoverable oil onshore and in State waters."[18] That's right — the U.S. has *at least* 112 billion barrels of proven oil reserves right here at home.

To put that in perspective, we have nearly half the reserves that Saudi Arabia has (267 billion barrels), and nearly as much as Iran itself has (136 billion barrels). As *Investor's Business Daily* noted in an editorial published while I was writing this book, 112 billion barrels of oil is enough oil "to power 60 million cars for 60 years," and "that's not counting the trillion barrels locked up in shale rock — three times the total oil reserves of Saudi Arabia."[19]

Why are we not doing everything we possibly can to drill for our own oil, in our own country, and build the necessary facilities to refine American oil, employing American workers to do the job? Such steps would move us in the right direction to bless our own people, safeguard our economy, and stop transferring hundreds of billions of dollars to countries owned or controlled by Islamic Radicals.

■ ■ ■ ■

Part Two:
The Reformers

■ ■ ■ ■

CHAPTER FOURTEEN: "ISLAM IS THE ANSWER, BUT JIHAD IS NOT THE WAY"

Who are the Reformers, and what do they want?

"Aren't there any Muslims out there who think the Radicals are crazy and are willing to fight back against the jihadists?" I am often asked. "Where are the Muslim leaders who are promoting freedom and opportunity and trying to create and expand democracy, as difficult as that may be in the modern Middle East?"

It is sad that such questions need to be asked so long after the 9/11 attacks. But the mainstream media has, frankly, done a terrible job examining the internal tensions and enormous diversity of beliefs and practices within the Muslim world.

So here are the answers: *"Yes, absolutely,"* and *"They're out there, but they don't get nearly enough attention or respect."*

My wife, Lynn, and I have met many Muslims who vehemently oppose the Radicals and seek only peace and prosperity for their people and the community of nations. We have befriended such Muslims. We have had them to our home for dinner. We have traveled around the world to have dinner in their homes. We have interviewed them at length, and though we do not agree with them theologically, we have grown to love and admire them in many ways. Indeed, they are a tremendously welcome breath of fresh air in a region being suffocated by the Radicals, and they deserve not only to be acknowledged by the free people of the West but to be appreciated, encouraged, and supported, for in many ways they represent our front line of defense in stopping the worst-case scenarios being planned by the Radicals.

Let there be no doubt, then, that throughout North America, Europe, North Africa, the Middle East, and Asia, there is an enormous and growing number of devout Muslims who read the Qur'an, pray to Allah, worship in mosques, respect Islamic culture, raise their children to follow Islamic tradition . . . and are moderates, not extremists.

Like the Radicals, moderate Muslims feel the Islamic world faces enormously serious and challenging social and economic problems. Like the Radicals, many of them feel dismay that for so long during the twentieth century and right up to the present, so many Islamic societies failed to substantially improve the quality of life for 1.3 billion Muslims on the planet, much less for the minority groups that live in Muslim-majority countries. Like the Radicals, they are largely dissatisfied with the political stagnation in the Middle East, even as they are deeply concerned about the deleterious effect of Western culture (movies, music, television, the Internet, pornography, etc.) on their children and grandchildren.

But unlike the Radicals, they are adamant that violence is not an appropriate avenue for political discourse for social change. Unlike the Radicals, they do not believe in imposing their view of Islam on anyone else. Unlike the Radicals, they do not see the West as a mortal enemy, whatever our faults. They do not seek the end of the world or a clash of civilizations. To the contrary, if you were to talk with them, they would tell you, as they have told Lynn and me, *"Yes, Islam is the answer, but jihad is not the way."*

Such devout Muslims represent a huge portion of the group I call "the Reformers."

And they are not alone. There also exists a large and growing number of Reformers who, while agreeing wholeheartedly that violent jihad is not the way, would not go so far as to say that Islam is *the* answer. They were raised as Muslims. They are respectful of traditional Muslims. But they themselves are not that religious. They have not abandoned Islam, per se, or converted to another religion. But they are primarily secular in their approach to political and social change. This group of Reformers would be more comfortable saying that Islam is *an* answer, but only one of many.

Together, these two strands make up the movement for reform in the Islamic world and seek a revolution that is no less dramatic than the Radicals' but that is far better for Muslims and for the rest of the world.

The Followers of Jefferson

What is so fascinating and compelling to me about this movement of Reformers is that while they see the world through the lens of the Qur'an — whether for religious reasons or merely cultural ones — they tend to simultaneously agree with Thomas Jefferson, who wrote in America's Declaration of Independence that all people have been "endowed by their Creator with certain unalienable Rights, that among these are Life, Liberty and the pursuit of Happiness." They argue, therefore, that the key to unleashing the true promise and potential of the people of their region is to provide Muslim men, women, and children with *more* freedom, *more* openness, *more* protection of human and civil rights, and *more* opportunities to participate in representative government — up to and including the creation of fully functional political democracies — whenever and wherever they can. Why? Because like Jefferson, they believe that these are God-given rights and that governments are created to protect them, not dispense with them or deny them at will. What's more, they believe in protecting the human and civil rights of ethnic, religious, and political minorities within their countries, again because they believe that God created all men with these unalienable rights and that because God celebrates differences and diversity, so should Muslim governments and societies.

In his first presidential inaugural address in 1801, Jefferson — one of the most highly respected and influential voices during the American Revolution — laid out fifteen principles of representational government, what would become known in time as "Jeffersonian democracy." Among these principles:

"Equal and exact justice to all men, of whatever state or persuasion, religious or political"

"Peace, commerce, and honest friendship with all nations, entangling alliances with none"

"A jealous care of the right of election by the people"

"Absolute acquiescence in the decisions of the

320

majority"

"The supremacy of the civil over the military authority"

"The diffusion of information and arraignment of all abuses at the bar of the public reason"

"Freedom of religion"

"Freedom of the press"

"Freedom of person under the protection of the habeas corpus, and trial by juries impartially selected"[1]

"These principles," Jefferson noted, "form the bright constellation which has gone before us and guided our steps through an age of revolution and reformation. The wisdom of our sages and blood of our heroes have been devoted to their attainment. They should be the creed of our political faith, the text of civic instruction, the touchstone by which to try the services of those we trust; and should we wander from them in moments of error or of alarm, let us hasten to retrace our steps and to regain the road which alone leads to peace, liberty, and safety."

Jefferson believed his country was "the world's best hope" for the spread of freedom and human dignity, and he openly and unashamedly appealed to the Almighty, "that Infinite Power which rules the destinies of the universe," for wisdom that the councils of government might do "what is best" for the people.[2]

In the same spirit, and sometimes using the same language, the Reformers are trying to lead their own revolution in the Muslim world, a revolution based on principles of freedom and opportunity, not fascism and oppression.

Building a Movement

While not all Reformers are full-blown "Jeffersonian democrats," a growing number of Muslim leaders are seeking to follow Jefferson's teachings and example in their own way, at their own pace, however haltingly and imperfectly.

Not all Reformers are willing to admit publicly that they are disciples of Jefferson. Some understandably fear they would be accused by their domestic critics — and especially by the Radicals — of trying to impose an "American model" on their citizens. Others, perhaps, are not even fully cognizant that the universal principles they are advocating and attempting to implement were articulated by America's third chief executive. But whether they admit to it or not, the most important and impressive of the Reformers are, in fact, followers of Thomas Jefferson.

And they are not simply teaching or talking about the power of representative government; they are actually gaining real political power and wielding game-changing influence in critical countries in the Middle East. In the process, they are representing and encouraging a vast and growing movement of Muslims who want to expand freedom and democracy throughout the region.

In Part 1, I referred to John Esposito and Dalia Mogahed, who in 2007 wrote a book entitled *Who Speaks for Islam? What a Billion Muslims Really Think*. Based on Gallup surveys conducted in thirty-five countries with Muslim-majority populations or substantial Muslim minorities, the book was described by the authors as "the largest, most comprehensive study of contemporary Muslims ever done."[3] The study found that the overwhelming majority of Muslims — more than nine in ten

— are traditional and quite moderate in their political views, meaning they are not inclined to violence and extremism, as are the Radicals. This does not necessarily make them all Reformers. But significant numbers of moderate Muslims are eager to embrace Jeffersonian notions of government.

For example, the authors found that "substantial majorities in nearly all nations surveyed" — 94 percent in Egypt, 93 percent in Iran, and 90 percent in Indonesia — said that if they had the opportunity to draft a constitution for a new country, "they would guarantee freedom of speech, defined as 'allowing all citizens to express their opinion on the political, social, and economic issues of the days.' "[4] The authors also found that large majorities in most Muslim countries support the right to vote not just for men but for women as well.

These figures, which indicate such a large number of reform-minded people in the Muslim world, were reinforced by a massive survey conducted throughout the Middle East by the Pew Global Attitudes Project, released in 2005. The Pew study found that 83 percent of Muslims in Kuwait believe democracy can work in their country, 68 percent of Muslims in Jordan, 68 percent in Lebanon, 64 percent in Morocco, and 58 percent in Pakistan, to name just a few.[5] Likewise, 83 percent of Muslims in Turkey believe it is "very important to live in a country where people can openly criticize the government." The same is true for 67 percent of the people of Lebanon, 63 percent of Pakistanis, and 56 percent of Indonesians.[6]

Could we wish there was 100 percent support

for Jeffersonian principles in these and other Muslim countries? Of course we could. But the point is that there are real and enormous numbers of Rank-and-File Muslims who describe themselves as ready, willing, and able to respond to the message of leaders who are perceived as bold and sincere Reformers. Indeed, some already have.

Snapshots from the Region

In this section of the book, I will take you inside the Muslim world to get an up-close-and-personal look at several of the most impressive Reformers. But first, we need to consider a few snapshots from the region to get the big picture.

Snapshot: Iraq

Iraq has been ground zero in the battle between the Radicals and the Reformers in the Arab world since 2003. It is still work in progress, but much progress has been made. And at the center of events has been Jalal Talabani, an intriguing warrior-turned-Reformer whom I will profile in the pages ahead.

"Jalal who?" you ask.

Don't worry. You're not alone. His face should be on the cover of *Newsweek.* His story should have made him *Time* magazine's "Person of the Year." He should be a household name for Americans who have invested so much blood and treasure into the liberation of Iraq. Yet the media has largely ignored him. Thus, few Americans have any idea who he is or why he matters.

In 2008, I had the privilege of making two trips inside the war-ravaged nation of Iraq to better understand who this man is and what makes him tick. His is an incredible story, and honestly, if I had not been there and heard it for myself, I might not have believed it.

Once the leader of a violent Kurdish guerrilla faction in the 1960s and 1970s, Talabani put down his arms, ordered his followers to do the same, and helped create a peaceful and prosperous democratic province in northern Iraq in the 1990s after the first Gulf War.

By 2005, after the fall of Saddam Hussein and the liberation of the entire country, Talabani emerged as the first democratically elected president of Iraq. He proceeded to wage a relentless and, I would say, heroic battle to defeat the Radicals and build a Jeffersonian democracy. In 2010, Talabani decisively won a second term, becoming the first democratically *re*elected president of Iraq, a testament to how widely trusted and admired he is throughout the country, in large part because of his reputation as an indefatigable Reformer.

He is not alone, of course, and the fate of the democratic experiment in Iraq certainly does not rest entirely on his shoulders. But what Talabani believes will astound you. What he has accomplished with the help of the Iraqi and American people, along with our Coalition allies, will amaze you. And his vision for his country's future will, I think, encourage you as it encouraged me and hopefully persuade you to pray daily for Iraq as you have never prayed before.

Snapshot: Morocco

Nearly unnoticed by the mainstream American media is King Mohammed VI of Morocco. He is almost never profiled, but he should be, for he has been one of the most intriguing and accomplished

Reformers in the Muslim world.

Upon assuming the throne in 1999, the impressive young North African monarch embarked on an initiative to turn Morocco into a model of moderation, cooperation with the West, and democratic reform. After the 9/11 attacks in the U.S. and a series of suicide bombings that rocked his own country in 2003, the king cracked down on al Qaeda and other Radical groups. He strengthened Morocco's political, economic, and military ties to the United States and the European Union. He allowed and encouraged dozens of political parties to compete in free and fair parliamentary elections, a relatively new experience for Moroccans. He expanded the role of the democratically elected government to run the day-to-day affairs of the country. He also dramatically expanded opportunities for women to serve in government.

Meanwhile, His Majesty quietly strengthened ties to Israel and the Jewish community. He completely revamped the training methodology for new Muslim clerics in the kingdom, requiring them to be schooled in the virtues of Christianity and Judaism and the theology of the Reformers. What's more, he dispatched top Muslim leaders to build bridges with evangelical Christians in the West and even invited well-known evangelicals to visit and speak in Morocco.

Since King Mohammed came to power, I have had the honor of traveling to Morocco four times and building friendships with close associates of His Majesty, including one of the country's top Islamic scholars. Along the way, Lynn and I have fallen in love with Morocco and pray for that nation often. If Morocco can stay on track and build on its recent record of reforms, its story could become vitally important to the rest of the Muslim world in the years ahead.

Snapshot: Jordan

King Hussein of Jordan was an impressive if imperfect Reformer in the twentieth century.

The king's family — descendants of Muhammad — hailed originally from the Arabian Peninsula, and for decades His Majesty was a leader in the fight to destroy Israel. But to his enormous credit, King Hussein eventually turned against the Radicals and the violent Arab nationalists in a dramatic and almost miraculous way.

In 1978, he married an American woman (Lisa Halaby, who became known as Queen Noor). He became an ally and close friend of Egyptian president Anwar Sadat, who in 1979 became the first Arab leader to forge a historic peace treaty with Israel. King Hussein also established a democratically elected parliamentary system responsible for the day-to-day governance of his tiny desert country. Then he himself agreed to a peace treaty with the Jewish state in 1994. And he did all this despite living in the shadow of Saddam Hussein in Iraq, his maniacal neighbor to the east, and in the shadow of the Assad regime controlling Syria, his despotic neighbor to the north, and despite the fact that Radicals tried to assassinate him numerous times.

When King Hussein succumbed to cancer in 1999, it was a sad day for Reformers in the region. But fortunately, his son King Abdullah II continued in his father's footsteps. He signed a free trade agreement with the U.S. in 2000. He became a critically important ally of the West in the battle against the Radicals after 9/11 and during the liberation of Iraq and its aftermath. In 2006 he became the first Muslim monarch to address the National Prayer Breakfast in Washington, D.C., speaking on the importance of Muslim-Christian relations before two thousand evangelicals from all over the world. And all the while, King Abdullah has tried to move Jordan step-by-step in a more moderate direction politically and socially, despite constant threats of assassinations, terrorist attacks, coups, and insurrections.

It has not been an easy journey, and there have been setbacks along the way. To be sure, no one would describe the Hashemite Kingdom of Jordan as a full-blown Jeffersonian democracy at this point. But having visited the country three times in recent years, I must tell you that I have fallen in love with Jordan, its people, and its leaders. As both a Jew and a believer in Jesus, I have never felt in danger in Jordan. To the contrary, I have had the honor of meeting safely with Reformers from one end of the country to the other. I have interviewed Prime Minister Abdelsalam al-Majali, the man who actually signed the peace treaty with Israel. I have stayed in the homes of Jordanians who have welcomed me with open arms, taught me about their history, and told me how hopeful they are about their future. As a result, I am deeply impressed with the significant progress the country has made over the past three decades.

Indeed, it is precisely because the Jordanians have made such progress that I am worried by the Radicals' determination to launch a jihad there, seize the capital, and create a new anti-Israel, anti-Western base camp for Iran and al Qaeda. Therefore, I pray often for Jordan's peace, prosperity, and continued progress. I pray for King Abdullah's health and safety, and I pray that God will grant him the wisdom to know how best to move forward in such challenging times.

Snapshot: Afghanistan

Another key theater in the battle between Radicals and Reformers, of course, has been Afghanistan, and thus far its recent leaders have a mixed track record at best. Still, it deserves attention and much prayer.

In October of 2008, I had the privilege of traveling to the Afghan capital of Kabul — a city on the front lines of the war between the Radicals and the Reformers — to meet tribal leaders, interview Rank-and-File Afghanis, and explore the story for myself. It is, I must say, an unforgettable saga.

In the early stages of Afghanistan's liberation from Taliban and al Qaeda tyranny, Hamid Karzai emerged as an intriguing, up-and-coming Reformer. Once a member of the mujahadeen against the Soviet occupation of his country in the 1980s, Karzai became a fierce critic of the Radicals and a powerful advocate for democracy in the 1990s. After the liberation of Afghanistan in the fall of 2001, Karzai emerged as the first democratically elected president of Afghanistan in more than five thousand years of recorded history. Against all odds, and in the face of repeated assassination attempts, Karzai began governing a country once thought ungovernable, vowing to build a truly Jeffersonian democracy in a land that it seems could not be less suited for the experiment.

After a compelling start, however, Karzai stumbled significantly. Can he get back on track?

Will his successors be more committed to being Reformers, or will they take the country back towards the Radicals? Only time will tell. The Afghan story is far from finished, as we will see in the pages ahead.

Snapshot: Turkey

The Muslim world's first big Reformer success story was led by a man named Mustafa Kemal Ataturk.

After the collapse of the Ottoman Empire and the fall of the caliphate in Istanbul in the 1920s, Ataturk founded the modern state of Turkey as a Muslim-friendly but essentially secular representative democracy. Many never expected his experiment to survive, much less work. But it did both for nearly a century.

After the sweeping reforms Ataturk put into motion — giving men and women the right to vote, separating the affairs of mosque and state, and establishing safeguards to prevent Radicals from gaining control of the military — Turkey became a trusted ally of the United States and a member of NATO. In fact, Turkey became so trusted that the U.S. actually placed ballistic missiles armed with nuclear warheads aimed at the Soviet Union on Turkish soil during some of the coldest years of the Cold War.

Decades later, Turkey pressed to become the first Muslim-majority country to join the European Union. Its leaders sent troops to Afghanistan to fight al Qaeda and the Taliban. They sent troops into northern Iraq to fight terrorist cells along the Turkey-Iraq border. They sent troops into Lebanon to participate in the U.N. peacekeeping force there. The country was long a haven and meeting place for Muslim moderates. For decades, Turkey was also so friendly to Israel that tens of thousands of Israeli Jews flocked there every year for gorgeous, low-cost Mediterranean vacations. It has been a country steadily modernizing its economy, its infrastructure, and its tourism industry.

I have been blessed with the opportunity to visit Turkey no fewer than a half-dozen times in recent years, and I have been simply amazed that this country — once the epicenter of Islam — has for so long been a model of moderation and Jeffersonian democracy.

That said, something is rapidly changing in Turkey, and not for the better. Turkey has all but officially been rejected from membership in the European Union. Its Islamist leaders have been deeply angered by the West's snub. As a result, these leaders appear to have concluded that Turkey's future lies in the East instead. In 2009 and 2010, the country's leaders made a series of troubling moves away from the Western alliance and Israel and towards Iran, Syria, and Hamas.

- On January 16, 2009, Turkish Prime Minister Recep Tayyip Erdogan (pronounced "air-do-wan") called for Israel to be barred from the United Nations after Israel launched a military operation into the Gaza Strip to stop Hamas from launching thousands of rockets and mortars at innocent Israeli civilians.
- On January 29, 2009, Erdogan stormed off the stage of a conference meeting in Davos, Switzerland, because Israeli President Shimon Peres was participating and defending Israel's operation in Gaza. The Turkish PM shouted at Peres, "When it comes to killing,

331

you know well how to kill."

- On April 27, 2009, Turkey and Syria held their first joint military exercises in modern history. What's more, "trade between the countries doubled between 2007 and 2008, and doubled again in 2009, to an estimated $4 billion, according to the Aleppo Chamber of Commerce."[7]
- In October 2009, Erdogan visited Tehran and met with Iranian President Mahmoud Ahmadinejad, calling him "our friend" and saying relations between Turkey and Iran were "very good." Trade between the two countries that year was about $12 billion, but the two leaders said they wanted that to grow to $20 billion over the next two years. That same month, Turkey canceled a NATO military exercise because Israel was invited to participate, later airing a drama on state-run TV that portrayed an Israeli soldier walking up to a Palestinian child and barbarically shooting her point-blank.
- On November 11, 2009, Erdogan accused Israel of committing war crimes in Gaza worse than the genocide in Sudan, even though Hamas's 12,000-plus rocket attacks against Israeli civilians are actually war crimes.
- On May 12, 2010, inspired by Iran's nuclear program and the West's inability to stop it, Erdogan's government agreed to pay Russia to build the first-ever nuclear reactor in Turkey.
- In May 2010, Turkey sent a flotilla of armed pro-Hamas activists and terrorists into the waters off of Gaza, presumably to bring

humanitarian relief to people in Gaza. The activists on one of the ships then attacked Israeli navy personnel who boarded the ship to make sure it wasn't carrying weapons or other illegal goods. Erdogan harshly condemned Israel and said the Jewish state should be "punished" for a "bloody massacre." He also withdrew Turkey's ambassador to Israel and canceled three joint military drills with Israel.

- On June 4, 2010, Erdogan said Hamas is not a terrorist group.
- On June 8, 2010, Erdogan met in Istanbul with Ahmadinejad and Russian Prime Minister Vladimir Putin to discuss how to form a closer alliance.
- By June 10, 2010, the London *Telegraph* editorialized: "Turkey's alliance with Iran is a threat to world peace."
- In August 2010, United Press International reported that "a secret meeting of Iranian and Turkish intelligence officials has led to a new weapons supply route for Hezbollah. . . . Iranian and Turkish intelligence officials recently signed an agreement that establishes territorial continuity for Turkey, Iran, Syria, and Lebanon, and guarantees a constant supply of weapons to Hezbollah, a report in the Italian newspaper *Corriere della Sera* said."[8]

These are not the moves of a Reformer country. So the big question now is: Where is Turkey headed? Does it want to be the world's leading Reformer country, or has it chosen to abandon its close ties with the West and make common cause with the Radicals? If the latter, it would make sense that Turkey would need to try to establish credibility ("street cred") with the Radicals (in Iran, for example) by turning most harshly against Israel. Does that mean Turkey will soon turn harshly against the U.S. and Western Europe, too? Could it become the base for hostile acts against Israel and the Western alliance? Will it withdraw from NATO membership, or be asked to leave? How could it remain as it becomes an ally of Iran, Syria, Hamas, and Hezbollah? We will soon see, but sadly — despite Turkey's rich history of reform — the current trends do not bode well.

CHAPTER FIFTEEN:
THE THEOLOGY
OF THE REFORMERS

What they believe, verse by verse

Make No Mistake: a ferocious battle is raging for the heart and soul of the Muslim world.

On one side is the theology of the Radicals, which as we have seen teaches that true Islam requires violent men to wage violent jihad against apostates and infidels in the name of Allah.

On the other side is the theology of the Reformers, which teaches that true Islam is a religion of peace, that the Qur'an is a book of peace, and that the Radicals are perverting Islam to their own fascist, power-hungry ends.

Few understood or could better explain this winner-take-all battle between the Radicals and the Reformers than Mrs. Benazir Bhutto, who served as the first *woman* ever elected prime minister of Pakistan (1988–1990) and later served as the *second* woman premier of that largely fundamentalist country (1993–1996).

Raised by a Sunni father and a Shia mother of Iranian-Kurdish descent, Bhutto considered herself fortunate to have been taught moderate theology from the Qur'an from an early age. "My parents taught me that men and women are equal in the eyes of God," she would later recall, "that the first convert to Islam was a woman, that the Prophet of Islam married a career woman, that the line of the Prophet was carried through his beloved daughter Fatima."[1]

Later, encouraged by her parents to study Jeffersonian democracy in the United States, she began attending Harvard University in the fall of 1969. Pakistan at that time was suffering under a military dictatorship, but in America, Bhutto came to appreciate firsthand the remarkable and enduring power of the American Revolution as well as the enormous challenges of creating and sustaining a free society.* "In America, I saw the power of the people to change and influence policies," Bhutto once wrote. "The struggle in Pakistan and the reality of the ability of people in America to assert themselves, to stand up without fear for what they believed in, were important influences in my life. I was positioned between two worlds,

*It should be noted that Benazir Bhutto's father, Zulfikar Ali Bhutto — educated at Berkley and Oxford — was a Sunni Muslim who married a Shia Muslim (his second wife). Benazir was born to Zulfikar's second wife. While Benazir was studying at Harvard in 1971, Zulfikar was elected president of Pakistan and served until 1973. His was an enormously controversial tenure, filled with charges of corruption and human-rights abuses. He was eventually arrested, convicted, and executed on charges of murder. During his time in office, however, he authored Pakistan's current constitution and made efforts to move his country bit by bit toward a Turkish-style democracy, Islamic-friendly but secular in nature.

the world of dictatorship and the world of democracy. I could see the power of the people in a democracy and contrast it to the lack of political power in my own country. I [also] saw people in America took their rights for granted: freedom of speech, freedom of association, freedom of movement. In my country people were killed or imprisoned fighting for these freedoms."[2]

Years later, during her two terms in office as premier, she came under withering criticism and fierce resistance from both the extremists and the moderates. The Radicals hated her for her bedrock belief that Islam is the answer but jihad is not the way. The Reformers despised her for being at best an imperfect executor of her convictions and at worst an outright hypocrite, having permitted rampant corruption during her administration.

After her second term, Bhutto took her family and went into a self-imposed exile in Dubai, the commercial capital of the United Arab Emirates — itself an emerging model of moderation and economic innovation — where she took nearly a decade to read, think, meet with Reformers, and more fully develop her own views of how to attack corruption, bring more accountability to government, and create a blend of Islamic tradition and Jeffersonian democracy in a country such as Pakistan.

"Islam Was Sent As a Message of Liberation"
In exile, Bhutto wrote a remarkable book entitled *Reconciliation: Islam, Democracy, and the West,* which could very well become the manifesto of the Reformer movement. In it she wrote: "Within the Muslim world there has been and continues to be an internal rift, an often violent confronta-

tion among sects, ideologies, and interpretations of the message of Islam. This destructive tension has set brother against brother, a deadly fratricide that has tortured intra-Islamic relations for 1,300 years. This sectarian conflict stifled the brilliance of the Muslim renaissance that took place during the Dark Ages of Europe, when the great universities, scientists, doctors, and artists were all Muslim. Today that intra-Muslim sectarian violence is most visibly manifest in a senseless, self-defeating sectarian civil war that is tearing modern Iraq apart at its fragile seams and exercising its brutality in other parts of the world, especially parts of Pakistan."[3]

She argued that the Qur'an "does not simply preach the tolerance of other religions" but "also acknowledges that salvation can be achieved in all monotheistic religions." Indeed, she insisted that "freedom of choice" — be it in what religion to follow or what spouse to marry or what school to attend or what leaders to elect — is "a cornerstone" of Islamic theology.

She noted further that "in contrast to other great religions' attitudes towards non-adherents, Muslims accept Jews and Christians as 'people of the Book.' Thus, Muslim global terrorists, including Osama bin Laden, display a striking ignorance of Islam. They distort Islam while at the same time using the name of religion to attract people to a path to terrorism. Bin Laden claims, 'The enmity between us and the Jews goes far back in time and is deep rooted. There is no question that war between the two of us is inevitable.' This comment contradicts 1,300 years of peaceful coexistence between Muslims and Jews."[4]

The bottom line, Bhutto concluded after years

of studying the Qur'an, is that "Islam was sent as a message of liberation." She blasted the Radicals for trying to "hijack Islam" for their own bloody purposes.[5] She praised Turkey as "one of the true success stories of democratic governance in the Muslim world" and praised Qatar for "struggling to build a democracy," noting that in 1999 the emir of the tiny Persian Gulf country "allowed local elections in which women could vote and run for office" and in 2005 created a new constitution that allowed for a unicameral legislature. She also noted that "in the pantheon of Muslim countries, Indonesia has also emerged as an example of one of the highest degrees of success in democratic governance," imperfect, to be sure, but moving in the right direction.[6]

Sadly, on December 27, 2007, just weeks after returning to her native Pakistan, planning to run again on a reinvigorated platform of bold and sweeping democratic reforms, Bhutto was assassinated by Radicals determined to silence her and send a message to all other Reformers that their days were numbered.

The People of the Book

We have seen the verses in the Qur'an that the Radicals point to in their claims that they are justified in waging violent jihad against those whom they view as apostates and infidels.

What, then, are the verses that Reformers point to as proof that Islam is a religion of peace and that Muslims should work together with Christians and Jews, known in the Qur'an as the "People of the Book"?

There are quite a few verses, actually. Consider the following examples:

339

"Those who believe [Muslims], or those who declare Judaism, or the Christians . . . whoever truly believes in God and the Last Day and does good, righteous deeds, surely their reward is with their Lord, and they will have no fear, nor will they grieve." — *Sura 2:62*

"Among the People of the Book there is an upright community, reciting God's Revelations in the watches of the night and prostrating (themselves in worship). They believe in God and the Last Day, and enjoin and promote what is right and good and forbid and try to prevent the evil, and hasten to do good deeds as if competing with one another. Those are of the righteous ones. Whatever good they do, they will never be denied the reward of it; and God has full knowledge of the God-revering pious." — *Sura 3:113–115*

"Surely We did send down the Torah, in which there was guidance and a light. Thereby did the prophets, who were fully submitted to God, judge for the Jews; and so did . . . the rabbis (teachers of law), as they had been entrusted to keep and observe . . . God's Book." — *Sura 5:44*

"In the footsteps of those (earlier prophets), We sent Jesus son of Mary, confirming (the truth of) the Torah revealed before him, and We granted to him the Gospel, in which there was guidance and light." — *Sura 5:46*

"Do not argue with those who were given the Book. . . . Say, 'We believe in what has been sent down to us and what was sent down to you, and your God and our God is one and the same.' " — *Sura 29:46*

"God does not forbid you, as regards those who do not make war against you on account of your Religion, to be kindly to them [Jews and Christians], and act towards them with equity. God surely loves the scrupulously equitable." — *Sura 60:8*

Reformers further argue that several key verses often cited by Radicals are quoted out of context.

Sura 8:60, for example, does say, "Make ready against them whatever you can of force and horses assigned (for war), that thereby you may dismay the enemies of God and your enemies and others besides them, of whom (and the nature of whose enmity) you may be unaware. God is aware of them (and of the nature of their enmity). Whatever you spend in God's cause will be repaid to you in full, and you will not be wronged." Radicals say this gives them justification to use any and all force possible — including weapons of mass destruction — against the infidels. Yet the very next verse says, "And if they (the enemies) incline to peace, incline to it also, and put your trust in God. Surely, He is the All-Hearing, the All-Knowing" (Sura 8:61). The Reformers say this proves that the Qur'an actually puts the emphasis on making peace between Islamic nations and the West, not on waging a violent, apocalyptic jihad against Judeo-Christian civilization.

Similarly, Sura 9:5 begins by saying, "Kill them [the infidels] wherever you may come upon them, and seize them, and confine them, and lie in wait for them at every conceivable place." But the second half of that verse says, "Yet, if they repent and (mending their ways) establish the Prescribed Prayer and pay the Prescribed Purifying Alms, let them go their way. Surely God is All-Forgiving, All-Compassionate." The Radicals argue that this verse suggests giving the infidels one last chance to convert or die. The Reformers, on the other hand, argue that this verse puts the emphasis on peacemaking and reconciliation, not violent jihad.

Reformers also argue with great moral force that suicide bombings are absolutely forbidden by the Qur'an and various hadiths and that committing such an evil act will send a Muslim to hell, not to paradise. "In the Quran, preserving life is a central moral value," Bhutto wrote. "It does not permit suicide but demands the preservation of life: 'And spend in the way of Allah and cast not yourselves to perdition with your own hands, and do good (to others); surely Allah loves the doers of good' " (Sura 2:195).[7] Other scholars of Islam cite hadiths such as this one to prove that suicide is forbidden in Islam: "The Prophet said: Whoever kills himself with a blade will be tormented with that blade in the fires of Hell. The Prophet also said: He who strangles himself will strangle himself in Hell. . . . He who throws himself off a mountain and kills himself will throw himself downward into the fires of Hell for ever and ever. . . . Whoever kills himself in any way will be tormented in that way in Hell."[8]

The Debate Within

Remarkably, the battle for the soul of Islam — to define the religion for current and future generations — is not just between the Radicals and the Reformers. The battle is increasingly being waged among the Radicals themselves as some Islamic theologians who have either been sympathetic to jihadists or actively cooperated with them have begun reexamining their core beliefs and concluding that men like Osama bin Laden and the Ayatollah Khomeini were not just wrong but evil and should be held criminally liable for their actions.

Consider, for example, this headline from the *Jerusalem Post,* published on January 8, 2008:

REFORMED AL-ZAWAHIRI DISCIPLE IN ISRAEL

In the article that followed, reporter David Horovitz profiled a man named Tawfik Hamid, a forty-seven-year-old Muslim who grew up in Cairo dreaming of becoming a *shaheed* — a martyr — perhaps by suicide bombing. Why? Because he wanted to go to paradise where, he was told, he could "eat all the lollipops and chocolates I wanted, or play all day without anyone telling me to study."

By the time he entered medical school at Cairo University, he was becoming a devout Radical. "I started to grow my beard. I stopped smiling and telling jokes. I adopted a serious look at all times and became very judgmental towards others. . . . My hatred toward non-Muslims increased dramatically, and Jihadi doctrine became second nature to me."[9]

Soon, Hamid met Dr. Ayman al-Zawahiri, a fellow Egyptian, and was entranced by his message and delivery, describing al Qaeda's chief strategist as "one of the fiercest speakers I had ever heard," whose "rhetoric inspired us to engage in war against the infidels, the enemies of Allah."

Hamid quickly became a follower of jihad. He was trained to blow up mosques and churches.

343

He was involved in plans to kidnap a police officer and bury him alive. He was eventually invited to an al Qaeda training camp in Afghanistan.

But he was developing a deep sense of unease. "The brutality didn't match my personality," he explained. Hamid began studying Islam more carefully. He found himself gravitating toward the verses about peace and pluralism, turned down the invitation to join the Radicals, and dedicated his life to teaching the theology of the Reformers, even moving to the United States and making his peace with the Israelis.

"Practically speaking," he explained on his first trip to the Jewish state, if young Muslims "don't have an alternative interpretation of the Koran, it's going to be impossible" to foster a moderate approach. And without it, he said, "we're essentially asking them to leave their religion" — and "that won't happen." Islam, he said, "could be followed and interpreted in a peaceful way, but the current dominant way of interpretation has many violent areas that need addressing. To say Islam is peaceful? It is not. But it can be taught peacefully. The texts allow you to do this."

One example: while the Qur'an does brand Jews as "monkeys," Hamid said this applied only to "the Jews who were resisting Judaism" — that is, apostate Jews who resisted the teachings of Moses and were unholy and idolatrous. As for the rest, Hamid said Muslims ought to be "incredibly respectful of the Jews on the basis of the Koran" since the text calls Moses and the descendants of Abraham and Israel the "chosen" people.

Sura 19:51, for example, says that Moses — the one who led the nation of Israel out of slavery in Egypt — "was one chosen, endowed with perfect sincerity and purity of intention in faith and practicing the Religion, and was a Messenger, a Prophet."

Sura 19:58, meanwhile, says, "God bestowed His blessings (of Scripture, Prophethood, authority with sound judgment, and wisdom)" on "the descendants of Adam" and "the descendants of Abraham and Israel (Jacob) . . . whom We guided and chose."

Consider, too, this headline from the *New York Sun,* published on December 20, 2007:

SENIOR [AL] QAEDA THEOLOGIAN URGES HIS FOLLOWERS TO END THEIR JIHAD

In the article that followed, reporter Eli Lake noted a stunning development: "One of al Qaeda's senior theologians is calling on his followers to end their military jihad and saying the attacks of September 11, 2001, were a 'catastrophe for all Muslims.' In a serialized manifesto written from prison in Egypt, Sayyed Imam al-Sharif is blasting Osama bin Laden" and "even calls for the formation of a special Islamic court to try Osama bin Laden and his old comrade Ayman al-Zawahiri." Lake noticed that the theologian's manifesto was "a renunciation of his earlier work, saying the military jihad or war against apostate states and America is futile" and read in certain parts "like a spicy Washington memoir by an embittered former official."[10]

The following are excerpts from Sayyed Imam al-Sharif's manifesto, as translated by the Middle East Media Research Institute:[11]

"I cut my ties with everyone [in al Qaeda] . . . when I saw that most of them were following their own desires. Allah said (Koran 28:50): 'Who is farther astray than he who follows his own desires without guidance from Allah? Allah does not guide unjust people.' "

"The events of September [11], 2001, were . . . a catastrophe for the Muslims. . . . Whoever approves of their action shares their sin."

"[Al-Qaeda] ignited strife that found its way into every home, and they were the cause of the imprisonment of thousands of Muslims in the prisons of various countries. They caused the death of tens of thousands of Muslims — Arabs, Afghans, Pakistanis, and others. The Taliban's Islamic Emirate was destroyed, and Al-Qaeda was destroyed. They were the direct cause of the American occupation of Afghanistan and other heavy losses which there is not enough time to mention here. They bear the responsibility for all of this."

"I think that a Shari'a court should be established, composed of reliable scholars, to hold these people [Osama bin Laden, Dr. Ayman al-Zawahiri, etc.] accountable for their crimes."

There were some other intriguing points in the manifesto as well. Among them:

- The lives and property of Muslims must be preserved.
- Jihad against the leaders of Muslim countries is not acceptable.
- It is forbidden to harm foreigners and tourists in Muslim countries.
- It is treachery to kill people in a non-Muslim country after entering that country with its government's permission (i.e., a legal visa).[12]

Though it was largely unnoticed by the mainstream media in the U.S. and Europe, the release of the manifesto made news in the Middle East and was a significant development in the raging battle between the Radicals and the Reformers. It represented a wholesale reassessment of the case for jihad by a senior al Qaeda theologian, one whose voice will certainly be widely listened to in the years ahead. And not just by the Rank-and-File processing the debate as if watching a championship tennis game at Wimbledon — turning their heads from one side to the other and back again — but among some Radicals as well, those whose consciences are burning and whose eyes reflect a growing horror as they see what they are doing in a new light and wonder if perhaps God is not in all this bloodshed and hatred after all.

CHAPTER SIXTEEN: THE DEFECTOR

A Khomeini heir's stunning call
for democracy and reform

On September 26, 2003, the grandson of the Ayatollah Khomeini — a highly respected Shia cleric in his own right — calmly stood up before an audience in Washington, D.C. He looked out over the crowd, took a deep breath, and then, speaking through an interpreter, denounced the Islamic Revolution, said it was time to usher in a new era of freedom and democracy in his country, and urged the Bush administration to mobilize the American people to overthrow the Iranian regime much as Winston Churchill had mobilized the British to destroy Adolf Hitler.

"As you know, the history of Iran in the nineteenth century was the history of a country under dictatorship," Hossein Khomeini, then forty-four, told the gathering at the American Enterprise Institute, just blocks from the White House. "But the Revolution and Mr. Khomeini promised to change the Iranian situation and bring democracy to Iran. But, unfortunately, as things turned out, Iran again became . . . [an] even worse dictatorship after the Revolution."[1]

The room was filled with over a hundred seasoned political professionals. They may have thought they had heard it all. But they had not heard this. Indeed, they could hardly believe it. This was no right-wing pundit speaking. This was no neoconservative policy wonk. This was a member of the ayatollah's own family. This was the son of the ayatollah's own firstborn son, Mostafa. And he had just become the Revolution's most outspoken opponent.

The AEI speech was not the first time Hossein Khomeini had spoken out publicly against his family and the Revolution. He had actually been speaking out for years, and at the time was living not in Iran but in exile in Iraq. Just before coming to the States, he had given an interview on an Arabic television network in which he called the current Iranian regime "the world's worst dictatorship" and argued that the mullahs in Iran were exploiting Islam "to continue their tyrannical rule." What's more, he called for "a democratic regime that does not make use of religion as a means of oppressing the people and strangling society" and insisted it was time "to separate the religion from the state."[2]

But this was the first time the Defector in Chief had spoken out against the Iranian regime on American soil. "At the beginning, the first few years of the Revolution, I was involved in that process," Khomeini, who was in his early twenties in 1979, explained. "However, about two years after the Revolution, I started questioning and doubting the practices and behavior of the Islamic Republic, especially in terms of the executions and pressures on the public. . . . At that time I still believed in the legitimacy of a theocratic regime. Yet my criticism was reflected in the papers, in the newspapers of the time, and I was somehow forced to retire from politics and devoted all my time to religious studies. . . . [In] the last few years, I've come to the belief that a theocratic regime, a religious government, is not compatible with Islamic tenets, because that should be established only after the reappearance of the absent [Twelfth] Imam."[3]

This last sentence was a fascinating point, and one whose significance, I must admit, I did not understand properly at the time. I had not spent time studying the coming of the Twelfth Imam. Mahmoud Ahmadinejad, after all, had not yet emerged as the president of Iran, and no Shia Muslim leaders that I was aware of were talking openly about the "imminent" arrival of the Mahdi, much less about the apocalyptic implications of such a development. Like many in Washington, in the fall of 2003 I was focused mostly on the exciting liberation of Iraq and what this meant for the rest of the region.

But Hossein Khomeini was ahead of the curve. He had been thinking long and hard about Shia theology and trying to come to logical conclusions about what his beliefs meant for his own life and the lives of his countrymen.

In the process, he had come to two conclusions: (1) the Islamic Revolution had been an unmitigated disaster, crushing the lives and dreams of millions of Iranians; and (2) as he noted to the AEI crowd, "religion cannot mix with government in the absence of the Messiah." That is, Khomeini believes that until the Mahdi comes and sets up his global caliphate, there is no place on earth for an Islamic government predicated on Sharia law.

Such a conclusion could have led him into Ahmadinejad's camp. Hossein Khomeini could have become a Radical, convinced it was his God-given mission in life to "hasten" the coming of the Mahdi by launching a genocidal jihad against the West. Instead, he concluded — as Thomas Jefferson did — that in the absence of a "perfect" government, a representational government with a built-in system of checks and balances was better than a violent dictatorship by far.

"The Iranian People Want Democracy"

"The Iranian people have become tired, fatigued, after . . . years of deprivation and suppression," Khomeini noted. "They have been deprived of the basic means of life. . . . They are not very hopeful. They're frustrated. They cannot come to the streets and fight the regime. . . . [But] we cannot remain silent and watch the further destruction of Iran and Iranian people. We cannot simply watch the young generation that is under tremendous pressure. . . . They have lost hope. They're all saddened. They are all melancholic, and in a sense, it's a . . . depressed generation."[4]

It was time, he insisted, for a new Iranian Revolution, one led by Reformers rather than Radicals. "Today, [the] Iranian people again want democracy; they want freedom," Khomeini explained. "Democracy is compatible with all the basic values of Shiism and Islamic law. . . . [The] establishment of freedom and democracy in Islamic countries is the guarantee of the international peace. It is the guarantee of security of the world. It's the guarantee that Americans and the Europeans — especially Americans — could live in peace and security in their own countries."

351

The big question, he said, was who would lead this new Revolution. "At the present time, the question is how we can get to democracy and freedom in our communities in the Middle East. Our nation is ready, but it cannot have any kind of activity because there is no leadership."

The event at which Khomeini was speaking had been organized by Michael Ledeen, then a resident scholar on Iranian issues at AEI and coauthor (with William Lewis) of *Debacle: The American Failure in Iran* and later *The Iranian Time Bomb: The Mullah Zealots' Quest for Destruction.* When I met with Ledeen in September 2008, I asked him how he had persuaded Khomeini to deliver such a landmark address just blocks from the White House.

"He showed up in Baghdad, and somebody in Baghdad with our armed forces told me about it and got me in touch with Khomeini," Ledeen told me. "It was just after the liberation of Iraq, and Khomeini had apparently told an American military officer, 'It's wonderful to be in a free country!' " Ledeen immediately followed up and contacted the Khomeini heir. "He intended to come to the U.S.," Ledeen recalled. "I told him we'd be delighted to host him if and when he came."[5]

After the address, Ledeen moderated a question-and-answer session. Khomeini was asked about the growing desire shared by many Iranians for a U.S.-led liberation of his country and whether he might support such a move. It was a question he might easily have dodged or even vehemently resisted, saying the last thing Iran needed was another "Operation Iraqi Freedom." Instead, he said carefully, deliberately, "One should think how deep the problem and the pressures are in Iran on the Iranian people, that there are so many of them who in fact crave for some sort of foreign intervention to get rid of this calamity." The response was diplomatic. It was nuanced. But it certainly was not a "no."

One guest at the event then asked the question more directly. "We don't have a tradition of four o'clock tea in the U.S., but if you were to be invited to the White House and you had a half-hour chat with the president of the United States, what, specifically, would you ask the president . . . to do to free your country?"

Khomeini considered that for a moment and then replied more directly as well: "I [would] ask the president to take the question of democracy, not only in the Middle East but especially in Iran, very seriously. As Churchill mobilized the laid-back British population against Hitler, the United States also could mobilize American public opinion for the freedom of Iranians."

It was a striking moment. Here was a member of the Khomeini family diplomatically but pointedly urging President Bush to mobilize the American people to support "regime change" in Tehran much as Prime Minister Winston Churchill once enlisted the British people to support "regime change" in Berlin.

But the Bush administration did not respond. The president occasionally spoke of his solidarity with the people of Iran, but he did little substantively to back up what little he said. Their hands full with the growing insurgency in Iraq, neither the State Department nor the Pentagon pursued any significant strategy to strengthen democratic opposition inside Iran, and they certainly did not launch military operations to overthrow the mullahs or build an international coalition to do so. Indeed, Secretary of State Condoleezza Rice essentially turned over the Iran portfolio to the Europeans.[6]

"Strength Will Not Be Obtained Through the Bomb"

Three years later, after watching the rise of Ahmadinejad and hearing the Iranian president's murderous, messianic rants — and seeing the doing nothing to stop him — Hossein Khomeini stepped up his criticisms. He unleashed another major salvo at the regime and the Revolution led by his family. He was no longer being polite or diplomatic. Rather, during an interview from Qom, Iran, with Al Arabiyah, the Dubai-based satellite television network, Khomeini called on the to overthrow Ahmadinejad's regime and liberate his country once and for all.

"Freedom must come to Iran in any possible way, whether through internal or external developments," Khomeini insisted when asked if he supported a U.S. military invasion of Iran. "If you were a prisoner, what would you do? I want someone to break the prison [doors open]."[7]

Coming from someone who as a teenager used to join millions of fellow Shia Muslims on the streets of Tehran shouting, "Death to America!" at his grandfather's rallies, these were tough words indeed. But Khomeini made no apologies. For him, becoming a Reformer was an act of moral obligation to his country and especially to the children of Iran.

"My grandfather's Revolution has devoured its children and has strayed from its course," Khomeini said. And making it clear how strongly he opposed Ahmadinejad's feverish efforts to obtain nuclear weapons, he noted, "Iran will gain real power if freedom and democracy develop there. Strength will not be obtained through weapons and the Bomb."

He described the Iranian regime under the mullahs as "a dictatorship of clerics who control every aspect of life." He was particularly critical of the treatment of women. "The Iranian regime shackles women by forcing [them to wear] the *hijab* in its ugliest form — namely a black [veil]. . . . Girls coming out of schools or out of the university [look] depressingly somber."

Then, underscoring just how completely he had broken with the Radicals, the grandson of the ayatollah revealed for the first time to the people of the Muslim world that when he visited the United States he had had a personal meeting with Reza Pahlavi, the son of the late shah of Iran. You could almost feel the air being sucked out of the lungs of Ahmadinejad and the Ayatollah Khamenei; both men regard the shah and his entire family as traitors and apostates.

Based in suburban Maryland, just outside of Washington, D.C., Reza Pahlavi has emerged over the past decade or so as a leading critic of the Radicals in his country and a staunch advocate of ending the mullahs' reign of terror and ushering in a new era of Jeffersonian democracy in the country of his birth. In 2002, Pahlavi published a manifesto entitled *Winds of Change: The Future of Democracy in Iran.* He also created a Web site (www.rezapahlavi.org) further explaining his case for democracy. He has traveled all over the U.S. and the world, trying to build a movement of fellow Reformers ready to overthrow the mullahs, though he has opposed U.S. military intervention as forcefully as Hossein Khomeini has advocated it. Not every Iranian Reformer has been convinced that Pahlavi is necessarily the man to lead the next Revolution, but he is certainly a key figure in the movement.

And now the grandson of the ayatollah was publicly describing a trip he had taken halfway around the world to meet the son of the shah, praising the common cause that had brought the two men together despite their histories and political differences.

It was "an ordinary meeting with a man who shares my suffering," Khomeini told the viewers of Al Arabiyah. "The [cause] of our suffering is one and the same, namely tyranny, though each of us has his own [political] orientation."[8]

Nevertheless, the Bush administration — so forceful and effective in bringing regime change to Afghanistan and Iraq — did nothing to help the people of Iran find their freedom.

The Tip of the Iceberg

By the time Hossein Khomeini made the shocking announcement about his meeting with Reza Pahlavi, the grandson of the ayatollah had become one of the most prominent defectors from the clutch of the Iranian Radicals, and he was becoming more so with each successive speech and interview. And he was not alone. Today, a growing number of Iranians — and Muslims throughout the region — are choosing to risk their lives to oppose the Radicals and pursue an entirely different kind of government and way of life.

There are many reasons for dissent, of course,

but if I had to sum those reasons up, I would say — based on interviewing hundreds of Muslim dissidents over the years and reading scores of their books, speeches, and blogs — that such dissidents and defectors feel betrayed. In their eyes, the Radicals made them and their family members and their friends and their countrymen a set of promises, and they have betrayed those promises in the worst possible way. Extremist, fundamentalist Islam did not bring about more freedom, more opportunity, and more hope and joy. Rather, the Radicals unleashed such horrific violence and oppression and psychotic behavior on their people that millions of Muslims were shocked into the realization that if they did not fight for change, they would drown in their own sorrow, if not their own blood.

Consider, for example, the case of Ali Rez Asgari. He was once Iran's deputy defense minister under President Khatami. He also once commanded the Iranian Revolutionary Guard Corps. But sometime in 2002 or 2003, he decided he could not take it any longer. He hated where the Ayatollah Khamenei was taking his country. He felt betrayed by the leaders of the Revolution. He saw no hope for reform and no end to Iran's support for violence against innocent civilians throughout the region and the world. So he began to spy on his country. He began turning over highly classified documents to Western intelligence agencies. And then, fearful of being found out, he finally defected to the West, most likely to the U.S., in 2007.

Ever since, sources say, he has been spilling his guts, telling intelligence officials everything he knows. Some published reports in the Middle East say Asgari even provided Israel with the key information they needed to attack and destroy a Syrian nuclear facility in the fall of 2007. What was particularly stunning about Asgari's defection was that Israeli intelligence believes he helped found and build Hezbollah in Lebanon at the direction of the Ayatollah Khomeini in the early 1980s.[9]

Is Asgari a Jeffersonian democrat? I do not know. But his defection is further evidence of how even the true believers in the Islamic Revolution are turning their backs and searching for change.

Or consider the case of Hamid Reza Zakiri. Born in 1962, Zakiri was just seventeen when the Revolution unfolded but soon became a true believer. He entered the military as the Iran-Iraq War was beginning and quickly rose through the ranks, eventually becoming the director of intelligence for the Iranian Revolutionary Guard Corps and later a senior intelligence official in the Security Ministry under President Khatami.

But in 2003, Zakiri had had enough. Having seen what the Radicals were really about — what they believed and how they behaved — he defected to the West and began spilling his nation's secrets, including the fact that Iran was working closely with North Korea on its nuclear weapons program and that al Qaeda had asked Iran for help in the 9/11 attacks. "Did you know about the plans to attack the World Trade Center in New York?" Zakiri was asked during an on-the-record interview by *Al-Sharq Al-Awsat*, a London-based Saudi daily, in 2003. "No," the defector replied, "but we had in our headquarters models of the two towers [of the World Trade Center], the White House, the Pentagon, and the CIA building at Langley."

Zakiri explained that a top Hezbollah operative had come to Iran before September 2001 and delivered a letter to senior Iranian intelligence officials from Dr. Ayman al-Zawahiri. The letter said, "We need your help to carry out a most important mission in the land of the 'Great Satan.' " The request was denied, but Zakiri described in detail how Iran assisted al Qaeda and other Sunni jihadist groups in many other ways.[10]

Consider, too, the case of Ahmad Rezai, an Iranian who escaped to the United States in the summer of 1998, requesting political asylum after becoming horrified by what he had seen in his home country. Rezai, however, was no ordinary defector. He was the son of General Mohsen Rezai, the former commander of the Iranian Revolutionary Guard Corps and a senior advisor to the Ayatollah Khamenei. Ahmad himself once served in the IRGC, Iran's elite fighting force, and later told U.S. intelligence officials that Iran was complicit in numerous terrorist attacks around the world, including the 1996 bombing of the Khobar Towers in Saudi Arabia.[11]

"We don't believe in the Iranian government," Rezai, then in his early twenties, said during a 1999 interview on the Voice of America radio network. "We believe that the Islamic Republic is a terrorist regime, the biggest terrorist government in the world. We don't want to be considered terrorists or to have anything to do with terrorism. We want to be free. We want to have a good life, democracy, freedom, but we have no freedom in Iran. . . . The Islamic Republic has taken our lives and sacrificed us to their goals. . . . They want us to work for them, to carry out their programs, their terrorist jobs around the world.

They want to control Israel. They want to control Muslim countries. They want to have power over the world like Hitler."[12]

Concluded the young defector: "Islam is not popular in Iran. No young people want to be Muslims today, not when they see what this regime does in the name of Islam."

Such stories are just the tip of the iceberg. Scores of defectors and political asylum seekers have fled Iran over the past decade. Not all are made public, of course. And not all are Jeffersonian democrats. But all feel betrayed by their government and its tyrannical ideology and criminal behavior. They have all had front-row seats to the nightmare, and the fact that they have risked their lives to find freedom in the West — usually in the United States — is a testament to how desperate they feel about the regime in Iran.*

★The danger to Iranian dissidents and defectors is real. Iran has been known to assassinate, kidnap, and torture such critics. A report by the Foundation for Democracy in Iran found that between 1979 and 1996 alone, "some 70 Iranian exiles and political activists [were] killed by Iranian government agents overseas." The group also noted that a U.N. subcommittee on human rights officially condemned Iran's extraterritorial killings in a resolution passed on April 24, 1996. The resolution stated that the international community "deplores the continuing violence against Iranians outside the Islamic Republic of Iran" and affirmed that governments "are accountable for assassinations and attacks by their agents." (See "FDI releases report on assassinations," Action Memorandum 011, Foundation for Democracy

The Despondent

Nearly 70 million people live in Iran today. Seven in ten are young — under the age of thirty. Nearly one in four Iranians are under fifteen.[13] They do not remember the heady days of the Revolution in 1979. They never experienced the thrill of overthrowing the shah. All they know are the broken promises. The ayatollahs pledged to their parents a society filled with hope, growth, and opportunity. Today, what they have instead is despair, unemployment, inflation, and chronic poverty. The vast majority of Iranians cannot defect, of course. Instead, they find themselves trapped and despondent.

Three decades after the Revolution, and despite the fact that Iran is sitting on a sea of oil and natural gas which should make for a robust export-driven economy, roughly a quarter of Iran's eligible workforce — about 6.5 million people — cannot find a job, though the government officially acknowledges an unemployment rate of only about 10 percent.[14] Inflation in 2008, meanwhile, hovered around 30 percent, making it difficult even for those with a job to keep up with the cost of essential goods and services.[15] At least one in five Iranians live below the poverty level,

---

in Iran, May 6, 1996.) In 2007, Bret Stephens of the *Wall Street Journal* reported that "Ahmad Rezai has . . . reportedly returned to Iran, though whether he did so voluntarily or under duress isn't clear." I e-mailed Stephens in September 2008. At that point, he said the trail on Rezai was still cold. I can only hope and pray that he is safe. (See Bret Stephens, "Iran's al Qaeda," *Wall Street Journal,* October 16, 2007.)

and 5 million Iranians survive on less than two dollars a day, according to the CIA and the U.N.[16]

Some Iranians, however, say that the situation is far worse. "Ninety percent of the population are living under the poverty level, and only ten percent of the people have access to social services provided by the government," said Mohammad Abbaspour, a member of the Iranian Majlis (parliament) who serves on the Social Affairs Committee, in 2005.[17]*

As the Revolution failed to deliver on its promises, drug use — particularly among young people — skyrocketed year after year. Despite the fact

*What is particularly offensive about the shambles of Iran's socialist and woefully mismanaged economy is that it squanders the value of Iran's greatest national asset — human capital. When free to develop their skills and reach their God-given potential, Iranian workers are some of the brightest and most resourceful in the world. In the free market environment of the United States, for example, American families of Iranian ancestry, on average, earn 20 percent more money than the average American family. Nearly one-third of Iranian-Americans earn $100,000 a year or more. No fewer than ten Iranian-Americans have been founders of or senior executives in U.S.-based businesses worth a combined $1 trillion, including Pierre Omidyar, founder of eBay, who had a net worth of $7.7 billion in 2008. (See Ali Mostashari, "Fact Sheet on the Iranian-American Community," Iranian Research Studies Group Series, Massachusetts Institute of Technology, April 2003, http://isg-mit.org/projects-storage/census/Factsheet.pdf)

that every Iranian government beginning with Khomeini's has cracked down on illegal drugs, today there are more than 4 million drug addicts in Iran, 11 million drug users, and half a million drug dealers. According to one top Iranian drug enforcement official, "every three minutes, one person in society becomes addicted to drugs."[18]

According to the U.N.'s *2007 World Drug Report*, Iran has the highest proportion of opium and heroin addicts on the entire planet — 2.8 percent of the population. No other country is even close; Afghanistan comes in second at 1.4 percent.[19] The director of the Iranian National Center for Addiction Studies told the *Washington Post* in 2005 that 20 percent of Iran's adult population is "somehow involved in drug abuse," while an Iranian doctor who treats drug abuse told the *Post* that 68 percent of his patients started using drugs before age twenty and said bluntly, "We have despair."[20]

Worst of all, experts say Iran has not reached the peak of the drug addiction epidemic.[21] Said Reza Sarami, a top Iranian antinarcotics official: "If nothing is done to reduce this increase in drug users, we will have some nine million addicts in less than twenty years," more than double the 4 million addicts Iran has now.[22]

The Disgusted

Despair is one response for those who cannot defect.

Another is sheer anger and disgust. Tens of millions of Iranians are furious at the Radicals. Individually, they have no political power. But they are increasingly repulsed by the jihadists and particularly by the Muslim-on-Muslim violence they see being perpetrated in Iran, in Iraq, in Afghanistan, in Somalia, in Pakistan, in Sudan, and in suicide bombings and other terrorist attacks from Casablanca to Istanbul to Riyadh. As a result, they are listening carefully to whatever Reformers they can find on the radio, on satellite television, and on the Internet, and they are moving steadily into the Reformer camp.

While I was researching this book, I interviewed a senior official working for a Western intelligence agency. This man spent many years in Iran and was once his agency's station chief in Tehran. The facts he shared with me about the magnitude of the Iranian leadership's cruelty against their own people floored me. But such statistics are certainly no secret to Iranians trapped inside the country or to the estimated 5 million Iranians who live in exile. Consider the following:

- Iran has executed more than 120,000 of its citizens on political grounds since 1979, including pregnant women, elderly women, and schoolchildren.
- Iran massacred 30,000 political prisoners in 1988 alone.
- Iran's secret police employ 170 forms of physical and psychological torture.
- The regime sends some 800,000 Iranians to prison every year.
- The regime employs stoning; public hangings; eye gouging; amputation of fingers, hands, and legs; beheading; and flogging in public as "punishment" for disobedience.
- Iran's government has engaged in no fewer than 450 terrorist operations around the world, including bombings, hijacking, abduc-

tions, and assassinations.

- At least eighty newspapers and periodicals have been closed down by the regime since April 2000, dozens of Iranians journalists are in jail, and some have called Iran "the world's biggest prison for journalists."
- Iran has the highest suicide rate in the world (200 fatal suicide attempts for every 100,000 people).
- Some 1,500 Iranians flee the country every day.[23]

With a burning desire to speak out against such atrocities — but with few means to talk to each other, much less the outside world — "the Disgusted" in Iran have turned to blogging. Today, there are at least eighty thousand Iranian blogs on the World Wide Web, electronic personal journals in which people write daily, and sometimes hourly, entries about their thoughts, feelings, political views, and the issues of the day. Farsi is actually the third most popular language on the Internet, after English and Mandarin Chinese.[24]

To scan such Farsi blogs is to take the temperature of the molten anger building up pressure underneath the regime in Tehran and threatening to explode like a volcano. Consider a sampling from a half dozen different Iranian bloggers:

"I [expletive deleted] the whole of Hezbollah [party of Allah] . . . and your distorted Islam and its ideology that you use to diminish a human being through torture. . . . This generation [of young people] finally . . . realize[s] what sort of hole it's in. . . . People put an ayatollah and the clergy on the same level as pimps and thugs."

"In my life there have been times when, consumed with rage, I have felt infinite helplessness and loss . . . a time when you feel that an injustice is crushing your mind. . . . You want to scream and shout and all you can see is the sneering face of your enemy . . . an opponent who seems only to get turned on even more at the spectre of your wet eyes and red cheeks. . . . [These are] times when you feel that God must feel ashamed to have created man."

"I have lived for 27 years . . . under revolution, repression, assassinations, hangings, and war. . . . My youth and childhood passed away during bombings . . . gazing at the trembling hands of my elders. . . . Sometimes I think this place is the land cursed by God."

"If only those Muslim idiots in our neighboring countries knew about our failed experiment with an Islamic government they would come to their senses, too. . . . [The Revolution] is finished . . . and when these mullahs are dethroned . . . it will be like the Berlin Wall coming down. . . . Soon we will be rid of them. . . . A little patience . . . our dawn is near."

"For me the most shocking aspect of 9/11 was that this was not some lone gunman but a group of people who voluntarily colluded in this evil act. . . . Didn't any of those involved have moments of sanity and say to themselves: 'What we are doing is pure evil'? . . . But it's no longer just 9/11. We are seeing so many acts of pure evil around the world committed by Muslims. . . . I have no doubt about the evil nature of our rulers and their

366

ability to perpetrate acts of pure wickedness. . . . I cannot stop feeling an enormous sense of shame, guilt, and helplessness."

"I keep a weblog so that I can breathe in this suffocating air. . . . In a society where one is taken to [prison] for the mere crime of thinking, I write so as not to be lost in despair . . . so that I feel that I am somewhere where my calls for justice can be uttered. . . . I write a weblog so that I can shout, cry, and laugh, and do the things that they have taken away from me in Iran today."[25]

It is not just millions of Iranians who are despondent and disgusted by the ideas and the acts of the Radicals. Hundreds of millions of Muslims around the world feel similarly.

Consider, for example, an intriguing trend in Pakistan in recent years. A 2004 Pew poll found that Osama bin Laden enjoyed a 65 percent favorable rating among Pakistani men.[26] Though profoundly disturbing in a country of 170 million people — and a nation that possesses nuclear weapons — this finding should not really be surprising. Pakistan has long been considered a hotbed of Radical Islam and, as noted earlier in this book, is very possibly the country where Osama bin Laden has been hiding since the liberation of Afghanistan.

But by September of 2007, after three years of highly publicized and at times spectacular al Qaeda violence against Muslims in Iraq, Afghanistan, and elsewhere, bin Laden's approval rating in Pakistan was down to 46 percent.[27]

Who was the most popular political leader in Pakistan at the time? Not bin Laden. Not President Musharraf, either, who had an approval rating of only 38 percent.

Rather, the leader of the pack was Benazir Bhutto, the former Pakistani prime minister who was promising to come home from exile and run for president on a bold and sweeping platform of reform. In September 2007, Bhutto had an approval rating of 63 percent.[28] Many intelligence and political analysts believe she was well poised to defeat Musharraf in the next elections and emerge as the next president of Pakistan. As noted in the last chapter, however, she was assassinated.

Did bin Laden's approval rating bounce back as a result? To the contrary, by January 2008, bin Laden's approval rating among Pakistanis had sunk to just 24 percent, a record low in seven years of polling. Al Qaeda's approval rating, meanwhile, dropped from 33 percent in August 2007 to just 18 percent in January 2008.[29]

Chapter Seventeen: Meet Hamid Karzai

The inside story of the first democratically
elected president of Afghanistan

It is hard to imagine a country less likely to
become a democracy. Indeed, Afghanistan is still
a work in progress, and it remains to be seen
whether democracy can truly take hold. But
Afghanistan and its fiercely independent people
have certainly had a knack for defying the odds.

Long ruled by kings, the landlocked and
poverty-stricken region became a nation-state in
1747 but held little interest for the West until the
Soviets invaded in 1979. That should have been
the end. To jaded Washington eyes, Afghanistan
seemed destined to be swallowed up by Moscow
to serve as another satellite state. But the Afghan
people refused to surrender. And Ronald Reagan
refused to let them.

By the early 1980s, Afghanistan was quickly
becoming the central front in the epic struggle
between the forces of freedom and the Communists of the Kremlin. With tremendous bravery,
unflinching resolve, and billions of dollars in
American aid and weaponry — including state-of-
the-art Stinger antiaircraft missiles — the Afghans

eventually defeated the mighty Red Army and, by the end of the 1980s, drove every single Soviet soldier out of their country. It was a stunning victory. One for the storybooks. And then, to our shame, we forgot about Afghanistan again.

The United States had built up significant goodwill inside Afghanistan. We had forged strong, albeit covert, relationships with national leaders, tribal chieftains, and well-educated young people eager to reclaim and rebuild their nation. We could have provided humanitarian relief for the 5 million refugees wasting away in squalid camps on the Afghanistan-Pakistan border. We could have helped the Afghans build schools and hospitals and farms and factories. We could have helped them build roads and electrical plants and drill thousands of wells to provide fresh water.

I'm not saying we should have done everything for them, but we could have helped. We should have helped. But we did not. Once the Soviets pulled out, we pulled out too.

A Radical "Paradise"

The provisional post-Soviet Afghan government collapsed in 1992, and into the vacuum rushed the Radicals, specifically Mohammed Omar — aka "Mullah Omar" — the ferocious and fanatical mujahadeen commander who once lost an eye in a firefight with the Russians but recovered and went on to found the Taliban, one of the most extreme jihadist organizations on the planet.

The Afghanis had been raped and pillaged by the Evil Empire from the North, Omar noted, and they had now been abandoned and betrayed by the infidels from the West.

But this was cause for celebration, not sadness,

Omar insisted. He argued that Allah had given the Afghan people a great victory in war and now it was time to give him thanks by constructing a purely Islamic country, governed by Sharia law, built on the sacred ashes of the past.

Not everyone was enamored of Omar's vision, much less wanted to see him in charge. But Omar was not about to take no for an answer. He believed he was chosen by God and was fighting for God and that God would give him victory. By the mid-1990s, after years of brutal, bloody tribal warfare and horrific sectarian violence, the fighters of the Taliban had successfully suppressed most of their opposition and had secured control of the country. In a world of blind men, a one-eyed man — literally — was now king.

It is difficult to put into words the reign of terror the Taliban unleashed on the people of Afghanistan. To talk to Afghans who suffered through the hellish conditions these Radicals created, as I had the opportunity to do on a research trip to Kabul in October 2008, is to wind up in tears at the nearly unbelievable stories they tell. Wives were beaten by their husbands without reason, with the regime's encouragement. Women were forbidden to style their hair. They were forbidden to wear nail polish. They were forced to wear blue burkas that covered them head to toe and were practically suffocating in hot weather.

Many children were beaten by their fathers and psychologically abused. Their schools were shut down. Their toys were taken from them. Movies were forbidden. Television was forbidden. Radio was forbidden, except for a station that continuously taught from the Qur'an. Games were forbidden. Kite flying was forbidden. Concerts were forbidden. Playing music in public was forbidden. New Year's celebrations were forbidden. Christmas decorations were forbidden. Christianity was most certainly forbidden.

Museums were closed. Zoos were closed. Dissenters were jailed. Others were murdered. Apostates were executed. "If you ever wanted to see Satan operating in the open, Afghanistan was it," said a friend of mine who used to travel to Kabul frequently before 9/11. "The Taliban was true evil, unmasked, unrestricted. I have never seen anything like it."[1]

It was into this Radical "paradise" that Mullah Omar invited Osama bin Laden.

Omar extended an invitation for the al Qaeda leader and his terror network to come back to Afghanistan after a season in Sudan, set up their training camps in the Hindu Kush Mountains, and enjoy a sanctuary far from the Americans, the British, and the Israelis, who were beginning to understand the threat they posed to the West. Bin Laden gladly accepted the offer. Sure, he would rather have overthrown the Saudi royal family, seized control of the Arabian Peninsula, and set up "the base" in Mecca or Medina. But the icon of Sunni jihadists considered Afghanistan holy ground, and a second home. And it was there that he and his colleagues began plotting the 9/11 attacks and trying to purchase weapons of mass destruction.

Once again, all seemed lost for the Afghan people. Yes, the vast majority were proud, traditional Muslims. Yes, most believed the Qur'an taught them to wage jihad in defense of their country, and they had done so to repel the Soviets. Yes, they had been grateful for outside help from

America and Saudi Arabia alike. But they had not signed up for this. They were not ethnically Arabs. They were not theologically Wahhabis. They were not politically Fascists. And yet now, suddenly, after all their sacrifice and suffering, here they were, slaves of the Salafists. Their children were being recruited for jihad or forced to do unspeakable things in the name of Allah. Hope was fading quickly. Depression was rising. Drug use was rampant. The country was becoming the world's number-one source for opium and heroin, and there seemed no way out.

Yet to their credit, the Afghans never gave up. In the north, an anti-Taliban resistance movement was recruiting, training, and building an army from a range of Afghan tribes known as the Northern Alliance. In the West, Afghan exiles — such as King Zahir Shah (no relation to the shah of Iran), who had been deposed in 1973 and was living in Rome — were trying to explain the enormous and growing danger posed by the Taliban and al Qaeda and appealing to the U.S. and the E.U. for financial and political assistance to push back and eventually take them down. In Pakistan, a young Afghan exile by the name of Hamid Karzai — once a member of the mujahadeen and briefly a Taliban sympathizer himself — was going through a remarkable personal and political transformation and emerging as the leader of the anti-Taliban opposition.

Then came 9/11. The West was suddenly awakened from its slumber. It suddenly remembered Afghanistan. It suddenly had to. And once the liberation of that ancient country began, its people and the international community turned to Karzai to lead the way.

A Family of Moderates

Hamid Karzai was born one of eight children — seven boys and one girl — in the village of Karz, in the Kandahar Province of Afghanistan, on Christmas Eve, 1957.

His family was prominent and well-off. His father was the educated and widely respected chief of the Popolzai tribe. A devout, traditional Muslim, Karzai's father had made his pilgrimage to Mecca but did not believe his country should be governed by Sharia law. To the contrary, he was a political moderate and a constitutional monarchist who was personally close to the king, who was then still in power. He continually encouraged the king to expand personal freedoms and give tribal leaders more opportunities to participate in the decision making of the country.

The elder Karzai also had great dreams for his children. He wanted them to receive world-class educations and become qualified to lead their country forward toward progress and modernization. He sent several of his sons to study in the United States. When Hamid was finished with high school, his father sent him to university in India to earn an undergraduate and a graduate degree and to become proficient in English, to go with his two native languages, Pashto and Dari (also known as Farsi, the language of the Persians).

Hamid Karzai was barely twenty-one years old in 1979, when the Ayatollah Khomeini launched the Islamic Revolution in Iran and the Soviets invaded his own country. Living in India, he felt lonely and far away from the dramatic events engulfing his people and his family. When he learned that his father had been imprisoned, he wanted to rush home, but his family said no. There was nothing he could do to help. He needed to stay alive, finish his studies, and plan for the future. Reluctantly, he agreed.

By 1982, however, Karzai was hearing dramatic stories of the mujahadeen fighting bravely against the Soviet forces. They were not yet achieving big successes (those would not really begin until 1984, when the Reagan administration dramatically accelerated aid to the Afghan "freedom fighters" through the CIA), but they were holding their own.

Karzai was inspired. He wanted to be part of it. He wanted to help, someway, somehow. Unable to contain himself any longer, he bought a train ticket and began the forty-eight-hour journey from Simla, India, to Quetta, Pakistan, where at least he could see the enormous and rapidly growing refugee camps along the Afghanistan-Pakistan border and get a clearer picture of what was really happening inside his country.

On the train, however, he overheard something that deeply disturbed him. Several men from one of Afghanistan's most radical political movements were talking about joining the jihad and killing the Russians, but they were also talking about their leaders' dream to one day seize control of Afghanistan and establish a Sunni theocracy, much as the Ayatollah Khomeini had seized control of Iran and established a Shia theocracy.

This was a new development, at least for Karzai. From his limited vantage point in India, all he had heard were positive stories of the jihadists defending their country from the infidels. He had not yet detected an extremist strain that might seek to use the conflict in Afghanistan to hijack

375

the country and take it into Khomeini-esque fascism rather than returning it to a constitutional monarchy.

"I became aware of a political and ideological movement that wanted to undermine the traditional Afghan value system and the Afghan way of life," Karzai told a biographer. "Over the months and years to come, I would see that this radical movement had many fathers. Everyone had a hand in its growth — the West, the neighbors [i.e., Iran, Pakistan, and the U.S.S.R.], everyone. And this movement was ultimately the cause of so much evil in Afghanistan and so much destruction in the United States and the rest of the world."[2]

Joining the Mujahadeen

Though he was now alert to and wary of a growing extremist strain in the anti-Soviet effort, Karzai was a devoted nationalist and still deeply committed to helping the mujahadeen succeed. Finished with his academic studies, he was now free to join the resistance and lend whatever skills he had to the cause.

Absent any military training, Karzai was asked by his father — living in exile in Pakistan — to help him with the logistics of moving food, medical supplies, weapons, and other goods to the fighters operating inside Afghanistan. Later he was asked to work in the refugee camps, teaching English to young people eager to prepare themselves for a better life one day. It was a job he loved and remains proud of to this day.

"Of all the things I did during those years, [teaching] that English course was one of my best contributions," Karzai would later recall. "It was a great, great work, and many young Afghans who learned English in that program went on to continue their educations, some to a very high level. I remember those people, and it gives me great happiness to know that I was able to help them with their educations."[3]

Eventually, however, Karzai became determined to go into battle against the Soviets. He wanted to participate in what his people were doing. He wanted to see what the Russians were doing. He wanted to feel like he was making a difference on the front lines. He believed that if Allah ever had a plan for him to provide leadership to the Afghan people, he was going to need the credibility of having served in forward areas.

The leadership finally gave him his chance. He went on numerous missions deep inside his homeland, conducting raids against Soviet convoys, engaging in firefights with Soviet patrols, and shooting down Soviet helicopters and fighter jets. It was exhilarating for Karzai, but he, his father, and the mujahadeen leaders all knew that ultimately this was not the best use of his gifts and abilities, including his language skills. He could be of far more use to the movement as a political leader, building relationships and alliances with the outside world and planning for the day when Afghanistan would be free and a new government would be formed.

When the Soviets finally left in 1989 and the caretaker regime they had left in place collapsed in 1992, the mujahadeen rose to power in an "interim government." Karzai was brought back to Kabul and appointed deputy foreign minister. It was a role that would have suited him perfectly, but it did not last for long. The coalition that made up the government was fragile at best. After more than a decade of intense combat, several of the most powerful tribes were not ready to stop fighting. They certainly were not ready to share power. They wanted to control the entire country for themselves, and a horrific civil war broke out.

It was kingdom against kingdom, tribe against tribe. Karzai watched in disbelief as the country he had just helped to liberate descended into what he called "a wilderness of savagery."[4] Kabul was being blown apart, house by house, street by street. What little the Soviets had left intact was being systematically obliterated. And thousands of Afghan Muslims were dying in the process.

By 1994, Karzai could not take it any longer. He had been spectacularly unsuccessful in persuading the Clinton-Gore administration to help his disintegrating country. The United Nations and the Europeans were similarly unhelpful. With the violence so bad he feared for his own life and the lives of his wife and children, Karzai pulled them out and returned to Quetta, Pakistan, to catch their breath and regroup.

Resisting the Taliban

In the early 1990s, Karzai began to notice the Taliban rising to power, though at first he — like many Afghans — thought the Taliban might be a positive force for change.

"As Karzai tells it," wrote Nick Mills, an associate professor of journalism at Boston University, in an excellent and thought-provoking biography of the Afghan leader, "a warlord in Kandahar kidnapped two girls from a rival group, and the girls were gang-raped at the warlord's base. A small group of Taliban attacked the warlord's base, freed the girls, and hanged him. Word of the dramatic rescue spread rapidly. The Pakistanis took notice as well and supplied the Taliban with weapons, vehicles, and military advisers."[5]

The goal at the time was to find someone — *anyone* — to restore some semblance of order and security to a country wracked by lawlessness and sectarian violence. The Taliban seemed to fit the bill. As Karzai has said, "We had hopes for the movement. We hoped the Taliban would bring peace and restore Afghanistan to the hands of the Afghan people."[6]

But as Mullah Omar and his forces steadily gained control of the country, Karzai kept hearing disturbing reports of wanton acts of cruelty against innocent civilians, and he began detecting that the Taliban was not really a homegrown movement. It was being heavily influenced by, if not directly run by, Arabs, not Afghans. Growing numbers of Saudis were seen entering and operating in Kabul, Kandahar, and other regions of the country. Radical Wahhabi Muslims, not traditional Muslims, were preaching in the mosques. And suitcases full of money were flowing into the country from the Arabian Peninsula.

In 1996, Taliban leaders asked Karzai to serve as Afghanistan's ambassador to the United Nations. But, deeply disturbed by where the movement was headed, Karzai declined. By 1999, the Taliban and its al Qaeda "guests" controlled 90 percent of the country, and they now believed that Karzai — still in Pakistan — was emerging as their main enemy.

They were right. Tribal chieftains were sending messengers to Karzai asking for help. Karzai was being interviewed on the BBC, the Voice of

America, Radio Liberty, and other international networks, and he was exposing the Taliban's cruelty and imploring the world to come to his country's aid once again.

"Islam?" Karzai would tell anyone who would listen. "The Taliban [are] not practicing Islam." He called them a "tool for defaming Islam." He accused them of being out "to destroy Afghanistan and Islam together" and insisted, "Humiliating women is not Islam. Depriving children of education is not Islam. Destroying lives is against Islam."[7]

To silence Karzai, the Taliban assassinated his father in 1999. This did not stop the Afghan idealist, however. Instead it deepened his resolve to do everything in his power to liberate his country from the Taliban.

Karzai accelerated his efforts to make the Clinton-Gore administration and the Western powers see the danger brewing in his country and to persuade them to take decisive action against the Taliban and al Qaeda before it was too late. Tragically, his pleas fell on deaf ears. "We kept telling the United States for the past five or six years . . . of the dangers that [these terrorists] could pose to the United States," Karzai would later say during an interview on American television not long after 9/11. "Unfortunately the incident in New York happened with such a tremendous loss of life, and that caused the reaction, which was right, which was on time. The only thing is that I'm sorry that it had to take that kind of a calamity for us to work against terrorism."[8]

Karzai is convinced that the U.S. government could have taken action during the 1990s to crush the threat posed by al Qaeda and the Taliban and that it had a moral obligation to the American people as well as to his own people to have done so. And he regrets that the price the U.S. paid for not listening was so enormous. "Should President Clinton have done more at the time?" Karzai said later, describing his disappointment at all the missed opportunities of the 1990s. "Yes, but not only he — the whole world should have done more. If the world had done more, the Twin Towers would be standing today."[9]

Destroying the Taliban

As the 9/11 attacks on the United States unfolded, Karzai was enraged but not surprised. This was what he had long feared could happen, and now it had.

When the Bush administration was ready to fight back, Karzai and his colleagues were ready too. After years of preparation, they had a network of insurgents in place to help the Americans, beginning with the forces of the Northern Alliance, which still controlled about 10 percent of the country. They had an extensive network of tribal leaders and informers that could provide intelligence on the whereabouts and movements of Taliban and al Qaeda forces. They had an extensive network of villagers willing to provide trucks, beds, food, and anything else they could to help the Americans and the mujahadeen oust these Radicals so they could again breathe free mountain air. They also had hundreds of local leaders ready and willing to form a representative government when the time was right.

In early October 2001, Karzai left his home in Quetta for the mountains near Kabul to rally his people against the Taliban. "I told everyone that I was going to a friend's memorial service in town," he said. "I didn't even tell my wife what I was really up to. I only said that if I weren't back in a few days, it was because I was busy and she shouldn't worry. She was surprised, of course, but I didn't give her the opportunity to discuss my trip. I hurried away."[10]

Once at the Afghan border, Karzai linked up with three close friends and trusted advisors who had agreed to help him get in and cover his back in the process. "They had two motorbikes and a couple of handguns," he recalled, adding that they donned Afghan-style turbans and hats, hoping to blend in to the local traffic and not attract attention. Gone was the natty Western clothing and distinguished lamb's-wool hat Karzai loved to wear and for which he would later become known.

Karzai was a wanted man. Given what had happened to his father, he knew that if the Taliban found him, they would slaughter him immediately. He was taking an enormous risk, but he felt he had no choice. If there was ever a chance to liberate his homeland, this was it, and his credibility with his own people as well as with the West hinged on his getting inside the country as quickly as possible.

"We stayed in a village near Kandahar's airport; then we moved to a house in the middle of town," Karzai would later recall. "That evening, American bombs began to fall around us. The war had begun. My cousins arranged for a taxi — an old Toyota station wagon — to take us into central Afghanistan. We stayed with a clergyman for several nights in the village of Tarin Kowt. His brother was a Taliban judge. In the afternoons, the brother would have tea with me and defend the Taliban. Yet he never told them I was staying in the house. That's when it sunk in that the Taliban were on the run, that Afghans wanted change."[11]

One night around nine o'clock, Karzai and his colleagues pulled together their first anti-Taliban organizational meeting inside Afghanistan, meeting with the local mullah and four tribal chiefs.

One of the chiefs asked if Karzai was in contact with the Americans.

Karzai said yes.

Were the Americans sending troops, or just bombs?

Karzai said he did not know for certain.

"You have a satellite telephone," the mullah noted. "Call the Americans and tell them to come and bomb the Taliban command center" in the village of Tarin Kowt.

Karzai hesitated. He said he could not call in American air strikes against his own people.

"In that case, you don't want to win," said the mullah. "You want to be a loser."

The words stung, and Karzai was stunned by the cleric's blunt manner.

"The population is fully with you," the mullah continued. "We will defend you to our deaths. But these are cruel people we are dealing with, and they have full backing from outside the country [i.e., bin Laden's money and international network of jihadists]. They will have no mercy on us. They will bomb us. They will send rockets into our homes and send the flesh of our women and children into the trees. Is this what you want?"

Karzai shook his head.

"We cannot win without the Americans," the

383

mullah concluded. "If you can't tell them to bomb, then at least ask them to drop weapons for us."[12]

Karzai finally agreed. He made the call, then rounded up about sixty men willing to head into the mountains to wait. Along the way, they encountered hundreds of other Afghan men — young and old — eager to join them. "The Americans dropped us weapons, ammunition, and sixteen members of the special forces," said Karzai. "Once, the Taliban and al-Qaeda came close to capturing us, setting up an ambush with about five hundred militiamen. But a village clergyman who had risen to call the early-morning prayers saw these armed men getting out of their vehicles and moving into the mountains. Instead of summoning the faithful to prayer, he ran to warn us. We put up stiff resistance, and we had help from American bombers. The Taliban announced that they'd caught and hanged me. I knew my wife was hearing this, but I couldn't call her because my satellite-phone batteries were running out."[13]

Soon U.S. and NATO forces were arriving, massive amounts of weapons and ammunition were flowing to Karzai's men and the Northern Alliance, and the bulk of the Taliban and al Qaeda were fleeing for their lives.

CHAPTER EIGHTEEN:
KARZAI'S MISSION

What he wants and what he has accomplished

It is almost impossible to convey the sense of elation that Hamid Karzai, his family, his colleagues, and his people felt when their country was liberated in late 2001.

Or when Karzai took office as interim president on December 22, 2001.

Or when national elections were held on October 9, 2004, and 8.1 million Afghans voted, 42 percent of whom were women.

Or when the votes were tallied and they learned that Karzai had received 55.4 percent of the vote and a stunning 3 million more votes than the closest of his eighteen challengers.

Or when Karzai was sworn in on December 7, 2004, for a five-year term as the first democratically elected president in Afghanistan's history.

Or when parliamentary elections were held in 2005, with some five thousand Afghan candidates running for the opportunity to represent their people.

The day they had the first opportunity to cast their ballots to choose their own leaders was a day no Afghan will ever forget. "It is a very important day," said a seventy-five-year-old toothless man in an old black turban as he voted in 2004. "We are very happy. It is like independence day, or freedom day. We are bringing security and peace to this country."[1]

"We are selecting our own president for ourselves," said a fifty-year-old headmaster of a local Afghan school. "That's important. There will definitely be changes after this election. There will be an end to the robberies and armed militias. People will cooperate with the government."[2]

"It is like a dream," one Afghan told the BBC, his eyes filled with tears. "Twenty-five years of displacement and life away from home have broken my back. Today I feel like I am reborn."[3]

An elderly woman who walked through mountain snows for four hours to find a polling station and cast her ballot told a reporter, "My life is almost over. [But] I am doing this for my children, and for my children's children."[4]

Not everyone outside the country fully understood what was happening in Afghanistan, however. Many in the West were — and remain — skeptical that representative government can firmly take root and bear fruit in an Islamic country such as Afghanistan, especially given its long history of bloodshed. But Hamid Karzai made the case that he was a proud and devout Muslim as well as a proud and determined democrat.

During a September 2003 forum at Princeton University, Karzai was asked point-blank by a student whether Islam was compatible with democracy. Absolutely, he insisted. The Taliban and al Qaeda used Islam "to justify murder and killing and destruction." But the Afghan people "joined hands" with the world's democracies "and drove them away." True Islam, he argued, calls for a just and fair society. "How can you have justice if you don't have people voting and choosing their governments?" he asked. "Islam is totally compatible with democracy."[5]

On July 4, 2004, President Karzai was honored at a ceremony in Philadelphia for being a true follower of Thomas Jefferson and a model for future Jeffersonian democrats. In presenting Karzai with the Philadelphia Liberty Medal, H. Craig Lewis, chairman of the Philadelphia Foundation, put it this way: "Like some very famous Americans who met in Philadelphia more than two centuries ago, President Karzai has pledged his life, his fortune, and his sacred honor to a cause and a country in which he deeply believes. He joins a distinguished roster of other Liberty Medal winners who have truly championed freedom and democratic values for the benefit of their nations and the world."[6]

Mayor John F. Street added, "President Hamid Karzai has tremendous faith in his country and its people and is a remarkable force in leading Afghanistan toward stability and democracy."[7]

In reply, Karzai said:

I am deeply honored to receive the Philadelphia Liberty Medal, on this momentous day, commemorating the Independence of America . . . in this great hall . . . which itself is a beacon, and a symbol of freedom. . . . I accept the Philadelphia Liberty Medal, with pride and a humble heart, on behalf of the Afghan people. This award is the Afghan people's award. The Declaration of Independence, signed in this very hall, led to the founding of this great nation . . . the United States of America. This historic and remarkable document . . . was based on basic, yet fundamental, beliefs of the founding fathers of America . . . that "God intended Man to be free"! That "life, liberty, and the pursuit of happiness" were inalienable rights, granted by God to all men . . . rights that must not be taken away. We, the Afghan people, have also enshrined these divine rights in our new Constitution. And we will protect and defend them. . . .

In November 2001, when I was conducting the campaign against the Taliban, a bomb hit an Afghan tribal leader's house and killed several members of his immediate family. A few days later, I was breaking fast with some Afghan elders, including this tribal leader, and some American officers. The tribal leader told the American officers that, "I have lost members of my family . . . and I wouldn't care if I lost more members of my family, provided Afghanistan is liberated." Ladies and gentleman, the Afghan people have sacrificed dearly to attain freedom. . . .

Ultimately, the Afghan people succeeded. With your help, we freed Afghanistan from the Soviet invasion . . . and with your support . . . we liberated Afghanistan from the rule of terrorism and extremism. As partners and defenders of freedom, both our nations are cognizant that liberty has its enemies. Where Liberty dies, evil grows. We Afghans have learned from our historical experiences that liberty does not come easily. We profoundly appreciate the value of liberty . . . for we have paid for it with our lives. And we will defend liberty with our lives. Here I quote the Afghan king of the early part of the last century . . . King Amanullah Khan, his words in pursuit of independence. "I will not stop seeking till I reach my heart's desire. Either the life in me gets to my beloved or the life in me leaves my body." For him "beloved" was liberty. And liberty is indeed beloved. Thank you. God bless you. God bless America and Afghanistan."[8]

This was not a case he made only in the West. Karzai addressed Muslim leaders in Doha, Qatar, in February 2008. Among his remarks were the following comments:

As a Muslim, I am greatly pained to see that, in contrast to the glory of our forebears, today we Muslims live in rather troubled times. It is unfortunate that many of the most violent conflicts today are taking place in our countries; or that, despite our immeasurable resources, too many of us are afflicted by poverty. It is painful to see that we make up one-fifth of the world's population, but only five percent of the world's economy. While the injunctions of our great faith are totally consistent with our duties as citizens of a single world which we share with the West, sometimes we do seem to have difficulty reconciling the two. . . .

As a Muslim, I think it is time we do better with the basic tenets of our great faith, Islam, and relive its glorious tradition of tolerance and progress. Fourteen hundred years ago, the benevolent God ordained to his Messenger

389

Muhammad (PBUH) in the Holy Qur'an that "all humans are equal in the sight of God," and that humans are born into different tribes and distinctions not to despise one another, but to know one another better. This Qur'anic verse is the earliest assertion ever about our shared humanity and about the basic elements we hold in common as members of a single human race. As Muslims, we must live up to the eminence of this divine truth.

And then, more than a millennium after the Holy Qur'an spoke about equality in the eyes of God Almighty, the founding fathers of what is today the United States of America adhered to the same principles as they set about founding a new great nation: "We hold these truths to be self-evident, that all men are created equal," they declared. The United States Constitution begins with "We the People" — a telling reminder of Islam's emphasis on the basic bondage of mankind. Thanks to the exemplary vision of its founding fathers, America today is a true beacon of prosperity, hope, and success. The American ideals of freedom, democracy, equality, and respect for the rights of the individual have inspired people around the world. I would say it is these ideals, much more than military prowess, that makes America attractive. . . .

The United States has also been one of the most successful nations in the world in terms of embracing and accepting multiplicity of religions and changing it to a social reality. Today, in the United States, Muslims live in peace and harmony with the followers of other religions, enjoying protection and full rights as citizens of that nation. . . . Today, no matter how divergent the views and interests of the United States and the Muslim world may appear on the surface, fundamentally, we aspire to the same ideals of freedom, peace, and prosperity."[9]

Confronting Poverty

Early on, I was encouraged not only by President Karzai's outspoken call for building a Jeffersonian democracy but by his commitment to tackling the enormous social and economic challenges facing his country and his devotion to improving the quality of life of every Afghan, particularly the lives of women and children. And while the country has a long, long way to go, Karzai and his team did make progress.

To begin with, Karzai was successful in persuading world leaders to support his country in a variety of ways. In January 2002, for example, just weeks after taking office, "Karzai swept onto the international stage . . . at an international donor's conference in Tokyo, where he managed to persuade donors to pledge more than $4 billion to help rebuild Afghanistan," reported the BBC, describing the new president as "charismatic" and a "shrewd statesman" with impressive diplomatic skills.[10]

By 2006, such skills had helped Karzai drive that number up to $10.5 billion in international aid pledges. In the summer of 2008, the U.S. government — impressed with the steady and significant progress that had been made so far — pledged an additional $10 billion in military and reconstruction assistance, while eighty other countries pledged an additional $5 billion.[11]

Such resources have been put to important use. More than four thousand kilometers of paved roads now crisscross the country, compared to only fifty when the Taliban was in charge. Nearly two thousand public schools have been built. Five universities are now operating. One hundred three hospitals are now running, along with 878 regional health clinics, and some 16 million vaccinations against childhood diseases have been administered.[12]

"Since the fall of the Taliban, Afghanistan's infant-mortality rate has been reduced by almost 25 percent," noted an impressed First Lady Laura Bush following a visit in June of 2008. "Its per-capita GDP has increased by 70 percent. In 2001, only 8 percent of Afghans had access to basic health care. Today, that number is 85 percent. In 2001, fewer than a million Afghan children were in school — all of them boys. Today, more than six million Afghan children are in school — about a third of them are girls."[13]

Perhaps it was not surprising that Karzai took a special interest in caring for the needs of women and children. He is married to a doctor who has spent many years caring for widows and orphans in Afghan refugee camps, and the couple had their first baby — a son — in 2007, when Karzai was forty-nine.[14]

Meanwhile, the Karzais have also been particularly focused on encouraging the participation of women in the political system. "We should do a lot more," Karzai said. "But the past five years have produced a lot of result, and a lot more will take place into the future. Out of 249 members in the Afghan Parliament, 68 are women. That's 27 percent of the Afghan Parliament."[15] By way of comparsion, in the 110th U.S. Congress (2007–2009), women held only 18 percent of the seats in the House and Senate combined.[16]

Asked in 2006 whether the Afghan people regarded the U.S. and NATO presence as invasion or liberation, Karzai said liberation without a moment's hesitation. "Five years ago," he said, "we were a country ruled by al Qaeda, ruled by their associates, the Taliban, and their sponsors from outside. Five years ago, we had more than five million of our people living outside of Afghanistan . . . the political leaders of our country [living] outside of Afghanistan. . . . I was outside of Afghanistan. . . . We had no schools in Afghanistan. We had no press in Afghanistan. We had no television in Afghanistan. People could not listen to their radios in their homes. . . . If you were caught listening to the BBC, you could be punished. Today we have Afghanistan once again as the home of all the Afghan people. . . . Four and a half million Afghan refugees have returned. We have Afghanistan's flag flying all over the world over our embassies, and we have sixty embassies represented in Afghanistan, some resident, some nonresident. We have the United Nations. We have the U.S. building a huge embassy there. . . . So for all good reasons, we are a liberated country with democracy. . . . Today we have . . . six television channels, private ones. And we have over 300 newspapers, all of them critical, by the way. And we have over thirty radio [stations]. So what do you call us, liberated or not?"[17]

Confronting the Radicals

From the very beginning, enormous challenges plagued the young president, who was a mere forty-four years old when he became the leader of his country. Among them: ongoing terrorism as Taliban and al Qaeda forces sought to destabilize and overthrow his regime; millions of widows and orphans; wrenching poverty; shortages of good housing and good jobs; illiteracy; psychological trauma; rampant drug production and drug use; budget shortages; government corruption; and an incredibly hostile neighborhood with the Radicals of the Iranian government on one side, an unstable Pakistan on the other, and the Russian Bear to the north.

Despite such challenges, Hamid Karzai initially seemed determined to build a healthy, functional democracy in his country, and I was moved by his personal determination to destroy the Radicals' stranglehold on his country despite at least four assassination attempts between 2001 and 2008 alone.

"Innocent life is the enemy of terrorism," Karzai argued with passion. "In other words, terrorism sees us all as enemies. Therefore, we have only one approach, one cause, one direction, one objective: to fight it, period. Playing with it is like trying to train a snake against somebody else. You don't train a snake. You cannot train a snake. It will come and bite you. Therefore, there's only one way: to fight terrorism, to fight extremism, in whatever form, wherever it may be, and to not use extremism as an instrument of policy. These are evils that the world has to get rid of. We have no choice there. If we adopt a complacent approach of having a choice there, you will see more destruction all around the world, without knowing when the next target would be."[18]

By and large, Afghans have appreciated U.S.

and NATO security assistance. They understood the stakes, and they understood the evil they were up against. In 2008, for example, some 70 percent of the Afghan population said they supported the presence of international forces to help them establish security. What was more, a stunning 84 percent said they supported their democratically elected government, compared to only 4 percent who said they wanted to go back to the rule of the Taliban.[19]

Afghans have not treated Osama bin Laden like a hero or a misunderstood genius. Rather, they have been determined to rid themselves of him and his al Qaeda tyrants. "In Afghanistan, people hate [bin Laden] because he has caused so much suffering to Afghans," Karzai told an American TV interviewer. "The Afghan people really see the pain that the American people went through [on 9/11] because they have experienced the same pain, so . . . there's hatred for [bin Laden] in Afghanistan."[20]

In his first years in office, Karzai not only strongly supported U.S. and NATO military efforts to root out the Radicals in his country; he actually urged the West to bring in *more* troops to finish the job.

Beginning in the winter of 2007 and continuing throughout the spring of 2008, terrorist attacks against the Karzai government and against innocent civilians spiked significantly. Karzai privately insisted to U.S. and NATO officials that a "surge" was needed in Afghanistan as it had been in Iraq. Only more troops could dramatically reduce violence in Kabul and the countryside and stabilize the government and society, he argued, while in the absence of more troops,

Afghanistan's future was in grave danger.

On June 13, 2008, Taliban forces underscored his point, pulling off a daring prison break in which scores of incredibly dangerous militants — including numerous would-be suicide bombers — were allowed to escape into the mountains. "Under the cover of darkness, nearly all of an estimated 1,150 prisoners, including some 400 Taliban inmates, fled from the jail," Reuters reported.[21]

By then, the Bush administration, the British, and other NATO countries had already been stepping up their efforts, but they noticeably accelerated after the jailbreak, increasing the number of foreign troops in Afghanistan from about forty thousand in 2007 to more than seventy thousand by the fall of 2008.[22]

Meanwhile, U.S.- and British-trained Afghan soldiers were defending their country as part of the Afghan National Army (ANA), a force that did not even exist before Karzai took office. Month by month, more Afghan troops graduated from the Kabul Military Training Center, preparing for the day that the country would have sufficiently trained and experienced forces to battle the Radicals without massive foreign assistance. At the same time, Karzai kept seeking to persuade countries from around the world to supply the Afghan forces, and such help was forthcoming. The Bulgarians provided mortars, ammunition, and binoculars. The Canadians provided small arms, ammunition, and other equipment. The Czechs provided helicopters. The Greeks provided tanks. The Romanians provided mobile kitchen trailers, while the Swiss have provided fire trucks, to name just a few examples of international assistance.[23]

When I visited Afghanistan in October of 2008, however, the big question was still whether the U.S. and NATO were doing enough to make Kabul and the rest of the country safe from the Taliban and from al Qaeda terrorists. Yes, much had been done. But many Afghanis told me the Taliban was regrouping, determined to unleash more chaos and carnage if the West did not do more to strengthen Karzai's hands.

Now, I have to say that when I was there, Kabul struck me as by far the most squalid and impoverished national capital I have ever visited — but not necessarily the most dangerous. Beggars were everywhere. Children covered with filth roamed the streets. Many destitute women wore suffocating blue burkas (despite the fact that it was over 95 degrees Fahrenheit) while carrying children and groceries, since they had no vehicles of their own. Most buildings were pockmarked with evidence of three decades of fighting, and many appeared to be in danger of collapsing. Nevertheless, my colleagues and I were able to travel around quite freely. We did not use an armored car. We did not wear flak jackets or helmets. The Afghanis who drove us and guided us from place to place had no weapons, and neither did we. Foreigners are not particularly encouraged to stroll about unaccompanied, as kidnappings by Taliban agents are still a concern. But there were no acts of terrorism in the five days we were on the ground. We never heard gunfire. We never heard explosions. And we never felt fear, despite the bloody history of the city.

Just days before my colleagues and I arrived, President Karzai and several Afghan governors and tribal leaders held a videoconference with President Bush and several senior U.S. diplomatic and military officials. Karzai briefed Bush on the latest evidence of progress. He specifically noted that the leaders of the Nangarhar province — located right on the border with Pakistan, in the heart of Taliban country — had over the past year successfully transformed itself from being the second biggest Afghan producer of poppy seeds for making opium and heroin to a province that was virtually drug free.[24]

Just days after we left, however, a Christian aid worker was murdered in Kabul by two members of the Taliban. Shortly after that, a suicide bomber shot his way into the entrance of a government building in the capital and blew himself up, killing five people and wounding twenty-one others. And that was just the beginning.

The hard truth is, the Taliban did not fold quickly or disappear into the night. Rather, in 2009 and 2010, they did regroup and then intensify their efforts to destroy Afghanistan's fledgling democracy and regain control of certain Afghan provinces. U.S., NATO, and Afghan forces increased their efforts to "clear, hold, and build" these areas — clear towns, villages, and provinces of Taliban and al Qaeda fighters; hold these areas and protect them from reinfiltration; and then invest significant funds to build schools, medical clinics, apartment buildings, and other sorely needed infrastructure. But it has not been as easy as many had hoped. Terrorist attacks against Afghan civilians — as well as attacks against U.S. and NATO forces — spiked in 2009 and 2010. Roadside bombings increased significantly. Suicide bombings began occurring every two or three days. Assassinations began averaging about one per day.

Upon taking office as president of the United States in January 2009, Barack Obama and his incoming national security team conducted a lengthy review of U.S. goals, objectives, and strategies in Afghanistan. By November of that year, Obama concluded that the Bush administration had been correct in putting more troops into the theater, but that it was still not enough. He ordered an additional thirty thousand American troops into Afghanistan to finish the job of stabilizing the country, bringing the total number of U.S. forces in the country to about one hundred thousand. This was wise.

The mistake President Obama and his team made, however, was saying publicly and repeatedly that they planned to begin withdrawing U.S. forces in 2011 and that they planned to have all or most U.S. forces out of Afghanistan by 2013. This artificial deadline for U.S. withdrawal sent precisely the wrong message to the Radicals, who concluded that the White House had no long-term stomach for the fight and that if the Taliban and al Qaeda could kill more civilians and more Americans in 2010 and beyond, they could eventually drive the U.S. and NATO out of Afghanistan and retake the country for themselves. I believe this artificial deadline also played a part in Karzai's stumbles.

Stumbling

In the first edition of this book, I noted, "Karzai is not a perfect leader. He should not be viewed as some kind of savior of, or panacea for, the Afghan nation. Honestly, only God knows whether he will survive in office, much less be reelected. But given the cards he has had to play with, there is no question in my mind that his first seven years running Afghanistan were remarkable. He has been a true Reformer swimming in a pool of Radical sharks and barracudas. For that, he deserves credit, and the American people have deserved the opportunity to get to know his views and accomplishments and just how dramatic his story has been."

I added, "Ultimately, the real test of his success will be whether Karzai can both create a stable, clean, accountable, and truly democratic national government and recruit, train, and inspire a new generation of democratic and corruption-free successors. If he allows himself to be seen as a one-man show — trying to solve Afghanistan's immense challenges essentially by himself — then a historic opportunity will be lost. But if he is able to recruit more tough, smart, ethical men and women to help him run the country, and if he can raise up more true Reformers who can establish and maintain security while simultaneously expanding freedom and democracy at home and abroad long after Karzai has retired or passed away from this earth, then he will earn his place as one of the truly remarkable game-changers of the twenty-first century. He started well. The question is, will he finish well?"

Unfortunately, Karzai made a series of unwise choices in recent years and has not lived up to his initial promise. For example, stories are rampant of his ignoring corruption throughout his government and not cracking down on it decisively. Among the most glaring examples: Karzai's half brother, Ahmad Wali Karzai, who is a wealthy businessman and the head of the Kandahar Provincial Council, is believed by some to be one of the country's biggest drug traffickers, allegedly overseeing huge heroin and opium distribution networks. It is a charge Ahmed has long denied, but the fact that President Karzai has done precious little to investigate his half brother — much less have him arrested or expelled from the country — has become symbolic in some Western capitals of the depth of the corruption problems plaguing the country and Karzai's inability or unwillingness to confront and change it.

The appearance of impropriety became so bad that upon President Obama's first official visit to Afghanistan as commander in chief in late-March 2010, he confronted Karzai directly and insisted that he tackle corruption as a top priority. The following day, Admiral Mike Mullen, chairman of the joint chiefs of staff, met with Karzai to reinforce the message that rooting out corruption was critical not only to the overall health of the country but to the effectiveness of the military campaign against the Radicals. Obama and Mullen were only the latest in a long line of U.S. officials to say the same thing, unfortunately to the same result. Nothing substantial changed in Karzai's behavior or that of his administration.

Also troubling was that as Obama's deadline for a full U.S. withdrawal from Afghanistan drew closer, Karzai began playing footsie with the leaders of Iran. In March 2010, not long before President Obama visited Kabul, Karzai invited Iranian president Mahmoud Ahmadinejad to Kabul for two days of talks and rolled out the red carpet for this high-profile and historic visit. At a press conference, Karzai heaped praise on Ahmadinejad, thanking Iran for investing in Afghan reconstruction projects and helping provide electricity. At the same press conference, Ahmadinejad gave a stridently anti-American speech while the Afghan president just stood there and smiled. Soon thereafter, Karzai traveled to Tehran to meet with Ahmadinejad again, as well as to celebrate the Afghan and Iranian New Year together.

Karzai first traveled to Tehran in 2005 to meet with the country's top leaders. At the time, it was perceived as a courtesy call from a new regional leader to another. By 2010, however, it was clear that Karzai was systematically strengthening ties with the anti-American regime, making numerous public statements calling Iran a "friend" as well as calling for closer ties between the two countries. Were Karzai and his government simply hedging their bets that when the U.S. is gone they might have to be nice to a very powerful (and possibly soon nuclear-armed) neighbor? Or were they using the U.S. and NATO to destroy their internal enemies while intentionally planning to join forces with Iran once the Western powers departed?

If all this were not disappointing enough, many U.N. and other Western observers accused Karzai of election fraud during his reelection campaign that culminated in the nationwide ballot on August 20, 2009. At first, Karzai claimed to have won 54 percent of the vote. Yet his challenger, Abdullah Abdullah, claimed Karzai's people were buying votes. Foreign election observers, reporters, and analysts corroborated Abdullah's claim, alleging as many as one million fraudulent votes. Some publicly accusing the Afghan president of trying to steal the election. Karzai himself eventually conceded there were irregularities but still claimed victory and took office for another five years. He did initially allow an independent panel to be created to investigate the serious and substantial charges of election fraud. But in February 2010, he effectively took over the panel and stripped it of its authority.

"Afghanistan's president has taken control of a formerly independent body that monitors election fraud, raising concern Tuesday that he's reneging on promises to clean up corruption and cronyism — a pillar of the Obama administration's plan to erode support for the Taliban," reported the *Washington Times*. "President Hamid Karzai signed a decree last week giving him the power to appoint all members of the Electoral Complaints Commission, a group previously dominated by U.N. appointees that uncovered massive fraud on behalf of Mr. Karzai in last year's presidential election. 'This is bad news for democracy,' said Gerard Russell, a former U.N. political adviser who resigned over disputes surrounding the August presidential election. 'Basically, if President Karzai wishes it, this could prevent free elections ever being held in Afghanistan.' "[25]

The Obama administration did little to protest Karzai's seizure of the election or the election fraud panel, effectively allowing Karzai to stay in power without serious opposition. This disappointed many who were hoping and praying for much better in Afghanistan, myself included.

"Karzai brazenly stole last year's presidential election," charged *New York Times* columnist Thomas L. Friedman. "But the Obama foreign policy team turned a blind eye, basically saying, he's the best we could get, so just let it go."[26]

Sadly, Friedman was right.

The question is: Why did Karzai make such choices? Did U.S. and Western leaders misread him from the beginning? Was he always an opportunist, not a true Reformer? Or did he begin to cut corners and cut deals with internal Afghan players and with Tehran as he anticipated the U.S. and NATO pulling out too fast?

Many more chapters are yet to be written in the Afghan saga, and my prayers are with the people of this blood-soaked, war-torn, poverty-stricken land. Suffice it to say at this point, Karzai began his presidency with real promise as a Reformer but became a disappointment. Maybe he can turn it around. Maybe his successors can. But one thing we must all keep in mind: being a Reformer isn't easy, especially in such rough neighborhoods as the Middle East and central Asia.

CHAPTER NINETEEN: "WE ARE FIGHTING ISLAMIC FASCISTS"

Nouri Al-Maliki and the battle for Iraq

My phone rang late on a Tuesday.

"Hey, Joel, what are you doing tomorrow?"

I recognized the voice immediately as a senior aide to U.S. House Speaker Denny Hastert.

"Not much. Why?" I asked.

"Want to come over and hear Maliki's speech?"

I certainly did. Three years after liberation, Nouri al-Maliki, the first democratically and constitutionally elected prime minister in the five-thousand-year history of Iraq, was coming to Washington to address a joint meeting of Congress the following day, July 26, 2006. Everyone in town wanted to hear this speech.

Maliki was a controversial figure, and a lot was riding on him. A Shia Muslim born in 1950, he had fled into exile in Iran and later Syria after Saddam Hussein ordered his execution in 1980, returning to Iraq only after liberation in 2003. This was causing not a few in Washington and European capitals to openly express suspicions about his core beliefs and independence. Was the somewhat shy, bespectacled one-time dissident a true democratic Reformer? Or was he an ideological ally — if not an actual agent — of Tehran and Damascus? With no track record of ever governing, could he become a serious game-changer, capable of both confronting and crushing the Radicals, such as Moqtada al-Sadr, head of the Iranian-funded, -supplied, and -encouraged Mahdi Army, the worst of the Shia militias? Or was he merely some sort of Bush-administration puppet, a figurehead whose mission was to appease Iraqi Shias while allowing the Pentagon and State Department to actually run the show?

Maliki had been elected by the parliament just three months before and had seemed to struggle to form a cabinet, not succeeding until late May. But to his credit, since then he and his team had seized the initiative. On June 7, U.S. and Iraqi intelligence forces tracked down and killed Abu Musab al-Zarqawi, the head of "Al Qaeda in Iraq" (AQI), and several of Zarqawi's top advisors, in a dramatically successful evening air strike that instantly electrified Reformers and the Rank-and-File alike as news spread throughout the country.

The Jordanian-born Zarqawi was, after all, the most feared man in Iraq at the time. A fully devoted follower of jihad, he had direct and personal ties to Osama bin Laden, and he had been in regular communication with the al Qaeda mastermind and his top deputies. He seemed to have plenty of funding and arms. He controlled thousands of indigenous and foreign-born fighters whose mission was to maim, kill, and destroy scores of Iraqi civilians in the hopes of turning them against Maliki's fledgling government and the very notion of democracy. And up until 6:11 p.m. that night, he had seemed invincible.

"We have declared a fierce war on this evil

principle of democracy and those who follow this wrong ideology," Zarqawi had said just before the first round of Iraqi elections in January 2005. "Anyone who tries to help set up this system is part of it." He called Iraqi parliamentary candidates "demi-idols" and denounced Iraqi voters as "infidels," pledging to kill as many of them as he possibly could.[1]

After the successful operation to take out Zarqawi, Maliki immediately held a press conference that was seen in homes throughout Iraq. "Today Zarqawi was defeated," Maliki had said, the relief palpable in his eyes and voice. "This is a message to all those who use violence, killing, and devastation to disrupt life in Iraq, to rethink within themselves before it is too late."[2] What is more, he added that those Iraqi citizens who had provided tips that led to the successful strike would, in fact, be eligible to receive the $25 million bounty that Coalition forces had put on Zarqawi's head, clearly trying to encourage more tips to the secure and anonymous telephone hotline that the U.S. and Iraqi authorities had established.

"The death of Abu Musab al-Zarqawi marks a great success for Iraq and the Global War on Terror. . . . I congratulate the Prime Minister," said Zalmay Khalilzad, the U.S. ambassador to Iraq at the time, standing at Maliki's side at the press conference. "Zarqawi was 'the Godfather' of sectarian killing and terror in Iraq. He declared a civil war within Islam and a global war of civilizations. His organization has been responsible for the deaths of thousands of civilians in Iraq and abroad." He added that while the terrorist leader's death would not "by itself end the violence," it was still "an important step in the right direction" and "a good omen for Iraq [and] for Prime Minister Maliki's new government."[3]

Moments later, President Bush stepped into the White House Rose Garden to praise the Maliki government, saying, "The ideology of terror has lost one of its most visible and aggressive leaders."[4]

The Zarqawi hit, however, was just the beginning. In the week that followed, Iraqi and U.S. forces conducted 452 raids (including 143 raids by Iraqi forces alone), captured 759 suspects, and killed 104 terrorists, based in part on intelligence gathered from the house the al Qaeda leader had been in when he was killed and in part on tips that began flowing in after Maliki's press conference.[5]

The prime minister's national security advisor noted that Coalition forces had uncovered a "huge treasure . . . a huge amount of information" from Zarqawi's computer, flash drive, and cell phone. "Now we have the upper hand," he said after the raids were complete. "We know their locations, the names of their leaders, their whereabouts, their movements, through the documents we have found in the last few days."[6]

Maliki then called on Radicals to give up violence and enter the political system. "There is," he said, "space for dialogue with insurgents who opposed the political process and now want to join the political process after offering guarantees" that they would fully renounce all use of violence. But he added that "we are not going to negotiate with the criminals who have killed the innocent."[7]

Though he was facing enormous challenges and worldwide questions about whether he was up to the task of governing Iraq, Maliki was at least able to come to Washington with a major success under his belt.

"We Are Building the New Iraq"

A hush settled over the great assembly.

The members of the House of Representatives and the Senate were now seated, as were members of the administration, the diplomatic community, and a full press contingent. Prime Minister Maliki cleared his throat and prepared to speak.

As he did, I said a silent prayer of thanksgiving that the Lord had given me the opportunity to be in the room for this historic moment. Thousands of Americans and allied forces had died to set Iraqis free and make this moment possible. Thousands more Americans and Coalition members had been wounded both in the 2003 war and in Operation Desert Storm in 1991, when we had helped liberate Kuwait from Iraqi tyranny.

I remembered a bitterly cold Saturday morning fifteen years earlier — January 12, 1991, to be exact — when I had had the privilege of sitting in this same chamber, in this same visitors' section. At the time, I was watching members of Congress debate whether or not to give President George H. W. Bush ("Bush 41") the authority to go to war against Iraq. It was a bitter and often brutal argument. The country and its democratically elected leaders were sharply divided as to whether to say yes to a war that would involve nearly a half million American soldiers, sailors, airmen, and Marines in a battle against the forces of Saddam Hussein, who controlled the fourth-largest army in the world.

But shouldn't it be so? I thought. *Going to war is*

a horrible act, even if sometimes it is necessary. It deserves a vigorous, full-throated, and very public debate, even if that debate is messy.

Messy it was. Passions ran as high as I had ever seen in this town. And then sometime late in the afternoon, I watched as the members of the House cast their ballots. By a margin of 250 to 183, President Bush got the authorization he requested, along with an even closer 52–47 Senate vote in favor of going to war.

Now, fifteen and a half years later, something I never imagined possible was unfolding before my very eyes. An Iraqi citizen who had been chosen by the democratically elected representatives of a free Iraq to be their prime minister was actually standing at the podium where great presidents and prime ministers throughout the last two centuries had stood before. I could barely believe it.

Nouri al-Maliki was a virtually unknown figure to most Americans, as he was to most people around the world. Yet now not only my eyes but the eyes of many nations were upon him. He represented our hopes and dreams for liberty and a more peaceful and secure relationship with the people of the epicenter. How would he fare? Was he up to the challenge? Only time would tell. But Maliki could not have arrived at a better moment. He and his team were on offense. They were making real and tangible progress. Tough times lay ahead, but the prime minister was on a victory lap, and he had earned it.

"In the name of God, the most gracious, the most merciful, Your Excellency, the Speaker of the House, Mr. Vice President, honorable ladies and gentlemen, members of Congress, it is with great pleasure that I am able to take this opportunity to be the first democratically and constitutionally elected prime minister of Iraq to address you, the elected representatives of the American people. And I thank you for affording me this unique chance to speak at this respected assembly. Let me begin by thanking the American people through you, on behalf of the Iraqi people, for supporting our people and ousting [Saddam Hussein's] dictatorship. Iraq will not forget those who stood with her and who continue to stand with her in times of need."

The room — virtually silent to that moment — erupted with sustained applause.

"Thank you," he eventually continued, "for your continued resolve in helping us fight the terrorists plaguing Iraq, which is a struggle to defend our nation's democracy and our people who aspire to liberty, democracy, human rights, and the rule of law. All of those are not Western values; they are universal values for humanity."

Again, the applause was deafening.

"I know that some of you here question whether Iraq is part of the war on terror," Maliki noted deeper into the address. "Let me be very clear: This is a battle between true Islam, for which a person's liberty and rights constitute essential cornerstones, and terrorism, which wraps itself in a fake Islamic cloak; in reality, terrorists are waging a war on Islam and Muslims and values and spread[ing] hatred between humanity. . . . The truth is that terrorism has no religion."

Maliki was making a point central to the Reformers: that Islam is a religion of peace, and that it had been hijacked by the Radicals.

"It is your duty and our duty to defeat this ter-

411

ror," the prime minister went on to say. "Iraq is the front line in this struggle, and history will prove that the sacrifices of Iraqis for freedom will not be in vain. Iraqis are your allies in the war on terror. . . . The fate of our country and yours is tied. Should democracy be allowed to fail in Iraq and terror permitted to triumph, then the war on terror will never be won elsewhere. Mr. Speaker, we are building the new Iraq on the foundation of democracy and are erecting it through our belief in the rights of every individual . . . so that future Iraqi generations can live in peace, prosperity, and hope. Iraqis have tasted freedom, and we will defend it absolutely. . . . Our people . . . defied the terrorists every time they were called upon to make a choice, by risking their lives for the ballot box. They have stated over and over again, with their ink-stained fingers waving in pride, that they will always make the same choice."

Suddenly, a protestor in the visitors' gallery jumped up and shouted, "Iraqis want the troops to leave! Bring them home now! Iraqis want the troops to leave! Bring them home now!"

The protestor was promptly removed from the chamber by security, and Maliki continued, directly challenging the notion that Iraqis wanted the American forces to leave soon, much less "now."

"Let there be no doubt," he insisted. "Today, Iraq is a democracy which stands firm because of the sacrifices of its people and the sacrifices of all those who stood with us in this crisis from nations and countries. And that's why — thank you — I would like to thank them very much for all their sacrifices. . . . The journey has been perilous, and the future is not guaranteed. Many around the world underestimated the resolve of Iraq's people and were sure that we would never reach this stage. Few believed in us. But you, the American people, did, and we are grateful for this."

I was suddenly on my feet, applauding the prime minister, as was everyone else in the room. It was a deeply emotional moment for me, and it was then that I realized how much it meant to me, and to many Americans, to be thanked by an Iraqi leader, on behalf of the Iraqi people, for what we had done for them.

And the prime minister was right. Many world leaders had not been willing to help liberate Iraq from tyranny. Indeed, many American political leaders in that very room had refused to help the Reformers in their epic struggle against the Resisters and the Radicals. But it had worked. It had not been easy. Much more sacrifice would be necessary. But tremendous progress was being made, and someone had had the decency to say thanks.

"I will not allow Iraq to become a launch pad for al Qaeda and other terrorist organizations," the prime minister insisted, to more well-deserved applause. "I will not allow terror to rob Iraqis of their hopes and dreams. I will not allow terrorists to dictate to us our future."

He closed by stating his heartfelt belief that Iraq and America "need each other to defeat the terror engulfing the free world," promising that Iraq, with America's help, would in time become "the graveyard for terrorism and terrorists for the good of all humanity."

After all, he said, the truth is that "God has made us free."

Maliki Vs. Clinton

Was it all just a show?

Numerous Washington critics said it was, that Prime Minister Maliki was no real Reformer and was just telling his country's chief financiers — Congress and the American people — what they wanted to hear while avoiding other important topics.

Democratic Party chairman Howard Dean accused Maliki of being an "anti-Semite" for failing to denounce Hezbollah by name in his speech or in private discussions on Capitol Hill because of the Lebanese terrorist group's repeated attacks against Israel.[8]

Senator Chuck Schumer, the New York Democrat, also sharply criticized Maliki for not singling out Hezbollah in his speech or in subsequent Hill meetings, as did Senator Richard J. Durbin, the Illinois Democrat, though the prime minister repeatedly denounced "terrorist" groups throughout the region.[9]

Senate Armed Services Committee chairman Carl Levin, the Michigan Democrat, became a particularly harsh critic following that speech, as did Senator Hillary Clinton of New York. Indeed, by the following summer, both were calling on the Iraqi parliament to dump Maliki in favor of someone more favorable to their political views and style.

"During his trip to Iraq last week, Senator Levin . . . confirmed that the Iraqi Government's failures have reinforced the widely held view that the Maliki government is nonfunctional and cannot produce a political settlement, because it is too beholden to religious and sectarian leaders," Senator Clinton said in a statement her office is-

414

sued on August 22, 2007. "I share Senator Levin's hope that the Iraqi Parliament will replace Prime Minister Maliki with a less divisive and more unifying figure when it returns in a few weeks."[10]

It was an extraordinary development. Here were two high-profile Americans interfering directly in the internal politics of a friendly democracy by calling for a democratically elected prime minister to be deposed because they didn't like his approach. Some speculated their real beef was that Maliki had strongly supported the Bush-McCain "surge" initiative to put more U.S. military forces into Iraq to help crush the insurgency, when both Senators Clinton and Levin had vehemently opposed the surge. Senator Clinton had said at the time, "Our best hope of fostering political progress in Iraq is to begin the immediate withdrawal of U.S. troops."[11]

This infuriated many senior Iraqi officials desperately trying to keep their country together, including Maliki, who feared a precipitous withdrawal of American forces could cause the nation to plunge into a full-blown civil war and destroy all the democratic gains they had made thus far.

Maliki wasted no time in punching back. "There are American officials who consider Iraq as if it were one of their villages, for example Hillary Clinton and Carl Levin," Maliki told Iraqi as well as American journalists. "This is severe interference in our domestic affairs. Carl Levin and Hillary Clinton are from the Democratic Party and they must demonstrate democracy."[12] He went on to urge Clinton and her colleagues to "come to their senses" and "respect democracy" and the will of the Iraqi people. What was more, he noted that "leaders like Hillary Clinton and Carl Levin have not experienced in their political lives the kind of differences we have in Iraq" and "when they give their judgment they have no knowledge of what reconciliation means."[13]

While the jury is still out on how successful Maliki will be as a Reformer, I must confess that, some of my own concerns about the prime minister's political toughness and savvy notwithstanding, in my mind Maliki's stock went up significantly that day. He had pushed back hard at two Washington masters of political deadlock and partisan bickering for having the audacity to criticize his difficulties in bringing about unity and political progress in Baghdad, of all places, when the U.S. Senate was getting so little done in its own backyard.

A True Hero of the Revolution

A few hours after Maliki's speech, my cell phone rang again.

It was a Jewish acquaintance of mine whom I had met in Israel. She had someone with her she thought I should meet.

"He's a member of the prime minister's delegation and helped write the speech," she explained. "He's also the only member of the Iraqi parliament who has ever been to Israel. I told him about you and your books and your interest in the future of his country. He would like to meet you, if you have some time."

I didn't, actually, but I made some.

Mithal al-Alusi and I met for breakfast the next morning at the Willard InterContinental hotel, just across the street from the White House. As a gift, I brought him a copy of my latest novel, *The*

416

Copper Scroll, which had just been released. He scanned the back cover, which read, in part, *"Saddam Hussein is gone. Yasser Arafat is dead. A new Iraq is rising. But so, too, is a new evil, and now White House advisors Jon Bennett and Erin McCoy find themselves facing a terrifying new threat triggered by an ancient mystery."*

He asked me questions about why my novels had such an uncanny track record of seeming to come true. I briefly shared with him the biblical prophecies upon which they were based, including the prophecies in the books of Daniel, Jeremiah, Isaiah, and Revelation that indicated Iraq would one day become the wealthiest, most peaceful and powerful nation on the face of the planet. Such prophecies intrigued him, particularly given the fact that as a Sunni Muslim, he had never heard of them before.

We turned to discussing the prime minister's speech. Alusi did not take credit for it, saying only that he had helped review and edit the speech with the prime minister. I suspect he was just being modest. But he did say that he believed strongly — as did I — that the address to Congress had gone well and had effectively communicated the vision of the new Iraqi leadership.

"I've written about such speeches for the fictional leader of Iraq in my novels," I told him. "But honestly, I'm not sure I ever had enough faith to believe I would see and hear one like that delivered by an actual Iraqi leader."

In the course of our morning together, and in tracking his career ever since, I have come to believe that Mithal al-Alusi is a true hero of the Revolution, a genuine Jeffersonian democratic Reformer who has pledged his life to build a new, free, and stable Iraq.

Born in 1953, Alusi was just twenty-six years old when Saddam Hussein and the Ayatollah Khomeini rose to power in Iraq and Iran, respectively. He knows firsthand what it feels like to live in a Republic of Fear. But now he has breathed free air, and he refuses to let it ever again be taken from him or his people. This is why he founded the Democratic Party of the Iraqi Nation with a fiercely liberal platform calling for free elections, free speech, freedom of worship, freedom of assembly, and other Jeffersonian ideals. And he is not just the first but, as of this writing, still the only Iraqi member of parliament ever to have visited Israel. This is a distinction in which he takes great pride, but it is also one for which he has paid a terrible price.

In September of 2004, Alusi was invited to speak at a conference in Herzliya, an Israeli city on the Mediterranean coastline just north of Tel Aviv, on how to fight radical Islamic terrorists. Despite objections by friends and colleagues who feared for his safety if the Radicals in Iraq learned about his trip, Alusi accepted, convinced that Iran — not Israel — was the real threat to the security of Iraq and the region. The trip went well. Alusi was warmly welcomed, and he met people he felt were ideological kindred spirits on many levels. He returned to Iraq after a few days feeling affirmed in his conviction that Iraq needed to build a quiet but strong relationship with the Israelis.

But on February 8, 2005, tragedy struck. Islamic extremists tried to assassinate Alusi for his prodemocracy views and his visit to Israel. Radicals ambushed his car in Baghdad. In the firefight that ensued, they murdered both of Alusi's sons —

Ayman, twenty-nine, and Jamal, twenty-two. They also murdered Haidar, his bodyguard. Alusi himself was shot multiple times and lost part of one of his thumbs, but miraculously he survived the attack.

"Again, the ghosts of death are going out," Alusi told Radio Free Iraq just hours after emerging from the bloody scene. "They are ready to kill a person, ready to kill the peace, ready to kill the victory of Iraqis and their right to life. Again, henchmen of the Ba'ath [Party] and dirty terrorist gangs, al Qaeda and others, are going out convinced that they can determine life and death as they desire. Iraq will not die. My children . . . died as heroes, no differently from other people who find their heroic deaths. But we will not, by God, hand Iraq over to murderers and terrorists. . . . As for the advocates of religious intolerance willing to kill . . . I tell them, 'Brothers, verily you have made a grave mistake.' I tell them, 'There can be no state in Iraq except for one founded on [democratic] institutions and [the rule of] law.' "[14]

In September 2005, Alusi was invited back to the Israeli counterterrorism conference, and remarkably, he accepted the invitation again.

"Why?" I asked him.

"Nobody can stop me," he said firmly. "I am not playing a game, my friend. I believe in my goals. To be a democrat doesn't just mean to go to the elections. To be a democrat, you have to have principles, and you have to be strong in them. For the majority of Iraqis, they believe Iran is the biggest threat in the region, not Israel. I agree with them. And I believe we must work together with the Israelis. I want peace with the

419

Israelis. I want peace with everybody — except the terrorists. There should be no peace with them."

The Anbar Awakening

In August 2008, I called Alusi to catch up.

So much had happened during the two years since I'd last spoken with him. Iraqi sectarian violence was way down. The threat of Iranian violence in the region was way up. The "surge" had worked. The government led by President Jalal Talabani and Prime Minister Maliki had not only lasted but seemed to be succeeding in a way that few had predicted.

But I wanted to understand it all from his unique vantage point, as a Sunni Muslim in a Shia-majority government, living in the heart of Baghdad, at the center of the battle between Radicals and Reformers.

"Are you feeling optimistic, my friend?" I asked as we began an hour-long call.

"I am," he said. "We are trying to find our way forward. We are trying to make progress, to give people a better life. We didn't succeed through the last eighty years. But I do believe we have the capacity to become a true democracy in the heart of the Middle East. We are willing. And we have the need — it's not just for fun — to play the role of free people in a clearly extremist atmosphere of Iran, al Qaeda, Hezbollah, the Mahdi Army, and others. The key is Baghdad. If Baghdad is strong and secure, we will have peace. If Baghdad is lost, all is lost."[15]

I asked him to tell me about the success of the "Anbar Awakening" during the summer and fall of 2006, in which hundreds of thousands of Sunnis in the Anbar Province in the western half of Iraq, along the Syrian and Jordanian border — once closely allied with Al Qaeda in Iraq (AQI) — chose to turn against AQI, turn in the terrorists to local and national authorities, and join the political progress. It was a remarkable development, and Alusi had been right in the middle of it.

"I'm secular, from a Sunni background, from Anbar, which is the biggest province in Iraq," he explained. "My people in Anbar, they were the real basis for Al Qaeda in Iraq. The religious fanatics there hate democracy. This was the real stronghold for the Sunni extremists. But the Anbar people understood after a while how dangerous Al Qaeda in Iraq really is. They saw the violence. They were horrified. It was Muslims killing other Muslims in the name of Islam that turned people's minds and hearts against al Qaeda."

I was familiar with some of the horrors Alusi was referring to. At one point in 2006, AQI forces murdered and then publicly burned the body of a Sunni cleric in Anbar who was encouraging people in his town to turn terrorists in to the local police. Iraqi Sunnis who had been strong supporters or at least sympathetic to AQI were horrified and began accelerating their assistance to the police. Prime Minister Maliki then visited Ramadi, a city of about four hundred thousand Sunnis in the heart of the Anbar Province, to call on the people to turn against AQI. To stop Maliki — remember, a Shia Muslim — and those listening to him, AQI began using chemical weapons in Anbar — notably bombs filled with chlorine gas — in the first half of 2007, trying to massacre Iraqi Sunni Muslim civilians and send a message that Sunni collaboration with the federal Iraqi government instead of with the Radicals would not be tolerated. But this only further inflamed Anbar residents against AQI and awakened more Sunnis to the urgent need to turn against AQI leaders and operatives for the sake of their own lives and those of their children and grand-children.[16]

More Iraqi and Coalition forces also moved into Anbar Province, hunting down key Radicals. And Maliki and other Shia leaders continued working with local Sunni tribal chiefs and community leaders, drawing them into the federal political process and showing them they really could have a voice and a significant role in the future of the country.

"What happened in Anbar means that now we have Iraqi experience to deal with a huge area that is controlled by al Qaeda and how to help turn people against the extremists and move in the direction of freedom and security," Alusi noted.

At the same time, he said, "the extremists were also trying to turn Sunnis against Shias and Shias against Sunnis. But you have to understand that in Iraq, there are no pure Sunni or pure Shia families. Everyone here is mixed. Some have a Shia father but a Sunni mother, or vice versa. Or you have a Sunni cousin or a Shia uncle, or whatever. So it's hard to divide people who are already so mixed and interwoven."

Standing Against Iran

I asked Alusi why Iraqi Shias aren't building an alliance with Iranian Shias to take over Iraq and drive out all Western influences, as so many have feared might happen.

"You have to understand, Joel, that Imam Ali [Grand Ayatollah Alial-Sistani] — the leader of the Shias in Iraq — is the father of liberal peace in Iraq. He is the head of the liberals. He's a force of moderation and democracy in Iraq. He tells people, 'Everybody has the right to think for themselves and come up with something new.' "

Alusi was absolutely right. Ayatollah al-Sistani has been a remarkable — and largely unexpected — voice of moderation and tolerance in Iraq. When U.S. forces were preparing to liberate his country in March 2003, Sistani told Shia Muslims — some 60 percent of the Iraqi population — to welcome, not oppose, them. When the time came to put together an interim government, Sistani encouraged full Shia participation. As the date approached for Iraqi elections, again Sistani encouraged full Shia participation. When sectarian violence by the Sunni-driven AQI was intensifying in the fall of 2004, Sistani called on Shia militias not to respond in kind. "Please be civilized," he said. "We don't want to start a civil war. This is the most important point."[17]

Sistani has not always been successful at keeping the Shia peaceful — restraining Moqtada al-Sadr, the fanatical leader of the Shia-driven Mahdi Army, from 2005 through 2007 was particularly difficult — but he has continued to try. Moreover, he has curiously but thankfully not been a voice of anti-Americanism, unlike his contemporaries in Iran. He does not evoke chants of "Death to America!" and "Death to Israel!" as the Ayatollah Khamenei does in Tehran. He does not want to be seen as being too cozy with the Americans, but to his credit, he certainly has not stirred Shia sentiment against U.S. leaders or the military.

"Iraqi Shia theology is peaceful here," Alusi noted. "They don't teach in Iran what Imam Ali is teaching here."

"But why is that?" I asked. "Isn't that counter-intuitive? Didn't we all think that Iran would be able to leverage Sistani against us, and against the rising Reformers in Baghdad?"

Alusi readily conceded that the Iranians have been able to enlist many Iraqi Shias into their cause. But by the grace of God, they have not been able to co-opt the entire movement or its leaders.

"The Shia here are open-minded, and they are Iraqis, not Iranians," he told me. "They are smart, and not stupid. They are human beings, and not killers. This is the space that we need to build on. The Shias are turning against Moqtada al Sadr. No one can control Moqtada if the Shia support him. But the Shia don't support the extremist ways. This means there is great hope for my country."

"Fair enough," I agreed. "But overall, how serious is the Iranian threat to the region and the world?"

"Iran is an exceptional problem," Alusi said categorically. "We are feeling that. The regime in Iran are fascists. They are trying to have crazy fascist propaganda to control the Shia people of Iraq. We believe they are trying to use Iraq as a tool to accomplish their goals. Iraq, Israel, and the United States have to stand against Iran. We have to work together. We are facing the same enemy, and we need each other. If Iran can destroy democracy here in Iraq, they will attack other countries — Turkey in the north, the Gulf states in the south, Jordan, and others. Iran is very smart to attack Iraq and not other countries. If they can win in Iraq, they will be able to control other countries too. Iran wants to build a Shia arc that starts with southern Iraq, goes into Syria, into Lebanon, and right to the borders of Israel. Iraq is the central player in stopping that."

"Do you believe Iran is trying to acquire nuclear weapons?"

"Yes, of course. We know this. Can they get an atomic bomb soon? Yes, I believe they can. But they need to test it, otherwise they won't be sure if it will work or not. But if they test it, the international community will wake up to the threat. So Iran is trying to use time to play games so they can build an atomic bomb. They will never test it until they have more that are ready to be used — five, six, seven, or eight. You have to realize, Joel, that all of the international intelligence agencies are worried that al Qaeda is trying to build an atomic bomb. The knowledge is out there. It's not hard to get. The problem is to have the uranium to actually make the bomb. What if Iran gets that uranium? What if they help al Qaeda build atomic bombs? What then?"

"What should we do about Iran?" I asked.

"If we want to stop them, we have to attack them," he replied without a pause. "Then we will have a major war. . . . I'm so upset to hear from some generals that 'We can't do it. We can't stop Iran. It would be too hard.' But we must do it. We don't have any other choice. It would actually be a short operation to stop the danger. Iran is not as strong as everyone thinks. Right now, they don't even have the Bomb yet, but they are taking everyone hostage. 'If you try to stop us,' they say, 'we will send terrorists to attack you. If you stop us, we will bomb your oil fields. If you stop us, we will set the region on fire.' They keep making threats, and no one in the free world is taking action. Now, imagine if they have the atomic bomb, how shall we ever stop them from their evil goals? The world should stop them. America should stop them, and Iraq should help, because there is no other alternative. Other politicians may not be able to say it yet, but who cares? It has to be done."

"How much time does the West and Iraq have to stop Iran before it is too late?"

"The Iranians have a time schedule," Alusi said. "I don't know what it is. They are playing a game. They are working full-time to get atomic bombs. From my point of view, they need one year at most. They are determined to get to their goal."

The Iraqi Model?

On September 10, 2008, Alusi returned to Israel. It was his third visit but his first as an actual member of Parliament. During his speech, he called for greater cooperation between Baghdad and Jerusalem. But when he got back to Iraq, he found himself facing a firestorm. Some MPs demanded he be arrested for traveling to an "enemy" state. Others demanded he be stripped of his parliamentary privileges and banned from the parliament building. Alusi received numerous death threats and could not travel for fear of being assassinated.

"Was it worth it to visit Israel not just once but three times?" I asked.

"Did you see President Talabani shaking hands with the Israeli defense minister [Ehud Barak] last month?" he asked in response. "If I had not gone, would that have happened? We are breaking the taboos, and they don't exist anymore. I will pay any price to keep Iraq safe and create a free society."

"Do you advocate a formal peace treaty with Israel at present?"

"Look, we Iraqis have respect for the Jewish people," he said. "There are more than three hundred thousand Israelis who were born in Iraq. But we are also politicians. We are trying to build a state, and we have to be careful. . . . So we don't want to move too far, too fast. . . . We need each other. We have tools that the Israelis need. They have tools we need. Staying alone we will be weak. Working together is very important, but a formal relationship is difficult right now."

This man is not only brave, I thought; *he is also quite shrewd.*

I had one more question for him.

"If Iraq gets it right," I asked, "if it can truly become a healthy, secure, fully functioning democracy, what kind of impact will this have on the rest of the region?"

"I am trying to learn from the international community how to build an Iraqi democracy," he replied. "If we succeed in Iraq, we — not as individuals, but as a whole, as an emerging democracy — we will have great influence on the whole region. Look at what has already happened since Iraq became free. Kuwait now allows women to be elected. There were elections in Bahrain. In the Emirates, they are trying small experiments with giving people more say in their governments. The Saudis, too. In Egypt, President Mubarak is having clear difficulties trying to install his son to succeed him. We are grateful to the American people for helping us become a free people. But it

427

is not that you are exporting Thomas Jefferson to us. It's not exporting. You cannot force people to embrace liberty and democracy. But if they want it, they will accept it and embrace it. And Iraqis, we want democracy. We want freedom. This is coming from our hearts and our souls. We are fighting Islamic fascists who want to rule our lives. But we want to be free, and I am very hopeful about how things are going."

CHAPTER TWENTY:
MEET JALAL TALABANI

The inside story of the first democratically elected president of Iraq

Few Reformers have intrigued or impressed me like Jalal Talabani. The first democratically and constitutionally elected president of Iraq, he is trying to govern a country devoid of any tradition of representative government in more than five thousand years of recorded history.

He is a Kurd in a nation where Kurds make up only about 15 percent of the population. And he is trying to govern a nation of Arabs, who make up some 80 percent of the population and have long ridiculed, hated, and even massacred the Kurds.*

He is a Sunni in a nation where Sunnis comprise only about 35 percent of the population. And he is trying to govern a nation of Shias, who comprise about 60 percent of the population.**

He is a Muslim, yet no national political leader

*Assyrians, Turkomans, and other minorities make up the other 5 percent.
**Christians, Zoroastrians, and other religious minorities make up the other 5 percent.

in Iraq has done more to protect Iraqi Christians from both Sunni and Shia Radicals. Nor has any Iraqi leader besides Mithal al-Alusi been so friendly to Jews and particularly to Israelis. It was Talabani who shook the hand of Israeli defense minister Ehud Barak at a conference they both attended in Athens in July of 2008, sparking calls for his resignation from some members of the Iraqi parliament.[1]

It was also Talabani who said in November of 2007 that Israeli president Shimon Peres was "an individual welcome in Iraqi Kurdistan" because Peres had long supported "the establishment of an independent Kurdish state or independent federal region for the Kurds in the north of Iraq."[2]

Looking closer, one finds that Talabani is a former guerrilla leader, yet he is trying to persuade Iraqis to give up sectarian violence as a political tool. He made his name as a Kurdish separatist, yet he is trying to persuade his nation to stick together, create a federal republic, and embrace national unity. He is the founder of a Socialist political party — the Patriotic Union of Kurdistan — yet since the early 1990s he has helped create a real, functioning market economy in the Iraqi Kurdish republics.

What's more, today he supports Iraq's flat tax, is doing what he can to attract more foreign direct investment into the country, is committed to U.S.- and British-style democracy, and is trying persuade his fellow Iraqis to embrace market economics and Jeffersonian democracy.

And if all that were not enough, Talabani is in his seventies, yet he is trying to govern a country where the average age is just twenty and nearly four in ten citizens are under the age of fifteen.

The task has been daunting, to say the least. Yet against all odds, it is now clear that Talabani has played a critical role in helping create a new Iraq that is increasingly peaceful and prosperous.

By the fall of 2008 an estimated 90 percent of Iraqi territory was considered safe for travel without much fear of kidnapping, assassination, or terrorist attack. Violence in Baghdad was down some 80 percent from its worst months in 2006. More than 70 percent of combat operations were being led by Iraqi military and security forces, with U.S. assistance, and Iraqi forces were increasingly battle-tested and successful, killing and capturing jihadists in impressive numbers. Iraqi civilians throughout the country were becoming so disgusted by Muslim-on-Muslim violence they were turning against the jihadist leaders, calling the tip lines and helping U.S. and Iraqi forces capture key leaders and huge caches of weapons.

As violence dropped, Iraq's economy began accelerating. Oil production and exports increased. Scores of foreign companies began arriving. Tens of thousands of Iraqis created their own small businesses. New jobs were created. Housing prices rose. New construction began. Cranes were everywhere, particularly in the north, as new high-rise office buildings and apartments were springing up. By the end of 2008, the Iraqi economy was doing so well that the government actually wound up with a budget surplus of about $80 billion, tangible evidence that the country was finally moving in the right direction.[3]

There is far more to be done, to be sure. Iraq is by no means out of the woods. But though it is seldom reported in the Western press, many good things have occurred in Iraq since Talabani came

431

to power. The question is, why?

The Rise of "Mam Jalal"

Who is Jalal Talabani? Where did he come from? Where does he want to take Iraq?

To understand the Iraqi president's remarkable rise to power and the vision he has for his country, several colleagues and I took the opportunity to travel to Iraq twice in 2008, once in February and again in late September. We traveled extensively throughout the Kurdish provinces where Talabani made his name, talking to people who have followed his career for decades and affectionately call him "Mam Jalal," or "Uncle Jalal." We visited the town where he was born and saw the home he still owns and visits along the shores of Lake Dukan, not far from the border of Iran. We interviewed several of his senior advisors. We also interviewed a number of U.S. diplomatic and military officials in Iraq and Washington who have known Talabani over the years.

Here is what we learned.

Talabani was born on November 12, 1933, during a time of tumultuous political change in Iraq. Just one year earlier, Iraq had gained its independence from British control after being carved out of the Ottoman Empire as a modern country by the League of Nations on November 11, 1920.

As a child, Talabani was raised in the village of Koya, near Lake Dukan, in the heart of Iraqi Kurdistan. Koya is surrounded by beautiful countryside whose geography reminded me of New Mexico or Arizona in the American Southwest — rugged mountains, arid deserts, and vast, painted skies that are particularly moving when the sun rises and sets. It is known by many Kurds to be a

432

"progressive" center, home of many well-known Kurdish poets, singers, and intellectuals.

As he grew older, Talabani went to high school in Erbil, a more modern and prosperous Kurdish city that today boasts a population of more than one million and is the official political and administrative capital of Iraqi Kurdistan.* It was there that Talabani became politically active, founding his own secret Kurdish student group at the age of thirteen and officially joining the Kurdistan Democratic Party (KDP) — headed up by Mustafa Barzani, the legendary Kurdish resistance leader — at the age of fourteen. Just four years later, Talabani had so impressed his elders with his intelligence and political savvy that he was actually elected to the KDP's central committee, helping shape future policy and strategy.

"Upon finishing his secondary education, he sought admission to medical school but was denied it by authorities of the then ruling Hashemite monarchy owing to his political activities," notes his official biography. "In 1953 he was allowed to enter law school but was obliged to go into hiding in 1956 to escape arrest for his activities as founder and secretary general of the Kurdistan Student Union. Following the July 1958 overthrow of the Hashemite monarchy, Mr. Talabani returned to law school, at the same time pursuing a career as a journalist and editor. . . . After graduating in 1959, Mr. Talabani performed national service in the Iraqi army, where he served in artillery and armor units and served as a commander of a tank unit."[4]

*In English, Erbil is also occasionally spelled "Irbil" or "Arbil." In Arabic, the city is known as "Hawler."

Ironically, it was in the Iraqi military that Talabani received the training in weapons, military strategy, and combat tactics that enabled him in 1961 to join Mustafa Barzani as one of the leaders of the "first Kurdish revolution," an armed and violent insurgency against the Iraqi government.

Talabani and Barzani's dream was to create a free Kurdistan, independent from Baghdad's control. Their plan was to recruit, train, mobilize, and deploy young Kurdish men to attack Iraqi military units and installations until Baghdad relented and recognized the Kurds' right of self-determination. Their chief allies were Iran, the U.S., and Israel.

Talabani and Barzani shrewdly exploited the Iranians' long-standing hatred for the Iraqi Arabs and successfully petitioned the shah to partially fund their rebellion against Baghdad. They also persuaded Washington and Jerusalem that in the spirit of the old Arab proverb "the enemy of my enemy is my friend," financially supporting the Kurds against the anti-America, anti-Israel government in Iraq and working in concert with the pro-Kurd shah was a wise investment. The CIA and the Mossad, therefore, became quite active in Kurdistan during this time.

A House Divided

By the early 1970s, the Kurdish insurgents had inflicted significant damage and casualties against the Iraqi central government, but serious cracks were growing within the resistance movement.

When the Ba'ath Party offered the Kurds a peace agreement and partial autonomy, the KDP under Barzani was inclined to accept the deal.

Many Kurds were exhausted from years of armed struggle. Talabani, however, fiercely opposed anything short of full independence.

By 1974, the KDP's negotiations with Baghdad had collapsed, but the strains between Barzani and Talabani were pronounced. The two men had developed two very different strategies to achieve their common goals. At the same time, they each had amassed a large and growing following of deeply devoted Kurdish supporters. A split was coming, and the events of 1975 became the turning point.

In March of 1975, Baghdad and Tehran signed what became known as the "Algiers Agreement." The accord — negotiated in secret in Algeria by Saddam Hussein, then Iraq's vice president — was designed to settle long-standing disputes over land and border demarcations between the two countries. As part of the deal, Saddam demanded that the shah cut off aid to the Kurdish rebellion against Baghdad.

The shah agreed. Funds stopped flowing from Tehran almost instantly. Saddam returned to Iraq, quickly marshaled his forces, and launched a massive counterattack against the Kurdish forces. Barzani was forced to flee for his life into exile, eventually ending up in Washington, D.C.

Talabani sensed his moment to seize the mantle of leadership. He broke with the KDP and formed his own political party, the Patriotic Union of Kurdistan, or PUK. And then, on June 1, 1976 — after working feverishly to procure sufficient foreign money and weapons — Talabani launched a "second Kurdish revolution" against Saddam and the Iraqi government.

By 1979, the Kurds were fully reengaged in their

bloody struggle with Baghdad, but rarely had they felt more isolated. The Ayatollah Khomeini — who for years had lived in exile in Iraq — now seized full control of the government of Iran. Saddam Hussein seized full control of the government of Iraq. The Carter administration cut off funding for the Kurdish rebels. And Mustafa Barzani died in Washington on March 1, 1979. His son, Massoud Barzani, picked up where his father left off, but tensions between the Talabanis and Barzanis continued unabated, and the Kurdish people entered the 1980s with little hope of achieving the freedoms for which they had fought so hard and so long.

Crimes Against Humanity

It is difficult to adequately describe the evils that Saddam Hussein and his regime inflicted upon the Kurdish people in the 1980s, but even a brief description helps explain why Talabani fought so hard to free his people from Saddam's reign of terror.

From 1986 to 1989, Saddam launched Operation Anfal, a military campaign designed to neutralize Kurdish opposition to him once and for all. Heading up the operation was Saddam's first cousin, a man named Ali Hassan al-Majid, who eventually became known as "Chemical Ali" because of his use of chemical weapons of mass destruction against the Kurds. After the fall of Saddam's regime in 2003, both Saddam and Chemical Ali were tried in an Iraqi court, convicted, sentenced to death, and hanged for crimes against humanity. Part of the charges against them: killing at least 180,000 Kurds using poison gas and mass executions.

"I smelled something dirty and strange," a fifty-six-year-old Kurdish woman testified during the trial, her voice cracking with emotion as she recalled with horror the events of June 5, 1987, the day that Iraqi forces dropped bombs filled with poison gas on her town. "People were falling to the ground. They vomited and their eyes were blinded. We couldn't see anything. We were all afraid."[5]

"I saw dozens of women and children walking with their eyes red; many were vomiting blood," a Kurdish doctor told the court. "Everything in the village was dead — the birds, the animals, the sheep. . . . I treated a man whose entire body was full of chemical bubbles, but he died a few days later."[6]

During the trial, which began on August 21, 2006, the court "heard more than seventy witnesses who described chemical air attacks, villages being burned, and Kurds being rounded up and tortured," the Reuters news service reported. The prosecution also presented the court with official Iraqi government documents authorizing the attacks.

"The first document was a 1987 memo from Iraq's military intelligence seeking permission from the president's office to use mustard gas and the nerve agent sarin against Kurds."[7] A second document proved that "Saddam had ordered military intelligence to study the possibility of a 'sudden strike' using such weapons against Iranian and Kurdish forces." A third document — an internal memo written by an Iraqi military intelligence officer — confirmed that Iraqi intelligence "had received approval from the president's office for a strike using 'special ammunition' and

437

emphasized that no strike would be launched without first informing the president."[8]

Betrayal

On August 2, 1990, Saddam ordered Iraqi forces to invade Kuwait, claiming Iraq was the rightful owner of Kuwait's territory and oil. This, in turn, triggered President George H. W. Bush ("Bush 41") to marshal an international coalition to protect Saudi Arabia and the other Gulf states from Iraqi aggression and to drive the Iraqis out of Kuwait. The president ordered U.S. forces to war on January 16, 1991. Operation Desert Storm turned out to be a dazzling success, but there were un intended consequences for the Kurds.

On February 16, as U.S. and Coalition forces augmented a punishing air campaign against Iraqi forces in Kuwait with a stunningly effective ground campaign, Bush 41 publicly called upon "the Iraqi military and the Iraqi people to take matters into their own hands, to force Saddam Hussein, the dictator, to step aside."[9] The theory in Washington was that while the U.N. Security Council had not authorized a U.S. overthrow of Saddam's regime during the liberation of Kuwait, perhaps the U.S. could inspire a successful coup in Baghdad anyway.

Talabani and Massoud Barzani saw their moment to achieve liberation with U.S. assistance. They immediately ordered their Kurdish paramilitary forces in northern Iraq into action against Saddam's forces, even as the leaders of Shia paramilitary groups in southern Iraq did the same. But when Saddam counterattacked and began killing Kurdish and Shia guerrillas and civilians in

438

large numbers, the U.S. refused to come to their aid.

"I made very clear that we did not intend to go into Iraq," Bush 41 said at the time. "I condemn Saddam Hussein's brutality against his own people. But I do not want to see U.S. forces who have performed with such skill and dedication sucked into a civil war in Iraq."[10]

Kurdish leaders were stunned by what they saw as an American betrayal. They implored Washington to protect their civilians from another Saddam-driven genocide. But at first, the White House turned a deaf ear to their pleas.

"I made clear from the very beginning that it was not an objective of the Coalition or the United States to overthrow Saddam Hussein," Bush 41 insisted. "So I don't think the Shiites in the south, those who are unhappy with Saddam in Baghdad, or the Kurds in the north ever felt that the United States would come to their assistance to overthrow this man. . . . I have not misled anybody about the intentions of the United States of America, or has any other coalition partner, all of whom to my knowledge agree with me in this position."[11]

It was winter and bitterly cold in the mountains of northern Iraq. But as Kurdish casualties mounted rapidly due to Iraqi air strikes, several million Kurdish civilians decided to brave the elements and flee into southern Turkey. Few of the refugees had food, water, tents, or warm enough clothing for themselves or their children.

News coverage of the mushrooming humanitarian crisis and the fervent and unrelenting pleas of the Kurdish leadership eventually moved the U.S. and the U.N. into action. The U.S. launched Operation Provide Comfort, creating a no-fly zone over the Kurdish provinces of Iraq — enforced by American fighter jets — to keep Saddam's air force from bombing the Kurds any longer. It also created an airlift operation to bring seventeen thousand tons of desperately needed humanitarian relief supplies to the Kurds in northern Iraq and southern Turkey.

The Silver Lining

By God's grace, there was a silver lining to the initial (and brief) American inaction on behalf of the Kurdish people. Though the delay was inexcusable, U.S. financial and political support for the Kurds finally did kick in and was a great blessing, saving many lives and eventually convincing the vast majority of the Kurdish refugees to return to their homes. What's more, the U.S.-designed no-fly zone operation effectively separated Iraqi Kurdistan from the rest of Iraq. No longer was Saddam Hussein able to attack the Kurdish people. Thus, in effect, Kurdish autonomy was established.

Talabani and Barzani wasted no time. Though there was no love lost between the two men, they knew they now had widespread international moral and political support. They also knew they had to leverage that support to create an independent enclave as quickly as they possibly could.

Their own internal tensions notwithstanding, they and their advisors soon created the Kurdistan Regional Government. They formed a parliament. They drafted a democratic constitution. They organized free and reasonably fair elections for the first time in Kurdish history. They began to encourage within Kurdistan everything that had not been possible when Saddam ruled them

— freedom of speech, freedom of assembly, freedom of worship, a free press. They also began building diplomatic ties with the rest of the world and trying to attract financial aid and direct foreign investment.

Was it messy? Yes, it was. Was it fractious? Yes, that too. But it was happening. With (belated) U.S. assistance, a new and real democracy was being born in the heart of the Muslim world.

Regime Change

Twelve years later, when President George W. Bush ("Bush 43") decided to liberate the rest of the Iraqi people and overthrow Saddam Hussein's regime, Talabani was ready to assist his American friends in every way he possibly could. He provided much-needed intelligence to U.S. military commanders. He provided political advice to CIA operatives trying to identify tribal leaders throughout Iraq who would be willing to help overthrow Saddam, neutralize the Iraqi military, and then govern the country in a post-Saddam world.

On March 20, 2003, Operation Iraqi Freedom commenced on the orders of Bush 43. U.S. ground forces entered Baghdad on April 5. Four days later the city was initially secure, and Iraqi citizens — with U.S. military assistance — tore down the statue of Saddam Hussein in the heart of the capital. As TV cameras beamed the remarkable images live around the world, ordinary Iraqis immediately leaped on the toppled icon of twenty-five dark and murderous years. They stomped on the statue's head and face. They cursed it, and the man in whose image it was created. They chanted, "Death to Saddam! Death to Saddam!"

"Mam Jalal was in Suly when Saddam's regime

fell," Talabani's spokesman, Mala Bakhtyar, told me during an exclusive eighty-minute interview in one of the president's offices in Sulymania (aka "Suly"). "It was a very dramatic moment for him, for all of us. He had tried for years to persuade Saddam to respect Kurdish rights and embrace democracy, but Saddam wouldn't listen."[12]

Bakhtyar revealed that Saddam had actually sent a private message to Talabani just weeks before the U.S. and Coalition forces arrived to liberate the country. The Iraqi leader was trying to buy off all of the opposition groups in an effort to keep them from working with the Americans. "Saddam wanted Mam Jalal to know that he was granting amnesty to all of the opposition groups in Iraq, except Talabani." Talabani sent a message back to Saddam saying, "History will not grant amnesty to you. History will remember that you used chemical weapons against your own people."

On April 22, 2003, just after arriving in Iraq to begin working on reconstruction and assembling a new government, the first two people U.S. Lieutenant General Jay Garner went to see were Jalal Talabani and Massoud Barzani. Talabani told Garner the Coalition needed to form an "advisory group" made up of leading Iraqi dissidents against the Saddam regime who could help lay the foundation of a new democracy.

Talabani laid out who the members of the group should be, who should not be included at the beginning, what religious backgrounds the members would need to have to make it truly representative, what their roles should be, and how they should interact with Garner and his team. He also insisted that the new Iraqi government have a federal structure that would give significant

442

freedom and autonomy to the Kurdish people, given all that they had been through over the years.

Garner was impressed.

"If this works, I'll make you a provisional government," he told Talabani and Barzani. "You'll still work for me, but I'll make you a provisional government."[13]

Garner then started going through his own to-do list.

"What are we going to do about a constitution?" he asked.

"We already thought about that," Talabani replied. "We'll have a big tent meeting, and we'll bring in somewhere between 200 and 300 people. Jay, this will be a mosaic of Iraq. It will be all the ethnic groups, all the religions, all the professions . . . the genders, [and together] we'll write this constitution."

"How quick can you do this?" Garner asked.

Talabani smiled and proposed the week of July 4.

A New Iraqi Leadership Emerges

Garner did not make it to July 4.

He was replaced by a far more experienced and savvy diplomat, Ambassador L. Paul "Jerry" Bremer III, who served as the presidential envoy to Iraq from May 2003 to June 2004.

It was Bremer who would turn Talabani and Barzani's suggestions into reality, creating an initial advisory group of seven Iraqi prodemocracy leaders he dubbed the "G-7."* It was Bremer

*The seven leaders were Jalal Talabani, Massoud Barzani, Ayad Allawi (a Shia who would later become the first appointed, though not elected, prime minister),

443

who would eventually turn the G-7 into the Iraqi Governing Council (IGC) with twenty-five senior Iraqi prodemocracy leaders, including both Talabani and Barzani. It was Bremer who created a rotating presidency so that each month a different member of IGC would preside over the group, minimizing tensions and preventing any one member from gaining too much power too quickly. It was also Bremer who over the course of the next twelve months helped the IGC make a series of essential decisions — from creating cabinet positions and filling them with the right people to laying the groundwork for an Iraqi parliament, an Iraqi constitution, and the country's first truly free and fair elections.

By the spring of 2004, the contours of the new Iraqi government were taking shape, and Talabani had his eye on the presidency, even traveling to Washington in an effort to rally support in Congress and among top Bush administration officials. But by early May of that year, the Coalition plan formulated by Bremer and approved by the White House, the State Department, and U.N. envoy Lakhdar Brahimi was to offer the presidency not to a Kurd but to a Sunni Arab. The role of prime minister was going to be offered to a Shia Arab, and Bremer strongly believed the Coalition needed to balance tensions between the two religious groups and give Sunnis a significant stake in the political process.

On Sunday, May 16, Bremer pulled Talabani

Ahmad Chalabi (a Shia), Naseer Chaderchi (a Sunni), Ibrahim al-Jaafari (a Shia), and Abdul Aziz Hakim (a Shia).

444

aside and tried to let him down gently. "For too long they [Arab Sunnis] have felt underrepresented in the new Iraq, Mr. Talabani," Bremer explained. "We have to use this government as an opportunity to broaden Iraq's political base."[14]

Searching for a President

Bremer's leading choice for the presidency was Adnan Pachachi, an eighty-one-year-old secular Sunni from a prominent Iraqi Sunni family. Educated in Egypt, Pachachi had served as Iraq's ambassador to the United Nations in the late 1950s and again in the late 1960s, while later serving as Iraq's foreign minister. During the Saddam Hussein years, he lived in exile in Abu Dhabi, returning to Iraq for the first time after the 2003 liberation, though he had actually opposed the U.S. invasion. Widely respected by U.S. officials, Pachachi was invited to serve as a member of the IGC upon liberation. He helped develop the Transitional Administrative Law — essentially a draft constitution — and served a rotation as president of the IGC.

To Bremer and his colleagues, Pachachi seemed like a perfect caretaker for the fledgling democracy until national elections could be held the following January and the first freely elected Iraqi president could emerge.

But when word leaked out that Pachachi was likely to be named president, sharp criticisms began throughout Baghdad. Religious Sunnis objected to Pachachi's secularism. And some leading Shias objected in principle to a Sunni Arab receiving so lofty a position. They could see a Sunni in the role of vice president, perhaps, but certainly not the presidency itself. Other members

445

of the IGC simply didn't trust Pachachi to be a strong enough leader. He had, after all, opposed the liberation of Iraq from the outset. Why should he now run the country?

Bremer needed to move forward. At the end of the month, he would be handing full sovereignty back to the people of Iraq and leaving the country for good. Iraq needed to have a new government in place and an orderly transition. So with the blessing of the White House, Bremer offered Pachachi the role in spite of the growing criticisms against him and scheduled a press conference for Tuesday, June 1, 2004, to announce Pachachi as Iraq's new president and Ayad Allawi as the new Iraqi prime minister.

But that morning, Bremer's military aide handed him a cell phone. It was Lakhdar Brahimi, the U.N. envoy.

"Astonishing news," Brahimi began. "Pachachi has declined the position. I'm dumbfounded and don't know what got into him. What do we do now?"[15]

Bremer was equally stunned. He and Brahimi considered delaying the press conference for several days, but in the end decided that would be a mistake, fearing internal rivalries on the Iraqi Governing Council would only intensify over time.

"We've got to close the whole deal" — the new prime minister and the new president — "or it will all unravel," Bremer concluded.

Emerging from the Shadows

In that moment of crisis, Bremer turned not to Talabani but to Sheikh Ghazi al-Yawer, who was serving as the IGC's president-of-the-month and had been actively pursuing the post.

446

Though he was the youngest member of the IGC — barely half Pachachi's age — Ghazi in every other way fit the image Bremer wanted for the first sovereign president of Iraq. He had been born in Mosul, the heart of Sunni Islamic fervency in Iraq. He was religiously devout but politically moderate. He had been educated in Saudi Arabia (the birthplace of Sunni Islam) as well as the U.S. (the birthplace of democracy) and held a master's degree in civil engineering from Georgetown University. His English was excellent, and he had a gift for television interviews. He was tech-savvy, having run a successful telecom business in the Saudi kingdom before returning to Iraq after liberation.

What's more, he had strongly supported the U.S. war of liberation. Despite his youth — or perhaps because of it — he was widely respected on the IGC as a passionate young Reformer.

Ghazi gratefully accepted the appointment. When Bremer officially transferred full sovereignty back to the Iraqi people on Monday, June 28, 2004, it was Sheikh Ghazi al-Yawer who became the president of Iraq's interim government.

His tenure was impressive. He was well liked and well trusted, and he was not afraid to speak his mind. He publicly denounced Sunni Radicals — such as Al Qaeda in Iraq, for example — as the "armies of darkness" trying to trigger a civil war in Iraq. What's more, he insisted these were not real Sunni Muslims, because they were killing Muslims when the Qur'an forbade such actions. The so-called Sunni Radicals were actually secular people with "sick minds." These insurgents were more like a "mafia" than a religious movement, he argued, power-obsessed fanatics with a deep-seated "hatred of democracy." Many, he noted, were not even Iraqis but had infiltrated from other countries. "This is not a battle between Iraqis," he said. "This is a battle between evil and good."[16]

On April 6, 2005, the first-ever free and fair elections in Iraq's history were finally held. And when the 275-member Iraqi National Assembly (parliament) was seated, it was Jalal Talabani who was chosen as president.

The following year, on April 22, 2006, after Iraq's constitution was completed and approved, Talabani earned the distinction of being Iraq's first democratically and constitutionally elected president.

Why? It was not complicated. Over more than seventy years, Talabani had earned the trust of the Iraqi people. He had devoted his life to opposing Saddam Hussein. He had been willing to die if necessary to fight for the liberation of his people. Everyone knew he was a real Reformer.

And he was certainly no Johnny-come-lately, just trying to grab power for power's sake or get his name in the papers. Over the decades, Talabani had built alliances all over the world with leaders and nations willing to help the Iraqi people gain their freedom, and he had impressed Iraqis with his diplomatic skills along the way. Moreover, he not only talked about building the first true democracy in the Muslim world; he was one of only a handful of leaders in Iraq that had actually helped create and run a true, healthy, functional, operational democracy — the Kurdistan Regional Government — comprising three of Iraq's eighteen provinces (Erbil, Sulymania, and Dohuk), 4 million people, and forty thousand square kilometers of territory, an area four times larger than

Lebanon.

"We will spare no effort to present Iraq as a model of democracy," Talabani said upon taking office. "We hope to consolidate national unity . . . regardless of religious and sectarian backgrounds. . . . [And we will ensure that] all Iraqis are equal before the law. It means that there [will be] no discrimination [and] that all Arabs, Kurds, and other nationalities have the same rights."[17]

CHAPTER TWENTY-ONE: TALABANI'S TEST

The insurgency, the surge, and the future

On September 13, 2005, President George W. Bush welcomed President Jalal Talabani to the White House for a series of private strategy meetings. When they were finished, the two leaders held a formal press conference.

"I'm proud to stand with a brave leader of the Iraqi people, a friend of the United States, and a testament to the power of human freedom," Bush began. "Mr. President, thank you for your leadership. Thank you for your courage. President Talabani has dedicated his life to the cause of liberty in Iraq. As a lawyer, journalist, and a political leader in northern Iraq, he stood up to a brutal dictator because he believes that every Iraqi deserves to be free. The dictator destroyed Kurdish villages, ordered poison gas attacks on a Kurdish city, and violently repressed other religious and ethnic groups. For President Talabani and his fellow citizens, the day Saddam was removed from power was a day of deliverance. And America will always be proud that we led the armies of liberation. The past two years, the Iraqi people have made their vision of their future clear. This past

January, more than 8 million Iraqis defied the car bombers and the assassins and voted in free elections. It was an inspiring act of unity when 80 percent of the elected national assembly chose the president, a member of Iraq's Kurdish minority, to lead the free nation."[1]

The Iraqi president beamed. "It is an honor to represent the world's youngest democracy," he said graciously. "In the name of the Iraqi people, I say to you, Mr. President, and to the glorious American people, thank you, thank you. Thank you because you have liberated us from the worst kind of dictatorship. Our people suffered too much from this worst kind of dictatorship. The signal is mass graves with hundred thousand of Iraqi innocent children and women, young and old men. Thank you. And thanks to the United States, there are now fifty million Muslims in Afghanistan and Iraq liberated by your courageous leadership and decision to liberate us, Mr. President. We agree with Mr. President Bush that democracy is the solution to the problems of the Middle East. Mr. President, you are a visionary, great statesman. We salute you. We are grateful to you. We will never forget what you have done for our people."

Talabani continued by declaring Iraq "partners" with the American people in the fight against the Radicals. "We are proud to say openly and to repeat it, that we are partners of the United States of America in fighting against tyranny, terrorism, and for democracy," he said without apology. "That's something we are not shy to say, and we'll repeat it everywhere, here and in Iraq and the United Nations and everywhere. Iraqis and Americans alike in the war against terrorism. Our soldiers now fighting side by side with your brave soldiers, now and every day. We have captured many senior elements of Al Qaeda. We killed many of them. And we had also many of them in our prisons. . . . Now Iraq is a free country. . . . With your support, we [will] create a society enjoying democracy for the first time of the history."[2]

What a remarkable moment. The world was watching the president of Iraq, of all countries, stand before a cynical White House press corps to thank the American people for their commitment to democracy and to suggest that Iraq could one day be a model of reform for other Middle Eastern countries.

More Troops, or Fewer?

To his enormous credit, the new Iraqi president was not just talk. As his entire life to date had demonstrated, he was a man of principle and a man of action. When he was tested, he rose to the challenge.

The first test came as the Sunni and Shia insurgencies accelerated. More and more Iraqis, Americans, and other Coalition members were being killed each and every day. A growing number of U.S. and foreign political leaders were urging President Bush to withdraw American forces and let the Iraqis fight on their own.

Talabani could not have disagreed more vehemently.

In November of 2006, Talabani met in Paris with then French president Jacques Chirac, who had strongly opposed the liberation of Iraq from the outset. Some may have expected Talabani to try to ingratiate himself to Chirac by agreeing with the French leader's sharp criticisms of American leadership and his insistence that President Bush pull U.S. forces out of Iraq as quickly as possible.

But Talabani would have none of it. He not only reiterated his gratefulness for the U.S.-led regime change in Baghdad but added that he wanted U.S. forces to stay at least three more years. "We need time," said Talabani. "Not twenty years, but time. I personally can say that two to three years will be enough to build up our forces and say to our American friends, 'Bye bye with thanks.' "[3]

Behind the scenes, Talabani went further, urging the White House and Pentagon to send more U.S. troops to help defeat the Radicals in Iraq. He was not alone. One of his key allies in Washington, Senator John McCain, the Arizona Republican, was also pressing the White House to implement a "surge" policy, putting an additional fifteen to thirty thousand U.S. troops on the ground in Iraq — and deploying them more effectively — despite the fact that polls showed only 15 to 18 percent of the American people supported such a policy.[4]

On January 10, 2007, President Bush formally embraced and announced his support for a surge, telling the American people that "it is clear that we need to change our strategy in Iraq. . . . Failure in Iraq would be a disaster for the United States. The consequences of failure are clear: Radical Islamic extremists would grow in strength and gain new recruits. They would be in a better position to topple moderate governments, create chaos in the region, and use oil revenues to fund their ambitions. Iran would be emboldened in its pursuit of nuclear weapons. Our enemies would have a safe haven from which to plan and launch attacks on the American people. On September the 11th, 2001, we saw what a refuge for extremists on the other side of the world could bring to the streets of our own cities. For the safety of our people, America must succeed in Iraq."[5]

Bush noted that "our past efforts to secure Baghdad failed for two principal reasons: There were not enough Iraqi and American troops to secure neighborhoods that had been cleared of terrorists and insurgents, and there were too many restrictions on the troops we did have. This will require increasing American force levels. So I've committed more than 20,000 additional American troops to Iraq. The vast majority of them — five brigades — will be deployed to Baghdad. . . . Our enemies in Iraq will make every effort to ensure that our television screens are filled with images of death and suffering. Yet over time, we can expect to see Iraqi troops chasing down murderers, fewer brazen acts of terror, and growing trust and cooperation from Baghdad's residents."[6]

Battle over the Surge

The Bush-McCain surge policy unleashed a torrent of opposition in Washington, and the attacks came from both Democrats and Republicans.

Senator Barack Obama, the Illinois Democrat, immediately went on MSNBC to declare his belief that the surge would make life in Iraq worse, not better. "I am not persuaded that 20,000 additional troops in Iraq [are] going to solve the sectarian violence there. In fact, I think it will do the reverse."[7]

Later that night on CNN's *Larry King Live,* Obama discounted the entire concept of creating a healthy, functional, representative government in Baghdad. "We know we are not going to have a Jeffersonian democracy in Iraq," the junior senator insisted. "We have to have a more realistic and constrained view of what's possible. . . . I don't think we advance that task [securing Iraq] — in fact, I'm certain we don't advance it — by putting more American troops at risk. . . . For us to simply think that by adding 15,000 or 20,000 more troops, as opposed to beginning a phased withdrawal, that we're sending that message, I think we're making a very bad mistake."[8]

Talabani, by contrast, strongly and publicly supported the surge, insisted in numerous interviews in the Muslim world as well as in the West that he was an optimist about the future of his country, and adamantly refused to surrender to the Radicals by encouraging the U.S. to cut and run. In an interview with an Arab newspaper in Damascus just days after Obama's comments, Talabani unleashed his fury against Islamic Radicals. He said he felt deep "resentment" toward them, especially toward al Qaeda, which he charged was "waging a war of extermination against the Iraqi people." He said al Qaeda does not "respect Islam" because they are "targeting innocent civilians."[9]

Talabani went on to reveal that in 2006, at least four thousand foreign-born terrorists — upward of 90 percent of whom enter his country through Syria — were killed inside Iraq by Iraqi and Coalition forces. Such terrorists were causing horrific damage inside his country, he said, noting that in 2006 some thirty-four thousand Iraqi civilians had been killed by Radical Islamic terrorists. "This is a form of genocide against the Iraqi people, carried out by people who came from outside Iraq," Talabani charged.

"Al-Qaeda has announced that the Shias are

Rafidites [infidels who reject legitimate Islamic authority and leadership] and therefore it is legitimate to kill them," he added. "It has also announced that the Kurds are traitors; therefore it is permissible to kill them, and that the Arab Sunnis, who do not follow them, are apostates whose punishment is also known. . . . This is a declaration of war on the Iraqi people."

Talabani was then asked by the Arab reporter conducting the interview, "Mr. President, are you afraid that there will be no way out of this situation?"

"No, I believe there is a way out," Talabani replied confidently.

First, he argued that as more Iraqi security forces were properly trained and equipped and able to take the leading role in defending their country, the Reformers would be able to crush the Radicals.

Second, he argued that as the population watched the horrific explosion of Muslim-on-Muslim violence — and, just as important, as they watched the Reformers showing courage, fighting back, and actually defeating the Radicals — many more Iraqis would start to feel a measure of hope, would begin participating in the political process, and would help the Iraqi security forces hunt down the terrorists and uncover arms caches. In fact, he argued that this was already beginning to happen.

"The people of the terrorism-plagued areas have begun to resist the terrorists," Talabani noted. "In certain areas, the people are completely ready to work with the government forces to put a lid on terrorist acts. This is a good phenomenon." Just as exciting, he said he was watching "a change in the mindset of almost all the Sunni community" who once thought that U.S. military forces were the enemy and that Iranian insurgents and their money and weapons were a blessing because they were helping kill the "infidels." But, Talabani said, "they now believe that Iran is the main danger, not the Americans," and "they have already started secret negotiations with the Americans" about how to work together to stop the Iranians from killing so many Iraqis.

Worst-Case Scenario

A year after the new surge policy was announced and set into motion, I sat down with Mala Bakhtyar, Talabani's spokesman, and asked him point-blank if the president still believed things were moving in the right direction.

Bakhtyar's answer was an adamant yes. He noted that all the evidence at that point reinforced the Iraqi leader's confidence that the surge was working. He said Talabani and other Iraqi leaders — including Prime Minister Maliki — believed Iraq was finally moving in the right direction, despite all the critics and naysayers in Washington.

"President Talabani is optimistic about the future of Iraq," Bakhtyar told me unequivocally. "He believes the forces of extremism will be defeated. He believes we will solve most of the problems Iraqis are suffering with and that democracy will go forward. . . . We think Iraq will eventually emerge as the central democratic country in the region. Other Middle East countries will look to Iraq as the model."

He added that Iraq could ultimately be more influential in the region than other moderate, pro-Western countries like Jordan, Morocco, the Gulf

States, and the like "because of the revenues" from accelerated oil exploration, production, and export over the next few decades that will give Iraq the ability to invest in other moderate states and strengthen the hands of fellow Reformers.

"What does President Talabani worry about most?" I asked.

"The worst-case scenario is a civil war," he said, one that is full-blown, engulfs the entire country (not just specific villages, cities, or regions), and leads to genocide. "If civil war had broken out, five hundred thousand to one million people would have been killed. . . . Many terrorist groups have worked and planned hard to create a civil war, supported by neighboring countries. . . . If the U.S. was not here, the civil war would have already happened. As a patriot, I hope foreign soldiers will not be in my country for long. But the reality is, they are necessary for now."

He quickly added that Talabani and his senior advisors fear that if the U.S. and Coalition military forces pull out of Iraqi too early or too recklessly, democracy could collapse, and a true, full-blown civil war could still erupt, leading to wholesale slaughter and chaos in the region. Having seen genocide happen to his people before, Talabani has no intention of letting it happen again.

During our conversation, Bakhtyar was very careful not to discuss the American presidential campaign that was well under way at the time. He knew full well that Senator McCain had been an early proponent of the surge strategy, while Senators Obama and Clinton — among many other American politicians — had been strong proponents of leaving Iraq as quickly as possible. Nevertheless, Bakhtyar made it clear that leaders

458

at the highest levels of the Iraqi government had grave concerns that the U.S. might abandon the Iraqi people in their time of need.

"President Talabani thinks the relationship with the United States is strategic and related to Iraq's destiny," Bakhtyar told me. "But a part of American public opinion is mistaken. They think Iraq is facing struggles because of the presence of American forces. On the contrary, 80 percent of those problems have been contained by U.S. and British forces. Look, Iraq has been around for eighty-plus years. We have fought against Israel four times. We fought Iran for eight years. We occupied Kuwait. We were under international embargo for thirteen years. There has been continual fighting throughout Kurdish history. From 1938 to 1945, there were three uprisings in the Barzan region. From 1961 to 1975, there was even more fighting in Kurdistan. From 1976 to 1991, there were many military operations and revolts. So what is Iraq? Is it a country or a butcher house? No one has experienced peace or happiness here. It's a country of bloodshed. So why do we blame America for our troubles? Terrorists are fighting against the democratic process in Iraq. The terrorists are frightened of what will happen if democracy wins in Iraq. They know the age of terror and [Radical Islamic] fundamentalism will be over."

"Aside from civil war and genocide," I asked, "what else concerns the president about what the terrorists could do to derail the creation of a new Iraq?"

"Joel, 8 million weapons were distributed by Saddam before he fell," Bakhtyar explained. "At the beginning of the insurgency, we estimated there were some eighty to ninety thousand volunteers to fight the U.S. Now we think that's down to between four and five thousand. This is still a big menace. The assassination of Talabani or al-Maliki would have a huge effect. . . . Talabani is not just the president of Iraq. He is, in many ways, seen as the real leader of Iraq, because none of the rest of the Iraqi politicians right now has the trust and confidence of the Shias, and the Sunni Arabs, and the Kurds, and the leftists. This is the courtyard of President Talabani, because he is most wise and experienced leader Iraq has had in a long time."

"Are you personally optimistic about the future of your country?" I asked.

"Yes," he said with a smile. "I believe the democrats in the Middle East will win this war in the next ten to fifteen years."

Stunning Results

Not everyone has been so optimistic.

In the spring of 2007, Senate majority leader Harry Reid, the Nevada Democrat, marked the fourth anniversary of the liberation of Iraq by declaring that "this war is lost, and this surge is not accomplishing anything."[10]

In the spring of 2008, Senator Hillary Clinton marked the fifth anniversary of the liberation of Iraq by denouncing the entire effort — a war she voted to authorize — as "a war we cannot win."[11]

That same spring, former U.S. secretary of state Madeleine Albright, who served in the Clinton-Gore administration, insisted that "Iraq will go down in history as the biggest disaster in American foreign policy."[12]

Talabani and his senior advisors say the exact

opposite is true. They say the "surge" has proved a stunning success. They say the war in Iraq not only *can* be won but *is* being won. Moreover, they say that Iraq will go down in history as one of America's greatest success stories. And they say they now have solid and compelling evidence to prove their claims.

As far as the "surge" is concerned, in just the first nine months of 2007, the number of U.S. boots on the ground in Iraq increased from 132,000 to 168,000. More troops and better tactics and strategies in using those troops had an immediate and powerful impact. During those first nine months, Iraqi officials note that 4,882 insurgents were killed by Iraqi and Coalition forces. That was a 25 percent increase from the same period the year before. It brought the overall total to nearly twenty thousand insurgents killed in Iraq in the first five years after liberation. More than twenty-five thousand insurgents were captured in the first five years as well.[13]

Over the course of the following year or so, the results were even more impressive. In August of 2008, Moqtada al-Sadr — the Radical Shia firebrand — effectively surrendered. He ordered his fighters to lay down their arms and transform their Mahdi Army into a social services organization. This was a dramatic development and is a key reason why violence levels continue to drop.

Could al-Sadr reverse course at any moment and launch a new and even more violent insurgency? Yes. Could Iran decide to invest even more heavily in such a revived insurgency? Absolutely. So Talabani and his team remain vigilant. But they certainly do not believe al-Sadr would have folded if the U.S. had unilaterally surrendered and left

461

the country as many in Washington and European capitals were strongly recommending.

By the end of August 2008, even the *New York Times* had to acknowledge how much progress was being made. "The surge, clearly, has worked, at least for now," wrote *Times* correspondent Dexter Filkins. "Violence, measured in the number of attacks against Americans and Iraqis each week, has dropped by 80 percent in the country since early 2007, according to figures [U.S. General David Petraeus] provided. Civilian deaths, which peaked at more than 100 a day in late 2006, have also plunged. Car and suicide bombings, which stoked sectarian violence, have fallen from a total of 130 in March 2007 to fewer than 40 last month. In July, fewer Americans were killed in Iraq — 13 — than in any month since the war began."[14]

Bremer's Perspective

In July of 2008, I called Ambassador L. Paul "Jerry" Bremer, who was appointed by President Bush as presidential envoy to Iraq from May 2003 to June 2004, and asked him for his assessment of the situation in Iraq. Bremer had been there essentially from the beginning. He knew Talabani well. He had seen the horrific violence al Qaeda, the Mahdi Army, and others had unleashed in the country over the previous several years. So I asked him, "Looking back on your time in Iraq and considering all that has happened since you were there, whom do you believe is winning — the Radicals or the Reformers — and why?"

The long-time diplomat — Bremer served in the State Department for twenty-three years — and confidant of the legendary Henry Kissinger thought about the question for a moment. Then he said he was finally cautiously optimistic that Iraq was going to turn out well. There had been a number of very painful years, he readily acknowledged, but now he believed there was light at the end of the tunnel, and it was not an oncoming train.

"The Sunni extremists are on the way to losing what they themselves define as the central battle — the battle in Iraq — after being thrown out of power in Afghanistan," Bremer told me. "They really have come close to losing in Iraq. This could certainly still change. But I think the Sunni Radicals overplayed their hand in Iraq."[15]

When I asked him to explain, Bremer said first that in his view, al Qaeda leaders and other Sunni extremists have overplayed their hand by talking incessantly about creating a Sunni-led Islamic caliphate. "When they talk about reestablishing the caliphate, average Iraqis," — 60 percent of whom are Shia Muslims — "hear, 'Gee, they're talking about Sunni domination. Didn't we just get rid of a thousand years of Sunni domination?' "

Second, Bremer said he believed Al Qaeda in Iraq had overplayed their hand by instigating Muslim-on-Muslim violence that Iraqis saw on their televisions — as well as in their streets — day after day, night after night, week after week. "The Sunni Radicals have killed so many innocent Shias, and almost succeeded into setting off a full-blown sectarian war," said Bremer. "But Iraqi Sunnis are now pushing back. The Anbar awakening was impressive, seeing tens of thousands of average, everyday Sunni citizens band together against al Qaeda."

Bremer also noted a third trend he found positive. He recently had a meeting with Sunni tribal leaders in Washington who told him, "We're close allies with you [the U.S.] because of our common enemy — Iran." After that meeting, Bremer concluded that "Sunni Arabs who were very hesitant to welcome us overthrowing Saddam [who himself was a Sunni] are finally coming to see they have a major stake in us succeeding because of what they see as the serious threat posed by Iran." Iraqi Sunnis do not want to be controlled by the Shias of Iran, and many have come to realize that if Sunnis force a civil war with Iraqi Shias, they could drive those Shias into the arms of Iran once and for all, a prospect they do not find appealing at all.

Confronting the Cynics

Not everyone, of course, believes it is possible to build a Jeffersonian democracy in the Muslim world, much less in a country as challenging as Iraq.

Barack Obama put it this way during his 2008 presidential campaign: "We were told this would make us safer and that this would be a model of democracy in the Middle East. Hasn't turned out that way. . . . This Administration's policy has been a combination of extraordinary naivety — the notion that, you know, we'll be greeted as liberators, flowers will be thrown at us in Iraq, we'll be creating a Jeffersonian democracy, that it's a model."[16]

Obama's running mate, Senator Joe Biden, the Delaware Democrat, readily concurred, dismissing President Bush's "wholesome but naive view that Western notions of liberty are easily transposed to that area of the world. . . . I think the president . . . thinks there's a Thomas Jefferson or a (James) Madison behind every sand dune waiting to jump up, and there are none."[17]

The Obama-Biden ticket was hardly alone. Anthony Zinni, the retired Marine Corps general who once led the U.S. Central Command, argued that "the Bush administration's idea that you could transplant a Jeffersonian democracy to Iraq and christen it with a single election and a lot of fingers dipped in ink was ridiculous. . . . Civics 101 should have alerted you that the region wasn't ready and that we first needed viable government structures, functioning political parties that everyone understood, and an educated electorate."[18]

Despite such critics, however, Jalal Talabani remains undaunted. He believes to the core of his being that Iraqis want freedom and democracy. He believes Iraqis are capable of creating a society of peace and prosperity. He also believes Iraqis are making great and steady progress. He does not claim it is easy. He does not claim there will not be setbacks. But one thing is clear: he is willing to live and fight and die, if necessary, to accomplish what is for him a lifelong dream.

In a sea of sadness and cynicism throughout the epicenter, I have to say, Talabani strikes me as a man of impressive integrity, courage, and hope for the future. As best as I can tell, he is a Reformer who is getting results, and that is no small thing anywhere in our world, but particularly in the heart of the Muslim Middle East.

A Conversation with Qubad Talabani

After these two chapters on President Talabani were largely completed, I was invited to meet with and interview Qubad Talabani, the son of the Iraqi president, on October 10, 2008, in his Washington, D.C., office. Naturally, I accepted without reservations.

Born in London in 1977, Qubad — whose name has Zoroastrian origins and means "upright and strong" — currently represents the Kurdistan Regional Government in Washington and serves as a personal advisor to his father, particularly on U.S.-Kurdish and U.S.-Iraqi relations. I found Qubad very engaging — intelligent, sophisticated, good-humored, passionate about his people and his country, and as optimistic as his father about the future. I also found him to be a strong believer that building a Jeffersonian democracy in Iraq is both possible and the right thing to do, no matter how long it takes.

"It would be unwise for the United States not to finish the job [in Iraq]," Qubad told an American journalist in 2006. "It is half complete. You are still democratizing society in America after a few hundred years. We cannot expect to turn from tyrannical dictatorship to Jeffersonian democracy in two or three years. We have been ruled by personalities for decades. We need to create institutions of government, with checks and balances within the political system that can protect people's civil liberties. A premature disengagement would lead to the collapse of our fledgling government, and would turn the situation into a full-scale civil war."[19]

To that I would simply add, "Amen."

What follows are excerpts of my conversation

with Qubad Talabani.

JOEL C. ROSENBERG: For many years, your father was really a guerrilla leader, wasn't he, fighting for Kurdish liberation from the Ba'ath Party and the Saddam regime?

QUBAD TALABANI: He was, but he was never a terrorist. His party, the PUK [Patriotic Union of Kurdistan], never attacked civilians. Their sole target was Saddam's military. In 1983, my father told the leaders of the PKK [a Kurdish militant faction in northern Iraq and southern Turkey fighting for liberation from the Turks] that they had to lay down their weapons and stop attacking civilians. But they didn't listen. . . . In 1991, during the Kurdish uprising against Saddam Hussein, the PUK forces had at one point captured 120,000 Iraqi troops. Not one of them was killed. All were treated humanely. They were fed, and eventually they were released and sent back to their homes. Compare that to the tens and tens of thousands of Kurds that were massacred by Saddam's forces.

ROSENBERG: Did you or your father ever imagine a Kurdish president?

TALABANI (laughing): No, I never imagined such a thing. Nor did my father. In fact, when I see him on TV and hear him introduced as the president of Iraq, it still makes me look twice. It sometimes doesn't seem real. It's even more remarkable when you realize that in 1983, Saddam Hussein gave amnesty to all the members of the Kurdish resistance movement — everyone except Jalal Talabani.

You should talk to Zalmay Khalilzad.* He will tell you about a meeting in 2002 in London. It was a conference of Iraqi opposition leaders. There was lots of squabbling going on. The meeting was completely disorganized. But finally my father pulled seven or eight key people in a room by themselves and calmed them down, and they were able to make progress on whatever issue was troubling them. At the end of the meeting, Zalmay took my father aside and said, "You know, you're the only one in this room who could be the president of Iraq one day." My father laughed. It was very kind what Zalmay said, but I'm not sure my father took it very seriously at the time. Years later, though, when my father was, in fact, elected president, one of the first calls he got was from Zalmay saying, "See, I told you so."

ROSENBERG: Where were you when you learned the news that your father had been elected president?

TALABANI: I was in D.C. I was alone. It was a very emotional moment for me. I could hardly believe it. I poured myself a glass of cognac, and I thought about Frank Sinatra's

*Zalmay Khalilzad served as the U.S. ambassador to Iraq from 2005 to 2007, after which he became the U.S. ambassador to the U.N. From 2003 to 2005, he served as U.S. ambassador to Afghanistan.

famous song "I Did It My Way," because that is exactly how my father has lived his life and risen to power — doing it his own way. And now he had succeeded.

You have to understand, I never saw my father until I was four years old. After I was born, my mother and I lived in London to be safe from all the troubles in Iraq. My father was back in Kurdistan and traveling constantly. And one day there was a knock at the door, and I opened the door and then I went running to mother, and I said, "Mom, there's a man at the door." And she said, "That's not just a man. That's your father." I was shocked. So I went back and let him in. But then I was being a little plucky and I said, "Where's my gift?" And he said, "Well, I don't have a gift. I'm sorry." And I said, "What kind of father comes to your door and claims to be your father and doesn't bring a gift?"

ROSENBERG: Now, at least, your father has given you and all the Kurdish people a gift — an Iraq free from Saddam Hussein and the Ba'ath Party.

TALABANI: That's true. I called him that day and I said, "Mr. President, congratulations." He got choked up, and he said, "Mr. Ambassador, congratulations." It was really quite a remarkable moment. After all, very few political [opposition] parties actually achieve the objective for which they were created. But my father's party has. They were founded in 1975 to remove Saddam Hussein from power and to create a federal, democratic Iraq. And

469

against all odds, they have succeeded.

ROSENBERG: What would you say are the biggest signs of progress since your father became the president of Iraq?

TALABANI: I think the biggest sign of progress has been that people have actually turned against the extremists — against al Qaeda and the Mahdi Army. In part, the extremists have brought this upon themselves with all of their attacks against innocent civilians. Eventually Iraqis said, "Enough is enough." And, of course, the surge policy [of more U.S. troops assisting Iraqi forces] has been very effective. Al Qaeda is now on the run. The Mahdi Army is laying low. So by and large we have a dramatically improved security situation.

Things are still fragile, of course. We still don't know how long things will stay quiet. But there's no question that right now the fact that Iraqis feel safer and more secure and want the Iraqi government and the Coalition to succeed in defeating the extremists is the single biggest sign of success since 2005.

ROSENBERG: Are there other successes you would point to that have occurred on your father's watch?

TALABANI: There are. I would call them mini successes. None are as important as crushing the terrorists, but they are still very important. The state of the Iraqi media is one success story. The media is very open now. There has been a proliferation of newspapers and radio stations and satellite TV channels and Web sites and blogs. Lots of Internet cafes have opened. News is being reported openly. People are able to voice their opinions openly about everything. That is a huge, positive change from life in Saddam's police state.

Another success has been the lifting of the [international economic] sanctions. Goods and services are now moving between Iraq and other countries. Iraq is no longer isolated from the international community. This is also in sharp contrast to the Saddam era.

A third success, I would say, would be political pluralism. There are many political parties operating freely in Iraq today, and they represent many different ideas and points of view. This is quite a change.

And then, of course, this is the first time in Iraqi history that we've seen the peaceful transition from one government to another — no coups, no bloodshed, no conspiracies. Well, maybe a little conspiracy (laughter).*

*On April 6, 2005, Iraq's initial interim president, Ghazi Mashal Ajil al-Yawer, peacefully handed over power to Jalal Talabani, the first democratically elected president of Iraq under the country's newly ratified constitution. Likewise, the following day — April 7, 2005 — Iraq's initial interim prime minister, Iyad Allawi, peacefully handed over the office to Ibrahim al-Jaafari, who became prime minister under the Iraqi Transitional Authority. Then, on May 20, 2006, al-Jafaari peacefully handed over power to Nouri al-

471

ROSENBERG: What are some of your major concerns going forward?

TALABANI: One of my concerns is that while there is more openness to discuss political ideas in Iraq, there hasn't emerged a real tolerance of different religious beliefs. As you can imagine, this is a real challenge in Iraq because we are so divided along sectarian lines — Shias, Sunnis, Christians, secularists, and others. I believe it is vital that we are able to develop a culture where people have strong religious views but can respect someone who disagrees with them without becoming violent. And we need to find ways to encourage religious tolerance at the national level as well as at the local and regional levels.

Let me give you an example of one way we should be doing this. The parliament recently debated the provincial elections law, but during the process they dropped Article 50 from the bill, which was a very important article. This article would mandate the representation of different ethnic and religious minorities in the local governments so that all religious groups have a voice and a say in local decisions. President Talabani and a number of his colleagues have sent the bill back for reconsideration, insisting that Article 50 be reinstated to protect minority religious views. The KRG [Kurdistan Regional Government, represent-

---

Maliki, who become the first democratically elected prime minister of Iraq under the country's newly ratified constitution.

472

ing five of Iraq's eighteen provinces] is also pressing for Article 50 to be put back into the final bill.

ROSENBERG: Well, this raises a very interesting point to me, Qubad. Because during all of my research about Iraq and my travels in the country, I have been struck by how tolerant the Kurdish people — most of whom are Sunni Muslims — are of Christians. When we drive through Kurdish military checkpoints, if the soldiers find out that we are Christians, they smile and wave us right through. There are many churches operating openly and safely throughout Kurdistan. Christians are able to freely talk about their faith in Christ. In fact, several colleagues and I had the opportunity to attend a conference of some 640 Iraqi pastors and Christian leaders near Lake Dukan, within sight of your family's presidential home. I personally cannot think of any other country in the Muslim world where hundreds of Christian leaders could openly gather for worship, prayer, and Bible teaching so close to a president's house.

TALABANI: You would be brave to have 640 pastors and Christians holding a meeting in front of King Abdullah's house in Jordan — and he's a very nice guy. You couldn't have such a gathering in Baghdad right now. You all would have been massacred. And this is what I'm talking about — we need to create a culture of true religious freedom and tolerance.

473

ROSENBERG: I absolutely agree. But why are the Kurdish people and President Talabani not just tolerant of Christians but actually supportive of them and even protective of them?

TALABANI: We [as Kurds] were always an oppressed people. Now that we're not, it's unthinkable to us to oppress a minority.

ROSENBERG: Well, you certainly could oppress other minorities if you wanted to. Many groups throughout history have found their freedom only to turn against those who previously oppressed them.

TALABANI: Well, we simply can't do it. That's not who we are. It's just not possible for us to turn against the Christians, for example. We've seen what the Christians have done in Kurdistan — helping grow the economy, bringing tourism, investments — and we're grateful for that.

One thing you should note, Joel, is that we as Kurds put our ethnic identity before our religious identity. The fact that most Kurds are Sunni Muslims never protected us as a minority under the Saddam regime. He was a Sunni Muslim, as were all of his advisors. But they never treated us well just because we were Sunnis. Just the opposite. He attacked us constantly. He used weapons of mass destruction against us. He killed thousands of Kurds despite the fact that we were the same religion as him.

I want American Christians to know that Jalal Talabani is the biggest champion they have in Iraq — more than the leaders of the Christian political parties — not because he cares more than the Christian [political] leaders but because he's able to use his authority more to ensure the rights of Christians. He's helping to protect churches. He's doing everything he can to protect and advance religious freedom for Christians. And he hopes that someday all of Iraq will be as safe and free for Christians as Kurdistan is today.

ROSENBERG: Qubad, do you believe Kurdistan could serve as a model for the rest of Iraq? After all, you have a sixteen-year head start, right? After the first Gulf War, the U.S. imposed a no-fly zone over northern Iraq, keeping Saddam's forces from being able to attack the Kurds. That newfound level of freedom led to the passage of a democratic constitution, the creation of a parliament, free and fair democratic elections. It certainly hasn't been easy for the Kurds. There were violent battles between various Kurdish political groups, including the one headed up by your father and another headed by the Barzani family. But eventually you all seem to have figured things out.

Your father is now the first truly democratically and constitutionally elected president in the history of Iraq. Massoud Barzani is the democratically elected president of the Kurdistan Regional Government. Nechirvan Barzani is the prime minister of the KRG. You are operating as an ambassador or representative of the KRG in Washington. The Kurdish economy is growing steadily. New homes are being constructed. New office buildings are being constructed. Foreign direct investment into Kurdish businesses is rising. Americans feel safe there. Christians feel safe there. Isn't it possible that Kurdistan looks today like what the rest of Iraq will look like in another ten to fifteen to twenty years?

TALABANI: I think Kurdistan could serve as a model. We went through the mistakes that the rest of Iraq is going through now. But we were able to figure things out eventually. We were able to set aside our political differences when we saw a larger goal — overthrowing Saddam. It did take time. And it did take the U.S. to bang our heads together and insist that we come together. But we finally saw the benefits of a united Kurdish front, and we have made an enormous amount of progress over the last sixteen years or so, and specifically over the last four or five years.

Will the rest of Iraq follow our lead? I don't know. There's still a lot of political immaturity in Iraq at large, much like we had in the nineties. But the fact that there is a Kurd serving as the president of the country — that, I think, is a hopeful sign.

In the winter of 2010, Iraq held a new round of national elections, as prescribed by the constitution. Violence in the country was way down. Turnout was strong at 62.4 percent. But the race for prime minister was too close to call. In fact, the vote was so close that month after month went by without the country knowing for certain whether Nouri al-Maliki and his party (the Shia

476

religious party known as the State of Law Coalition) would once more gain control, or whether one of the rival parties (such as Iraqiya, run by Dr. Ayad Allawi, a secular Shia leader who served as an appointed prime minister of Iraq just after the liberation in 2003 and before full national elections had been held) would gain control instead.

Even as President Obama pulled U.S. combat forces out of Iraq by August 31, 2010 (due to the enormous success of the "surge" policy), it still was not clear who would lead the fledgling Iraqi democracy into the future as prime minister. After recounts and close election scrutiny from all sides, al-Maliki's party appeared to control 89 seats. But Dr. Allawi's party appeared to control 91 seats. However, both were vigorously asserting their right to form a new government, and neither showed any interest in compromising or forming a national unity government.

One thing was clear, though: despite Jalal Talabani's serious health issues, he was going to receive a second term as president. He was, therefore, going to be the first democratically *re*-elected president of Iraq. Such an accomplishment was a testament to how widely trusted and admired Talabani was throughout the country and across political, religious, and ideological lines. He was broadly perceived as a consensus builder and a man all sides could trust, in large part because of his reputation as an indefatigable Reformer. His future, and the future of Iraq, will be worth watching closely.

Chapter Twenty-Two:
The King and I

Meet Mohammed VI and
the Reformers of Rabat

In the spring of 2006, I received a phone call from a friend in Casablanca.

My friend explained that he was coming to Washington with Dr. Ahmed Abaddi, who works for Moroccan king Mohammed VI who had read my novel *The Ezekiel Option* and was interested in meeting me. Moreover, they were wondering if Lynn and I would be willing to put on a small dinner party at our home with some journalists and key policy makers to discuss Morocco's efforts to fight Islamic Radicalism, promote democracy, and build bridges of friendship and cooperation with Jews and evangelical Christians.

We certainly were, I told him. Indeed, it would be an honor.

To say the resulting evening was fascinating would be putting it mildly.

Dr. Abaddi was not simply a soft-spoken, gentle-mannered professor of comparative religion who had been a visiting Fulbright scholar at the University of Chicago and DePaul University and learned excellent English. As Morocco's director

478

of Islamic affairs, he was also a man of considerable influence, responsible for overseeing more
than thirty-three thousand Sunni mosques
throughout his country.* His wife, Fatiha, was
also impressive — a gracious, well-read, devoutly
religious wife and mother who, like Lynn, had
devoted herself to raising four sons (though the
Abaddi boys were a little older than the Rosenberg boys, ranging in age from seven to seventeen).

In their late forties, the Abaddis were warm and
engaging, and from the moment they entered our
home, Lynn and I immediately felt a real affection
for them both.

We encountered only one small problem: Fatiha
spoke far more Arabic and French than English,
and we spoke *no* Arabic and *bad* high school

*Most Moroccan Sunnis, Dr. Abaddi included, are Sufi
Muslims, as opposed to Wahhabi Muslims. That is, they
practice something called "Sufism." This is defined by
the Encyclopedia Britannica as a "mystical movement
within Islam that seeks to find divine love and knowledge through direct personal experience of God."
Sufism began probably in Morocco sometime after the
death of Muhammad in AD 632 and later migrated to
Iraq. Though scholars disagree on the exact nature of
the movement's origins — whether it was a spiritualiza-
tion of Islam, an evolution toward mysticism, an attempt to escape a stifling religiosity, etc. — and despite
heavy resistance over the years both from inside and
outside Islam, "the importance of Sufism in the history
of Islam is incalculable." Today Sufism is practiced
worldwide in numerous variations. See http://
www.answers.com/topic/sufism.

French. Fortunately, Lynn had invited some dear friends who could translate, and that made all the difference.

Also joining us were about two dozen other friends and acquaintances, including writers for the *Washington Times, National Review, Weekly Standard,* and National Public Radio; several administration officials, including Fred Schwien, senior advisor to Homeland Security Secretary Michael Chertoff; Jack and Kathy Rusenko, who founded the George Washington Academy, Morocco's foremost K–12 private school, and who had first suggested the evening; a diplomat from the Moroccan Embassy helping coordinate the trip; and the board of the Joshua Fund, the nonprofit educational and charitable organization Lynn and I founded "to bless Israel and her neighbors in the name of Jesus, according to Genesis 12:1–3."

Once we were all properly introduced, Lynn served her famous (and my favorite) "chicken puffs," asparagus, and salad, and we settled in for an intimate yet on-the-record discussion.

A Monarch on the Move

At a time when Osama bin Laden and Mahmoud Ahmadinejad were breathing their murderous threats against Christians and Jews and attempting to incite Muslims around the world to annihilate the U.S. and Israel, Dr. Abaddi was a welcome and wonderful breath of fresh air. He reminded us that in 1777, Morocco was the first country in the world to officially recognize the United States as an independent nation. Ever since, he said, Morocco has not only been the most western Muslim nation geographically; it has also been among the most pro-Western ideologically and operationally.* And in Abaddi's view, King Mohammed VI was quietly emerging as one of the boldest Reformers in the Muslim world.

The story of Morocco's king was not one the American mainstream media was reporting, but it was one Abaddi felt they should be. After all, he explained, ever since ascending to the throne in July 1999 — just hours after the death of his father, King Hassan II — the young monarch had been on the move, steadily and systematically transforming Morocco into a model of moderation.

After 9/11 the king could have shown sympathy to the terrorists and the plight of the Muslim people, as many in the Islamic world had done. He was, after all, a direct descendant of Islam's founder. Instead, the king immediately ordered his security forces to work closely with the U.S. to round up al Qaeda operatives, with tremendous success. On June 16, 2002, Moroccan intelligence and the CIA intercepted a sleeper cell of bin Laden agents who were in the advanced stages of planning major terrorist attacks against U.S. and British warships and commercial container ships

*"Moroccans recognized the Government of the United States in 1777," says the U.S. State Department. "Formal U.S. relations with Morocco date from 1787, when the two nations negotiated a Treaty of Peace and Friendship. Renegotiated in 1836, the treaty is still in force, constituting the longest unbroken treaty relationship in U.S. history" (see State Department country profile of Morocco, November 2003).

in the Strait of Gibraltar.[1] A few days later, Moroccan police rounded up still more al Qaeda operatives, and the arrests have continued every few months ever since.[2] By 2006, Moroccan authorities had arrested nearly three thousand terror suspects — some homegrown, some from Saudi Arabia and other Islamist countries — and busted up at least fifty terror cells.[3]

Simultaneously, His Majesty dispatched Abaddi and his colleagues in the Ministry of Islamic Affairs to embark upon a public information campaign of speeches, sermons, and interviews in the Moroccan media condemning al Qaeda's teachings and tactics and laying out the theology of the Reformers. The king ordered this campaign to be accelerated and intensified after a series of suicide bombings ripped through several Muslim- and Jewish-owned restaurants and a Jewish community center in Casablanca on May 16, 2003, leaving forty-five dead (including twelve of fourteen bombers) and more than a hundred wounded.

It was clear that the Radicals posed a clear and present danger to the safety and security of the 34 million citizens of the kingdom, as well as to the stability of the regime itself. And as the eighteenth heir to the Alaouite dynasty, which has ruled Morocco since 1649 — as well as the "Commander of the Faithful," guardian of all Muslims, Jews, and Christians in Morocco — the king was not about to let the Radicals succeed.

Nor, for that matter, were the Moroccan people, the majority of whom were outraged by the attacks. That month, Abaddi and his team helped mobilize more than one million Moroccans who took to the streets of Casablanca to denounce radical Islamic terrorism, a march in which more than a thousand Moroccan Jews openly participated and were warmly embraced by the Muslim community as kindred spirits against a common enemy.

As if all this were not enough, the king also began advancing a series of significant legislative reforms designed to open up the democratic process and allow all Moroccans — including women — the right to participate. The reforms sought to protect the rights of women and children and rectify a number of human rights abuses for which the king's father had been widely blamed. Moreover, His Majesty ordered Abaddi and his colleagues to launch an aggressive new theological training program to ensure that all new Imams coming out of Moroccan seminaries would be prepared to promote a moderate, peaceful, progressive version of Islam, not turn mosques into hotbeds of Radical recruitment and incitement as in Egypt and Saudi Arabia.

"We need our people to know the real West . . . to understand that the West ain't no angel, but it ain't no demon, either," Abaddi, attempting a Western accent, told those gathered at our home for dinner that night. "This effort is not a luxury. We are trying to train responsible people to live in dangerous times."[4]

He went on to say he was worried about the apocalyptic rhetoric coming out of Tehran, Iran's nuclear program, radical Islamic terrorism, AIDS, and severe global poverty. "Morocco can help bring about peace. I think the Moroccan model is practical and helpful. It communicates an entirely different concept of Islam to the rest of the world. . . . I personally can't sit back and do nothing. There is an Arab proverb that says, 'Don't be a mute Satan.' I feel compelled to do everything I can to make a better world."

An Invitation to the Kingdom

In the years that followed that first meeting, Dr. Abaddi and I developed a friendship that I have grown to appreciate a great deal. Among other things, he has helped me to go inside the minds of the Reformers and better understand who they are, what they want, when they started, where they are going, and how they plan to get there. We keep in contact by phone. We e-mail each other. He has been back to our home for more chicken puffs and more in-depth conversations. Along the way, he graciously invited me to visit his country and see the Moroccan model for myself. In January of 2008 I accepted.

I had been to Morocco before, as a tourist with Lynn and the boys in 2001 and 2002, and again in 2005 as I was researching and writing *Epicenter.* I had already come to love Morocco, with its beauty and rich history and wonderfully hospitable people. But this was a particularly special visit as it afforded me the opportunity to meet with men and women who worked for King Mohammed VI, knew him well, advised him, and understood what made him tick.

Abaddi himself had been promoted since I had seen him last. He was no longer responsible for overseeing the day-to-day affairs of the nation's mosques. He now had been personally appointed by His Majesty to head up a strategic studies center whose explicit mission was to engage all of the top Islamic scholars in the country in a sweeping effort to map out and passionately advance a

Reformer agenda for the twenty-first century. What's more, Abaddi was teaching the Qur'an to an estimated audience of 6 million Muslims every night in a television program broadcast on Moroccan television and on an Arabic satellite network throughout North Africa and the Middle East. He had essentially become the Dr. James Dobson or the Chuck Swindoll of the moderate Muslim world, one of the most thoughtful and most listened-to religious teachers in the region.

It was a remarkable trip, to say the least. Joining me as part of our delegation were several dear friends, including John Moser, executive director of the Joshua Fund; Fred Schwien from Homeland Security (traveling as a private citizen); and Chip and Larissa Lusko, producers of the *Epicenter* documentary film who again had a film crew with them as we compiled material for a future *Inside the Revolution* documentary.

Together, we visited the palace, met with members of parliament, and were briefed by a top security official at the Interior Ministry. We talked with Islamic scholars, spent several days with Dr. Abaddi, and were invited to a wonderful dinner party in our honor at the Abaddis' home in the capital city of Rabat. We also spent an engaging (though off-the-record) afternoon with U.S. Ambassador Thomas Riley and his wife at their home and visited Jack and Kathy Rusenko in Casablanca at the George Washington Academy, where they and their staff have the privilege and responsibility of helping to prepare some five hundred students from Morocco, the U.S., and two dozen other countries to become future leaders of their respective nations, most of them in North Africa or the Middle East.

My Impressions of the King

What I saw and heard and learned during that visit to Morocco, together with my observations from the last eight years of closely watching the country, could fill a book in its own right. But I would have to say that what has impressed me most has been the character and vision of King Mohammed VI. We have not met personally. He was hosting a summit with King Abdullah II of Jordan while we were there, and rarely gives interviews, particularly to foreigners. Nevertheless, I have come to believe that he is someone to keep a close eye on.

Born on August 21, 1963, His Majesty is one of the youngest leaders in the Muslim world. Though he began moving slowly and cautiously upon first becoming king, over time he has put his own peers into positions of power to replace his father's generation. He has consolidated his support within the military and the ruling class, and he has impressed the citizens as a ruler who truly cares for the poor and is determined to improve their lives. In the process, he has seemed to gain confidence, become more assertive, and become more willing to take Moroccans toward a future in which they have more freedom to make their own choices about how to live their lives, raise their children, build their businesses, and interact with the outside world. Indeed, in many ways, His Majesty has come to exemplify a new generation of regional leaders.

The king is religious, having begun memorizing the entire Qur'an at the age of four, but he is by no means a Radical. He is a monarch but not a megalomaniac, harboring no delusional visions of grandeur and all-encompassing power as some leaders in the region do. He is authoritative but not an authoritarian, as some have criticized his father for being. He is clearly open to expanding democracy, but he is deeply (and wisely) opposed to allowing extremists to hijack the electoral process and seize power once and for all.

What is more, he is mindful and respectful of Arab history and tradition yet is also pro-Western in his outlook and approach. He is committed to protecting and advancing the human rights of the Palestinian people, but he has also developed excellent relations with Jews in general and Israelis in particular. Likewise, he is cognizant of the enormous sensitivities within the region to the notion of Muslims converting to Christianity, but he has demonstrated a sincere and consistent interest in fostering better relations with Christians in general and with evangelicals in particular.

Understanding the Reformers of Rabat

Most impressive to me was the fact that the king and his advisors truly understand the magnitude of the epic struggle they are facing and seem fully committed to victory.

"This is a battle about defining the soul and spirit of Islam itself," Abaddi told me as we sat in his spacious but modestly decorated office one afternoon, sipping tea and overlooking Rabat, with its population of 2 million. "And we dare not fail. His Majesty believes the stakes are very high. We have no right to make the mistakes of previous generations, because we should have learned from previous mistakes and because we are very efficient today. And our mistakes could be very expensive. Look at Pearl Harbor. Look at Hiroshima and Nagasaki. World War II was very expensive in terms of human life. But the next war could mean the extermination of the planet."

I asked him to expand on that, particularly in light of the apocalyptic talk coming out of Tehran.

"Nowadays," he said, "one can discern a lot of apocalyptic seeds in our thinking in the Middle East. There has been an explosion of apocalyptic literature in the Muslim world beginning in the 1980s — after 1979, actually. There have been hundreds of books about the end of the world and the coming of the Mahdi and messianic prophecies and ideologies. Ahmadinejad is preparing for the coming of the Mahdi. Osama bin Laden is preparing for the Mahdi. He is trying to use his version of Islam to recruit an army, and he is very dangerous. That's why I say this is a battle for the soul of the Muslim world. Because there are two completely different visions. One is peaceful, and one is apocalyptic. And Morocco can be an answer to this because His Majesty is leading a reform plan that touches the forces and the understandings and renews the souls and spirits of Islam.

"But we need to act. We need to face this. We need to be able to make intellectual and theological arguments that convince people that the Radicals are wrong. We need coordinated actions in the media, in the world of art, in the universities, in the think tanks, at the United Nations. We also need to be able to speak in a language that regular people, including those without much education, can understand and respond to. The Reformers need to engage in actions that will drag the carpets from under the Radicals' feet."

"What do you see as the worst-case scenario if the Reformers don't seize the moment, or if they do seize the moment but lose the argument with the Rank-and-File of the Muslim world?" I asked.

"Millions of new recruits to radicalism," he replied. "More war. More terrorism. But, Joel, the worst is not material disasters, as bad as they would be. The worst would be the missed opportunities to live as brothers in harmony and beauty. The worst would be the missed appointment with destiny."

Abaddi pointed again and again to passages in the Qur'an saying that God created all of humankind, men and women from every nation. Such passages prove, he said, that "we are all one family, an extended family, and we need each other to survive and succeed." This, he argued, was the Islamic doctrine of "complementarity," the notion that we all complement and complete each other.

Moreover, he said, the Qur'an teaches that since we were all created as brothers and sisters, we need to perform "mutual recognition." This goes "beyond tolerance," he insisted. To tolerate someone is merely to put up with him. That is not good enough. "People who think they are self-sufficient with their own ideas and their own views of the world are in danger." What we need, he said, is to recognize that other people, other religions, other races have good in them, have richness and beauty, and we need to be wise enough to find such qualities, appreciate them, and build upon them.

"These ideas exist in the Qur'an," he told me, speaking specifically of complementarity and mutual recognition. "But honestly, they have been on 'pause mode' for too long. They have not been activated enough. They have not been taught or practiced enough. It is time to push the 'play' button. Wisdom is like pieces of a puzzle. Did you know that Eskimos have forty-three different words for snow? Why? Because they really understand snow. They understand its shades and its nuances. They have wisdom we don't have. And if we're living in a snowstorm, wouldn't it be good to draw on the wisdom of the Eskimos?

"What if you were putting together a puzzle of Cyrano de Bergerac. What if you put together the whole puzzle, but you were missing a piece? What if you were missing the nose? You would miss the whole point, would you not? We need to see the missing pieces in the world around us to get the whole picture, to really understand how the world works. And the only way to get those missing pieces is to recognize that someone else from some other culture or religion might understand something we don't understand today."

I cannot think of a better way to sum up the way Reformers see the world. Yes, they believe Islam is the answer. But no, they do not believe violent jihad is the way. Yes, they look to the Qur'an for wisdom. But no, they do not reject the outside world, even the world of the Christians and the Jews. Rather, they believe now is the time to teach Muslims to revere their own religion but also reach out to other cultures and other religions and look for wisdom they might not have.

CHAPTER TWENTY-THREE: THE MOROCCAN MODEL

One nation's twelve-step program
to combat the Radicals

It is not just talk, though. It's not just theory.

King Mohammed VI and his team have a plan. Indeed, they have developed what amounts to a twelve-step program to battle the Radicals and spread Morocco's message of reform throughout the region and around the world. The steps are:

1. Know the enemy
2. Stop the enemy
3. Embrace the East
4. Embrace the West
5. Teach the theology of the Reformers
6. Expand democracy
7. Empower women
8. Combat poverty
9. Let the voiceless speak
10. Build and maintain strong relations with the Jewish community
11. Reach out to evangelical Christians in the West
12. Counter the "Hollywood stigma"

Allow me to explain.

Step 1: Know the Enemy

First and foremost, the king and his team believe that good intelligence is critical to identifying terrorist threats *before* they materialize. They are absolutely right.

This involves building effective networks of human agents and electronic surveillance to monitor extremist groups and individuals. And it requires close cooperation with other intelligence agencies in the region and around the world to monitor subversives that may be planning to enter or traverse Moroccan territory.

But it also involves understanding the mind-set of the enemy. And given that the main enemy today involves followers of an extreme interpretation of Islam, religious scholars like Ahmed Abaddi have emerged as key players in helping the king and his court understand more deeply and completely what they are up against.

"When you study the extremists' literature and you visit their Web sites and watch their DVDs and what they produce, you see that there are six repetitive items that come back all the time," Abaddi explained.

The first issue, he said, is that of colonialism, in which the West is demonized because, as the Radicals say, "They came in and colonized our countries and killed our people!" While it is true that Morocco was a protectorate of France for nearly a century, little violence ensued. But in Algeria, Abaddi noted, some 1.5 million Muslims were killed by French colonialists, to say nothing of numerous other cases of violence committed throughout North Africa and the Middle East by the British, the Italians, and others. Add to this what Abaddi calls the "Afghani-Iraqi cocktail" in which the Radicals say that the Americans and the Europeans are occupying Islamic territory as colonialists, imperialists, and oppressors, and you have a highly charged emotional issue that resonates deeply within the Muslim world and helps the Radicals recruit vast numbers of new jihadists.

The second issue is the belief that the West is "draining the wealth of the Islamic world" by exploiting the region's natural resources, notably oil. The West, of course, is paying Muslims enormous sums of money for these resources. Each year, the U.S. alone sends hundreds of billions of dollars to Muslim countries in return for oil, in addition to what the Europeans are paying. We hardly see ourselves as "exploiting" anyone. But Abaddi notes that as one might expect, such facts are never mentioned by the Radicals; thus the exploitation issue has great populist appeal.

The third recurring theme among extremists is the "Hollywood stigma," a widespread and deep-rooted feeling of humiliation throughout the region due to the belief that major American motion pictures are constantly showing Arabs and Muslims as being stupid, dirty, and evil.

Fourth, Abaddi said, is the historic "conspiracy" by the West "against the Ottoman Empire," which was the seat of the caliphate and represented the unity of Muslims. Radicals constantly repeat facts about the 1915 attack by the British, French, and Germans to reclaim control of Istanbul. Even though the Allies actually lost the Battle of the Dardanelles and the Gallipoli campaign, the conflicts resulted in a quarter of a million Turkish casualties, and the Radicals have vowed never to forget. Moroccans, Abaddi conceded, were not as concerned with this issue because they were never a part of the Ottoman Empire. Still, he added, "this is what is being said in Radical literature," and it has been working to recruit more jihadists.

The fifth issue is the perceived double standard Westerners have regarding Israel versus the Arabs. The Radicals say that the Jews possess advanced major weapons systems, weapons of mass destruction, and even nuclear weapons, and the West says nothing. But when Iraq or Iran or other countries in the region seek such weapons, "then everybody tries to get rid of those nations," say the Radicals.

The sixth issue is the existence of Israel in the first place. Radicals insist that a great injustice was done to the Muslim people when the Jews began flooding into the Holy Land, buying up land and driving out the local population. The Jews, of course, say that the rebirth of Israel — aside from being a prophetic event — was specifically designed to correct a great injustice: the Holocaust. In response, the Radicals say, "There was no Holocaust! And even if there was, let the Jews have a state in Europe, where the alleged atrocities were committed, not in Palestine, which was not directly involved!" It is a vicious cycle, compounded by all the deaths and dislocation experienced by the Muslims of the area since 1948.

Step 2: Stop the Enemy

It is one thing to know the enemy. It is another thing to stop the enemy, and here having crack security services able to intercept terrorists and dismantle jihadist cells before they can strike is essential. Morocco has excelled in this arena, and to understand why, Fred Schwien, John Moser, and I took some time to visit the headquarters of the Ministry of the Interior. There we met with Khalid Zerouali, a senior official in Morocco's equivalent of the U.S. Department of Homeland Security.

I took a liking to Zerouali, who was in his early forties and thus similar in age to me, right away — and not simply because he began our meeting by telling me that he had read and appreciated *Epicenter.* I also appreciated his passion for his job and how well he understood the nature of the evil Morocco is facing.

"The threat to us is real and serious," Zerouali told us. "We were the first Arab country to stand with you after 9/11. His Majesty was in Mauritania and sent condolences to the U.S. from there. Then we began to work closely with the U.S. to stop al Qaeda. It was the right thing to do, but the fact is it made us a target. We are still a target. So far we have been successful. But we can't rest for a moment."[1]

Zerouali noted that bin Laden and Zawahiri have established a new branch known as "Al Qaeda in the Islamic Maghreb,"* or AQIM, a clandestine network of sleeper agents and infiltrators whose mission is to kill innocents, overthrow moderates, and ultimately establish new regimes that can create new base camps for the original al Qaeda operation, on the run since the liberation of Afghanistan. "Al Qaeda leaders are looking for new harbors," he said matter-of-factly. "And the Sahara region historically has had all the right

*"Maghreb" is an Arab and French term generally referring to the Western half of North Africa, including Morocco, Mauritania, Algeria, Tunisia, and Libya.

conditions — poor people, porous borders, states that cannot control their own territories. His Majesty recognized this right away and ordered us to take actions to safeguard our people. Our strength is intel — knowing who is in our country, what they are doing, whether they pose a threat, and stopping them in time."

"What keeps you up at night?" I asked him.

"Self-radicalization," he said. "We can find people when they are acting in a group. We can pick up their calls or intercept their e-mails or recruit an informer. But the Internet today is posing a real challenge. You can go on there and learn to build a bomb. You can find jihadist teachings. You can learn how to be a terrorist. . . . How can you stop that? How can you prevent the chemistry in the mind to prevent the fatal work of terrorism?" He calls this problem "disposable terrorism," lone wolves who can prepare to blow up themselves and lots of other people and then be gone without a trace. "You can't detect them. You can't track them. You can't infiltrate them. You can rarely stop them. This is what I worry about."

The good news: ever since the Casablanca bombings in 2003, the Moroccan security forces are getting a lot of tips from citizens watching for guerrillas in their midst. A few months before we arrived, for example, police raided a house to bust up a cell of suicide bombers preparing to strike. During the raid, several of the bombers blew themselves up, killing only themselves. But in the commotion, one of the terrorists slipped away, unnoticed by the police. He tried to blend into the crowd, but several people saw him. They didn't know he was one of the terrorists. They thought he was simply a thief. But they pounced

496

on him, captured him, and turned him over to the police. "The population is against all this extremism, all these suicide bombings," Zerouali explained. "This is not Islam, they say; this is not human."

Border protection is one of Zerouali's top priorities. "My main concern is not airports or seaports," he said, though his department has worked hard to shore up security procedures at all such entry points, including making Morocco the first country in the region to have biometric passports that are nearly impossible to counterfeit. "My main concern is open land." Mindful of this threat a generation ago, King Hassan II ordered a 2,700 kilometer "berm" or security wall to be built in the Sahara along Morocco's (disputed) southern border, beginning in 1982. The goal at the time was to stop illegal immigrants, drug smugglers, and gun runners from entering the country. The security fence was completed in 1988, long before the U.S. government decided it needed to build such a fence along its southern border with Mexico. Today, the wall is the first line of defense against al Qaeda operatives and other Radicals hoping to slip across the border unnoticed.

But it is not a perfect system. As evidenced by how many foreign-born terrorists Moroccan authorities have rounded up in recent years, much more needs to be done.

Step 3: Embrace the East

Judging it wiser, safer, and more effective to build strong strategic alliances with other moderate Islamic nations rather than to go it alone against the Radicals, King Mohammed VI — positioned at the farthest western edge of the Islamic world

— has made it a priority to embrace the East.

He has built strong ties with Turkey over the years. In March of 2005 he welcomed Turkish prime minister Recep Erdogan to Rabat for a state visit in which the two countries signed a historic free trade agreement. The king has also been very supportive of Turkey's bid to join the European Union, believing that would be a huge step forward in healing long-standing tensions between the Islamic world and the West, particularly given Europe's conflict with Istanbul in 1915.

The king has also been strongly supportive of democratic reforms in Afghanistan. He sent humanitarian aid to the Afghan people immediately after the fall of the Taliban, and Morocco was one of the first Islamic countries to endorse and support the government of President Karzai from the earliest days of his administration. "Morocco . . . has been constantly following up with interest developments experienced by Afghanistan, a Muslim country . . . hails the major step [of] the agreement concluded between Afghan parties to form an interim government to manage public affairs . . . and considers this event as a major step in the path leading to restoring peace, security, and serenity for the Afghan people after the conflicts and misfortunes they underwent," said a statement by the Moroccan Foreign Ministry on December 24, 2001. Since then, the king and President Karzai have established and maintained regular diplomatic contact.

Morocco was also the first Arab state to condemn Saddam Hussein's invasion of Kuwait and sent troops to help liberate the moderate Gulf state in 1991 as well as to defend the Saudis. On the other hand, the king and his aides have taken a "wait and see" approach to the newly democratic government in Iraq. After the abduction and murder of two Moroccan diplomats in Baghdad in the fall of 2005 and repeated reports that al Qaeda has been recruiting Moroccans to launch terrorist attacks inside Iraq, the issue of democracy in Iraq and U.S. and European military involvement there apparently have been simply too sensitive for the Moroccan government to tackle thus far.[2]

The king's closest ally in the East has been the Hashemite Kingdom of Jordan. As I noted earlier, His Majesty was holding a bilateral summit with Jordan's King Abdullah II while I was in Rabat. Indeed, the two monarchs actually meet regularly and are considered good friends.

And it makes sense; they share many similarities. Aside from being among the region's leading Reformers, they are also close in age (Mohammed was born 1963, Abdullah in 1962) and thus have a similar generational outlook. They are both married with children (Mohammed has a son and a daughter; Abdullah has two of each). They both love adventure and high speeds (Mohammed loves racing his Mercedes and his Jet Ski, earning him the nickname "His Majetski"; Abdullah loves racing his Harley and skydiving). Their fathers — King Hassan II and King Hussein, respectively — were friends and allies and were both sympathetic to the West and to Israel. Their fathers also passed away within months of each other, turning power over to their sons with little notice (Mohammed's father passed away on July 23, 1999; Abdullah's father passed away on February 7, 1999).

Most important, they both face the same enormous challenge — trying to move their monarchies in the direction of representative democracies, knowing all the while that al Qaeda is gunning for them and that the Radicals would love to overthrow them or use the electoral process to seize control. Both kings are walking a tightrope without a net, and neither can afford to slip.

Step 4: Embrace the West

Continuing his belief in not going it alone in the world, King Mohammed VI has clearly chosen to strengthen strategic alliances with Europe and the U.S.

Morocco has even expressed a desire to join the European Union after Turkey is accepted — *if* Turkey is ever accepted.* Given that Ankara's bid appears to be a long shot at this point, the king has agreed to join the new "Mediterranean Union" made up of twenty-seven E.U. states and twelve other nations bordering the Mediterranean Sea, an initiative launched by French president Nicolas Sarkozy at a July 2008 summit in Paris.[3]

His Majesty has cooperated with Washington on a wide range of security, economic, and cultural issues. He made his first state visit to the U.S. in the summer of 2000 and returned in the summer of 2004 when the Bush administration gave Morocco the designation of "major non-NATO ally."

The king also regularly welcomes high-level delegations to Rabat, including Secretaries of State Colin Powell and Condoleezza Rice, and his

*Morocco actually applied in 1987 to join the European Communities, the precursor to the E.U., but was turned down.

government signed a historic free trade agreement with the U.S. in 2005, the second such agreement the U.S. signed with an Arab country (Jordan was first), and the first in North Africa. The agreement eliminated 95 percent of all tariffs on goods flowing between the two countries and made arrangements to phase out the remaining 5 percent over the next decade.

Moreover, Morocco agreed in 2002 to allow the U.S. government to build a $225 million transmitter in its country for Radio Sawa, which broadcasts news, information, music, and some entertainment programming in Arabic to young people throughout North Africa and the Middle East who have few other sources of accurate news reporting from around the world and few other sources of pro-American commentary and analysis.

Step 5: Teach the Theology of the Reformers

This is one of Dr. Abaddi's main assignments from the king, and it is one he takes very seriously. The strategy has two key components.

First, Morocco believes it must train a new generation of moderate Islamic preachers.

After the 2003 bombings, the king ordered the Ministry of Islamic Affairs to launch a theological training program for new imams to teach them how to promote moderation within Islam, to educate them about Western history and the importance of Christianity and Judaism to Western social and political development, and to help them identify and oppose extremist forces and trends within Islam. Participants take thirty-two hours of instruction each week for a full year. The first class graduated 210 new clerics, including fifty-five women, in 2006.

Abaddi and his team also helped organize the "World Congress of Rabbis and Imams for Peace" in Brussels (January 2005) and Seville (March 2006), where some 150 Muslim and Jewish leaders "sit beard to beard" to explore common ground, denounce extremists, and "write declarations of peace." They are publishing books and producing Web sites, tapes, and DVDs to drive moderate theology deep into the culture.

Abaddi has also placed under the supervision of the Ministry of Islamic Affairs some nine thousand mosques that had not previously been subject to government oversight, raising the total number from thirty-three thousand to forty-two thousand.

Second, Morocco believes it must train a new generation of moderate Islamic scholars.

The king is not concerned just about those who teach the Qur'an day by day. He is also concerned about those who would shape Islamic theology for the next century to come. To help me understand the king's long-term approach, Abaddi sent my colleagues and me across town to meet a man named Dr. Ahmed Khamlichi (pronounced "Hahm*lee*-shee"), director of Dar Al Hadith Al Hassania, the most famous religious institute in Morocco.

Now in his seventies, Dr. Khamlichi has trained scores of imams, professors, and judges since founding the institute in 1965. But at the king's insistence, he oversaw a dramatic transformation of his entire operation after the Casablanca bombings of 2003. Neither he nor his staff had been teaching anything close to Radicalism before the bombings. But neither had they been intentionally and proactively developing future leaders who would be ready to *combat* extremism and make a clear, principled, well-researched, and theologically persuasive case of Islamic moderation throughout Morocco, much less to the rest of the Arab world. Now, using a completely revamped curriculum, this is precisely their mission.

Sitting in Khamlichi's ornate Rabat office, covered with exquisite, hand-painted tiles and handsome wooden shelves holding hundreds of tomes by Islamic scholars across the ages, we sipped sweet mint tea as he explained what he is doing and why.

"The situation is urgent," he told us in no uncertain terms. Morocco, he said, cannot rely on the police rounding up all the Radicals and putting them in prison. Nor should it even think of executing Radicals en masse, as other Arab states have done in recent decades. He pointed to the executions of thousands of Radicals, including Sayyid Qutb, in Egypt. "Did it work?" he asked. "Were the Radical movements" — such as the Muslim Brotherhood and Egyptian Islamic Jihad — "stopped?" To the contrary, he noted, "human rights violations have been deplorable in this region. This gives rise to revolutions, not peace." The only way to win the battle for the soul of Islam and thus establish lasting peace and prosperity in the region, he insisted, is to fight and win a battle of ideas. "Extremism is gaining new ground," he warned us. "It is urgent to develop a new generation of scholars to counteract these Radical ideas."[4]

His approach: recruit the best and the brightest Muslim students — true up-and-coming leaders — and turn them into scholars who are fully devoted to teaching the theology of the Reformers and applying their moderate theology at every

503

level of Moroccan society.

Today, some 160 students a year take classes from Khamlichi's handpicked staff, studying Islamic history, society, and jurisprudence, but also studying comparative religion, including the merits of Christianity and Judaism. The students also take English and even Hebrew.

After spending most of a day talking with the director and his staff, touring the urban campus, sitting in on a few classes — including a Hebrew class in progress — and chatting with several students, I must say I came away impressed. Obviously, we do not share the same theology. But like Khamlichi, I would much rather see a young Muslim become a Reformer than a Radical, and thus I am grateful for what he and his team are doing. They are not playing games. They are true Reformers. They have a sense of mission. They understand the stakes could not be higher. And they are not afraid of Christianity and Judaism. Indeed, they believe now is the time for Muslims to understand both faiths better than ever before.

My only disappointment when the day was done was that there was only one Arabic copy of the Bible in the library for the students to use in their comparative religion classes. I asked the librarian if she thought they needed more.

"Oh, absolutely," she replied. "We just don't have the funds in the budget."

When I asked whether the Joshua Fund could supply a case of Arabic Bibles to help the students study it in their own heart language, her eyes lit up. "Well, that is very kind," she said, and in a small but telling sign of the true openness of the institute's leaders, she quickly got approval. By the time we left the country, the Bibles had been ordered and were soon delivered.

When Abaddi told me that "Dr. Khamlichi is one of the most prominent men in Morocco," I had no difficulty understanding why. Nor was it a stretch to believe that "his is a very sensitive office" in Morocco's overall strategy because, as Abaddi put it, Khamlichi "is training the gatekeepers of tomorrow."

Step 6: Expand Democracy

In a rare interview with *Time* magazine in the summer of 2000, King Mohammed VI agreed that "Morocco has a lot to do in terms of democracy." He went on to say that "the daily practice of democracy evolves in time — trying to apply a Western democratic system to a country of the Maghreb [North African countries], the Middle East, or the Gulf would be a mistake. We are not Germany, Sweden, or Spain. I have a lot of respect for countries where the practice of democracy is highly developed. I think, however, that each country has to have its own specific features of democracy."[5]

"People speculate that the Moroccan monarchy will evolve like the Spanish one," noted *Time*'s Cairo bureau chief Scott MacLeod. He was referring to the fact that after the 1975 death of General Francisco Franco, Spain's longtime Socialist dictator, Franco's handpicked and personally educated and groomed successor, King Juan Carlos, came to power. No one expected the young monarch — then only thirty-seven — to buck the system Franco had created. But to everyone's shock, that is precisely what he did. Beginning in 1976, the king slowly but surely began helping the country make the transition to

505

a full-blown and robust constitutional democracy without violence or massive social upheaval. He legalized political parties. He authorized the creation of a constitution. And then he actually relinquished absolute power, putting control of the country in the hands of the people and their elected representatives, while still serving as the head of state.

It was a perceptive point, and the king's reply was interesting.

"I have a lot of respect for His Majesty Juan Carlos," said the Moroccan monarch. "I call him 'Uncle Juan' because he is an extraordinary person whom I have known for a long time. He is a relative almost. We often speak on the phone, and I ask him for his guidance. But Moroccans are not Spaniards, and they will never be. Democracy in Spain was very good for Spain. There should be a Moroccan model specific to Morocco."[6]

That was nearly a decade ago. Today, I believe the Moroccan king knows precisely where he is headed. He knows precisely how he is going to get there. And he has a proven leader in King Juan Carlos to answer his questions and advise him along the journey. He may not have known exactly how to proceed back in 2000. But he does now. And personally I believe he is following the Spanish approach. Not so precisely. Not so quickly. He does not want to frighten the Rank-and-File. He does not want to alarm the rest of the Muslim world. He does not want to enrage the Radicals, if he can help it, or give them an opening to seize control of his country and turn back the clock on democracy and progress as Hamas has done in Gaza after the West unwisely pressured the

Palestinian Authority to hold elections before building a truly free and civil society. But he knows where he is going, he is going in the right direction, and he is learning how to persuade people to follow him step-by-step.

Today, Moroccans enjoy far more freedom to say what they want, write what they want, and organize their political parties, labor unions, human-rights organizations, and social reform groups than they did under the current king's father — and far more than almost anywhere in the Islamic world. The country has a functioning bicameral legislature. It has held several successful, transparent, and relatively corruption-free elections for parliament — including as recently as 2007 — in which thirty-four democratic political parties openly competed.

Still, more must be done. Prodemocracy and human-rights organizations should not lessen their pressure for more change. Indeed, they should accelerate such pressure.

Step 7: Empower Women

According to Ms. Fatiha Layadi, among the king's most impressive moves has been his commitment to improving conditions for women and children and expanding democratic opportunities for women to run for political office and serve in positions of power and authority. Layadi was a well-known newscaster in Morocco before being elected to Parliament in 2007, where she has quickly emerged as one of the most influential women in the country. I interviewed her in the gardens of the Rabat Hilton and was immediately impressed.

"How many other women are in the Moroccan

parliament?" I asked.

"Thirty-four," she said.

"Out of how many seats?"

"Out of 325," she replied — more than 10 percent, one of the highest percentages in the Islamic world. "Four women were elected in direct election, and thirty were elected under what we call here in Morocco the 'National List,' which is a list for women that was agreed on six years ago, to make access to Parliament easier for women, so that 20 percent of the House of Representatives should be made of women."[7]

But even that is not enough for Layadi. Now she and her colleagues are pressing for legislation that would make a full third of the representatives women.

"Had there ever been a woman elected in Morocco prior to the changes encouraged by the king in 2002?" I asked.

"Yes, four of them," she said.

"Four total, in all of history?"

"Oh yes. Women have been running for election since the very first elections in Morocco in the '60s. But the very first ones to be elected — there were two of them — were in 1992."

"So this is real progress," I noted, even more impressed after learning that a Moroccan Jewish woman ran for a seat in Parliament in 2007, making news all throughout the Islamic world.[8]

"Yes, it's a historical trend in Morocco. We have to keep in mind that in his very first address to the nation, the new king said that the country could not move forward on only one leg, since women did not have their whole rights, political and also civil rights. Since the king came to power in 1999, there have been major reforms that have

508

been conducted. The first and most important one for me is the 'Family Law.' "

On October 10, 2003, the king delivered a major address laying out eleven reforms he wanted the legislature to pass. Known as the "Family Code" or "Family Law," they included giving men and women equal rights before the law, giving wives living in abusive and destructive marriages the right to divorce their husbands, giving wives equal rights to the couples' financial property, and making polygamy — hotly debated by Islamic scholars but still very common in the Muslim world* — nearly impossible by requiring the husband to obtain not only his first wife's written permission but also a judge's assent that "the husband will treat his second wife and her children on an equal footing with the first [and] provide the same living conditions for all" before being legally permitted to marry another woman.[9]

The landmark legislation passed on January 25, 2004, and was a shot heard around the Muslim world. Layadi readily conceded it made the

*A portion of Sura 4:3 reads, "When you marry the orphan girls (in your custody), you can marry, from among other women (who are permitted to you in marriage and) who seem good to you, two, three, and four." Muhammad had multiple wives, and this verse is believed to be a justification for it. But those Islamic scholars who oppose polygamy (or who severely discourage its practice) note that the very next portion of the very same verse says, "However, if you fear that (in mutual obligations) you will not be able to observe justice among them, then content yourselves with only one."

509

Radicals unhappy, but she did not care. She was convinced that the kind of social and political reforms the king has been pursuing are absolutely essential to helping Morocco become a model of Muslim moderation in an age of Muslim radicalism.

"May 16, 2003, was a terrible day for me as a journalist and for me as a Moroccan," she told me. "I could never imagine that Moroccans would kill Moroccans. I could not imagine that young Moroccans — sixteen of them — could just go all over Casablanca and explode themselves, blow themselves up, and kill forty-four people with them. It was a shock. And 9/11 was a shock to me too. I remember staying all day stuck to my TV, trying to understand, trying to feel what these people in the Twin Towers felt when they saw the planes coming to strike the towers. Terrorism is something crazy. Terrorism is something — I don't know how to say it in English — I'm shocked. . . . It's something incredible."

"But it is driven by those who say they are fighting in the name of Islam," I noted.

"Osama bin Laden is not a Muslim for me," she shot back.

"What is he?" I asked. "How would you define bin Laden?"

"I don't know, a sort of monster," Layadi replied. "All these people are sort of monsters, creatures coming from out of nowhere. The people who killed Benazir Bhutto — why? The lady came to speak about democracy. The lady was coming to speak about reform in her country. And they came and blew themselves up. What does it mean? They are creatures of chaos. . . . I just cannot understand where they are coming from and

510

where they want us to go. We have nothing in common as Muslims. They say they are Muslims, but I am a Muslim and I have nothing in common with them.

"My parents used to have Jewish friends. I used to play with Jewish friends of mine. I had no problems going to Jewish houses, no problem going to Christian houses. I think most Moroccans are like me. Islam in Morocco has always been different. I think Morocco and Jordan are trying to show themselves — the two young monarchs are trying to show themselves — as models for the other Arab countries. I'm cautious because I think both countries have to consolidate their own affairs before trying to turn the others. There are reforms here in Morocco and there in Jordan that have been under way less than ten years, don't forget. We have to consolidate all this . . . but I hope we can make a true difference."

Step 8: Combat Poverty

In 2000, *Time* magazine asked the new monarch what Morocco's most important problems were.

"First of all, there is unemployment, and agriculture, drought," he replied. "There is the fight against poverty. I could talk about this endlessly: poverty, misery, illiteracy."[10]

Ever since, the king has taken a series of positive steps to boost Morocco's economy and increase national wealth and individual wages. In addition to providing political stability and taking strong measures to prevent terrorists from driving away tourists and investment, he has also privatized state-owned businesses, reduced taxes, and encouraged diversification from an agriculture-based economy to more manufacturing and technology-related industries.

Though there is still a long way to go, progress has been noticeable. In 1999, the gross domestic product was $108 billion, or about $3,600 per person, and there was absolutely no growth that year. Over the next few years, the economy grew between 4 percent and 8 percent a year. By 2007, the GDP was $125 billion, or about $4,100 per person. Annual foreign direct investment has more than quadrupled. There is a construction boom under way in Casablanca, the country's commercial capital. And unemployment has fallen from 14 percent in 1999 to just 10 percent today.[11]

Step 9: Let the Voiceless Speak

One of the most distinctive reforms the king has pursued is creating a national forum to allow those Moroccans who suffered injustices at the hands of judges, generals, and security officials under his father the right to be heard, to be valued, and to be compensated. In 2004, victims of past government oppression were actually invited to testify on live national television about what happened to them, and they were provided with financial reparations as a sign of goodwill.

"It was striking," Layadi recalled, and it sent an unprecedented message of change in an Islamic nation. "I mean, it was the new way of government in Morocco. Everybody knew that these things had happened. So why not talk about them? Why not have a real catharsis? Why keep them quiet like something that you are ashamed of?"

"It was the king's way of saying he did not agree with the previous generals, judges, and others who were responsible for the oppression," Abaddi told me.

Obviously, the harm could not be undone. But at least it was no longer hidden, and people could begin to reclaim some sense of dignity by telling the nation what they had experienced, why it was wrong, and how they felt about it.

Step 10: Build and Maintain Strong Relations with the Jewish Community

The current king, like his father, has been second to none in the Middle East in terms of honoring and respecting Jews and treating them as equal citizens. Few people understand this remarkable relationship better than Serge Berdugo, a man who holds a unique place in the Islamic world. From 1993 to 1995, he served in government as Morocco's minister of tourism. Yet since 1987, he has also served as the secretary-general of the Council of Morocco's Jewish Communities.

That's right — Berdugo is Jewish.

When I visited Casablanca and Rabat in the fall of 2005, I had the privilege of meeting Berdugo in his home, and he gave me some fascinating insights. He noted that the first thing King Mohammed V (the current king's grandfather) did when he returned from exile in 1956 and led his country to independence from France was to declare that "Jews are equal citizens." From 1956 to 1961, the king made a point to install at least one or two Jewish leaders into senior-level positions in each cabinet ministry. The king also allowed Jews to freely emigrate when they wanted, and there are now around six hundred thousand Moroccan Jews living in Israel.

Berdugo also told me it was King Hassan II (the

513

current king's father, who came to power in 1961) who initiated a relationship with Israel in the late 1960s through a series of top secret meetings with Yitzhak Rabin and Moshe Dayan, then two of Israel's leading defense officials.

By 1984, the king had decided to make such contacts public. He invited fifty Jewish and Israeli leaders to Rabat for an interfaith conference. As expected, this sparked controversy in the region. The Syrian government under then president Hafez al-Assad was particularly vocal in their outrage — so vocal that King Hassan decided to push back. He ordered that the entire senior leadership of the Moroccan government, including the crown prince, attend the conference's gala dinner. The following year, the king helped create the World Council of Moroccan Jews. In 1986, he invited Israeli prime minister Shimon Peres to Morocco for a highly publicized visit, a move that stunned most of the rest of the Muslim world.

King Mohammed VI has certainly continued in this remarkably positive tradition. One of his most senior foreign policy advisors is a Moroccan Jew by the name of Andre Azoulay. After the 2003 bombings in Casablanca, the king personally blessed a series of candlelight vigils and later a rally in which one million Moroccans, including more than a thousand Jews, marched in unison to denounce the radical jihadists and called for peace. "We were applauded as Jews," Berdugo told me. "We were kissed. People came up to us and said, 'You are our brothers.' It was extraordinary."[12]

A few years later, several Moroccan officials confirmed to me rumors swirling about in the Arab press that the king had been quietly laying the groundwork with Israeli and Palestinian leaders to hold a new round of high-level peace talks as soon as the climate is right. "This king is a new generation," one official who requested anonymity told me. "He is ready to help make peace between the Israelis and Palestinians. The deal is easy to do. We are now in a supermarket, not in the *souk*. We all know the price of peace. There is no more need to haggle. It is time to get the deal done."[13]

Step 11: Reach Out to Evangelical Christians in the West

To his enormous credit, the king launched an initiative in late 2004 to build a "bridge of friendship" to evangelical Christians in the U.S., despite long-standing sensitivities about Islamic-Christian relations throughout the Arab world. Abaddi and his colleagues have established ongoing dialogues with prominent evangelists and church leaders such as author Josh McDowell, Richard Cizik of the National Association of Evangelicals, and Rob Schenck of the National Clergy Council. They have invited evangelical pastors, business leaders, and authors to visit Morocco and meet with Muslim leaders. They have even organized a series of concerts in Marrakech where Christian and Muslim rock bands have performed together for tens of thousands of Moroccan young people.

"Why is the king doing something so few leaders in the Islamic world are doing?" I asked Abaddi during his first visit to my home.

"The king knows the real America is not Hollywood and the pornography industry but people of faith," he told me. "Historically, it has been the Christians who have held America together. Anyone who traces the history of America knows

515

that evangelicals are behind it."

"But why would Morocco specifically reach out to evangelicals when one of our central goals is to *evangelize,* a practice frowned upon in the Muslim world?"

Abaddi told me he feels evangelicals are "gentlemen" who can be trusted. "We are trying to reach out to the real America. Evangelicals are serious people, helpful people." Abaddi acknowledged that the idea of Muslims converting to Christianity is a very sensitive subject in his country. But he also told me that he has written and spoken about the importance of encouraging religious freedom within Islam, including ensuring that "Muslims have the right to change their religion" if they so desire. "Islam cannot be a prison," he stressed when I saw him in Rabat. "People shouldn't feel trapped, like they're in jail and they can't get out. What kind of religion is that?"

These were remarkable steps, and they should be lauded. Hopefully the king and his court will take other positive steps in the years ahead. Among them: hosting major conferences (perhaps nationally televised) in Morocco where prominent evangelical and Muslim leaders discuss areas of theological agreement and disagreement in an open, kind, and candid manner; inviting Western evangelicals as well as Moroccan believers to freely publish books, DVDs, and other material inside the kingdom; and having His Majesty address major evangelical gatherings in the United States, including the annual National Prayer Breakfast in Washington, D.C., as Jordan's King Abdullah II did in February 2006.[14]

However, it must be noted that since the publication of the first edition of this book, the government of Morocco has taken some deeply disturbing steps in the wrong direction. In 2010, some one hundred American and European Christian workers were unfairly and inexplicably expelled from Morocco by the government, accused of being "missionaries." What's more, an accredited American school in Casablanca was legally attacked by a parent of a sixth grade boy enrolled in the school, accused of trying to convert minors.

Regarding the expulsions, I was amazed and disappointed that so many followers of Jesus Christ could be so hastily deported or refused entry to Morocco without due process of any kind. It appeared that Morocco's own immigration laws were not even respected. This action sent shock waves into the American business community, raising concern over doing business there if due process is no longer respected in Morocco. It certainly also sent shock waves through the American Christian community, as it suddenly appeared that evangelical Christians — particularly those running orphanages and doing other humanitarian relief work among the poor and needy — were no longer welcome in Morocco.

In regards to the court case, here is the background: several sixth-grade classmates shared their Christian faith with a Moroccan Muslim boy, and the boy decided to put his faith in Jesus Christ as his Savior and Lord. The legal complaint stated the names of fourteen people associated with the school and accused them all with "shaking the child's [Islamic] faith." The problem is that only a few of the fourteen people cited had ever even met the boy. The only evidence the lawyer provided was that these fourteen people have membership in Christian churches and organizations

517

and are in some way connected to the school. At one point, the lawyer cited that a certain individual made charitable contributions through a well known Christian foundation. The lawyer cited an "army of evangelists" in Morocco from "extremist denominations" (Baptist, Community Church, United Bible Society, etc).

It was noteworthy that the lawyer representing the boy was also the parliamentary leader of the Muslim fundamentalist political party in Morocco (PJD). He was turning the decision of one young boy into a political debate pitting Christians against Muslims. This has potentially far-reaching implications and reminded me of the largest complaint of al Qaeda dating back to 1991. Osama bin Laden was incensed at the time because there were hundreds of thousands of "Christian" soldiers in Saudi Arabia. This was the rallying cry that led to most of the terrorist attacks leading up to September 11, 2001. Are the members of the Moroccan PJD party now bringing this same logic to Morocco? Do they want to rid Morocco of all evangelical Christians? Do they want to turn the tolerant Muslim kingdom into a new Iran or Saudi Arabia?

Were these developments anomalies, or did they represent a new policy for the Moroccan government? It appears the king and his government are at a crossroads. They have been reaching out to Christians in the West and seeking to promote the Moroccan model. But if they continue expelling foreign Christians who love Morocco and refusing to allow back in those Christian workers they have already expelled, they will be reversing course and tragically undermining the progress they have made in recent years. If they furthermore convict people of shaking the faith of a Muslim — even those have never even met that person — it will be clear that merely holding the evangelical faith would be a crime in Morocco. Let us be watching and praying.

Step 12: Counter the "Hollywood Stigma"
Finally, Morocco has decided not to whine and complain about Hollywood's unfair depiction of Muslims and Arabs. Instead, they are actively encouraging Western directors to come to Morocco to shoot major motion pictures that deal with Islam fairly and respectfully.

They are not looking for "puff pieces" or hagiographies. Rather, they are looking for a little balance. Officials in Rabat do not expect to see lots of scripts coming across their desks that tell the story of Muslim Reformers. But at the very minimum, the kingdom does look for scripts that have examples of Muslims being mistreated by the West, and have examples of Muslims working with the West to hunt down the Radicals.

Among the recent films that have been shot in Morocco are *Black Hawk Down* (the story of America's fight against the Radicals in Somalia); *Charlie Wilson's War* (the story of America's assistance to the mujahadeen against the Soviets in Afghanistan); *Kingdom of Heaven* (about the European Crusades against the Muslims); *The Bourne Ultimatum* (in which, in part, former CIA agent Jason Bourne chases an assassin through Tangier, Morocco); and *Body of Lies* (the story of a CIA operative who hunts down a terrorist in Jordan).

Reflections

Bottom line: I have been impressed in recent years by the Moroccan model and by the king and his team who have set it into motion. The jury is still out on whether these steps will turn Morocco into a full-blown Jeffersonian democracy over time, or whether Morocco will continue moving in the right direction. If they do choose to continue bravely going down this path, it remains to be seen whether other Muslim leaders or nations will embrace the model as their own. I am praying for the king and for the future of this wonderful country that my family and I love so dearly. I hope you will join us in praying as well.

■ ■ ■ ■

PART THREE:
THE REVIVALISTS

■ ■ ■ ■

Chapter Twenty-Four:
"Islam Is Not the Answer, and Jihad Is Not the Way; Jesus Is the Way"

Who are the Revivalists,
and what do they want?

Tass Saada was a killer.

He and his friends murdered Jews in Israel. They murdered civilians and soldiers alike. They attacked Christians in Jordan. Sometimes they tossed hand grenades at Christians' homes. Other times they strafed houses with machine-gun fire. They once tried to assassinate the crown prince of an Arab country. They nearly succeeded. And they did all this willingly. They did it eagerly. Saada certainly did. His nickname was once *Jazzar* — "butcher." It was a moniker he relished.

Born in Gaza and raised in Saudi Arabia and the Gulf in a world of radical Islam and violent Palestinian nationalism, by his teenage years Saada was a cauldron of seething, roiling hatred. His family was close to the Saudi royal family. He once met Osama bin Laden. He became personal friends with Yasser Arafat, a man he long regarded as a hero and in whose name he happily killed. He served as a sniper in the Palestine Liberation Organization and for a time was Arafat's driver and one of his bodyguards.

523

But in 1993, God gave Tass Saada's life drama a second act.

After marrying an American and moving to the United States — a country he had long hated — this jihadist found Jesus. This violent Radical was one day radically transformed by the power of the Holy Spirit. This killer became a man of peace and compassion.

"Jesus, Come Into My Life"

Saada was not expecting to become a follower of Jesus Christ.

To the contrary, when an evangelical friend tried to share the gospel with him, he became enraged. When his friend encouraged him to read the New Testament for himself, every fiber of his being resisted.

"I must not touch that book!" he said.[1]

"Why not?" his friend said. "It's just paper."

"No!" Saada replied. "It's God's Word!"

The two men just stood there for a moment. "Do you really believe that?" his friend asked in shock.

"Yes, I do," Saada replied, hardly understanding the words that were coming out of his mouth. As a Muslim, he had not been raised to believe the Bible was God's Word. He certainly had not been trained to believe that as a Radical. But he soon heard his friend saying, "Well, if you believe that, then let me read you what the Bible says about Jesus Christ. Fair enough?"

Saada nodded.

His friend began reading from the book of John, chapter one, verse one: "In the beginning was the Word, and the Word was with God, and the Word was God."

The moment his friend said, "Word," Saada began to shake. He suddenly flashed back to a line in the Qur'an that said, "The Messiah, Jesus son of Mary, was . . . the Messenger of God, and His Word that He committed to Mary, and a Spirit from Him."*

"Hearing the Bible say essentially the same thing, that Jesus was the Word of God, struck deep to the core of my being," Saada would later recall. "Before I knew it, I was on my knees. I didn't consciously decide to kneel. It just happened. I lost all awareness that my friend was in the room. A light came into my field of vision — a talking light. Now I know this sounds really odd, but this is what happened that Sunday afternoon, March 14, 1993. The light said to me, 'I am the Way, the Truth, and the Life. No one comes to the Father except through Me.' I didn't know at that moment that those words were what Jesus said during the Last Supper [in John 14:6]. As far as I was concerned, they were a message from Jesus solely for me."

Suddenly, Saada said, he just knew beyond the shadow of a doubt that the triune God — the Father, the Son, and the Holy Spirit — existed. He knew with certainty that this triune God loved him. And sobbing with shame at his sin and with thankfulness for God's mercy, he cried out, "Oh, Jesus, come into my life! Forgive me and be my Lord and Savior!"

"I felt as if a heavy load went flying off my shoulders," he said. "A sense of peace and joy rushed into my heart. The presence of God was so real it seemed I could almost reach out and

*Sura 4:171.

525

touch it."

His friend was in shock. He too was in tears. To be sure Saada really understood what he was doing, he explained the gospel in some detail. And then, to be sure Saada was really committing his life fully and completely to Jesus Christ, he led Saada in the following prayer:

Lord Jesus, I am a sinner, and I am sorry for my sins. I ask you to forgive me and wash away my sins by your precious blood. Lord, I can't save myself. I can't take away my sins, but you can. You are the Savior of the world — the only Savior — and I want you to be my Savior. I ask you to forgive me and come into my life. Change me and give me a new heart. I will forever love you and follow you. Now I thank you for hearing my prayer and saving my soul. I know you have, because you promised you would. Now I am yours, and you are mine. I will serve you the rest of my life.

Saada not only willingly and eagerly prayed that prayer, he become a dedicated follower of Jesus Christ from that moment forward.

A Minister of the Gospel

"I was a Palestinian sniper," Saada would later tell me. "But then I fell in love with a Savior who loves Arabs as well as Jews."

In his remarkable book, *Once An Arafat Man,* Saada explained his realization that the God of the Bible loves us all with an unfathomable, everlasting, unquenchable love. He explained that God's love is so amazing, so divine, that He actually offers all of us — Jew and Gentile alike — the

526

free gift of salvation through the death and resurrection of His Son, Jesus Christ. And he explained that God wants to adopt each one of us into His own family. He wants to bless us. He wants to take care of us. He wants to heal us and change us and make us more like Him. And He wants to empower us to be a blessing to others.

Given Saada's upbringing and life experiences, it is remarkable that he said yes to that divine love. Indeed, it is miraculous, but that is exactly what happened, and in the process, Saada was changed forever. Before long, his whole immediate family had come to faith in Christ. Eventually, God called him to be a minister of the gospel and even gave him the opportunity to share the message of salvation with his old boss, Yasser Arafat, before the PLO chairman's death in 2004.

Saada also humbly shared the message of Christ's love and forgiveness with his parents and brothers, still living in the Gulf area, many of whom wanted to kill him for converting away from Islam. And eventually, he and his wife, Karen, began a ministry to reach out to the poor and needy in Gaza and the West Bank — especially children — with God's love through the distribution of humanitarian relief supplies in the name of Jesus.

That is how Saada and I met.

It was a Saturday night in January 2008, and I had been invited to preach at a church in Jerusalem. My sermon title was "What God Is Doing among the Muslims." This was not a typical message for an audience of Jewish and Gentile Christ-followers in Israel. But after much prayer, I felt the Lord wanted me to share with my Israeli friends what He had told me to share with my

Jordanian friends when I preached in Amman several years earlier:

> We need to get serious about obeying Jesus' command to love our neighbors and our enemies. We can only do this when we have the power of the Holy Spirit flowing through our lives. But when we do — when we truly obey Jesus' teachings and the model He set for us — heads will turn. People will be shocked when they see us love those who hate us. Then they will ask questions. Their hearts will be softened. They will be curious to know more about the God we serve. And then, hopefully, they will want to know this God personally for themselves.

I had told the Jordanian followers of Jesus that this meant it was time to start loving their Jewish neighbors and enemies. That night in Jerusalem, I told the Israeli believers that this meant loving their Muslim neighbors and enemies and believing that the God of the Bible truly loves all people everywhere, including those who hate Him and His children.

I explained that behind the headlines of all the Middle Eastern wars and rumors of wars and revolutions and acts of terror, God is actually moving in an incredibly powerful way. People in the epicenter are coming to Christ in record numbers. Millions in Iran. Millions in Sudan. Millions in Pakistan. Millions in Egypt. And many more throughout the rest of the region. It is truly stunning to behold. The question I posed for Israeli believers is the question I pose for all of us who claim to be followers of Jesus: what role does the Lord have for *us* in strengthening our brothers and sisters who come to Christ from a Muslim background, and how can we actively love our neighbors and our enemies when, humanly speaking, this is impossible?

That was the message I had come to Jerusalem to share, and who was the first couple I was introduced to that night as I came through the front door of the church? Tass and Karen Saada.

I had never met them before. When they told me their story, I was deeply moved. Here we were, a former aide to PLO Chairman Yasser Arafat and a former aide to Prime Minister Benjamin Netanyahu, hugging each other — not trying to kill each other — in the heart of Jerusalem. All because of the work Jesus had done to give us hearts of love rather than hatred.

I had a sense that this was the beginning of a story, not the end. And sure enough, the very next day, the Saadas and my team and I decided to travel together with several Israeli colleagues to the Israeli city of Ashkelon. There we visited the Barzilai Medical Center, a hospital that treats Jews and Arabs wounded in the ongoing border skirmishes that have plagued that region for so long.

As we met with the hospital administrators, Tass and I both presented checks from our respective ministries to help finance the purchase of much-needed medical equipment. When the doctors and staff asked why we had come to bless them, we both told them our stories. Tass explained that he had been born just a few miles south of where we were gathered and had been raised with a desire to kill everyone in the room where we were sitting.

"You really worked for the PLO?" asked one doctor.

Tass nodded.

"Then what happened? What changed you?" another asked.

Tass gave all the credit to Jesus Christ. He briefly explained how God had changed his heart and given him a love for the Jewish people.

And then he stunned us all. He asked the hospital staff to forgive him for what he and the Palestinian people had done over the years to harm them. It was a powerful moment. Everyone was in tears. These Israelis had never seen anything like it. Honestly, few people have.

The Rise of the Revivalists

Tass Saada is no longer a Radical — he is a Revivalist.

He no longer believes that Islam is the answer. He no longer believes jihad is the way. He believes that Jesus is the Way, the Truth, and the Life and that no one — Jew or Gentile, Radical or Reformer — can have a personal relationship with God without accepting that Jesus is the Messiah, just as the Bible teaches in John 14:6.

Though Saada would certainly prefer to see Reformers in power in the Middle East rather than Radicals, I have not found him to be a particularly political person by nature. He believes he is part of a much greater and more important revolution — a spiritual revolution to save souls and change lives. He believes passionately that the only way for the people of the Middle East to move forward and make real and lasting social, economic, and spiritual progress is to make a choice to skip back in their history and revive what once was so prevalent in the region before Islam — first-century, New Testament, biblical Christianity.

Saada has completely dedicated his life to making sure that all the people in the Middle East — especially all Muslims — have the opportunity before they die to hear and understand the claims of Jesus Christ in their own language and make their own decision to follow Him or reject Him.

Revivalists like Saada argue with great conviction that biblical Christianity is not a Western, colonialist, or imperialist religion. Nor is it some foreign ideology imposed on the Muslim world to enslave or hinder it. Rather, Revivalists assert that biblical Christianity is a movement that was born in the Middle East, one that spread rapidly to all corners of the Middle East, one that then spread all over the globe, and one that is destined by biblical prophecy to be dramatically revived in the Middle East just before Jesus Christ returns to set up His Kingdom on earth, based in the Holy City of Jerusalem.

They believe that Christianity is a spiritually and personally liberating force, the most powerful liberating force in human history. They believe that a personal relationship with God through faith in Jesus Christ changes hearts so that the violent become men and women of peace and reconciliation. And they believe this not because someone told them about it but because they have experienced it for themselves.

As you will see in this final section — as you will hear in their own words — the Revivalists know firsthand that the gospel changes the hearts of the fearful into hearts filled with courage and hope, that it changes those who were wracked with sin and guilt into those who experience the joy of forgiveness and a new life. And again, they know it because they have experienced it themselves.

If you travel through the Middle East, you will meet many ex-Muslims who will tell you, as they have told me, that they have seen dreams and visions of Jesus, who personally told them to follow Him. They readily identify with the apostle Paul, who described his own conversion in his letter to the Galatians saying, "I neither received [the gospel] from man, nor was I taught it, but I received it through a revelation of Jesus Christ" (Galatians 1:12). These former Muslims are stunned by the way God has changed their lives, especially given the fact that many of them, like Paul, used to "persecute the church of God beyond measure and tried to destroy it." Like Paul, they were "extremely zealous" for their "ancestral traditions" (Galatians 1:13–14). Like Paul — the greatest apostle in the history of Christendom, a man who wrote much of the New Testament — they, too, were once religious extremists who hated Jesus and all of His followers.

Yet they also personally and deeply identify with Paul's words in Galatians 1:15–24: "But when God, who had set me apart even from my mother's womb and called me through His grace, was pleased to reveal His Son in me so that I might preach Him among the Gentiles, I did not immediately consult with flesh and blood, nor did I go up to Jerusalem . . . but I went away to Arabia, and returned once more to Damascus. . . . Then I went into the regions of Syria and Cilicia [Turkey and Armenia] . . . [and the people] kept hearing, 'He who once persecuted us is now preaching the faith which he once tried to destroy.' And they were glorifying God because of me."

The Revivalists say that what happened in the early Church two thousand years ago is happening again today.

What Revivalists Want

When asked what they want, Revivalists like Saada and others point to Matthew 28:18–20, where Jesus told His disciples, "All authority has been given to Me in heaven and on earth. Go therefore and make disciples of all the nations, baptizing them in the name of the Father and the Son and the Holy Spirit, teaching them to observe all that I commanded you; and lo, I am with you always, even to the end of the age."

They say that because Jesus is God, He has all power. He is the King of kings and the Lord of lords. Thus, when He gives His disciples an order, it must be followed. And that order, they note, is to preach the gospel to the whole world and make disciples — not just "Christians" but truly dedicated and devoted Christ-followers — of "all the nations."

Not just the safe nations.

Not just the democratic nations.

Not just the free market nations.

Jesus told His disciples to go make more disciples in *all* the nations.

Even the difficult nations.

Even the dangerous nations.

Even the Radical nations.

Indeed, the Revivalists say the Bible provides a specific geographic game plan. In Acts 1:8, Jesus told His disciples, "You will receive power when the Holy Spirit has come upon you; and you shall be My witnesses both in Jerusalem, and in all Judea and Samaria, and even to the remotest part of the earth."

The directive is clear, the Revivalists say. Jesus told them to start the Church in the epicenter, in Jerusalem, where He died and rose again. Then He commanded His disciples to take the gospel to the West Bank and Gaza and beyond in a series of concentric circles radiating out from Jerusalem and extending even to the remotest and most desolate parts of the world. By definition, this includes the entire Islamic world.

Reaching the entire world — and particularly the world of Islam — with the gospel is an enormously challenging mission. Many Revivalists readily concede that humanly speaking they feel overwhelmed by the task. Often they feel physically weak, or emotionally frail, or intimidated by the Radicals, or not nearly educated enough to make the most intellectual case for why a Muslim should become a follower of Christ.

Yet they say their encouragement and strength come from biblical promises like Matthew 28 and Acts 1, in which Jesus promises to be with them always. He also promises to give them access to God's supernatural power, the power of the Holy Spirit, as they obey Him in reaching the people of all nations — including Muslims — with the gospel. He promises to guide them. He promises to strengthen them. He promises to give them the right words to say and sufficient courage in the face of danger. And they say they have seen God keep His promises time and time again.

So these Christ-followers say they intend to fulfill the "Great Commission" that Jesus has given them, whatever may befall them, even persecution, torture, and death. They ask, "If Jesus loved us so much that He gave up His life for us at the hands of His enemies, shouldn't we be willing to die in His service if that is necessary?"

Unlike the Radicals, the Revivalists are not seeking death or trying to become martyrs. They want to live as long as possible to reach as many Muslims with the gospel as possible. They point to Deuteronomy 30:19, where God instructs His followers to "choose life in order that you may live, you and your descendants." They point to Romans 12:1, where the apostle Paul says, "I urge you, brethren, by the mercies of God, to present your bodies a living and holy sacrifice, acceptable to God, which is your spiritual service of worship." They have no intention, therefore, of blowing themselves up as suicide bombers or doing other kinds of violence to kill "infidels." They are commanded to be *living* sacrifices — people devoting their very lives to serve and to save the lives of others.

Nevertheless, they know full well that Jesus also taught His disciples there will be fierce opposition. They know they need to be ready to die at any moment. "If anyone wishes to come after Me, he must deny himself, and take up his cross daily and follow Me," Jesus said in Luke 9:23–24. "For whoever wishes to save his life will lose it, but whoever loses his life for My sake, he is the one who will save it."

Two Different Approaches

It should be noted at the outset that not all Revivalists operate alike.

There are hundreds of different creative strategies being used to win Muslims to Christ and help them grow in their faith, but in terms of philosophy of ministry, there are two basic approaches, and they are distinctly different. This was a point driven home to me as I interviewed Salim, the director of one of the largest ministries in the Middle East, a man with several thousand Arab, Iranian, and other national believers working with him as paid staff and volunteers in every Islamic country in North Africa, the Middle East, and central Asia.

"Joel, I see two groups among the Revivalists," Salim told me. "First, there are those who say, 'Islam is wrong and is not the answer,' and they are preaching that Jesus is the way. And there is a second group that says, 'We're preaching Jesus alone, not criticizing Islam.' For example, our ministry preaches simply that Jesus is the Son of God and the only way of salvation. We explain His teachings. We explain His miracles. We explain His death on the cross and His resurrection from the dead. We teach His love for the poor and the needy and women and the outcasts. As Paul said in 1 Corinthians 2:1–2, 'When I came to you, brethren, I did not come with superiority of speech or of wisdom, proclaiming to you the testimony of God. For I determined to know nothing among you except Jesus Christ, and Him crucified.' We never mention Islam. We never mention Muhammad. We just preach Christ. Period. There are other ministries that specifically teach that Muhammad is not a prophet and that Islam is wrong to say that Jesus is not the Son of God. And then they explain why Jesus really is the Son of God. . . . I wouldn't say that one is more effective than the other, but we find there is a huge benefit to simply preaching Christ's love as the positive, hopeful message it is to those Muslims who are hungering for truth and have become disillusioned and disenchanted with Islam."*

Salim noted that the ministries that are confronting Islam directly are, for the most part, waging an "air war" through radio and satellite television (as well as the Internet) for Muslim hearts and minds that have typically been closed to — and sometimes violently opposed to — the gospel message. For security reasons, the leaders of these ministries typically operate from outside the region or from its perimeters, so they are not in immediate danger of being killed by Muslims enraged by their criticisms of Muhammad and the Qur'an.

By contrast, those ministries that are preaching the gospel without ever mentioning Islam are typically waging a "ground war" inside hostile Muslim territory. Their leaders — and, more important, their disciples and volunteers — are talking to Muslims face-to-face, one-on-one and in small groups. They are distributing copies of the *Injil* (the Arabic word for New Testament). They are distributing gospel literature. They are distributing CDs and DVDs with the gospel message and information about how to become a fully devoted follower of Jesus Christ. They are holding Bible studies and house churches in the privacy of people's homes. In short, they are operating inside the fire and focusing their efforts on Muslims who are already close to leaving Islam and open to hearing and receiving the gospel message.

I asked Salim if there was room for both ap-

*Author interview in the spring of 2008. Salim is a pseudonym.

proaches.

"Absolutely," he said. "There is room for both. The benefit of those ministries that confront Islam directly is that they create controversy. They generate conversation among Muslims about what is wrong with Islam, the hypocrisy of its leaders, and the contradictions in its texts, as well as who Jesus is and what he taught. Jesus attacked the Pharisees, the religious leaders of His day. He didn't attack the common Jews, but He faced the Jewish leaders directly with their hypocrisy. So those ministries that are confronting the Islamic leaders today have an important place. They are definitely rocking the boat. We are too. It just needs to be remembered that we are paying a price on the inside by the anger being generated from the outside."

Two Different Kinds

Just as not all Revivalist strategies are identical, it should also be noted that not all Revivalists themselves are alike.

I have had the wonderful privilege of meeting with and befriending Revivalists all over the world during the past two decades. In the course of researching and writing this book over the past several years, I have spoken with and interviewed at length more than 150 Christian leaders operating in and ministering to the Muslim world. Whether they were ethnically Arab, Iranian, Turkish, Kurdish, Afghan, Berber, or from some other background, I found their stories absolutely amazing and profoundly inspiring, in part because they are leading a spiritual Revolution as significant and consequential as those led by the Radicals and the Reformers. I would even say more so.

In the next chapter, I will share with you the trend lines indicating how rapidly Christianity is growing in the Muslim world. But first, let me briefly define two different kinds of Revivalists so you will better understand who they are and where they are coming from.

Some Revivalists are known as "MBBs," which stands for Muslim Background Believers. These are true, born-again, fully devoted followers of Jesus Christ, commonly known in the West simply as "Christians." Their distinction is that they were born into Muslim families and were raised as Muslims. But at some point in their lives, they converted to Christianity and away from Islam. Because of that decision, MBBs face persecution, torture, and death from their families, their neighbors, and sometimes their governments for leaving Islam in general and for becoming Christ-followers in particular. MBBs face tremendous social and legal pressure to keep quiet about their faith and not seek out fellowship with other believers and certainly not try to share their faith with other Muslims. They need a tremendous amount of prayer, therefore, for wisdom and courage and for Christian friends who can help them grow and mature in their faith and know how best to handle themselves in a godly way. This is true wherever an MBB lives, but it is particularly true for MBBs who still live in a Muslim country.

The other kind of Revivalist is someone known as an "NCBB," which stands for Nominal Christian Background Believer. These, too, are true, born-again, fully devoted followers of Jesus Christ. Their distinction is that while they are true believers today, they were born into families with parents who called themselves Christians but did not actually have real, active, life-changing, personal relationships with Jesus Christ. Their families may have identified themselves culturally or religiously as Christians as opposed to Muslims or Jews or Hindus or atheists. Perhaps they went to church often. Perhaps they went rarely, only on Christmas and Easter, for example. But the key is that while a nominal Christian may describe himself as a Christian by name, he has not actually been transformed — born again — on the inside.

Once they make a decision to follow Christ and become NCBBs, such believers face the threat of persecution, torture, and death from neighbors and sometimes their governments if they want to share their faith with Muslims and become engaged in ministries to help MBBs grow in their faith. They also face ostracism from family members and friends who remain nominal Christians and don't understand the life change they are undergoing. Sadly, many NCBBs face persecution even from the churches they grew up in because their passion for Jesus and for fulfilling the Great Commission of Matthew 28:18–20 now threatens their childhood pastors or priests who oppose rocking the boat in any way, shape, or form in a Muslim community. Therefore, like MBBs, these believers need a tremendous amount of prayer for wisdom and courage and fellow Christ-following friends who can help them grow and mature in their faith and know how best to handle themselves in a godly way wherever they live, but particularly if they still live in a Muslim country.

The very notion of an NCBB can be confusing for many people, particularly Muslims, to whom a person is a Muslim simply if he is born to Muslim parents, not just if he converts to Islam. But the Bible teaches that just being physically born into a so-called Christian family does *not* bring about salvation. Indeed, even if a person's parents or siblings really are true followers of Jesus, being born into such a family *still* does not save that person. The only way a person can be forgiven of his sins and saved from eternal damnation, according to the Bible, is to personally repent and receive Jesus Christ as Savior by faith and in the process be spiritually reborn.

In John 3:3, Jesus told a religious leader from Jerusalem, "Truly, truly, I say to you, unless one is born again he cannot see the kingdom of God." One's physical birth into a religious family, Jesus was saying, is not enough. Nor is being a very "religious" person. Or even a religious leader. Something else has to happen on the inside. Thus, as you read the New Testament, it becomes clear that the term "born again" is a biblical term referring to a person who (1) is fully convinced that faith in Jesus Christ's death on the cross and resurrection from the dead is the only way to be forgiven of his sins and adopted into God's family; and (2) has consciously, willfully, and purposefully asked God through prayer to wash his sins away and save him through the death and resurrection of Jesus Christ.

John 1:12 tells us that "as many as received Him [Jesus Christ], to them He gave the right to become children of God."

Jesus said in John 3:16 that "God so loved the world, that He gave His only begotten Son, that whoever believes in Him shall not perish, but have eternal life."

In Romans 10:9–10, the apostle Paul explains how to be born again: "If you confess with your mouth Jesus as Lord, and believe in your heart that God raised Him from the dead, you will be saved; for with the heart a person believes, resulting in righteousness, and with the mouth he confesses, resulting in salvation."

Then in 2 Corinthians 5:17–18, Paul tells us the result of being born again: "If anyone is in Christ, he is a new creature; the old things passed away; behold, new things have come. Now all these things are from God, who reconciled us to Himself through Christ and gave us the ministry of reconciliation."

My own family's spiritual journey has helped me understand how this process works. Though my mother is not from the Middle East, she is actually an NCBB. She was born into a Protestant family. She attended church when she was growing up in Rome, New York. As such, she thought she was a Christian. But the truth is she was a nominal Christian. Her heart had not been transformed, for until 1973, no one had ever explained to her that going to church was not enough. She did not know she needed to individually receive Jesus Christ to be her Savior and Lord. All she knew was that despite calling herself a Christian, she was filled with enormous loneliness and anxiety, and she had no idea how to change or how to find relief and hope for her life.

Then she visited a different church in Rochester, New York, where several couples simply and patiently answered her questions. They read to her the key verses in the Bible that explain how to know God in a real and personal way, and once they had, she knew immediately that what they

542

were saying was true. She knew that was what she wanted. That very Sunday morning, she chose to follow Jesus and prayed a prayer very similar to the one Tass Saada prayed.

In that moment, she was born again. Her troubles didn't all immediately melt away. But from that day forward, she began seeing God change her life as He gave her peace and joy and a sense of calm that she had never had before.

My father, on the other hand, is not an MBB, but you might say that he is a "JBB" — a Jewish Background Believer. With a name like Rosenberg, you can guess that he was not raised in a Christian home. Rather, he was raised in an Orthodox Jewish home, though he would have described himself more as an agnostic during his twenties. In 1973, about six months after my mother became a follower of Jesus Christ, my father prayed to receive Jesus as the Messiah, and he too was born again. His troubles did not disappear either. Some of them increased, even. But over the next few years, though I was young, I could see my father changing in very positive ways. He was no longer the bitter man with a quick temper that I had feared. He was becoming gentle and kind, a man who loved to study the Bible and to teach it — especially to kids.

My point is simply this: in my own home, I have personally witnessed — and been blessed by — God's love for Jews and Gentiles, and I am grateful that He does not show favoritism and restrict His loving-kindness to one group or another.

Likewise, in my travels through the epicenter I have personally witnessed — and been blessed by — God's love for Muslims and for nominal Christians. He is reviving them both. He is awaking

Muslims to the truth of the Scriptures, and He is breathing new spiritual life into people who were raised in churches but were long unaware of the life-changing power of Jesus Christ.

And He is doing so in numbers few could ever have imagined.

CHAPTER TWENTY-FIVE:
THE BIG, UNTOLD STORY —
PART ONE

*The greatest spiritual awakening in the history
of the Middle East is under way.*

You rarely hear about it on the news.

You rarely even hear about it in churches in the West, in the East, or even in the Middle East. But the big, untold story is that more Muslims are coming to faith in Jesus Christ today than at any other time in history.

For many Muslims, despair and despondency at what they see as the utter failure of Islamic governments and societies to improve their lives and give them peace, security, and a sense of purpose and meaning in life are causing them to leave Islam in search of truth. Some have lost their way entirely and become agnostics and atheists. Others, as we have seen, have sadly turned to alcohol and drug abuse. But millions are finding that only Jesus Christ heals the ache in their hearts and the deep wounds in their souls.

For other Muslims, it is not depression but rage that is driving them away from the Qur'an and the mosque. They are seeing far too many Muslim leaders and governments and preachers both advocating and acting out cruelty toward women and children and violence even against fellow Muslims. Not all of these find Jesus in their journey away from Islam, but millions do, especially since the 9/11 attacks against the United States. In fact, while this backlash against the theology and practice of Radicalism has been building since 1979, I first began to detect it during my travels in Europe, North Africa, and the Middle East soon after 9/11. Again and again, I would meet people who had long been devout and traditional Muslims who told me that they had watched with horror as Arabic television networks constantly replayed the images of commercial airliners hijacked by radical Islamic jihadists flying into the World Trade Center.

First they found themselves weeping. But then they saw other Muslims cheering, and their sadness turned to anger as they asked themselves, "Is this who we really are? Is this what it really means to be a Muslim? To fly planes into buildings and kill thousands of innocent civilians? Because if it is, then count me out. How could I possibly be part of a religion or a political movement that glorifies and celebrates death?"

Many of these former Muslims hear the message of the Reformers but believe that it is actually the Radicals who are reading the Qur'an correctly. They say that if a person truly studies the Qur'an carefully, he will become a Radical and will engage in violent jihad, because that is what the preponderance of verses tell Muslims to do. They say that the verses that speak about Muslims being peaceful to the "People of the Book" were written mostly when Muhammad was trying to win Jews and Christians to his side but that once Muhammad realized he could not convert these "infidels," he turned against them and wrote verses that the Radicals now embrace in pursuit of jihad.

Whether such claims are correct theologically or historically is, of course, a matter of debate. The point, however, is not whether these people are accurate in their interpretation of the Qur'an. The point is that they have had enough. They are furious about the atrocities being done in the name of Islam. And their outrage has only intensified as month after month, year after year, they have watched the Radicals blow up mosques, blow up women, blow up children, blow up the disabled and the mentally handicapped, and in the process, blow up their dreams.

And as their anger has risen, so too has their determination to disassociate themselves with Islam and find the truth someplace else.

The Christian Surge

That said, what intrigues me is not simply that the Revivalists say the greatest spiritual awakening in the history of the Middle East is under way. What intrigues me is that Islamic leaders are worrying in public that a Christian surge is taking place in the region.

In 1993, a Saudi sheikh by the name of Salman Al-Odeh delivered a sermon entitled "Christian Missionaries Sweeping the Islamic World." He argued that "in Spain [Christians] have the biggest center of missionaries to Africa. They are trained really well, and their efforts lead many Moroccans to convert." He then cited the *World Christian Encyclopedia* — which he described as a "dangerous survey" — and warned his fellow Muslims that "the number of Christians in Africa was 9 million only in 1900 AD, or . . . 9 percent of the whole population. In the year 1980 they became 200 million! . . . They jumped from 9 to 200 million in 80 years [and the survey's authors] expected them to reach 390 million in the year 2000, or 48 percent of the whole population of Africa."[1]*

Eight years later, in December 2001, Sheikh Ahmad Al Qataani, another significant Saudi cleric, appeared in a live interview on Aljazeera satellite television to confirm that, sure enough, Muslims were turning to Jesus in alarming numbers. "In every hour, 667 Muslims convert to Christianity," Al Qataani warned. "Every day, 16,000 Muslims convert to Christianity. Every year, 6 million Muslims convert to Christianity."

Stunned, the interviewer interrupted the cleric. "Hold on! Let me clarify. Do we have 6 million converting from Islam to Christianity or converting from Islam *and* other religions?"

Al Qataani repeated his assertion.

"So 6 million Muslims a year convert?" said the interviewer.

"Every year," the cleric confirmed, adding, "a tragedy has happened."[2]

I cannot confirm these precise numbers. I can,

---

*Al-Odeh was apparently citing the 1982 edition of the *World Christian Encyclopedia*. The updated figures in the 2001 edition found that the number of Christians in Africa had jumped from 9.9 million in 1900 to 360 million in 2000, still an enormous growth and a significant percentage of it from Muslim converts. See David B. Barrett et al, *World Christian Encyclopedia* (New York: Oxford Press, 2001), p. 5.

however, confirm the trend lines. During the course of interviewing more than 150 Christian leaders in the epicenter over the past several years, I have been able to assemble enough data and anecdotal evidence to paint a picture — albeit an imperfect and incomplete one — that provides a sense of how powerfully the God of the Bible is moving to draw Muslims into His family. Given the threat of jail or death facing all believers in the region, it is simply not possible to take a complete Christian census or conduct accurate polling to know for certain how many Muslims and nominal Christians have come to faith in Jesus Christ in a given year or even over the last few decades. But again, there is now no question that so many people are becoming Christians in the region that Muslim leaders are becoming nervous and angry.

Revival in Iran

"It's ironic that when the Ayatollah Khomeini took power in Iran with his style of Islamic Shiite extremism that the true face of Islam was finally exposed not just to the Christian populace, but to the Muslims themselves," one of the region's leading evangelists — a man named Taheer — once told me. "Before 1979, the demand for Bibles in Iran was never that great. Today, Iranians can't get enough of the Bible or biblical teaching. It is counterintuitive, I know, but it's as if God used that man, the Ayatollah . . . to expose Islam for what it is and for Muslims to say to themselves, 'That's not what we want; we want something else. We want something better.' "[3]

One Iranian Muslim woman was barren for many years. Praying to Allah in the mosque was not working. Knowing several MBBs, she asked them to pray for her to be healed. They agreed and began reading her passages from the Bible. They specifically taught her James 5:14–16, which says, "Is anyone among you sick? Then he must call for the elders of the church and they are to pray over him, anointing him with oil in the name of the Lord; and the prayer offered in faith will restore the one who is sick, and the Lord will raise him up, and if he has committed sins, they will be forgiven him. Therefore, confess your sins to one another, and pray for one another so that you may be healed. The effective prayer of a righteous man can accomplish much." Then the believers prayed for the Muslim woman and anointed her with oil. Soon she was pregnant, and she secretly prayed with her friends to become a follower of Christ. She had a baby boy and named him Shah — the Persian word for "king" — saying, "Jesus is the King. He healed me and gave me a son as a miracle!"

"If you are working in Iran, you feel like you are working with God," a top Iranian ministry leader told me. "He is with us in Iran. Jesus Christ is revealing Himself to people in Iran. A big revival is under way and more is coming. Friends keep telling me to leave the country for my own safety. 'The government will arrest you,' they say. 'They will kill you.' But if you leave, you are losing a big, historical chance. If you stay and serve, you will see a big revival and see prophecy fulfilled. You feel so small. But God is so big!"[4]

"In Iran," another Iranian Christian told me, "you don't go after people with the gospel. They are coming to you to ask you about the Lord. Let me give you an example. I went to the doctor's office because I was feeling very ill. I asked the receptionist if I could see the doctor right away, but she was a veiled woman and a fanatical Muslim. She had no intention of making life easier for an 'infidel,' and she told me I would have to wait for two hours. 'You will regret that,' I said with a smile, and then sat down in the crowded waiting room. A few moments later, the doctor walked by to pick up a file. 'Hello, Reverend,' he said to me. I greeted him back. Then everyone in the waiting room asked me, 'Are you really a reverend?' I said I was. 'How can I know Jesus?' they asked. I told them and five Muslims prayed with me in the waiting room to receive Christ as their Savior. 'See how you will regret making me wait?' I told the receptionist, again with a smile. She has never made me wait again."[5]

The Avalanche Is Still Coming

"Let me give you another example," the same Iranian Christian told me. "There was an abused Muslim woman who tried to commit suicide by swallowing a bunch of sleeping pills. But as she was fading into unconsciousness, she had a vision of something called the 'Living Water.' She had never heard of 'Living Water.' But something made her want to know more. She woke herself up, vomited out the pills, found a Bible, and read the entire Gospel according to John.

"When she got to chapter 4, she read the story where Jesus asked a sad and troubled woman for a drink of water from a well in Samaria. The woman is surprised that this Jewish man is talking to her. Then Jesus says to her, 'If you knew the gift of God, and who it is who says to you, "Give Me a drink," you would have asked Him, and He

551

would have given you living water.' And the woman said to Jesus, 'Sir, You have nothing to draw with and the well is deep; where then do You get that living water?' And Jesus replied, 'Everyone who drinks of this water will thirst again; but whoever drinks of the water that I will give him shall never thirst; but the water that I will give him will become in him a well of water springing up to eternal life.'

"The Muslim woman was astonished by Jesus' love and compassion for this troubled Samaritan woman. She wanted that Living Water. By the time she finished reading the book of John, she had prayed to accept Christ as her Savior. Then she came to our church asking for help to grow in her faith. We did not lead her to Christ. She came already convinced. We simply encouraged her, taught her God's Word, and taught her how to share her faith with others. And she listened. She has led her four sisters and her parents to Christ. And a house church of twenty secret Iranian believers now meets in her home."

"Before the [Islamic] Revolution, there was a very small response to the gospel," one Iranian pastor told me. "In the summer of 1975, our ministry shared Christ with nearly five thousand people. Only two people showed any interest. But in 2005, ninety-eight out of every one hundred people we shared with showed interest, and we saw many decisions for Christ."[6]

"In the last 20 years, more Iranians have come to Christ [than in] the last 14 centuries," said Lazarus Yeghnazar, an Iranian-born evangelist now based in Great Britain. "We've never seen such phenomenal thirst. . . . I believe this phenom- enon [will] snowball into a major avalanche. This

552

is still a rain. This is not the avalanche coming. . . .
But it will be happening very, very soon."[7]

At the time of the Islamic Revolution in 1979, there were only about five hundred known Muslim converts to Jesus inside the country. By 2000, a survey of Christian demographic trends reported that there were 220,000 Christians inside Iran, of which between 4,000 and 20,000 were Muslim converts.[8] And according to Iranian Christian leaders I interviewed for this book, the number of Christ-followers inside their country shot dramatically higher between 2000 and 2008.

The head of one leading Iranian ministry, who agreed to speak on the condition of anonymity, told me: "Based on all the things we are seeing inside Iran today, I personally believe that if every Iranian who secretly believes in Jesus could come forward right now and declare his or her faith publicly, the number would top a million."[9]

A leading Iranian political dissident in the West who also happens to be a Muslim convert to Christianity told me he believes there are as many as 4.5 million Iranian converts.[10]

An Iranian who directs one of the largest ministries of evangelism and discipleship to Shia Muslims in his country — and is one of the most trusted Iranian ministry leaders in the world — tells me he believes the real number is closer to 7 million believers, or roughly one out of every ten people in Iran.[11]

Government Crackdown

Keep in mind, such numbers are impossible to verify given the current political conditions, but again, the trend lines are clear, and the increasingly panicked reaction of Iranian authorities in recent years seems to support the notion of unprecedented growth of the Iranian church.

In April 2004, for example, an Iranian Shiite cleric by the name of Hasan Mohammadi delivered a stunning speech at a high school in Tehran. He urged the students to "safeguard your beloved Shi'ite faith" against the influence of the evangelicals and other so-called apostate religions, and warned: "Unfortunately, on average every day, fifty Iranian girls and boys convert secretly to Christian denominations in our country."[12]

Mohammadi had been hired by the Ministry of Education to teach fundamental Shiite Islam to the country's youth, who are increasingly dissatisfied with the Islamic Revolution and are looking elsewhere for fulfillment. But as one father whose son was in the audience told a reporter, Mohammadi "unknowing admitted the defeat of the Islamic Republic of Iran as a theocratic regime in promoting its Islam."

By September of that year, the Iranian regime had arrested eighty-six evangelical pastors and subjected them to extended interrogations and even torture. In October 2004, Compass Direct, an international Christian news agency, reported that "a top [Iranian] official within the Ministry of Security Intelligence spoke on state television's Channel 1, warning the populace against the many 'foreign religions' active in the country and pledging to protect the nation's 'beloved Shiite Islam' from all outside forces." The news service went on to report that this security official had helped interrogate ten of the arrested evangelical pastors, had complained that Christian activities in Iran had gone "out of control," and was "insisting that their church do something to stop the flood of Christian literature, television, and radio programs targeting Iran."[13]

The rise of Mahmoud Ahmadinejad led to a dramatic acceleration of government-directed persecution of Iranian Christians — particularly pastors, many of whom have been arrested, interrogated, beaten, and even worse. "An Iranian convert to Christianity was kidnapped last week from his home in northeastern Iran and stabbed to death, his bleeding body thrown in front of his home a few hours later," Compass Direct reported in November 2005. "Ghorban Tori, 50, was pastoring an independent house church of covert Christians in Gonbad-e-Kavus, a town just east of the Caspian Sea along the Turkmenistan border. Within hours of the November 22 murder, local secret police arrived at the martyred pastor's home, searching for Bibles and other banned Christian books in the Farsi language. By the end of the following day, the secret police had also raided the houses of all other known Christian believers in the city. According to one informed Iranian source, during the past eight days representatives of the Ministry of Intelligence and Security (MOIS) have arrested and severely tortured ten other Christians in several cities, including Tehran."[14]

Just a few days before the pastor's murder, Ahmadinejad met with thirty provincial governors and vowed to shut down the country's growing house-church movement, reportedly saying: "I will stop Christianity in this country."[15]

Nevertheless, evangelical leaders inside Iran say they are seeing the words of Matthew 16:18 come true before their very eyes: "I will build my church," Jesus said, "and the gates of hell shall not prevail against it" (KJV).

Dreams and Visions

Ultimately, I'm told that most Iranian MBBs are not coming to Christ primarily through *The Passion of the Christ* or the *JESUS* film, or through radio and satellite TV ministries, or even through the work of the mushrooming house-church movement. These resources are vitally important. They are giving many unbelievers initial exposure to the gospel, and they are certainly strengthening the faith of new believers as well as those who have been following Christ for some time. But they are not enough to bring many Iranians to a point of decision. What is bringing these Iranians to Christ are dreams and visions of Jesus.

One Iranian Muslim woman had a dream in which God told her, "Whatever the two women you are going to meet with tomorrow tell you, listen to them." Startled, she went through the next day curious who she would meet. She had no plans to meet anyone, but sure enough, at one point two Iranian Christian women came up to her and explained the message of salvation to her. She obeyed the Lord's directive from the dream, listened carefully, and then bowed her head and prayed to receive Christ as her Savior.

Several years ago, an Iranian pastor I know met a twenty-two-year-old Iranian Shia woman who had become a Christian after seeing a vision of Jesus Christ. She just showed up in his church one day, hungry to study the Bible for herself. The more she studied God's Word, the more deeply she loved Jesus. Soon, she discovered that God had given her the spiritual gift of evangelism. That is, not only did she have a passion to share

556

her faith with others; the Holy Spirit had also blessed her with a supernatural ability to lead Muslims to Jesus. Today, she leads an average of fifteen people to Christ every day — that's right, *fifteen a day.* She told my pastor friend that Iranian Muslims are so desperate for the gospel that typically it takes about five minutes to share the story of her conversion and how God has changed her life before the listener is ready to also receive Christ. "Difficult" conversations, she says, with several questions or concerns, take fifteen to twenty minutes. Her prayer: to lead seven thousand Iranian Muslims to Christ over the next five years.[16]

In my third novel, *The Ezekiel Option,* I tell the story of two Christians driving through the mountains of Iran with a car full of Bibles. Suddenly, their steering wheel jammed and they had to slam on the brakes to keep from driving off the side of the road. When they looked up, they saw an old man knocking on their windows and asking if they had the books.

"What books?" they asked.

"The books about Jesus," the old man replied. He went on to explain that an angel recently came to him in a vision and told him about Jesus. Later he found out that everyone in his mountain village had had the same vision. They were all brand-new followers of Jesus, but they did not know what do to next. Then the old man had a dream in which Jesus told him to go down the mountain and wait by the road for someone to bring books that would explain how to be a Christian. He obeyed, and suddenly two men with a car full of Bibles had come to a stop right in front of him.

This was one of my favorite passages in *The*

Ezekiel Option, but it's not fiction. I didn't make it up. It's true. I got it directly from a dear friend of mine who is the head of a ministry in the Middle East. He personally knows the men involved. I simply asked if I could change their names for use in the novel, and my friend agreed.

Chapter Twenty-Six:
The Big, Untold Story —
Part Two

More evidence of a dramatic
revival in the Middle East

What God is doing in Iran is extraordinary.

But it is just the beginning. As you travel through the rest of the Islamic world, you find miracles happening everywhere and accelerating as never before.

Revival in North Africa

Senior pastors and ministry leaders in Egypt estimate there are more than 2.5 million followers of Jesus Christ in their country. A growing number of these are Muslim converts, and there is also an enormous revival going on among nominal Christians inside the historic Coptic church, whose members number about 10 million.[1]

Lynn's mom, our boys, Lynn, and I lived in Egypt for nearly three months in late 2005 and early 2006 when I was researching and writing *Epicenter.* During that time, we had the opportunity to see this enormous surge of Christianity firsthand. We met with Egyptian MBBs and NCBBs engaged in satellite television ministry, in radio ministry, in Internet ministry, in gospel literature distribution, and in all manner of evangelism outreaches and discipleship programs. We visited a variety of churches, including the famous "garbage church" in the caves above Cairo, located right next to the biggest "city" of trash and waste products I have ever seen in my life.

To get to the "garbage church," you must first drive through this "city" of badly built brick and cement apartment buildings teeming with an estimated fifteen to thirty thousand "garbage people" — no one knows for sure, and the numbers are always changing — living amid literally thousands of tons of trash. Everywhere you look you see people picking through it, sorting it, rebagging it, looking for objects of value and hoping to sell plastic bottles and the like to recyclers. The stench is unbelievable.

But then you come through it to the other side, to a paved parking lot and a lovely little Christian chapel, nestled against huge cliffs. Carved into the cliffs are the most amazing scenes of Jesus walking on water, Jesus on the cross, Jesus ascending to heaven, and so forth, each with a Bible verse inscribed below it in Arabic and English, all done by a Polish artist. Inside the six caves are six chapels, the largest of which holds twenty thousand people.

Our guide that day was an MBB named Addel. He shared with us (by translation) how he was lost in drugs and alcohol and the depression of living in the garbage village. He also shared with us how he came to hear an audiocassette of one of the priests at the church and how God used that sermon to convict him of his sin and point him to what Jesus did on the cross to pay the penalty for his sins and offer him forgiveness. Now Addel greets visitors who come to see this extraordinary ministry and tells them the story of what God is doing there.

The church was planted, he said, in 1978 by a Coptic priest with a burden for reaching people many consider, as Paul called himself, "the scum of the world, the dregs of all things"* with the Good News that they could be adopted by the King of kings. So many people became Christians in the years that followed that in 1992 they had to convert the largest cave into a worship amphitheater. On an average weekend, some ten thousand new and growing believers from the garbage community come to sing and hear the message of the gospel and learn how to be true disciples of Jesus Christ. Services are held on Thursday nights (the most popular service), Friday mornings, and Sunday evenings.

In May of 2005, more than twenty thousand Arab believers gathered for a day of prayer for their unsaved Muslim friends to become followers of Christ. The event was broadcast throughout the Middle East on a Christian satellite television network, allowing millions more to see God powerfully at work.

The number of believers in Libya is not currently known. In Tunisia, I am told, there are less than a thousand MBBs. But in neighboring Algeria — the birthplace of St. Augustine, one of the early Church fathers, but for many centuries almost devoid of a Christian presence — more than eighty thousand Muslims have become followers of Christ in recent years. The vast majority

*1 Corinthians 4:13.

of these believers are young people under the age of thirty.[2]

The surge of Christianity has become so alarming to Islamic clerics that in March of 2006, Algerian officials passed a law banning Muslims from becoming Christians or even learning about Christianity. Christians trying to share their faith with Muslims face two to five years in jail and fines of five thousand to ten thousand euros for "trying to call on a Muslim to embrace another religion." In a move to stamp out the rapidly growing house-church movement, the law also forbids Christians from meeting together in any building without a license from the government.[3]

Christianity is also growing in Morocco. On a 2005 trip to Casablanca and Rabat, I found the Moroccan media up in arms about the "phenomenon of Moroccans converting to Christianity," suggesting that between 20,000 and 40,000 Muslims have become Christ-followers. The *Morocco Times,* for example, ran an article on March 12, 2005, entitled, "Why Are Moroccans Converting to Christianity?" Then on January 24, 2006, the *Times* published a story entitled "Evangelical Missionaries Back in the Limelight."*

Local pastors and ministry leaders have told me that the kinds of numbers cited in these stories may be overstated, but they readily acknowledge that God is on the move in their country. During my visits there, I have personally had the privilege of meeting many MBB leaders who shared with me the dramatic stories of their own conversions.

*Other Moroccan publications, including *Attajdid, Le Journal Hebdomadaire, Le Matin,* and *La Gazette Du Maroc,* have run similar stories.

Some of these leaders were actually "hajjis" — meaning they were once such devout Muslims that they made the pilgrimage to Mecca known as the *Haj* to worship Allah — before leaving Islam and turning to Christ. Now they are evangelists, disciple makers, and church planters overflowing with exciting stories of how other Moroccans are coming to Christ. Let me share just one with you.

A young Muslim woman from Morocco — let's call her Abidah (which means "worshiper") — saw the *JESUS* film while living and working in Europe and became a follower of Jesus. After two years of being discipled in the faith by an older and wiser believer, Abidah went home on vacation to visit her family in Morocco. For five days she prayed about how to tell her family that she had become a Christian, but she was too scared. On the sixth day, her sister also returned home from Europe. "Hey, look what I got for free!" the sister said to her family, showing them a copy of the Injil (New Testament) and the *JESUS* film a Christian had given her as a gift on the ferry ride across the Mediterranean.

"Hey, look, the film is about Isa!"★ exclaimed the father, a traditional Muslim. "He's our prophet. Let's all watch it."

Abidah was in shock.

The family sat down together in front of the television. About halfway through the film, the whole family was asking one question after another, trying to understand who Jesus was, why He taught the way He did, and how He could do miracles and show such love and compassion to everyone, including His enemies.

★Isa is the Arabic name for Jesus.

Abidah saw her opening. She started answering the questions. Now it was her family who was in shock. "Why do you know all these things?" asked her father.

"Because I saw this movie two years ago and I became a Christian. But I've been afraid to tell you."

A cloud covered her father's face. He looked angry. But when he spoke, he did not yell at Abidah. Instead, he said, "What! You made us wait five days to hear about Jesus?"

Revival in Sudan

In Sudan, meanwhile, one of the biggest stories in modern Christendom is unfolding — a spiritual awakening of almost unimaginable proportions amid civil war, radical Islam, rampant persecution, and outright genocide. Some three hundred thousand Sudanese have been killed in recent years in Darfur alone. More than 2.5 million Sudanese have been displaced by all the fighting. Yet the God of the Bible is moving powerfully there to draw these dear people into His family.

In *Epicenter,* I reported that one million Sudanese had turned to Christ just since the year 2000 — not in spite of persecution, war, and genocide, but *because* of them. "People see what radical Islam is like," one Sudanese Christian leader told me, "and they want Jesus instead."[4]

Since the book's release in the fall of 2006, more than a quarter of a million additional Sudanese have given their lives to Christ, bringing the estimated total number of believers in the country to more than 5.5 million.[5] The crying need now is for more trained pastors, Bible teachers, disciple makers, and humanitarian relief workers.

When Sudan received independence in 1956, there were only five or six born-again Anglican priests in the entire country. Today there are more than 3,500 Anglican priests there, along with scores of pastors and ministry leaders from other denominations.[6] But this is simply not enough to keep up with the demand. Students are attending seminary classes in caves. The government is preventing Christians from building adequate ministry training facilities. And, of course, hundreds of churches have been destroyed by years of fighting.

Revival in Iraq

In the fall of 2008, several colleagues and I had the privilege of traveling to Iraq and participating in a conference of prayer, worship, and Bible teaching attended by 640 Iraqi pastors, worship leaders, Bible study leaders, and young people. It was, we were told, the fourth such annual conference, and this one constituted by far the largest gathering of Iraqi believers in the modern history of the country.

It was an incredibly special time, and I wish every one of my readers could have a similar opportunity. The believers and their pastors came from every province in the country. They were filled with joy and excitement to worship God and to be together as brothers and sisters in Christ. They literally sang songs of praise and adoration to their Lord Jesus Christ for two — and sometimes three — hours at a time before settling down for a pastor to teach from the Bible. After each session, they would huddle together to compare notes about what God was doing in their cities, towns, and villages. They would tell stories of miracles they were seeing happen in their midst. They would pray with and for each other. They would exchange e-mail addresses and promise to stay in touch with each other. They also asked the Western pastors and ministry leaders, of which there were a few in attendance, to pray about coming back and helping to lead future conferences and retreats to train Iraqi believers how to study the Bible for themselves.

Without a doubt, the hunger for Christ inside Iraq is also at an all-time high, say the numerous Iraqi pastors and ministry leaders I interviewed. Several million Arabic New Testaments and Christian books have been shipped into Iraq since the liberation. Millions more are being printed inside the country, and pastors say they cannot keep up with the demand. What's more, Iraqis today are turning to Christ in numbers unimaginable at any point during Saddam Hussein's reign of terror.

Before 2003, senior Iraqi Christian leaders tell me, there were only about four to six hundred known born-again followers of Jesus Christ in the entire country, despite an estimated 750,000 nominal Christians in historic Iraqi churches. By the time *Epicenter* was published in 2006, the number of known believers inside Iraq had grown to more than five thousand. And God has continued moving powerfully since then. By the end of 2008, Iraqi Christian leaders estimated that there were more than seventy thousand born-again Iraqi believers — some ten thousand actively worshiping in above-ground Bible-teaching churches inside Iraq, at least another ten thousand worshiping in secret house churches inside Iraq, and another fifty thousand living as refugees outside the country, mostly in Jordan, Egypt, Europe, and the U.S.[7]

In addition to Muslims converting to Christianity in large numbers, there is also a significant spiritual awakening under way inside the traditional Iraqi churches. "Catholic and Orthodox Christian priests are seeing their faith in Christ revitalized," one Iraqi pastor, who asked not to be named, told me. "They want to see their churches restored to the first-century kind of activity — evangelism, discipleship, and miracles."[8]

Why such spiritual hunger? Every Iraqi Christian I have interviewed has given me the same two answers: war and persecution. Though the security in Iraq was deteriorating from 2003 to 2007, one of the top leaders of the Revivalist movement there told me he had never seen so many Iraqis praying to receive Christ and wanting Bible teaching.

I asked him how he accounted for such developments.

"It's not that complicated really, Joel," he replied. "When human beings are under threat, they look for a strong power to help them — a refuge. Iraqis look around and when they see believers in Jesus enjoying internal peace during a time of such violence and fear, they want Jesus too."[9]

But, I asked, how did he and his disciples share their faith and lead people to Christ with all the suicide bombings, car bombings, snipers, and other troubles of the past few years?

"We did what we could," he said, "but God is not dependent upon us. This is something He is doing on His own. He is drawing Muslims to Christ. We are just His servants, helping where we can. The truth is, God is healing Muslims of sicknesses and diseases. He's also giving Muslims visions of Jesus Christ. He is coming to them and speaking to them, and they are repenting and giving their lives to Him. I'm saying that Shiites are seeing visions of Christ and repenting. When we meet them, they already believe in Jesus. We don't have to share the gospel with them. We want to, but it's not necessary. They're already convinced that Jesus is the Savior. They're already convinced that the Bible is the Word of God. So we help them study the Bible. We help them grow in their faith and get into a good church so they can meet other believers and learn to worship the Lord as part of the Church. But you see, Joel, it is God who is at work. He is making this happen — not us."

Revival in the Holy Land

In the heart of the epicenter itself — Jerusalem, Judea, Samaria, and Gaza — signs of revival are finally noticeable after centuries of spiritual drought.

In 1967 there were only a few hundred NCBBs and only a handful of MBBs in the Holy Land. Today, when you include Israeli Arab believers and Palestinian believers living in the West Bank and Gaza, there are about five to six thousand born-again followers of Jesus Christ walking where He once walked. What's really exciting is that just since 2007, nearly one thousand Muslims have come to Christ in the West Bank alone, most of them converted through dreams and visions of Jesus. What's more, the quality of the converts is exceptional. Indeed, Jesus appears to be handpicking spiritual game-changers out of His backyard and raising them up to be enormously influential in reaching the rest of the epicenter with the gospel.

One of the most influential Revivalists I have ever met is a Palestinian Arab. Born to a nominal Christian family in Jerusalem in 1947, Taheer (whom I cited in the last chapter)* was barely six months old when the first Arab-Israeli war broke out. His mother died soon thereafter. Nevertheless, God was incredibly gracious to him, bringing him to saving faith in Jesus Christ at the age of eighteen as he wept on his knees with repentance after finally reading the New Testament for himself.

"I will not leave you as orphans," Jesus said in John 14:18–19. "I will come to you. After a little while the world will no longer see Me, but you will see Me; because I live, you will live also." These verses were suddenly coming true in this man's life, and he soon developed a passion for reaching Muslims and nominal Christians with God's amazing grace. When I met him, he was running the Arab-language division of one of the world's most effective radio ministries, broadcasting the gospel and hour after hour of solid Bible teaching to millions of Muslims scanning their radio dials for hope and truth.

Several years ago, Lynn and I met three young Palestinian men from Bethlehem who had become believers from nominal Christian backgrounds. Not long before we had met them, they were teenage boys throwing stones at Israeli soldiers and participating with PLO activists and Hamas Radicals in violent demonstrations against what they denounced as "Israeli occupation of Pales-

*Taheer is a pseudonym.

tine." But after coming to faith in Jesus Christ, they had changed completely. Now they were sharing their new faith with anyone and everyone who would listen, enrolling in intensive Bible and evangelism training classes, and doing everything they could to train younger Palestinian believers to become effective in ministry as well.

"The Church is really growing here — finally," one of them told me. "I remember just a few years ago there was a church in Bethlehem where there was just the pastor and one believer. But the pastor conducted services as if the little worship hall was full, like a regular church. He would stand up at the pulpit and read announcements. He would preach his sermon. Then he would tell the congregation to stand for a closing song. The congregation was just this one guy. But the guy would stand up and sing, and then sit back down. Before I became a believer, I thought it was funny. But now that little church has more than one hundred new believers in it. I don't think it's funny anymore. It's very exciting!"[10]

Revival in Syria, Lebanon, and Jordan

In 1967, there were no known born-again followers of Jesus Christ from a Muslim background in the entire country of Syria. But after the humiliating loss to the Israelis and all the casualties and carnage wrought by the war, spiritual interest in the gospel began to grow. By 1997, there were about one thousand known believers in Syria. Today, there are between four and five thousand born-again believers in the country, both MBBs and NCBBs combined.

Does more need to be done? Absolutely. But as one Arab ministry leader there told me: "I am so excited because God is doing a miracle in Syria." Women, he said, are particularly receptive to the gospel. About two hundred fifty women attended one conference his wife organized — *and ninety-six prayed to receive Christ.* "Some of the first churches in the world were in Syria in the first century," he reminded me. "Then it became a spiritual desert. But now the Church is coming back here." What's more, he says that "because Paul received Christ on the road to Damascus, we have a vision for this to become a sending country" — that is, a country that sends trained disciples from Syria to other Muslim countries in the region to share the gospel.[11]

Arab Christian leaders in Jordan tell me that in 1967, there were fewer than one thousand born-again believers in this entire biblically historic country — only about ten known Muslim Background Believers and only five to eight hundred Nominal Christian Background Believers. But God has been reviving the Church in the last four decades, and particularly in the past few years. Conservative estimates say the number of believers in the country is now between five and ten thousand. The head of one major Jordanian ministry, however, believes there may be as many as fifty thousand believers in the country — about fifteen thousand NCBBs and more than thirty-five thousand MBBs.[12] Again, the precise numbers are not as important as the trend, and the trend is that the Church is definitely bearing fruit again after centuries of spiritual barrenness.

In Lebanon, sources tell me, there are about ten thousand truly born-again followers of Jesus Christ today, though nearly four in ten of the country's 4 million residents describe themselves as "Christian." Most of the believers are NCBBs, but Muslims are starting to show an openness to the gospel that has been lacking for centuries.

As the Second Lebanon War erupted in July of 2006, Lebanese Revivalists huddled together to fast and pray for their country, even as rockets and bombs were falling all around them and the mood of the people was quickly darkening. "The Lebanese find themselves in a very dark tunnel, and they feel there is no light," a local Arab ministry leader told me later. "We asked God for wisdom to know how to love our neighbors and our enemies."

The believers soon found themselves drawn to Matthew 5:14–16, in which Jesus said, "You are the light of the world. A city set on a hill cannot be hidden; nor does anyone light a lamp and put it under a basket, but on the lampstand, and it gives light to all who are in the house. Let your light shine before men in such a way that they may see your good works, and glorify your Father who is in heaven."

They decided they needed to spring into action, not wait for the war to be over. They mobilized dozens of teams of twenty believers each to begin doing relief work among the Shia families from southern Lebanon who had fled to the Beirut area for safety. In just a few short weeks, with financial help from the Joshua Fund, they delivered forty thousand packages of food, cooking supplies, New Testaments, and the *JESUS* film on DVD to these displaced and terrified families. They also drove trucks filled with relief supplies and gospel literature to Shia families hunkered down in the south as well as those in the Bekaa Valley, near the border with Syria.

"Food they need, but Jesus they need more," said an Arab Christian ministry worker. Through that outreach alone, more than 1,100 Lebanese Muslims prayed to receive Christ as their Savior.

Revival in Saudi Arabia

In Saudi Arabia — the epicenter of Islam due to its status as the home of Mecca and Medina — a dramatic spiritual awakening is taking place. In 1967, Arab Christian leaders tell me, there were only a handful of Muslim Background Believers in the entire country. By 2005, they estimated there were more than one hundred thousand Saudi MBBs. They believe the numbers are even higher today, and they say that thousands more Saudis have come to Christ in Europe and elsewhere around the world. Most are coming to Christ through dreams and visions, though often they first hear about the claims of Christ through gospel radio broadcasting, satellite television, the Internet, or through Christians befriending them and giving them a Bible or a book or film about the life of Christ.

Consider one example. A Saudi woman — let's call her Marzuqah (which means "blessed by God") — secretly converted to Christianity. But she had a brother who was dying of a terrible disease, and Marzuqah was deeply grieved. She loved her brother very much, and she wanted to spend eternity with him in heaven. So she prayed fervently for God to heal and to save her brother.

One day, Jesus appeared to Marzuqah in a dream. "Your prayers have been answered," He told her. "Go tell your brother about Me." She did.

To her astonishment, her brother prayed with

her to receive Christ. Then his health improved briefly. The family — seeing his physical improvement but not knowing about his conversion — asked, "Why is this happening?"

The brother said, "It is because I accepted Jesus as my Savior. And He is my healer, not physically but spiritually. You must take Him too."

After explaining why he had given his life to Christ, he died the next day. But first, he made the family promise not to harm Marzuqah for her faith. They agreed.

Though her family has not yet followed her lead, Marzuqah has become a devoted disciple. She studies her Bible two hours a day. She has found other secret believers to meet with for prayer and Bible study. And she is sharing the gospel with her Muslim friends. "There are so many people I must tell about Jesus!" she says.[13]

Revival in Afghanistan

Before September 11, 2001, I am told, there were fewer than one hundred MBBs in all of Afghanistan. By 2006 I reported in *Epicenter* that there were 10,000 MBBs, based on the reporting of several trusted sources. However, after traveling to the country in the fall of 2008 and meeting with senior pastors and ministry leaders there, I am inclined to revise that figure downward to a range of between 3,000 and 5,000.

Is God moving powerfully in Afghanistan? He most certainly is. Has the Church grown significantly since 9/11? Absolutely. The question is simply by how much. Some sources told me the number of Afghan believers is now between 20,000 and 30,000. That could be true, but I honestly did not see enough evidence to convince

574

me with any certainty that there are even 10,000 at present. There is not a single Afghan MBB church that can operate safely above ground. There are no prayer or worship conferences that Afghan MBBs can attend in any significant numbers. Persecution of the believers is intense. Indeed, a thirty-four-year old foreign Christian aid worker was martyred in Kabul just after we left, shot in the head by two members of the Taliban.[14]

"The greatest need now is leadership development," one Afghan ministry leader told me. "We need to train pastors to care for all these new believers."[15]

An illiterate Afghan Muslim man came to Christ a few years ago and began to be discipled by an older and wiser man in the faith. He then enrolled in a series of training classes for secret believers to grow in their faith. After graduating from the fifth level of Bible and ministry training, he shared the gospel with his town, and almost everyone prayed to receive Christ. Together, they built the first Afghan Christian church without any outside help.

Ministry leaders in Afghanistan say the spiritual liberation of the country began as soon as the political liberation did. The Revivalists began distributing humanitarian relief supplies — food, clothing, medical supplies, and the like — to their neighbors and even to their enemies to show the love of Jesus Christ in a real and practical way. They set up medical clinics and English-language schools and job-training programs. Their goal was not to convert people but simply to love people.

At the same time, they began using radio and satellite television to beam the gospel to Afghans hungry to hear the truth after decades of oppression. They began distributing copies of the New Testament and other pieces of gospel literature by the hundreds of thousands. Perhaps more important, they began showing and distributing copies of the *JESUS* film translated into local languages and dialects to reach the illiterate.

And Afghans began responding.

The enormous controversy over the case of Abdul Rahman, a Muslim convert to Christianity facing execution by a court in Kabul for apostasy, became the talk of the nation in the spring of 2006, with saturation coverage by Afghan TV, radio, and newspapers. The event shone a huge spotlight on the fact that Afghans are turning to Christ in such numbers that Islamic leaders are furious. It also showed the fledgling Afghan church that fellow believers around the world are praying for them and eager to see them grow and flourish.

By God's grace, and with pressure from American, Canadian, British, Italian, and other leaders, the case against Rahman was dropped. He was set free and left the country.

But persecution of believers in Afghanistan has hardly diminished. Just days after Rahman's release, two more Afghan believers were arrested, and according to Compass Direct news service and Open Doors, a Christian ministry to the "closed" countries of the Middle East, one young Afghan convert to Christianity "was beaten severely outside his home by a group of six men, who finally knocked him unconscious with a hard blow to his temple. He woke up in the hospital two hours later" but was discharged before morning. Compass and Open Doors also reported that "several other Afghan Christians have been subjected to police raids on their homes and places of work in the past month, as well as to telephone threats."[16]

Revival in Central Asia

During the summer of 1986, I had the privilege of traveling to Tashkent, the capital of Uzbekistan, to share Christ with Muslims. At the time, there were only a few Uzbek believers in a country of 27 million people. Today, there are some thirty thousand Uzbek followers of Christ, and hunger for the gospel is at an all-time high. "Hundreds and hundreds of churches were planted after the Soviet Union broke down," one Uzbek Christian leader told me. "And now these churches are growing."[17]

On that same trip, I also had the opportunity to travel to Alma-Ata (now Almaty) in southern Kazakhstan, near the Chinese border, on a ministry trip to share the gospel with Muslims. At the time there were no known Kazakh believers in Christ in the entire country of 15 million people. By 1990, there were only three known believers. But today evangelical leaders in the country report that there are more than sixteen thousand Kazakh Christians, and more than one hundred thousand Christians of all ethnicities.

The stories I hear from Kazakhstan today are extraordinary. One young Kazakh Muslim man, for example, was severely persecuted after he converted to Christianity and began preaching the gospel in village after village. The leaders of his own village cursed him and said terrible things about him. But several years later, two Muslim tribal leaders came to his home with a lamb. They said they had come to apologize because their crops were failing, their livestock were dying, and they knew God was punishing them.

"Will you forgive us?" they asked.

The evangelist said yes.

Then the leaders sacrificed the lamb as a sign of their repentance. This opened a new door for the young man to bear witness for Christ in that village, explaining verses from the Bible like John 1:29, which describes Jesus Christ as "the Lamb of God who takes away the sin of the world" because of His death on the cross. The tribal leaders did not immediately come to Christ. But having asked the evangelist for forgiveness and being willing to listen respectfully to the Word of God, they found that their crops suddenly began to grow and their livestock began to flourish again.

And then something really unexpected happened. The evangelist's father would not speak to his son or visit his home for ten years because of his son's conversion to Christianity. But after watching how calmly and patiently his son had endured the village's persecution, and how God had withdrawn his favor from the village and now was giving it back again, the father sat up all night with his son asking him questions about his faith, about the Bible, and about the power of his son's God to hear prayers and answer them.

In the morning, the Holy Spirit moved in the father's heart and the son had the privilege of praying with him to receive Jesus Christ as his personal Savior and Lord.[18]

Revival in Pakistan

Senior Pakistani Christian leaders whom I have great trust in tell me there is a "conversion explosion" going on in their country, comparable in many ways to what is going on in Iran, Sudan, and Egypt. Despite the fact that Pakistan is a base camp for the Radicals, God is moving powerfully, and there are now an estimated 2.5 million to 3 million born-again believers worshiping Jesus Christ amongst the jihadists. Whole towns and villages along the Afghan-Pakistani border are seeing dreams and visions of Jesus and are converting to Christianity.

One young Pakistani Muslim who converted to Christianity became a bold minister of the gospel to Taliban refugees. Over the course of two to three years, the thirty-one-year-old evangelist personally led eight hundred Taliban extremists to faith in Christ before he was captured and murdered and his car set ablaze by a bloodthirsty mob.

The spiritual climate is so ripe for harvest that even Indian evangelists are seeing record numbers of Pakistanis come to Christ. My friend Dr. T. E. Koshy, a senior elder in one of India's largest evangelical church-planting movements, began traveling to Pakistan in 1993 to preach the gospel and strengthen the local believers. In 2006, he addressed a conference in the city of Lahore on the topic "Jesus Christ, the Healer."

He told the gathered crowd of more than ten thousand people, "Sin is the worst sickness of all. And only Christ can heal us of this sickness." He pointed to passages like Matthew 4:23–24, which tells us that "Jesus was going throughout all Galilee, teaching . . . and proclaiming the gospel of the kingdom, and healing every kind of disease and every kind of sickness among the people. The news about Him spread throughout all Syria; and they brought to Him all who were ill, those suffering with various diseases and pains, demoniacs, epileptics, paralytics; and He healed them." He pointed to passages like Matthew 14:14, which tells us that when Jesus "went ashore, He saw a large crowd, and felt compassion for them and healed their sick."

Koshy also pointed to passages like Matthew 9:1–8, which tells the story of Jesus healing a paralyzed man. "Take courage, son; your sins are forgiven," Jesus told the man. The religious leaders were angry when they heard this, saying privately to each other, "This fellow blasphemes." Jesus, however, knew exactly what they were thinking. So He said to them, "Which is easier, to say, 'Your sins are forgiven,' or to say, 'Get up, and walk'?" Then, in a stunning display of His authority, Jesus said to the paralytic, "Get up, pick up your bed and go home." And the paralyzed man jumped to his feet, completely healed physically and completely healed spiritually. The text tells us that "when the crowds saw this, they were awestruck, and glorified God, who had given such authority to men."

When Koshy was finished preaching, more than a thousand Pakistanis — all of them weeping over their sins — made decisions to receive Jesus Christ as their Savior and their Healer. For the next four nights, Koshy preached the power of Christ to heal and forgive, and when the conference was over, more than three thousand Pakistanis had become followers of Jesus Christ.[19]

I asked Koshy why so many Pakistanis — Muslims and nominal Christians — are giving their lives to the Lord in this post–9/11 world.

"Today, with so many Christians in Pakistan, many are seeing the believers demonstrate Christ's love in real and practical ways," he said. "When the massive earthquake struck several years ago, it was the Christians who responded with relief supplies, love, and compassion. One Muslim told me, 'No one else but the Christians came to give us hope.' Pakistanis now are able to see the difference between hard-core radical Islam and hard-core Christianity, and they are choosing Jesus. You can see the hand of God moving so powerfully. The restlessness of the masses is created by the Enemy, and Pakistanis are coming to realize that they can only find rest and healing and forgiveness through Jesus Christ."

CHAPTER TWENTY-SEVEN:
THE AIR WAR

How the Revivalists use TV and radio
to reach Muslims with the gospel

You have probably never heard of Father Zakaria Botros.

But you need to know his story. He is far and away the most watched and most effective Arab evangelist operating in the Muslim world, and he is by far the most controversial. I think of him as the Rush Limbaugh of the Revivalists — he is funny, feisty, brilliant, opinionated, and provocative. But rather than preaching the gospel of conservatism, he is preaching the gospel of Jesus Christ. And his enemies do not simply want to silence him. They want to assassinate him.

An Arabic newspaper has named Botros "Islam's Public Enemy #1."[1] The week I interviewed Botros by phone from a secure, undisclosed location, he told me that he had just learned that an al Qaeda Web site had posted his photograph and named him one of the "most wanted" infidels in the world.[2] The Radicals have even put a bounty on his head. The Christian Broadcasting Network reported the figure was as high as $60 million.[3] Botros does not know for certain. But just to put that in context, the U.S. bounty on Osama bin Laden's head is $25 million.

Why are the Radicals so enraged by a Coptic priest from Egypt who is in his seventies? Because Botros is waging an air war against them, and he is winning.

Must-See TV

Using state-of-the art satellite technology to bypass the efforts of Islamic governments to keep the gospel out of their countries, Botros is directly challenging the claims of Muhammad to be a prophet and the claims of the Qur'an to be God's word. He systematically deconstructs Muhammad's life, story by story, pointing out character flaws and sinful behavior. He carefully deconstructs the Qur'an, verse by verse, citing contradictions and inconsistencies. And not only does he explain without apology what he believes is wrong with Islam; he goes on to teach from the Bible why Jesus loves Muslims and why He is so ready to forgive them and adopt them into His family, no matter who they are or what they have done.

If Botros were doing this in a corner, or on some cable-access channel where no one saw him or cared, that would be one thing. But his ninety-minute program — a combination of preaching, teaching, and answering questions from (often irate) callers all over the world — has become "must-see TV" throughout the Muslim world. It is replayed four times a week in Arabic, his native language, on a satellite television network called Al Hayat ("Life TV"). It can be seen in every country in North Africa, the Middle East, and central Asia. It can also been seen throughout North America, Europe, and even as far away as

Australia and New Zealand. And not only *can* it be seen in so many places, it *is* seen — by an estimated 50 million Muslims a day.

At the same time, Botros is getting millions of hits on his multiple Web sites in multiple languages. There, Muslims can read his sermons and study through an archive of answers to frequently asked questions. They can also enter a live chat room called "Pal Chat," where they are not only permitted but encouraged to ask their toughest questions to trained online counselors, many of whom are Muslim converts to Christianity who understand exactly where the questioners are coming from and the struggles they face.

As a result, "Father Zakaria" — who has been on the air only since 2003 — has practically become a household name in the Muslim world. Millions hate him, to be sure, but they are watching. They are listening. They are processing what he is saying, and they are talking about him with their friends and family.

When Botros challenges Radical clerics to answer his many refutations of Islam and defend the Qur'an, millions wait to see how the fundamentalists will respond. But they rarely do. They prefer to attack Botros rather than answer him.

Yet the more the Radicals attack him, the more well-known he becomes. The more well-known he becomes, the more Muslims feel compelled to tune in. And as more Muslims tune in, more are coming to the conclusion that he is right and are in turn choosing to become followers of Jesus Christ.

Botros estimates at least a thousand Muslims a month pray to receive Christ with his telephone counselors. Some of them pray to receive Christ live on the air with Botros. And this surely is the tip of the iceberg, as it represents only those who are able to get through on the jammed phone lines. There simply are not enough trained counselors to handle all the calls.

Many leading Arab evangelists I interviewed for *Inside the Revolution* said they believe God is using Botros to help bring in the greatest harvest of Muslim converts to Christianity in the history of Christendom. Botros refuses to take any credit, saying he is just one voice in a movement of millions. But he is certainly excited by the trend lines. He does see more Muslims turning to Christ than ever before, and he told me he has cited *Epicenter* at least three times as evidence of the enormous numbers of conversions taking place.

What's more, he vows to keep preaching the gospel so long as the Lord Jesus gives him breath. John 3:16 — "For God so loved the world, that He gave His only begotten Son [Jesus], that whoever believes in Him shall not perish, but have eternal life." — is the verse that drives Botros. He believes passionately that God loves the whole world, including each and every Muslim. He believes that "whoever" believes in the lordship of Jesus Christ — Jew, Muslim, or otherwise — will, in fact, receive eternal life. He does not believe all Muslims are Radicals, but he does believe all Muslims are spiritually lost, and he desperately wants to help them find their way to forgiveness and reconciliation with the God who made them and loves them.

"I believe this is the hand of God," Botros told me when we spoke by phone in September 2008. "He is directing me. He shows me what to say. He shows me what to write on the Web sites. He is showing me more and more how to use technology to reach people with his message of redemption."

Twice Imprisoned

Zakaria Botros was born in Egypt in 1934 to a Christian family that raised him to love Christ with all of his heart, soul, mind, and strength and to study the Bible for himself. "Since I was a child I loved Jesus and loved to worship Him," he said.

Sadness struck at a young age, however, when his older brother, Fuad, was murdered by members of the Muslim Brotherhood. "But it did not cause me to be against Muslims," Botros said. "I know he was a believer. I will see him again in heaven."

What did affect Botros was a high school teacher who was "a very fanatic Muslim." The teacher was "always asking me difficult questions about the Bible" and mocking Christianity. "I started to study Islam to answer him. I read the Qur'an and other books. And then I became a Sunday school teacher in my church, and I began teaching the youth about what was wrong about Islam and what was right about the Bible."

In 1959, at the age of twenty-five, Botros was ordained as a priest in the Egyptian Coptic church, one of the oldest Christian Orthodox denominations in the Middle East, started in Alexandria, Egypt, by the apostle Mark. "After I became a priest, I began to print lectures and essays explaining how to refute Islam and lead people to Jesus," Botros said. By the time he was arrested and imprisoned for his faith in 1981, he had baptized five hundred MBBs.

But it was not enough. Botros wanted to have

more impact. When he was released from prison after a year, he went back to preaching the gospel and refuting Islam. By 1989, the Egyptian authorities had had enough. They not only arrested him; they sentenced him to life in prison.

After much prayer — his own and the prayers of many of his disciples and friends — Botros was surprised when the authorities made an offer he could not refuse: they would set him free, but only if he left Egypt and went into exile, never to return. He agreed and moved to Melbourne, Australia, where he practiced his faith freely until moving in 1992 to England, where he lived eleven years.

It was there, amid a British society that was rapidly becoming home to Muslim immigrants from all over the world, that Botros began praying about ways to reach more Muslims. He could not bear the thought of speaking to only a few at a time. But he also knew that for security purposes he needed to have a way to get "in the face" of a Muslim without literally being in his face.

In early 2001, the Lord answered his prayers. Someone suggested he set up an Internet chat room where he could have online conversations with Muslims without subjecting himself to physical danger. In April of that year, "Pal Talk" was born.

Soon a producer for Al Hayat heard the growing buzz about Botros and invited him to be a guest on the network. The interview went well. Botros was asked back again and again. In time, Al Hayat executives asked him to host his own weekly program, teaching the Bible and challenging the Qur'an. After much prayer, Botros agreed.

"Truth Debate" debuted on September 1, 2003.

At first, the show was taped. "We used to record twenty episodes in a week and they would air them later," Botros recalls. But in February 2008, the decision was made to go live for ninety minutes every Friday night during prime time (9 p.m.) in the Middle East. While a tape of the show was replayed multiple times throughout the week, it was the live broadcast airing on the Muslim Sabbath when families are home sitting around their televisions that changed everything. The audience grew rapidly, and so did the controversy.

"It is much more effective now," Botros said with palpable excitement in his voice. "Now I'm in direct contact with people. They ask me questions in front of the whole Muslim world. They debate me. They challenge me. And then they accept Christ on air. Just this morning, a man named Ahmed prayed with me to become a follower of Jesus. He said, 'I need You, God. I accept You now.' . . . What a joy! That is why I do this."

Directly Challenging Islam

Botros pulls no punches on the air or off. He tells Muslims what he believes is wrong with their religion, no matter how painful it may be to hear.

During a 2005 show, for example, he blasted Muslims for abusing children by telling them lies. "Children are brainwashed that Islam is the truth, that Mohammad is the last prophet, that the Christians are infidels, and that the Jews are infidels," he said. "They repeat it constantly."

In that same show, he blasted Islamic leaders for historically spreading their religion by violence rather than by persuasion. "Islam, as portrayed in *The Encyclopedia of Islam*, in the Qur'an and the Hadith, was spread by means of the sword,"

Botros said on the show. " 'The sword played a major role in spreading Islam in the past, and it is the sword that preserves Islam today. Islam relies upon jihad in spreading the religion.' This is very clear in the encyclopedia. This appears in section 11, page 3,245. It says: 'Spreading Islam by means of the sword is a duty incumbent upon all Muslims.' Thus, Islam is spread by means of the sword."[4]

At the same time, Botros also tells Muslims the truth about just how costly it can be in human terms to convert to Christianity, even though that is precisely what he wants them to do. "Another thing [you need to know] is the punishment for apostasy," he said. "[*The Encyclopedia of Islam* says that] 'the punishment of killing any Muslim who abandons Islam is one of the most important factors terrifying all Muslim. He does not dare question the truth of Islam, so that his thoughts will not lead him to abandon Islam. In such a case, he would receive the punishment for apostasy: He would lose his life, and his property.' "

Botros said this reminded him of a true story he once heard about a Muslim cleric trying to spread Islam throughout Africa. "They reached a certain place in order to spread Islam, and they asked one of the locals, 'Do you prefer to worship one god and have four wives, or to worship three gods and have one wife?' We, of course, don't worship three gods, but that's what they said. The African said, 'I like four women, and I don't care which god. I want four women.'

"So they told him to say the *shahada* [the prayer to become a Muslim], and he did. Then they told him he had to be circumcised in order to become a Muslim. He asked, 'Do I really have to? I am a grown man.' They answered, 'Yes, you have to, in order to get the monthly stipend, and you can marry four wives.'

"The man agreed and underwent the pains of circumcision despite his advanced age. They began to pay him the monthly stipend, but after a few months they canceled the stipend. The man went and asked, 'Where's the money?'

"They told him, 'Now [that] you are deep in Islam, you don't need the monthly stipend anymore.'

"He threatened, 'I will abandon Islam.'

"They said, 'If you leave Islam, we will carry out the apostasy punishment on you.' He asked what it was, and they said, 'We will chop off your head and cut you into pieces.'

"This African man began to mumble, 'What a strange religion: when you go in they cut off a little piece of you, and when you go out, they cut you into little pieces.' "

Botros concluded, "This is the punishment for apostasy that keeps people afraid. Even when they reach the truth, they're afraid to express their opinion."

Is It Effective?

I asked Botros whether it was really effective to be so "in your face" with Muslims. "Some people believe the best evangelism with Muslims is to preach the love of Christ alone, not to deconstruct Islam," I noted. "But you have said that you like to use provocative ideas and language to shock Muslims into thinking about Jesus. You once said, 'This is my way: short, sharp, shock.' Isn't that right?"

"Yes," he laughed, grateful for the question, not

defensive. "Short, sharp, shock — absolutely."

"So why do you do that?" I asked. "Is that really the best way to show the love of Christ?"

"I will tell you, Joel," Botros said with the tone of a kindly old grandfather sitting his grandson down to explain to him how the world works. "If you are speaking to a person who is deep in thought, and you say to him so sweetly, 'Oh, I love you, my friend. You are wonderful. I really appreciate you,' does he hear you? No. He cannot hear you because he is so focused on his own thoughts. So how do you get his attention? Throw some water in his face? Hit him in the face? That would wake him up, right? Then maybe he gets mad. Maybe he insults you. 'What are you doing?' he says. 'Why did you throw water in my face?' But now he is paying attention.

"Now, if you go up to a Muslim and say, 'God loves you,' will he really hear you? No. He will say, 'Which of your three gods loves me?' If you say to a Muslim, 'The Bible has all the answers for life,' will he believe you? No. He will say, 'Oh, you mean the Bible that was changed and can no longer be trusted?' They do not listen. They are so focused on believing that Islam is the strongest religion in the world, that Muhammad is the best prophet, they are so focused on how wonderful their own beliefs are that they refuse to even consider the claims of Christ. They are brainwashed. Their conscience is dead. So I have to awaken them first by a shock — by an electric shock. I try to wake Muslims up by throwing some water in their face. I'm not doing it to be mean. I'm doing it because I love them."

"Do Muslim scholars and clerics ever call in or write in to answer you?" I asked.

"No one in five years has really answered my questions," he said.

"I'm guessing that is what makes Muslims so mad at you," I noted.

Botros laughed. "It causes people to want to kill me."

"I Want Them to Read the Bible"

"How, then, do you pivot from making provocative statements to sharing the love of Christ with Muslims?" I asked.

"Once I have their attention, I say to them, 'I read to you from your books about Muhammad and what he had done. If you are searching for the truth — if you are really searching — then compare between Muhammad and Jesus. See what Jesus said about purity and love. But you have to read the Bible to know more. And say to God, "If Islam is the truth, let me stand firm in it until eternity. If it is not, and if Jesus is the Truth, please let me know".' "

"You are trying to provoke them into reading the Bible to prove you are wrong?" I clarified.

"Yes," Botros said. "I want them to read the Bible, which is the true Word of God. I want them to study the Bible for themselves, because I know it will open their eyes to who Jesus is and how He can change their lives forever."

He was making a point I have heard from Revivalists all over the world, from Morocco to Afghanistan: A Christian cannot in and of himself convince a Muslim (or a Jew, or an atheist, or anyone for that matter) of the truth of the gospel and thus "convert" or change him. Only God Himself can do that, through the power of the Holy Spirit. The best that a follower of Jesus can

592

do is to encourage a person to read the Bible and consider the life and claims of Jesus Christ and then encourage him or her to ask God for wisdom to know what the truth is and how to follow it.

This is, in fact, precisely what the Bible tells us to do. Psalm 119 tells us that God's Word "is a lamp to my feet and a light to my path" that will "make me wiser than my enemies" and give a person who studies it carefully "more insight than all my teachers."

The Gospel of John, chapter one, tells us that "in the beginning was the Word, and the Word was with God, and the Word was God." John goes on to make it clear that the Word of God "became flesh" in the form of Jesus Christ "and dwelt among us, and we saw His glory, glory as of the only begotten from the Father, full of grace and truth."

Paul told us in 2 Timothy 3:15–17 that the Scriptures "are able to give you the wisdom that leads to salvation through faith which is in Christ Jesus" and that "all Scripture is inspired by God and profitable for teaching, for reproof, for correction, for training in righteousness; so that the man of God may be adequate, equipped for every good work."

Hebrews 4:12 says that "the word of God is living and active and sharper than any two-edged sword, and piercing as far as the division of soul and spirit, of both joints and marrow, and able to judge the thoughts and intentions of the heart."

And James 1:5 tells us that "if any of you lacks wisdom, let him ask of God, who gives to all generously and without reproach, and it will be given to him."

Ten Demands

Given his provocative style and powerful success, I asked Botros if he was worried for his safety. He is, after all, married and has four grown children and nine grandchildren.

"I have many guards who care for me day and night," he replied. "They are with me without ceasing — twenty-four hours a day, seven days a week, 365 days a year. And they don't take from me any penny." Botros was speaking of angels. While he is careful not to take unnecessary risks, he has entrusted his fate to the Lord.

Once, during an interview in Arabic, Botros was asked, "What should the Muslims do to make you stop saying these things?"[5]

Botros thought about it for a moment, and then said he had "ten demands" for Muslim clerics and authorities. If they would agree to all ten and truly implement them, then he would stop preaching the gospel and refuting the Qur'an. During our conversation, I asked Botros to recount his top-ten list in English. He graciously agreed.

1. Strike out all of the Qur'anic verses that deny the divinity of Jesus and the revelation of God in Him.
2. Acknowledge that Jesus is the Spirit and Word of God, as they truly believe, without hiding this fact.
3. Strike out the Qur'anic verses and hadiths that incite Muslims to kill Christians.
4. Strike out the Qur'anic verses and hadiths that incite Muslims to terrorism and oppression.
5. Delete all the Qur'anic verses that traduce the truth of Christ's crucifixion, creating

doubt about God's plan of salvation.

6. Stop the attacks on Jesus and the Holy Book in mosques and in all the media.

7. Give Muslims the freedom to choose their religion and the freedom to express their belief.

8. Abolish the punishment for apostasy, which is death; stop torturing people who convert to Christianity; and stop imprisoning them.

9. Make formal apologies by leaders throughout the Arab world for the murder of Christians in countries invaded by Islam.

10. Make formal apologies by leaders throughout the Arab world for the insults directed against the Christian faith throughout Islamic history.

Needless to say, there's no need to hold your breath waiting for Muslim authorities to comply with these demands. I suspect Father Zakaria Botros will be preaching the gospel nonstop until the Lord Jesus Himself decides to take him home, or until the Rapture.

The Billy Graham of Iran
While "Father Zakaria" is by far the most watched and best known evangelist to the Muslim world at large on the air today, he is by no means the only one.

I consider my friend Hormoz Shariat to be the Billy Graham of Iran. He is without question the most recognizable and most influential Iranian evangelist in the world. Every night in prime time, Shariat broadcasts by satellite a live program in which he shares the gospel in his native Farsi, teaches in-depth Bible studies, and takes phone calls from Muslims who have sincere questions or simply want to attack him on the air. And given that he is hosting a program unlike anything on Iranian state-run television, Shariat draws an enormous audience, an estimated 7 to 9 million Iranians every night.

The pastor of a fast-growing congregation of Iranian Muslim converts, Shariat also broadcasts his weekly worship service and teaching into Iran. Many secret believers in Iran are too scared to go to a church for fear the secret police might catch them. Many are also too scared to play Christian music in their homes or sing too loudly for fear their neighbors might hear them. For some of them, Shariat's Sunday service is the only time of worship and fellowship they have. And for Muslims who are curious about Christianity but equally fearful of anyone knowing about their interest, such services give them a safe window into a world of ideas to which they feel increasingly drawn.

Several years ago, Shariat became interested in my novels and in *Epicenter* and invited me to visit his congregation and TV production facility in another secure, undisclosed location. I gratefully accepted his offer and am so glad I did.

For me, a Jewish believer in Jesus, it was incredibly moving to meet such a remarkable Iranian believer in Jesus, his family, and his staff. It was amazing to see how God is using them to reach the Iranian people they love so much with the life-changing message of the gospel.

Most remarkable to me is that Shariat did not grow up hoping to be an evangelist. In 1979, he and his wife were actually part of the Iranian Revolution. Along with millions of other Iranians,

596

they were out on the streets of Tehran shouting, "Death to America! Death to Israel!" But once the shah fell and Khomeini came to power, Shariat decided he did not want death to come to America too quickly. Why? He wanted to go to graduate school here. Indeed, the desire proved to be a turning point that would change their lives forever.

In the early 1980s, the Shariats obtained the necessary visas and came to the U.S. to study. But they quickly grew homesick, lonely, and despondent. Their marriage was fraying. They were getting into fights. They were seriously contemplating a divorce.

Then Shariat's wife was invited by an American friend to go with her to visit an evangelical church. For some reason, she said yes, and there she began hearing Bible verses like Jeremiah 31:3, where God says, "I have loved you with an everlasting love." She heard John 10:10, in which Jesus said, "I came that they might have life, and have it abundantly" — that is, that life might be full and meaningful.

She also heard verses about God's willingness to forgive all of her sins, verses like 1 John 1:7–9, which says, "If we walk in the Light as He Himself is in the Light, we have fellowship with one another, and the blood of Jesus His Son cleanses us from all sin. If we say that we have no sin, we are deceiving ourselves and the truth is not in us. If we confess our sins, He is faithful and righteous to forgive us our sins and to cleanse us from all unrighteousness."

Something happened inside of her. She suddenly knew that Jesus was, in fact, the Messiah and the only way of salvation, and she prayed to receive

597

Christ into her heart. Then she encouraged her husband to attend church with her. He did, and before long, he too had become a follower of Jesus, drawn in part by God's love and in part by the notion that God would actually forgive him and give him the assurance of salvation, something he could not get from Islam.

The Shariats' problems did not evaporate, but they did begin a true, deep relationship with the God who had rescued them and adopted them into His family. To their surprise, they also began falling more deeply in love with each other. They began experiencing joy and peace that welled up from within them. Their circumstances had not really changed — they were still far from home and struggling through school — but their lives had changed. Soon they felt that God was calling them to devote their lives to reaching all of Iran with the gospel, and today they are part of the greatest evangelical air war in the history of Christendom.

Shariat told me, "Joel, I'm often asked, 'What does Christianity have to offer Muslims?' I can only report from my own experience and from personally witnessing the effects on thousands of others that have come to Christ from Islam through our ministry. By far, the most expressed benefits are peace and joy — which are direct results of salvation. As Jesus says in John 14:27, 'Peace I leave with you; My peace I give to you; not as the world gives do I give to you. Do not let your heart be troubled, nor let it be fearful.'

"Muslims do not enjoy the assurance of salvation. I have heard the prayers of devout Muslims begging God to deliver them from torture in the grave and the fires of hell. Unlike Muslims, Christians have the assurance of salvation. After all, the Bible tells us that salvation is a free gift of God's grace. It is not something we can earn. It is not something we can buy. It is something God gives us for free. All we have to do is accept it. Acts 16:31 says 'Believe in the Lord Jesus Christ, and you will be saved.' Romans 6:23 says, 'For the wages of sin is death, but the free gift of God is eternal life in Christ Jesus our Lord.' 1 John 5:13 says, 'These things I have written to you who believe in the name of the Son of God, so that you may *know* that you have eternal life' (emphasis added). Christians can really know beyond the shadow of a doubt that we are saved and going to heaven. Muslims cannot.

"When I accepted Christ as my Savior, Joel, my heart was filled with peace and joy. It was the most extraordinary thing. And now, one of the greatest rewards of my ministry is to hear Iranian Muslims tell me that they, too, are experiencing peace and joy because they have accepted Jesus Christ as their personal Savior and have come to understand His assurance of salvation."[6]

An Explosion of Satellite Evangelism

While other media continue to work powerfully, today it is satellite television that has become the breakthrough strategy to advance the gospel in the Muslim world. And what is amazing to me is just how many people in the epicenter have satellite dishes, even if they own almost no other material possessions.

"Satellite television dishes are sprouting like mushrooms on rooftops in post–Saddam Hussein Baghdad," one news report noted shortly after the Iraqi liberation in 2003. "The trade in TV gear is flourishing, and enterprising Iraqi entrepreneurs see bright prospects for this business. . . . People are buying satellite equipment for two reasons. The first one is that satellite television was illegal in Iraq under Saddam Hussein's rule, and people now want to 'taste a forbidden fruit.' The other reason is that . . . people want access to news and entertainment of any kind."[7]

In Iran, satellite TV is still technically illegal, but no one seems to care. Millions of dishes can be seen throughout big cities like Tehran as well as in small villages and mountain hamlets.

Over the last decade or so, I have had the privilege of traveling through countries with a combined population of over a quarter of a billion Muslims, and everywhere I have gone I have seen satellite dishes sprouting up like weeds. In Bedouin tents in the most barren and isolated sections of the Sinai desert. In the filthiest slums in Cairo. In the remotest mountain villages in Morocco. In the tiniest towns in Iraq and Afghanistan. In the poorest Palestinian neighborhoods of the West Bank. In teeming tenement buildings in Turkey. Friends from Iran and Saudi Arabia and Sudan and Yemen and Pakistan and elsewhere say dishes are ubiquitous there as well.

Why? Because Muslims in the twenty-first century — regardless of age or income — desperately want to be connected to the outside world. They want news and information that does not come from their state-run television networks. They want religious teaching that does not come solely from their state-run mosques. They are hungry for new ideas, different ideas.

Not everyone with a satellite dish has the purest motives, of course. Many are searching for pornography and other forms of cultural pollution pouring out of Europe and Hollywood. But as people flip through the channels searching for something they want in the privacy of their own home or room, sometimes they stumble upon a channel showing something they need, a channel that provides them a completely different perspective on the God of the universe and a completely different take on how we can interact with Him.

With the explosion of satellite dish sales has come an explosion of satellite evangelism. Al Hayat is one of the premier sources of Christian programming, but it is certainly not the only network beaming biblical messages into the region.

The Egyptian-based "Nilesat" and the Gulf-based "Arabsat" systems refuse to carry any Christian programming, but today there are no fewer than sixteen different Christian television channels operating on the "Hot Bird" satellites run by the European telecommunications company Eutelsat.* These channels are widely diverse in Christian doctrine, style, and impact. Nevertheless, they all share the same objectives: to communicate the gospel; to broadcast sermons and church services in Arabic, Farsi, Turkish, and other regional languages and dialects; and to show

*Christian channels in the epicenter include: Al Hayat; SAT-7 in Arabic, Persian, Turkish, and North African dialects; Miracle TV; Three Angels Broadcasting Network; the God Channel; the Spirit Channel; Smile (a Christian channel for children in the Middle East); and five networks run by the Trinity Broadcasting Network.

Christian feature films and miniseries, including the famous *JESUS* film, which was produced in 1979 by Warner Brothers and Campus Crusade for Christ International and has had some 6 billion viewings worldwide in the last three decades. And these channels are succeeding beyond anything the Radicals can imagine.

One Christian network known as SAT-7 is regularly seen by at least 9 million viewers throughout North Africa and the Middle East, according to Dr. Graham Mytton, research consultant and former director of audience research for the BBC World Service, based on a survey of eight sample Muslim countries. This number includes 2 to 3 million viewers who watch daily or at least once a week: 319,000 people in Morocco, 201,000 in Syria, and 118,000 in Saudi Arabia. It also includes 5 to 6 million "occasional" viewers: 1.2 million people in Morocco, 464,000 in Syria, and 309,000 in Saudi Arabia.[8]

Not long ago, the head of one Middle East ministry told me a remarkable story he knew firsthand, one that is indicative of the kind of impact satellite evangelism in general — and SAT-7 in particular — is having.

An elderly woman in Iran was watching the *JESUS* film in Farsi in the privacy of her little apartment, he recalled. She had always been fascinated with the person of Jesus Christ, but she knew so little about Him. She did not have a Bible. She did not know any Christians. She had never been to church. She was not even particularly seeking out a film about Jesus that night. She just stumbled onto it while flipping through the channels coming into her satellite receiver.

But as the story unfolded, she began to respond

to the love of Christ. She was intrigued by His teachings, amazed by His compassion and miracles, and moved by His love and forgiveness even for His enemies, even for those who had condemned Him to death and nailed Him to the cross.

When she saw the depiction of Jesus rising from the dead, she found herself in tears.

At the end of the film, the narrator explained how a viewer could pray to become a follower of Jesus Christ. In doing so, he read a Bible verse — Revelation 3:20 — in which Jesus says, "Behold, I stand at the door and knock; if anyone hears My voice and opens the door, I will come in to him and will dine with him, and he with Me."

Unfamiliar with the passage and thus not aware that Jesus was speaking metaphorically — saying that if a person opens the door of his or her heart and welcomes Him in, then He will come in and save that person — the woman thought, *I guess I had better open the door.* So she got up from her chair, walked over to the front door of her apartment, and opened it.

She was suddenly blinded by a bolt of light emanating from a figure in the doorway. "Who is it?" she asked.

"It is I," Jesus said.

"Come in, my Lord," she said, and Jesus entered her home.

For the next few minutes, Jesus spoke to her about Himself, told her He loved her and had forgiven her, and told her to get a Bible and begin reading it. And then, as suddenly as He had appeared, He was gone.

The woman, startled but excited, looked back at the television screen and noticed there was a phone number she could call for more information. She picked up the phone and dialed it immediately.

The call was routed from Iran to an overseas number through a secure telephone system that terminated at a secret call center — one Lynn and I have visited — where Iranian converts who are trained as counselors answer calls such as these and help those wanting more information about becoming a Christian or growing in their faith.

"I just saw Jesus," the elderly woman told a counselor, her voice trembling.

"That's great," the counselor replied. "Isn't it a wonderful film?"

"No, no, you don't understand," the woman said. "I just *saw* Jesus — in person, in my home. He appeared to me. He told me I am now His follower. Can you help me get a Bible and understand what I should do next?"

The Power of Radio

Before the advent of satellite TV broadcasting, radio was the main way Arab evangelists brought the gospel to millions of Muslims — many of whom were illiterate — in closed countries. Even today, radio is still a powerful weapon in the evangelical air war in the epicenter. Trans World Radio, for example, broadcasts biblical programming in Arabic for twenty-eight hours a week (roughly four hours a day) from two stations, one in Cyprus and one in Monte Carlo, targeting the Middle East and North Africa, respectively. As a result, they receive more than two hundred thousand letters a year from listeners asking for answers to their many questions, requesting Arabic Bibles, requesting Bible correspondence courses, and sharing their stories of how they came to faith by listening to TWR's programs. Other radio ministries have similar approaches and results.

As I was researching this book, a dear Arab evangelist friend of mine shared with me a great example of the impact of gospel radio. A few years ago, he received a letter from a man named Mohammed who was the assistant to an imam in Saudi Arabia. Though the young man lived in the most extreme Wahhabi country on the planet — and worked in a mosque every single day — he would go home after work and listen to Christian radio, which came on late at night.

One night he tuned in to a fifteen-minute broadcast that was focusing on Egyptian illiterates. The language of the program was a dialect used by impoverished people from upper Egypt, and the broadcaster spoke slowly and with very simple vocabulary. He began by sharing three or four testimonies of Muslims who had come to Christ. Then he shared a short message focused on one simple truth: Jesus Christ is powerful, and He answers prayer. That was all.

Now, the Saudi man was well educated and deeply religious. He could have been turned off by this simple presentation and angered by all this talk of Jesus penetrating the airwaves of Mecca and Medina. But he had a need in his own personal life, a very specific and unique need.

For a long time he had prayed to Allah and to Muhammad to help him meet that need. But nothing happened. And then he heard on the radio that "Jesus Christ is powerful, and He answers prayer."

As an assistant mosque leader, he believed that

605

he could not pray to Jesus, that Jesus was not omnipresent, that Jesus was not God to be prayed to. But he said to himself, "I have nothing to lose if I do."

So as he went to bed, he started repeating that phrase again and again. He fell asleep with the words in his mouth: "O Christ, the powerful."

At five the next morning, there was a knock on his door. His brother was at the gate, saying, "Good news, good news, Mohammed."

Mohammed said, "What's going on? Why do you wake me up now?"

His brother said, "I don't know what happened, but your need, your request, has been met."

Mohammed was stunned. He remembered what he had gone to bed saying: "O Christ, the powerful." And right there in front of his brother, he said, "I'm a Christian now. I am a Christian."

He quit his job at the mosque. He went underground. He received biblical discipleship and ministry training. And today he is a Christian evangelist in Saudi Arabia.

"So, Joel, who worked?" my Arab evangelist friend asked me. "Who changed this young man? Christ the Lord. That's very simple. He went in faith to Christ, and Christ delivered. And that's the story of scores and scores of people. God has used radio to open the eyes of anyone, including Muslims, if they are willing to have their eyes opened to Him."

CHAPTER TWENTY-EIGHT:
THE GROUND WAR — PART ONE

How the Revivalists are making disciples
despite extreme persecution

All of the true followers of Jesus Christ in the Muslim world that I have met are deeply burdened for their neighbors and their countrymen. Often when they pray, they are in tears because they know that hundreds of millions of Muslims go to bed every night without any hope, without any peace, without having their sins forgiven, without the assurance that they are going to heaven when they die. This grieves the Revivalists and motivates many of them to take enormous risks to get the good news of God's love and plan of salvation to those who have never heard the gospel or never accepted Christ as their Savior.

What comforts the Revivalists, they say, is Jesus' message in Matthew 16:18, when he said, "I will build my church; and the gates of hell shall not prevail against it" (KJV). This passage is a great source of relief and consolation for pastors and ministry leaders in the epicenter because it means that at the end of the day, they are not responsible for the success of the church in the epicenter. That's Jesus' job. He said that *He* is building His

Church in the epicenter and around the world, and nothing and no one can stop Him.

What, then, is the job of the Revivalists?

Simple: to obey the Lord Jesus Christ in whatever He tells them to do. "If you love Me," Jesus said in John 14:15, "you will keep My commandments."

So what does Jesus tell them to do? Love Him enough to preach the gospel, make disciples, plant churches, and teach and equip others to do the same.

To some the notion of *doing* the work of God even while *trusting* God to ultimately accomplish that work may seem contradictory. But not to the Revivalists. They say the distinction is that the burden of *obedience* lies with individual followers of Jesus Christ, while the burden for *success* lies with Jesus Christ Himself. As one ministry operating very effectively in the Muslim world likes to teach its members: "Your job is to share Christ in the power of the Holy Spirit and leave the results to God."

To men and women trying to serve the Lord in very dangerous and difficult circumstances, these are liberating principles. The Bible teaches that Jesus loves His true followers regardless of their performance. He wants them to obey Him, whatever the cost, but He is not grading them based on their results. The results are dependent on Him, not them, and this, many Revivalists have told me, helps them sleep peacefully at night despite the enormous task that lies before them.

"Boots on the Ground"

As we saw in the last chapter, the leaders of the Revivalists are deeply grateful to the Lord for providing radio, satellite television, and increasingly the Internet as powerful and effective new ways of reaching vast numbers of Muslims with the gospel and biblical precepts.

Still, most are not convinced that they can win the battle for the souls of the Muslim people through an "air war" alone. That is, they do not feel that they can merely beam in the evangelistic programming and Bible teaching — however strong the quality of those programs — from afar and make the revolutionary impact they believe is needed. What is vital, they insist, is waging a massive and historic "ground war" to complement the "air war." As God directs them, therefore, they are steadily and systematically putting "boots on the ground" all throughout the Muslim world — men and women trained to make disciples, who will be qualified to make other disciples, who will be able to make other disciples as well.

Ultimately, the Revivalists say, their hope for transforming the Muslim world is not in technology but in human beings who have been "revived" — spiritually transformed by faith in Jesus Christ and filled with the power of the Holy Spirit of God.

Jesus, they note, used no technology when He came to a dusty corner of Roman-occupied Palestine. Rather, He preached to the masses, sometimes five to ten thousand at a time. He also recruited individuals, built a team, and invested His time in teaching this small band of brothers how to live like God-chosen global game-changers. He walked with His twelve disciples. He ate with them. He traveled with them. He spent time with their friends and family members. He gave them projects and assignments to test the content of their character and the quality of their faith. He forgave them when they made mistakes. He encouraged them. He prayed for them. He prayed with them. And He loved them to the last moment of His life on earth.

What was the result? Admittedly, one — Judas Iscariot — failed disastrously, betraying them all. But look at the other eleven disciples. They started as worldly, fearful, jealous, petty, competitive, small-minded, uneducated, and untrained men. But after a few years of walking and talking with Jesus and observing His life, His purity, and His supernatural power in action, these men became such bold, decisive, and fearless preachers, pastors, evangelists, and apostles that even their opponents had to admit that they had soon "turned the world upside down" (Acts 17:6, KJV). This is the model believers in Christ must follow, the Revivalists say, if they are to change the Muslim world.

The key is the personal touch. The Muslim culture is an Eastern culture, not a Western one. It is based on relationships and storytelling and on people spending long periods of time with one another. People in Eastern cultures are not so worried about schedules and quotas and sales figures and returning e-mails and phone calls quickly. They are interested in personal contact. They are interested in firm handshakes and good food and strong coffee and sweet tea and looking in a man's eyes to see if he is a good man or a bad man and whether he can be trusted or not.

In such a culture, a spiritual revolution cannot all be waged or won by remote control. It cannot all be done from radio and TV studios in Europe or the U.S., or via e-mail and Web sites. Some of it — much of it — must be done face-to-face, person-to-person.

Can that be dangerous? Absolutely. But the Revivalists say there is no other way.

Never before in human history have there been so many followers of Christ living in North Africa, the Middle East, and Central Asia. The mission of the Revivalists, they tell me, is to focus on helping mere followers turn into *fully devoted disciples* who are willing to do whatever Jesus tells them to do, go wherever Jesus tells them to go, and say whatever Jesus tells them to say. They want to do so in every city, every town, every village, and every neighborhood in their countries and region.

What's more, they are trying to identify, train, and mobilize leaders. They are prayerfully seeking out men and women who are ready to help new converts study the Bible for themselves. They are looking for people who are willing to lead new and young believers in worshiping their risen Savior. And they are hoping to find people who are able to plant new churches, often in the privacy and secrecy of their own homes, since renting or buying or building a church facility would draw too much attention and buildings could be attacked by Radicals and blown to smithereens. This, the Revivalists stress, is how movements are made.

Waging a Spiritual War, Not a Physical One

In the pages ahead, I will profile some of the most effective "ground commanders" I have met in the Middle East. But first, let me be crystal clear about an extremely important point. When I use the terms "air war" and "ground war," I do not mean to suggest in any way, shape, or form that the Revivalists are violent people or that they would ever resort to military weapons to force their beliefs on others. To the contrary, the Revivalists abhor violence as much as the Radicals embrace it. Their deeply rooted conviction not to use violence to advance the Kingdom of Jesus Christ comes directly from the teachings of the Bible.

On the night of His arrest in the garden of Gethsemane, Jesus told Peter not to attack Roman soldiers with his sword, noting that "all who draw the sword will die by the sword" (Matthew 26:52, NIV). Likewise, the apostle Paul wrote to those he was discipling, saying, "For though we live in the world, we do not wage war as the world does. The weapons we fight with are not the weapons of the world. On the contrary, they have divine power to demolish strongholds" (2 Corinthians 10:3–4, NIV).

Paul made an even more detailed case to this effect in Ephesians 6:10–17: "Finally, be strong in the Lord and in the strength of His might. Put on the full armor of God, so that you will be able to stand firm against the schemes of the devil. For our struggle is not against flesh and blood, but against the rulers, against the powers, against the world forces of this darkness, against the spiritual forces of wickedness in the heavenly places. Therefore, take up the full armor of God, so that you will be able to resist in the evil day, and having done everything, to stand firm. Stand firm therefore, having girded your loins with truth, and having put on the breastplate of righteousness, and having shod your feet with the preparation of the gospel of peace; in addition to all, taking up the shield of faith with which you will be able to

612

extinguish all the flaming arrows of the evil one. And take the helmet of salvation, and the sword of the Spirit, which is the word of God."

Revivalists do not use pistols, rifles, machine guns, explosives, or bombs of any kind to advance their objectives. They understand that a physical war as well as a spiritual war is being waged against them, but the Bible teaches them to wage *only* a spiritual war, a war of ideas and beliefs, not a physical war.

Thus, they say they thank God every morning for a new day and for continued life. Then they pray that God would fill them with the Holy Spirit, suit them up in the full armor of God, give them the strength and the courage to do and say whatever He commands them, and accomplish His divine purposes for that day in and through their lives.

Recruited by a Pakistani

Hamid is one of the most wanted Iranian Revivalists in the world.*

Precisely because he is so effective in recruiting and training Iranian evangelists, disciple makers, pastors, and church planters, the Iranian secret police have hunted him for years. They nearly assassinated him in 1994, but by God's grace he and his family narrowly escaped with their lives.

While I have known of Hamid for nearly two decades, I finally met him for the first time several years ago in a secure, undisclosed location. I have

---

*Hamid is not his real name; it is a pseudonym to protect this Iranian Christian leader. For security reasons, I cannot disclose when or where I interviewed him, but I can say it was within the last two years.

no idea where he actually lives, but I have enjoyed the privilege of staying in touch with him, and I was deeply grateful when he allowed me to interview him for this project. His story deserves an entire book, not just a portion of a chapter. Nevertheless, allow me to share with you a few highlights and some of his observations of how the ground war is being waged inside Iran.

"I was born in 1943 in Isfahan, Iran, and at the age of seventeen I became a follower of Jesus Christ," Hamid recounted. "I am not from a Muslim background. I am from a nominal Christian background. But before I was born, my mother had a dream in which she was told, 'You will have a boy, and this will be his name. He will serve the Lord.'

"From the age of three, I loved God. My grandmother was a Catholic, and she taught me to pray before bed. As a teenager, I began to serve in the Orthodox Church. But at seventeen, I just had an inexplicable love for Jesus. I believe He chose me even before I was formed in the womb. He just decided I would be His follower, His servant. He is God. He doesn't always explain. I just had a passion to serve the Lord. I went to the priest and said, 'I want to preach!' It was like what the apostle Paul wrote in Ephesians 1:4: 'He chose us in Him before the foundation of the world, that we would be holy and blameless before Him.' "

"Did your friends love Jesus the way you did?" I asked. "Did they also want to preach the gospel in Iran?"

Hamid laughed. "No, I had no other friends like this."

The Catholic and Orthodox churches in Iran

did not even believe in preaching the gospel back in the 1960s and 1970s, he said. They were not trying to lead Muslims to Christ. To do so was illegal, anyway. So Hamid got little encouragement and no training.

"The turning point," he told me, "happened in 1974. I had already graduated from college. I was a mechanical engineer, and I was working for an oil company. But one day I met a Christian leader from Pakistan who was traveling through Iran looking for someone to start a nationwide ministry in that country." Hamid said he had little interest in helping the Pakistani. After all, "the economy in Iran was thriving at the time," OPEC was battling the West, the price of oil was soaring, and Hamid had a comfortable life.

"Three months later, the Pakistani returned to Iran and invited me to attend a conference outside the country about evangelism and discipleship," Hamid said. "I was curious, so I agreed to go. While I was there, a voice in my heart asked me, 'What do you want to do with the rest of your life?' I wasn't sure. I liked working for the oil company. But the voice said to me, 'Every day, thousands are going to hell.'

"For three days and nights I struggled with God. Finally I knew what I had to do. I went back to Tehran and resigned from the oil company. The Pakistani arranged for me to receive nine months of ministry training. Then in 1975, I started a ministry to reach all of Iran with the gospel."

Launching A Ministry to Reach All of Iran
"Did you think it was possible to reach every Iranian with the gospel?" I asked.

Not really, Hamid conceded. He wanted to see

God do something great in his country, but the task seemed overwhelming.

Then I asked, "Did you see the Islamic Revolution coming?"

"No," he said. "Even three months before the Revolution, no ordinary citizen in Iran that I knew would have thought that this would happen, that the Ayatollah Khomeini could topple the shah and change Iran forever."

"How then did you and your wife launch a national ministry by yourselves?"

"We concentrated on five things from the beginning," he said. "First, we identified men and women from many churches who displayed a passion for the Lord, and we asked them if they would like us to disciple them." If they said yes, Hamid and his wife would teach them the Bible. They would teach them what it meant to walk in the power of the Holy Spirit and not try to live the Christian life in their own limited strength and knowledge. They taught people to share their faith and to serve the Lord completely, in every area of their lives.

"Second, we took our disciples to parks to practice witnessing [telling people about their faith in Christ]. Third, we recruited and trained four disciples to become full-time staff members with our ministry, because we knew we couldn't do it on our own, and we didn't want to do it alone. Fourth, we started a Bible school by correspondence." This provided an opportunity for Iranian Christians all over the country to study the Bible on their own, using the lessons Hamid sent them, and to do so in the privacy and safety of their own homes. The students would then mail in their completed homework, and Hamid and his team would correspond with them, correct their homework, answer their questions, and help them grow in their faith as best they could.

"Fifth, we held conferences and special meetings," Hamid added. This provided Iranian believers the opportunity to gather together for more intensive Bible study, prayer, worship, and fellowship. Hamid believed it was very important for the Christ-followers in the country to have time together, to get to know one another, to know that they were not alone, to pray with and for one another, and to be encouraged to go back to their towns and villages to share their faith in Christ and help fellow believers grow in their faith.

The Ground War in Iran

Not many Muslims came to Christ in the early years of the ministry, Hamid admitted. The believers were growing bolder in their faith, and that was good. But there was very little interest among Iranian Shias.

That all changed in 1979.

"I thank God for the Ayatollah Khomeini," Hamid said with a big smile, "because he did something that all the believers and all the missionaries in Iran put together for a hundred years could not do. He presented the true color of Islam. Iranians could suddenly see what Islam really is. And they began to turn against it because it's not what they thought it would be."

Violence. Torture. Imprisonments. Executions. Rapes. Corruption. An eight-year war with fellow Muslims in Iraq.

"You see, Joel, for Muslims, it's not hard to love Jesus," Hamid continued. "The hard part is leaving Muhammad. There is an Islam in people's

617

minds that does not exist in reality. The Islam of their minds is Utopia. Islam is complete, they think. So why should they leave and go to another faith? Plus, they think if you leave Islam bad things will happen to you. Muslims are very superstitious. They believe if you read the Bible you will go to hell. Some believe that if you leave Islam, your face will turn into a monkey face — all kinds of things like this. Before the Revolution, we would start sharing the gospel with Muslims by talking about God. 'Do you believe He exists? What do you think about Him?' That kind of thing. But after the Revolution, we could not start by talking about God because people were so angry. They would say, 'If this is God, then I don't want this God.' So I realized that we have to start with Jesus. 'Have you heard of Jesus? Have you read His teachings? What do you think of Him?' "

People started responding. They wanted to read about Jesus in the New Testament. They wanted to see films about Jesus. They wanted to read Christian literature explaining how to follow Jesus.

By 1980, there were a few thousand MBBs in Iran, Hamid said. Now he believes there are a few million. The challenge today is that there are not nearly enough pastors and other ministry leaders to help all these believers grow and mature in their faith. This is why Hamid and his team have focused so much time, attention, and resources on identifying believers who could become wise, loving, and caring leaders. That's why they are helping to train and develop such leaders. They see God bringing great "flocks of lost sheep" into His Kingdom, and the Lord has shown them that the desperate need in Iran is to train up more "shepherds" to care for these sheep and guide them in biblical truth.

The Hit List

It is not easy to be a shepherd in Iran, however. The price for serving Christ in full-time ministry is very high. Many ministry leaders have been arrested, tortured, and even executed or assassinated.

In late 1979, for example, an Anglican priest was beheaded in the Iranian city of Shiraz. Around the same time, five bullets were fired at Iranian pastor Hassan Dehghany. Though he miraculously survived, his twenty-four-year-old son, Bahram, was soon found dead, martyred for his faith in Christ. In 1990, the Iranian government hanged a man named Hoseyn Soodmand for turning from Islam to Christianity. In 1994, three key Iranian Christian leaders were assassinated one after another — Bishop Haik Hovsepian, Mehdi Dibaj, and Tateos Michaelian. Then in 1996, another Christian, Mohammed Yousefi, met the same fate.

During the killing spree in the 1990s, an Iranian secret police official fled the country and gave a media interview saying that more murders of Christian leaders were coming. A crumpled-up hit list was actually found with the body of Tateos Michaelian after his death. The list contained the names of those Christian leaders who had already been murdered and a list of names of pastors who had not yet been killed. Hamid's name was on that list. As it turned out, he and his family were able to get out of the country, leaving all their worldly possessions behind, just hours before assassins came to his home to kill him.

I asked Hamid why he thought the systematic killing of pastors had begun in the early 1990s.

"Three reasons, I think," he said. "First, the war with Iraq was over, and the concentration of the government was shifting to domestic problems and threats. Second, more people were coming to Christ than ever before. Many had become believers in the 1980s, certainly. But in the early 1990s, a real spiritual awakening began in Iran, a real acceleration in the numbers of Muslim converts, and the government was noticing this. And third, the leader levels were rising too high. The quality of the leaders we were recruiting and training was too high. They were older and more educated and very effective. It was no longer poor and uneducated people coming to Christ. Now the educated were coming to the Lord — doctors, engineers, philosophers, rich people. And they weren't just converting from Islam, they were giving their money to the cause of Christ. They were giving their gold jewelry to the Church to help fund more ministry work. The government and the mullahs are scared of Christian leaders because they are very high quality and the Lord can use them to lead many people very effectively."

"Do you miss your life in Iran?" I asked Hamid.

He sat back and sighed. "Yes," he said. He misses his country, and he misses his friends. But he has no regrets. He said he believes God is using him far more now that he is living on the outside where he can study and teach and preach and travel freely without fear of arrest, or worse.

"Just look what God is doing in Iran today," he said. "How can I not be grateful to the Lord? I wouldn't have believed in 1974 that we could see millions of believers in Iran, because people were so secular and so rich back then, compared to today. Women used to fly to Paris to get their hair done and fly back to attend a wedding. During the time of the shah, my team and I shared the gospel with more than five thousand people one summer, but only two people showed interest. Now, there are too many calls coming into our offices from people who have accepted Christ or want to know more about Jesus. We don't have time to answer them all."

And that, Hamid says, is why he focuses on training leaders capable of responding to the spiritual revolution Jesus has unleashed in Iran. "Like Jesus said, 'The harvest is plentiful, but the laborers are few; therefore beseech the Lord of the harvest to send out laborers into His harvest.' "*

*Luke 10:2

CHAPTER TWENTY-NINE:
THE GROUND WAR — PART TWO

More accounts of leaders on the front lines

For the past several decades, the most effective and influential pastors and ministry leaders operating on the front lines of the Christian ground war in the Muslim world have been those who, like Hamid, were born into nominal Christian families. But as more Muslims have come to faith in Christ, grown in their faith, and begun to gain practical ministry experience, a rising number of Muslim Background Believers have emerged as effective spiritual leaders in the epicenter as well.

Samir is one example. I met him on my first trip to Iraq in February 2008 and was immediately impressed with his love for Jesus Christ and his passion for ministry.*

Born in 1968 in a southern Iraqi village, Samir, an Arab, was raised a devout Shia Muslim. While his forefathers were Shia imams (high-ranking Islamic clerics) and his parents were devout,

*Samir is not his real name. It is a pseudonym to protect this Iraqi Christian leader. These sections are based on an author interview with Samir in February 2008.

Samir said, "Nobody pushed me to be very religious. I chose that. I was about eleven or twelve. I started going to the mosque and meditating on many things. There was something special between me and my God, I believed. I felt God was very near to me. I was so close to God that I used to try to do funny things to make God laugh. And I felt He did laugh, and I felt He was happy . . . and I was happy."

After he graduated from college, trained to be an electrician, Samir was arrested. "I was perceived by Saddam's police as a Shia activist or a subversive," he told me.

"Were you a rebel?" I asked him.

"Yes, I was," he conceded. "I was against the government and against the Sunnis. But I was not violent."

Samir spent seven months in jail. When he was released, he was required to serve in the Iraqi Army, but he refused and was sent back to jail. A special court released him from army service — Saddam's Sunni-dominated army had no interest in training Shias to use weapons — but Samir was fired from his job. With his growing reputation as a Shia activist, he found it difficult to find work.

By the end of 1994, Samir decided that if he was going to be tagged as a Shia Radical anyway, he might as well become a Shia Radical. So he moved to the Iraqi city of Najaf and applied to study at the *Hawza,* the most elite Shia Muslim seminary in all of Iraq, second in prestige and influence only to the main seminary in Qom, Iran. Once accepted, Samir plunged himself into his studies and received high marks from his professors.

In time, Samir not only completed his studies

but was greatly honored by being invited to become a professor at the seminary to teach Shia doctrine to the fresh, eager students. Samir eagerly agreed.

Visions and Trances

"There are two areas of teaching at the *Hawza*," Samir told me. "The first concerns knowledge — that is, teaching students Islamic theology and Sharia law. The second concerns one's spiritual life — that is, helping students develop their relationship with God. I was fascinated with both, but especially with getting closer to God and helping others do the same.

"Shia Islam is very mystical, and we taught the students that there are higher and higher levels of spiritual growth that they need to attain and lead other people to. One of these levels is discovering God's love for you and building your love for God until you become consumed by God. The challenge is that Shia doctrine teaches that God's love is not available for everyone, only for those who go through this very specific spiritual journey that we were teaching at the *Hawza.*

"We taught our Shia seminary students to do various spiritual exercises. In these exercises you are supposed to meditate until you are in, essentially, a trance. In that trance, you will begin to see visions or revelations of ancient imams and the various prophets and other historical figures. But Shias consider actually seeing such visions a very low level of revelation, because seeing these ancient figures could hinder a person from going higher and seeing God Himself. But these visions and revelations are indications that you are going in the right direction.

"Now, please understand, Joel, that I was teaching this all to my students. I was one of only four professors at the seminary teaching this form of meditation. But one day something unexpected happened."

"What was that?" I asked.

"One day I was meditating, and it was almost as if I was flying in an airplane," Samir explained. "I was climbing up from the ground, higher and higher, and then I started passing through the clouds, and I was climbing higher and higher and then suddenly it was as though I was slipping away from the atmosphere and entering another reality, and then I saw Jesus. He was smiling at me. He looked just like the one I had seen in the *JESUS* film that I had once seen on television, but with a darker face, an Eastern face. In the first vision, I had no communication with Jesus, but I felt very peaceful. Then, over the course of the next few days, He appeared a second, third, fourth, and fifth time. He began to speak to me. He gave me answers to the many questions I had."

The Qur'an, Samir noted, teaches Muslims that Jesus is to be highly revered. It says Jesus was born of a virgin, was a wise teacher, and did miracles. But it does not give many more details than this. Yet Samir had become intensely hungry to understand this Jesus who kept appearing to him. He could not tell the two hundred Shia students he was teaching about the visions he was having. But as a scholar, he knew he had to do more research. So one day he told one of his students to go to Baghdad and find a complete Arabic copy of the Bible for him, though he did not say why. The student complied, and Samir, in the privacy of his own room, began reading the Bible voraciously.

The more he read, the more intrigued with Jesus he became. So he would pray more, hoping to see Jesus again, and he did. For a certain period in the mid-1990s, Samir said, Jesus was appearing to him every day.

"The Lord in some of these appearances would give me homework assignments. He would tell me where to read in the Bible, specific verses. He would give me a verse, without a specific address. For example, He would tell me to find where it says, 'But you, when you pray, go into your inner room, close your door and pray to your Father who is in secret, and your Father who sees what is done in secret will reward you.' But He wouldn't tell me where in the Bible that verse is. So I would have to read the whole Bible to find the verses."

Other times, there were specific events that Jesus would tell Samir would happen, and they would come to pass. Once, for example, Jesus told Samir that he would see a certain person in Beirut, and sure enough, the next time Samir was in Beirut he saw that person, even though that person did not live in Beirut and rarely traveled to Lebanon.

"From the first homework assignment that He gave me," Samir told me, "He called me to follow Him alone. He made it clear that He had a very big work to do and that He was calling me to be part of it."

The Transforming Power of the Bible

Samir, the Shia seminary professor, had fallen in love with Jesus Christ. He had become convinced that Jesus was the One True God and the only way to salvation. He had become convinced that Islam was wrong, that the Qur'an was not the word of God, and that only the Bible contained the true words of the living God. The process he went through to reach such conclusions was not a classic conversion process, to be sure. But there was no question: Samir had become a fully devoted follower of Jesus Christ. And as soon as he realized his calling to serve Christ by teaching the Bible and not the Qur'an, he fled the *Hawza* for his life.

Samir told me that when he thinks about his salvation, he remembers the story of Joseph in the book of Genesis. Joseph was captured by his brothers and sold into slavery. But eventually God set him free, made him a leader in Egypt, and used him to save his brothers and all the people of the Middle East from a terrible famine. Joseph could have been angry with his brothers for forcing him into slavery, but he wasn't. "You meant evil against me," Joseph told his brothers, "but God meant it for good in order to bring about this present result, to preserve many people alive" (Genesis 50:20).

Similarly, Samir believes he was enslaved in Shia Islam, but he is not angry with his Shia brothers. Rather, he believes God took him to the *Hawza* to help him better understand the Shias and to learn how to reach them with the gospel of Jesus Christ and teach them through the transforming power of the Bible.

"I am so grateful to God, and I am so fortunate," Samir told me. "By entering all those visions and trances I could have been trapped by Satan forever and sent to hell. But I think that God, in His amazing love and grace, respected the innocence of my childhood, when I wanted to know Him and make Him laugh. So God protected me from getting trapped. He pulled me close to His heart through Jesus Christ and taught me His Word. I was so lost, but He came and saved me just because He loved me so much."

Samir is convinced a great revival is under way in the Shia world and that God is revealing Himself in supernatural ways to many devout Muslims who were lost and trapped in their own sins like he once was. In Iran to his east, millions of Shias are coming to faith in Jesus Christ, and tens of thousands are entering full-time Christian ministry to preach the gospel, make disciples, and plant churches. Samir believes that in time millions of Iraqi Shias will come to Christ too, and he is committed to teaching the Bible to young Iraqi disciples to prepare for that day to come to fruition. "The Lord has a special work to be done among the Shias of Iraq," he said with great passion and confidence. "God is working directly here, just like in the first century when Jesus chose the disciples directly."

Samir's story inspires almost everyone who hears it. In fact, while he was sharing his testimony with me, another Iraqi — in this case a former Sunni Wahhabi Muslim who had his own miraculous encounter with the Lord and is now in full-time Christian ministry — was sitting beside me and listening as well. Deeply moved by Samir's faith, this MBB turned to me and said, "Jesus has removed the hatred for the Shias from my heart. When I see the intense, passionate devotion of the Shias to God, I am moved. They are wrong. They don't yet know that Jesus is the King of kings and the Lord of lords, as my brother Samir now does. But they are so devoted. I want to understand this devotion better and help reach them with God's truth so they can be devoted to Jesus instead. And now, when I see for myself that God has chosen a Shia person to follow Jesus Christ and serve Him in ministry, I know that He is really powerful and is really moving in this country."[1]

A Kurdish Jihadist Becomes a Revivalist

God is drawing not only Iranians and Arabs into His Kingdom; He is drawing Kurds to Christ as well and is appointing them to be courageous "ground warriors" for His name.

During my first trip to Iraq, I had the privilege of meeting a particularly passionate and effective Kurdish Christian leader by the name of Kerem.* Today, he is sharing the gospel, discipling new Muslim converts, and training up future church leaders. But not that long ago, Kerem was a foot soldier in a much different war.

"I was born in 1969 in a Sunni religious family," Kerem told me one cold winter night in Kurdistan as we sipped coffee together. "Because my family was religious and committed to religion and I was going regularly to mosque, I met members of a Radical religious group. And gradually I found that those people believed in jihad. I was so excited with them. I had faith in jihad like them. My terrorist group that I was a member of was worse than al Qaeda."

"In what way was it worse?" I asked.

"Al Qaeda in Iraq is a known organization with a known leader and with clear intentions of attacking the U.S. and Israel, as well as Muslim

---

*Kerem is not his real name. It is a pseudonym to protect this Kurdish Christian leader. These sections are based on a series of author interviews with Kerem in February 2008.

apostates, with suicide bombers and other terror-ist means," he explained. "But our group [*Al Haraka Al Islamia Fe Kurdistan,* or the Islamic Movement of Kurdistan] was brainwashing simple people to become time bombs in their own homes — to become radicalized Muslims who reject every norm and custom in their home if it is not pure, fanatical, Islamic teaching, to create a spirit of rebellion. We trained people to think of them-selves as true, pure holy men and then to attack their families as infidels."

Kerem became a teacher of the Qur'an and received terrorist training to kill infidels. "But from 1988 until the beginning of 1991," he told me, "I had many questions inside myself about God. I hated serving God by force. I hated pray-ing by force, fasting by force, and I did not feel right about forcing others to follow God and destroy their families. When I asked my leaders — religious leaders or political leaders — if this was right, if we were doing the just thing, they told me don't ask these questions. I was prohibited from asking questions."

After Saddam Hussein's invasion of Kuwait in 1990 and the subsequent Gulf War in 1991 in which the U.S.-led coalition defeated Saddam's forces and liberated Kuwait, there was a revolu-tion in Iraq. The Kurdish Muslims in the north and the Shia Muslims in the south rose up in hopes of overthrowing Saddam's government. "We declared jihad against Saddam and his regime," Kerem explained. "We carried weapons and started to fight."

One day, Kerem and several of his colleagues led an attack against an Iraqi military unit and in the process captured four prisoners. "The emir, or the prince, of our group told us to go and kill those prisoners. There was a river nearby. Other prisoners captured by fellow terrorists were killed there and thrown into the river. We took our prisoners there, and they knew that we were about to start shooting them. But they were begging for their lives, and they started praying parts of the Qur'an because they noticed that we were Muslims."

Kerem was deeply conflicted. As a Kurd, he hated Saddam's regime and was dedicated to liberating the Kurdish people. But he had been developing doubts for some time about the violence he and his friends were engaged in. Now he kept telling himself, "These are Muslims. As a Muslim, I cannot kill them."

At that point Kerem threw down his weapon and refused to join in the executions. "One of my group told me that I would be shot because I had disobeyed the emir," Kerem recalled. "But I prefered to be murdered instead of being a murderer!"

The executions proceeded. All four of the prisoners were killed. When Kerem and his colleagues got back to their headquarters, sure enough, Kerem was denounced by the leaders of the group for disobeying orders. But he shot back, "I will do worse than disobey your orders. I divorce Islam from this moment." He repeated the words three times. "They thought I was giving excuses for my behavior. They threatened to kill me because I had left the religion."

Fearing for his life, Kerem fled from the headquarters and eventually escaped to Iran for safety.

"Wow," I said. "Things must have really been bad for an Iraqi to escape to Iran for safety."

He laughed and agreed. But he said he didn't know what else to do. He was a wanted man inside Iraq. He was a wanted man inside his own terrorist organization. What's more, he was wracked with guilt and anxiety and confusion and desperate to find peace.

The Turning Point

"Inwardly I knew there was a God," Kerem told me. "But I also knew He was a different God from Allah."

The Qur'an, he said, was teaching him to hate and to kill. He, in turn, was teaching such violent suras from the Qur'an to young, impressionable Muslims, and he was recruiting others to wage jihad against Saddam's regime as well as against Muslim families that weren't as Radical as his terrorist organization thought they should be. He knew this was wrong, but he had no idea where to turn or what to do next. "When I left this terrorist group, I left also the praying and everything," Kerem said. "I hated God. I hated praying. I hated everything called religion. I liked only one thing: myself, my life."

Years later, Kerem was able to slip back into Iraq. He decided to move to Baghdad and lose himself in the vastness of the big city. Gifted with artistic talents, he enrolled in a fine arts academy, and completely unexpectedly, this proved to be the turning point in Kerem's life.

"There was a painting on the wall of one of the classrooms with a cross on it and the words, in Arabic, 'God is love.' I was curious about this, but I was also confused. It was a very strange thing to me to think of God as love. The god I knew had no love. There was a Christian girl in my class, so one day I asked her, 'What does that saying mean?' "

The girl told him that this was a verse from the Bible, from 1 John 4:16, which says plainly, "God is love."

"I had no idea what she was talking about," Kerem said. "So I asked her if she could get me a copy of an Arabic Bible — there was no Bible in the Kurdish language at the time. After two days she brought me one book, the book of Matthew. I went back home and started reading. I couldn't sleep. I read it three times. As I read, I knew it was all true. I just knew it. And I felt a peace that I couldn't explain come over me. I felt angels all around me. I felt that there was a burden on my chest that was gone. I felt that I had discovered someone called Jesus. The next day I went back to the college, and I was smiling. Most of the students noticed that, and they asked me why I was happy. I couldn't tell them why. Not yet."

That night, Kerem turned on his radio and happened to tune in to Trans World Radio, a Christian broadcasting network operating out of Monte Carlo. "The man on the program was repeating the same verses of the Sermon on the Mount that I had just read in Matthew.* I was so moved by the Sermon on the Mount. It was so beautiful. I had never heard any teaching like it, and I knew it was true. I knew in my heart that these words were spoken by the One True God. After finishing his program, the man on the radio offered the opportunity to pray to receive Jesus Christ as my Savior. I didn't hesitate. I accepted this lovely

*Jesus' Sermon on the Mount is found in Matthew 5–7.

God. And from that day my life started changing. I had been hating God, but then I started loving God. I had been hating people of all religions, but then I started loving all, even people in Islam. Once I became a follower of Jesus, then Jesus just gave me a love for people I had never experienced and could hardly explain."

Kerem not only found himself filled with a divine love; he also had an insatiable hunger to know God personally and study the Bible more and more for himself. He read the book of Matthew constantly, as it was the only portion of the Bible that he had at that point. As he read, he developed an intense desire to obey Jesus because he loved Him so much.

He learned about the importance of being baptized as an act of repentance — that is, turning away from one's own way of doing things and choosing to follow Christ — and as a simple act of publicly professing one's love for and devotion to the living God. He saw that John the Baptist told the people to "repent, for the kingdom of heaven is at hand" (Matthew 3:2). He saw that Jesus was baptized in order to "fulfill all righteousness." He saw that this made the Father say He was "well-pleased" with Jesus (Matthew 3:13–17). He also saw that Jesus told His disciples to "go therefore and make disciples of all the nations, baptizing them in the name of the Father and the Son and the Holy Spirit, teaching them to observe all that I commanded you" (Matthew 28:19–20).

Kerem decided that he, too, should be baptized. He quietly visited one church after another, but they were filled with nominal Christians — not true followers of Jesus Christ — who refused to baptize him because he had been a Muslim. He insisted that he had been changed by God, but they refused to listen. "They were afraid to baptize me," Kerem explained. "They were afraid of the secret police. They were afraid of informants. They were afraid for many reasons. But they forgot the 366 times in the Bible it says, 'Do not be afraid.' "

Kerem refused to give up, and eventually, by God's grace, he found a brave Catholic priest who baptized him in the early 1990s.

This is one of the things I love most about Kerem: he has no fear. He believes in the greatness of his God. He knows how powerful his God is because of how dramatically God changed his life, from jihad to Jesus. Now, Kerem says, he is willing to go wherever Jesus tells him to go, do whatever Jesus tells him to do, and say whatever Jesus tells him to say, no matter what happens.

And he is not all talk. Kerem, I have found, is a man of action. First he led his brother to faith in Jesus Christ. Then he helped translate the New Testament into the Kurdish language. Now he is helping translate the Old Testament into Kurdish. He is also training young men to read and study and be able to teach the Bible, because he has seen the power of God's Word to change lives, beginning with his own. What's more, he is absolutely convinced that Kurdish MBBs are going to be used by God to take the gospel all throughout the Middle East — through regions of Iraq, Turkey, Syria, and Iran — and he is determined to stay engaged in the spiritual battle for the souls of Muslims until God takes him home to heaven.

"The truth is, I did not really decide to follow Jesus," Kerem told me. "Jesus called me to follow Him, and I was not able to resist that call. Like when Jesus called Matthew and said, 'Follow Me,' Matthew left all to follow Jesus. He couldn't resist. This is a divine calling."

One Last Question

The apostle John concluded his account of the life of Christ with this thought: "And there are also many other things which Jesus did, which if they were written in detail, I suppose that even the world itself would not contain the books that would be written" (John 21:25).

I feel these chapters on the Revivalists could be concluded the same way. Having met with and interviewed more than 150 Revivalist leaders, I could not possibly include all of their stories in these pages. And I must confess this pains me, because I find each of their testimonies of God's love and power utterly amazing and deeply encouraging, especially in light of the extreme persecution and pressures that these leaders face on a daily basis.

Once when I was in Iraq, I had the privilege of having dinner with the first known Shia Muslim convert to Christianity in the entire modern history of Iraq. He became a follower of Jesus Christ in 1967. He was baptized in 1972. He began to share his faith and make disciples and plant churches in 1985. He has been kidnapped by Radicals multiple times. But he loves Jesus more than ever. And he is absolutely convinced that the Iraqi church will eventually be led by MBBs, even though most pastors there now are NCBBs.

Another time, I had the honor of dining with arguably the most influential ministry leader in Iraq, an NCBB who told me the story of how he went into full-time ministry. He had been an ordinary professional business man. One day, his village was attacked by Radical Islamic terrorists, one of whom ran up to his house, leveled an AK-47 at him, and pulled the trigger. But the gun didn't fire. The terrorist pulled the trigger again. It still didn't fire. The terrorist pointed the gun in the air and pulled the trigger to test the gun. This time it did fire. So once more the terrorist pointed the gun at this Christian man and pulled the trigger. But again, the gun didn't fire. The terrorist ran off, and the Christian man knew that God had miraculously spared his life. The next day, he quit the Iraqi oil company he was working for and committed himself to serving the Lord full-time, making disciples and training church leaders.

In Afghanistan, I had the privilege of meeting a senior Afghan church leader who had been living in the United States in 2001. That summer, he saw a documentary film on television about the horrors the Taliban was inflicting on the people of his home country. He prayed, "Lord, if You get rid of the Taliban, I will quit my job and move back to Afghanistan to serve You there." Two months later, the 9/11 attacks happened. Two months after that, this man saw a breaking news story on CNN announcing that U.S. military forces were on the ground in Afghanistan to destroy al Qaeda and the Taliban. He gasped. The Lord had kept His end of the bargain. Now it was his turn. Keeping his promise, he quit his job and moved to Afghanistan, where God is now using him in a mighty way.

In talking to these and a host of other Christian leaders in the epicenter, I had one question that continued nagging at me. They were describing millions of people coming to Christ throughout the region through dreams and visions. And they were noting that those who come to faith in Christ through visions are fruitful immediately, meaning they start living holy, pure lives and are completely dedicated to Christ from the moment of conversion. They compared these conversions to Paul's conversion on the road to Damascus in Acts 9. Paul never doubted his decision to follow Jesus later on. He never wavered. He never faltered. He was bold and devout right away, because his experience with Christ was so personal and so powerful that it changed him forever.

What, then, I asked, is the role of sharing the gospel, preaching the gospel, showing people the *JESUS* film, using radio and satellite broadcasting, and so forth if God is drawing these people to Himself supernaturally?

"That's a great question," one dear Iraqi Christian brother replied. "It's true that every single Shia MBB I know or have ever heard of has come to faith in Christ directly, without apparent human persuasion. It's not always a dream or vision, although it often is. Sometimes it is simply that the Lord speaks to them directly in their heart, sometimes audibly, sometimes not. The key is that one day they don't believe in Jesus, and the next day they do. But it's not because someone sat down and persuaded them. It's that God just did a supernatural work in their heart."

"Okay," I said, "but again, why are so many Revivalists risking their lives to communicate the gospel to Muslims if the Muslims who are coming to Christ are not being persuaded by the Revivalists?"

"Because, Joel, the Bible tells us to teach the Word of God and to preach the gospel, and so we obey," he replied gently. "And actually, when you look closer at the stories of these MBBs, you will find that each of them has had some exposure to the name of Jesus and the story of Jesus in his or her past. Think of what the apostle Paul said: 'Whoever will call on the name of the Lord will be saved. How then will they call on Him in whom they have not believed? How will they believe in Him whom they have not heard? And how will they hear without a preacher? How will they preach unless they are sent? Just as it is written, "How beautiful are the feet of those who bring good news of good things!" . . . So faith comes from hearing, and hearing by the word of Christ.'*

"Likewise, in Matthew 13, Jesus teaches the parable of the seed and the sower. He insisted that His followers sow seeds — that is, preach the gospel and teach the Word of God — everywhere. We don't know whose hearts will be like good soil and receive God's Word and bear the fruit of changed lives. Only God knows that. We are simply supposed to obey. Just like the farmer — he just plants the seeds; it is God who makes them grow and bear fruit. Arguing with Muslims about Christ will not lead people to Christ. But we are supposed to teach them about Jesus whenever possible, and encourage them to read the Bible, and love them, and pray for them; and somehow God uses this as part of His mysterious plan to adopt Muslims into His Kingdom."

I had my answer, and it wasn't complicated. If you love Me, Jesus said, you will obey Me. It was not an easy answer, but it was simple.

*See Romans 10:13–17.

Chapter Thirty:
The Theology
of the Revivalists

What they believe, verse by verse

I met Shakir during my first trip to Iraq in February of 2008.*

Another fearless and effective evangelist, church planter, and pastor in his war-torn country, Shakir (pronounced "Shah-*keer*") has a tremendous passion to care for the poor and needy, preach the gospel — especially in villages and rural areas — and help young converts from Islam study the Bible and become fully devoted followers of Jesus Christ.

But this was not always the case. Indeed, how Shakir became a Christian and entered full-time ministry is one of the most fascinating testimonies I have personally had the privilege of hearing firsthand. What's more, spending time with him helped me understand more fully the theology of the Revivalists.

*Shakir is not his real name. It is a pseudonym to protect this Iraqi pastor. This chapter is based on a series of author interviews with Shakir in February 2008.

Heading to Nineveh

As it happened, Shakir and I and several others took a road trip together in northern Iraq to meet some Muslim Background Believers not far from the city of Mosul.

I had been advised not to take this trip.

Yes, friends said, Mosul is the site of the ancient biblical city of Nineveh, the very city to which God sent the prophets Jonah and Nahum. Certainly both the city and the province by the same name are exceedingly rich in history, they conceded. But the city is also exceedingly violent — one of the most dangerous cities in modern-day Iraq and a key hub for terrorists allied with "Al Qaeda in Mesopotamia" and other Radical Sunni insurgent groups.

My friends were right, of course. Innocent civilians die in Mosul every day — Arabs, Kurds, and occasionally foreigners, if they are foolish enough to enter the city limits. Some are stabbed to death. Some have their heads cut off. Others are riddled with bullets from AK-47s or other automatic weapons. Still others are murdered by suicide bombers. Some have their houses burned to the ground. Some see their wives raped before they are murdered. And some see their young children kidnapped and killed. It is a vicious, cruel, unforgiving place, as it has been from time immemorial.

The prophet Nahum once wrote of Nineveh, "Woe to the city of blood, full of lies, full of plunder, never without victims! . . . Many casualties, piles of dead, bodies without number, people stumbling over the corpses" (Nahum 3:1–3, NIV). That was 2,600 years ago. But Nahum could have written it yesterday.

A few days before we headed to Nineveh, the media reported that a series of suicide bombings launched there by al Qaeda had destroyed a hundred houses, killed at least sixty people, and wounded more than 280 others. Said the Iraqi defense minister after touring the city following the attacks: "The situation in Mosul is worse than imagined by far."[1]

Still, after much prayer, I had a sense of peace that it was God's will for me to go with Shakir and several other Iraqi Christian leaders to a village just minutes away from Mosul. Our destination was not actually within the "city of blood," and it was a village where — to their knowledge — not a single American had ever been. More importantly, it was a village where some three hundred of the seven hundred or so residents had come to faith in Christ over the last several years, mostly through dreams and visions of Jesus.

"This is a village where God is moving very powerfully," Shakir told me. "All this violence by Muslims against Muslims is causing many people to reconsider whether Islam is true. And now Jesus is appearing to people, and they are becoming His followers. I will take you to meet the first family to whom Jesus appeared. They were the first Christians in the whole village, and now everything is changing there. It is very exciting. I think, by God's grace, you will be very safe. It should be no problem."

It did sound exciting. It was exactly what I had come to see for myself. So I agreed to go.

Shakir's Remarkable Spiritual Journey

Our journey was long and dusty and required our little team, traveling in an old Chevy Impala, to pass through numerous military checkpoints, each manned by heavily armed Iraqi soldiers and policemen checking passports and asking questions, all on high alert for members of al Qaeda and the Mahdi Army.

Along the way, I found myself staring out at a landscape that was often as barren as the surface of the moon, covered with rocks, nearly devoid of vegetation, and only scarcely populated. During a lull in the conversation with an Iraqi in the car whom I had known for several years, I asked the meek-looking and mild-mannered Pastor Shakir how he had become a Christ-follower and a pastor.

"Were you raised in a Christian home?" I asked through our translator.

"No," he replied quietly. "I was raised a Muslim."

"Really?" I said. "What did you do before becoming a pastor?"

"I was a jihad cell commander."

I gulped. *You don't say,* I thought. He certainly had my full attention now. "Please, tell me your story," I said eagerly, pulling out my notebook.

Shakir graciously agreed.

He explained that he was born in 1975 to a devout Sunni Muslim family and that as he grew up he became deeply religious. Even at an early age, he loved going to the mosque regularly, and by the age of seventeen, he had joined a secret Radical Islamic movement. He studied hard and learned quickly, and before long he was teaching the Qur'an in various mosques.

"My leaders then sent me to a military training camp where I was trained to use light weapons — pistols, machine guns, and RPGs [rocket propelled

643

grenades] — against the infidels," he told me. "I was so excited because I wanted to do jihad for God. I was fully convinced that the Shias and the Christians were blasphemers and that if I killed them I would be blessed."

After successfully completing "Terrorism 101," Shakir was made a jihad cell commander and was ordered to quietly recruit other jihadists. "I soon had a group of my own followers," he explained. "I would put them through this military training and then help them get jobs in different government offices and other shops and businesses so they could spy for me and be in position to do great damage when we launched the overthrow of Saddam and his regime."

One day, one of Shakir's Radical Muslim disciples came to him and said that someone was distributing Bibles to everyone in the machine shop where he worked. The disciple was very angry and told Shakir that he had cursed out everyone in the shop, collected all the Bibles, and promptly destroyed them. All but one.

"He brought one Bible — a New Testament — to me and said I should read it and see how to react to it and counter it," Shakir explained. He said he praised his disciple for acting quickly and decisively. Then he sent the disciple away and took the Bible home, and that night he began to read the Gospel according to Matthew.

The Parade of Prophets

"I read the book very fervently to find all the blasphemies and corruption," Shakir said. "But I discovered the words started affecting my mind, and my heart started changing. These were powerful words, not human words. They seemed to me like God's words. But I thought, 'How could this be?' "

Shakir became deeply troubled. He kept reading through Matthew but was ashamed of himself because rather than finding fault with these Christian Scriptures, he found himself completely intrigued. He had so many questions. But whom could he ask? He couldn't very well start discussing the life and teachings of Jesus with the members of the terrorist cell group he was leading. He couldn't very well ask questions of the terrorist leaders above him. He didn't dare seek out any Christians. So night after night he kept reading the Gospels, searching for answers. The more he did, the more troubled and anxious he became.

"After reading the Bible in a deep way, I began comparing it with the Qur'an," he told me. "I was so confused, and in my confusion, I began pleading with God, 'Please show me Yourself.' I begged God, 'Please, show me the right way — are you the God of the Qur'an or the God of the Bible?' "

This went on for several nights.

"One night," he said, "I was pleading with God fervently to show me the true, straight path. And that night I had a dream. I found myself standing on the side of a road. There was a large crowd gathered on both sides of the road, and they were cheering and very excited. And I realized that they were awaiting a parade to go by. So I looked down the road to see who was coming, and I saw many prophets riding on horses coming towards us. Suddenly Jonah was riding by. And then David. And Abraham. And Moses — riding on high, strong horses. Everyone was cheering and I was cheering. It was so exciting to see these prophets."

645

Shakir kept waiting for Muhammad to come riding by as well, but Muhammad never came. He was not in the parade of prophets. Instead, Shakir said that "at the end of the procession, I saw another person riding, but He was riding on a donkey instead of a horse. He was wearing a white robe, and His face was covered by a white shroud. When this person approached, for some reason I heard myself calling out to Him and asking, 'Are you Jesus?' Like I said, His face was covered by a white cloth. So I couldn't really see His face at that moment. But when He heard my question, the man pulled the cloth away from His face and smiled at me and nodded yes.

"Something came from His face that filled me with a joy I had never felt in my whole life. I started shouting, 'I saw Jesus! I saw Jesus!' I was so happy and so joyful and I was laughing. But as soon as I woke up, I realized that my pillowcase and my sheets were all wet around my head. I realized that at some point during my dream I had been crying — sobbing — in shame for all of my sins, for all of my hatred."

Shakir found himself overcome with the realization that he had been so wrong about God, about Islam, about terrorism. He also found himself incredibly grateful and humbled that Jesus would come and rescue him and forgive him of all of his sins and set him on the true path to heaven.

A Complete Transformation

"I felt a strong joy, and I wanted to find my Muslim disciples and tell them that I loved them and that Jesus loved them," Shakir explained. "After that dream, my life was completely changed. I was eager to evangelize — to tell people about the love of Jesus Christ. I couldn't hide that joy. The more I read of the Gospels, the more I felt I had to tell people about this love of God, even people that I had hated. This was not easy. I was mocked and persecuted by many. Once I was beaten by eight people. I was nearly assassinated three times. But it is okay. Since I came to know the Lord Jesus as my Savior, I am ready to put my life — and my family — as a sacrifice for Jesus."

What a remarkable transformation, I thought as Shakir finished his story. A few days later, I asked him to repeat the story before a video camera for a future documentary film we were working on. He graciously agreed, and when the interview was over, Shakir stood up, looked me straight in the eye, and without any expression on his face said, "Joel, you are very lucky."

"I think that's true," I said. "But why do you say it?"

He took a deep breath. "Because if I had met you in 1993, I would have killed you immediately."

My pulse quickened. There was a silence. And then he added, "But now you are my brother in Jesus, and I love you!"

A huge smile flashed across his face. He threw his arms around me and gave me a bear hug. I breathed a big sigh of relief, and — laughing — gave him a hug as well.

Five Core Convictions

After spending time with Pastor Shakir and dozens of other ministry leaders like him throughout the region, I have concluded that while Revivalists hold many important theological beliefs, they have at least five common core theological convictions based on their steadfast belief that the Bible is the holy Word of God.

These are not unique convictions. Indeed, they are shared by fully devoted followers of Jesus Christ all over the world. Nevertheless it is both important and remarkable that former Muslims — not a few of whom are former Radicals — hold such convictions.

Allow me to explain.

Core Conviction No. 1: God Loves All of Mankind

Each and every one of the Revivalists I interviewed — including Shakir — noted with deep conviction that according to the Bible, God's defining character trait is love. The Bible teaches that God loves every man, woman, and child on the face of the earth — regardless of race, nationality, tribe, or language.

God loves all of us with an everlasting love. He loved all of us before we loved Him. He loves us so much that He wants to adopt us into His family as His children and let us live with Him in heaven forever. He loves us so much that if we let Him, He will be a Shepherd to us, guiding us, providing for us, protecting us, giving us rest, and taking care of us in every possible way. He loves us so much that if we follow and obey Him, we can actually become friends with Him and develop a personal, intimate relationship with Him.

Here are some of the verses the Revivalists point to in describing the love of this incredible God:

"God is love." — *1 John 4:16*

"For God so loved the world, that He gave His only begotten Son, that whoever believes in Him shall not perish, but have eternal life." — *John 3:16*

648

"I have loved you with an everlasting love; therefore I have drawn you with lovingkindness." — *Jeremiah 31:3*

"Give thanks to the LORD, for He is good, for His lovingkindness is everlasting. Give thanks to the God of gods, for His lovingkindness is everlasting. Give thanks to the Lord of lords, for His lovingkindness is everlasting." — *Psalm 136:1–3*

"We love, because He first loved us." — *1 John 4:19*

"See how great a love the Father has bestowed on us, that we should be called children of God." — *1 John 3:1*

"The LORD is my shepherd, I shall not want. He makes me lie down in green pastures; He leads me beside quiet waters. He restores my soul; He guides me in the paths of righteousness for His name's sake. Even though I walk through the valley of the shadow of death, I fear no evil, for You are with me; Your rod and Your staff, they comfort me. You prepare a table before me in the presence of my enemies; You have anointed my head with oil; my cup overflows. Surely goodness and lovingkindness will follow me all the days of my life, and I will dwell in the house of the LORD forever." — *Psalm 23:1–6*

[Jesus said,] "You are My friends if you do what I command you. No longer do I call you slaves, for the slave does not know what his master is doing; but I have called you friends, for all things that I have heard from My Father I have made known to you." — *John 15:14–15*

"Do not envy a man of violence and do not

choose any of his ways. For the devious are an abomination to the LORD; but He is intimate with the upright." — *Proverbs 3:31–32*

The Revivalists note with equal conviction that the Bible also teaches that because God loves all mankind, He also has a wonderful plan and purpose for every man, woman, and child. Consider these verses:

> "For I know the plans I have for you," says the LORD. "They are plans for good and not for disaster, to give you a future and a hope. In those days when you pray, I will listen. If you look for me wholeheartedly, you will find me." — *Jeremiah 29:11–13, NLT*
> [Jesus said,] "I came that they may have life, and have it abundantly." — *John 10:10*
> "And we know that God causes all things to work together for good to those who love God, to those who are called according to His purpose." — *Romans 8:28*
> "God . . . desires all men to be saved and to come to the knowledge of the truth." — *1 Timothy 2:3–4*
> "We are His workmanship, created in Christ Jesus for good works, which God prepared beforehand so that we would walk in them." — *Ephesians 2:10*

Such truths astounded Shakir as he began reading the Bible, first as a Radical Muslim and even after his conversion and decision to follow Jesus Christ. He had never seen God as someone who loved him. He had never thought of God as hav-

650

ing a positive plan and purpose for his life. He certainly never imagined that God wanted to count him as a friend and even as a member of His own family.

Core Conviction No. 2:
All Mankind Is Sinful and Thus Separated from God
Another truth that floored Shakir as he read the New Testament and when he was in the presence of Jesus in his dream was the realization that he — Shakir — was a sinner, that he had been on a terribly wrong path, that not only had he disobeyed God but he was making God grieve because of his sins. This is why Shakir awoke from his dream to find his pillow and sheets drenched in his tears. They were tears of shame and remorse that were triggered as soon as he realized just how sinful he really was.

Most of us are not terrorists, of course. Most of us have not been trained to kill "infidels" and recruit others to do the same. Nevertheless, the Bible teaches that every man, woman, and child has sinned against God. We have either generally disregarded Him — paying Him and His Word scant interest or attention — or we have actively disobeyed Him. Either way, this is sin.

Some of us may have committed more sins than others, but none of us is innocent before God. According to the Scriptures, every single one of us has broken God's laws. We have lied, or stolen, or cheated, or been guilty of lust, or coveted something of our neighbor's. We have tried to live our own lives in our own way, not following God's ways, and this is further evidence of what the Bible calls sin.

The problem, the Bible makes clear, is that our

sins separate us from a close, loving, personal relationship with God. Our sins also condemn us to eternal death where we will be separated from God in hell forever and ever and ever. Why? Because God is holy and we are not. God cannot allow a person with even one sin into heaven; if He did, that person would taint and thus destroy the holiness of God and His Kingdom. As a result of our sinful nature, then, the Bible teaches that we cannot know and experience God's love and plan for our lives.

Consider the following verses:

"All have sinned and fall short of the glory of God." — *Romans 3:23*

"The LORD has looked down from heaven upon the sons of men to see if there are any who understand, who seek after God. [But] they have all turned aside, together they have become corrupt; there is no one who does good, not even one." — *Psalm 14:2–3*

"The wages of sin is death." — *Romans 6:23*

[Jesus said,] "If your foot causes you to stumble, cut it off; it is better for you to enter life lame, than, having your two feet, to be cast into hell, where . . . the fire is not quenched." — *Mark 9:45–46*

[Jesus said,] "I say to you, My friends, do not be afraid of those who kill the body and after that have no more that they can do. But I will warn you whom to fear: fear the One who, after He has killed, has authority to cast into hell; yes, I tell you, fear Him!" — *Luke 12:4–5*

Jesus said, "But when the Son of Man comes in His glory, and all the angels with Him, then He will sit on His glorious throne. All the nations will be gathered before Him; and He will separate them from one another, as the shepherd separates the sheep from the goats; and He will put the sheep [His true followers] on His right and the goats [those who refused to follow and obey Him] on the left. Then the King will say to those on His right, 'Come, you who are blessed of My Father, inherit the kingdom prepared for you from the foundation of the world. . . .' Then He will also say to those on His left, 'Depart from Me, accursed ones, into the eternal fire which has been prepared for the devil and his angels. . . . These will go away into eternal punishment, but the righteous into eternal life." — *Matthew 25:31–34, 41, 46*

Core Conviction No. 3:
Jesus Christ Is Mankind's Only Hope of Salvation
The fact that we are all sinners separated from God now and for eternity is terrible, depressing, devastating news, of course. Fortunately, however, the Bible teaches that God in His unending love and kindness made a way for us to be forgiven and to be saved from going to hell. He made a way for us to enter an intimate and personal relationship with Him.

As one reads the New Testament, the Revivalists note, one learns that God sent Jesus to die on a Roman cross to pay the penalty for our sins. He died in our place, to rescue us from hell and restore us to a right relationship with God. He not only died on the cross, the Bible teaches, but He rose from the dead, thus proving that He is the only way to God.

Consider the following verses:

"While we were still helpless, at the right time Christ died for the ungodly." — *Romans 5:6*

"God demonstrates His own love toward us, in that while we were yet sinners, Christ died for us." — *Romans 5:8*

"The wages of sin is death, but the free gift of God is eternal life in Christ Jesus our Lord." — *Romans 6:23*

"Christ died for our sins . . . He was buried . . . He was raised on the third day according to the Scriptures . . . He appeared to [Peter], then to the twelve. After that He appeared to more than five hundred." — *1 Corinthians 15:3–6*

It is no wonder Shakir was so confused when he first began reading the Bible. On the one hand, he was learning that God loved him deeply and wanted to be his friend, something he had never heard before and was not learning from reading or teaching the Qur'an. On the other hand, he was coming to realize that he was a sinner and was therefore eternally separated from this kind and loving God.

The questions that Shakir had to wrestle through at that point came down to this: What was the right way to proceed? What was the right way to be forgiven of his sins — by his own death as a martyr in pursuit of jihad, or by accepting Jesus' death on the cross as the payment for his sins? What was the right way to be saved from going to hell — by killing innocent people in the name of God, or by accepting the fact that God allowed His own innocent Son, Jesus, to be killed to pay the penalty for Shakir's sins and the sins of all mankind?

The answer to all these questions, Shakir knew, had to be found in determining which book was true, the Qur'an or the Bible. If the Qur'an was right, then Islam was indeed the answer, and jihad was indeed the way to God and eternal salvation. But if the Bible was right, then Jesus was speaking the truth when He said, "I am the way, and the truth, and the life; no one comes to the Father but through Me" (John 14:6).

How, then, can one know which book is right? By doing exactly what Shakir did, say fellow Revivalists, many of whom have had similar experiences. Study the New Testament, and then earnestly ask God to make it clear what the truth is.

Not everyone who asks God for wisdom will receive a dream or a vision. While millions of Muslims are having such dreams and visions convincing them that the Bible is the true book of God, there are many other ways that God can and has convinced people as well. The point is not how God explains Himself. The point is honestly and sincerely pleading with God to make Himself and His will clear. He will most certainly answer such sincere requests. Why would He not?

Consider the following promises found in the Bible:

" 'You will call upon Me and come and pray to Me, and I will listen to you. You will seek Me and find Me when you search for Me with all your heart. I will be found by you,' declares the LORD." — *Jeremiah 29:12–14*

"Call to Me and I will answer you," [says the

Lord,] "and I will tell you great and mighty things, which you do not know." — *Jeremiah 33:3*

[Jesus said,] "Ask, and it will be given to you; seek, and you will find; knock, and it will be opened to you. For everyone who asks receives, and he who seeks finds, and to him who knocks it will be opened." — *Matthew 7:7–8*

[Jesus said,] "Come to Me, all who are weary and heavy-laden, and I will give you rest. Take My yoke upon you and learn from Me, for I am gentle and humble in heart, and you will find rest for your souls. For My yoke is easy and My burden is light." — *Matthew 11:28–30*

[Jesus said,] "Truly, truly, I say to you, he who believes has eternal life. I am the bread of life. . . . I am the living bread that came down out of heaven; if anyone eats of this bread, he will live forever." — *John 6:47–48, 51*

I believe it is important to note here what a beautiful portrait of God's love we see in Jesus' appearing to Shakir. Think about it for a moment. Shakir honestly wanted to know God, serve God, please God. In his ignorance and sin, Shakir did not realize that as a Sunni terrorist he was on the wrong path. But because Jesus loved Shakir so much, He sent someone to give him a Bible to read. Because Jesus loved Shakir so much, when Shakir was troubled, Jesus came directly to him to answer his fervent, heartfelt prayer and make it clear that He really was the One True Way.

Shakir asked, and he received. Shakir sought,

and he found. He knocked, and the door was opened, just as Jesus promised.

Core Conviction No. 4:
A Person Must Individually Choose to Follow Jesus Christ as Personal Savior and Lord

It was not enough for Shakir simply to realize that God loved him, that he was a sinner, that the Bible was the only true book of life, and that Jesus was the only true path to salvation. Shakir had to do more than just come to the intellectual realization of these truths.

Shakir had to individually receive Jesus Christ as his own personal Savior and Lord. He had to believe in his heart that Jesus died on the cross to pay for his sins. He had to believe that Jesus rose again from the dead, thus proving Himself to be the Messiah. He had to choose by faith to become a Christ-follower and accept God's free gift of salvation, acknowledging the fact that he could not pay for his salvation or earn it by doing enough good works to outweigh the bad.

He also had to be willing to declare out loud his allegiance to Jesus Christ and to tell others that Jesus is the King of kings and the Lord of lords. Only then, the Bible teaches, could Shakir — or anyone else — truly know and experience God's love and plan for his life.

That, of course, is exactly what Shakir did, and it changed his life forever.

Consider the following verses:

"But as many as received Him [Jesus Christ], to them He gave the right to become children of God, even to those who believe in His name." — *John 1:12*

"If you confess with your mouth Jesus as Lord, and believe in your heart that God raised Him from the dead, you will be saved; for with the heart a person believes, resulting in righteousness, and with the mouth he confesses, resulting in salvation. . . . Whoever will call on the name of the Lord will be saved. . . . Faith comes from hearing, and hearing by the word of Christ." — *Romans 10:9–10, 13, 17*

"For by grace [unmerited favor] you have been saved through faith; and that not of yourselves, it is the gift of God; not as a result of works, so that no one may boast." — *Ephesians 2:8–9*

"Behold, I [Jesus] stand at the door and knock; if anyone hears My voice and opens the door, I will come in to him and will dine with him, and he with Me." — *Revelation 3:20*

To his eternal joy, Shakir heard Jesus knocking at the door of his heart. He opened that door and asked Christ to come into his heart and adopt him into God's family, and Jesus answered that prayer and transformed Shakir from a preacher of hatred and violence to a preacher of love and forgiveness.

Would you like to make the same decision? If you are willing to repent — turn away from your own sins and from living your life as you see fit — and turn around to actually follow the God of the Bible, you can receive Jesus Christ as your Savior and Lord right now, just as Shakir did. Here is a suggested prayer that has been helpful to many Muslims, Jews, and others — including my parents and me — in becoming followers of Christ. The key is not so much the precise words as the attitude of your heart.

Lord Jesus, thank You for loving me. Thank You for having a wonderful plan and purpose for my life. I need You today — I know I need You to forgive me for all of my sins. Thank You for dying on the cross to pay the penalty for my sins. Thank You for rising again from the dead to prove that You are the Way, the Truth, and the Life and the only way to get to heaven. Jesus, I confess right now with my mouth that You are the King of kings and the Lord of lords. And I believe in my heart that God raised You from the dead. And now I open the door of my heart and my life right now. I receive You as my Savior and Lord. Thank You for forgiving my sins and giving me eternal life. Please change my life. Please fill me with your Holy Spirit. Please take control of my life and make me the kind of person that You want me to be, so that I can serve You and please You forever. Thank You so much. I love You, and I want to follow You. Amen.

If you just prayed that prayer with sincere faith in Jesus Christ's death and resurrection, then congratulations and welcome to the family of God. The Bible teaches that several wonderful things have just happened:

1. You have a new spiritual life. According to the words of Jesus in John chapter 3, you have been spiritually "born again" and have been adopted into the family of God. Your physical body has not changed, of course. But inside, your soul and spirit (the part of you that really is *you* — your thoughts, your beliefs, your feelings) have been supernaturally regenerated. What was spiritually dead inside of you because of sin has been made alive because of the resurrection power of Jesus Christ.

The apostle Paul put it this way in 2 Corinthians 5:17: "Therefore if anyone is in Christ, he is a new creature; the old things passed away; behold, new things have come." In Romans 6:11 we are told, "Consider yourselves to be dead to sin, but alive to God in Christ Jesus." In Ephesians 2:4–6 we are told, "God, being rich in mercy, because of His great love with which He loved us, even when we were dead in our transgressions, made us alive together with Christ (by grace you have been saved), and raised us up with Him, and seated us with Him in the heavenly places in Christ Jesus." And, as we read earlier from John 1:12, "But as many as received Him [Jesus Christ], to them He gave the right to become children of God."

2. You have made everyone in heaven happy. According to the words of Jesus in Luke 15:10, there is great rejoicing in heaven because you have become a follower of the living God. "I tell you," Jesus said, "there is joy in the presence of the angels of God over one sinner who repents."

3. You are going to heaven when you die. According to the words of Jesus in John 3:16, you now have eternal life. You will *not* go to hell and perish eternally when you die physically. Rather, you will go to heaven and live forever with God and all those who have been adopted into His family by faith in Jesus Christ.

In fact, the New Testament was written precisely to show people how to find eternal life through faith in Jesus Christ and to give true followers of Jesus solid assurance of their salvation. As we see in 1 John 5:13, "These things I have written to you who believe in the name of the Son of God, so that you may know that you have eternal life." God wants you to know — beyond the shadow of a doubt — that you are now forever safe in His family. Take confidence in His promises.

4. You have the Holy Spirit living within you. According to the words of the apostle Paul in Ephesians 1:13–14, your salvation has been sealed and secured forever by God's Holy Spirit now living within you. "In Him [Jesus Christ], you also, after listening to the message of truth, the gospel of your salvation — having also believed, you were sealed in Him with the Holy Spirit of promise, who is given as a pledge of our inheritance, with a view to the redemption of God's own possession, to the praise of His glory."

5. You have access to a supernatural sense of peace. According to Philippians 4:7, you now have access to a supernatural peace with God and internal peace of mind, regardless of whatever external circumstances come your way. "The peace of God, which surpasses all comprehension, will guard your hearts and your minds in Christ Jesus." This does not mean you won't face times of stress, anxiety, panic, or fear. Indeed, you may actually experience persecution and other severe challenges now that you are willing to follow Jesus with all your heart. But as a child of the living God and a follower of Jesus Christ, whom the Bible calls the "Prince of Peace" (Isaiah 9:6), you can now pray and ask your Father in heaven to give you the "peace which surpasses all comprehension" — an overwhelming sense of calm that may not even make sense to you — and He promises to give you such peace.

6. You have access to a supernatural sense of hope. According to the words of Hebrews 6:18–19, all followers of Jesus Christ are encouraged to "take hold of the hope set before us" and to view "this hope we have as an anchor of the soul, a hope both sure and steadfast." We no longer need to be discouraged, depressed, or despairing. Regardless of how poor we might be, or how endangered, or how persecuted, or how sick, God is ready and willing to give us a supernatural sense of hope and optimism about the future. And the more we study the Bible and understand how much God loves us and wants to care for us — and that He promises never to leave or forsake us — the more hopeful we will become.

7. You also have access to God's supernatural wisdom. According to James 1:5, "If any of you lacks wisdom, let him ask of God, who gives to all generously and without reproach, and it will be given to him." Whenever we face situations or decisions that confuse or perplex us, we can turn to our Father in heaven and ask for help. When we do, He promises to provide us with supernatural guidance and direction.

Core Conviction No. 5:
Christ-Followers Are Commanded to Love Their
Neighbors and Their Enemies and to Make Disciples
of All Nations

The day Pastor Shakir and I met, we were not only going to visit Muslim Background Believers in a village near Mosul. We were also, at his suggestion, going to do a project to care for poor and needy Muslim children near Mosul. It was an amazing thing to see a former terrorist loving a group of underprivileged children and their parents, and doing so unconditionally. They did not believe what he believed. Indeed, they lived in a region where many hate Christians and seek to kill them.

He did not try to force his belief in Jesus Christ on any of them. Despite the fact that he is a gifted evangelist, Pastor Shakir did not even share the gospel that day. He simply demonstrated God's love for these Muslim families by bringing relief supplies and giving them out freely, without the expectation that these families were going to convert to Christianity and certainly without the expectation that he was going to gain personally in any way, least of all financially.

In this way, Pastor Shakir was following the model that Jesus set for us in the New Testament. Jesus taught His disciples to love their neighbors and their enemies.

What's more, Jesus practiced what He preached. He loved people whether they deserved it or not, whether they wanted His love or not, whether they said thank you or not, whether they chose to follow Him or not, whether they blessed Him or whether they cursed Him. Even in the last moments of His life on earth, while hanging on the cross — after having been beaten and mocked and tortured in the cruelest and most inhumane ways — Jesus demonstrated His love even for His worst and most violent enemies by saying, "Father, forgive them; for they do not know what they are doing" (Luke 23:34). And this is what He expects from His followers, in the Middle East and around the world.

Consider the following words of Jesus:

"You shall love your neighbor as yourself." — *Matthew 19:19*

"You have heard that it was said, 'You shall love your neighbor and hate your enemy.' But I say to you, love your enemies and pray for those who persecute you." — *Matthew 5:43–44*

"Blessed are you when men hate you, and ostracize you, and insult you, and scorn your name as evil, for the sake of the Son of Man. Be glad in that day and leap for joy, for behold, your reward is great in heaven. For in the same way their fathers used to treat the prophets. . . . Woe to you when all men speak well of you, for their fathers used to treat the false prophets in the same way. But I say to you who hear, love your enemies, do good to those who hate you, bless those who curse you, pray for those who mistreat you. Whoever hits you on the cheek, offer him the other also; and whoever takes away your coat, do not withhold your shirt from him either. Give to everyone who asks of you, and whoever takes away what is yours, do not demand it back. Treat others the same way you want them to treat you. If you love those who love you, what credit is that to you? For even sinners love those who love them. If you do good to those who do good to you, what credit is that to you? For even sinners do the same. If you lend to those from whom you expect to receive, what credit is that to you? Even sinners lend to sinners in order to receive back the same amount. But love your enemies, and do good, and lend, expecting nothing in return; and your reward will be great, and you will be sons of the Most High; for He Himself is kind to ungrateful and evil men. Be merciful, just as your Father is merciful." — *Luke 6:22–36*

To be sure, loving one's neighbors — and particularly loving one's enemies — can be difficult if not impossible in the Muslim world, humanly speaking. But Jesus commanded that we follow His example and do it anyway. He knew that only someone supernaturally transformed — born again — by God's love and empowered by the Holy Spirit could obey such commands. Thus, when we obey these commands in the power of the Holy Spirit, we demonstrate that we are, in fact, true followers of a living and all-powerful God.

CHAPTER THIRTY-ONE:
MAKING WAY FOR THE MESSIAH

Biblical eschatology is a
hot topic in the epicenter

In 2007, I was invited to speak at a conference of
two hundred Christian leaders from Iraq, Iran,
Egypt, Syria, and a host of other countries in the
Muslim world. For security reasons, I cannot say
what country the conference was held in, but I
can say it was one of the most fascinating events I
have ever been privileged to attend.

The hall was packed with Revivalists — MBBs
and NCBBs — each of whom was doing heroic
work to advance the gospel and make disciples
under extreme conditions in some of the most
difficult and dangerous countries on the planet.
All had amazing stories of what God was doing in
their countries, and I counted it a great privilege
to spend time with them and to soak in as much
information as I possibly could. It was in many
ways like being transported back to the book of
Acts, when God first began miraculously building
His Church in the epicenter. Today, He is at work
miraculously rebuilding that Church and breathing new life into the people of that region. Meeting servants that Jesus Christ has personally

chosen to lead such important work was like meeting people right out of the book of Acts. I almost felt like I was talking with Peter, Paul, Barnabas, Timothy, and Priscilla and Aquila, among others.

What made the conference particularly remarkable for me, however, was not simply learning from these dear Revivalist leaders but also seeing their eagerness for Jesus Christ to return to earth and set up His Kingdom, and their hunger to understand what the Bible teaches about the end of days. All of them believed without a doubt that they were living in the last days before the return of Christ. But few of them had ever had any in-depth teaching on biblical eschatology, or end times theology.

That said, given their own sense that Christ's return could be soon — and given the buzz in the Muslim world in recent years about Mahmoud Ahmadinejad's eschatology — they had lots of questions, and I counted it an honor to answer them from the Scriptures as best I could. The following year, they invited me back to go deeper and answer more questions.

Bible prophecy and current events are increasingly a hot topic in the epicenter. Wherever I travel in North Africa, the Middle East, or central Asia these days, I find deep and growing curiosity about such subjects. During my first trip to Iraq, for example, I met with a group of thirteen Iraqi Christian leaders to interview them about what God was doing in their country. They graciously answered all of my questions but then insisted that I extend my visit with them for several hours so they could ask me questions about what the Bible teaches about the future of Iraq, the future of Iran, and the future of other neighboring countries.

On that same trip, I was invited to preach at an Iraqi congregation that didn't even exist before the 2003 liberation. It was planted by a young pastor and is now filled to standing room only with new converts to Christianity, many of whom are from a Muslim background and most of whom had to flee the violence against and persecution of Christians in Baghdad. What did the pastor want me to speak on? "Are We Living in the Last Days?"

When I returned to Iraq in September 2008, I again found enormous interest from pastors and other Christian leaders there in Bible prophecy. The same was true when I traveled to Afghanistan in October 2008.

Unfortunately, too few pastors and Christian leaders in the epicenter have been taught much if anything about biblical eschatology. Too few feel equipped to study the subject on their own. But in my experience, it is certainly not for a lack of interest. At the same time, many Muslim leaders in the region are also interested in biblical eschatology, if for no other reason than that they want to compare it with what the mullahs and political leaders in Iran are teaching and what millions of Muslims are discussing in the streets and in their homes.

Here are my answers to the some of the questions I am asked most frequently.

What Does the Bible Teach About the Second Coming of Jesus Christ?

The Bible describes two separate and distinct future events, both of which are often described as the Second Coming.

668

The first event is what Bible scholars call the Rapture. In 1 Thessalonians 4:16–17, the apostle Paul writes that "the Lord Himself will descend from heaven with a shout, with the voice of the archangel and with the trumpet of God, and the dead in Christ will rise first. Then we who are alive and remain will be caught up together with them in the clouds to meet the Lord in the air, and so we shall always be with the Lord." In this passage, Paul is describing an event in which Jesus Christ will not physically, literally touch down on the earth but will first come "in the clouds" and snatch away His true followers from the earth in an instant of time. Those who have not chosen to follow Christ, those who have not been "born again," will remain behind on the earth and will have to go through a terrible time of wars, famines, natural disasters, and divine judgments known as the Tribulation.

The second event occurs at the end of the Tribulation. This is when the Bible teaches that Jesus will physically, literally return to earth, destroy His enemies, and set up His own righteous government based in Jerusalem. He will reign on earth for one thousand years. In Revelation 19:11–20:6, the apostle John writes, "I saw heaven opened, and behold, a white horse, and He who sat on it is called Faithful and True, and in righteousness He judges and wages war. His eyes are a flame of fire, and on His head are many diadems; and He has a name written on Him which no one knows except Himself. He is clothed with a robe dipped in blood, and His name is called The Word of God. . . . He will rule [the nations]. . . . And [an angel] laid hold of the dragon, the serpent of old, who is the devil and Satan, and

669

bound him for a thousand years; and he threw him into the abyss. . . . And I saw the souls of those who had been beheaded because of their testimony of Jesus and because of the word of God . . . and they came to life and reigned with Christ for a thousand years. . . . Blessed and holy is the one who has a part in the first resurrection; . . . they will be priests of God and of Christ and will reign with Him for a thousand years."

Are There Any Signs That Will Indicate When the Return of Jesus Christ Is Close at Hand, and If So, What Are They?

One day while Jesus and His disciples were sitting on the Mount of Olives, overlooking the city of Jerusalem, the disciples asked Him this very question. Their query is recounted in Matthew 24:3.

"Tell us," they said, "what will be the sign of Your coming, and of the end of the age?"

Jesus could have refused to answer the question. Instead, He answered them at great length and detail. His answers are recorded in Matthew chapter 24 and in Luke chapter 21, and they provide a checklist of signs to watch for. Among them:

- Revolutions (Luke 21:9, NIV)
- The rise of false prophets and false messiahs (Matthew 24:4–5, 11, 23–27)
- Wars and rumors of wars (Matthew 24:6)
- Nations rising against nations (Matthew 24:7)
- Kingdoms rising against kingdoms (Matthew 24:7)
- Famines (Matthew 24:7)
- Plagues (Luke 21:11)

- Earthquakes (Matthew 24:7) and "great earthquakes" (Luke 21:11)
- "Terrors" that lead to "men fainting from fear" (Luke 21:11, 26)
- Persecution of the believers (Matthew 24:9)
- Apostasy and betrayal of one another (Matthew 24:10)
- Increasing lawlessness (Matthew 24:12)
- People's love for one another growing cold (Matthew 24:12)
- "The roaring of the sea and the waves" (Luke 21:25)
- The good news (the gospel) of Christ's love and forgiveness will be preached "in the whole world as a testimony to all the nations" — even Muslim nations, even Radical nations — "and then the end will come" (Matthew 24:14)

Jesus cautioned His followers not to speculate on the exact time of the Rapture or the Second Coming. In Matthew 24:36, He said that "of that day and hour no one knows, not even the angels of heaven, nor the Son, but the Father alone." But "day and hour" is a very narrow slice of time. By giving us at least fifteen other specific signs that would be happening in the last days, Jesus clearly wanted us to know when the time of His return was rapidly approaching.

Why did He want His disciples to understand such signs? Jesus gave the answer in Matthew 24:42, when He said, "Therefore, be on the alert." He reinforced the point in the next verse, when again He urged His followers to be "on the alert." In Matthew 24:44, He stressed this critical point for a third time. "You also must be ready," He insisted, "for the Son of Man is coming at an hour when you do not think He will."

Revivalists who study these signs are coming to the conclusion that they are being fulfilled today and that we are, in fact, living in the last days. They are, after all, living through revolutions, wars and rumors of wars, and horrifying persecution, for starters.

They have no idea precisely when Jesus will return, of course. But given how closely world events are tracking with Bible prophecy, they find themselves increasingly motivated to "be ready" and "be prepared" for His arrival by living lives of holiness, by sharing the gospel with Muslims and nominal Christians, by making disciples of all nations, and by planting new church congregations throughout the region.

Is It Possible that We Will See the Emergence of an Actual Figure that Shia Muslims Will Point to As the Mahdi?

While I would not go so far as to predict that this will happen, I do believe followers of Jesus Christ should be on guard for such a possibility. Jesus repeatedly warned of false prophets and false messiahs in the last days before His own return. Therefore, we cannot rule out the possibility that someone claiming to be the Islamic messiah could appear, possibly even doing "great signs and wonders, so as to mislead, if possible, even the elect," as Jesus specifically warned about in Matthew 24:24.

If such an alleged "Islamic Messiah" does appear, a media feeding frenzy will ensue. People from all over the world will want to travel to the Middle East to see this false messiah. But Jesus warned His followers not to join the crowds. "For just as the lightning comes from the east and flashes even to the west, so will the coming of the Son of Man be," Jesus promised in Matthew 24:27. In other words, the Rapture of the Church will come fast and dramatically, like a bolt of lightning. True followers of Christ won't need to wander into the desert to find Jesus. The true Messiah will find them and snatch them away from this world in the twinkle of an eye.

Are These All the Signs of What Will Happen in the "Last Days," or Does the Bible Speak of Others?

There are actually a number of other noteworthy signs of the last days.

One very important sign can be found in the Old Testament book written by the Hebrew prophet Joel. The Lord God said through this prophet, "It will come about [in the last days] that I will pour out My Spirit on all mankind; and your sons and daughters will prophesy, your old men will dream dreams, your young men will see visions. Even on the male and female servants I will pour out My Spirit in those days" (Joel 2:28–29). Revivalists note the millions of Muslims coming to faith in Christ through dreams and visions as evidence that this sign is currently coming to pass as well.

Another set of important signs that will occur in the last days can be found in Ezekiel 36–39. I explored the details and implications of this series of prophesies at some length in my first nonfiction book, *Epicenter.* In these passages, the Hebrew prophet Ezekiel, writing more than 2,500 years ago, prophesied that:

- Israel will be reborn as a country (chapters 36–38)
- The Jews will return to the Holy Land after centuries in exile (36:10–11, 24, 37–38; 37:12, 21; 38:8, 12)
- The ancient ruins in Israel will be rebuilt (36:36)
- Israel's desolate, desert lands will again blossom and produce abundant food, fruit, and foliage (36:8–9, 30–35)
- Israel will have an "exceedingly great army" (37:10)

Many Arabs, Iranians, and others in the Middle East are not happy that Israel became a country on May 14, 1948, that millions of Jews have moved to Israel, and that the Israeli military has become powerful and highly effective. Nevertheless, a growing number of Revivalists are beginning to realize that these recent historical events — as difficult and as painful as they have been for themselves, their families, and their fellow countrymen — are actually the fulfillment of ancient biblical prophecies and thus further evidence that we are living in the last days.

What's more, a growing number of Revivalists are beginning to consider the possibility that other prophecies described by Ezekiel may not be far from fulfillment. Ezekiel wrote that when Israel is a country again and the Jews are feeling more secure in their ancient homeland than ever before, several dramatic events will occur. Among them:

- **A dictator known as Gog will rise to power in Russia, referred to in the Bible as Magog (Ezekiel 38:1–4).** This is raising eyebrows, since some believe a dictator has been rising to power in Russia in recent years.

- **This Russian dictator will then form an alliance with Iran (Ezekiel 38:5).** This was odd given that for most of the last several thousand years the Russians and Iranians have hated each other. In recent years, however, Moscow and Tehran have aggressively developed military, diplomatic, and economic ties.

- **The Russian leader will then form other regional alliances with countries such as Sudan and Ethiopia (the territories known in ancient Bible times as "Cush"), with Libya and Algeria (ancient "Put"), with Turkey (ancient "Gomer"), and with the Turkic-speaking peoples of central Asia (ancient "Beth-togarmah") (Ezekiel 38:5–6).** Geopolitical analysts note that Russia has been forming these very alliances over the past decade or so and selling billions of dollars' worth of weapons to these countries.

- **The Russian leader will then "devise an evil plan" and marshal Iran, Libya, and these other countries to form a military coalition to surround Israel and try to destroy her (Ezekiel 38:10).** Iran has been steadily preparing to attack Israel. Sudan and Libya have demonstrated hostility towards the Jewish state as well. Russia's invasion of Georgia in the summer of 2008 raised new questions about whether it is developing hostile intentions toward other states to its south.

- **The bulk of this Russian-Iranian military coalition will come against the mountains of Israel from the north (Ezekiel 38:8–12, 15; 39:1–2).** This indicates either that the governments of Lebanon and Syria will be actively engaged in the "evil plan" to wipe the Jews off the map and seize Jewish wealth or that they will have been overrun by Russian and Iranian forces. Curiously, Russia has accelerated its efforts to develop a stronger military alliance with Syria in recent years, selling billions of dollars' worth of weapons to Damascus and even building a massive new port for the Russian Navy on the Syrian coast. Hezbollah, meanwhile, continues to maintain strong ties to Iran and Syria.

- **Egypt, one of Israel's most fearsome historic enemies, is never mentioned in Ezekiel 38–39, suggesting that this great power does not play an active role in these prophecies.** This is particularly intriguing given that Egypt signed a peace treaty with Israel in 1979. It is a cold peace, to be sure, but it is peace nonetheless, meaning that we are living in the first sliver of time in some five thousand years that Egypt is not likely to go to war against the Jews in the near future.

- **Iraq, another major enemy of Israel throughout history and the Saddam era, is also not mentioned in Ezekiel 38–39, not by any of its ancient names, including Babel, Babylon, Babylonia, Mesopotamia, or Shinar.** Since the fall of Saddam Hussein and the rise of Prime Minister

Nouri al-Maliki and President Jalal Talabani, Iraq has posed no strategic threat to Israel at all. The Iraqi government has shown little interest in making a formal peace treaty with Israel to date. But Iraq currently has too many internal troubles and weaknesses to launch a war or join a war against the Jewish state any time soon. This is significant in that not once in the 2,500-plus years since Ezekiel wrote down the prophecies have *both* Egypt and Iraq not been an immediate strategic threat to the Jewish people.

- **Ezekiel tells us that all of these events "shall come about in the last days" (Ezekiel 38:16).**

Let me be clear: As I wrote in *Epicenter,* I have no idea whether this prophetic war — known to Bible scholars as the "War of Gog and Magog" — will come to pass in our lifetime, much less soon. Nevertheless, the trajectory of events over the past ten years or so has been curious, to say the least. What's more, we have seen most of the prophecies in Ezekiel 36 and 37 (the rebirth of Israel and the return of Jews to the Holy Land) come true since 1948. This raises the distinct possibility that Ezekiel 38 and 39 could come to complete fulfillment in our lifetime as well. In my view, we certainly cannot rule it out.[1]

What Are the Implications of the War of Gog and Magog for the People of the Middle East?

First, the bad news. The War of Gog and Magog will be unlike any other war in human history. Ezekiel clearly indicates that no country comes to the aid of Israel as she finds herself surrounded by the Russian-Iranian-Libyan alliance. Rather, Ezekiel explains that the God of the Bible will actually go to war on behalf of Israel and against her enemies, with supernatural and devastating results. Ezekiel 38:18–20 indicates that "on that day, when Gog comes against the land of Israel" the Lord God says, "My fury will mount up in My anger. In My zeal and in My blazing wrath I declare that on that day there will surely be a great earthquake in the land of Israel. The fish of the sea, the birds of the heavens, the beasts of the field, all the creeping things that creep on the earth, and all the men who are on the face of the earth will shake at My presence." The earthquake will be epicentered in Israel, but its shock waves will be felt around the world.

This massive earthquake, however, is only the beginning. "I shall call for a sword against him on all My mountains," declares the Lord God in Ezekiel 38:21. "Every man's sword will be against his brother." In other words, in the ensuing chaos, the enemy forces arrayed against Israel will begin fighting one another. The war will begin all right, but Russian and Muslim forces will be firing at one another, not at the Jews. "With pestilence and with blood I will enter into judgment with him," the Lord God continues in Ezekiel 38:22, referring to the Russian dictator known as Gog. "And I will rain on him and on his troops, and on the many peoples who are with him, a torrential rain, with hailstones, fire and brimstone."

This will be the most terrifying sequence of events in human history to date. On the heels of a terrifying supernatural global earthquake that will undoubtedly take many lives will come a cascading series of other disasters. Pandemic diseases,

678

for example, will sweep through the troops of the Russian coalition as well as through "the many peoples" who support these troops in their war of annihilation against Israel. And the attackers will face other judgments such as have rarely been seen since the cataclysmic showdown in Egypt between Moses and Pharaoh (Exodus 7–11). Deadly and devastating hailstorms will hit these enemy forces and their supporters (reminiscent of Exodus 9). So, too, will apocalyptic firestorms that will call to mind both the terrible judgment of Sodom and Gomorrah (Genesis 19) and the most frightening of Hollywood's long list of disaster films. But such events will be neither ancient history nor fiction. They will be all too immediate, real, and tragic.

The firestorms will be geographically widespread and exceptionally deadly. In Ezekiel 39:6, the Lord says, "I will rain down fire on Magog and on all your allies who live safely on the coasts. Then they will know that I am the Lord" (NLT). This suggests that targets throughout Russia and the former Soviet Union, as well as Russia's allies, will be supernaturally struck on this day of judgment and partially or completely consumed. These could be limited to nuclear missile silos, military bases, radar installations, defense ministries, intelligence headquarters, and other government buildings of various kinds. But other targets could very well include religious centers, such as mosques, madrasses, Islamic schools and universities, and other facilities where hatred against Jews and Christians is preached and where calls for the destruction of Israel are sounded. Either way, we will have to expect extensive collateral damage; many civilians will be at severe risk.

679

Ezekiel 39:12 tells us that the devastation will be so immense that it will take seven full months for Israel to bury all the bodies of the enemies in her midst, to say nothing of the dead and wounded back in the coalition countries. What's more, the process would actually take much longer except that scores of bodies will be devoured by carnivorous birds and beasts that will be drawn to the battlefields like moths to a flame. "Call all the birds and wild animals," the Lord God tells His prophet in Ezekiel 39:17–19 (NLT). "Say to them: Gather together for my great sacrificial feast. Come from far and near to the mountains of Israel, and there eat flesh and drink blood! Eat the flesh of mighty men and drink the blood of princes as though they were rams, lambs, goats, and bulls. . . . Gorge yourselves with flesh until you are glutted; drink blood until you are drunk. This is the sacrificial feast I have prepared for you."

A more gruesome sight is hard to imagine, but again, this is not the stuff of fiction. Ezekiel is giving us an intelligence report of the future, a future that is steadily approaching.

Is There Any Good News That Will Come Out of the War of Gog and Magog?

Fortunately, there is some good news.

First, while none of us wishes these events would happen at all, at least God in His love and mercy has chosen to give the whole world advance warning of what is coming. Through the Bible, God is urging people to repent and become followers of Jesus Christ before these terrible events come to pass.

Second, in Ezekiel 39:21, God says, "I will set

My glory among the nations; and all the nations will see My judgment." In Ezekiel 39:29, He says that He will pour out the Holy Spirit on His chosen people.

What does this tell us? It certainly tells us that these events will be a judgment of God's enemies in keeping with Genesis 12:1–3, where God says He will bless those who bless Israel and curse those who curse Israel.

But it also says that the War of Gog and Magog will be a key moment in a great spiritual awakening that will sweep through the epicenter and the entire world. The God of the Bible will literally and metaphorically shake people out of spiritual apathy and lethargy to help them realize that there is a God in heaven who loves them and has a wonderful plan for their lives if they will repent, turn from their wicked ways, and follow His ways. When God pours out His Holy Spirit, many will suddenly realize that the only way to find peace with God — and peace with their neighbors — is through faith in Jesus Christ.

Moreover, God will shake both those who are nominal Christians and those who are born-again followers of Christ but have not been particularly serious about or devoted to their faith. He will awaken them spiritually. He will revive them and cause them to live their lives wholly and completely to please Jesus Christ and to make disciples of all nations, just as He commanded.

True, the lead-up to this prophetic war, the war itself, and its immediate aftermath will be very dark days for the people of Russia, Iran, Libya, Sudan, Turkey, and their Muslim allies. But the Bible tells us that this will also be a new birth of freedom for all the people of the region, an opportunity to actually see for themselves the glory of the living God.

What Else Does the Bible Tell Us About the Future of Iran?

We learn more about God's ultimate plan for Iran (sometimes referred to in the Old Testament as "Elam") from the book of Jeremiah. Jeremiah 49:34–39 says:

That which came as the word of the LORD to Jeremiah the prophet concerning Elam, at the beginning of the reign of Zedekiah king of Judah, saying:

"Thus says the LORD of hosts,
'Behold, I am going to break the bow of Elam,
The finest of their might.
I will bring upon Elam the four winds
From the four ends of heaven,
And will scatter them to all these winds;
And there will be no nation
To which the outcasts of Elam will not go.
So I will shatter Elam before their enemies
And before those who seek their lives;
And I will bring calamity upon them,
Even My fierce anger,' declares the LORD,
'And I will send out the sword after them
Until I have consumed them.
Then I will set My throne in Elam
And destroy out of it king and princes,'
Declares the LORD.
'But it will come about in the last days
That I will restore the fortunes of Elam,'
Declares the LORD."

Allow me to draw out several key points from this passage:

- Verse 39 is important because it tells us that these events are going to happen in "the last days."
- The passage tells us that in the last days, God will scatter the people of Iran all over the earth (verse 36). This actually happened in 1979. For the first time in history, Iranians have been scattered all over the globe. An estimated 5 million Iranians now live outside of their home country.
- God says He is going to "break" the current structure of Iran (verse 35).
- God says that He will "shatter Elam [Iran] before their enemies" (verse 37).
- God says He will bring His "fierce anger" against the leaders of Iran (verse 37).
- God says, "I will send out the sword after them until I have consumed them" (verse 37).
- God says He will specifically "destroy" Iran's "king and princes" (verse 38).
- Despite all this terrible judgment, God specifically promises to "set My throne in Elam" — that is, be the God and King of the people of Iran (verse 38).
- God also promises to "restore the fortunes of Elam" (verse 39).

One view of the promise in verse 39 to "restore the fortunes" of Iran is that after judging Iran's leaders and military, God will allow the people of Iran to become politically peaceful and economically prosperous. I, however, lean toward the view

683

held by many Iranian Revivalists who believe that God specifically means He will bless the people of Iran spiritually.

Iranian Christians believe that God is going to pour out His love and forgiveness and His Holy Spirit on the people of Iran, open the eyes of their hearts, and help them to see clearly that Jesus Christ is the only Savior of the world and that through faith in Him they can know and experience God's love and plan for their lives. They also believe that Iran will then become a "sending country," a base camp, as it were, from which thousands — perhaps tens of thousands — of Iranian followers of Christ will fan out throughout the epicenter, preaching the gospel, making disciples, and planting churches.

What Does the Bible Tell Us About the Future of Iraq?

As I wrote in the first edition of *Epicenter* back in 2006 — during the height of the terrorist insurgency in Iraq — a careful study of Bible prophecy indicates that in time Iraq will form a strong, stable, and decisive central government. Iraq's military and internal security forces will be well trained, well equipped, and increasingly effective. The insurgency will be crushed, support for it will evaporate, and foreign terrorists will stop flowing into the country.

As the situation stabilizes, Iraqi roads and airports will become safe, and people will finally be able to move freely about the country. Tourists will come in droves to visit the country's many ancient archeological sites and national treasures. Business leaders will pour into the country, as will foreign investment, particularly to get Iraq's oil fields, refineries, and shipping facilities up to twenty-first-century standards.

Once these things happen, Iraq will emerge as an oil superpower rivaling Saudi Arabia. Trillions of petrodollars will flood the country, making Iraq a magnet for banks and multinational corporations that will set up their regional and international headquarters in the country. High-rise office buildings, luxury apartments, and single-family homes will be constructed. Theaters, concert halls, parks, and malls will be built. The ancient city of Babylon will emerge virtually overnight like a phoenix rising from the ashes to become one of the modern wonders of the world.

Iraq is about to see a political and economic renaissance unparalleled in the history of the world. The people of Iraq are about to experience a level of personal and national wealth and power they have never dreamed possible. The pundits who have written the country off to failure and chaos will be absolutely stunned by such a dramatic turn of events, much as those who said the Berlin Wall would never come down and the Soviet empire would never collapse found themselves scratching their heads in disbelief just a few years later.

How can I be so sure? By studying Bible prophecy.

Iraq is described by the Hebrew prophets Ezekiel, Isaiah, Jeremiah, and Daniel, as well as by the apostle John in the book of Revelation, as a center of unprecedented wealth and power in the last days before the return of Christ. The Bible teaches that the city of Babylon will be resurrected from the dead in the last days. In Revelation 18 (NLT), Babylon is described as "a great city" and a center of "extravagant luxury." What's more, Iraq is described as one of the world's great commercial hubs, where "the merchants of the world" come to trade "great quantities of gold, silver, jewels, and pearls" along with all kinds of other "expensive" goods and services that entice "the kings of the world" and draw ships from everywhere on the planet. When the people of the world think about the great wealth of Iraq's future capital, they will ask themselves and each other, "Where is there another city as great as this?"

We also learn from the book of Revelation that Iraq will eventually become a center of great evil as well as wealth and at the end of history will face a judgment similar to the War of Gog and Magog. But before that, the Scriptures are clear: Iraq will be rich and powerful.

What's more, the judgment of Russia, Iran, and other Middle Eastern countries will work to Iraq's advantage. Oil and gas exports from those countries will be slowed or halted altogether because of the terrible destruction described by Ezekiel. Iraq, meanwhile, as one of the few Middle Eastern countries not having participated in the attack on Israel, will be one of the few oil powers left intact when the smoke clears. As oil and gas prices skyrocket due to severe shortages, the world will become increasingly dependent upon Iraq for energy, and money will pour into the country's coffers like never before.

Before Iraq can be so wealthy, however, the nation must become stable, peaceful, and free. Only then can the physical and financial infrastructure necessary for such dramatic economic growth be set in place. Only then will international oil companies invest heavily in refurbishing Iraq's drilling, refining, and export equipment and facilities. Only then will the merchants of the world begin establishing headquarters in Iraq, dramatically increasing the level of trade done in and through Iraq.

In my view, we are seeing the early stages of these biblical prophecies come to pass right now in Iraq. Tremendous — almost miraculous — military, political, and economic progress has been made in Iraq since 2006. It has not been easy to get through the birth pangs. It has not been painless. It has not been without mistakes, some tragic and costly.

But a new Iraq has been born. It is now growing, developing, and moving in the right direction. I have seen it with my own eyes, and it is quite the sight to behold. The U.S. and our Coalition allies have played a critical — and I would say heroic — role in making such progress possible. Real credit is also due to Reformers such as President Talabani and Prime Minister Maliki and their staff and advisors. The U.S. and European naysayers who said the "surge" would not work in Iraq were wrong. Those who said al Qaeda and the Mahdi Army could not be defeated were wrong. Those who said Talabani and Maliki could not help move their country forward were wrong. Iraq is a success story now, and it will be even more so in the days ahead.

That said, if you really want to know what Iraq will look like in the not-too-distant future, allow me to recommend that you do what I did in the fall of 2008: visit Dubai, the high-tech, high-finance city in the United Arab Emirates, on the southern shores of the Persian Gulf. I was absolutely blown away when I visited the city in 2008.

Twenty years ago, the city was almost entirely a desert. Today, it is a metropolis that boasts some of the most expensive and elite malls, hotels, office buildings, banks, and resorts in the world. It has designer islands built from scratch, holding some of the most expensive homes in the region. Private jets and private yachts frequent the city constantly. High-priced American and European designer clothing shops and jewelry stores and car dealers are everywhere. Starbucks is ubiquitous. Dubai even has an indoor ski resort that operates year-round despite outdoor temperatures often averaging well over 100 degrees Fahrenheit. Its motto: "The coolest thing to do in Dubai."

Perhaps most remarkably, Dubai is home of the famed $4 billion Burj Dubai, which at nearly half a mile high is the tallest man-made structure on the face of the planet. I can personally attest that it is a breathtaking sight, soaring far above anything else on the horizon in any direction. Engineers and architects have come from all over the world to marvel at it.

In fact, the Burj is now triggering competition. An engineering company in Wales says it has been retained to build an even bigger structure, the Mile High Tower in Jeddah, Saudi Arabia, which executives say will be at least 5,250 feet high. Meanwhile, the Russian press is reporting plans for a *two-mile-high* skyscraper in Moscow known as the Ultima Tower, complete with parks, gardens, artificial rivers and hills, apartment houses, schools, kindergartens, and all manner of stores, all built inside the tower.[2]

Can it be long before engineers announce plans to build new towers of Babel like these in Iraq, even in the new city of Babylon itself?

Chapter Thirty-Two:
Join the Revolution

Christians have the "love your enemy"
strategy all to themselves

Judeo-Christian civilization today faces the most
dangerous moment in the history of the Islamic
Revolution.

Three decades after the rise of the Ayatollah
Khomeini in Iran, the millions of Radical Islamic
jihadists he inspired — both Shias and Sunnis —
are determined to finish what he began. Some are
driven by apocalyptic eschatology. They are using
genocidal rhetoric. They are building alliances
with nuclear-armed nations. And they are feverishly trying to build, buy, or steal weapons of mass
destruction to accomplish their maniacal dreams.

Yet far too many in both the West and the East
— political, military, and intelligence leaders as
well as everyday citizens — are asleep to the
gathering storm. In my judgment, this lack of
awareness poses the greatest danger of all. An
intellectually honest, spiritually strong, morally
courageous, politically united global alliance
against the Radicals could be enormously successful. We have more people, more money, better
technology, and better ideas than the Radicals.

689

But should we succumb to the ignorance, apathy, callousness, hubris, and fear already so pervasive among many of our leaders, we will find ourselves facing cataclysms of biblical proportions that will make the attacks of September 11, 2001, pale by comparison.

It is time to wake up.

It is time to awaken our neighbors.

It is time for every citizen who values life, liberty, and the pursuit of happiness to shake off lethargy and join the Revolution to defeat the Radicals, encourage the Reformers, and strengthen the Revivalists — now, while there is still time.

My prayer is that some of you who read this book will be inspired to follow the powerful examples set by men like Jerry Boykin, Fred Schwien, Porter Goss, and others — men who have devoted their lives, their fortunes, and their sacred honor to the defense of their nation. Free nations of the world urgently need more of such selfless public servants. We need men and women who willingly choose to serve in the military, in government security agencies, and in various intelligence agencies. We need men and women who will run for and serve in public office — and do so for the good of the country, not for their own personal gain. Might you join them?

My prayer, too, is that some of you who read this book will be inspired to follow the example set by leaders like Hamid Karzai, Jalal Talabani, King Mohammed VI, and Benazir Bhutto — leaders who have devoted their entire lives to fighting the Radicals and expanding freedom and opportunity for the people of the nations they serve. The Muslim world urgently needs more Reformers like these, men and women prepared to protect the poor, defend widows, care for orphans, provide justice for the downtrodden, and protect and advance the human rights of every single man, woman, and child in their countries, regardless of their race, religion, or political beliefs.

At the same time, the Muslim world needs hundreds of millions of sincere and selfless friends in both the West and the East who choose to help the Reformers succeed against the Radicals in every possible way. We need people who will invest in the economies of Reformer countries. We need people who will set up and run successful businesses in Reformer countries. We need people who will direct humanitarian relief organizations that serve people in Reformer countries. We also need people willing to advise and counsel Reformer leaders in areas of democratic change, religious freedom, science, technology, economic development, and the like. Now is the critical time to raise up a new generation of people to help the Reformers succeed against the Radicals. Will you be among them?

As you may have guessed by now, my deepest heartfelt prayer is that each of you who read this book will be inspired to follow the example set by the Revivalists, men and women who — regardless of their past religious beliefs — ultimately have chosen to follow Jesus Christ as the only way of salvation and in so doing have found true peace and forgiveness and personal transformation by His death on the cross in Jerusalem and His resurrection from the dead three days later. What's more, I pray that you will be inspired by the Revivalists' commitment to love their neighbors and love their enemies through the power of the Holy Spirit — just as Jesus did — and that you

691

will be moved to stand with them and help them in this dramatic yet dangerous hour.

A Personal Journey

I did not grow up thinking I would write novels or nonfiction books about Muslims. I am the son of a Gentile mother and a Jewish father. Both of them became followers of Jesus in 1973, and I became a follower of Jesus in 1975. My wife is a Gentile with a deep love for the Jewish people, and she also became a Christ-follower in the early 1970s. When we fell in love in the late 1980s and married in the summer of 1990, we had a great passion to travel to Israel and bless the Jewish people in real and practical ways. But the Lord took us down an unexpected path.

For the first thirteen years of our marriage, the Lord prevented Lynn and me from traveling to Israel. Instead, He took us to Muslim countries and brought one Revivalist leader after another into our lives to befriend us and help us understand God's heart of compassion for the Muslim people.

These Revivalists shared with us firsthand stories of how they had seen the God of the Bible transforming the lives of Muslims through the love of Jesus Christ. They taught us how to love Muslims by praying for them. They showed us how to love Muslims by providing food for the hungry, water for the thirsty, and comfort for the afflicted. They shared with us the sorrows and joys they had experienced serving Muslims in the name of Jesus while under the constant threat of persecution, arrest, torture, and death.

Along the way, their hearts became our heart. Lynn and I developed an overwhelming — and, honestly, unexpected — love for the Muslim people that has come to complement our love for Jews. We found ourselves wanting to bless Muslims as we had always wanted to bless the Jews. We certainly were not born with such love. We had to be born again first. And then we had to see such supernatural love in action. When we did, our lives were forever changed.

Love in Action in Iraq

In Iraq, I once met a dear follower of Jesus Christ who had nearly been killed for his faith. Several years ago, death threats forced him to flee the city where he was engaged in a very effective ministry, and he resettled in a city he had never lived in before. He began to pray, *Lord, how would You have me serve You in this new city? How can I love my neighbors and my enemies? Please give me the wisdom and the courage to serve You faithfully.*

The Lord loves to answer prayers like that, and soon He told this man to go meet with the mayor of the city and offer to bring several trucks filled with humanitarian relief supplies to the needy Muslims in that community. The man obeyed. Yet when he arrived in the mayor's office and asked if he and his Christian colleagues could distribute such relief supplies, the mayor looked puzzled and for a moment just sat there saying nothing, seemingly unsure how to respond.

Rather than give the man an answer, the mayor pressed the intercom on his desk and ordered his secretary to summon the local mullah.

The Christian leader grew scared. He had no desire to meet with a mullah. He was, after all, on the run from Radical mullahs. Nevertheless, a few minutes later, the Islamic cleric arrived.

The mayor said, "This man is a Christian. He has trucks filled with food, clothing, Bibles, and DVDs about the life of Jesus. Go back to the mosque and tell all the people to gather because the Christians have come to bless us."

My friend was stunned. In all his years of ministry in Iraq, he had never experienced such a moment. Yet to his shock, the mullah agreed. He went back to the mosque, and a few minutes later, my friend heard an announcement booming from the loudspeakers on the minarets. "Come to the mosque," the mullah declared. "The Christians are here to bless us!"

My friend made a quick phone call and told his colleagues to bring the trucks filled with relief supplies to the mosque. Before long, hundreds of local Iraqi Muslims had gathered. Rather than attacking the Christians, however, the Muslims were happy and excited. And when the trucks arrived, most wanted the copies of the New Testaments and the DVDs about Jesus first. Only afterward did they seek out the rest of the relief supplies.

When this Iraqi Christian leader told me his story, I found myself moved to tears. I was not raised to hate Muslims. But it had never dawned on me while I was growing up to specifically find ways to bless Muslims in the name of Jesus. Nor, for that matter, had it ever occurred to me that I might live in a period of human history when Rank-and-File Muslims might actually respond positively to practical expressions of Christlike love.

I immediately pledged to this Iraqi brother that I would go back to the U.S. and raise money through the Joshua Fund to help him and his team acquire more Bibles, more films about Jesus, and more humanitarian relief supplies to bless more Muslims. By the grace of God, this is exactly what we have done, and by the grace of God, we hope to do more and to mobilize others to do more as well.

Love in Action in Afghanistan

In Afghanistan, I once met a man who told me he had been a Radical Muslim growing up in the 1980s and '90s but had been imprisoned by the Taliban in 1999 for not being Radical enough. His beard wasn't long enough to suit the Taliban fighters. Moreover, they thought he was a spy for the Northern Alliance, though he was not.

"There were 350 of us in the wing of the prison that I was assigned to," he told me. "The Taliban didn't feed any of us. It was winter, and they didn't give us blankets or warm clothes. They wanted to starve us to death or let us die of exposure."

He feared for his life. He feared he would never see his wife and children again. And his fears were well founded. Eighty men died over the next few weeks.

Then one day the Taliban guards permitted representatives from the Red Cross to visit the prison. "They brought some bread, shoes, jackets, blankets," the man recalled. It wasn't much, but the aid was desperately needed.

"I started asking myself, why are these people helping me?" he told me. "These Red Cross people are not Muslims. They are Christians. Yet they are showing me more love than my fellow followers of Islam. Why?"

This simple act of compassion set into motion a chain of events that would change this Afghan man's life forever. It led this Radical Muslim to question whether Islam was even true. It caused him to ask himself, "Why do the people who love Jesus love me?" It made him hunger to know whether Jesus Christ was the One True God.

Looking back, the man told me he doesn't even know if the Red Cross volunteers who came to his prison were actually born-again Christians. But they showed him compassion in the name of the cross, and this had a profound effect on him. Eventually he was released. He moved to Islamabad, Pakistan. He found his brother, who had become a follower of Jesus Christ. He found other Muslim converts to Christianity. And in time, he too became a fully devoted follower of Jesus.

Today this man is an effective MBB ministry leader on the front lines of the most dramatic spiritual Revolution of our time. He has a passion for demonstrating the love of Christ to other Afghans, and he prays that because of his efforts, they will be drawn to the love of the Savior and find forgiveness and new hope in His name.

The Road Ahead
These stories — and countless others like them — have led me over the past two decades to one fundamental conclusion: Jesus' strategy of "love your neighbors" and "love your enemies" is the key to winning the hearts and minds of the Muslim people, and Christians have this strategy all to themselves.

No one else in the Islamic world is teaching people to show love, mercy, and compassion to those who hate them and want to destroy them. No one else in the Islamic world is offering forgiveness to those who have committed acts of evil against them. Only the true followers of Jesus are doing these things, because only people who have been born again and truly transformed by the Holy Spirit have the capacity to love their enemies. None of us have that ability in and of ourselves as normal human beings. So when we demonstrate Christlike love to our enemies, we show the Muslim world that we serve a different God, the One True God, the God of love and power and forgiveness.

Imagine if more of the Church around the world were mobilized to love our neighbors and our enemies in the name of Jesus. Already, Muslims are becoming Revivalists in record numbers. What if God wants to accelerate this trend? What if He wants us to be part of that acceleration?

Lynn and I and the Joshua Fund team believe that is exactly what the Lord wants, and we have dedicated ourselves to helping mobilize the Church to pursue four simple strategies: learn, pray, give, and go. Let me close, therefore, by sharing a few thoughts with those of you who want to know more about these strategies and who may already be considering joining the Revolution and aiding the Revivalists.

Strategy No. 1: Learn
"Look among the nations! Observe! Be astonished! Wonder! Because I am doing something in your days — you would not believe if you were told." — Ha-bakkuk 1:5

First and foremost, I would encourage you to study the Bible for yourself and discover God's plan and purpose for all the people of the Middle East. You will, of course, find much about the

Lord's great love for the Jewish people and the nation of Israel. At the same time, a careful reading will help you discover God's tremendous love for Iraqis, Iranians, Egyptians, Kurds, Arabs, Turks, and many others in the epicenter as well.

The Iraqi people, for example, are central players in the Bible, from Genesis to Revelation. Many Bible scholars and archaeologists believe that the Garden of Eden was likely in Iraq. Genesis 11 and 12 indicate that God chose Abraham from Ur of the Chaldeans — a town in Iraq, located south of Baghdad — to bless all the peoples of the earth.

The Lord told the Hebrew prophet Daniel critical details about the promised Messiah and about events that would occur in the last days while Daniel was living in Iraq. Though Daniel and his friends were Jews, they were actually raised in Iraq, had a great love for the people of Iraq, and served the king and people of the Babylonian empire in the name of the God of the Bible.

The Hebrew prophet Ezekiel likewise received his visions of events in the last days while he was living in Iraq. And the Hebrew prophets Jonah and Nahum were sent by God to speak to the people of Iraq and urge them to repent of their sins and cry out for God's love and forgiveness.*

What's more, 1 Peter 5:13 suggests that the apostle Peter may have actually written his first letter to the Church from Iraq. Finally, the book of Revelation (chapters 17 and 18) indicates that

*Nahum is actually buried in the Iraqi town of Elkosh, and my Joshua Fund colleague Jeremy Grafman and I have had the privilege of visiting his tomb and seeing the ancient Hebrew writing on the walls of the ancient facility enclosing the tomb.

all the eyes of the nations will be riveted on Iraq in the last days.

All told, of the sixty-six books in the Bible, fully twenty-two mention Iraq, referring to Babylon, Mesopotamia, Chaldea, or Shinar, the ancient names for the modern-day country we call Iraq.

The Bible is clear that the Iranian people are dear to God's heart as well. After serving the Babylonian leaders, Daniel later served the leaders of Persia and spoke God's Word to the Persian people. Daniel is even buried in Iran. I have Iranian MBB friends who have visited his tomb. The Hebrew prophets Jeremiah and Ezekiel were also used by God to speak directly to the Iranian people. The book of Esther describes how God raised up a young woman to become the queen of Persia and use her lofty position to bless both the Jewish people and the people of Iran. Many Bible scholars believe that at least two of the "wise men" who came "from the East" to visit baby Jesus were from Iran. All told, no fewer than eleven books of the Bible refer to Persia or Elam, the ancient names for Iran.

The Bible also teaches that God loves the Egyptian people. Abraham's son Ishmael was born to an Egyptian mother. Moses was born in Egypt. The entire nation of Israel was, of course, sent to live in Egypt for 430 years. What's more, many of the great men and women of Scripture were sent by God to Egypt. Among them: Abraham and Sarah; Joseph and his brothers; and later Joseph, Mary, and the baby Jesus.

One of Lynn's and my favorite passages about God's love for the Egyptians and how He will bless them in the last days comes from Isaiah 19:18–25, which reads in part: "In the land of

Egypt . . . they will cry to the LORD because of oppressors, and He will send them a Savior and a Champion, and He will deliver them. Thus the LORD will make Himself known to Egypt, and the Egyptians will know the LORD in that day. . . . They will return to the Lord, and He will respond to them and will heal them. In that day, there will be a highway from Egypt to Assyria, and the Assyrians will come into Egypt and the Egyptians into Assyria, and the Egyptians will worship with the Assyrians. In that day, Israel will be the third party with Egypt and Assyria, a blessing in the midst of the earth, whom the LORD of hosts has blessed, saying, 'Blessed is Egypt My people, and Assyria the work of My hands, and Israel My inheritance.' "

The Kurdish people are also beloved by God. They are mentioned prominently and repeatedly in the Bible — in the Old Testament and the New — as the Medes and the Median Empire. (The Medes joined with the Iranians in ancient times to create the Media-Persian Empire, which took over the Babylonian Empire about six hundred years before Christ.) The prophet Jeremiah describes the Kurds as key end times players whom God will use to bring judgment on the forces of the Antichrist in a revived Babylonian empire (see Jeremiah 51). The book of Acts indicates that there were actually Kurdish people present in Jerusalem when the good news of Christ's love and forgiveness was preached on the Day of Pentecost (Acts 2:9).

What's more, the Kurds may have been among the first to realize that Jesus was the Jewish Messiah and the Savior of the world. When I made my first trip to Iraq, I had the privilege of having a several-hour meeting with Mr. Falakaddin Kakaye, the minister of culture for the Kurdistan Regional Government. Mr. Kakaye was enormously generous in helping me understand the historic contributions of the Kurds. What fascinated me most, however, was that for the first ten minutes, the minister made a compelling case that at least one of the three "magi" or wise men who came to find and worship Jesus as the "King of the Jews" in Matthew 2 was a Kurd. "You've convinced me," I replied. "Apparently, wise men from Kurdistan have been seeking to worship Jesus from the beginning."

I am, of course, just scratching the surface in explaining how often the Bible describes God's love for *all* the people of the epicenter, not just the Jews. In Matthew 4:24–25, you will find the news of Jesus' love and forgiveness spreading throughout all of Syria and Jordan. In Matthew 15:21–28, you will find Jesus in southern Lebanon, showing mercy to the people of Tyre and Sidon and healing the daughter of a woman imploring Him to show kindness to those who want to serve Him. In Acts 2, you will read that God poured out the Holy Spirit on the apostles, who immediately began preaching the good news of Christ's love and forgiveness to the Parthians (from northern Iran); the Medes (the Kurds); the Elamites (from southern Iran); the Mesopotamians (Iraqis); those from Cappadocia, Pontus, Asia, Phrygia, and Pamphilia (Turks); Egyptians; Libyans; people from Crete; and Arabs.

The bottom line: I have no doubt that the more you study the Bible for yourself, the more you will learn about God's great love for all the people of the epicenter — and the more you will be inspired to love them too.

Strategy No. 2: Pray
"Be joyful in hope, patient in affliction, faithful in prayer." — Romans 12:12, NIV

As you become more knowledgeable about the people of the Muslim world, let me encourage you to begin praying faithfully and consistently for them, because this is what the Bible teaches us to do. Here are ten specific ideas you might use in praying for the people of the epicenter:

1. Praise God that He loves *all* the people of the world and sent His Son to rescue *anyone* who will repent and turn to Him for salvation. (John 3:16)
2. Pray for the peace of Jerusalem and for the peace of all the people in the region. (Psalm 122:6)
3. Pray for God's blessing on Israel and her neighbors. (Genesis 12:1–3)
4. Pray for open doors for the gospel so that everyone in the epicenter can hear and respond to Christ's offer of salvation to anyone who believes. (Colossians 4:2–6; Revelation 3:20)
5. Pray for Christ-followers in the epicenter to have the courage to "fearlessly make known the mystery of the gospel" despite intense persecution that may accelerate in the years ahead. (Ephesians 6:19–20, NIV)
6. Pray for the Radicals and those who persecute the Church, that God would change their hearts and draw them into His Kingdom. (Matthew 5:44)

702

7. Pray that the Lord would open the hearts of the Christ-followers in the region so that they might know Christ even more fully than they do now. (Ephesians 2:15–23)
8. Pray that the Lord of the harvest would raise up and send out more laborers because "the harvest" of souls "is plentiful." (Luke 10:2)
9. Pray without ceasing, and do so with thanksgiving, "for this is God's will for you in Christ Jesus." (1 Thessalonians 5:16–18)
10. Pray in the name of Jesus, for this is where the real power lies. (Matthew 18:19–20)

We who are followers of Jesus Christ serve a prayer-hearing and a prayer-answering God — a wonder-working God. This is what the Bible clearly teaches, even if we do not fully understand why a sovereign God should respond to our entreaties. So as you pray for the people of the epicenter, let me also encourage you to gather others around you as part of a prayer team. The members of the early Church often gathered together for prayer, as we read about in the Gospels and in the book of Acts. This is a wise model for us to follow. We need more than individuals engaged in prayer. We need to see a global movement of "prayer warriors" raised up by God, interceding on behalf of the persecuted Church in the Islamic world and for the spiritual and political liberation of all the people in the epicenter.

For more information on how to pray knowledgeably and consistently, you may want to sign up for my Flash Traffic e-mails at www.joelrosen berg.com. These e-mails provide updates every week or so on the geopolitical, economic, and spiritual trends in Israel and the Muslim world. They also provide updates on Joshua Fund projects and will provide specific (and often urgent) prayer requests that you and your family and friends can focus on as well. You can find more prayer resources on our Web site and blog at www.joshuafund.net.

In order to give you a sense of how we are trying to help educate and mobilize this movement of prayer, here are a few sample updates we have sent out in recent years:

April 26, 2007: "Last week saw the brutal murder of three evangelical Christians — two Turks and a German — working at a Bible publisher" in Turkey, we noted, quoting press accounts. "According to Turkish newspaper reports, the five young males arrested at the scene told investigators they committed the crime in defense of Islam. . . . Violent attacks against Christian targets are becoming more frequent. Last year, several evangelical churches were fire-bombed, and a Protestant church leader in the city of Adana was severely beaten by a group of assailants. Last February, Andrea Santoro, a Catholic priest working in the Black Sea city of Trabzon was shot and killed by a 16-year-old."[1]

We urged people to pray for:

- Turkish Christians to have wisdom to know how the Lord wants them to operate effectively and fruitfully in this hostile environment, knowing that historically the Church grows in strength and numbers amid persecution.

704

- The Holy Spirit to move among Turkish Muslims and bring them to faith in Jesus Christ in record numbers.
- The Western church to know how to stand with our brothers and sisters in Turkey as well as followers of Christ throughout the Muslim world.

October 9, 2007: "Here's the latest e-mail we've received from our friends at the Palestinian Bible Society: 'Rami Ayyad, 30, manager of the Bible Society bookshop in Gaza, was kidnapped on Saturday near his home in Gaza City. His body was later found near the Islamic University on Sunday morning. It is not known who is responsible for the killing. The attack comes six months after the Palestinian Bible Society bookshop was bombed, causing significant damage. Mr. Ayyad leaves a pregnant widow . . . and two children. . . . The believers in Gaza face the threat of attack daily. But they are dedicated to demonstrating the Bible's life-changing message to the Palestinian people. Rami was no different, and the bookshop he ran was an oasis in Gaza City.' "

We urged people to pray for Rami's family, and that all the Palestinian believers in Gaza would have supernatural courage and love amid such trials, and for the Church outside Gaza to know how best to strengthen and encourage our embattled brothers and sisters.

August 15, 2008: "A huge story broke first in Israel in *Haaretz* about a week ago, and now on the Fox News Channel. The son of the leader of Hamas has renounced his affiliation with the terrorist group, has renounced Islam, and has become a follower of Jesus Christ. The full-length interviews are absolutely fascinating."

We urged readers to pray:

- That this young man's faith deepens and grows and that he can be discipled by an older, wiser man of God.
- That the Lord keeps this young man safe from those Radical jihadists who would try to take his life.
- That the Lord would answer his prayers for his family's eyes and hearts to be opened and that they would all come to faith in Jesus as well.
- That other Hamas leaders and Muslims throughout the West Bank and Gaza — as well as all Israelis who are hearing this story — would be moved by this young man's spiritual journey and begin asking why he did it.
- That the Lord would continue to build His Church in the Holy Land and not allow the gates of hell to prevail against it.

October 21, 2008: "Please be praying for courage, protection, and wisdom for Christians in the Iraqi city of Mosul (ancient Ninevah), where violence and persecution has worsened dramatically in recent weeks. . . . 'More than 15,000 Iraqi Christians, or 2,500 families, have been driven out of Mosul over the past two weeks,' reports the *Christian Post*. 'The number skyrocketed from last week's estimate of some 3,000 Christians that fled the northern Iraq city, which is said to be the last urban stronghold of Al-Qaeda. Officials in Mosul also reported that some 13 Iraqi Christians have been killed in the past four weeks, and at least three Assyrian Christian homes were bombed on Saturday alone, according to the Assyrian International News Agency.'[2] Please also pray for comfort for those affected by the violence, and for God's peace and tranquility to descend on that city and the entire country of Iraq.

"Please be praying for courage, protection, and wisdom for Christians in Afghanistan. A Christian aid worker was just murdered in the capital city of Kabul, only a week or so after Jeremy Grafman and I visited there. Please also pray for comfort for the family and friends of Gayle Williams, 34, who was shot dead by two gunmen. Please pray for God's peace and tranquility to descend on Kabul and the entire country of Afghanistan."

Strategy No. 3: Give
"Do not store up for yourselves treasures on earth, where moth and rust destroy, and where thieves break in and steal. But store up for yourselves treasures in heaven . . . for where your treasure is, there your heart will be also." — Matthew 6:19–21

Once you begin to understand God's plan and purpose for the people of the epicenter and become devoted to prayer, please consider investing your time, your talents, and your treasure in the work God is doing in the Middle East, as the Scriptures command.

We need to strengthen our brothers and sisters on the front lines of this spiritual Revolution in tangible and practical ways. The Revivalists can't do the work all by themselves. They don't want to do the work all by themselves. And it's not biblical for them to have to do the work all by them-

707

selves. They need our help.

They need Bibles and Bible study materials that are translated into the local languages. They need DVDs and CDs that tell Jesus' story and communicate the teachings of the Scriptures. They need funding to run satellite, radio, and Internet ministries. They need retreats and training conferences to encourage and better equip pastors and ministry leaders. They need food, clothing, medical equipment, and other supplies that they can distribute in the name of Jesus to the poor and needy and to victims of war and terrorism.

This is exactly what we established the Joshua Fund to do. Should you be interested in helping us, we would be deeply honored. You can learn more about our work at www.joshuafund.net. If you would like to make a tax-deductible contribution, you can do so securely online, or you can send a check payable to "The Joshua Fund" to:

The Joshua Fund
18940 Base Camp Road
Monument, Colorado 80132-8009

Strategy No. 4: Go
"Go therefore and make disciples of all the nations, baptizing them in the name of the Father and the Son and the Holy Spirit, teaching them to observe all that I commanded you; and lo, I am with you always, even to the end of the age." — Matthew 28:19–20

Learning, praying, and giving are biblical responses, but they are not enough. To truly obey the teachings of the Bible and follow the model Jesus set for us, we need to be willing to turn off

708

our TVs, get up off the couch, put away our iPods, and go love Muslims in the name of Jesus in real and practical ways.

I asked an MBB friend of Lynn's and mine to give me a list of ten practical ways readers of this book can show the love of Jesus Christ to their Muslim neighbors. Here's what she came up with:

Before you approach your Muslim neighbors, pray that the Holy Spirit would show you ways you might be able to love them the way Christ Himself would love them. Of course the Holy Spirit is the expert in this matter, but here are my suggestions.

1. Take your Muslim neighbor a "welcome to the neighborhood" gift, like a box of home-made cookies, a basket of fruits, chocolate, a card, a plant, or just flowers. If you are invited to their home, never go empty-handed. Take a plant, flowers, chocolate, pastries, cookies, or any presentable sweet treat.

2. Invite your Muslim neighbors to your home for dinner. As you invite them, ask them what they would like to eat. Make sure they understand that you are sensitive to their diet (no pork or alcohol).

3. When they come to your home, be very respectful. They may take off their shoes when they enter your home, as it is a tradition. You may ask them to keep their shoes on or you may take off your shoes as well. (On the other hand, when you enter their home, please always take off your shoes.) Then, offer them a nonalcoholic drink. Out of respect, refrain from drinking alcoholic beverages in front of them. When seating them at the dinner table,

if possible seat them at the head of the table away from the door or any entrance.

4. At dinner, pray for your new friends individually. Pray for the couple, their children, or whatever situation they may be in. And don't be afraid to pray in the name of Jesus.

5. At dinner, get to know your new Muslim friends. Ask about their culture, traditions, food, interests, etc. It is fun to learn about other cultures. Also ask if you could meet again another time to have a cup of coffee or tea and continue building the friendship.

6. When you meet with them for coffee or tea, offer to pray for them individually regarding whatever is on their hearts.

7. Invite them to spend time with you and your Christian friends doing something fun and "safe" — that is, nonthreatening to their faith — so that they can see the love of Christ in His followers. This is very attractive to Muslims. Eventually, you may want to ask them to a church function, like a Christmas or Easter service.

8. When you make dinner for your own family, consider making extra and taking the extra meal to your Muslim neighbor. Middle Easterners really appreciate this gesture. Again, no pork, please!

9. When any member of their family is ill, pray for that person with your Muslim neighbor. Take them chicken soup. Offer to do some of their chores, like picking things up for them at the grocery store or the pharmacy. Offer to babysit if they need to go to a doctor's appointment, or — if you have time — offer to drive them to their appointment. Or just offer

to babysit their kids so that the couple can have a date night.

10. If you go on vacation, bring back a souvenir for your neighbor. In the Middle East, that is very much appreciated. Remember their birthdays, and surprise them with a card, a gift, a cake, or flowers. In all things, follow the teachings of Jesus to "do to others as you would have them do to you" (Luke 6:31, NIV).

Loving your Muslim neighbor is the right way to begin, but we should not stop there. Jesus teaches us to "go" and make disciples of "all the nations." I would encourage you, therefore, to prayerfully consider going on a prayer and vision trip to a Muslim country, perhaps a trip organized by an evangelical Christian ministry with a heart for the Muslim people. Prayerfully consider, too, going on a short-term mission trip — for a week or two, or even for a few months — to a Muslim country to work alongside Revivalists and to learn how to serve the Church operating in the Islamic world. From there, prayerfully consider serving a Christian ministry in the epicenter for a year or two. The key is to start small, learn as you go, and constantly seek the Lord's will and direction for your life.

Along the way, keep in mind that the Lord may be calling you to serve Him full-time in the Muslim world. That may seem scary at first. But if it is God's will for your life, there can be no greater joy than obeying Christ's call. Seek wise counsel from pastors, ministry leaders, and friends who know you and who have experience doing ministry in cross-cultural environments, particularly in the Muslim world. Get as much training as you possibly can. Build a team of friends and allies who will pray faithfully for you and support you financially. Whatever you do, don't be a "lone ranger" and head into the Muslim world by yourself. Such an approach is neither biblical nor wise.

Courage and Compassion

Have you ever read the book of Jonah in the Old Testament?

If you haven't, let me encourage you to do so. It's a short, interesting book, and it won't take long. If you have read it, could I convince you to reread it today? As you read, notice that God told Jonah to leave his home (which happened to be Israel), travel to Ninevah (one of the most wicked cities on the planet at that time), and tell the people that God was about to punish their wickedness by sending a terrible judgment upon them.

As you probably know, Jonah disobeyed.

Now, it is easy for us to be pious and say to ourselves or our children, "Oh, that silly little Jonah! He should have known better. He should have obeyed God and not jumped on that ship heading far away from Ninevah! Then he never would have been swallowed up and spit out by the whale."

But imagine for a moment that tonight, as you lay your head down on your pillow, the Lord speaks to you. Imagine that He tells you to go to Mosul — modern-day Ninevah, one of the most dangerous cities on the face of the planet — and stand on the street corner and preach a message of repentance at the risk of your life. Would you obey? Or would you jump on a Disney cruise and head in the opposite direction?

On February 9, 2006, I had the privilege of interviewing a young woman named Carrie McDonnall, who served as a Christian worker for the Southern Baptists in Iraq. After the fall of Saddam, God told Carrie, her husband, David, and three colleagues to go to Mosul to do relief work, share the gospel with Muslims, and encourage local believers in a house church there.

They obeyed.

But on March 15, 2004, they were ambushed by terrorists. Carrie's three colleagues died instantly. She sustained more than twenty gunshot wounds. Every bone in her arms and legs was shattered. She couldn't move. She was hemorrhaging massive amounts of blood. She could see only blood and bone where three of her fingers had just been ripped off.

David was shot in the chest but refused to go down. By the grace of God, he was able to drag her out of the bullet-riddled SUV and, with the help of Iraqi bystanders, get her to a hospital, where she immediately blacked out.

When she woke up eight days later, she was in Dallas, only to find that David had not made it. Yet two years later, she told me she still loved the Iraqi people. She had forgiven her attackers. And she was traveling the U.S. trying to mobilize young people to invest their lives as missionaries to "reach the nations," even in Iraq, no matter what the cost.

Carrie's story of faith and courage is amazing to me. It is evidence of what a great God we have, a God who is sending His servants to penetrate the darkness of Islam with the light of Jesus. And it brings me back to the central question provoked by the book of Jonah: If God clearly told you to go to Mosul, would you do it? For many today, the answer is no, and the reason is fear. But look more closely at the biblical text. Was it fear that prevented Jonah from obeying the Lord's call? No. It was racism. It was prejudice. Jonah did not want the people of Ninevah to repent. He did not want the enemies of Israel to experience God's love and forgiveness.

Today, there is no question that fear is preventing many followers of Jesus Christ from obeying His call to love the Muslim people. But others share Jonah's animosity toward the people of the epicenter. We need to repent of such views. We need to ask God to change our hearts and give us His supernatural love. If we are ever going to join the Revolution — much less win it — the Church is going to need both courage and compassion.

The exciting news is that many around the world are responding to God's call to love and bless the people of the Islamic world. In China, for example, the "Back to Jerusalem" movement is on the rise. Chinese house-church leaders are praying that God will raise up at least one hundred thousand believers to reach every person in every country between China and Israel — including Buddhists, Hindus, and Muslims — with the gospel of Jesus Christ, regardless of the cost.

Remarkably, thousands of Chinese believers are responding to that call. So are Mexican believers. And African believers. And South Korean believers. And believers from the Philippines and India and Pakistan and the United States and Canada.

What about you? Are you willing to join the Revolution?

Jesus Is With Us

Jesus tells us not to be afraid to serve Him. He promises to always be with us. He promises never to forsake us. Perhaps we should take Him at His word.

On my second trip to Iraq, I met a wonderful MBB named Daniel. He is a businessman who came to faith in Jesus Christ in 1986 after seeing six visions in one night telling him to follow Jesus. In March of 2008, however, Daniel was kidnapped in Baghdad by five members of the Mahdi Army. They took him to a warehouse, stripped him, beat him mercilessly, and demanded he pay them $200,000.

He told them he did not have such money. They didn't believe him, so they beat him some more. Eventually they forced him to call a friend who was able to come up with $20,000 as a ransom. When the Radicals got their money, they took Daniel to the edge of town and promised to set him free. Instead, they put a pistol to his head and pulled the trigger.[3]

Daniel told me that everything went black. He never heard the gunshot. Nor did he feel it. Suddenly he saw his sister — agitated and distressed — trying to get to him. But she could not; she went away. Then Daniel saw his daughter trying desperately to get to him. But she, too, was unable. Then it dawned on him that he was dead, that there was a barrier between life and death, and his sister and daughter were unable to cross it. He told me that he fell on his face weeping. But at that moment, he said the two most beautiful and gentle hands that he had ever seen took him and picked him up. When he was standing, he suddenly realized that he was looking directly into the eyes of Jesus. A tremendous sense of peace and calm came over him. Jesus embraced him, put Daniel's head on His shoulder, and told him, "I will never leave you or forsake you."

At that moment, Daniel said, he was alive again. He was lying on the side of the road, covered in his own blood. A passerby stopped, put him in the back of his car, and raced him to the hospital. It took months of medical treatment — in Iraq and in Jordan — but today, Daniel is not only alive but well. Though he is blind in one eye, he is convinced he can see more clearly than ever, and he is testifying with conviction and humility to the greatness of our great God.

"The Lord, He cares for us, Joel," Daniel told me as he showed me the wounds where the 9 mm bullet entered his left temple and exited his right cheek. "He never leaves us or forsakes us."

I do not tell this story to suggest that God will immediately resurrect every believer who is killed for his faith in a Muslim land. Obviously that's not the case. But once God adopts us into His family, He will stay with us forever, in this life and in the life to come.

My friends, I am in awe of this God who makes promises and keeps them, who hears our prayers and answers them. Jesus wants to embrace us. Should we not embrace Him? Should we not follow Him, no matter what the cost? Should we not join the Revolution that He is leading in the epicenter?

I have. My wife has. Our boys have. Not because we are brave but because we are in love with the Jesus who loved us so much that He gave Himself for us. At the end of time, we want to hear Him say to us, "Well done, good and faithful servant!

You have been faithful with a few things; I will put you in charge of many things. Come and share your master's happiness" (Matthew 25:21, NIV).

Will you join us?

APPENDIX:
20 TERROR PLOTS AGAINST
AMERICA FOILED SINCE 9/11

Why has the United States not been hit by terrorists inside our country since September 11, 2001? It is not because the Radicals are not trying. Al Qaeda and other extremist individuals and organizations have tried repeatedly to launch murderous attacks against innocent American civilians and military personnel. But they have failed by God's grace and the hard work of U.S. and foreign law enforcement, intelligence, and military officials. The following is a list of twenty known terror plots thwarted by the U.S. government since the attacks on the World Trade Center and the Pentagon in 2001:[1]

1. December 2001 — Richard Reid: British citizen attempted to ignite shoe bomb on flight from Paris to Miami.

2. May 2002 — Jose Padilla: American citizen accused of seeking radioactive-laced "dirty bomb" to use in an attack against America. Padilla was convicted of conspiracy in August 2007.

3. September 2002 — Lackawanna Six: American citizens of Yemeni origin convicted of supporting al Qaeda after attending jihadist camp in Pakistan. Five of six were from Lackawanna, New York.

4. May 2003 — Iyman Faris: American citizen charged with plotting to use blowtorches to collapse the Brooklyn Bridge.

5. June 2003 — Virginia Jihad Network: Eleven men from Alexandria, Virginia, trained for jihad against American soldiers, convicted of violating the Neutrality Act.

6. August 2004 — Dhiren Barot: Indian-born leader of terror cell plotted bombings on financial centers.

7. August 2004 — James Elshafay and Shahawar Matin Siraj: Sought to plant bomb at New York's Penn Station during the Republican National Convention.

8. August 2004 — Yassin Aref and Mohammed Hossain: Plotted to assassinate a Pakistani diplomat on American soil.

9. June 2005 — Father and son Umer Hayat and Hamid Hayat: Son convicted of attending terrorist training camp in Pakistan; father convicted of customs violation.

10. August 2005 — Kevin James, Levar Haley Washington, Gregory Vernon Patterson, and Hammad Riaz Samana: Los Angeles homegrown terrorists who plotted to attack National Guard, LAX, two synagogues, and the Israeli consulate.

11. December 2005 — Michael Reynolds: Plotted to blow up natural gas refinery in Wyoming, the Transcontinental Pipeline, and a refinery in New Jersey. Reynolds was sentenced to thirty years in prison.

12. February 2006 — Mohammad Zaki Amawi, Marwan Othman El-Hindi, and Zand Wassim Mazloum: Accused of providing material support to terrorists making bombs for use in Iraq.

13. April 2006 — Syed Haris Ahmed and Ehsanul Islam Sadequee: Cased and videotaped the Capitol and World Bank for a terrorist organization.

14. June 2006 — Narseal Batiste, Patrick Abraham, Stanley Grant Phanor, Naudimar Herrera, Burson Augustin, Lyglenson Lemorin, and Rotschild Augustine: Accused of plotting to blow up the Sears Tower.

15. July 2006 — Assem Hammoud: Accused of plotting to bomb New York City train tunnels.

16. August 2006 — Liquid Explosives Plot: Thwarted plot to explode ten airliners over the United States.

17. March 2007 — Khalid Sheikh Mohammed: Mastermind of 9/11 and author of numerous plots confessed in court to planning to destroy skyscrapers in New York, Los Angeles, and Chicago. Also plotted to assassinate Pope John Paul II and former president Bill Clinton.

18. May 2007 — Fort Dix Plot: Six men accused of plotting to attack Fort Dix Army base in New Jersey. The plan included attacking and killing soldiers using assault rifles and grenades.

19. June 2007 — JFK Plot: Four men accused of plotting to blow up fuel arteries that run through residential neighborhoods at JFK Airport in New York.

20. September 2007 — German authorities disrupt terrorist cell planning attacks on military installations and facilities used by Americans in Germany. The Germans arrested three suspected members of the Islamic Jihad Union, a group that has links to al Qaeda and supports al Qaeda's global jihadist agenda.

ENDNOTES

Introduction: Not "If" But "When"

1. Jim Michaels, "19,000 insurgents killed in Iraq since '03," *USA Today,* September 27, 2007.

Chapter 1: Worst-Case Scenario

1. Lt. General (ret.) William G. Boykin, author interview, February 11, 2008.
2. "Mission Backgrounder: Somalia UNOSOM I," United Nations Office of Public Information, March 21, 1997.
3. "Fact Sheet on Dirty Bombs," U.S. Nuclear Regulatory Commission, February 20, 2007, http://www.nrc.gov/reading-rm/doc-collections/factsheets/dirty-bombs.html, accessed July 31, 2008.
4. E-mail from General Boykin to the author on August 2, 2008.
5. Kamal Saleem, author interview, February 12, 2008.
6. Walid Shoebat, interview for *Epicenter* documentary film, March 10, 2008.
7. Porter Goss, author interview, February 12, 2008.
8. Alireza Jafarzadeh, spokesman for the National Council of Resistance of Iran, author interview,

March 24, 2008.

9. Alireza Jafarzadeh, see remarks at the National Press Club, August 14, 2002, http://www.iran watch.org/privateviews/NCRI/perspexncri-topsecretprojects-081402.htm, accessed August 21, 2008.

10. See transcript, NBC's *Meet the Press,* April 2, 2006.

11. General Moshe Ya'alon, author interview, March 9, 2007.

12. Former prime minister Benjamin Netanyahu, author interview, March 2007.

Chapter 2: "Islam Is the Answer; Jihad Is the Way"

1. Sen. Barack Obama was speaking at a town hall in Oregon on May 18, 2008. See "Obama Flip-Flop on Iran," *The Weekly Standard,* "The Blog," May 19, 2008; see also "McCain Criticizes Obama Over Iran Comments," Associated Press, May 19, 2008.

2. Ibid.

3. Ibid.

4. "Russia Warns over U.S. Missile Defense, Says Iran Is Not a Threat," Associated Press, October 23, 2007.

5. Scott Ritter, "The Big Lie: 'Iran Is a Threat,' " CommonDreams.org, October 8, 2007, http://www.commondreams.org/archive/2007/10/08/4404, accessed July 26, 2008.

6. Nikki R. Keddie, *Modern Iran: Roots and Results of Revolution,* p. 346.

7. Ted Koppel, "Let 'Em Have Nukes. But . . ." *New York Times/International Herald Tribune,* October 3, 2006.

8. Daniel Trotta, "Ted Turner Says Iraq War

among History's 'Dumbest,' " Reuters, September 19, 2006.

9. Cited by V. S. Naipaul, *Among the Believers,* pp. 81–82; and by Robin Wright, *Sacred Rage,* p. 21.

10. Cited by Hamid Algar, translator, *Islam and Revolution: Writings and Declarations of Imam Khomeini (1941–1980),* p. 286. Dr. Algar's compilation of Khomeini's writings was extraordinarily helpful to me in understanding the ayatollah. The book also begins with an excellent summary of Khomeini's biography and basic religious philosophy.

11. Cited by Alireza Jafarzadeh, *The Iran Threat: President Ahmadinejad and the Coming Nuclear Crisis,* p. 208.

12. See bin Laden's "Declaration of War Against the Americans," cited by Randall Hamud, *Osama bin Laden: America's Enemy in His Own Words,* pp. 32–58

13. Broadcast on Palestinian Authority TV, May 13, 2005. See transcript of translation by the Middle East Media Research Institute, http://www.memritv.org/clip_transcript/en/669.htm, accessed July 6, 2008.

14. The publication was called *Risalat al-Ikhwan.* The slogan was removed from future printings after September 11, 2001. Cited by Lt. Col. (res.) Jonathan Dahoah-Halevi, "The Muslim Brotherhood: A Moderate Islamic Alternative to al-Qaeda or a Partner in Global Jihad?" Jerusalem Center for Public Affairs, November 1, 2007, http://www.jcpa.org/JCPA/Templates/ShowPage.asp?DBID=1&T MID=111&LNG ID=1&FID=379&PID=0&IID=1920, accessed on June 23, 2008.

15. Cited by Kasra Naji, *Ahmadinejad: The Secret History of Iran's Radical Leader,* p. 144.
16. Cited by Naji, p. 143.
17. "Rafsanjani says Muslims Should Use Nuclear Weapon against Israel," *Iran Press Service,* December 14, 2001.
18. Cited by Naji, p. 139.
19. Cited by Jafarzadeh, p. 31.
20. "Ahmadinejad Says Israel Will Soon Disappear," Agence France-Presse, June 2, 2008.
21. *Beirut Daily Star,* October 23, 2002; cited by Deborah Passner, "Hassan Nasrallah: In His Own Words," research paper produced by the Committee for Accuracy in Middle East Reporting in America, July 26, 2006, http://www.camera.org/index.asp?x_context=7&x_issue=11&x_article=1158, accessed July 6, 2006.
22. Cited by Passner, "Hassan Nasrallah: In His Own Words."
23. Cited by Steven Stalinsky, executive director of the Middle East Media Research Institute (MEMRI), "Palestinian Authority Sermons 2000–2003," MEMRI, Special Report - No. 24, December 26, 2003.
24. Ibid.
25. Cited by Jafarzadeh, p. 25.
26. "Ahmadinejad Says Israel Will Soon Disappear," Agence France-Presse, June 2, 2008.
27. "Ahmadinejad: Iran, Japan Should Be Prepared for a World without U.S.," Islamic Republic News Agency, June 4, 2008.
28. Osama bin Laden, "Jihad Against Jews and Crusaders," World Islamic Front statement, February 2, 1998; cited by Wright, p. 256.
29. Cited by Wright, p. 257
30. Cited by Peter Bergen, *The Osama Bin Laden I*

Know, p. 339.

31. BBC Monitoring: Al-Manar TV, September 27, 2002; cited by Passner, "Hassan Nasrallah: In His Own Words."

32. Cited by MEMRI, Special Dispatch Series - No. 1791, December 21, 2007.

33. Cited by Stalinsky, "Incitement Official," FrontPageMagazine.com, May 26, 2005.

34. Cited by Stalinsky, "Palestinian Authority Sermons."

35. Cited by Mansfield, pp. 200–201.

36. Cited by Bergen, p. 347.

37. Bernard Lewis, *What Went Wrong? The Clash Between Islam and Modernity in the Middle East,* and *The Crisis of Islam: Holy War and Unholy Terror.*

38. See "Islam and the West: A Conversation with Bernard Lewis," event transcript, Pew Forum, April 27, 2006, Washington, D.C.

39. Pervez Hoodbhoy, "Islamic Failure," *Prospect* magazine, February 2002.

40. From a series of essays Mr. al-Akhdar posted in June 2003; cited by Barry Rubin, editor of the *Middle East Review of International Affairs (MERIA)*, in "What's Wrong: The Arab Liberal Critique of Arab Society," *MERIA,* Vol. 9, N. 4, Article 5, December 2005.

41. Jamal Bittar, "What's Wrong With The Arab World?" *The Arab American News,* January 19, 2008.

42. Zaffar Abbas, "Musharraf Berates Muslim World," BBC News, February 16, 2002.

43. Ehsan Ahrari, "Musharraf's Clarion Call to the World of Islam," *Asia Times,* March 5, 2002.

44. Pervez Musharraf, *In the Line of Fire: A Memoir,* p. 149.

45. Cited by Bergen, pp. 6–7.
46. Sheik Yussef Al-Qaradhawi, interview on Al-Jazeera Television, "The Prophet Muhammad as a Jihad Model," June 19, 2001, cited by MEMRI, Special Dispatch Series - No. 246, July 24, 2001.
47. Cited by Mansfield, pp. 50, 51, 54.
48. Cited by Wright, p. 44.
49. Cited by Naji, p. 98.
50. Yossef Bodansky, *Bin Laden: The Man Who Declared War on America* (Roseville, Calif.: Prima Publishing, 2001), 110.
51. Cited by Sadanand Dhume, "Indonesian Democracy's Enemy Within: Radical Islamic Party Threatens Indonesia with Ballots more than Bullets," column for *Yale Global Online,* December 1, 2005.
52. Cited by Mansfield, p. 205.
53. Cited by Mansfield, pp. 346–347.

Chapter 3: The Theology of the Radicals

1. George W. Bush, remarks at Islamic Center of Washington, D.C., transcript made available by the White House, Office of the Press Secretary, September 17, 2001, http://www.whitehouse.gov/news/releases/2001/09/20010917-11.html, accessed August 4, 2008.
2. See "Backgrounder: The President's Quotes on Islam — In the President's Words, Respecting Islam," White House Office of the Press Secretary, http://www.whitehouse.gov/infocus/ramadan/islam.html, accessed August 4, 2008.
3. Transcript, "Bush, Blair News Conference," Associated Press, November 20, 2003.
4. "Tony Blair: 'Wake Up' to Iran's Extremism," Associated Press, December 21, 2006.

5. " 'Islam Is also France,' Sarkozy Says at Iftar," Al Arabiya TV, October 2, 2007, http://www.alarabiya.net/articles/2007/10/02/39829.html, accessed August 4, 2008.

6. For more information on specific citations, see Sh. G. F. Haddad, "Documentation of 'Greater Jihad' Hadith," www.livingislam.org, February 28, 2005, http://www.livingislam.org/n/dgjh_e.html, accessed August 16, 2008. See also "Religion & Ethics — Islam," BBC, http://www.bbc.co.uk/religion/religions/islam/beliefs/jihad_2.shtml, accessed August 16, 2008.

7. Douglas E. Streusand, "What Does Jihad Mean?" *Middle East Quarterly,* September 1997, http://www.meforum.org/article/357, accessed August 16, 2008.

8. Cited by Yossef Bodansky, *Bin Laden: The Man Who Declared War on America,* p. xiii.

9. Abdullah Azzam, *Join The Caravan,* a tract originally published on www.alhaqq.org in December 2001, retrieved from http://www.religioscope.com/info/doc/jihad/azzam_caravan_6_conclusion.htm, accessed August 16, 2008.

10. Cited by Hamid Algar, *Islam and Revolution: Writings and Declarations of Imam Khomeini (1941–1980),* pp. 387–388.

11. *Jihad* magazine, Issue 1, December 28, 1984, published by Osama bin Laden and his mentor, Sheikh Azzam; cited by Peter Bergen, *The Osama Bin Laden I Know,* p. 33.

12. Cited by Randall Hamud, *Osama bin Laden: America's Enemy in His Own Words,* pp. 50–51.

13. Ibid, p. 54.

14. Cited by Steven Stalinsky, "Palestinian Authority Sermons 2000–2003," MEMRI, Special

Report - No. 24, December 26, 2003.

15. Ibid.

16. Sheik Yussef Al-Qaradhawi, interview on Al-Jazeera Television, "The Prophet Muhammad as a Jihad Model," June 19, 2001, cited by MEMRI, Special Dispatch Series - No. 246, July 24, 2001.

Chapter 4: "We Were Asleep"

1. Cited by Baqer Moin, *Khomeini: Life of the Ayatollah,* p. 186

2. Jimmy Carter, *Keeping Faith: Memoirs of a President,* p. 437; see also Dr. Hamid Algar, translator, *Islam and Revolution: Writings and Declarations of Imam Khomeini (1941–1980),* p. 23, citing the *New York Times,* January 2, 1978.

3. Cited in "American Experience: Jimmy Carter," transcript from the PBS documentary film, http://www.pbs.org/wgbh/amex/carter/filmmore/pt_2.html, accessed August 13, 2008.

4. See Michael Ledeen, *The Iranian Time Bomb: The Mullah Zealots' Quest for Destruction,* p. 4.

5. See Algar, p. 16.

6. Cited by Moin, p. 75.

7. Moin, p. 174.

8. Moin, p. 175.

9. Algar, pp. 217–218.

10. See Yossi Melman and Meir Javedanfar, *The Nuclear Sphinx of Tehran: Mahmoud Ahmadinejad and the State of Iran,* p. 79.

11. Ibid, p. 79.

12. Cited by Algar, p. 120.

13. Cited by Algar, pp. 18, 182, 187.

14. See full speech in Algar, pp. 181–188.

15. See Kasra Naji, *Ahmadinejad: The Secret His-*

tory of Iran's Radical Leader, p. 115.

16. Cited by Moin, p. 122.
17. Cited by Algar, pp. 228–230.
18. Cited by Kenneth M. Pollack, *The Persian Puzzle: The Conflict Between Iran and America,* p. 129.
19. Cited by Algar, p. 231.
20. See Amir Arjomand, *The Turban for the Crown: The Islamic Revolution in Iran,* p. 190.
21. Admiral Stansfield Turner, *Burn Before Reading: Presidents, CIA Directors and Secret Intelligence,* p. 180.
22. Cited by Carter, p. 438.
23. Cited by Christopher Andrew, *For the President's Eyes Only: Secret Intelligence and the American President from Washington to Bush,* p. 440.
24. Pollack, p. 131.
25. Tim Weiner, *Legacy of Ashes: The History of the CIA,* p. 428.
26. Mark Bowden, *Guests of the Ayatollah,* p. 120.
27. Pollack, p. 130.
28. Pollack, p. 134.
29. Cited in "Man of the Year: 1979," *Time* magazine, January 7, 1980.
30. See Moin, pp. 200–201.
31. "Declaration upon Arrival at Tehran," full text of Khomeini's speech, cited by Algar, pp. 252–243.
32. See "On This Day: February 1, 1979. Exiled Ayatollah Khomeini Returns to Iran," BBC News, http://news.bbc.co.uk/onthisday/hi/dates/stories/february/1/newsid_2521000/2521003.stm, accessed August 9, 2008.
33. Cited in "Man of the Year: 1979," *Time* magazine, January 7, 1980.

34. Cited by William Daugherty, *In The Shadow of the Ayatollah: A CIA Hostage in Iran,* p. 4.

35. "The First Day of God's Government," full text of Khomeini's statement, cited by Algar, pp. 265–267.

36. Cited by Bowden, p. 14.

37. See Robert Gates, *From the Shadows: The Ulimate Insider's Story of Five Presidents and How They Won the Cold War,* pp. 129–130.

38. See Zbigniew Brzezinski, *Power and Principle,* pp. 475–476.

39. Cited by Gates, p. 130.

40. See President Jimmy Carter, "Daily Diary," November 3, 1979, document archived on Carter Presidential Library Web site, http://www.jimmycarterlibrary.org/documents/diary/1979/d110379t.pdf, accessed June 21, 2008.

41. Cited by Bowden, p. 52.

42. Cited by Bowden, pp. 69–70. See also Massoumeh Ebtekar, *Takeover in Tehran: The Inside Story of the 1979 U.S. Embassy Capture,* p. 70.

43. See Amir Taheri, "America Can't Do a Thing," *New York Post,* November 2, 2004.

44. Turner, p. 180.

Chapter 5: Tragedy at Desert One

1. Unless otherwise noted, most of this chapter relies on the author's interview with General Jerry Boykin and on Boykin's book, *Never Surrender,* written with the help of *World* magazine journalist Lynn Vincent.

2. Bowden, *Guests of the Ayatollah,* p. 230.

3. See Boykin, pp. 122–123.

4. See Bowden, p. 468.

Chapter 6: "We Must Export Our Revolution"

1. See Hon. Royce C. Lamberth, United States District Judge, District of Columbia, "Memoradum Opinion" in the case of *Plaintiffs v. The Islamic Republic of Iran,* May 30, 2003, p. 16.
2. Ibid, p. 16.
3. Ibid, pp. 7–19.
4. Ibid, pp. 18–19.
5. Ibid, p. 10.
6. Ibid, pp. 24–25.
7. Ibid, p. 29.
8. See "Iran Must Pay $2.6 Billion for Attack on U.S. Marines, Judge Rules," CNN, September 7, 2007.
9. Cited by Daniel Byman, "Should Hezbollah Be Next?" *Foreign Affairs,* November/December 2003, http://www.foreignaffairs.org/20031101faessay82606/daniel-byman/should-hezbollah-be-next.html?mode=print, accessed August 24, 2008.
10. Cited by BBC Monitoring: al-Manar TV, September 27, 2002; see Deborah Passner, "Hassan Nasrallah: In His Own Words," research paper produced by the Committee for Accuracy in Middle East Reporting in America, July 26, 2006, http://www.camera.org/index.asp?x_context=7&x_issue=11&x_article=1158, accessed July 6, 2006.
11. Cited by Nicholas Noe, editor, *Voice of Hezbollah: The Statements of Sayyed Hassan Nasrallah,* p. 32.
12. Ibid, p. 50.
13. Ibid, p. 54.
14. Ibid, p. 54.
15. Cited by Mohamad Shmaysani, "Al-Sayyed Nasrallah: Drill Shows Resistance Full Readi-

ness," al-Manar, August 11, 2007.

16. See Noe, pp. 95, 128.
17. See "Analysis: Hezbollah a Force to be Reckoned With," Agence France-Presse, July 18, 2006.
18. See *Patterns of Global Terrorism,* "State Sponsors of Terrorism Overview," Office of the Coordinator for Counterterrorism, U.S. Department of State, April 30, 2008.
19. Ibid.
20. See "U.S. Official Says Hezbollah Aiding Iraqi Shiites," Associated Press, November 28, 2006; Michael R. Gordon and Dexter Filkins, "Hezbollah Said to Help Shiite Army in Iraq," *New York Times,* November 28, 2006; "Iraqis: Hezbollah Trained Shiite Militants," Associated Press, July 2, 2008.
21. Cited by Nizar Latif and Phil Sands, "Mehdi Fighters 'Trained by Hizbollah in Lebanon,' " *The (U.K.) Independent,* August 20, 2007.
22. See "Hezbollah's Shi'ite Youth Movement, 'The Imam al-Mahdi Scouts,' Has Tens of Thousands of Members," fact sheet produced by the Intelligence and Terrorism Information Center at the Center for Special Studies, September 11, 2006, http://www.intelligence.org.il/eng/eng_n/html/hezbollah_scouts_e.htm, accessed July 6, 2006.

Chapter 7: Christmas in Kabul

1. See MacNeil/Lehrer Report, PBS, August 14, 1979, cited by James A. Phillips, "The Soviet Invasion of Afghanistan," Backgrounder No. 108, The Heritage Foundation, January 9, 1980, http://www.heritage.org/Research/RussiaandEurasia/upload/86944_1.pdf, ac-

cessed August 16, 2008.

2. Cited by Tim Weiner, *Legacy of Ashes: The History of the CIA,* p. 423.

3. Cited by Weiner, p. 423.

4. See Robert Gates, *From the Shadows: The Ulimate Insider's Story of Five Presidents and How They Won the Cold War,* pp. 146–147.

5. Ibid, p. 132.

6. Ibid, pp. 132–133.

7. Weiner, p. 424.

8. Ibid.

9. Text of President Carter's State of the Union address, January 23, 1980, http://www.jimmy carterlibrary.gov/documents/speeches/su80jec .phtml, accessed August 19, 2008.

10. Weiner, p. 425.

11. See Gates, p. 134.

12. See Lawrence Wright, *The Looming Tower,* p. 85.

13. See Peter Bergen, *The Osama Bin Laden I Know,* p.71.

14. See Gary M. Sevold, "The Muslim Brotherhood and Islamic Radicalism," in *Know Thy Enemy: Profiles of Adversary Leaders and Their Strategic Cultures,* ed. Barry R. Schneider and Jerrold M. Post (U.S. Air Force Counterproliferation Center, 2003), pp. 45–48.

15. See Wright, p. 87.

16. Ibid, p. 110.

17. Cited by Yossef Bodansky, *Bin Laden: The Man Who Declared War on America,* p. 20.

18. Cited by Bergen, p. 27.

19. Cited by Wright, p. 110.

20. Ibid, p. 111.

21. See Bodansky, p. 14.

22. See Wright, p. 116.

23. Ibid, pp. 116–117.
24. Cited by Bodansky, p. 19.

Chapter 8: Declaring War on America

1. Cited by Lawrence Wright, *The Looming Tower,* p. 151.
2. See Wright, pp. 152–153, and Bodansky, *Bin Laden: The Man Who Declared War on America,* p. 12.
3. See Wright, p. 157.
4. Ibid, p. 162.
5. See Bodansky, p. 28.
6. John Miller, interview with ABC News, May 1998, cited on PBS *Frontline* Web site, http://www.pbs.org/wgbh/pages/frontline/shows/binladen/who/interview.html, accessed June 21, 2008.
7. See James Phillips, "Somalia and al-Qaeda: Implications for the War on Terrorism," Backgrounder No. 1526, Heritage Foundation, April 5, 2002.
8. Ibid.
9. See Miller, interview with ABC News.
10. Excerpts from full text of bin Laden's 1996 fatwa, multiple sources based on multiple translations; see http://www.pbs.org/newshour/terrorism/international/fatwa_1996.html as an example.
11. Excerpts from bin Laden's 1998 fatwa.
12. See *The 9/11 Commission Report,* Section 2.5.
13. Ibid.
14. Ibid.
15. See "Al Qaeda's Global Context," *Frontline* Web site, PBS, http://www.pbs.org/wgbh/pages/frontline/shows/knew/etc/cron2.html, accessed August 19, 2008. See also George Tenet, *At the*

Center of the Storm, p. 125.

16. See *The 9/11 Commission Report,* Section 6.3.

Chapter 9: Unleashing the Islamic Bomb

1. See "Verbatim Transcript of Combatant Status Review Tribunal Hearing for ISN 10024," March 10, 2007, http://www.defenselink.mil/news/transcript_ISN10024.pdf, accessed August 20, 2008.
2. Cited by Warren Richey, "The Self-Portrait of an Al Qaeda Leader," *Christian Science Monitor,* March 16, 2007.
3. See *The 9/11 Commission Report,* Section 5.1.
4. See *The 9/11 Commission Report,* Section 5.1.
5. See "Substitution for the Testimony of Khalid Sheikh Mohammed."
6. *The Secret History of 9/11,* Canadian Broadcasting Company, aired September 10, 2006. The documentary drew on material from previously classified interrogation notes.
7. Cited by Walter Pincus, "New Bin Laden Tape Transcript Offers More Details," *Washington Post,* December 21, 2001.
8. See "Bin Laden Claims Responsibility for 9/11," Canadian Broadcasting Company, October 29, 2004.
9. See "Substitution for the Testimony of Khalid Sheikh Mohammed."
10. Cited by George Tenet, *At the Center of the Storm,* p. 260, citing a *Time* article from December 24, 1998.
11. Ibid, p. 269.
12. See Sheikh Nasir bin Hamd al-Fahd, "A Treatise on the Legal Status of Using Weapons of Mass Destruction Against the Infidels," May 1, 2003; cited by Tenet, p. 274. Also cited by

Michael Scheuer, *Marching Toward Hell: America and Islam after Iraq,* p. 74.

13. See Robert S. Mueller, III, Director, Federal Bureau of Investigation, "Global Initiative Nuclear Terrorism Conference," Miami, Florida, June 11, 2007.

14. See Tenet, pp. 259–260.

15. Ibid, p. 279.

Chapter 10: Terror High

1. See Josh Meyer, "Student Allegedly Talked of Assassination Plots," *Los Angeles Times,* March 2, 2005.

2. See David Stout, "Arab American Convicted of Plot to Kill Bush: Virginia Student Linked to Operatives of al Qaeda Network," *New York Times,* November 23, 2005.

3. See Department of Justice press release, September 8, 2005, http://www.usdoj.gov/usao/vae/Pressreleases/09-SeptemberPDFArchive/05/20050909alinr.pdf, accessed July 16, 2008.

4. See FBI press release, March 29, 2006, http://washingtondc.fbi.gov/dojpressrel/pressrel06/wfo032906.htm, accessed August 13, 2008.

5. See "Court Upholds Conviction in Bush al Qaeda Plot," Reuters, June 6, 2008.

6. See Stout, "Arab American Convicted of Plot."

7. See Jerry Markon and Dana Priest, "Terrorist Plot to Kill Bush Alleged," *Washington Post,* February 23, 2005.

8. Fred Schwien, interview with the author.

9. See Jerry Markon and Ben Hubbard, "Review Finds Slurs in '06 Saudi Texts," *Washington Post,* July 15, 2008.

10. See transcript of report on Al Jazeera, June 17, 2008; see "Al-Jazeera TV Report on the

Controversy over the Islamic Saudi Academy in Virginia," MEMRI, clip 1799, June 17, 2008, http://www.memritv.org/clip_transcript/en/1799.htm, accessed July 16, 2008; see also "Critics Dubs Saudi Islamic School 'Terror High,' " Associated Press, November 24, 2007.

11. See Markon and Hubbard, "Review Finds Slurs in '06 Saudi Texts."

12. See R. James Woolsey, testimony delivered before the U.S. House Committee on International Relations Subcommittee on the Middle East and South Asia, May 22, 2002.

13. Ibid.

14. See Stephen Schwartz, Director of the Islam and Democracy Program of the Foundation for the Defense of Democracies, "Wahhabism and Islam in the U.S.," testimony before the U.S. Senate Subcommittee on Terrorism, Technology and Homeland Security, June 26, 2003.

15. See findings from the Hartford Institute for Religion Research, http://hirr.hartsem.edu/research/quick_question20.html, accessed July 7, 2008. The data are drawn from "Mosque in America: A National Portrait," a survey released in April 2001. This was part of a larger study of American congregations called "Faith Communities Today," coordinated by Hartford Seminary's Hartford Institute for Religious Research in Connecticut. Muslim organizations cosponsoring the survey are the Council on American-Islamic Relations, the Islamic Society of North America, the Ministry of Imam W. Deen Muhammed, and the Islamic Circle of North America. See http://usinfo.state.gov/products/pubs/muslimlife/demograp.htm, ac-

cessed July 7, 2008.

16. See "New Dearborn Mosque to Be the Nation's Largest," Associated Press, January 7, 2004. See also Joanne Viviano, "Muslim Worshippers Say Dearborn Mosque Was Overdue," *Detroit News,* October 22, 2005.

17. See "Saudi Publications on Hate Ideology Invade American Mosques," Special Report released by the Center for Religious Freedom, Freedom House, 2006, p. 2, http://www.freedomhouse.org/uploads/special_report/45.pdf, accessed July 7, 2008.

18. Ibid, p. 38.

19. Ibid, p. 48.

20. Ibid, p. 57.

21. Ibid, pp. 19–20.

22. See Andrew Kohut, "Muslims in America: Middle Class and Mostly Mainstream," Pew Research Center, May 22, 2007, http://pewresearch.org/assets/pdf/muslim-americans.pdf, accessed June 24, 2008.

23. For an excellent and more detailed analysis of the Islamist threat to Great Britain and the British society's state of denial of the problem, see Melanie Phillips's *Londonistan.*

24. See Jason Bennetto, "MI5 Conducts Secret Inquiry into 8,000 al-Qa'ida 'Sympathisers,' *The (UK) Independent,* July 3, 2006.

25. Ibid.

26. See Robert Winnett and David Leppard, "Leaked No. 10 Dossier Reveals al-Qaeda's British Recruits," *The Sunday Times* of London, July 10, 2005.

27. See "Young Muslims and Extremism," U.K. Foreign and Commonwealth Office/Home Office, April 2004, presented to Prime Minister

Tony Blair.

28. See "Sharia Law in UK is 'Unavoidable,' " BBC, February 7, 2008, http://news.bbc.co.uk/ 2/hi/uk_news/7232661.stm, accessed July 6, 2008.

29. See David Machlis and Tovah Lazaroff, "Muslims 'About to Take Over Europe,' " *Jerusalem Post,* January 29, 2007.

30. Simon Kuper, "Europe Can Feel at Home with 16m Muslims," *Financial Times,* September 16, 2007.

31. Cited in Kohut, "Muslims in America."

32. "Muslims in Europe: Economic Worries Top Concerns about Religious and Cultural Identity," Pew Global Attitudes Project, July 6, 2006, http://pewglobal.org/reports/display.php ?ReportID=254, accessed August 14, 2008.

33. See John Esposito and Dalia Mogahed, *Who Speaks for Islam? What a Billion Muslims Really Think,* pp. x–xi.

34. Ibid, pp. 47–51.

35. Ibid, pp. 69–70.

36. Ibid, pp. 70–71.

Chapter 11: Revolution 2.0

1. Cited by Karim Sadjadpour, *Reading Khamenei: The World View of Iran's Most Powerful Leader,* p. 7.

2. Cited by Steve Stalinsky, "The Iranian Threat: Ayatollah Ali Khamenei," *New York Sun,* February 9, 2005

3. Cited by Naji, *Ahmadinejad: The Secret History of Iran's Radical Leader,* p. 259.

4. Cited by Sadjadpour, p. 15.

5. Cited by Nasser Karimi, "Iran Leader: Bush

Will Be Tried," Associated Press, February 14, 2007.

6. See Fars news, August 2, 2006, cited by MEMRI, Special Dispatch Series - No. 1230, August 4, 2006.

7. Ibid.

8. Cited by Stalinsky.

9. Ibid.

10. Cited by Naji, p. 144.

11. Cited by Kenneth R. Timmerman, *Countdown to Crisis: The Coming Nuclear Showdown With Iran,* p. 42.

12. Cited by Sadjadpour, pp. 21–22.

13. In writing this chapter, I am deeply indebted to Kasra Naji, author of *Ahmadinejad: The Secret History of Iran's Radical Leader;* Yossi Melman and Meir Javedanfar, authors of *The Nuclear Sphinx of Tehran: Mahmoud Ahmadinejad and the State of Iran;* and Alireza Jafarzadeh, author of *The Iran Threat: President Ahmadinejad and the Coming Nuclear Crisis.* They provided a treasure trove of biographical information, historical background, and geopolitical and cultural context.

14. See Naji, pp. 61–62.

15. Ibid, p. 62.

16. Cited by Melman and Javedanfar, p. 23.

17. See "Iran Hardliner To Contest Runoff," BBC News, June 18, 2005, cited by Melman and Javedanfar, p. 35.

18. See "Hardline Win in Iran Sparks Fears on Nukes and Extremism," Agence France-Presse, June 25, 2005.

19. Cited by Naji, p. 85.

20. Cited by Naji, p. 86.

21. See "Iran Official Alleges Election Fraud,"

CNN, June 25, 2005; Michael Slackman, "Iran Moderate Says Hard-Liners Rigged Election," *New York Times,* June 19, 2005; "Iranian Reformer Alleges Election 'Rigged,' " Agence France-Presse, June 18, 2005; "Iran's Rafsanjani Renews Firestorm Over Election Fraud," *Iran Focus,* July 18, 2005

22. See Iran News, October 15, 2006, cited by MEMRI, Special Dispatch Series - No. 1328, October 19, 2006, http://memri.org/bin/latestnews.cgi?ID=SD132806, accessed on August 24, 2008.

23. Ibid.

24. See Naji, pp. 4–5; Melman and Javedanfar, pp. 1–2.

25. See Naji, p. 15.

26. See official biography on the president's Web site, http://www.president.ir/en/, accessed August 24, 2008.

27. See Jafarzadeh, p. 16; also see biography on GlobalSecurity.org's Web site, http://www.globalsecurity.org/military/world/iran/ahmadinejadbio.htm, accessed August 24, 2008; see Dan Diker, "President Bush and the Qods Controversy: Lessons Learned," Jerusalem Center for Public Affairs, March 6, 2007, http://www.jcpa.org/JCPA/Templates/ShowPage.asp?DRIT=1&DBID=1&LNGID=1&TMID=111&FID=443&PID=0&IID=1516&TTL=President_Bush_ and_the_Qods_Force_Con troversy:_Lessons_Learned, accessed August 24, 2008.

28. See Colin Freeman, "The Rise of Prof 'Crocodile' — A Hardliner to Terrify Hardliners," *London Telegraph,* November 19, 2005; Colin Freeman and Kay Biouki, "Ayatollah

who backs suicide bombs aims to be Iran's next spiritual leader," *London Telegraph,* November 19, 2006.

29. Cited by Naji, p. 99.

30. Ibid, p. 98.

31. Cited by Colin Freeman and Philip Sherwell, "Iranian Fatwa Approves Use of Nuclear Weapons," *London Telegraph,* February 18, 2006. See also "New Iranian Fatwa: Religious Law Does Not Forbid Use of Nuclear Weapons," MEMRI, Special Dispatch Series - No. 1096, February 17, 2006.

32. Cited by Naji, p. 102.

33. Cited by Jafarzadeh, p. 25.

34. Cited by Jafarzadeh, p. 22.

35. See Jafarzadeh, pp. 22–23.

36. Cited by Naji, p. 47.

37. Cited by Jafarzadeh, p. 22.

38. See Naji, p. 49.

39. Cited by Naji, p. 98.

40. See Melman and Javedanfar, p. 50.

41. Cited by Naji, p. 92.

42. See Jafarzadeh, p. 31; see also Vali Nasr, *The Shia Revival: How Conflicts within Islam Will Shape the Future,* p. 134.

43. Cited by Melman and Javedanfar, p. 51.

44. Cited by Melman and Javedanfar, p. 46 and Naji, p. 93.

45. See Melman and Javedanfar, pp. 46–47.

46. See Naji, p. 96.

47. President Mahmoud Ahmadinejad, address to the United Nations General Assembly, New York City, September 17, 2005, translated and distributed by the Islamic Republic News Agency, posted on www.globalsecurity.org.

48. See accounts by Amir Taheri, "The Frighten-

ing Truth of Why Iran Wants a Bomb," *Sunday Telegraph,* April 16, 2006; see also "Claims of Communication with Imam Mahdi," *Emrouz,* December 12, 2005; Arash Motamed, "The Appearance of Imam Mahdi in 2 Years," Rooz online, a popular Iranian dissident Web site, October 18, 2005; Hossein Bostani, "Ahmadinejad in Touch with 12th Imam," Rooz online, November 5, 2005; Melman and Javedanfar, pp. 55–57.

49. See Hossein Bostani, "Ahmadinejad in Touch with 12th Imam," Rooz online, November 5, 2005; and Amir Taheri, "The Frightening Truth of Why Iran Wants A Bomb," Sunday Telegraph, April 16, 2006.

50. Cited by Melman and Javedanfar, p. 41.

51. Mahmoud Ahmadinejad, text of address to "A World Without Zionism" conference, Tehran, reported by the Iranian Students News Agency, October 26, 2005, cited by MEMRI, Special Dispatch Series - No. 1013, October 28, 2005.

52. See Y. Carmon, "The Role of Holocaust Denial in the Ideology and Strategy of the Iranian Regime," MEMRI Special Dispatch Series - No. 307, December 15, 2006.

53. "Iran's Ahmadinejad Declares Holocaust Is a Myth," Reuters, December 14, 2005.

54. See "Russia Agrees to Sell Missiles to Iran," Associated Press, December 2, 2005; Lyuba Pronina, "Moscow Inks Arms Deal with Tehran," *Moscow Times,* December 5, 2005.

55. "Iran Received 12 Cruise Missiles with a 3,000-Km Range from Ukraine, Capable of Carrying Nuclear Warheads," *Ha'aretz,* December 21, 2005.

56. Ali Akbar Dareini, "Iran Votes to Block

Nuclear Inspections," Associated Press, November 20, 2005.

57. "Iran's Army Takes Control of Nukes," *Pakistani Daily Times,* October 6, 2005.

58. For this quote, as well as an excellent and detailed analyis of the behind-the-scenes political tensions created by Ahmadinejad's rise to power and devotion to the Mahdi, see the paper by A. Savyon, "The 'Second Islamic Revolution' in Iran: Power Struggle at the Top," MEMRI, Special Dispatch Series - No. 253, November 17, 2005.

59. Ibid.

Chapter 12: Making Way for the Mahdi

1. Mahmoud Ahmadinejad, "Iranian Leader Opens Up," interview with Mike Wallace, CBS News, August 13, 2006, http://www.cbsnews .com/stories/2006/08/09/60minutes/main187 9867.shtml, accessed August 25, 2008; Scott MacLeod, "A Date with a Dangerous Mind," *Time* magazine cover story, September 17, 2005 issue, http://www.time.com/time/ magazine/article/0,9171,1535827,00.html, accessed August 25, 2008; Ahmadinejad, "NBC Exclusive: Ahmadinejad on the Record," interview with Brian Williams, NBC News, September 20, 2006, http://www.msnbc.msn.com/id/ 14911753/, accessed August 25, 2008; Ahmadinejad, "Interview with Iranian President Mahmoud Ahmadinejad," interview with Anderson Cooper, CNN, September 20, 2006, http://transcripts.cnn.com/TRANSCRIPTS/ 0609/20/acd.01.html, accessed August 25, 2008.

2. See Joel C. Rosenberg, "Mesmerized Media:

When Will Ahmadinejad's Radical Religious Beliefs Get Covered?" National Review Online, September 20, 2006, http://article.national review.com/?q=Zjg2MjgxZmVkNDkxOGZiN2 RiMWNiZjUwYjhjOTMxZWU, accessed August 25, 2008. See also Joel C. Rosenberg, "60 Minutes's Missed Opportunity: What Mike Wallace Should Have Asked Ahmadinejad," National Review Online, August 14, 2006, http:// article.nationalreview.com/print/?q=MjZmMW FkNTE2YTRiZGQ4YTliZTllMzg2MTM3N zIyOWQ, accessed August 25, 2008.

3. Ibid, August 14, 2006 story.

4. See Mehdi Khalaji, *Apocalyptic Politics: On the Rationality of Iranian Policy*, p. 35; Melman and Javedanfar, *The Nuclear Sphinx of Tehran: Mahmoud Ahmadinejad and the State of Iran*, p. 43; Naji, *Ahmadinejad: The Secret History of Iran's Radical Leader*, p. 92; Vali Nasr, *The Shia Revival: How Conflicts within Islam Will Shape the Future*, p. 67.

5. See Khalaji, p. 34.

6. Cited by Khalaji, p. 4.

7. See Khalaji, p. 4; Melman and Javedanfar, p. 44.

8. See the Institute's Web site, http://www.intizar .org/en/.

9. Interviews with teachers at the Bright Future Institute; see Melman and Javedanfar, pp. 43–44.

10. Ayatollah Ibrahim Amini, *Al-Imam al-Mahdi, the Just Leader of Humanity*, trans. Dr. Abulaziz Sachedina (Qum, Iran: Ahul Bayt Digital Islamic Library Project, electronic online version), http://www.al-islam.org/mahdi/nontl/ Toc.htm, accessed April 15, 2006.

11. The World Towards Illumination, Islamic

Republic of Iran Broadcasting, http://
english.irib.ir/IRAN/Leader/Illumination.htm,
accessed January 2, 2007 (as of June 2008, the
Web posting had been removed); see posting
on Joel C. Rosenberg's blog: "Iran Says 2007
Could Bring Islamic Messiah, Possibly This
Spring," January 2, 2007; see also, "Waiting for
the Mahdi: Official Iranian Eschatology Out-
lined in Public Broadcasting Program in Iran,"
MEMRI, Special Dispatch Series - No. 1436,
January 25, 2007.
12. See Yaakov Lappin, "Iran: Mahdi Will Defeat
Archenemy in Jerusalem," YnetNews.com,
December 31, 2006.
13. The World Towards Illumination, Islamic
Republic of Iran Broadcasting.
14. Cited by A. Savyon and Y. Mansharof, "The
Doctrine of Mahdism: In the Ideological and
Political Philosophy of Mahmoud Ahmadinejad and Ayatollah Mesbah-e Yazdi," MEMRI
Special Dispatch Series - No. 357, May 31,
2007.
15. Cited by Y. Mansharof and A. Savyon, "Escalation in the Positions of Iranian President Mahmoud Ahmadinejad — A Special Report,"
MEMRI Special Dispatch Series - No. 389,
September 17, 2007.
16. Ibid.
17. Ibid.
18. See transcripts of President Ahmadinejad's
speeches to the U.N. and Columbia University
as reported in the *Washington Post,* September
24, 2007.
19. See *The Iraq Study Group Report,* p. 32.
20. See Kathleen Ridolfo, "Analysis: Iraqi Defense
Minister Continues Accusations against Iran,

Syria," RFE/RL, January 19, 2005.

21. See "Most Foreign Insurgents Come from Iran," *Al-Taji,* May 8, 2006, cited by IranFocus-.com, May 9, 2006.

22. Cited by Jafarzadeh, *The Iran Threat: President Ahmadinejad and the Coming Nuclear Crisis,* p. 85.

23. See "Report: 70 Percent of Insurgents in Iraq Come from Gulf States via Syria," Associated Press, May 23, 2007.

24. Cited by Ali Akbar Dareini, "Iran Ready to Fill Any Vacuum in Iraq," Associated Press, August 28, 2007.

25. See "Iraqi Forces Discover 'Largest' Iranian EFP Cache," IranFocus.com, April 9, 2008.

26. Cited by Peter Spiegel, "Petraeus Calls Iran-Backed Groups Biggest Threat in Iraq," *Los Angeles Times,* April 10, 2008.

27. "Hayden: Killing Americans Is Iran's Policy," Associated Press, May 1, 2008.

28. Mark Mazzetti, "U.S. Report Says Iran Halted Nuclear Weapons Program in 2003," *International Herald Tribune,* December 3, 2007.

29. Sen. Richard Shelby, interview with PBS *NewsHour,* June 3, 1998. See also "CIA Caught Off Guard on India Nuclear Test," CNNInterctive.com, http://www.cnn.com/WORLD/asiapcf/9805/12/india.cia/index.html, accessed March 24, 2008; and "U.S. Intelligence and the Indian Bomb: Documents Show U.S. Intelligence Failed to Warn of India's Nuclear Tests Despite Tracking Nuclear Weapons Potential Since 1950s," National Security Archive Electronic Briefing Book No. 187, George Washington University, available online at: http://www.gwu.edu/~nsarchiv/NSAEBB/NSAEBB187/

index.htm, accessed March 24, 2008.

30. For examples, see Amb. John Bolton, "The Flaws in the Iran Report," *Washington Post,* December 6, 2007; and Gerald M. Steinberg, "Decoding the U.S. National Intelligence Estimate on Iran's Nuclear Weapons Program," Jerusalem Center for Public Affairs, www .jcpa.org, December 5, 2007.

31. "Good and Bad News about Iran," *New York Times* editorial, December 5, 2007.

32. " 'High Confidence' Games: The CIA's Flip-Flop on Iran Is Hardly Reassuring," *Wall Street Journal* editorial, December 5, 2007.

33. "Intelligence on Iran," *Washington Post* editorial, December 5, 2007.

34. "Iran Hands IAEA Nuclear Blueprints," Associated Press, November 14, 2007.

35. See Patricia McNerney, Principal Deputy Assistant Secretary, International Security and Nonproliferation, "Testimony before the Senate Homeland Security and Governmental Affairs Committee; Subcommittee on Federal Financial Management, Government Information, Federal Services, and International Security," April 24, 2008.

36. "IAEA 'Alarmed' by Iran's Alleged Nuclear Weapons Work: Diplomat," Agence France-Presse, May 29, 2008.

37. "Report: Iran Says It Now Has 6,000 Centrifuges," Associated Press, July 27, 2008.

38. See David Morgan, "U.S. Says Iran Has Missile That Could Hit Europe," Reuters, July 15, 2008.

39. "Iran Launches Satellite Carrier into Space," Press TV, August 17, 2008.

40. "Abizaid: We Can Live with a Nuclear Iran,"

ABC News.com, September 17, 2007, http://blogs.abcnews.com/politicalradar/2007/09/abizaid-we-can-.html, accessed June 26, 2008.

41. Cited by Tom Curry, "Would Deterrence Work against Nuclear Iran?" MSNBC, July 6, 2007.

42. Hillary Clinton, interview on *Good Morning America,* ABC, April 22, 2008.

43. Joe Biden, speech delivered at the Iowa City Public Library, December 3, 2007, http://www.cfr.org/publication/14976/joe_bidens_speech_on_iran.html, accessed August 26, 2008.

Chapter 13: The Road Ahead

1. See Paul McGeough, "Down Syndrome Youth Used as Suicide Bomber," *The Age* (Sydney, Australia), February 2, 2005.

2. "Minister: Suicide Bomber a Handicapped Child," Associated Press, January 31, 2005.

3. Kim Gamel, "Female Bombers Strike Markets in Baghdad," Associated Press, February 1, 2008.

4. "U.S.: 'Demonic' Militants Sent Women to Bomb Markets in Iraq," CNN, February 2, 2008.

5. Porter Goss, interviews with the author. I submitted twenty-five written questions to Goss by e-mail. He sent written answers to those questions — cleared by the CIA — on February 11, 2008. I then conducted a video-taped interview with Goss on February 12, 2008, for use in this book, at our Epicenter Conference in Jerusalem in April 2008, and for a documentary film based on this book.

6. See Michael Ledeen, "Iran Is at War with Us," National Review Online, March 28, 2006, http://www.nationalreview.com/ledeen/

ledeen200603280728.asp, accessed August 23, 2008; see "Iran's Supreme Ruler Ayatollah Ali Khamenei, 68, Appeared on State TV Monday Looking Pale and Feeble, after Suffering a Cerebral Stroke Last Wednesday Jan. 3," Debka File report, January 13, 2007, http://www.debka.com/headline.php?hid=3708, accessed August 23, 2008; see "Iran Denies Reports on Khamenei Death," *Al Bawaba,* January 7, 2007, http://www.albawaba.com/en/countries/Iran/208173, accessed August 23, 2008.

7. For a detailed and excellent analysis of the Saudi threat, see Dore Gold's book *Hatred's Kingdom: How Saudi Arabia Supports the New Global Terrorism.*

8. See J. Michael McConnell, director of national intelligence, "Annual Threat Assessment of the Intelligence Community," testimony to the Senate Armed Services Committee, February 27, 2008.

9. Cited by James Pethokoukis, "So How Goes Bin Laden's War on the U.S. Economy?" *U.S. News & World Report,* September 11, 2007.

10. Ibid.

11. Cited by Randall Hamud, *Osama bin Laden: America's Enemy in His Own Words,* pp. 163–164.

12. Cited in "Ahmadinejad: Doom Will Befall US Economy," Press TV, April 23, 2008.

13. Cited in "Iran Threatens to Close Strait of Hormuz if Attacked," MEMRI, Special Dispatch Series - No. 2029, August 19, 2008.

14. For historic oil prices, see Lawrence Kumins, "Oil Prices: Overview of Current World Market Dynamics," CRS Report for Congress, Con-

gressional Research Service, October 26, 2001. For historic gas prices, see "Crude Oil Production and Crude Oil Well Productivity: 1954–2006," Annual Energy Review, Table 5.2, U.S. Energy Information Administration, http://www.eia.doe.gov/emeu/aer/pdf/pages/sec5_7.pdf.

15. See "Iran Threatens to Stop Oil Flow via Hormuz Strait," *Jerusalem Post,* January 8, 2007; "Iran Threatens to Close Straits of Hormuz with Missile Launch," *Oil and Gas Journal,* August 4, 2008; "Iran Threatens US Ships in Hormuz," *Al Arabiya,* January 7, 2008, http://www.alarabiya.net/articles/2008/01/07/43906.html, accessed August 23, 2008.

16. See "Crude Oil Production and Crude Oil Well Productivity: 1954–2006."

17. See Charles Krauthammer, "McCain's Oil Epiphany," *Washington Post,* June 20, 2008.

18. See Dr. Suzanne Weedman, energy program coordinator for the U.S. Geological Survey, U.S. Department of the Interior, testimony before the Energy Subcommitte of the House Science Committee, May 3, 2001.

19. See "It's Domestic Energy, Stupid" editorial, *Investor's Business Daily,* June 11, 2008.

Chapter 14: "Islam Is the Answer, but Jihad Is Not the Way"

1. See text of President Jefferson's first inaugural address, March 4, 1801, http://www.yale.edu/lawweb/avalon/presiden/inaug/jefinau1.htm, accessed August 31, 2008.

2. Ibid.

3. See John Esposito and Dalia Mogahed, *Who Speaks for Islam?* pp. x–xi.

4. Ibid, p. 47.
5. See "Iraqi Vote Mirrors Desire for Democracy in the Muslim World," press release, Pew Global Attitudes Project, February 3, 2005.
6. Ibid.
7. Robert F. Worth, "Relations With Turkey Kindle Hopes in Syria," *New York Times,* December 14, 2009.
8. "Arms from Turkey, Syria, Iran to Hezbollah," *UPI,* August 12, 2010.

Chapter 15: The Theology of the Reformers

1. See Benazir Bhutto, *Reconciliation,* p. 270.
2. Ibid, pp. 269–270.
3. Ibid, p. 2.
4. Ibid, pp. 31, 37–38.
5. Ibid, pp. 79–80.
6. Ibid, pp. 132, 134, 142.
7. Ibid, pp. 26–27.
8. Bernard Lewis, *The Crisis of Islam,* p. 153.
9. See David Horovitz, "Reformed al-Zawahiri Disciple in Israel," *Jerusalem Post,* January 8, 2008.
10. See Eli Lake, "Senior al Qaeda Theologian Urges His Followers to End Their Jihad," *New York Sun,* December 20, 2007.
11. See "Major Jihadi Cleric and Author of Al-Qaeda's Shari'a Guide to Jihad: 9/11 Was a Sin," MEMRI Special Dispatch Series - No. 1785, December 14, 2007; http://memri.org/bin/articles.cgi?Page=archives&Area=sd&ID=SP178507, accessed July 9, 2008.
12. See Abdul Hameed Bakier, "Imprisoned Leader of Egypt's Islamic Jihad Challenges al-Qaeda," *Terrorism Monitor,* The Jamestown Foundation, December 10, 2007.

Chapter 16: The Defector

1. Hossein Khomeini, event hosted by Michael A. Ledeen, American Enterprise Institute, September 26, 2003, http://www.aei.org/events/filter.,eventID.630/transcript.asp, accessed July 25, 2008.

2. *Al-Sharq Al-Awsat* (London), August 4, 2003; cited in MEMRI Special Dispatch Series - No. 548, August 6, 2003.

3. See Khomeini transcript.

4. See Khomeini transcript.

5. Michael Ledeen, interview with author, September 2, 2008.

6. See "Bush: U.S., Europeans Speaking with 'One Voice' on Iran," CNN, March 11, 2005; Anne Gearan, "Rice Praises European Plan on Iran," Associated Press, May 10, 2006; "Secretary of State Condoleezza Rice Backs European Nuclear Talks on Iran," Associated Press, September 27, 2006.

7. Interview on Al Arabiyah, cited in "Ayatollah Khomeini's Grandson: Grandfather's Revolution Devoured its Children, Strayed from Original Course," *Iran Press News*, June 15, 2006; see also, Philip Sherwell, "Ayatollah's Grandson Calls for U.S. Overthrow of Iran," *London Telegraph*, June 19, 2006.

8. See interview on Al Arabiyah, cited in "Ayatollah Khomeini's Grandson: Grandfather's Revolution Devoured its Children"; see also Eli Lake, "Unlikely Pair Emerges as Foe of Iran Regime," *New York Sun*, June 13, 2006.

9. See Dafna Linzer, "Ex-Iranian Official Talks to Western Intelligence: Deputy Defense Minister Instrumental in Founding of Hezbollah, Officials Say," *Washington Post*, March 8, 2007;

"Defector Spied on Iran for Years," Ynet News, March 11, 2007; "Iranian Defector Enabled IAF Syria Strike," *Al Jerida* (Kuwait), cited by Arutz Sheva, September 28, 2007; "Report: Defecting Iranian Official Gave Info before Alleged Syrian Foray," *Jerusalem Post,* September 28, 2007; "Israel: Asghari Gave Syrian Intelligence," *Stratfor,* September 28, 2007.

10. See "Top Iranian Defector on Iran's Collaboration with Iraq, North Korea, Al-Qa'ida, and Hizbullah," MEMRI Special Dispatch Series - No. 473, February 20, 2003.

11. See "Son of Iranian General Defects to US," BBC News, July 3, 1998. See also Voice of America interview, February 24, 1999, available at http://www.fas.org/news/iran/1999/990224iran.htm, accessed June 26, 2008

12. Ibid, VOA interview.

13. See *World Fact Book,* Central Intelligence Agency, updated July 24, 2008, https://www.cia.gov/library/publications/the-world-factbook/geos/ir.html, accessed July 26, 2008; and "Population and Growth," *Iran Daily,* March 15, 2006.

14. "Unemployment Ffalls to 10.3 — Minister," Reuters, March 31, 2008.

15. "Khamenei Urges Ahmadinejad to Rein In Soaring Inflation," Agence France-Presse, August 25, 2008.

16. See *World Fact Book,* Central Intelligence Agency; Human Development Reports: 2007–2008, U.N. Development Program, http://hdrstats.undp.org/countries/data_sheets/cty_ds_IRN.html, accessed June 26, 2008.

17. See "90 Percent of Population Under Poverty Line: MP," *Iran Focus,* January 21, 2005.

18. Hamid Sarami, Iranian Office to Combat Drugs, Education and Prevention Unit; quoted in "In Iran, One New Person Gains Drug Addiction Every 3 Minutes," *Iran Focus*, July 7, 2005; see also "Iran Tops World Drug Addiction Rate," *Iran Focus*, September 24, 2005; see also Karl Vick, "Opiates of the Iranian People: Despair Drives World's Highest Addiction Rate," *Washington Post*, September 23, 2005.

19. See *2007 World Drug Report*, U.N. Office on Drug and Crime, p. 241, http://www.unodc.org/pdf/research/wdr07/WDR_2007.pdf, accessed June 26, 2008.

20. See Vick, "Opiates of the Iranian People."

21. Ibid.

22. See "Nine Million Drug Addicts Nationwide by 20 Years," Agence France-Presse, October 31, 2002.

23. Interview with a senior Western intelligence official, on the condition of anonymity, fall of 2005.

24. See Vali Nasr, *The Shia Revival*, p. 213.

25. All cited from a wonderful book by an Iranian dissident whose pseudonym is Nasrin Alavi. The book is entitled *We Are Iran: The Persian Blogs*.

26. Cited by Peter Bergen, *The Osama Bin Laden I Know*, p. 400.

27. See "Poll: Bin Laden Tops Musharraf in Pakistan," CNN, September 11, 2007.

28. Ibid.

29. "Pakistani Support for al Qaeda, bin Laden Plunges," polling report conducted for Terror Free Tomorrow, January 2008, http://www.terrorfreetomorrow.org/upimagestft/TFT%20

Pakistan%20Poll%20Report.pdf, accessed
August 4, 2008; see also Griff Witte and Robin
Wright, "Musharraf's Approval Rating Plum-
mets," *Washington Post,* February 11, 2008.

Chapter 17: Meet Hamid Karzai

1. Author interview with a Christian relief worker
   on the condition of anonymity, summer 2008.
2. Cited by Nick B. Mills, *Karzai,* pp. 50–51.
   Mills's biography, based on extensive interviews
   with the Afghan president and a personal
   relationship between the two men dating back
   to 1987, was an enormously helpful resource
   in drafting this chapter. I highly recommend it
   to anyone interested in understanding Karzai's
   thinking and the tremendously challenging
   geopolitical environment in which he is operating.
3. Ibid, p. 64.
4. Ibid, p. 91.
5. Ibid, p. 98.
6. Ibid, p. 99.
7. Ibid, p. 105.
8. Hamid Karzai, interview, PBS *NewsHour* with
   Jim Lehrer, January 28, 2002.
9. See Mills, p. 112.
10. Hamid Karzai, "Home Free," *Time* magazine,
    August 18–25, 2003 issue.
11. Ibid.
12. See Mills, pp. 154–155.
13. See Karzai essay in *Time* magazine.

Chapter 18: Karzai's Mission

1. Cited by Carlotta Gall, "At the Polls in a
   Southern Village, Afghans Vote with Confidence
   and Yearn for Security," *New York Times,*

October 10, 2004

2. Ibid.

3. Cited by Mills, *Karzai,* p. 201.

4. Ibid.

5. Cited by Eric Quiñones, "Karzai Lauds International Cooperation in Rebuilding Afghanistan," Princeton University news Web site, September 26, 2003, http://www.princeton.edu/pr/home/03/0926_karzai/hmcap.html, accessed July 6, 2008.

6. See John Fischer, "Hamid Karzai, President of Afghanistan to Receive Award," About.com, http://philadelphia.about.com/od/history/a/liberty_medal_b.htm?p=1, accessed July 6, 2008.

7. Ibid.

8. See address by His Excellency President Hamid Karzai, National Constitution Center, Philadelphia, Pennsylvania, July 4, 2004, http://www.constitutioncenter.org/libertymedal/recipient_2004_speech.html, accessed August 30, 2008.

9. See transcript of keynote address by President Karzai at the U.S.-Islamic Forum, Doha, Qatar, February 16, 2008.

10. See "Hamid Karzai: Shrewd Statesman," BBC, June 14, 2002.

11. See Arshad Mohammed, "U.S. Expected to Pledge Some $10 Billion for Afghans," June 10, 2008; "Donors to Give Billions in Afghan Aid," Agence France-Presse, June 12, 2008.

12. For more, see NATO report.

13. See Laura Bush, "What I Saw in Afghanistan," *Wall Street Journal,* June 12, 2008.

14. "Hamid Karzai Becomes Father at 49," BBC, January 26, 2007.

15. See transcript of open forum discussion with President Karzai, Council on Foreign Relations, September 21, 2006, http://www.cfr.org/publication/11507/, accessed June 27, 2008.

16. From 2007–2009, women held 94 of 535 total seats in the U.S. House and Senate. See http://womenincongress.house.gov/data/wic-by-congress.html?cong=110.

17. See Council on Foreign Relations transcript.

18. See transcript from an interview with Hamid Karzai, Council on Foreign Relations, September 26, 2006.

19. See Council on Foreign Relations transcript.

20. See transcript from an interview with Hamid Karzai, Council on Foreign Relations, September 26, 2006.

21. "Massive Prison Break in Afghanistan," Reuters, June 13, 2008.

22. See Weblog posting by Joel C. Rosenberg, "U.S. to Launch New 'Surge' — This Time in Afghanistan,' " June 18, 2008, http://joelrosenberg.blogspot.com/2008/06/us-to-launch-new-surge-this-time-in.html; Steven Lee Myers and Thom Shanker, "Pentagon Considers Adding Forces in Afghanistan," *New York Times,* May 3 2008; "Progress in Afghanistan," NATO report, April 2008, http://www.nato.int/isaf/docu/epub/pdf/progress_afghanistan.pdf; "U.S. Troops in Afghanistan Number More Than 32,000," Associated Press, April 10, 2008; "Canada to Boost Troops in Afghanistan," Xinhua news agency, July 26, 2008; "UK to Send More Troops to Afghanistan," Afghanistan News Network, August 8, 2008; "Pentagon Plans to Send More Than 12,000 Additional Troops to Afghanistan," *U.S. News*

& *World Report,* August 19, 2008.

23. See NATO report, p. 9.

24. Information based on author interviews with U.S. and Afghan officials on the condition of anonymity, conducted in October of 2008.

25. "Karzai Takes Over Afghan Vote-Fraud Panel," *Washington Times,* February 23, 2010.

26. Thomas L. Friedman, "This Time We Really Mean It," *New York Times,* March 30, 2010.

Chapter 19: "We Are Fighting Islamic Fascists"

1. "Purported al-Zarqawi Tape Vows to Fight [Iraqi] Election," MSNBC, January 24, 2005, http://www.msnbc.msn.com/id/6855496/, accessed August 2, 2008.

2. Cited by Ellen Knickmeyer and Jonathan Finer, "Insurgent Leader al-Zarqawi Killed in Iraq," *Washington Post,* June 8, 2006.

3. "Statement by U.S. Ambassador Zalmay Khalilzad on the Killing of Abu Musab Al-Zarqawi," U.S. Embassy in Iraq, June 8, 2006.

4. See "Insurgent Leader al-Zarqawi Killed in Iraq," *Washington Post,* June 8, 2006.

5. See Cesar Soriano, "Iraqi Leaders: Memo Details al-Qaeda Plans," *USA Today,* June 15, 2006; see also "Officials Give Details on al-Zarqawi Strike," U.S. Multi-National Force Iraq news service, June 18, 2006.

6. "Iraq Announces Info from al-Zarqawi Raid," Associated Press, June 15, 2006.

7. Ibid.

8. See Jonathan Weisman, "Iraqi Prime Minister Presses for More Aid," *Washington Post,* July 27, 2006.

9. Ibid; see also David Stout, "Maliki Expresses Thanks in Address to Congress," *New York*

Times, July 26, 2006.

10. "Statement of Senator Hillary Rodham Clinton Calling for Political Change in Iraq," http:// clinton.senate.gov/news/statements/details.cfm ?id=281188&& (accessed October 24, 2008); "Clinton Urges Ouster of Iraq's al-Maliki," Associated Press, August 23, 2007.

11. Ibid.

12. "Iraq PM Hits Out at Critics," Aljazeera TV, August 26, 2007.

13. "Maliki Returns Fire at US critics," BBC News, August 26, 2007.

14. "Interview: Iraqi Official Mourns Sons, Vows to Fight 'The Ghosts of Death,' " transcript of interview by Radio Free Iraq, posted on the Web site of Radio Free Europe/ Radio Liberty, February 8, 2005, http://www.rferl.org/content/ article/1057351.html, accessed August 1, 2008.

15. Mithal Al-Alusi, member of the Iraqi parliament, interview with author, August 1, 2008.

16. See Kimberly Kagan, "The Anbar Awakening: Displacing Al-Qaeda from Its Stronghold in Western Iraq," *The Weekly Standard,* March 30, 2007, http://www.weeklystandard.com/ weblogs/TWSFP/IraqReport03.1.pdf, accessed August 2, 2008.

17. Cited by Vali Nasr, *The Shia Revival,* p. 178. For an excellent analysis of Sistani, see Nasr's entire chapter "The Tide Turns," which was very helpful to me in writing this section.

Chapter 20: Meet Jalal Talabani

1. See "Barak Shakes Hands with Iraqi President," Ynet News, July 1, 2008; "Iraq: MPs Slam Talabani-Barak Handshake," Ynet News, July 4, 2008

2. See "Iraqi President Jalal Talabani says Israeli President Peres 'welcome in Iraqi Kurdistan,' " *Yaqen News Agency*, November 14, 2007.

3. Data in this section are based on the author's interviews with senior Iraqi and U.S. government officials throughout 2008.

4. See official biography of President Jalal Talabani, Web site of the Patriotic Union of Kurdistan, http://www.puk.org/web/htm/about/talab.html, accessed October 29, 2008.

5. "Woman Testifies on Alleged Saddam Attack," *Associated Press*, September 11, 2006.

6. Cited by Bushra Juhi and Jamal Halaby, "At Saddam's Trial, Kurdish Doctor Describes Gas Attack," *Associated Press*, December 8, 2006.

7. See Ahmed Rasheed, "Saddam Says Responsible for Any Iran Gas Attacks," *Reuters*, December 18, 2006.

8. Ibid.

9. Cited by Ross Colvin, "Iraq Trial Revives Bitter Memories of 'U.S. Betrayal,' " *Reuters*, August 21, 2007.

10. Cited by Dian McDonald, "U.S. Won't Intervene in Iraq's Civil War," U.S. Information Agency report, April 4, 1991.

11. Ibid.

12. Mala Bakhtyar, spokesman for President Jalal Talabani, interview with the author, February 25, 2008.

13. See Bob Woodward, *State of Denial,* pp. 174–176.

14. See Amb. L. Paul Bremer III, *My Year in Iraq,* pp. 355–356.

15. Ibid, p. 376.

16. See "An Hour with Iraqi President Ghazi al-Yawar," *Charlie Rose Show,* December 6, 2006,

763

http://www.charlierose.com/shows/2004/12/06/
1/an-hour-with-iraqi-president-ghazi-al-yawar,
accessed July 3, 2008.

17. Cited in "Kurd Leader Talabani New Iraq President," Dawn News Service (Pakistan), April 7, 2005. See also "Iraq Parliament Elects Jalal Talabani as President," Bloomberg, April 6, 2006.

Chapter 21: Talabani's Test

1. See transcript, President Talabani's first White House press conference with President Bush, www.whitehouse.gov, September 13, 2005.
2. Ibid.
3. Cited in "Talabani: U.S. Troops Should Stay 3 More Years: Iraqi President Denies Civil War in Iraq but Asks for Help Defeating Terrorists," Reuters, November 2, 2006; see also Katrinn Bennhold, "Talabani: U.S. Troops Should Stay 3 More Years," International Herald Tribune, November 2, 2006.
4. See "McCain: Deploy More Troops to Iraq," Associated Press, December 14, 2006.
5. See transcript of President Bush's address to the nation, CNN, January 10, 2007.
6. Ibid.
7. See transcript of interview with Sen. Obama on MSNBC's "Response to the President's Speech on Iraq," January 10, 2007.
8. See transcript of interview with Sen. Obama on CNN's Larry King Live, January, 10, 2007, http://transcripts.cnn.com/TRANSCRIPTS/0701/10/lkl.01.html, accessed July 18, 2008.
9. See "Interview with Iraqi President Jalal Talabani," Dar al-Hayat (Lebanon), January 22, 2007.

10. Cited in "Iraq War is 'Lost': US Democrat Leader," Agence France-Presse, April 19, 2007.
11. Cited by Jeff Mason, "Clinton Says 'We Cannot Win' Iraq War," Reuters, March 17, 2008.
12. Cited by Ivan Moreno, "Albright Visits University of Denver, Slams Bush," Associated Press, May 28, 2008.
13. Based on author interviews with Iraqi officials. Also see "U.S. Ground Forces End Strength," fact sheet, GlobalSecurity.org, http://www .globalsecurity.org/military/ops/iraq_orbat_es .htm, accessed July 18, 2008; Jim Michaels, "19,000 Insurgents Killed in Iraq Since '03," *USA Today,* September 27, 2007.
14. See Dexter Filkins, "Exiting Iraq, Petraeus Says Gains Are Fragile," *New York Times,* August 21, 2008.
15. Ambassador L. Paul Bremer III, interview with author, July 10, 2008.
16. See ABC News and *Time* magazine transcript of press availability with Sen. Obama, Watertown, South Dakota, May 16, 2008, http:// thepage.time.com/transcript-of-obama-presser-2/, accessed June 27, 2008.
17. Cited by "Iraq Study Group Chairs Defend Report," Reuters, December 11, 2007.
18. Cited by James Kitfield, "Democracy Stalled," *National Journal,* May 3, 2008.
19. Cited by John Bersia, "Iraq President's Son: U.S. Role Half-Complete," *Orlando Sentinel,* March 29, 2006.

Chapter 22: The King and I

1. See "CIA Helps Defuse al Qaeda Bomb Plot in Morocco," CNN, June 16, 2002.
2. See "Morocco Makes More Al Qaeda Arrests,"

CBS News, June 25, 2002; "Morocco Dismantles 'Terrorist Network': Police," Agence France-Presse, August 29, 2008; "Morocco Arrests 17 Terror Suspects," Associated Press, November 20, 2005; "Morocco Arrests Four Female Terrorist Suspects," Deutsche Presse Agentur, September 1, 2006; "Dozens Held Over Morocco Plot," Aljazeera, February 21, 2008.

3. See "Morocco Holds 14 over Suspected al Qaeda Links," Reuters, October 27, 2006.

4. Dr. Ahmed Abaddi, interview with author, May 2006; see also Joel C. Rosenberg, "A Different Sort of Radical Muslim: Ahmed Abaddi Is Helping Muslims to Understand the West," *National Review,* May 9, 2006; Joseph Loconte, "The Moroccan Model: A Beacon of Hope in the Islamic World," *The Weekly Standard,* May 16, 2006; James Morrison and Julia Duin, "Moroccan Model," *Washington Times,* April 27, 2006.

Chapter 23: The Moroccan Model

1. Khalid Zerouali, interview with the author, January 16, 2008.

2. See "Morocco Hails Formation of Interim Government in Afghanistan," Arab News, December 24, 2001; see also "A List of Foreign Diplomats Attacked in Iraq," Associated Press, October 3, 2007; "Moroccan Suspect [in Iraq] Named in 60 Shiite Deaths," Associated Press, November 1, 2005; "Moroccan Charged with Helping al-Qaida," Associated Press, December 20, 2007.

3. See "Morocco Waits Its Turn Following Turkey's EU Membership," *Turkish Weekly,* March 31,

2005; "Morocco's Quest to be European," BBC, April 3, 2000; "Morocco Wants Closer Ties to the E.U.," *EU Business,* October 4, 2007; "Morocco 'to Strongly Adhere to Mr. Sarkozy's Mediterranean Union Initiative,' Minister," Maghreb Arab Presse, June 7, 2008; "Paris Summit for the Mediterranean," fact sheet, July 2008, http://www.ue2008.fr/webdav/site/PFUE/shared/import/07/0713_sommet_mediterranee/Press%20Kit%20Paris%20Summit_EN.pdf.

4. Dr. Ahmed Khamlichi, interview with the author, January 14, 2008.

5. See Scott MacLeod, "An interview with King Mohammed VI of Morocco," *Time* magazine, June 26, 2000.

6. Ibid.

7. MP Fatiha Layadi, interview with the author, January 2008.

8. See Ahmed El Amraoui, "Jewish Woman in Morocco Poll Fray," Aljazeera, September 7, 2007; see also "Jewish Woman Runs for Moroccan Parliament," Jewish Telegraphic Agency, September 7, 2007.

9. See "King of Morocco Calls for Fundamental Reform in Family Law," MEMRI Special Dispatch Series - No. 604, November 7, 2003, http://www.memri.org/bin/latestnews.cgi?ID=SD60403.

10. See MacLeod, *Time* magazine.

11. See "FACTBOX: Morocco's Economy: Trade, Tourism Check Poverty," Reuters, September 7, 2007; CIA *World Fact Book;* and World Bank data.

12. Serge Berdugo, interview with the author, November 2005.

13. Author interview with senior Moroccan official who requested anonymity, January 2008.
14. See "King Abdullah of Jordan Participates in U.S. 'National Prayer Breakfast' Events," press release, Embassy of Jordan, February 1, 2006, http://www.jordanembassyus.org/new/pr/pr02022006.shtml; see also "Jordan's king urges moderates to unite," *Washington Times,* February 2, 2006.

Chapter 24: "Islam Is Not the Answer, and Jihad Is Not the Way; Jesus Is the Way"

1. This section is adapted from the foreword I wrote for *Once an Arafat Man: The True Story of How a PLO Sniper Found a New Life,* written by Saada and Dean Merrill. It is based on my conversations and e-mails with Saada and material drawn from his book.

Chapter 25: The Big, Untold Story — Part One

1. Sheikh Salman Al-Odeh, "Christian Missionaries Sweeping the Islamic World," transcript, Lesson 66, Monday 12th of Safar, 1413 Hijra (1993), from www.islamworld.net/tanseer.htm, accessed February 3, 2006.
2. Interview with Sheikh Ahmad Al Qataani on Aljazeera, December 12, 2000. Transcript available from Ali Sina, Iranian dissident, on his Web site, www.faithfreedom.org/oped/sina31103.htm, accessed February 3, 2006.
3. Author interview with a senior Mideast Christian leader, spring 2008. Taheer is a pseudonym.
4. Author interview with an Iranian Christian leader on the condition of anonymity, 2007.
5. Author interview with an Iranian Christian

768

leader on the condition of anonymity, 2007.

6. Author interview with Iranian pastor, name and date withheld.

7. Cited by Julian Lukins, "Behind the Black Veil," *Charisma,* June 2004 issue.

8. Patrick Johnstone et al., *Operation World* (Waynesboro: Authentic Media, 2001), p. 353.

9. Author interview with Iranian evangelical leader, name and date withheld.

10. Author interview with Iranian political dissident on the condition of anonymity, summer of 2008.

11. Author interview with senior Iranian ministry leader on the condition of anonymity, fall of 2007.

12. Ramin Mostaghim, "Ruling Shiites Influence Eroded by Other Faiths," Inter Press Service, May 5, 2004.

13. See "Government Officials Admit Christianity 'Out of Control,' " Compass Direct, October 7, 2004.

14. See "Iran: Convert Stabbed to Death," Compass Direct, November 28, 2005; see also World Watch List 2006, Open Doors, http://www .opendoorsuk.org/downloads/wwl_downloads/ WorldWatchList.pdf, accessed April 3, 2006.

15. See "Iran Convert Stabbed," Compass Direct. See also Nina Shea, "The Real War on Christmas: Being a Christian Can Be Deadly," *National Review,* December 19, 2005. Shea cited Rev. Keith Roderick, an Episcopal priest representing Christian Solidarity International. The Voice of the Martyrs news agency also reported Ahmadinejad's quote.

16. Author interview with an Iranian pastor on the condition of anonymity, 2007.

Chapter 26: The Big, Untold Story — Part Two

1. Author interviews with Egyptian pastors and ministry leaders beginning in 2005 and continuing through the fall of 2008.
2. Author interview with an Arab pastor, name and date of interview withheld.
3. "Algeria Bans Muslims from Learning about Christianity," www.ArabicNews.com, March 21, 2006.
4. Author interview with a Sudanese evangelical leader, name and date withheld.
5. Author interviews with numerous Sudanese Christian leaders, 2008.
6. See Stan Guthrie, "Hope amid the Ruins: Anglican Bishop Sees Massive Church Growth," *Christianity Today,* January 2004.
7. Interviews with Iraqi and Jordanian Christian leaders, 2008.
8. Author interview with an Iraqi pastor, name and date withheld.
9. Author interview with Iraqi evangelical leader, name and date withheld.
10. Author interview with a Palestinian evangelist, name and date withheld.
11. Author interview with an Arab Christian leader from Syria on the condition of anonymity, 2007.
12. Interviews with several senior Jordanian Christian leaders on the condition of anonymity, 2008.
13. The story was relayed to me by an Arab ministry leader who has interacted with this woman personally, name and date of interview withheld.
14. Author interviews with numerous Afghan ministry leaders on the condition of anonym-

ity, summer and fall of 2008.

15. Author interview with Afghan evangelical Christian leader, name and date withheld.
16. "More Christians Arrested in Wake of 'Apostasy' Case," Open Doors USA Web site, http://www.opendoorsusa.org/Display.asp?Page =AfghanArrests, accessed April 3, 2006. See also www.compassdirect.org.
17. Author interview with an Uzbek Christian leader on the condition of anonymity, 2007.
18. Author interview with a Kazakh Christian leader on the condition of anonymity, 2007.
19. Interview with Dr. T. E. Koshy, June 15, 2008.

Chapter 27: The Air War

1. Cited by Raymond Ibrahim, "Islam's 'Public Enemy #1,' " *National Review,* March 25, 2008.
2. Father Zakaria Botros, interview with the author, September 5, 2008.
3. Steve Little, "Talking Truth to the Muslim World," *Christian World News,* CBN, September 29, 2006.
4. See "Coptic TV Show Causes Controversy in Egypt," MEMRI Special Dispatch Series - No. 943, July 27, 2005.
5. See "Coptic TV Show."
6. Hormoz Shariat, interview with the author, January 2007.
7. See "Iraq: Once-Outlawed Satellite Dishes Sprouting Like Mushrooms on Baghdad's Rooftops," Radio Free Europe/Radio Liberty, May 28, 2003.
8. See "Christian Television Succeeding in Middle East: 9 Million Viewers in Middle East Watch SAT-7 Christian TV According to New Research," press release, SAT-7, May 3, 2005.

Chapter 29: The Ground War — Part Two

1. Author interview with an Iraqi ministry leader from a Sunni Muslim background, February 2008.

Chapter 30: The Theology of the Revivalists

1. "Iraq Minister Says Mosul 'Worse Than Imagined,' " Agence France-Presse, January 28, 2008.

Chapter 31: Making Way for the Messiah

1. For a more detailed and complete analysis of Ezekiel's prophecies described by Bible scholars as the "War of Gog and Magog," please see Joel C. Rosenberg's book *Epicenter: Why the Current Rumblings in the Middle East Will Change Your Future* (Tyndale, 2006 hardcover edition, or 2008 softcover updated edition).
2. See Joel C. Rosenberg, "Arabs Building New Tower of Babel," Weblog posting, May 1, 2008, www.joelrosenberg.com.

Chapter 32: Join the Revolution

1. Cited by Yigal Schleifer, "Turkey's Christians Face Backlash," *Christian Science Monitor,* April 25, 2007. See also Suna Erdem, "Christians at Bible Publishers Have Their Throats Cut," The *Times* of London, April 19, 2007.
2. See Ethan Cole, "15,000 Iraqi Christians Driven Out of Mosul," *Christian Post,* October 20, 2008.
3. Author interview with Daniel — not his real name — October 2008.

Appendix: 20 Terrorist Plots Against America Foiled Since 9/11

1. See Joseph Abrams and Jonathan Passantino, "Foiled Terror Plots Against America Since 9/11," Fox News, September 11, 2008, http://www.foxnews.com/printer_friendly_story/0,3566,335500,00.html.

ACKNOWLEDGMENTS

Looking back, it now seems clear this book was set into motion in 1986, when the Lord first began to stir in my heart a curiosity about the Muslim world and gave me the opportunity to travel for a month to several Islamic cities in what was known then as Soviet Central Asia.

The following year, He gave me the wonderful privilege of traveling for the first time to Israel and the West Bank. While studying at Tel Aviv University for a semester, I witnessed firsthand the beginning of the Palestinian Muslim uprising known as the first intifada and its effect on Israel, on the U.S., and on world opinion.

By the next year, back at Syracuse University — my alma mater — Lynn and I began dating and volunteering in an international student ministry on campus run by our dear friend and pastor, Dr. T. E. Koshy. It was there that we developed so many special friendships with students from Iran, Gaza, and Algeria; and it was there that we began to learn how to love Muslims in real and practical ways.

What a journey it has been since. Lynn and I have been blessed by so many men and women who went out of their way to teach us, encourage us, challenge and inspire us. Though we wish we could, it would be impossible to acknowledge and thank them all by name. Still, we are compelled to honor a handful who deserve special recognition and appreciation.

Our families: Len and Mary Rosenberg; June "Bubbe" Meyers, the hero of November Communications; Dan and Susan Rebeiz; Michael and Patricia Meyers; the extended Meyers team; Steve and Kate Scoma; Jim and Emily Urbanski. We love you all so much. Thank you for loving us and helping us in countless and deeply appreciated ways.

Our sources: thanks so much to each and every person cited in this book, as well as to hundreds more who provided useful facts, insightful analysis and candid observations that we found enormously helpful and without which this book would have been impossible to write. Special thanks to Tom and JoAnn Doyle for an amazing trip to Afghanistan.

Our amazingly wonderful, courageous, and deeply loved Joshua Fund team: Tim and Carolyn Lugbill, Edward and Kailea Hunt, Steve and Barb Klemke, Amy Knapp, John and Cheryl Moser, Jeremy and Angie Grafman, Nancy Pierce, Dr. Chung Woo and Dr. Farah Woo, and Dr. T. E. Koshy. Though words are our living, Lynn and I confess that we simply cannot find words adequate enough to express to each of you how grateful we are that you have joined the Revolution at great personal cost and chosen to help us when we have needed it most.

Our supporters and prayer warriors: all the individuals, families, pastors, congregations, ministries, and business leaders in the U.S.,

Canada, the epicenter, and around the world who are praying with and for us and who are faithfully and generously investing in the work of the Joshua Fund. We are humbled by your confidence and deeply committed to being wise stewards of the trust you have bestowed upon us. May the Lord richly bless you for blessing Israel and her neighbors in the name of Jesus, according to Genesis 12:1–3.

Our publishing team: Mark Taylor, Ron Beers, Becky Nesbitt, Jan Stob, Jeremy Taylor, Cheryl Kerwin, Beverly Rykerd, Dean Renninger, and the entire Tyndale family. You each are such a joy to work with. Thank you so much for helping us share this message.

Our literary agent: Scott Miller of Trident Media Group, the best in the business. Thanks for being such a dear friend and providing consistently wise counsel.

Our continuing heroes: all those whom we thanked in our previous books and who continue to bless our family and our team in countless and unexpected ways.

Our children: Caleb, Jacob, Jonah, and Noah, for whom we are so grateful. May you walk faithfully with Jesus, come what may.

Most of all, I want to thank my precious wife, Lynn, with all of my heart. You are my hero and my best friend, Lynn, and I love you more than I can possibly explain. Promise me you'll let me kneel beside you when we worship together at the feet of Jesus.

ABOUT THE AUTHOR

Joel C. Rosenberg is the founder of the Joshua Fund and the *New York Times* best-selling author of *The Last Jihad, The Last Days, The Ezekiel Option, The Copper Scroll, Dead Heat,* and *Epicenter,* with more than 1.5 million copies in print. As a communications strategist, he has worked with some of the world's most influential leaders in business, politics, and media, including Steve Forbes, Rush Limbaugh, and former Israeli prime minister Benjamin Netanyahu. As a novelist, he has been interviewed on hundreds of radio and TV programs, including ABC's *Nightline, CNN Headline News,* FOX News Channel, The History Channel, MSNBC, *The Rush Limbaugh Show,* and *The Sean Hannity Show.* He has been profiled by the *New York Times,* the *Washington Times, World* magazine, and the *Jerusalem Post.* He has addressed audiences all over the world, including Russia, Israel, Iraq, Jordan, Egypt, Turkey, and Belgium, and has spoken at the White House, the Pentagon, and the U.S. Capitol.

The first page of his first novel — *The Last Jihad* — puts readers inside the cockpit of a hijacked jet, coming in on a kamikaze attack into an American city, which leads to a war with Saddam

Hussein over weapons of mass destruction. Yet it was written before 9/11 and published before the actual war with Iraq. *The Last Jihad* spent eleven weeks on the *New York Times* hardcover fiction best-seller list, reaching as high as #7. It raced up the *USA Today* and *Publishers Weekly* best-seller lists, hit #4 on the *Wall Street Journal* list, and hit #1 on Amazon.com.

His second thriller — *The Last Days* — opens with the death of Yasser Arafat and a U.S. diplomatic convoy ambushed in Gaza. Two weeks before *The Last Days* was published in hardcover, a U.S. diplomatic convoy was ambushed in Gaza. Thirteen months later, Yasser Arafat was dead. *The Last Days* spent four weeks on the *New York Times* hardcover fiction best-seller list, hit #5 on the *Denver Post* list, and hit #8 on the *Dallas Morning News* list. Both books have been optioned by a Hollywood producer.

The Ezekiel Option centers on a dictator rising in Russia who forms a military alliance with the leaders of Iran as they feverishly pursue nuclear weapons and threaten to wipe Israel off the face of the earth. On the very day it was published in June 2005, Iran elected a new leader who vowed to accelerate the country's nuclear program and later threatened to "wipe Israel off the map." Six months after it was published, Moscow signed a $1 billion arms deal with Tehran. *The Ezekiel Option* spent four weeks on the *New York Times* hardcover fiction best-seller list and five months on the Christian Bookseller Association (CBA) best-seller list, reaching as high as #4. It won the 2006 Christian Book Award for fiction.

In *The Copper Scroll,* an ancient scroll describes unimaginable treasures worth untold billions buried in the hills east of Jerusalem and under the Holy City itself — treasures that could come from the Second Temple and whose discovery could lead to the building of the Third Temple and a war of biblical proportions. One month after it was released, *Biblical Archaeology Review* published a story describing the real-life, intensified hunt for the treasures of the actual Copper Scroll. *The Copper Scroll* spent four weeks on the *New York Times* hardcover fiction best-seller list, two weeks on the *Wall Street Journal* best-seller list, two weeks on the *Publishers Weekly* hardcover fiction list, and several months on the CBA best-seller list. It won the 2007 Logos Bookstores Best Fiction Award.

In *Dead Heat,* America is in the midst of a heated presidential election when the Secret Service learns of a catastrophic terrorist plot to assassinate one of the candidates. U.S. forces attempt to stop the terrorists before millions lose their lives, but events threaten to spin out of control. *Dead Heat* debuted at #4 on the *New York Times* hardcover best-seller list. It also became a *USA Today, Wall Street Journal, Publishers Weekly,* and CBA hardcover best seller.

Epicenter, Joel's best-selling nonfiction title, gives readers the headlines before they happen. It explains what is happening in the Middle East and how it will impact our world. It contains exclusive interviews with top political, military, intelligence, business, and religious leaders in Israel, Iran, Iraq, and Russia. It also contains previously classified documents from the CIA, Pentagon, and White House. *Epicenter* is available in hardcover and a 2.0 updated and expanded softcover edition. *Epicenter* has appeared on the

New York Times political list, as well as the CBA and *Publishers Weekly* Religion lists. It also appeared on the Top 100 list in *Christian Retailing.*
www.joelrosenberg.com
www.joshuafund.net

RECOMMENDED READING

Islam

Bernard Lewis. *What Went Wrong? The Clash Between Islam and Modernity in the Middle East*

Bernard Lewis. *The Crisis of Islam: Holy War and Unholy Terror*

John L. Esposito and Dalia Mogahed. *Who Speaks for Islam?: What a Billion Muslims Really Think*

Sayyid Qutb. *Milestones*

Vali Nasr. *The Shia Revival: How Conflicts within Islam Will Shape the Future*

V. S. Naipaul. *Among the Believers: An Islamic Journey*

Melanie Phillips. *Londonistan*

Ambassador Marwan Muasher. *The Arab Center: The Promise of Moderation*

Queen Noor of Jordan. *Leap of Faith: Memoirs of an Unexpected Life*

Benazir Bhutto. *Reconciliation: Islam, Democracy, and the West*

Ayaan Hirsi Ali. *Infidel*

Jim Murk. *Islam Rising*

Brigitte Gabriel. *Because They Hate: A Survivor of Islamic Terror Warns America*

Nonie Darwish. *Now They Call Me Infidel: Why I Renounced Jihad for America, Israel, and the War* on Terror

Karen Armstrong. *Muhammad: A Biography of the Prophet*

Robert Spencer. *The Truth about Muhammad: Founder of the World's Most Intolerant Religion*

Maulana Muhammad Ali. "Founder of the Ahmadiyya Movement": A Short Story

Terrorism and Al Qaeda

Yaroslav Trofimov. *The Siege of Mecca: The Forgotten Uprising in Islam's Holiest Shrine and the Birth of al-Qaeda*

Lawrence Wright. *The Looming Tower: Al-Qaeda and the Road to 9/11*

Peter Bergen. *The Osama bin Laden I Know: An Oral History of al Qaeda's Leader*

Yossef Bodansky. *Bin Laden: The Man Who Declared War on America*

Randall B. Hamud. *Osama Bin Laden: America's Enemy in His Own Words*

Richard A. Clarke. *Against All Enemies: Inside America's War on Terror*

Richard Miniter. *Losing Bin Laden*

Laura Mansfield, editor. *His Own Words: A Translation of the Writings of Dr. Ayman al Zawahiri*

National Commission on Terrorist Attacks. *The 9/11 Commission Report: Final Report of the National Commission on Terrorist Attacks upon the United States*

Dore Gold. *Hatred's Kingdom: How Saudi Arabia Supports the New Global Terrorism*

Michael A. Sheehan. *Crush the Cell: How to Defeat Terrorism Without Terrorizing Ourselves*

Nicholas Noe, editor. *Voice of Hezbollah: The Statements of Sayyed Hassan Nasrallah*

Naim Qassem. *Hizbullah: The Story from Within*

United States Politics

President Dwight Eisenhower. *Mandate for Change: The White House Years, 1953–1956*

President Jimmy Carter. *Keeping Faith: Memoirs of a President*

Admiral Stansfield Turner. *Burn Before Reading: Presidents, CIA Directors, and Secret Intelligence*

Zbigniew Brzezinski. *Power and Principle: Memoirs of the National Security Adviser, 1977–1981*

Henry Kissinger. *The White House Years*

Robert Gates. *From the Shadows: The Ultimate Insider's Story of Five Presidents and How They Won the Cold War*

Tim Weiner. *Legacy of Ashes: The History of the CIA*

Christopher Andrew. *For the President's Eyes Only: Secret Intelligence and the American Presidency from Washington to Bush*

George Tenet. *At the Center of the Storm: My Years at the CIA*

Bob Woodward. *State of Denial: Bush at War, Part III*

Bob Woodward. *The War Within: A Secret White House History 2006–2008*

Islam and the United States

Mark Bowden. *Guests of the Ayatollah: The First Battle in America's War with Militant Islam*

His Majesty King Abdullah II. Address to the National Prayer Luncheon, February 2, 2006

Daniel Pipes. *Militant Islam Reaches America*

Stephen Kinzer. *All the Shah's Men: An American Coup and the Roots of Middle East Terror*

International Politics
Jerrold Post. *Leaders and Their Followers in a Dangerous World: The Psychology of Political Behavior*

Israel
Tom Doyle. *Two Nations Under God: Why You Should Care about Israel*

Iraq
Ambassador L. Paul Bremer III. *My Year in Iraq: The Struggle to Build a Future of Hope*

James A. Baker III and Lee H. Hamilton, co-chairs. *The Iraq Study Group Report: The Way Forward — A New Approach*

Central Asia — Afghanistan and Pakistan
Nick B. Mills. *Karzai: The Failing American Intervention and the Struggle for Afghanistan*

John Weaver. *Inside Afghanistan: The American Who Stayed Behind after 9/11 and His Mission of Mercy to a War-Torn People*

Pervez Musharraf. *In the Line of Fire: A Memoir*

Iran and the Islamic Revolution
Baqer Moin. *Khomeini: Life of the Ayatollah*

Dr. Hamid Algar, translator. *Islam and Revolution 1: Writings and Declarations of Imam Khomeini (1941–1980)*

Nikki R. Keddie. *Modern Iran: Roots and Results of Revolution*

Said Amir Arjomand. *The Turban for the Crown: The Islamic Revolution in Iran*

Michael Ledeen. *The Iranian Time Bomb: The Mullah Zealots' Quest for Destruction*

William J. Daugherty. *In the Shadow of the Ayatol-lah: A CIA Hostage in Iran*

Ali M. Ansari. *Confronting Iran: The Failure of American Foreign Policy and the Next Great Conflict in the Middle East*

Mehdi Khalaji. *Apocalyptic Politics: On the Ratio-nality of Iranian Policy,* Policy Focus #79, Washington Institute for Near East Policy, January 2008

Karim Sadjadpour. *Reading Khamenei: The World View of Iran's Most Powerful Leader*

Alireza Jafarzadeh. *The Iran Threat: President Ah-madinejad and the Coming Nuclear Crisis*

Yossi Melman and Meir Javedanfar. *The Nuclear Sphinx of Tehran: Mahmoud Ahmadinejad and the State of Iran*

Kasra Naji. *Ahmadinejad: The Secret History of Iran's Radical Leader*

Kenneth M. Pollack. *The Persian Puzzle: The Conflict between Iran and America*

Reza Pahlavi. *Winds of Change: The Future of Democracy in Iran*

Nasrin Alavi. *We Are Iran: The Persian Blogs*

Azar Nafisi. *Reading Lolita in Tehran*

Tom White, et al. (Voice of the Martyrs). *Iran, Desperate for God: An Oppressive Islamic State Drives Its People into the Arms of Christ*

Former Muslims and Christian Evangelism

Ibn Warraq, editor. *Leaving Islam: Apostates Speak Out*

Susan Crimp and Joel Richardson, editors. *Why We Left Islam: Former Muslims Speak Out*

Brother Andrew and Al Janssen. *Light Force: A Stirring Account of the Church Caught in the*

Middle East Crossfire

Brother Andrew and Al Janssen. *Secret Believers: What Happens When Muslims Believe in Christ*

Brother Yun, Peter Xu Yongze, and Enoch Wang (with Paul Hattaway). *Back to Jerusalem: Three Chinese House Church Leaders Share Their Vision to Complete the Great Commission*

Walid Shoebat. *Why I Left Jihad: The Root of Terrorism and the Return of Radical Islam*

Tass Saada. *Once an Arafat Man: The True Story of How a PLO Sniper Found a New Life*

William McElwee Miller. *Ten Muslims Meet Christ*

Carrie McDonnall. *Facing Terror: The True Story of How an American Couple Paid the Ultimate Price for Their Love of the Muslim People*

The employees of Thorndike Press hope you have enjoyed this Large Print book. All our Thorndike, Wheeler, and Kennebec Large Print titles are designed for easy reading, and all our books are made to last. Other Thorndike Press Large Print books are available at your library, through selected bookstores, or directly from us.

For information about titles, please call:
(800) 223-1244

or visit our Web site at:
http://gale.cengage.com/thorndike

To share your comments, please write:
Publisher
Thorndike Press
295 Kennedy Memorial Drive
Waterville, ME 04901